Macroprudential Banking Supervision & Monetary Policy

Luca Amorello

Macroprudential Banking Supervision & Monetary Policy

Legal Interaction in the European Union

palgrave
macmillan

Luca Amorello
Cleary Gottlieb Steen & Hamilton LLP
London, UK

ISBN 978-3-030-06805-9 ISBN 978-3-319-94156-1 (eBook)
https://doi.org/10.1007/978-3-319-94156-1

Cover illustration: Achim Thomae / Getty Images
Cover design by Akihiro Nakay

This Palgrave Macmillan imprint is published by the registered company Springer Nature Switzerland AG
The registered company address is: Gewerbestrasse 11, 6330 Cham, Switzerland

Acknowledgments

This book is dedicated to my mentor Prof. Mauro Bussani (University of Trieste and University of Macau), whom I greatly admire.

Throughout the process of writing this book, many law and economics scholars and practitioners have taken time out to help me. Special thanks go to my supervisor, Prof. Helmut Siekmann (Goethe University of Frankfurt), for his patience and guidance. In addition, I would like to give a special thanks to Dr. Francesco Papadia (Bruegel), and Dr. Francesco Mazzaferro (ESRB Secretariat), for providing precious feedback and contributions to this book. For valuable comments and inputs, I also thank Avv. Giuseppe Napoletano (Banca d'Italia), Prof. Isabel Feichtner (Goethe University of Frankfurt), Prof. Brigitte Haar (Goethe University of Frankfurt), Prof. Rosa Lastra (Queen Mary Law School), Prof. Katerina Pistor (Columbia Law School), Olaf Weeken (ESRB Secretariat), Dr. Norbert Metiu (Deutsche Bundesbank), Frank Dierick (ESRB Secretariat), Mario Marangoni (Banca d'Italia), Kosmas Kaprinis (Oxford University), Jurgita Abisalaite (ESRB Secretariat), and Giovanni Di Balsamo (ESRB Secretariat). I would also like to thank all my colleagues in the PhD/Doctoral Program in Law and Economics of Money and Finance for their help and encouragement. I would like to thank Banca d'Italia for the financial support provided through the 'Menichella Scholarship Award', which helped me finance my doctoral program, and the ESRB Secretariat for the theoretical and practical teachings in in the field of macroprudential policy and regulation. Finally, very special thanks to my parents, Paolo and Rosamaria, for their love, understanding, and financial support during these years abroad.

Contents

List of Tables

CHAPTER 1

Introduction

1.1 Reasons for a Research

It is not a revelation that the 2008 global financial crash considerably distressed the European Union and its members leading to the worst recession in Europe since World War II. A fundamental lack of understanding of system-wide risk and the failure to appreciate the threat posed by aggressive risk-taking behaviors of financial institutions led to underestimate the consequence of excessive accumulation of growing debt and leverage which resulted from booming credit and asset prices.[1]

Defaulting loans secured by mortgages[2] and securities mispricing[3] in a deregulated environment played a key role in catalyzing the eruption of the banking system's failure that ultimately resulted in an impairment of the real and financial transmission channels.[4] Further, the soft touch supervision helped amplifying the externalities related to financial shocks.[5] Attempts made by some European governments to bail out the banking system eventually triggered a dramatic increase of public debt

[1] Galati and Moessner (2013), p. 846.

[2] For a better understanding on the role of mortgages defaults in 2007 crisis, see Mayer, Pence, and Sherlund (2008).

[3] See Levitin and Wachter (2012), pp. 1177–1258. See also Ball (2009).

[4] For a better insight of the real and financial transmission channels, see BCBS (2011).

[5] Enoch, Everaert, Tressel, and Zhou (2013), p. 8.

L. Amorello, *Macroprudential Banking Supervision & Monetary Policy*, https://doi.org/10.1007/978-3-319-94156-1_1

across many EU countries, leading to the outbreak of the Eurozone Debt Crisis.[6]

Among different views upon the reasons behind the European financial turmoil, the law & economics literature acknowledges that a prominent fraction of responsibilities lies on the institutional features and competences of the European Monetary Union and, more broadly, of the European Union as a whole.[7] As a result, the European debt crisis brought about not only a change in the EU statutory framework[8] but also a shift in the institutional competences of the European institutions with the establishment of new supervisory authorities and institutional powers.[9]

One of the key attributes of the institutional response against the financial turmoil lies in the unconventional reaction of both monetary and prudential authorities seeking to restore the sustainability of the financial markets. For decades mainstream central banking has been dominated by the target of price stability, and conventional operating instruments have been implemented rather straightforward.[10]

The struggle for price stability (and/or full employment) through the influence of the short-term interest rate represented the ultimate objective of monetary policy, while open market operations were the artillery used to meet the desired interest rate target. Simultaneously, separate prudential agencies have relied mainly on microprudential regulatory instruments aimed at protecting the soundness and prudent management of private

[6] Inter alia, see on the issue: Reinhart and Rogoff (2011), pp. 1676–1706; Mody and Sandri (2011). More generally, about the transmission from banking sector stress to sovereigns, see Correa and Sapriza (2014).

[7] On this topic, see Dabrowski (2009); Avgouleas and Arner (2013); Vourloumis (2012). Besides, see also the Communication from the Commission—From financial crisis to recovery: A European framework for action, COM/2008/0706 final, Brussels, 29 October 2008 where the Commission stated the 'need to redefine the regulatory and supervisory model of the EU financial sector, particularly for the large cross border financial institutions'.

[8] We refer, in particular, to the approval of the 'EU Stability and Growth Pack', designed to ensure that countries in the European Union pursue sound public finances and coordinate their fiscal policies, and the following 'EU Six Pack', containing five regulations and one directive intended to tighten economic coordination and macroeconomic surveillance among Eurozone countries.

[9] For example, we refer to the establishment of the European Stability Mechanism (ESM), and of the European System of Financial Supervision (ESFS) comprising the European Supervisory Authorities (ESAs) and the European Systemic Risk Board (ESRB). See also the creation of the Single Supervisory Mechanism (SSM), the Single Resolution Mechanism (SRM), and the Single Resolution Fund (SRF).

[10] For details, see Wachtel (2011).

market participants by influencing their risk-taking decisions[11] and reducing the overall agency costs surrounding the investors-managers relationship.[12]

Against this backdrop, the European experience seems to suggest that the efforts made to achieve an efficient trade-off between monetary policy and prudential supervision for financial markets ultimately failed. The severity and scope of the global crisis have pushed central banks to explore innovative tools and discover new functions—within or beyond their statutory constraints—capable of restoring the smooth functioning of the financial cycle. The ideal of price stability as unique mandate of central banking has been increasingly under scrutiny, and at least one further macro-objective seems to take root in the worldwide current discussions among central bankers,[13] that is, financial stability. Such central bank's policy enlargement proposal has found the support of a number of academics and practitioners whose main concern is to prevent further systemic disruptions of the lending transmission channels by limiting excessive credit growth and borrowing.[14]

Under this perspective, the outbreak of the crisis has suggested the inclusion of some macroprudential policy instruments in the overall regulatory toolkit employed by financial supervisors to be deployed worldwide in order to safeguard certain structural features of the financial systems as a whole.[15] Consisting in a combination of old practices and new perspectives,[16] these macroprudential proposals have mainly involved ad hoc regulatory interventions through a litany of tools and strategies unable to provide any concrete guidance for an overall macroprudential assessment of financial stability.[17]

[11] Zhou (2010), p. 2. See also Suarez (1988), pp. 307–336.

[12] Inter alia, see Schwarcz (2015).

[13] For example, see Buch (2014), arguing that safeguarding financial stability is now to be deemed as part of the operational responsibilities of Deutsche Bundesbank. See also the speech of Vítor Constâncio, Vice-President of the ECB, at the FT Banking Summit 'Ensuring Future Growth', held in London on 26 November 2014, and the remarks of Jeremy C. Stein, FED Governor, 'Incorporating Financial Stability Considerations into a Monetary Policy Framework', presented at the International Research Forum on Monetary Policy, Washington, DC, 21 March 2014.

[14] Inter alia, see Jácome and Mancini-Griffoli (2014); Bayoumi, Dell'Ariccia, Habermeier, Mancini-Griffoli, Valencia, and others (2014); Aucremanne and Ide (2010), pp. 7–20.

[15] Hockett (2013), p. 3.

[16] Wall (2010), p. 12.

[17] See Schwarcz (2015), p. 26.

Albeit this weakness in the macroprudential dimension seems well recognized, further concerns arise when dealing with its implementation. In particular, some questions become pivotal: 'which are the legal boundaries of the macroprudential instruments?'; 'where are located powers and competences of the macroprudential supervision?'; 'according to the findings obtained, is there any inconsistency in the architecture of the current macroprudential framework?'

Besides, our concern becomes deeper when seeking to investigate the relationship between macroprudential supervision and the scope of central bank's monetary policy. As a matter of fact, a legal analysis of this relationship requires the development of a new analytical framework aimed at reconciling the macroeconomic outcomes of these policies within their legal boundaries. By doing so, this law and economics analysis will disclose an economic interdependence and a legal interaction that calls for rethinking the institutional arrangements of EU competences and supervisory powers.

1.2 The Problem at Issue

Financial stability plays a major role in ensuring an efficient monetary environment, while the smooth functioning of the monetary policy transmission channel is a crucial requirement for effective prudential policies.[18] The economic literature is unanimous in affirming this cross dependence, while a number of studies have provided empirical evidences for most of these interactions.[19]

However, these interactions are not necessarily consistent. It is not irrational to find scenarios where macroprudential and monetary policies go after different directions: one might be restrictive while the other is expansive. This is the case when a country experiences low nominal growth that requires the intervention of the central bank to lower interest rates.

Although this monetary intervention is deemed as necessary, it is also capable to foster banks towards additional risk-taking and search for yield.[20] One can also envisage a different scenario where low interest rates are consistent with low inflation: under these circumstances, low rates may

[18] Borio and Shim (2007), p. 1.

[19] For example, see Angelini, Neri, and Panetta (2011); Angeloni and Faia (2009); Willem van den End (2010); De Paoli and Paustian (2013).

[20] On the issue, in general, see Altunbas, Gambacorta, and Marques-Ibanez (2009).

contribute to excessive credit growth and the build-up of asset bubbles,[21] thereby sowing the seeds of systemic risk and financial instability. In brief, central bank's monetary policy, in the pursuit of price stability, may contribute to systemic risk via its risk-taking channel.[22] From a supervisory perspective, the emergence of this externality claims for the need of restrictive macroprudential measures to counter the materialization of possible shocks.

The contrary also holds true. Restrictive macroprudential policies are capable to influence credit conditions, thereby affecting the overall economy and the outlook for price stability.[23] As argued in the next chapters, the macroprudential instruments may provide a constraint on borrowings and expenditure in one or more sectors of the economy[24] that may burden the overall output and inflation rate.[25]

To put it briefly, macroprudential and monetary policies, by sharing multiple transmission channels, may interact—*and conflict*—with each other although pursuing different objectives. This statement would entail that when a national authority (or body) decides to use one policy to effectively achieve its statutory target, the *side effects* affecting the other policy must be taken into account.[26] This stated interdependence provides a convincing rationale for why monetary and prudential authorities are currently showing interest in ensuring effective macroprudential assessments.[27]

A similar rationale holds with regard to the efforts made by the same authorities to establish a harmonized macroprudential framework within a coordinated institutional environment.[28] However, despite these interdependencies look genuine and easily understandable, the consequences for the institutional legal framework could be overwhelming.

This is particularly true for the Eurozone where the responsibility for conducting macroprudential policies is statutorily separate from the ECB's

[21] See Borio and Zhu (2008). For details, see also IMF (2014), p. ix.

[22] Among others, see Angeloni, Faia, and Lo Duca (2011); Bianchi (2014).

[23] See the speech of Vítor Constâncio, Vice-President of the ECB, at the Third Conference of the Macro-prudential Research Network, held in Frankfurt-am-Main, 23 June 2014.

[24] IMF (2013a), p. 9.

[25] Idem, p. 9.

[26] Smets (2014), p. 265.

[27] IMF (2013b), p. 9.

[28] Idem, p. 9.

monetary policy tasks.[29] Macroprudential instruments are certainly of primary importance in the Eurozone because of the statutory constraints on monetary policy and the absence of a fiscal union capable to provide rebalancing transfers at the national level to relieve the impact of financial shocks.[30] But, if the Eurozone is characterized by a financial environment where monetary and macroprudential policies are able to mutual affect each other's target, questions of legal consistency of the European Monetary Union's framework will eventually arise.

The point is that if such inconsistencies in the regulatory developments of the EU macroprudential and monetary frameworks are found, this would represent not only an economic challenge in the pursuit of price and financial stability but also a legal uncertainty to be kept under severe scrutiny. In analyzing the legal framework behind this interdependence at national and EU levels, the aim of this book is to provide evidence, if any, of the legal inconsistencies associated with the structural separation of macroprudential and monetary framework. Further intent is to establish a clearer rational understanding of basic concepts of macroprudential supervision and monetary policy such as systemic risk, price stability, et alia, under a so far little-developed law and macroeconomic perspective.

By doing so, the ultimate goal of this work is to offer an institutional proposal to policymakers and practitioners that may likely reconcile conflicts existing in Europe between financial and monetary stability through a broader reconsideration of the institutional tasks and responsibilities.

1.3 The 'Legal Interaction' in a Nutshell

This book is organized as follow. Chapter 2 explores the law and economics of macroprudential banking supervision: in particular, the key concepts of macroprudential policy are defined through a theoretical overview of its legal components. The chapter lays out a set of strategies, indicators, and

[29] This separation can be immediately inferred from the EU primary law. In fact, while the primary objective of the ESCB is to maintain price stability pursuant to Article 127(1) TFEU and Article 3(3) of the ESCB Statute, the ESCB is mandated to contribute only to the conduct of supervisory policies carried out by other competent authorities. In accordance with Article 127(5) TFEU, these policies related to the prudential supervision of credit institutions and the stability of financial system (i.e. microprudential and macroprudential policies) are therefore not considered basic tasks of the ESCB. For details, see Lastra (2012), p. 1274.

[30] Enoch, Everaert, Tressel, and Zhou (2013), p. 386.

tools that best describe the channels of systemic instability. Further, the investigation includes an overview of the institutional and regulatory framework at the European level to classify the principal macroprudential instruments available within the constraints of national and EU competences and tasks.

Chapter 3 proposes a 'legal approach to monetary policy'. Starting from a prospective synopsis of the main historical developments in monetary policy, it seeks to define in legal terms fundamental notions such as price stability, inflation, and monetary policy transmission mechanism. In the second part of the chapter, the monetary system is reconstructed by means of the principles established by this legal analysis of monetary policy. At last, this part explores the economic interactions between law and monetary policy channels, considering also the major components of an effective monetary supervisory framework.

Chapter 4 investigates interactions and conflicts between macroprudential and monetary policies under the current regime. More precisely, it provides an impact assessment of the current calibrations of powers and competences, providing some evidences of the economic interactions existing between financial and monetary stability. This chapter also sheds light on the risk of conflict between macroprudential supervision and monetary intervention under particular scenarios. The risk of negative interactions between the two policies is further discussed in consideration of the current EU financial environment. In addition, the chapter scrutinizes the institutional models that may permit the alignment of the two policies.

Chapter 5 explores the EU legal framework. The chapter firstly defines how the law is capable to constrain the financial and business cycles and address the crossed effects of monetary and macroprudential policies. It explains that constitutional constraints, political pressure, and the characteristics of the financial cycle at the national level determine the institutional model addressing the interaction between the two policies. Against this backdrop, the relationships between the ESCB, the ECB in its capacity of banking supervisor within the SSM, and the national authorities entrusted with macroprudential authorities are examined. The EU institutional architecture is analyzed considering, in particular, the legal arrangements set by the Union law to mitigate the risk of policy conflicts and inconsistencies. Moreover, in the light of the constitutional constraints posed onto the ESCB and ESRB by the EU primary law, this chapter analyzes the lack of a European integrated framework between monetary and macroprudential policies. The existence of such constitutional constraints can have negative implications for the cooperative conduct of the two policies and for the operationalization of additional macroprudential instruments. In line with these findings, the chapter tests the legal limits of the ESRB as European macroprudential body and questions its capacity to fully capture—and mitigate—the systemic risks arising due to the monetary policy conduct of the ESCB.

Finally, Chap. 6 provides some concluding—but not conclusive—remarks.

References

Altunbas, Yener, Gambacorta, Leonardo, Marques-Ibanez, David (2009). An Empirical Assessment of the Risk-Taking Channel, Paper prepared for the BIS/ECB Workshop on '*Monetary Policy and Financial Stability*'. Basel, 11 September 2009.

Angelini, Paolo, Stefano Neri, and Fabio Panetta (2011). Monetary and Macroprudential Policies, *Banca d'Italia Working Papers*, No. 801, March 2011.

Angeloni, Ignazio, Faia, Ester (2009). A Tale of Two Policies: Prudential Regulation and Monetary Policy with Fragile Banks, *Kiel Institute for the World Economy Working Paper*, No. 2.

Angeloni, Ignazio, Faia, Ester, Lo Duca, Marco (2011). Monetary Policy and Risk Taking, *Journal of Economic Dynamics and Control*, Vol. 52.

Aucremanne, Luc, Ide, Stefaan (2010). Lessons from the Crisis: Monetary Policy and Financial Stability, *Economic Review*, Issue I.

Avgouleas, Emilios, Arner, Douglas W. (2013). The Eurozone Debt Crisis and the European Banking Union: A Cautionary Tale of Failure and Reform, *University of Hong Kong Faculty of Law Research Paper*, No. 2013/037.

Ball, Ray (2009). The Global Financial Crisis and the Efficient Market Hypothesis: What Have We Learned?, *Journal of Applied Corporate Finance,* Vol. 21, No. 4.

BCBS (2011). The transmission Channels between the Financial and Real Sectors: A Critical Survey of the Literature, *BIS Working Paper*, No. 18.

Bayoumi, Tamim, Dell'Ariccia, Giovanni, Habermeier, Karl, Tommaso Mancini-Griffoli, Fabián Valencia, and An IMF staff (2014). Monetary Policy in the New Normal, *IMF Staff Discussion Note*, No. 14/3.

Bianchi, Javier (2014). Discussion of "The Risk Channel of Monetary Policy", *International Journal of Central Banking,* Vol. 10, No. 2.

Borio, Claudio, Shim, Ilhyock (2007). What Can (Macro-)Prudential Policy Do to Support Monetary Policy?, *BIS Working Papers*, No. 242.

Borio, Claudio, Zhu, Haibin (2008). Capital Regulation, Risk Taking and Monetary Policy: A Missing Link in the Transmission Mechanism?, *BIS Working Paper*, No. 268.

Buch, Claudia M. (2014). Presentation of the 2014 Financial Stability Review, *Speech Delivered at the Unveiling of the Deutsche Bundesbank's Financial Stability Review*, Frankfurt am Main, 25 November 2014.

Correa, Ricardo, Sapriza, Horacio (2014). Sovereign Debt Default, *Board of Governors of the Federal Reserve System International Finance Discussion Papers*, No. 1104.

Dabrowski, Marek (2009). The Global Financial Crisis: Lessons for European Integration, *CASE Network Studies and Analyses*, No. 384.

De Paoli, Bianca, Paustian, Matthias (2013). Coordinating Monetary and Macroprudential Policies, *Federal Reserve Bank of New York Staff Report*, No. 653.

Enoch, Charles, Luc Everaert, Thierry Tressel, and Jianping Zhou (2013). From Fragmentation to Financial Integration in Europe, Washington, DC, (ed.) *International Monetary Fund*.

Galati, Gabriele, Moessner, Richhild (2013). Macroprudential Policy – A Literature Review, *Journal of Economic Surveys*, Vol. 27, No. 5.

Hockett, Robert C. (2013). The Macroprudential Turn: From Institutional "Safety and Soundness" to "Systemic Stability" in Financial Supervision, *Cornell Law Faculty Working Papers*, No. 108.

IMF (2013a). The interaction of Monetary and Macroprudential Policies, 29 January 2013.

IMF (2013b). Key Aspects of Macroprudential Policy, 10 June 2013.

IMF (2014). Risk Taking, Liquidity, and Shadow Banking Curbing Excess While Promoting Growth, *Global Financial Stability Report (GFSR)*, October 2014.

Jácome, Luis; Mancini-Griffoli, Tommaso (2014). A Broader Mandate, *IMF Finance & Development*, Vol. 51, No. 2, June 2014.

Lastra, Maria Rosa (2012). The Evolution of the European Central Bank, *Fordham International Law Journal*, Vol. 35, Spring Issue.

Levitin, Adam J., Wachter, Susan M. (2012). Explaining the Housing Bubble, *Georgetown Law Journal*, Vol. 100, No. 4.

Mayer, Christopher J., Pence, Karen M., Sherlund, Shane M. (2008). The Rise in Mortgage Defaults. Divisions of Research & Statistics and Monetary Affairs, Federal Reserve Board, Washington, DC, *Finance and Economics Discussion Series*, No. 58-2008.

Mody, Ashoka, Sandri, Damiano (2011). The Eurozone Crisis: How Banks and Sovereigns Came to Be Joined at the Hip, *IMF Working Paper*, No. 269.

Reinhart, Carmen M., Rogoff, Kenneth S. (2011). From Financial Crash to Debt Crisis, *American Economic Review*, Vol. 101.

Schwarcz, Steven L. (2015). Regulating Financial Change: A Functional Approach, *Minnesota Law Review*, Vol. 100 (forthcoming).

Smets, Frank (2014). Financial Stability and Monetary Policy: How Closely Interlinked? *International Journal of Central Banking*, Vol. 10, No. 2.

Suàrez, Javier (1988). Risk-Taking and Prudential Regulation of Banks, *Investigaciones Economicas*, Vol. 22, XXII, No. 3.

Vourloumis, Stavros (2012). Reforming EU and Global Financial Regulation: Crisis, Learning and Paradigm Shifts, *Paper Presented at the 4th Biennial ECPR Standing Group for Regulatory Governance Conference 'New Perspectives on Regulation, Governance and Learning 2012'*, University of Exeter, 27–29 June 2012.

Wachtel, Paul (2011). The Evolving Role of the Federal Reserve, *NYU Working Paper*, No. 2451/31339.

Wall, Larry D. (2010). Prudential Discipline for Financial Firms: Micro, Macro, and Market Structures, *Federal Reserve Bank of Atlanta Working Paper*, No. 2010-09.

van den End, Jan Willem (2010). Trading Off Monetary and Financial Stability: A Balance of Risk Framework, *DNB Working Papers*, No. 249.

Zhou, Chen (2010). Why the micro-prudential regulation fails? The impact on systemic risk by imposing a capital requirement, *DNB Working Paper*, No. 256/July 2010.

CHAPTER 2

Law and Economics of Macroprudential Banking Supervision

2.1 Defining Macroprudential Policy

A legal analysis on the interactions between macroprudential supervision and monetary policy requires at first some definitions. The term 'macroprudential' was little used before the outbreak of the crisis.[1] Policymakers felt confident in the pursuing of monetary, fiscal, and prudential policies that would have ensured financial stability and steady growth without the need of any macroprudential consideration.[2]

The concept dates back to the 1970s in the context of the analysis of the macroeconomic risks posed in the banking sector by common exposures to risky debt of developing countries.[3] The term 'macroprudential', in fact, was firstly used in 1979 at the meeting of the Cooke Committee, the precursor of the Basel Committee on Banking Supervision (BCBS), held in Basel.[4] During the discussions of 28–29 June 1979 about the macroeconomic risks caused by the rapid growth then under way in international bank lending to developing countries,[5] the Committee's Chairman W. P. Cooke, the then head of banking supervision at the Bank of England, affirmed that 'microeconomic problems [...] began to merge

[1] Clement (2010), p. 59.
[2] Caruana and Cohen (2014), p. 16.
[3] IMF (2013c), p. 53.
[4] Clement (2010), p. 60.
[5] IMF (2013c), p. 53.

L. Amorello, *Macroprudential Banking Supervision & Monetary Policy*, https://doi.org/10.1007/978-3-319-94156-1_2

into macroeconomic problems [...] at the point where microprudential problems became what could be called macroprudential ones'.[6]

According to the minutes, 'the Committee had a justifiable concern with macroprudential problems and it was the link between those and macroeconomic ones which formed the boundary of the Committee's interest'.[7] Worried about the rapid increase of the exposure to developing countries and the related consequences for financial stability, the Cooke Committee was seeking policy options to counter possible financial shocks.[8]

The following year, the term macroprudential appeared for the second time in a background document, signed by the Deputy Chief of the Bank of England Overseas Department David Holland and prepared for a working party chaired by Alexandre Lamfalussy.[9] By examining possible prudential measures to constrain bank lending,[10] this document emphasized the need to take a broader perspective in prudential policies with a macroprudential approach that 'considers problems that bear upon the market as a whole as distinct from an individual bank, and which may not be obvious at the microprudential level'.[11] In the same year, the term macroprudential was found in the final report of the Lamfalussy Working Party to the G10 meeting of April 1980, which called for an 'effective supervision of the international banking system, from both the microprudential and the macro-prudential points of view'.[12]

Besides these earlier references, the term macroprudential became public domain for the first time only on April 1986 with the publication of the

[6] See Informal Record of the 16th meeting of the Committee on Banking Regulations and Supervisory Practices held in Basel on 28–29 June 1979. (BS/79/42). BIS Archives—Banking Supervision, Informal Record, file 2.

[7] Idem.

[8] Clement (2010), p. 60.

[9] See The use of prudential measures in the international banking markets, 24 October 1979, pp. 1–2. BIS Archives 7.18(15)—Papers Lamfalussy, LAM25/F67.

[10] Clement (2010), p. 61.

[11] The report submitted to Lamfalussy acknowledged three examples of macroprudential issues that could not be solved by a microprudential approach: (1) the growth of the overall market, (2) the perception of risk, and (3) the perception of liquidity. For better insights on this relevant issue, see Willke, Becker, and Rostásy (2013).

[12] Report for the Working Party on possible approaches to constraining the growth of banks' international lending, 29 February 1980, BIS Archives 1.3a(3)J—Working Party on constraining growth of international bank lending, vol. 2. For more details, see also Clement (2010), p. 61.

report 'Recent Innovation in international banking (Cross Report)' by the Euro-currency Standing Committee (ECSC).[13] The Supervisors' Committee was mainly concerned with the threat posed by the process of financial innovation and structural changes that had resulted in a rapid growth of off-balance-sheet activity of credit institutions, such as securitization and credit derivatives. The vulnerabilities associated with these trends would have required, according to central bankers, substantial adjustments in regulation and other policies, among which macroprudential policy would have been pivotal.[14]

Following a period in which the term remained unmentioned, in October 1992, the ECSC published a report on recent developments in international interbank relations[15] where central governors were asked 'to focus on the role and interaction of banks in non-traditional markets, [...], to examine the linkages among various segments of the interbank markets and among the players active in them, and to consider the macro-prudential concerns to which these aspects might give rise'. The ECSC reiterated the use of the term three years later when a report on 'issues related to the measurement of market size and macroprudential risks in derivatives markets' was published to identify the principal macroeconomic and macroprudential information requirements of central banks in relation to global derivatives market activity.[16]

Subsequently, the term macroprudential appeared in November 1996 when the Board of Governors of the Federal Reserve System decided to dispose a supervisory program for a risk-based inspection of top 50 bank holding companies[17] with the purpose of analyzing macroprudential information on movement, conduct, and risk profiles of the major US banks.[18] Further, in 1997, the Bank for International Settlement (BIS) referred to the term 'macroprudential' in a special chapter of its 67th Annual Report to describe the two-level strategy used to safeguard financial stability.[19]

[13] We refer to BIS (1986).

[14] Idem, p. 2. For further details cf. Clement (2010), p. 62.

[15] The report is BIS (1992).

[16] This report is CGFS (1995). For details, see Clement (2010), p. 63.

[17] A bank holding company is a parent company of a banking group that does not necessarily provide banking services itself. In the United States, the prudential regulation of such entities is laid down in 12 CFR Part 225 (Regulation Y).

[18] Banerjee (2011), p. 4.

[19] We refer to BIS (1997), p. 147.

In September 2000, Andrew Crockett, General Manager of the BIS and Chairman of the 1997 Financial Stability Forum, released a speech before the 11th International Conference of Banking Supervisors, held in Basel. In his remarks,[20] Crockett sought to explain the distinction between the micro- and macroprudential dimensions of financial stability, arguing that while 'the micro-prudential objective can be seen as limiting the likelihood of failure of individual institutions', 'the macro-prudential objective can be defined as limiting the costs to the economy from financial distress, including those that arise from any moral hazard induced by the policies pursued'. For Crockett the objective of macroprudential policy is to limit the likelihood of the failure, and corresponding costs, of significant portions of the financial system, that is, the *systemic risk*.[21] Only a few months later, it is the turn of David Clementi, Deputy Governor of the Bank of England, to point out at a Bank of England Conference held in London that the 'fragility at individual banks can turn into system-wide fragility and in turn into system wide crisis', while 'a macro-prudential shock or policy error can impact on individual institutions, revealing underlying systemic weakness and triggering a crisis'.[22]

The financial crisis of 2007 has shacked up the intellectual foundations of the policy disciplines,[23] requiring a reassessment of the institutional framework for financial stability. The financial turmoil thus may be seen as a turning point for the use of the term 'macroprudential' in the regulatory proposals. Although there is no general agreement on a single definition of what constitutes a macroprudential policy,[24] the financial crisis has demonstrated the need to renew the common approach to financial system regulation by complementing the older regulatory framework with a new macroprudential perspective. In light of this, previous conceptual discussions on macroprudential policies have been operationalized and many countries have started assigning a macroprudential mandate to a national authority, providing it with a specific range of tools and competences.[25]

[20] For the whole speech, see Crockett (1997).

[21] For insights, see Clement (2010), pp. 63–64.

[22] David Clementi (2001), p. 4.

[23] We paraphrase Tarullo (2014), p. 48.

[24] Noyer (2014), p. 7. According to Caruana and Cohen (2014), p. 16, 'debates about correct definition of "macroprudential" sometimes border on the theological', and 'it can be counterproductive to strive for too much precision'.

[25] Knot (2014), p. 25.

This section aims at introducing the key elements of what is nowadays deemed as macroprudential policy. To this purpose, we seek to identify in the scholarship of Hyman Minsky, a well-known American economist and professor of economics at Washington University in St. Louis,[26] the theoretical underpinnings of the macroprudential dimension. Next, a brief outline of the economic literature on the concept of macroprudential policy is described. Ultimately, the legal sub-components of macroprudential policy are defined.

2.1.1 Minsky and the Theoretical Foundation of the Macroprudential Dimension

Prior to outlining the legal components of macroprudential policy, a brief investigation on the theoretical underpinnings of macroprudential policy seems necessary. Although there is no general consensus on the meaning of macroprudential policy, the earliest economic foundations for the macroprudential architecture are to be found in the *Financial Instability Hypothesis* of Hyman P. Minsky.[27] The 'Minskian' perspective on financial stability, provided the rationale for the earliest proposal of what is now recognized as macroprudential regulation. By incorporating his analysis in a new dynamic regulatory approach,[28] the intent of Minsky was to challenge the mainstream economic theory of self-adjusting equilibrium[29] which leaves little room for investigating the dynamic of systemic crisis. Under this conventional view, the only theoretical basis for prudential regulation relied on the assessment of the activities of individual banks (so-called idiosyncratic approach) without any reference to the interdependence with other credit institutions and the financial system as a whole.[30]

The general framework of this theory appeared for the first time in 1974 but popularized only after the recent financial crisis as model-based

[26] For a biography of Minsky and a thorough analysis of his scholarship, see Mehrling (1999), pp. 129–158.

[27] For a better explanation of the theory, see Minsky (1992). For an academic analysis of Minsky's theory, see also Mehrling (1999); Wolfson (2001); Papadimitriou and Wray (1997).

[28] Kregel (2014), pp. 224–226. See also Esen and Binatlı (2012).

[29] We refer to the '(*Neo-*)Classical Theory of Economics' according to which the economy is capable of self-regulating. For a detailed historical overview of the Classical Theory of Economics, see Sowell (2007). In addition, an interesting overview from an 'Austrian Perspective' is given by Rothbard (1995).

[30] Kregel (2014), p. 219.

explanation of the reasons behind the 2008 financial turmoil.[31] According to Minsky,

> the past, the present, and the future in a capitalist economy are linked not only by capital assets and labor force but also by financial relations. The key financial relationships link the creation and the ownership of capital assets to the structure of financial relations and changes in this structure. Institutional complexity may result in several layers of intermediation between the ultimate owners of the communities' wealth and the units that control and operate the communities' wealth.[32]

All units are deemed as a banker who maximizes profits under liquidity and solvency constraints. Any unit can operate as a hedge, speculative, or Ponzi investor and switch from one type to the other according to the credit and macroeconomic conditions of the economy.[33] For Minsky, hedge, speculative, and Ponzi financing units alike are vulnerable to events which reduce the cash flow from assets.[34]

On the one hand, in fact, a decrease in income from operations, or a 'default' or 'restructuring of the debt owed to a unit', can transform a hedge financing unit into a speculative one. On the other hand, speculative and Ponzi finance units are vulnerable to changes in interest rates. Increase in interest rates will increase cash flow commitments without increasing receipts. As they must continuously refinance their positions, they are vulnerable to financial market disruptions.[35] Thus, the greater the weights of speculative finance in the total financial structure, the greater the fragility of the financial structure itself.[36]

In the light of these assumptions, Minsky argued that a capitalist economy is inherently fragile because its investment and financing process

[31] On the issue, see Nersisyan and Wray (2010), where the authors identify the reasons of the financial crisis in the shift to the shadow banking system and the creation of what Minsky called the money manager phase of capitalism with a rapid growth of leverage and speculative financing.

[32] Minsky (1992), p. 4.

[33] Minsky defines the economic units as *hedge* when they can fulfill all of their contractual payment obligations by their cash flow; the *speculative* units, instead, are those units that cannot repay the principle out of income cash flows and need to roll over their existing liabilities, while *Ponzi* units are those unable to cover neither the repayment of principle nor the interest due on their own outstanding debts. Ponzi units must either sell assets or borrow. For details, see Minsky (1992), p. 7.

[34] Minsky (1976), pp. 8–9.

[35] Idem, p. 9.

[36] For further insights, see Siqiwen (2010), pp. 256–258.

introduce such endogenous destabilizing forces. A positive economic trend generates optimism among investors, thereby increasing the volume of investments. These aggregate investments feed economic growth generating further optimism and readiness to accumulate debt. In this scenario, the accrual continues until it reaches a breaking point and the painful debt-deleveraging strikes down the whole system.[37] This fragility depends upon the number of things that can amplify initial disturbance.

But this brings to the conclusion that normal functioning of the capitalist economy inherently leads to financial trauma and crises.[38] To state it simply, it is the stability itself that may breed instability[39]: the financial fragility is an inner attribute of the financial systems[40] and provides fertile ground for financial instability, leading to a process of debt deflation and full-blown crises.[41] Under this approach, Minsky sought to define the cyclical nature and the systemic interactions within the economic system, thereby providing a theoretical rationale for a macroprudential approach to regulation.[42]

Minsky not only came to a reexamination of the capitalist system in its systemic interactions, but he also sought to rethink the appropriate type of bank supervision and examination in the light of his works on the Financial Stability Hypothesis. In his article on the economics of disaster,[43] Minsky stated that the typical outcome of a bank examination by supervisors is a balance sheet, which places prices on assets, though many banks' assets (such as at that time loans) do not have an active market.[44] By examining this balance sheet, the measures of adequacy of bank's capital and liquidity are derived.[45] However, as argued by Minsky, the examiners' balance sheet is the result of many arbitrary rules to the extent that valuation is divorced from current market prices.[46] In order to address this weakness, Minsky

[37] Schmidt and Thatcher (2013), p. 216.

[38] Minsky (1992), p. 4.

[39] See Minsky (1986), p. 237, according to which: 'success breeds a disregard of the possibility of failure'.

[40] Minsky (1976), p. 3.

[41] For details, see Esen and Binatlı (2012).

[42] Kregel (2014), p. 224.

[43] We refer to: Minsky (1970).

[44] Idem, p. 63.

[45] Idem, p. 64.

[46] Idem, p. 64. On the issue at hand, see also Phillips (1997).

presented a proposal on a 'cash flow approach' to bank examination,[47] based upon the assumption that liquidity is a time-related characteristics of an ongoing, continuing economic institution embedded in an evolving financial system.[48]

Under this approach, the practical purpose of the proposal was not only to offer a more precise source of information on liquidity and solvency of particular institutions, but also to assess the likelihood of threats to the stability of financial markets.[49] To this end, Minsky designed the cash flow examination to focus upon the actual and potential position making operation of a bank, so that the supervisory authorities would have been aware of the actual or threatened financial fragility.[50] In addition, through the establishment of a regular reporting procedure, the supervisory authorities would have been forced to inquire those institutional changes and developments that could affect the overall stability of the financial system.[51]

This stability evaluation was to be made by assessing the adequacy of cash flows from income relative to debt, the adequacy of refinancing possibilities relative to position, and the ratio of unprotected to protected financial assets. As a result, the likelihood of financial stability would have depended upon the trend and the evolution of these financial ratios.[52]

From this point of view, Minsky's proposal for a cash flow-oriented bank examination recognized for the first time the need for integration of the microeconomic and macroeconomic perspective in bank examinations and supervision.[53] Both of these intuitions can be considered as a first attempt to outline the economic foundation for the establishment of a rational macroprudential supervisory framework for the banking sector. Yet, despite a general agreement by regulators on the importance of such 'systemic' macroprudential approach to regulation and supervision, these early ideas have been hardly recognized in practice, and, until the 2008 financial turmoil, few substantial changes in supervision and examination procedures have been carried out.

[47] This proposal is contained in Minsky (1967). In this regard, see also his final proposal included in Minsky (1975).

[48] Minsky (1975), p. 1.

[49] Idem, p. 1.

[50] Idem, p. 1.

[51] Idem, p. 2.

[52] Minsky (1970), p. 20.

[53] Phillips (1997), p. 513.

2.1.2 *The Concept of 'Macroprudential' in the Economic Literature*

If Minsky's intuitions are certainly the primary cornerstone for the establishment of a theoretical macroprudential framework, the economic literature only recently has opened up the debate on the implementation and the effectiveness of macroprudential policy. Due to a lack of understanding of system-wide risks, in fact, the analytical research on the development of macroprudential tools until the 2008 financial breakdown has been rather limited.[54] Even today, despite a deeper insight into the dynamics of system-wide risks and a fast growing research in this field, the literature on macroprudential policy remains fragmented, as scholars maintain different views upon objectives, scope, and instruments of the macroprudential dimension.[55]

Undoubtedly, the earliest stage of this debate turns around the macroprudential policy's objectives. The economic literature draws up a clear distinction between the 'macroprudential' and the 'microprudential' dimension, as to reconcile the economic policy objective with a specific range of instruments to be deployed. It can be easily assumed that both macroprudential and microprudential policy play a complement role in safeguarding the financial system; however, the conventional wisdom is unanimous in recognizing different goals for each policy.

According to Borio (2003),[56] the dividing line is to be found in terms of (proximate and ultimate) objectives, models used to describe risk and calibration of prudential controls.[57]

In terms of proximate objective, the *microprudential* policy aims at limiting the risk of episodes of financial distress at the individual level, while the core objective of macroprudential policy focuses on limiting the risk of financial distress for the economy as a whole (the so-called system-wide distress).[58] From a different angle, the macroprudential dimension acknowledges the idea that the stability of the financial system does not depend solely on the soundness of its individual components, as for the microprudential approach; instead, this stability relies to some extent on a complex set of interactions and interdependencies between the components of the whole financial system.[59]

[54] Galati and Moessner (2013), p. 847.
[55] Idem, p. 847.
[56] See Borio (2003).
[57] Idem, p. 2. For further details, see also Table 1 in Galati and Moessner (2013), p. 849.
[58] Idem, p. 2.
[59] Noyer (2014), p. 7.

However, despite this common understanding in distinguishing the microprudential and macroprudential policies, the economic literature is not unanimous in describing what is meant for financial stability. Yet, it can be argued that if the proximate objective of macroprudential policy is to safeguard the financial stability of the financial system, it seems possible to rationalize the notion of financial stability in terms of absence of systemic externalities that may arise once certain events of disruption in the financial intermediation channels occur.[60] In the light of this approach, macroprudential policy should address all market failures—due to the inefficiencies of the financial systems—that can generate correlated losses, risks, and fire sales of assets.[61]

In this respect, at least three positive definitions of financial stability can be outlined in the international scholarship.[62] On the one hand, a first group of economists emphasizes the resilience of the financial systems as a key component of financial stability.[63] This resilience is interpreted in terms of robustness against external shocks 'in order to maintain a stable supply of financial intermediation services across the credit cycle'.[64] On the other hand, a second group of scholars defines financial stability in terms of resilience from shocks originating within the financial systems, thereby highlighting the endogenous nature of systemic distress.[65] Finally,

[60] Angeloni (2014), p. 73.

[61] Knot (2014), pp. 26–27. On the issue, see also Noyer (2014), pp. 9–10.

[62] For an analytical insight of the literature investigating the concept of ***financial stability***, among others, see Alawode and Al Sadek (2008).

[63] Galati and Moessner (2013), p. 848. Among the economists of the first group, Crockett (1997) recognizes financial stability in 'that the key institutions in the financial system are stable, in that there is a high degree of confidence that they continue to meet their contractual obligations without interruption or outside assistance; and that the key markets are stable, in that participants can confidently transact in them at prices that reflect the fundamental forces and do not vary substantially over short periods when there have been no changes in the fundamentals'. According to Padoa-Schioppa (2002), 'financial stability is a condition where the financial system is able to withstand shocks without giving way to cumulative processes, which impair the allocation of savings to investment opportunities and the processing of payments in the economy', thereby posing the emphasis on the shock-absorbing capacity of the financial system. Laker (1999) further suggests that 'the objective of financial system stability could therefore be defined, in broad terms, as the avoidance of disruptions to the financial system that are likely to cause significant costs to real output'. He went on to say that 'such disruptions might have their origins in difficulties facing financial institutions or in disturbances in financial markets'.

[64] Bank of England (2009), p. 10.

[65] Galati and Moessner (2013), p. 848. See also Schinasi (2004).

a third academic approach ties the meaning of financial stability to situations with asset price stability without particular reference to banking crises.[66] This third approach takes advantage of the more directly observable variables that can be used for the stability assessments but offers no guide for measuring the relative strength of the financial system.[67]

Due to the absence of unanimous definitions in positive terms, many economists prefer a negative definition by referring to the broader concept of *financial instability*.[68] Along this line, some scholarship used to define the notion of *financial instability* in terms of disruption of the credit channels with serious negative consequences on the economic activity and performance.[69] Other economists give weight to the disturbance of the funds channeling following the breakdown of the information flow within the financial system.[70] A last group of scholars, instead, is still committed to incorporate the distortion of asset prices in a broader definition of financial instability.[71] What remains apparent, however, is that even the negative notion of financial instability is not able to provide a clear guidance for a shared understanding of the macroprudential target.

Far more relevant to mark a distinctive line between macroprudential and microprudential dimensions are their objectives. While the consumer/investor protection is recognized as an intermediate objective of the microprudential framework, the economic literature generally acknowledges the assumption that the proximate target of macroprudential policy is to limit

[66] Das, Quintyn, and Chenard (2004), p. 6.

[67] Das, Quintyn, and Chenard (2004), p. 6.

[68] For more details on the concept of financial instability, see Alawode and Al Sadek (2008); Houben, Kakes, and Schinasi (2004); Borio and Drehmann (2009).

[69] In this regard, see Davis (2001); Chant (2003).

[70] For example, Mishkin (1999) argues that 'financial instability occurs when shocks to the financial system interfere with information flow so that the financial system can no longer do its job of channeling funds to those with productive investment opportunities'. Also Davis (2001) notes that financial instability means 'a major collapse of the financial system, entailing inability to provide payments services or to allocate credit to productive investment opportunities'.

[71] This is the case of Ferguson (2003) that refers to financial instability as 'a situation characterized by [...] three basic criteria: (1) some important set of financial asset prices seem to have diverged sharply from fundamentals; and/or (2) market functioning and credit availability, domestically and perhaps internationally, have been significantly distorted; with the result that, (3) aggregate spending deviates (or is likely to deviate) significantly, either above or below, from the economy's ability to produce'.

risks and costs of systemic crises.[72] The costs of financial stability in terms of outputs and fiscal balances can be substantial and their incidence highly extensive.[73] The macroprudential tools are therefore deemed to reduce to some extent the impact and the incidence of such costs providing large economic benefits for the smooth functioning of the credit cycle.[74]

Thus, while microprudential policy aims at ensuring the safety and soundness of specific financial institutions,[75] the intermediate objective of macroprudential policy can be defined instead as to 'limit systemic or system-wide financial risk, thereby limiting the incidence of disruptions in the provision of key financial services that can have serious consequences for the real economy'.[76] But, if the intermediate objective of macroprudential policy is to avoid output costs related to systemic crisis, it is essential at this point to clearly describe when such risks are deemed *systemic*.

As for the notion of financial stability and instability, there is no mutual agreement in the economic literature on the definition of systemic risk.[77] On the one hand, some authors define systemic risk as 'any set of circumstances that threatens the stability of or public confidence in the financial system',[78] in particular when a series of correlated defaults and liquidity shortage occur among financial institutions over a short time period.[79] On the other hand, a number of other economists seek to understand the very essence of systemic risk by focusing on more specific crisis events, such as imbalances, contagion, or asset bubbles.[80]

Systemic events can be scrutinized under a narrow or a broader perspective. In a narrow sense, the events are systemic 'where the release of

[72] Galati and Moessner (2013), p. 848. See also Berger, Molyneux, and Wilson (2009), pp. 674–675.

[73] See Borio (2003), p. 4, who quotes Hoggarth, Reis, and Saporta (2001). As argued by the latter authors, the cumulative output losses incurred during a banking crisis may be large, roughly 15–20% of annual GDP, on average. On the issue, *cf.* also Schuknecht (2002) who conducts a comprehensive analysis of the fiscal costs of financial instability.

[74] For details on the issue, see Arregui, Beneš, Krznar, Mitra, and Santos (2013); Galati and Moessner (2014). For a macroeconometric inquiry, see Kawata, Kurachi, Nakamura, and Teranishi (2013).

[75] Caruana and Cohen (2014), p. 16.

[76] FSB, IMF, and BIS (2011), p. 2.

[77] Smaga (2014), p. 2. For an overview of the relevant literature, see also Galati and Moessner (2013), pp. 854–856.

[78] Billio, Getmansky, Lo, and Pelizzon (2012), pp. 535–559.

[79] Billio, Getmansky, Lo, and Pelizzon (2010), p. 1.

[80] Inter alia, see Bisias, Flood, Lo, and Valavanis (2012), p. 1.

"bad news" about a financial institution, or even its failure, or the crash of a financial market leads in a sequential fashion to considerable adverse effects on one or several other financial institutions or markets'.[81] Alternatively, in a broader perspective, systemic events are considered not only the ones included in the narrow definition but also those having 'simultaneous adverse effects on a large number of institutions or markets as a consequence of severe and widespread […] shocks'.[82]

In both senses, these events can be triggered by either an exogenous shock (idiosyncratic or systemic) or an endogenous shock arising within the financial system or the economy at large.[83]

More importantly, in the narrow sense, a systemic event is deemed strong 'if the institution(s) affected in the second round or later actually fail as a consequence of the initial shock, although they have been fundamentally solvent ex ante, or if the market(s) affected in later rounds also crash and would not have done so without the initial shock'.[84] This latter scenario provides a conceptual background to describe the additional concept of *systemic crisis* which refers to 'a systemic event that affects a considerable number of financial institutions or markets in a strong sense, thereby severely impairing the general well-functioning (of an important part) of the financial system'.[85] From this, it can be assumed that systemic risk is the risk of experiencing systemic events in the strong sense[86] and its severity can be measured in terms of effect that these events may have on consumption, investment, growth, or economic welfare.[87]

Another relevant distinction regards the model used to describe risk.[88] The microprudential approach characterizes risk as *exogenous* (*i.e.* independent of individual agents' behaviors); the macroprudential dimension, instead, assumes to some extent risk as *endogenous* (*i.e.* dependent on collective behavior of the financial system) with respect to the aggregate behavior of the market.[89]

[81] De Bandt and Hartmann (2000), p. 10.
[82] ECB (2009), p. 134.
[83] De Bandt and Hartmann (2000), p. 10.
[84] Idem, p. 11.
[85] Idem, p. 11.
[86] Idem, p. 11.
[87] ECB (2009), pp. 134–135.
[88] Borio (2003), p. 3.
[89] Idem, p. 3. For example, see Martinez-Miera and Suarez (2012), analyzing the role of banks in generating endogenous systemic risk.

By modeling the responses of individual banks to exogenous risk, the microprudential dimension does not take into account the systemic effects of collective behaviors. Differently, the macroprudential approach, in describing financial stability, incorporates in its risk model the variability of the participants' behavior to the financial system. A number of factors drive heterogeneous market participants to behave homogeneously, that is, by selling at the same time or buying at the same time.[90] This homogeneous response is determined by endogenous factors that are capable to cause systemic risk. Under this assumption, systemic risk is seen as an endogenous product, and the macroprudential policy is thought to identify the endogenous processes that turn heterogeneity into homogeneity, thereby affecting the overall resilience of the financial system.[91]

Finally, the last difference between macroprudential and microprudential banking supervisions relies on the calibration of prudential controls. Contrary to the microprudential approach which assumes a bottom-up approach in calibrating prudential measures,[92] the macroprudential dimension is characterized by a top-down approach in setting prudential requirements. First, the macroprudential supervisor sets the relevant thresholds of acceptable aggregate losses that the entire system is capable to undertake.[93] Second, once the key risks to the financial sector are identified, the macroprudential analysis moves to the individual level.[94] Finally, after measuring the marginal contribution of each entity in the calculation of the aggregate risk, the relevant macroprudential tools are selected. In this respect, the measurement of correlations across financial assets becomes of primary importance.[95]

The stance of this volume is that the nature of macroprudential policy key components should be analyzed under a legal standpoint within the institutional framework in which they are set up. The economic modeling of such concepts should be accompanied by a thorough analysis of their legal and institutional settings. A legal analysis of macroprudential fundamentals can help identifying the very nature of its ultimate and

[90] See The Warwick Commission (2009), p. 13.

[91] Idem, p. 13.

[92] Borio (2003), p. 2. For additional insights, see also de Haan, Oosterloo, and Schoenmaker (2012), p. 394.

[93] Borio (2003), pp. 2–3.

[94] Kellermann, de Haan, and de Vries (2013), p. 214.

[95] Borio (2003), p. 3.

intermediate objectives, providing a better view on how macroprudential and monetary policies may concretely interact and cooperate.

Before moving to such an analysis, an additional topic, that is, the channels of financial instability, needs however to be discussed. Having acquaintance with these transmission channels is instrumental in analyzing how the legal features of macroprudential policies are developed and to what extent the macroprudential dimension of banking supervision has impact on monetary policy.

2.1.3 *Exploring the Channels of Instability*

A well-established literature today acknowledges the idea that financial markets are to be analyzed as a complex agent-based dynamic network, where the agents are highly interrelated from both the asset and the liability sides of their balance sheets.[96] More precisely, these connections result directly from mutual exposures in the interbank lending market and indirectly through similar holdings in their own portfolios and the same mass of depositors.[97]

The use of network theory is particularly important today because it allows analyzing systemic risk—*and financial stability*—by looking at how resilient the system is to contagion and identifying the major triggers and channels of contagion affecting the entire system.[98] As a complex adaptive system,[99] the financial system became over time progressively more complex and less diversified, resulting in greater fragility for the system as a whole.[100] However, the structure of the system led to homogeneity in the behavior of financial institutions, particularly among the compositions of their portfolios. For example, in July and August 2007, the market of asset-backed commercial papers collapsed when investors realized that money market mutual funds had massively invested in paper backed by

[96] Allen and Babus (2009), p. 368. See also Galati and Moessner (2013), p. 856. For a survey of the literature, see Hüser (2015).

[97] Allen and Babus (2009), p. 859.

[98] See Tumpel-Gugerell (2009). As a prominent example of this interdependence of the financial system, see the overview of the risk network of the US financial system drawn in Hautsch, Schaumburg, and Schienle (2014).

[99] About the notion of 'complex adaptive systems', see Chan (2001). In addition, see Ahmed, Elgazzar, and Hegazi (2005).

[100] Haldane (2009), p. 2. See also Allen, Babus, and Carletti (2010), p. 2; Yellen (2013).

subprime assets.[101] Suddenly, the investors' trust in all forms of private credit—from plain vanilla products to structured and opaque products—broke down, thereby drying up the funding source for structured investment vehicles and special-purpose vehicles.[102]

This unstable dynamic increases the probability that the failure of one institution is likely to coincide with the failure of other similar institutions. This is also the case when a bank experiences serious troubles and investors may fear that other banks with similar portfolio may also be in trouble.[103] The investors' reaction is a pessimistic mood capable to affect their confidence and their investment choices. If investors decide to withdraw their money, the financial market immediately dries up pushing the banking sector into a paralysis.

It follows that the interconnections of financial market, because of this 'robust-yet-fragile' property of complex networks, may serve as shock amplifiers,[104] leading an idiosyncratic event to turn into a systemic crisis. Thus, the inner nature of this fragility may cause a variety of externalities that may fluidize the transmission channels[105] for the propagation of the financial instability.

On the one hand, the tendency of the financial system to amplify adverse aggregate shocks may result in asset shrinkage from new lending by banks.[106] This asset shrinkage has two immediate and interconnected costs: the risk of credit crunch and fire sale of assets. If banks decide to cut new lending, the cost of credit for the corporate sector sharply increases, so affecting investment and employment. The ultimate result is the contraction of the economy.

Further, if a large fraction of the banking industry decides to shrink their assets at the same time by selling out a large quantity of the same illiquid securities, the price of such assets—given the following lower demand—fall down accordingly causing a risky fire sale.[107] Ultimately, such fire sale causes a further depression of price and a weakening of the

[101] See Tumpel-Gugerell (2009). For a better understanding of the role of commercial papers in the 2007–8 crisis, *see* Kacperczyk and Schnabl (2010), pp. 29–50.

[102] See Tumpel-Gugerell (2009).

[103] Allen, Babus, and Carletti (2010), p. 2.

[104] See Haldane (2009).

[105] For a general explanation of these transmission channels, in particular, see Kaufman (2000). See also IMF (2013a).

[106] See IMF (2013b), pp. 6–7.

[107] For insights, see Hanson, Kashyap, and Stein (2011), pp. 5–7.

banks' balance sheets with serious negative consequences in terms of prudential capital requirements. Indeed, the fire sale of assets reduces the capital ratios of banks and their availability of collaterals, thereby causing a further liquidation of underpriced assets with new losses. All these events trigger a systemic crisis.

On the other hand, the economic literature suggests that financial intermediaries tend to assume over-exposure in the upswing of the financial cycle. In boom times, banks have fewer incentives to scrutinize potential borrowers' creditworthiness due to the stronger competitive pressure within the credit market.[108] It follows a reduction in monitoring and an increase in lending to bad borrowers that fuels even further the credit booms.[109] The over-borrowing may lead to excessive leverage and inflated asset prices, increasing the vulnerability of the system as soon as the contractionary stage of the business cycle appears reversing asset prices' trend.[110] In this respect, the higher asset price volatility and the erosion of the lending standards may enhance the likelihood of macroeconomic shocks.

Moreover, when credit is growing rapidly, there is an excessive reliance on short-term wholesale funding provided by banks and non-banks. Despite its importance in the funding structure of banks, wholesale funding may be a major source of instability.[111] In particular, this source of short-term financing make banks more interconnected because banks and non-banks provide liquidity to each other. Banks are incentivized to rely on wholesale funding because it results cheaper than other funding sources.[112]

However, the interbank market is not adequately monitored by the liquidity providers because they know they can easily decide not to roll over their funding should negative information on the creditworthiness of borrowers come out. Yet, if the asset value of a particular bank declines on negative public news, the complex interconnections of the interbank market may

[108] De Nicolò, Favara, and Ratnovski (2012), p. 8. See also Gorton and He (2008), pp. 1181–1214.

[109] De Nicolò, Favara, and Ratnovski (2012), p. 8. See also Dell'Ariccia and Marquez (2004), pp. 185–214, where the authors argue that if the borrowers' pool is sufficiently correlated, an increase in the competitiveness of uninformed lenders can worsen the informed lender's overall loan portfolio.

[110] See De Nicolò, Favara, and Ratnovski (2012), p. 8. On the issue, *cf.* IMF (2013b), p. 7.

[111] On the issue in general, see IMF (2011a), p. 113.

[112] Brunnermeier and Oehmke (2013), pp. 484–485.

hamper its ability to obtain new funds. As a result, this bank could have excessive incentives to obtain new liquidity by an asset fire sale triggering a potential contagion with adverse real consequences.[113]

All these externalities have been of primary importance in the outbreak of the 2007–8 financial crises questioning the legal foundations of the financial system. When the mainstream view on the adequacy of microprudential instruments to ensure the soundness of the banking sector proved erroneous, policymakers felt the need to renew the approach on the global regulatory framework. Whatever the transmission channel considered, the severity and the scope of the crisis proved that the systemic vulnerabilities related to the financial system require a new regulatory response under a broader macroeconomic perspective. It is precisely at this point that macroprudential regulation comes into play.

2.2 Legal Components of the Macroprudential Policy Definition

The economics behind macroprudential key concepts is of primary importance to understand the theoretical underpinnings of macroprudential policies whose development at the EU level (and abroad) is still an ongoing process.[114] Any economic insight onto this field of research suffers from a lack of precision in establishing a common language[115] that policymakers and regulators may adopt to define the core components of macroprudential regulations.

One of the main criticalities today when discussing macroprudential policy is that an operational definition of its ultimate and intermediate objectives is still missing. Moreover, despite the establishment of a large variety of indicators and early warning methodologies to signal system-wide shocks, a coherent framework to interpret, assess, and measure data on the need of macroprudential intervention is currently not available.[116]

Against this backdrop, we take a different approach in defining what macroprudential policy is and what an effective macroprudential framework entails. The basic idea is that a stricter legal inquiry on macroprudential

[113] For details, see Acharya, Philippon, Richardson, and Roubini (2009), pp. 89–137. See also Huang and Ratnovski (2010).

[114] See Borio (2014).

[115] Caruana and Cohen (2014), p. 16.

[116] See Visco (2011).

policy may shed some light on the blurred policy perimeter envisioned by the economic literature. The goal of this section is therefore to deconstruct the economic concepts explained in the previous section in light of a pure legal interpretation. Deconstructing and reconstructing objectives and the scope of macroprudential supervision by looking at its legal components will allow us to establish one broad definition of macroprudential policy that may best reconcile its economic foundations and the corresponding regulatory instruments.

2.2.1 *Objectives of Macroprudential Policy: Deconstructing Financial Stability and Systemic Risk*

A legal analysis of macroprudential policy should start from the recognition of its fundamental elements. Any policy decision regarding a matter of regulation must be informed to certain criteria capable to differentiate whether a specific regulatory measure may be deemed as falling within the domain of one policy or another. To put it in a nutshell, we need to identify a methodology that allow us to understand whether an instrument can be considered as really *macroprudential* in nature. This identification can be easily performed if the general categories of *objectives*, *competences*, and *instruments* are used.

A legal reconstruction of the macroprudential policy definition can rely on the concepts laid down in the relevant legislation that define what *objectives*, *competences*, and *instruments* of macroprudential supervision are. The objectives represent pivotal elements of this analysis as they allow determining the purpose of the policy actions, acting as legislative bases to set up functions, powers, and tasks of the competent authorities. Explicit objectives also help competent authorities to guide their decision-making processes and strengthen their accountability by limiting the likelihood of abuse of power.[117]

It is worth noting that a number of national central banks and supervisory authorities in Europe are statutorily entrusted with a 'financial stability objective' whose meaning reflects to various degrees the purpose of generally ensuring, contributing, or promoting the stability of the financial system as a whole.[118] As explained in the previous section, the definition of

[117] IMF (2013b), pp. 6–7.

[118] For a survey of central bank law and on the assignment of financial stability objectives, see Gianviti (2010), pp. 454–463; Lastra (2015), pp. 318–323.

this financial stability objective is backed by a segment of the economic scholarship that used to justify in this way the existence of the macroprudential dimension in banking supervision.

But the use of legal reasoning allows us to question whether the 'financial stability objective' by itself permits a clear recognition of what tasks, instruments, and powers constitute macroprudential policy. If this is not the case, other legal elements should be considered in order to clarify the realm of this policy.

The problem with the notion of financial stability and, thus, with the 'financial stability objective' set out in many jurisdictions is that it does not provide a rigorous definition that may guide the decision-making processes of public authorities in macroprudential policy. This definition is not capable by itself to support public actions in banking supervision given its ambiguity, making it difficult to set up a proper accountability framework for the authorities involved.

One national authority entrusted with the financial stability objective could take a number of actions that can 'promote the stability of the financial system as a whole'. The vagueness of this provision does not permit however to clearly recognize whether the actions taken were consistent with the competences statutorily assigned to the central bank. National authorities could eventually take whatever action they deem necessary without any clear constraints.

The concept of financial stability is inherently multidimensional.[119] For example, the protection of depositors,[120] the protection of public confidence in the financial markets,[121] the protection of public funds,[122] the resilience of the banking sector,[123] and the resolution of a failing credit institution[124] are all dimensions of financial stability requiring a wide range of different prudential (both *micro-* and *macro-*) and non-prudential measures.

[119] Jeanneau (2014), pp. 48–49.

[120] For example, see the Recital (3) of the Directive 2014/49/EU on Deposit Guarantee Schemes. On this issue, see also Bank of England, HM Treasury, FSA (2008).

[121] For example, see Aziz (2007).

[122] Among others, see Section 4 of the UK Banking Act (2009).

[123] See BCSB (2009), p. 11. See also the Proposal for a Regulation of the European Parliament and of the Council on structural measures improving the resilience of EU credit institutions COM/2014/043 final—2014/0020 (COD), whose aim is to enhance the financial stability in the Union by means of structural reform of large banks.

[124] See the Recital (18) of the Directive 2014/59/EU establishing a common framework for the recovery and resolution of credit institutions (BRRD).

These dimensions not only involve different instruments, scope, and powers rowing in the same direction, but they may also involve instruments and powers conflicting with each other, striking down any proposal to establish a coherent macroprudential framework based on the objective of financial stability.[125] An example may be found in the bail-in instrument for the orderly resolution of banks. While the bail-in instrument serves the primary purpose to protect public funds by reducing the potential public cost of possible bank failure,[126] it could also create instability in other parts of the financial network, as, for example, among insurers, asset management firms, or other bank holding bonds that are wiped out.[127] From a legal perspective, this means that the proper objective of the macroprudential regulation cannot be the *financial stability objective*.

Consequently, the legal foundation of the macroprudential dimension in banking supervision is to be found in another key notion. In particular, it can be assumed that the ultimate objective of macroprudential banking supervision is to be found in preventing and mitigating systemic risk.[128]

At the global level, the FSB, the IMF, and the BIS have clearly affirmed that the objective of macroprudential policy is to limit systemic risk, which is defined as 'the risk of widespread disruptions to the provision of financial services that have serious negative consequences for the economy at large'.[129]

Looking at the US experience, the Dodd-Frank Act of 2010[130] established a new regulatory framework of macroprudential oversight whose prime objective is to identify, analyze, and discipline systemic risk.[131] In the

[125] Jeanneau (2014), pp. 48–49. The author provides a list of examples in which the multiple dimensions of financial stability may conflict with each other.

[126] See the Recital (67) of the BRRD on the bail-in tool.

[127] See Finance Watch (2015). For details, see also Dombret and Lucius (2013).

[128] FSB, IMF, and BIS (2011), p. 3. See also IMF (2011b).

[129] FSB, IMF, and BIS (2011), p. 4.

[130] Dodd-Frank Wall Street Reform and Consumer Protection Act. Public Law, No. 111–203. H.R. 4173 (2010).

[131] For details, see Murphy (2013), pp. 4–9. Although the Dodd-Frank Act does not provide any general definition of systemic risk, it uses this notion several times when attributing the tasks of the newly established macroprudential agency, which is the Financial Stability Oversight Council (FSOC). For example, Section 112 (b) (1) requires member agencies of the FSOC to submit a signed statement to Congress if the agency believes that all reasonable steps are being taken 'to ensure financial stability and to mitigate systemic risk that would negatively affect the economy'. It seems therefore clear that even in the United States, the primary objective of the macroprudential oversight is to assess and mitigate systemic risk. On this issue, see also Napoletano (2014), pp. 42–47.

United Kingdom, the Financial Services Act of 2012,[132] in assigning macroprudential supervisory functions to the newly formed Financial Policy Committee of the Bank of England (FPC),[133] states that the prime responsibility of the FPC is to identify, monitor, and take action to remove or reduce systemic risks with a view to protect and enhance the resilience of the UK financial system.[134]

At the European level, the TFEU does not mention the concept of systemic risk. Instead, the main reference to this notion can be found in Regulation (EU) No. 1092/2010 of the European Parliament and of the Council of 24 November 2010 establishing the European Systemic Risk Board (ESRB),[135] which states the objective of macroprudential oversight is to 'contribute to the prevention or mitigation of systemic risks to financial stability in the Union that arise from developments within the financial system and taking into account macroeconomic developments, so as to avoid periods of widespread financial distress'.[136] In this respect, the primary purpose of macroprudential supervision is to mitigate the exposure of the system to the risk of failure of its systemic components, thereby enhancing the resilience of the whole financial system against the likelihood of future shocks.[137]

As a matter of fact, the notion of systemic risk seems to be explicitly recognized by the national and international lawmakers as a cornerstone of the legal macroprudential framework. On the issue, the European legislator provides a basic legal definition of systemic risk which is recognized as the 'risk of disruption in the financial system with the potential to have serious negative consequences for the internal market and the real economy'.[138]

Despite its broad and challenging nature,[139] it is reasonable to assume that a policy measure—or instrument—can be considered 'macroprudential' only if its primary objective is to help mitigate the risk of disruption in

[132] See Financial Services Act 2012 (Chapter 21).

[133] With respect to the role of the FPC in the macroprudential policy management see Sharp (2014); Tucker, Hall, and Pattani (2013), pp. 192–200.

[134] See Section 9 (C2) of the Financial Services Act 2012.

[135] A general description of mandate, tasks, and governance arrangements for macroprudential policy is provided in the next section of this volume.

[136] See Article 3 of the Regulation (EU) No. 1092/2010.

[137] See the Recital (10) of the Regulation (EU) No. 1092/2010.

[138] See Article 2(c) of the Regulation (EU) No. 1092/2010. In addition, see Article 3(10) of the Directive 2013/36/EU. On the issue, see also Głuch, Škovranová, and Stenströmp (2013), p. 2.

[139] See Visco (2011), p. 129, arguing that systemic risk presents a number of challenges to the policymaker given its difficulty in being measured and spotted ex ante.

the financial market caused by the failure of its systemic components that may affect to some extent the real economy.

That said it is necessary to clarify whether it is possible to give more precise substance to the legal concept of systemic risk. If key elements highlighted in the legal definition of systemic risk are the likelihood of a systemic event (trigger or shock) and its domino effect into the real economy,[140] a way to specify more clearly the legal content of such basic components is found.

2.2.2 *The Reconstruction of Financial Stability: Insights into the Cross-Sectional Dimension of Systemic Risk*

The economic literature suggests that the notion of systemic risk cannot be fully captured without recognizing its Janus-faced emerging nature.[141] Under this perspective, the concept of systemic risk is traditionally characterized by both a time and cross-sectional dimension whose understanding is necessary to allow for recognition of the regulatory instruments available within the macroprudential framework. This *de facto* distinction acknowledges that any dimension is characterized by own features and criticalities, thereby requiring a specific set of tools deemed to manage the system-wide shocks associated to it.[142]

On the one hand, in its time dimension, systemic risk relates to the intrinsic procyclicality of financial system which is likely to lead over time to the materialization of dangerous financial imbalances.[143] Consequently, major role of macroprudential policy is to increase the resilience of the financial system by setting out a wide range of *countercyclical* instruments[144] designed to assess, monitor, and, if possible, mitigate the extremes of the financial cycles.[145]

[140] A primary investigation on the concept of systemic risk under a legal standpoint is offered by Schwarcz (2008), pp. 193–249.

[141] Inter alia, see Borio (2003), pp. 10–11; Galati and Moessner (2013), p. 847; Caruana and Cohen (2014), pp. 17–18. See also Krishnamurti and Lee (2014).

[142] Caruana and Cohen (2014), p. 17. See also Servén (2010), p. 131.

[143] Idem, p. 17. There is an extensive literature on the role of procyclical behaviors in financial stability. For a general overview, see Borio, Furfine, and Lowe (2001); Landau (2009); Rochet (2008). In addition, see Borio (2012).

[144] With respect to the rationale of countercyclical regulatory instruments, see Goodhart (2009), pp. 9–20. For a comprehensive list of countercyclical instruments, see BIS (2010), pp. 91–97.

[145] Caruana and Cohen (2014), p. 17.

Within this category, countercyclical capital buffers, countercyclical accounting standards, funding liquidity requirements, and risk concentration measures are dominant.[146] These instruments initially are intended to signal, on an ongoing basis, the fluctuations of the financial cycle and assess the risk concentration and the likelihood of shocks across the system. Afterward, they ***should*** work as cushion and constrain the credit and asset price booms should a bust materialize over the financial cycle.[147]

On the other hand, in its cross-sectional dimension, systemic risk is characterized by common exposures, risk concentrations, and balance sheet interlinkages across entities and markets at any point in time.[148] Accordingly, the focus of this dimension is on correlated exposures of financial intermediaries and their behavioral responses which require tools to measure, monitor, and mitigate risks primarily associated to the 'Global Systemically Important Institutions' (GSIIs) and the banking sector as a whole.[149]

Under this perspective, the size and complexity of bank's balance sheet assume a dominant role: larger institutions are expected to have higher risks and, thus, require tighter prudential standards to counter possible distress spillovers across the system.[150] Among the instruments designed under the cross-sectional dimension, the systemic capital surcharges and higher loss absorbing capacity standards are of primary importance.[151]

This traditional distinction of systemic risk is useful, even under a legal standpoint, to design a range of macroprudential instruments that may help monitor and mitigate the vulnerabilities arising in any of such dimension. But it does not seem to help very much in providing deeper legal significance to the concept of systemic risk. In contrast, this concept should be deconstructed by its smaller components that can be legally defined. Once these components have been established, they may serve as

[146] See Galati and Moessner (2013), p. 851. See also on the issue Financial Stability Forum (2009). For a list of these instruments *cf.* ESRB (2014a).

[147] Caruana and Cohen (2014), p. 17.

[148] Idem, p. 17.

[149] Idem, p. 18.

[150] See Borio (2003), p. 10.

[151] Caruana and Cohen (2014), p. 18. For a survey on capital surcharges, see Board of Governors of the Federal Reserve System, *Draft Notice of Proposed Rulemaking—Capital Surcharge for Systemically Important U.S. bank Holding Companies*, 9 December 2014; On the concept of 'loss-absorbing capacity', see BIS (2013) and FSB (2014).

legal foundations for the establishment of the macroprudential policy mandate and its related instruments.

At the European level, the taxonomy for the sources of systemic risk recognized by the ESRB in its recommendation on the intermediate objectives of macroprudential policy[152] and by the European Banking Authority (EBA) in one of its legal opinions[153] seems to be tailored for our reasoning. Both authorities recognize seven categories of systemic risk, namely, (1) structural risks, (2) cyclical risk, (3) risks caused by SII, (4) systemic funding risks, (5) structural exposure-based risk, (6) cyclical exposure-based risks, and (7) other systemic risks.[154]

All of these systemic risk categories have been accurately defined by the ESRB and EBA, thereby providing a concrete background for the recognition of what systemic risk is under a legal perspective. In particular,

1. 'Structural and cyclical risks'[155] are qualified as the risk of excessive credit growth and leverage. This risk materializes in particular 'when excessive credit growth coincides with unsustainable developments in real estate markets that lead to a build-up of leverage in the private sector'.[156]

[152] In detail, see the ESRB Recommendation of 4 April 2013 on intermediate objectives and instruments of macro-prudential policy (ESRB/2013/1). Section I—Recommendation A. See also ESRB (2014a), pp. 7–9.

[153] See EBA (2014).

[154] It must be noted that the same legal categories have been established in a number of EU countries. For example, the *Ausschuss für Finanzstabilität*, the German national macroprudential authority, published in 2013 its macroprudential strategy including five risk factors which are close to the ESRB's proposed risks. The list of these systemic risk factors is laid down in paragraph 2(8) of the macroprudential policy strategy and includes (a) excessive credit growth and leverage (in the financial system or other sectors); (b) excessive maturity/currency/liquidity transformation; (c) excessive direct and indirect exposure concentrations (the latter owing to interconnectedness), including disruptions caused by the disorderly market exit of systemically important financial institutions as a risk factor; (d) systemic impact of misaligned incentives and moral hazard—this includes insufficient resilience of systemically important financial intermediaries as a risk factor; (e) systemic impact of disruptions to financial market infrastructures.

[155] The EBA prefers to distinguish between structural and cyclical risks, putting them into two separate categories. However, since there is no clear distinction between them, we prefer to use only one category for both risks. The ESRB uses the same approach, considering both within the same category.

[156] ESRB (2014a), p. 8.

2. 'Risks caused by SII' are defined as the risks posed by the systemic impact of misaligned incentives aimed at reducing moral hazard.[157] This is the risk of moral hazard related to the presence of 'to-big-to-fail' financial institutions which requires greater resilience to counterbalance the negative effects of implicit government guarantees.[158]
3. 'Systemic funding risks' are caused by maturity mismatch and market illiquidity. As explained by the ESRB,[159] both sides of banks' balance sheets are subject to liquidity risk: market illiquidity on the asset side and funding risk on the liability side. Both risks may be source of fire sales and contagion.[160]
4. 'Exposure-based risks' are those risks related to common exposures, contagion, and interconnectedness.[161] More precisely, these are risks arising from large exposures to individual counterparties or groups of connected counterparties which are kept to an acceptable level.[162] As explained by the ESRB, they can be direct or indirect. Direct concentration risks arise from large exposures to specific sectors or asset classes. Indirect concentration risks arise when a shock weakens banks through contagion channels, such as interconnectedness, asset fire sales, and a general dry-up of liquidity.[163]
5. 'Other systemic risks' is a general category[164] that regards those risks that are not captured by other sources and/or we are not aware of. An example of these risks is the interest rate risk from the banking book which is the risk to the bank's capital and earnings arising from adverse movements in interest rates that affect the institution's banking book.[165] Another example is the sovereign risk,[166] due to the growing bank-sovereign nexus and caused by the zero risk-weighting treatment of sovereign exposures in the calculation of banks' capital requirements.

[157] ESRB (2014a), p. 13.
[158] Narodna Banka Slovenska (2014), p. 4.
[159] ESRB (2014a), p. 10.
[160] ESRB (2014a), p. 10.
[161] Idem, pp. 11–12.
[162] On the issue, see the EBA Technical Standards and Guidelines on large exposure, for example, CEBS Guidelines on the implementation of the revised large exposures regime (11 December 2009). For further insights, see also Tucker et al. (2013), pp. 193–194.
[163] ESRB (2014a), p. 12.
[164] See EBA (2014), p. 11.
[165] For details, see BCBS (2016), p. 3.
[166] For a thorough analysis, see ESRB (2015).

As a matter of fact, each category of risk listed above presents all the essential elements of the legal definition of systemic risk laid out in the EU legal framework. In particular, the disruption of the financial system as a whole and the domino effect for the internal market and the real economy are common characteristics for any of the types recognized by the European authorities.

This leads to the consideration that the broad nature of the legal definition of systemic risk may be restricted and refined through the recognition of the different categories of risk that are institutionally recognized as *systemic*. As a result, this taxonomy not only provides the sources of systemic risk that the macroprudential instruments are thought to deal with, but it also allows, from a legal standpoint, to spot the key components of its legal dimension. As such, the different categories of systemic risk represent not only the intermediate objectives of macroprudential policy[167] but also the legal foundations for the assignment of the macroprudential supervisory objective and the development of the regulatory macroprudential toolbox.[168]

Accordingly, a legal definition of macroprudential banking supervision can be established, at this point, as a set of institutional powers and regulatory tools specifically assigned to assess, prevent, or mitigate the different categories of risk arising in the banking sector institutionally recognized as *systemic* because of their capacity to disrupt the financial markets and affect the real economy.[169] The macroprudential legal objective so defined is consistently narrow and, thus, constrains the discretionary use of powers.[170]

[167] ESRB (2014a), p. 7.

[168] For details, see EBA (2014), p. 14, arguing that 'the instrument's purpose with respect to is macro and micro use should be unambiguous and not subject to interpretation, but also that the risks addressed (structural/cyclical risks) and the scope of the instrument (bank specific/systemic wide) are adequately specified'. The EBA also states that 'the goal and purpose of each macroprudential rule should be clearly defined. [...] all markets participants and regulators (competent and designed) should have the same understanding of the risks and exposures that can be covered by the rule, and about the situations in which the rule may be applied'.

[169] Of the same opinion, see Nier (2011) pp. R2–R3. A different perspective on the definition of macroprudential banking supervision is instead provided by Tröger (2015), p. 576.

[170] Although the macroprudential objectives hereafter proposed are not entirely satisfactory, see also Nier (2011), pp. R7–R8.

2.2.3 *The Macroprudential Framework: Indicators, Strategies, and Tools*

The above reasoning centered upon the recognition of the legal objective of macroprudential policy, identified, as argued above, in assessing, monitoring, and mitigating risks deemed as systemic. From the recognition of this objective and its legal foundations, it can be easily assumed that the macroprudential authority has specific supervisory powers, expectations, and tasks.[171] This authority is supposed to conduct the macroprudential surveillance on systemic risks in an effort to avoid the disruption of the financial system as a whole and prevent spillovers to the real economy. This surveillance requires instruments for a rapid and effective diagnosis: to this purpose, the macroprudential objective should include the responsibility to monitor and measure the emergence of systemic risks on an ongoing basis.[172] Moreover, should systemic risks materialize, this would require a prompt intervention as to contain and alleviate the related negative externalities.[173]

The construction of the macroprudential framework requires the establishment of a proper menu of indicators, strategies, and regulatory tools which are deemed to comply with the scope of this objective[174] and that may permit to concretize the achievement of the macroprudential objective.

In detail, the macroprudential framework should firstly comprise a specific set of indicators capable to signal the emergence of potential categories of systemic risk and assess its severity. Once the uprising of a specific category of systemic risk is detected, the macroprudential framework should provide a range of strategies designed to mitigate it. Any strategy would imply the application of specific macroprudential powers designed to address the externalities related to that peculiar category of risk.[175] The macroprudential framework so designed becomes simple enough to understand the underlying dynamics of the regulatory interventions,

[171] Kawai and Pomerleano (2010), p. 7.

[172] See FSB, IMF, and BIS (2011), pp. 3–4.

[173] On this important topic, see Domanski and Ng (2011), p. 89, according to which elements of a macroprudential policy framework should be 'an objective, diagnostic tools, instruments, an operating strategy, and governance arrangements'.

[174] See Collin, Druant, and Ferrari (2014), p. 87.

[175] According to ESRB (2014a), a macroprudential policy strategy follows four stages and is designed to link together objectives to indicators and instruments.

offering clear guidance to policymakers in the applications of strategies and tools.[176] The aim of this section is to provide a brief overview of how this macroprudential framework is consistently tailored.

2.2.3.1 Indicators for Tracking Systemic Risks

To begin with, the macroprudential framework must comprise a set of systemic risk indicators. Any macroprudential policy intervention has to be grounded upon detailed information on when and where systemic risks are appearing and on the transmission channels that are supposed to carry on the disruption of the real economy.[177] Given the complexity of interlinkages in the financial system and the difficulty to measure systemic risks, multiple methodologies and various categories of quantitative and qualitative indicators have been proposed.[178]

A prominent work in this regard is represented by the 'Financial Soundness Indicators', developed by the IMF in 2006 as a body of economic statistics aimed at supporting macroprudential analysis and assessing the vulnerabilities of financial systems.[179] Since then, the ECB has monitored the development of the IMF initiative, and, along with the FSB and ESRB, it is currently developing its own systemic risk indicators and early warning signals in order to strengthen the macroprudential oversight in the EU.[180]

However, despite the number of frameworks available at the global level, common features can be recognized. In particular, the diagnostic of systemic risks must signal the different phases of systemic risk cycle which

[176] For a discussion of the ideal macroprudential framework, see Angelini, Neri, and Panetta (2011), p. 9.

[177] Blancher, Mitra, Morsy, Otani, Severo, and Valderrama (2013), p. 4.

[178] The literature concerning this subject is quite broad. For details, inter alia, see Rodríguez-Moreno and Peña (2013); Patro, Qi, and Sun (2013); He and Krishnamurthy (2014); De Nicolò and Lucchetta (2010); Acharya, Pedersen, Philippon, and Richardson (2010).

[179] See IMF (2006). On the issue, see also Xingyuan Che and Shinagawa (2014).

[180] See Agresti, Baudino, and Poloni (2008); Schwaab, Koopman, and Lucas (2011). See also the final results of the *Report on the Macro-prudential Research Network (MARS)*, published by the ECB on 23 June 2014. This report is available online at http://www.ecb.europa.eu/press/pr/date/2014/html/pr140623.en.html. Instead, for an overview of the international and European developments of systemic risk indicators, see Israël, Sandars, Schubert, and Fischer (2013).

can be summarized as follows: (1) the build-up phase, (2) the shock materialization phase, and (3) the amplification and propagation phase.[181]

1. Indicators signaling the build-up phase can be divided into two broad categories: macroeconomic/macro-financial indicators and aggregate balance sheet indicators. The former are thought to assess the systemic risk at the aggregate level; the latter are designed to signal a build-up of risks in banks and potential spillovers to the real economy.[182]
2. Indicators relevant for the second phase are aimed at capturing the different possible sources of systemic risk and measuring the probability and size of shocks to the financial system and the rest of the economy.[183]
3. The amplification and propagation phase requires indicators capable to capture the amplification mechanisms, such as interconnections between financial institutions, potential fire sales, as well as the degree of exposures to particular assets.[184]

In order to monitor and measure any risk development, all the above indicators should consider, in particular:

1. the total credit growth and macroeconomic drivers of imbalances;
2. financial interrelations between the financial and real sectors; and
3. the structure of the banking system and linkages across key classes of intermediaries and market infrastructures.[185]

More importantly, the indicators must be selected and calibrated in order to capture the different categories of systemic risk as defined above.[186] This means that for any source of systemic risk a proper set of targeted indicators, assessing and monitoring each phase of its cycle, is required. To provide some examples, the following table (Table 2.1) offers a non-exhaustive set of indicators for each category of systemic risk during the three stages of its cycle.

[181] IMF (2013a), p. 16.
[182] ESRB (2014a), pp. 39–40.
[183] For details, see IMF (2011c), p. 1.
[184] Blancher, Mitra, Morsy, Otani, Severo, and Valderrama (2013), p. 7.
[185] IMF (2013a), p. 16.
[186] See Jahn and Kick (2012), p. 1.

Table 2.1 Example of indicators for typology of systemic risk

Systemic risks	*Indicators*		
	Build-up	*Shock materialization*	*Amplification and propagation*
Structural and cyclical risks	Credit/GDP gap, real estate price-based indicators; current account/GDP ratio; aggregate bank balance sheet-based indicators; household debt/income	Leverage ratios; structural profitability indicators, asset price booms; sectoral credit concentration; non-performing loans and provisions; sectoral indebtedness	Financial market correlations; trade spillovers
Risks caused by SII	Market-based probability of default; SII indicators on size, interconnectedness, substitutability, complexity	Conditional value-at-risk (CoVaR); returns spillovers; stress tests	Distress spillovers; cross-border network contagion
Systemic funding risks	Liquid assets/total assets; central bank lending; weighted average maturity of assets and liabilities; funding ratios; net open position in foreign currencies/total assets	Financial market liquidity indicator; market liquidity metrics; interbank interest rate spreads; CDS spreads; segmentation of interbank rates; maturity structure of assets and liabilities	Indicators of secondary market liquidity
Structural and cyclical exposure-based risks	Mortgages/total assets; asset-backed securities/ total assets; cross-border interconnectedness; financial corporate debt/ GDP	Concentration indicators, large exposure indicators	Intra-financial assets/total assets; joint distress indicators; number of banks failing due to contagion; financial network indicators
Other risks (i.e. sovereign risk)	Country-risk models, debt sustainability indicators, fiscal stress indicators	Crisis prediction models	Macro stress tests, funding shock scenarios

The quantitative indicators mentioned in this table are picked up from different sources. Inter alia, see ESRB (2014a); Blancher, Mitra, Morsy, Otani, Severo, and Valderrama (2013); Evans, Leone, Gill, and Hilbers (2000)

2.2.3.2 *Macroprudential Policy Strategies*

Another key element of the macroprudential toolbox is the existence of operating strategies within a well-settled institutional architecture.[187] As a matter of fact, a coherent macroprudential strategy is to be clearly defined in order to support accountability and credibility of the macroprudential supervisory actions.[188] The purpose of this operating strategy is to link together the various sources of systemic risk, the indicators, and their assessments along with a proper set of macroprudential instruments.[189]

For this reason, the choice of the proper strategy must take fully into account the category of systemic risk that may arise in the different stages of the financial cycle. When the indicators identify and assess the build-up of one systemic risk typology, the related strategy should comprise a set of instruments designed to mitigate it prior to its materialization.[190]

After the risk materializes, the policy strategy should require the exercise of sound judgment in the application of the macroprudential tools and accurate oversight of the risk transmission channels.[191] In addition, it should be noted that multiple stages characterize the operating strategy: in the first stage, the typology of risk must be detected and measured; in the second stage, the proper instruments are chosen and calibrated to the specific source of risk; in the third one, the macroprudential instruments are expected to be activated.

At last, an ex post assessment on the impact of the instrument activation completes the implementation of the operating strategy.[192] Following the ex post assessments, the macroprudential authority should always have the option to adjust or deactivate its strategy according to the sensitivity of the financial systems and the outcome obtained.[193]

Of primary importance in the development of the operating strategy are a centralized and transparent decision-making process and a simple

[187] For example, see Deutsche Bundesbank (2013), p. 39.

[188] *Inter alia*, see Banco De Portugal (2014a), p. 72; Banka Slovenjie (2015), p. 4.

[189] Houben, van der Molen, and Wierts (2012), p. 14.

[190] Banco De Portugal (2014a), p. 63.

[191] ESRB (2014b), p. 6.

[192] See Idem, p. 14.

[193] Oet, Ong, and Gramlich (2013), p. 1. See also Recommendation of the European Systemic Risk Board of 4 April 2013 on intermediate objectives and instruments of macroprudential policy (ESRB/2013/1), sub-recommendation C(2).

communication policy.[194] In particular, transparency is required both ex ante and ex post the implementation of the strategy.

Ex ante transparency allows policy decisions to be better informed as macroprudential authorities may obtain more information to better understand whether policy decisions are effective and how credit institutions can respond to changes in policy.[195] By contrast, ex post transparency ensures the accountability of its internal decision-making process and the administrative legality of the policy decisions.[196]

2.2.3.3 The 'Macroprudential Toolkit'

The macroprudential framework is completed by a wide range of regulatory tools. The reconnaissance of the different typologies of systemic risk is pivotal in designing and choosing this toolkit, given that each tool is supposed to prevent or mitigate the emergence of one specific risk category.[197] More in detail, when the macroprudential authority recognizes the build-up of one systemic risk typology, it can select the appropriate tool from the range of instruments available within the operating strategy to help prevent its materialization and/or amplification. Table 2.2 categorizes some of the macroprudential instruments available according to both the different typologies of risk they are supposed to address and possible policy strategies undertaken by the macroprudential authorities.

Capital instruments are generally thought to increase the resilience of the banking sector against structural and cyclical risks. SII buffers and capital surcharges are designed to address risks caused by SII. Liquidity instruments are instead supposed to address systemic funding risks. Ultimately, large exposures restrictions and sectoral capital requirements prevent the build-up of exposure-based risks.

On the one hand, multiple instruments—*or a combination of them*—can be used to deal with a specific source of systemic risk, reflecting the coexistence of different macroprudential policy strategies. Against this backdrop, using a combination of macroprudential instruments may have the advantage of targeting different aspects of the same risk, reducing the

[194] Houben, van der Molen, and Wierts (2012), p. 22. About the role of communication strategies, see Ng (2012). See also Osiński, Seal, and Hoogduin (2013), p. 21.

[195] See Coglianese, Kilmartin, and Mendelson (2009), pp. 927–928.

[196] For details, see Idem, p. 928.

[197] Knot (2014), p. 27.

Table 2.2 Lists of macroprudential tools classified by systemic risk typology and strategy

Systemic risks						
		Structural and cyclical risks	*Risks caused by SII*	*Systemic funding risks*	*Structural and cyclical exposure-based risks*	*Other systemic risks*
Strategies	Increase resilience of banking sector	Countercyclical capital buffers; sectoral capital requirements; loan-to-value (LTV) cap; credit tools (LTI/DSTI)	SII buffers; O-SII buffer; capital surcharges; systemic risk buffer; own funds; conservation buffer	Liquidity coverage ratio (LCR); net stable funding ratio (NSFR); loan-to-deposit ratio (LTD); liquidity charge	Sectoral capital requirements; systemic risk buffer; large exposure limits	All tools
	Dampening excessive credit growth	Countercyclical capital buffers; sectoral capital requirements; loan-to-value (LTV) credit tools (LTI/DSTI)	SII buffers; O-SII buffer; capital surcharges; systemic risk buffer; own funds; conservation buffer	Loan-to-deposit ratio (LTD); margin and haircut requirements	Systemic risk buffers; large exposures limits	All tools
	Limit leverage and increase funding costs	Leverage ratio; own funds; conservation buffer	SII buffers; O-SII buffer; additional liquidity requirements for SII	Liquidity coverage ratio (LCR); liquidity charge; other liquidity buffers	Systemic risk buffers; large exposure limits; own funds; conservation buffer	All tools
	Increase market discipline and reduce information uncertainty	Pillar 2 instruments; disclosure through stress tests, additional disclosure requirements	Pillar 2 instruments; disclosure through stress tests; additional disclosure requirements	Pillar 2 instruments; disclosure through stress tests; additional disclosure requirements	Pillar 2 instruments; disclosure through stress tests; additional disclosure requirements	Pillar 2 instruments; disclosure through stress tests; additional disclosure requirements

This table is partially derived from Grace, Hallissey, and Woods (2015), p. 95. The strategies listed in this table are not exhaustive, and macroprudential authorities may choose to diversify or combine their strategies to better pursue their tasks

incentives for credit leakages[198] and ensuring greater effectiveness.[199] On the other hand, one tool can be used to address different categories of systemic risk.

The international experience shows that macroprudential instruments can be developed in two fashions: firstly, it is possible to adapt existing microprudential tools and standards, such as stronger capital and liquidity buffers, in order to increase the aggregate resilience of the banking sector against exposures and vulnerabilities of systemic shocks.[200] Secondly, the macroprudential toolkit can be composed of innovative dynamic tools, such as countercyclical measures, acting as automatic stabilizers in response to the fluctuations of the financial cycle.[201] In addition, it would also be possible to use under the macroprudential umbrella some instruments typically belonging to other public policies, such as fiscal, monetary, and administrative ones.[202] This is the case, for example, of some housing-related taxes or tax relief on mortgage interest payments that may work as macroprudential credit tools to dampening credit demand of borrowers.[203]

Finally, a last reference to the ongoing debate between a rule-based approach and a discretion-based approach in developing and calibrating macroprudential instruments seems necessary.[204]

In the first case, macroprudential authorities use rules to lay out the key features of macroprudential tools and offer some guidance for implementing the policy strategy. This option offers several advantages for the achievement of the macroprudential objective. In particular, the reduction

[198] Credit leakages occur when regulatory interventions are able to influence the aggregate supply of credit in the banking sector, thereby incentivizing other less regulated credit suppliers to substitute banks in the supply of credit. On the risks associated with credit leakages after the implementation of macroprudential rules, for example, see Jeanne and Korinek (2014), pp. 166–167. See also Arregui, Beneš, Krznar, Mitra, and Santos (2013), pp. 30–33; Aiyar, Calomiris, and Wieladek (2014).

[199] Lim, Columba, Costa, Kongsamut, Otani, Saiyid, Wezel, and Wu (2011), p. 4. The authors argued that 'Caps on the LTV and DTI [...] are frequently applied together by country authorities to curb rapid credit growth in the real estate sector (p. 12)'.

[200] CGFS (2010), p. 2.

[201] Idem, p. 3. In this regard, part of the recent economic literature acknowledges the difference between structural and time-varying macroprudential instruments, thereby overcoming the traditional distinction, as seen above, between cross-sectional and time dimension of macroprudential policy. On this topic, see also Constâncio (2014); Tarullo (2014).

[202] Lim, Columba, Costa, Kongsamut, Otani, Saiyid, Wezel, and Wu (2011), p. 8.

[203] For details, see Caruana (2014), pp. 3–4.

[204] For a discussion between economists and policymakers on this particular topic, see Knot (2014), pp. 29–31.

of regulatory uncertainties, the prevention of inertia, and the mitigation of political bias about future policy interventions of macroprudential authorities make the rule-based approach desirable.[205]

Conversely, a small part of the law and economics scholarship assumes that the macroprudential policy would be better off by using a discretionary-based approach, claiming that inflexible rules are not capable to target the changing circumstances characterizing the financial cycle.[206] Under this approach, design and calibration of macroprudential instruments become a learning-by-doing process in which mistakes, trials, and forecasts play a pivotal role.[207]

As a matter of fact, not only the legal macroprudential framework is designed to take into account the structural and cyclical differences in the financial cycles of the various countries,[208] but also it acknowledges an intrinsic flexibility due to the continuing calibration of the rule-based instruments. In this case, it is the law that enables the macroprudential strategies to be flexibly adjusted in accordance with the different circumstances arising along the financial cycle.[209] As a result, the discretion-based approach is not to be considered as opposed to the rule-based one. Instead, discretion and judgment complement the rule-based framework by leaving room for a discretionary calibration of the strategies dealing with the build-up and the materialization of systemic risks.[210]

This supports the idea that an optimal macroprudential policy is to be necessarily rule-bound, but it must also allow for some sort of discretionary elasticity—constrained by the law—in the strategic calibration of the instruments, with particular regard to the market circumstances and the sources of systemic risk arising along the cycle.

[205] Idem, p. 29.

[206] For example, see Kannan, Rabanal, and Scott (2009), p. 20, according to which the 'inflexible use of rigid macroprudential rules could sometimes result in policy errors'.

[207] Lim, Columba, Costa, Kongsamut, Otani, Saiyid, Torsten, and Wu (2011), p. 14. This is the case, for example, of the Indian experience, where the Reserve Bank's macroprudential policy has been rather judgmental. On the issue, see Sinha (2011), p. 1063.

[208] Banco de Portugal (2014b), p. 9.

[209] For example, to deal with risks caused by SIIs, national authorities may use systemic risks buffers to address systemic risks that cannot be sufficiently mitigated through the standard capital requirements. On the issue, see ESRB (2014b), p. 13.

[210] This view is shared by Agur and Sharma (2013). See also ESRB (2014a), pp. 21–22, stating that the 'new prudential rules for the EU banking sector combine elements of the rules-based approaches and the need for judgment into a principle of guided discretion'.

2.3 The EU Regulatory Archipelago

After looking at the legal foundations of macroprudential policy and giving a preliminary insight into the core components of macroprudential banking supervision, this section aims at exploring the macroprudential regulatory framework available in the EU. Therefore, the preliminary examination of the EU regulatory framework for macroprudential policy is essential.

During the financial crisis of 2007, the standard entity-based financial regulation, that is, 'microprudential', and the whole banking supervisory framework failed to achieve the goal of maintaining the stability of global financial system.[211] The whole supervisory regime was not able to detect the widespread mispricing of debt contracts,[212] assess the negative impact of the overreliance on credit rating agencies,[213] and target the growing risk appetite of credit institutions particularly due to the pervasive incentives to shadow banking activities.[214] The prudential requirements of credit institutions were insufficient to internalize risks associated to these practices,[215] while the legal instruments available were notably deficient in responding to the rapid changes characterizing the financial markets at that time.[216]

One of the weaknesses of microprudential regulation is that it is not capable to detect, measure, and mitigate the inherent procyclicality of financial system and its associated risks.[217] Conversely, it follows a procyclical path: it tends to loosen in times of booms and strengthen after the financial meltdown occurred.[218] Such a structural failure of traditional

[211] On the issue, see in particular Zhou (2010).

[212] For details, see Goodhart (2008), pp. 331–334. See also Begg (2009), p. 1110.

[213] For a thorough analysis of credit rating agencies and the role in the financial crisis, see Hunt (2009), pp. 109–209; Partnoy (2010), pp. 116–131. See also Dennis (2009), pp. 1111–1150, where the author proves the underestimation of the risks of securities by credit rating agencies was a rational response to legal, regulatory, and market incentives prevalent at that time.

[214] For details on shadow banking activities, see Adrian and Shin (2009). See also Schwarcz (2012), pp. 632–641. The author argues, in particular, that regulation on shadow banking should focus on minimizing banking's potential to create systemic risk.

[215] See Kern (2014), pp. 347–349.

[216] Alexander and Moloney (2011), p. viii.

[217] Gohari and Woody (2014), p. 8. See also Kero (2011), p. 3.

[218] McDonnell (2014), p. 125. See also Repullo (2013), pp. 452–490; Turner (2000).

prudential regulation requires a broader overture to banking supervision that can take into account the procyclical nature of financial behaviors.[219]

To do that, macroprudential regulation should tighten capital and liquidity standards when booms start and market euphoria can turn into speculative financing and excessive credit growth; by contrast, when the crisis begins, macroprudential regulation should become more lenient in order to maintain sufficient credit for borrowers and investors in bad times.[220] In one word, the macroprudential regulation should be, by its own very nature, 'countercyclical'.[221] That being the case, macroprudential regulation is intended to intervene where microprudential regulation has been proven to fail, leaning against the wind and limiting the severity of the financial cycle.[222]

In spite of the acknowledgment of the weaknesses related to the microprudential approach, after the financial crisis, the regulatory interventions put forward since the operationalization of Basel III capital and liquidity requirements have been almost exclusively microprudential.[223] The target of Basel III has been first to require banks to put aside additional capital to reduce the likelihood of possible defaults.

These rules were primarily designed to strengthen resilience and soundness of individual financial institutions by raising capital and liquidity ratios to higher standards[224] and considering the dynamics of financial system as given.[225] However, Basel III also sponsored a number of regulatory initiatives, such as the adoption of countercyclical capital buffers, which marked the starting point for the operationalization of proper macroprudential rules at national and international levels. Since then, the regulatory proposals on macroprudential policy improved every year.

The European macroprudential regulation is not intended to replace the traditional microprudential rules for financial institutions. Instead, while microprudential rules are aimed at ensuring the continuing performance of the economic functions carried out by each component of the

[219] For evidences of strong procyclicality among financial players, see Papaioannou, Park, Pihlman, and van der Hoorn (2013).

[220] Idem, p. 125. On the issue, *cf.* also McDonnell (2013), pp. 1597–1651.

[221] With respect to the 'countercyclical' approach to regulation, see Ren (2011); Ryoo and Hong (2011), pp. 97–106.

[222] In general, see Crockett (1997).

[223] Tarullo (2014), p. 52. See also Shin (2011), p. 5.

[224] Goodhart and Perotti (2014), p. 34.

[225] Angeloni (2014), p. 73.

financial system against its market failures,[226] this new holistic approach to regulation complements the microprudential tools available, by enabling competent authorities to take actions ex ante to counter the growing threats posed by systemic risks.[227]

One of the most interesting cases for such a policy expansion is the regulatory archipelago constructed as of 2009 in Europe, where the EU and Member States' competences and responsibilities overlap in an under-development framework. An analytical overview of this regulatory construction is essential to understand how the macroprudential and monetary policy may interact within the EMU and what legal consequences should follow.

Starting from the proposal made immediately after the financial crisis, the following section outlines the macroprudential innovations made in the European legal framework both at EU and Member State levels. By doing so, we will next define the macroprudential toolkit available in Europe to counter systemic risks.

2.3.1 From the de Larosière Report to Basel III

In October 2008, as immediate response to the financial collapse of 2007, José Manuel Barroso, the then President of the European Commission, invited Jacques de Larosière—former Governor of the Banque de France and former Director of the IMF—to chair a High-Level Group of experts to review the scope for regulatory and supervisory reform of the financial system in the EU.

After a few months, the Group published its final report (so-called the *de Larosière Report*) in February 2009. The Report is divided in four chapters: (1) Causes of the Financial Crisis, (2) Policy and Regulatory Repair, (3) EU Supervisory Repair, and (4) Global Repair. The Report recognizes as premise that the financial crisis of 2007 has been due 'complex interaction of market failures, global financial and monetary imbalances, inappropriate regulation, weak supervision and poor macro-prudential oversight'.[228] In particular, one of the main issues highlighted by the crisis was that 'regulators and supervisors focused on the micro-prudential

[226] Schwarcz (2014), p. 5.
[227] See Jácome and Nier (2011).
[228] de Larosière Report (2009), p. 13.

supervision of individual financial institutions and not sufficiently on the macro-systemic risks of a contagion of correlated horizontal shocks'.[229]

Against this backdrop, the second chapter of the Report first acknowledges that the ECB must be more involved in macroprudential overseeing of banking activities; further it recommends banks 'to hold more capital [...] not only to cover idiosyncratic risks but also to incorporate the broader macro-prudential risks [...] in order to avoid procyclical drawbacks and an aggravation of the present credit crunch'.[230]

The third chapter of the Report presents a new architecture for banking supervision in the EU: in particular, in order to organize the macroprudential supervision, the experts call for the creation of an European Systemic Risk Council (ESRC), having the responsibility to issue risk warnings, recommendations, and observations on macroprudential policy, and giving advice on the proper measures to be adopted among EU Member States.[231]

Yet, the responsibility for implementing macroprudential policy remains allocated to the central banks of EU members.[232] According to the Report, the new ESRC should pool and analyze all information pertaining to macroeconomic conditions and to macroprudential developments in all the financial sectors.[233] Despite the great emphasis on the institutional aspects of EU macroprudential policy, the Report provides few details about the macroprudential regulatory tools and strategies that should be operationalized in Europe.

Nonetheless, the experts suggest strengthening the cooperation between monetary and regulatory authorities 'with a view to defining and implementing the policy- mix that can best maintain in a stable and balanced macroeconomic framework'.[234] To do that, the Report recommends a more proactive role of the ECB in the macroprudential aspects of banking activities.[235]

[229] Idem, p. 11.

[230] Idem, pp. 16–17.

[231] Idem, p. 44.

[232] For an in-depth analysis of the Larosière Report, see Nagy, Pete, Benyovszki, Petru, and Györfy (2010), pp. 5–20.

[233] de Larosière Report (2009), p. 46.

[234] Idem, p. 15.

[235] See Whelan (2009), p. 2, where the author favors in addition a regulatory structure in which monetary policy and macroprudential supervision are conducted under the same roof.

As a proof of general consensus on the Report, in March 2009, the EU Commission welcomed the main findings and recommendations of the High-Level Group, setting an action plan for reforming the European regulatory and supervisory architecture.[236] In May 2009, the EU Commission issued a communication on European financial supervision setting the technical details of the new European financial supervisory framework.[237]

This communication, in particular, proposed the enhancement of the supervisory framework in the EU by establishing two new bodies: the ESRB and the European System of Financial Supervisors (ESFS).[238] Significantly more important, the communication signaled a change in the attitude of the European regulatory framework towards a broader macroprudential approach.[239]

For the legal construction of a macroprudential framework in Europe, significant efforts have been made not only at EU but also at international level. Since late 2009, the BCBS issued a number of reforms having a macroprudential focus, including the proposal made to introduce countercyclical capital buffers that may help dampen financial and economic shocks.[240]

As a corollary of these efforts, in November 2010, the G20 leaders called upon the FSB, IMF, and BIS to do further work on macroprudential tools to mitigate the impact of excessive capital flows and deal with systemic risks in the financial sector.[241] Accordingly, in December 2010, the BCBS issued the 'International Regulatory Framework for Banks' (Basel III) which lay out global regulatory standards on capital and liquidity adequacy for banks.[242] Amid these standards, Basel III includes

[236] See European Commission (2009a).

[237] See European Commission (2009b).

[238] The European System of Financial Supervision (ESFS) is the European supervisory network comprising the three ESAs, the Joint Committee of the European Supervisory Authorities, and the national supervisors. It also includes the ESRB (see Article 2(2) of ESAs Regulation). The objective of this network is to ensure the adequate application of the rules to the financial sector is adequate as to preserve the financial stability, ensure confidence in the financial system as a whole, and enhance protection for the customers of financial services.

[239] Beroš (2010), p. 49.

[240] See BCBS (2009).

[241] See G20 Seoul Summit Document, 11–12 November 2010, paragraph 41. Available online at https://g20.org/wp-content/uploads/2014/12/Seoul_Summit_Document.pdf.

[242] See BCBS (2010a).

measures to put in place global liquidity standards, such as the 'liquidity coverage ratio' (LCR) and the 'net stable funding requirement' (NSFR), the capital conservation buffer, and a specific countercyclical capital buffer for banks, designed to reduce procyclicality in financial markets.

With the aim of implementing the Basel III standards in the EU banking legislation, in 2013 the EU Commission and the Council decided to adopt a new legislative package comprising the Regulation (EU) No. 575/2013 (Capital Requirement Regulation or CRR) and the Directive 2013/36/EU (Capital Requirement Directive IV or CRD IV).[243]

This new package was intended to substitute the previous EU Directives (2006/48 and 2006/49) on capital requirements in order to create a sounder and safer financial system that could overcome the criticalities exposed by the financial crisis. More importantly, with the implementation of the Basel III instruments and further macroprudential tools not previously defined in the Basel framework, the EU legislator introduced for the first time a limited set of harmonized rules for the operationalization of macroprudential policy in the EU.[244]

2.3.2 *The EU Framework: CRD IV, CRR, and Pillar 2 Instruments*

As argued above, the CRD IV and the CRR introduced a number of new macroprudential instruments at the EU level to address systemic risks.[245] The instruments introduced by the CRR are immediately effective in all member jurisdictions. By contrast, the instruments laid out by the CRD IV have to be transposed into national laws to become effective. All of

[243] For a critical discussion on the implementation of Basel III standards in the EU banking framework, see Atik (2014), pp. 287–345. See also Greenwood and Roederer-Rynning (2014), pp. 325–338, where the authors discuss the role of the European Parliament in the process of adopting the Basel III framework, along with the Europeanization of the relevant banking standards.

[244] Although this harmonization process seems to be consistent across Europe, this cannot be considered an accomplished project. Several provisions leave room to national discretion in the implementation phase that could eventually harm the uniformity of the macroprudential measures across the EU Member States. For a critical discussion of this issue, see Babis (2015), pp. 779–803.

[245] For an overview of the main instruments laid down in the CRR/CRD IV package targeting system risks, see Amorello (2016), pp. 137–171; Tröger (2015), pp. 579–581. For a critical appraisal, see also Masera (2014), pp. 381–422.

the instruments defined by the CRR/CRD IV package have different degrees of flexibility in their implementation, and Member States may decide to impose stricter requirements to fulfill their macroprudential responsibilities.[246]

2.3.2.1 Capital-Based Macroprudential Instruments

The CRD IV defines essentially macroprudential instruments based on capital buffers. Article 130 CRD IV enables Member States to require credit institutions to maintain an institution-specific countercyclical capital buffer. This buffer is intended to target procyclicality in the financial system. In practice, when structural and cyclical risks are deemed to be increasing, banks should accumulate capital to foster the resilience of the banking sector following a shock.[247]

As set out by the article, the buffer must be equivalent to the bank's total risk-weighted assets (RWAs) multiplied by the weighted average of the countercyclical buffer rates[248] calculated on an individual and consolidated basis.[249] In simple terms, the countercyclical capital buffer constitutes an additional Common Equity Tier 1 (CET 1) buffer requirement on domestic exposure[250] whose rate is set between 0% and 2.5% calibrated in steps or multiples of 0.25% points.

The buffer rate may be set even higher by Member States if the related risks are deemed to be particularly high.[251] Such a regime under the CRD IV follows a principle of 'guided discretion': this means that Member States in deciding the appropriate buffer rate shall combine a rule-based approach with the exercise of discretionary powers.[252] To this purpose, the designed or competent authorities of Member States must calculate for

[246] See ESRB (2014b), p. 18.

[247] See Recital (9) of ESRB Recommendation on guidance for setting countercyclical buffer rates of 18 June 2014 (ESRB/2014/1). For a discussion of the use of the countercyclical capital buffer, see Detken, Weeken, Alessi, Bonfim et al. (2014).

[248] According to Article 140 CRD IV, the institution-specific countercyclical capital buffer rate is the weighted average of the countercyclical buffer rates that apply in the jurisdictions where the relevant credit exposures of the institution are located or are applied.

[249] See Article 130(1) CRD IV.

[250] ESRB (2014a), p. 29.

[251] Article 136(4) CRD IV.

[252] See Recital (3) of ESRB Recommendation on guidance for setting countercyclical buffer rates of 18 June 2014 (ESRB/2014/1).

every quarter a 'buffer guide' as a reference to guide their judgment in setting the countercyclical capital buffer rates.[253]

In addition, by taking into account the buffer guide, the ESRB recommendations, and other relevant variables, each authority assesses and sets the appropriate rate on a quarterly basis.[254] After an increase of the countercyclical capital buffer rate is announced, banks have usually 12 months to meet the new requirements. In exceptional circumstances, however, a shorter deadline can be established.[255] At last, it is worth mentioning that the CRD IV allows for an exemption to the general rule stating that a member state may exempt small and medium investment firms from the countercyclical capital buffer requirements if such an exemption does not threaten the stability of the financial system of that member state.[256]

To counter systemic risks caused by systemically important institutions, the CRD IV introduced the so-called G-SII and O-SII buffers.[257] In particular, as of 1 January 2016, each G-SII shall maintain, on a consolidated basis and in relation to the sub-category to which the G-SII belongs, a G-SII buffer consisting of additional CET 1 capital.[258] To this purpose, at least five sub-categories of G-SII are identified with respect to the size, interconnectedness, substitutability of the services or of the financial infrastructure, complexity, and cross-border activity of the group.[259]

The rate of the G-SII buffers varies in accordance with the sub-categories and ranges from 1% to 3.5% of RWAs. These G-SII buffers are to be implemented gradually, and G-SIIs are expected to be fully compliant as of 2019.[260] While in the light of the CRD IV the G-SII buffer is mandatory, the Directive provides a slightly different discipline for the so-called O-SII buffer. Indeed, once the O-SIIs have been identified according to the criteria of size, importance, significance of cross-border

[253] Article 136(2) CRD IV. According to this provision, 'the buffer guide shall reflect, in a meaningful way, the credit cycle and the risks due to excess credit growth in the Member State and shall duly take into account specificities of the national economy. It shall be based on the deviation of the ratio of credit-to-GDP from its long-term trend'.

[254] Article 136 (3) CRD IV.

[255] Article 136 (5) CRD IV.

[256] Article 130 (2) CRD IV. If adopted, this exemption must be notified to the Commission, the ESRB, EBA and the national competent authorities concerned.

[257] For a more comprehensive examination of the G-SII and O-SII buffers, see ESRB (2014a), pp. 77–86.

[258] Article 131 (4) CRD IV.

[259] Article 131 (2) CRD IV.

[260] Article 162 (5) CRD IV.

activities, and interconnectedness, national macroprudential authorities may discretionally require each O-SII, on a consolidated, sub-consolidated, or individual basis, to maintain an O-SII buffer, consisting of supplementary CET 1 capital, of up to 2% of the RWAs.[261]

This national discretion may be exercised only if the O-SII buffer does not entail disproportionate adverse effects of the financial system of other Member States or of the Union as a whole affecting the smooth functioning of the EU internal market. As for the case of the G-SII buffer, the O-SII buffer must be reviewed by the national macroprudential authority at least annually.[262]

The CRD IV also acknowledges the possibility for EU Member States to introduce a systemic risk buffer for all banks, or one or more subset of them. This additional buffer is designed to prevent and mitigate long-term non-cyclical systemic risks and other risks not covered by the CRR.[263] It is designed as an additional CET 1 capital requirement of at least 1% on an individual, consolidated, or sub-consolidated basis.[264]

As for the O-SII buffer, the systemic risk buffer may be applied only if it does not entail disproportionate adverse effects on the financial system; yet, differently from the O-SII buffer discipline, the national macroprudential authority has the duty to review the systemic risk buffer at least every second year.[265] Peculiarity of the discipline is that no maximum limit is set for the buffer; anyway, the higher the buffer, the higher the level of scrutiny exercised by the European Commission, ESRB, and EBA on the reasons and justifications of its calibration.[266]

The additional capital-based instrument that can be deemed as a proper macroprudential tool, albeit the CRD IV refers vaguely to its macroprudential nature,[267] is the capital conservation buffer. Article 129 CRD IV provides that Member States must require banks to maintain in addition to their CET 1 a capital conservation buffer of CET 1 capital equal to 2% of RWAs on an individual and consolidated basis.[268] Member States may

[261] Article 131 (5) CRD IV.
[262] Article 131 (6) CRD IV.
[263] Article 133 (1) CRD IV. On the issue, see also ESRB (2014a), p. 80.
[264] Article 133 (3) CRD IV.
[265] Article 133 (10) CRD IV.
[266] See Article 133 (13)–(15) CRD IV.
[267] See Recitals (80) and (85) CRD IV.
[268] Article 129 (1) CRD IV.

discretionally exempt small- and medium-sized investment firms from the capital conservation buffer if such an exemption does not threaten the stability of the financial system of that Member State.[269]

The macroprudential nature of this instrument is revealed by Article 101 of Regulation (EU) No. 468/2014 of the ECB[270] which lists the instruments recognized as macroprudential under the ECB framework. In particular, Article 101 (1)(c) recognizes as macroprudential 'any other measures to be adopted by NDAs [national designed authorities] or NCAs [national competent authorities] aimed at addressing systemic or macroprudential risks provided for, and subject to the procedures set out, in Regulation (EU) No 575/2013 and Directive 2013/36/EU in the cases specifically set out in relevant Union law'. As a matter of fact, the capital conservation buffer falls within this category as Member States must designate the authority in charge of the application of this buffer.[271]

Moreover, its macroprudential nature can be also recognized by reading the Recital (24) of the Council Regulation (EU) No. 1024/2013[272] where a non-exhaustive list of instruments aimed at absorbing losses in stressed periods and addressing systemic or macroprudential risks is provided.[273] Finally, the possibility to raise the capital conservation buffer above its fixed 2.5% rate, pursuant to Article 458 (2)(d)(iv) CRR, implicitly features a macroprudential dimension in its construction.[274]

2.3.2.2 *Macroprudential Pillar 2 Instruments*

As a corollary of the above capital-based tools, Articles 104 and 105 CRD IV set out a variety of powers that national supervisory authorities with

[269] Article 129 (2) CRD IV.

[270] This is the Regulation (EU) No. 468/2014 of 16 April 2014 establishing the framework for cooperation within the Single Supervisory Mechanism between the European Central Bank and national competent authorities and with national designated authorities (SSM Framework Regulation).

[271] See Article 129 (3) CRD IV.

[272] This is the Council Regulation (EU) No. 1024/2013 conferring specific tasks to the European Central Bank relating to the prudential supervision of credit institutions and establishing the Single Supervisory Mechanism.

[273] According to Recital (24): 'Additional capital buffers, including a capital conservation buffer, a countercyclical capital buffer to ensure that credit institutions accumulate, during periods of economic growth, a sufficient capital base to absorb losses in stressed periods, global and other systemic institution buffers, and other measures aimed at addressing systemic or macroprudential risk, are key prudential tools.'

[274] EBA (2014), p. 24.

responsibilities for banking supervision are allowed to use under the so-called 'Pillar 2 framework'.

On the issue, it must be noted that the organization of the banking supervisory framework, from the Basel II Accord onward, has been organized around three main pillars, namely, (1) minimum capital requirements, (2) supervisory review process, and (3) market discipline. While Pillar 1 defines the banks' capital requirements in order to address credit, market, and operational risks and Pillar 3 introduces disclosure requirements to encourage market discipline, the aim of Pillar 2 is to address risks that are not sufficiently covered by Pillar 1 and incentivize banks to develop better risk management techniques in monitoring and managing these risks.[275]

To this purpose, Pillar 2 has been operationalized in the EU via the *Internal Capital Adequacy Assessment Process* (ICAAP), the *Internal Liquidity Adequacy Assessment Process* (ILAAP), and the *Supervisory Review and Evaluation Process* (SREP). While the ICAAP and ILAAP require banks to have sound, effective, and complete strategies and processes to assess and maintain adequate internal capital and liquidity commensurate to their risk profiles,[276] the SREP compels credit institutions to have adequate arrangements, strategies and processes, as well as capital and liquidity as to ensure a sound management and coverage of their risk exposures.[277]

The SREP permits supervisory authorities to impose additional requirements in order to strengthen the internal procedures, controls, and risk management of banks. More importantly, these requirements can be also used for macroprudential purposes.[278] To this end, Articles 97 and 98 CRD IV provide that national competent authorities for banking supervision in carrying out their supervisory review and evaluation must take into account and assess systemic risks threatening the financial system.[279]

[275] For details, see BCBS (2003).

[276] See Article 123 of Directive 2006/48/EC of the European Parliament and of the Council of 14 June 2006 relating to the taking up and pursuit of the business of credit institutions.

[277] See Article 97 CRD IV. For details on the SREP, see also EBA Guidelines on common procedures and methodologies for the supervisory review and evaluation process (SREP) of 19 December 2014 (EBA/GL/2014/13). For a general overview, see also Kern (2014), pp. 354–358.

[278] On the issue, see ESRB (2014a), pp. 134–137.

[279] Articles 97 (1)(b) and 98 (1)(j) CRD IV.

According to Article 104 CRD IV, where these risks are identified, competent authorities may require credit institution to:

1. hold additional own funds (i.e. *capital surcharges*);
2. improve internal capital adequacy assessment and internal governance arrangements;
3. require institutions to apply a specific provisioning policy or treatment of assets in terms of own funds requirements;
4. restrict or limit the business, operations, or network of institutions or to request the divestment of activities;
5. require the reduction of the risk inherent in the activities, products, and systems of institutions;
6. require institutions to limit variable remuneration;
7. require institutions to use net profits to strengthen own funds;
8. impose additional or more frequent reporting requirements;
9. impose specific liquidity requirements (i.e. *liquidity surcharges*); and
10. require additional disclosures.

The Pillar 2 framework provides therefore a set of instruments that can further help competent authorities to counter and mitigate the various categories of systemic risk not fully captured by the macroprudential tools already available under the CRR/CRD IV framework. Under this perspective, SREP measures can be applied to institutions with similar risk profiles that might be exposed to similar risks or pose similar threats to the financial system as a whole.[280]

When using Pillar 2 measures under a macroprudential approach, competent authorities can discretionarily tailor their own intervention to particular circumstances at stake, taking immediate action against possible shocks that can spread to the financial system and the real economy: for instance, if excessive credit growth materializes in one specific sector of the market, for example, residential real estate, the national competent authority may decide to raise own funds requirements or the capital conservation buffer. Instead, if systemic funding risk is building up, the same authority may decide to tighten liquidity requirements or impose further liquidity surcharges based on its supervisory assessments.

It must be noted, however, that the macroprudential nature of Pillar 2 measures will be likely ruled out, at least partly, by the implementation of

[280] EBA (2014), pp. 20–21.

the so-called CRD V/CRR II package, a set of proposed amendments from the EU Commission to the CRR/CRD IV now in consultation.[281] To ensure effectiveness and efficiency of other macroprudential instruments, the EU Commission has advanced a new Article 104a(1) providing that additional own funds requirements under the Pillar 2 framework shall not be imposed to cover macroprudential or systemic risk.[282]

2.3.2.3 *The 'CRR National Flexibility Measures'*

Beyond the capital-based instruments and SREP measures included in the CRD IV, the EU macroprudential framework is enriched by the CRR provisions enabling Member States to address systemic risks by applying certain macroprudential measures—so-called 'CRR national flexibility measures'—at the national level that are considered more effective than other tools.[283] Article 458 CRR states that, where national authorities identify the build-up of systemic risks that may harm the financial system and the real economy, they can impose stricter prudential requirements to domestic institutions, upon notification to the European Parliament, the Council, the Commission, the ESRB, and the EBA of the relevant information and approval of the Council.[284]

[281] We refer to Proposal for a Directive of the European Parliament and of the Council amending Directive 2013/36/EU as regards exempted entities, financial holding companies, mixed financial holding companies, remuneration, supervisory measures and powers, and capital conservation measures, Brussels, 23.11.2016 COM (2016) 854 final 2016/0364 (COD); and Proposal for a Regulation of the European Parliament and the Council amending Regulation (EU) No 575/2013 as regards the leverage ratio, the net stable funding ratio, requirements for own funds and eligible liabilities, counterparty credit risk, market risk, exposures to central counterparties, exposures to collective investment undertakings, large exposures, reporting and disclosure requirements, and amending Regulation (EU) No. 648/2012, Brussels, 23.11.2016 COM (2016) 850 final 2016/0360 (COD).

[282] It is worth noting the position of the ECB on this amending proposal. Although supportive, the ECB states that removing Pillar 2 requirements should not result in authorities having insufficient tools to carry out their mandate and achieve their policy objectives. In particular, the ECB requires the macroprudential toolkit to be broadened and rendered since its effectiveness is especially important in a monetary union where macroprudential policies are needed to address country-specific or sector-specific imbalances, thereby playing a key complementary role in addressing the heterogeneity in financial and business cycles across EU Member States. For details, see Opinion of the European Central Bank of 8 November 2017 on amendments to the Union framework for capital requirements of credit institutions and investment firms (CON/2017/46), p. 5.

[283] See Recital (16) CRR.

[284] The procedure for notifying the relevant information and obtaining the approval by the Council is laid out in Article 458 CRR.

These national measures may consist in: (1) an increase of own funds requirements above the level laid down by the CRR[285]; (2) tightening large exposure requirements[286]; (3) additional disclosure requirements[287]; (4) an increase of the capital conservation buffer above the level described above[288]; (5) tightening prudential measures for intra-financial sector exposures[289]; (6) tightening risk-weights for targeting asset bubbles in real estate sector[290]; and (7) further liquidity requirements.[291]

2.3.2.4 Macroprudential Liquidity Requirements

The CRR does not set out only capital-based instruments. Additional rules are in fact devoted to discipline the liquidity management of credit institutions. Against this backdrop, two instruments are particularly relevant since they can be conceptualized in essence as macroprudential tools[292]; the LCR and the NSFR.

[285] This means that a CET 1 capital ratio may be increased above 4.5% of RWA, a Tier 1 capital ratio above 6% of RWA, and a total capital ratio above 8% of RWA. For further details, see ESRB (2014a), pp. 145–146.

[286] According to definition set out in Article 392 CRR, an institution's exposure to a client is considered a large exposure where its value is equal to or exceeds 10% of its eligible capital. However, a cap for large exposures is provided by Article 395 CRR which states that institution's large exposures to client or a connected group of clients must not exceed 25% of its eligible capital; for exposures to other banks, the value must not exceed 25% of the bank's eligible capital or 150 million. Against this backdrop, the national macroprudential measure tightening large exposure requirements may be designed to (a) reduce the threshold of 10% to identify an exposure as 'large'; (b) reduce the limits to large exposures or remove the exemptions; or (c) tighten the accounting rules to calculate large exposures. For more details, see ESRB (2014a), pp. 151–154.

[287] According to the ESRB, this implies higher frequency or granularity of disclosure. For details, see ESRB (2014a), pp. 154–157.

[288] This means an increase of the capital conservation buffer above 2.5% of RWA.

[289] This would imply the possibility to tighten all CRR/CRD microprudential capital requirements to target sectoral risks that may pose a threat to financial stability. On the issue, see ESRB (2014a), pp. 148–151.

[290] In particular, under this provision, the national macroprudential authority can temporarily increase risk-weights to target asset bubbles in the residential and commercial real estate sector. This may also be requested by national authorities pursuant to Article 103 CRD IV. Further, under Article 124 (2) CRR, competent authorities may require banks to apply higher risk-weights or stricter criteria for exposures fully secured by mortgages on immovable property, on the basis of financial stability considerations.

[291] As explained further below, these are the liquidity buffer requirements and the stable funding requirements.

[292] It must be noted, however, that the macroprudential nature of the LCR and NSFR is questionable. For example, Willem van den End and Kruidhof (2013), pp. 91–106, argue

These instruments are primarily designed to address systemic funding risks which arise when the normal funding and refinancing channels of banks no longer work, thus requiring the intervention of the central bank to act as lender of last resort.[293] This is the lesson learned by policymakers in the early stage of the 2007 financial crisis when many credit institutions, albeit largely capitalized, experienced significant losses because of their imprudence in managing liquidity risk.[294]

Based on the Basel III standards[295] and in order to take into account the European Union and national specificities, Article 412 CRR introduces a LCR for credit institutions. Banks are required to hold a certain amount of liquid assets whose summed values shall cover the liquidity outflow less the liquidity inflows under stress conditions.

that the LCR is a microprudential instruments and in extremes scenarios the LCR can become a binding constraint that may hamper the stability of the financial system. Of the same opinion, Hartlage (2012), pp. 453–483, argues that the LCR may undermine effective liquidity management and thus foster system risk. Albeit praiseworthy, these considerations do not consider the flexibility provided by the CRR and the CRD IV in calibrating the LCR and the NSFR. National competent authorities, if deemed necessary, could always increase the minimum liquidity thresholds by using the Pillar 2 instruments or the CRR national flexibility measures. The static liquidity instruments laid down in the CRR therefore can be adjusted dynamically in accordance with the macroeconomic circumstances of credit institutions. For an overview of how this can be done with respect to the NSFR, see Bicu, Bunea, and Wedow (2014), pp. 118–129. For further insights, see also ESRB (2014a), pp. 105–107. It is therefore possible to reconsider these ratios under a macroprudential perspective by calibrating time-varying liquidity and stable funding buffers that banks have to apply beyond their standard prudential requirements. This is evidenced by some European countries, such as Sweden. As of January 2013, the Swedish Financial Supervisory Authority has adopted new regulation (FFFS 2012/6) requiring domestic credit institutions of relevant dimensions to apply a LCR with anti-cyclical properties to be used under stress scenarios. These new rules are based on Basel III framework and require a LCR of at least 100%. For details, see Finansinspektionen's regulation regarding requirements for a liquidity coverage ratio and reporting of liquid assets and cash flow (FFFS 2012:6), published on 19 November 2012.

[293] ESRB (2014a), p. 102.

[294] See BCBS (2010b), p. 1.

[295] See BCBS (2010a), p. 9. The BCBS published some principles for sound liquidity risk management and supervision in order to provide guidance for risk management and supervision of funding liquidity risk. Moreover, Basel III introduced a LCR aimed at enhancing bank's resilience in the short term by ensuring sufficient high-quality liquid assets to survive a significant stress scenario of at least 30 days—and a NSFR—designed to reduce funding risk over a longer period by requesting banks to fund their own activities by sufficiently stable sources of funding.

Credit institutions need this way to maintain sufficient levels of liquidity buffer to cover any potential imbalance between liquidity inflows and outflows under stressed conditions over a period of 30 days.[296] Further, banks have to maintain a LCR of at least 100%.[297] During periods of severe stress, credit institutions are allowed to cover their net liquidity outflows by selling their liquid assets, even if such a use of liquid assets may result in their LCR falling below 100%.[298] To operationalize this LCR, the composition of the liquidity buffer and the criteria for liquid assets are accurately defined by the Commission.[299]

With respect to the NSFR, Article 413 CRR requires banks to ensure as of January 2016 that long-term obligations are adequately met with a diversity of stable funding instruments under both normal and stressed conditions. Although this provision sets out a net stable funding requirement for credit institutions, the content of this instrument is very general. Unlike the LCR, the Commission has not come out, so far, with any detailed proposal for a harmonized application of this ratio, and its implementation is currently a national matter.[300]

That said, it must be noted however that Article 413 CRR allows Member States to maintain or introduce national provisions in the area of stable funding requirements before binding minimum standards are introduced at the EU level.[301] In addition, the Pillar 2 framework gives national competent authority the possibility to put in place macroprudential LCR and NSFR to institutions sharing similar liquidity risk profiles. Moreover, as already mentioned, stricter requirements on liquidity can be adopted by national competent authorities under Article 458 CRR, if justified by changes in the intensity of systemic risks.

[296] Article 412 CRR.

[297] See Articles 4(1) and 4(2) of Commission Delegated Regulation (EU) No. 2015/61 of 10.10.2014 to supplement Regulation (EU) No. 575/2013 with regard to liquidity coverage requirement for Credit Institutions.

[298] Idem, see Article 4(3).

[299] Idem, see Title II, Chapters 1 and 2.

[300] In order to implement the NSFR contained in Basel III, the BCBS published in October 2014 definitions, minimum requirements, and operational issues of the funding ratio. See BCBS (2014). This ratio is defined as the amount of available stable funding relative to the amount of required stable funding, and it should be equal to at least 100% on an ongoing basis.

[301] Article 413(3) CRR.

2.3.3 *Member States' Own Tools Outside the CRR and CRD IV*

Beyond the instruments harmonized at the EU level, a number of other macroprudential tools may be found by looking at the EU Member States' experiences. Not only Member States may use the *CRR national flexibility measures* as discretional framework to target systemic risks, but they can also operationalize instruments yet to be considered by the EU lawmakers or not fully developed at the international level.

The most important of these national-based instruments are thought to target the borrower's demand of credit, thereby curbing the credit growth in the real estate sector.[302] Among these tools, most relevant are the loan-to-value (LTV), the loan-to-income (LTI), and the debt-to-income (DTI) caps, which are designed as caps on the amount that can be borrowed in relation to the value of collateral or income of the borrowers.[303] More in detail, the LTV cap is a cap on the value of the loan relative to the value of the underlying real estate collateral.[304] This instrument is intended to increase the borrower's equity stake in the property and create incentives for borrowers to meet their repayment, so decreasing the bank's losses should the borrower default.[305]

As of 2010, the LTV cap is operative in Sweden and has contributed to decreasing the volume of mortgage in the country.[306] Since then, other EU countries such as Finland, Denmark, Hungary, Latvia, Lithuania, the Netherlands, Poland, Romania, and Slovakia have decided to operationalize the same cap.[307]

Slightly different from the LTV cap, the LTI cap is a cap on the value of the loan or a set of a borrower's loans relative to the disposable income of the borrowers.[308] Similar to the LTV cap, the LTI cap is designed to restrict the availability of mortgage loans and reduce the risks associated with excessive household indebtedness and unsustainable credit boom. An

[302] For an overview of the macroprudential measure introduced by Member States to curb the real estate sector, see Ciani, Cornacchia, and Garofalo (2014). See also Tröger (2015), pp. 581–582, where these instruments are discussed in light of their capacity to influence specific conditions for lenders and borrowers.

[303] For a legal definition of these instruments, see Recommendation ESRB/2013/1.

[304] This definition is provided in ESRB (2014a), p. 62. In this respect, see also Recommendation ESRB/2013/1.

[305] ECB (2014), p. 116.

[306] For a survey of the LTV in Sweden, in particular, see Finanspektionen (2012); Finanspektionen (2013); Finanspektionen (2014).

[307] See ECB (2014), p. 116.

[308] ESRB (2014a), p. 64.

example of its implementation in Europe is the recommendation laid out by the UK FPC in 2014 which requires mortgage lenders to not extend more than 15% of their total number of new residential mortgages at loan-to-income ratios or greater than 4.5 times.[309]

An additional tool of this set is the DTI cap, which is defined as a cap on the total debt of borrower relative to his disposable income.[310] Aimed at reducing vulnerabilities arising from highly geared borrowing,[311] this instrument has been so far implemented in Greece, Romania, as well as Poland.[312] Despite the strong support received from the Liikanen Group[313] and ESRB,[314] until now, all such tools remain out of the EU macroprudential framework and, their application, as noted above, is left to national discretion.

At last, it is worth mentioning a couple of other macroprudential tools which are out of the EU macroprudential framework and are left once again to national discretion.[315] These tools are the loan-to-deposits (LTD) and the loan-to-stable-funding (LTSF) caps which are deemed to limit customer loans relative to customer deposit or other source of bank's stable funding.[316] A macroprudential design of these tools, in terms of LTD and LTSF ratios, is viable, and currently some EU countries are experiencing the macroeconomic effects of their operationalization.[317] These experiences

[309] See Records of the Financial Policy Committee Meetings held on 17 and 25 June 2014. Available online at http://www.bankofengland.co.uk/publications/Documents/records/fpc/pdf/2014/record1407.pdf. For further details, see also FCA (2014) and PRA (2014).

[310] Deutsche Bundesbank (2013), p. 51.

[311] See The World Bank (2014), p. 208.

[312] See ECB (2014), p. 116.

[313] The Liikanen Report acknowledges, at p. 81, that 'the support to the inclusion of a loan-to-value (LTV) cap and/or loan-to-income (LTI) cap into the macro-prudential toolkit'. In addition, the Report states the harmonization at the EU level 'of the actual definition and use of such restrictions should be a priority in the further development of an effective set of macro-prudential tools'.

[314] In 2011 and in 2013, the ESRB has recommended to introduce the LTV, LTI, and DTI caps in the national macroprudential toolbox. In this respect, see the Recommendation of the European Systemic Risk Board of 21 September 2011 on lending in foreign currencies (ESRB/2011/1) and the Recommendation of the European Systemic Risk Board of 4 April 2013 on intermediate objectives and instruments of macroprudential policy (ESRB/2013/1).

[315] ESRB (2014a), p. 116.

[316] Idem, p. 116.

[317] In particular, an LTD cap has been established in Portugal in the context of the Portuguese Financial Assistance Programme negotiated with the European Commissions, the European Central Bank, and the International Monetary Fund in 2011. In particular, the eight largest banking groups had to gradually reduce their loan-to-deposit ratios to about

represent a promising example to pave the way towards a more complete macroprudential framework in Europe.

2.4 A European Institutional Overview

After looking at the macroprudential tools currently available within the EU and national frameworks, it is now necessary to describe how the macroprudential mandate has been institutionalized in the EU and what are the European and national bodies entrusted with macroprudential supervisory competences. The institutional architecture of the EU bodies plays a pivotal role for the functioning of the EU internal market, and the attribution of competences and powers is capable to affect the policy response against the emergence of possible financial and economic shocks.

The de Larosière Report had already recognized the importance of setting out appropriate institutional arrangements for an effective macroprudential supervision ensuring that the assessment of systemic risks could be translated into immediate policy action.[318] The lack of an adequate macroprudential analysis and warning system associated with the incompleteness of the EU institutional framework due to the lack of a single banking supervisory dimension has been one of the major reasons for the ineffective response of the European and national authorities against the financial spillover of 2007.[319]

The build-up of large private financial imbalances between 1999 and 2007 primarily affected the European banking sector which had become in the meanwhile much more integrated as a result of the EMU.[320] These

120% by the end of 2014. A similar measure has been adopted also in Ireland as a component of the Irish Financial Assistance Programme. See Banco De Portugal (2011) *Explanatory note by Banco de Portugal: loan-to-deposit ratio in the context of the Portuguese Financial Assistance Programme*, 29 September 2011. By contrast, a slightly different version of LTFS ratio—a loan-to-local stable funding ratios (LLSFRs)—has been introduced in Austria for the subsidiaries of the three largest banks as a monitoring tool and early warning indicator for non-sustainable lending growth in boom periods. This ratio aims at strengthening 'the stability of the local funding base of banking subsidiaries and to improve the quality and sustainability of future credit growth'. See Österreichische Finanzmarktaufsicht & Österreichische Nationalbank (2012), pp. 1, 4–5.

[318] See de Larosière Report (2009), pp. 39–40.

[319] Constâncio (2013), pp. 3–4. See also Mawdsley (2014), pp. 209–229.

[320] Idem, p. 3. For a survey of the European integration with respect to financial services industry, see Allen and Song (2005), pp. 7–24. For a historical perspective on the European financial integration after the EMU, see Thalassinos and Dafnos (2015), pp. 15–37.

imbalances—due to the sharp growth in a number of EU Member States of public and private debt intermediated by credit institutions—affected the sustainability of banks' balance sheets, ultimately endangering their viability and, as a consequence, the real economy.[321]

At that time the national authorities were the sole institutions responsible to identify the growing threat posed by the build-up of risks in the banking sector. However, they were unable to capture the new cross-border dimension of the systemic risks arising in the Euro area given the national scope of their tasks.[322] The prudential instruments available were insufficient to counter the excessive leverage of banks' balance sheets and the concentration risks were neglected. The increasing financial integration of credit intermediaries was therefore accompanied by a fragmentation of the European banking supervision[323] that proved ineffective in addressing the new financial challenges posed by the EMU.[324]

Against this backdrop, the members of the de Larosière Group were the first to recommend a challenging structural reform of the EU supervisory architecture aimed at establishing a new centralized banking union and advocating the need to assign specific macroprudential responsibilities to the ECB.[325]

From an institutional perspective, the de Larosière Report outlines the new EU supervisory framework, building its architecture around two pillars. On the one side, the European System of Financial Supervision (ESFS),

[321] For details, see Constâncio (2015), pp. 250–259.

[322] Constâncio (2013), p. 4.

[323] For an early evaluation of the costs related to this supervisory fragmentation in Europe, see Schüler and Heinemann (2005); see also Ferrarini and Chiodini (2009), p. 2, where the authors argue that pre-crisis banking regulation did not fully recognize and support the role of cross-border firms in financial market integration.

[324] As pointed out by Baker (2013), p. 43, immediately after the height of the crisis, there was a radical and immediate intellectual shift towards a macroprudential approach to banking supervision. Policymakers laid down new constituents concepts, such as procyclicality, herding, and systemic externalities, that should now inform and guide the regulatory agenda and the legislative reforms.

[325] In particular, the de Larosière Report recommended the ECB to be entrusted with macroprudential supervision responsibilities, without assuming, however, microprudential supervisory tasks. This is because such an assignment could have resulted in political pressure and interference, thereby jeopardizing the independence of the ECB. On the issue, see also Hennessy (2014), p. 156.

designed as an integrated network of three European Supervisory Authorities (ESAs), would perform the microprudential supervision.[326]

These new European agencies, replacing the already existing Committee of European Banking Supervisors (CEBS), Committee of European Insurance and Occupational Pensions Supervisors (CEIOPS), and Committee of European Securities Regulators (CESR),[327] would coordinate the application of supervisory standards and ensure strong cooperation between national supervisors which are to carry out day-to-day microprudential supervision.[328]

On the other side, the second pillar would rely on a new body—replacing the Banking Supervision Committee (BSC) of the ECB[329]—called the European Systemic Risk Council (ESRC), established as an integral part of the ECB with some macroprudential supervisory tasks.

Chaired by the ECB President, the ESRC would be composed of the members of the General Council of the ECB; the chairpersons of CEBS, CEIOPS, and CESR; as well as one representative of the European Commission.[330] With respect to its competences, the new body was intended to pool and analyze all macroeconomic information relevant for financial stability and ensure a proper flow of information between the ESRC itself and all the microprudential supervisors.[331]

[326] de Larosière Report (2009), p. 48.

[327] As part of the so-called Lamfalussy process, the Commission established the CERS in 2001, the CEIOPS in 2003, and the CEBS in 2004, as independent level 3 committees with the purpose of promoting debate and advising the Commission in the field of banking, insurance, and securities regulation and supervision. For details, see Final Report of the Committee of Wise Men on the Regulation of European Securities Markets (Lamfalussy report), Brussels, 15 February 2001. The Lamfalussy process was an agreement that re-established the financial rule-making procedures and the coordination mechanisms for implementation and enforcement of European financial legislation. The broad framework legislations were introduced through normal co-decision procedures, while technical standards and detailed rules were created through committees of experts, national regulators, and European Commission officials. This process therefore led to the creation of the ESAs. See Posner (2007), pp. 141–142; De Meester (2008), pp. 129–131. For a critical discussion on the Lamfalussy process, see also Alford (2006), pp. 389–435; Schaub (2005), pp. 110–120.

[328] de Larosière Report (2009), p. 48.

[329] The BSC was established in Frankfurt immediately after the creation of the ECB. It assisted the ECB in drafting banking legislation and supported the ESCB in the field of prudential supervision of credit institutions and financial stability.

[330] de Larosière Report (2009), p. 44.

[331] Idem, p. 45.

For this purpose, along with the ESCR, an effective risk warning system would be established in order to issue macroprudential risk warnings and facilitate immediate actions in the events of risk materialization.[332] The expert group recognized that all central banks, and in particular the ECB, should receive 'an explicit formal mandate to assess high-level macro-financial risks to the system and to issue warnings where required'.[333]

This new mandate would have entailed new macroprudential tasks for the ECB in terms of financial stability analysis, development of early warning systems, macro-stress testing exercises, as well as definition of reporting and disclosure requirement.[334] The call for such an extension of the ECB's tasks was based on the idea that the ECB would be the only institution capable to detect macroprudential risks, compare outcomes of the assessments on macroeconomic and prudential developments, and give recommendations on these issues.[335]

However, in spite of this acknowledgment for new macroprudential tasks to be assigned to the ECB, the content of this supervisory function, as intended by the expert group, was more in the nature of mere oversight of the EU financial stability.[336] Evidence of this is that the ECB was supposed to have at its disposal only soft-law instruments—such as warnings, recommendations, and exercises—while the translation of these tools into hard law would be competence of the ESAs through the establishment of a legally binding mechanism via the national supervisory authorities.[337]

[332] these: de Larosière Report (2009), p. 45.

[333] de Larosière Report (2009), p. 44.

[334] Idem, p. 43.

[335] On the issue, see Tröger (2014), p. 464, arguing that a number of reasons suggest that the ECB should be primarily responsible for microprudential and macroprudential supervision. Similarly, see Garicano and Lastra (2010), p. 612.

[336] For details, see Napoletano (2014), p. 88.

[337] Idem, p. 88. According to de Larosière Report (2009), p. 49, 'the level 3 committees should prepare the modalities with the ESRC for a legally binding mechanism, including for the transfer of information, whereby the identification of risks by the ESRC translates into expeditious regulatory, supervisory or monetary policy examination at EU level'. In relation to macroprudential issues, 'the Authorities would have binding cooperation and information sharing procedures with the ESRC to allow the latter to perform its macro-prudential supervision task. The Authorities should create and lead groups of national supervisors to deal with specific events affecting several Member States (p. 54)'. For an analysis of the concepts and uses of soft law for disciplining the European financial markets, with further literature, see Möllers (2010), pp. 386–392; Arner and Taylor (2009), pp. 505–509. For a definition of soft law and its problematic relationship with hard law, see Shaffer and Pollack (2010), pp. 706–799.

According to the Report, the new institutional architecture of the EU supervision was to be implemented in two stages. In the first stage, national supervisory authorities would be strengthened with a view to upgrading the quality of supervision in the EU.[338] As a result, the EU financial sector would be equipped with a consistent set of core harmonized rules in order to identify and remove differences among national legislations.[339] In the second stage, the level 3 committees would be transformed legally into the three authorities, that is, a European Banking Authority, a European Insurance Authority, and a European Securities Authority, thereby establishing an integrated ESFS.[340]

With respect to macroprudential policy, in addition to the competences already exercised by the level 3 committees, these authorities would play a role in setting up cooperative arrangements and information sharing procedures with the ESRC to allow the latter to perform its macroprudential supervision tasks and creating and leading groups of national supervisors, or acting as a mediator to deal with specific systemic events affecting several Member States.[341] Eventually, the functioning of the ESFS should have been reviewed within three years for considering further reforms.[342]

The outcomes of the de Larosière Report have been a fundamental stimulus to improve the European framework dealing with systemic risks and, more generally, with financial stability. Most of the recommendations issued by the expert group have been integrated in the European framework,[343] while the new proposed authorities coping

[338] de Larosière Report (2009), p. 49.

[339] Idem, p. 50.

[340] Idem, p. 52. For a discussion of the ESFS as designed by the de Larosière Report, see Lannoo (2009).

[341] de Larosière Report (2009), p. 54. As pointed out by Ferrarini and Chiodini (2009), p. 4, cooperation and access to information are fundamental to ensure effective consolidated supervision. The information sharing between home and host authorities failed many times, and prudential supervision of institutions on a consolidated basis has been rather difficult.

[342] de Larosière Report (2009), p. 58.

[343] The recommendations included in the de Larosière Report were subject to consultation with the ECB and were considered by the European Parliament and the Council of the European Union before adoption. Despite the general support, some of the relevant proposals were controversial and intensive negotiations followed. Finally, the Economic and Financial Affairs Council (ECOFIN) adopted the reform plan in November 2010. With respect to the ECB's position on the recommendations, see Opinion of the European Central Bank of 11 November 2009 on a proposal for a Regulation of the European Parliament and of the Council on Community macroprudential oversight of the financial system and establishing a European Systemic Risk Board and a proposal for a Council decision entrusting the

with macroprudential supervision have been established. Since then, the political, economic, and regulatory process of reform for further financial integration and better banking supervision in EU never ended and is still underway.

2.4.1 The Macroprudential Mandate in the EU

Following the recommendations set out by the de Larosière Report, in late 2010 the European Parliament and the Council issued five regulations which constitute the institutional pillars of the ESFS.[344] As part of this

European Central Bank with specific tasks concerning the functioning of the European Systemic Risk Board (CON/2009/88) (OJ C 270, 11.11.2009, p. 1); opinion of the European Central Bank on three proposals for regulations of the European Parliament and of the Council establishing a European Banking Authority, a European Insurance and Occupational Pensions Authority, and a European Securities and Markets Authority (CON/2010/5) (OJ C 13, 20.1.2010, p. 1). For details, see also Głuch, Škovranová, and Stenströmpp (2013), pp. 3–4, Ferran and Alexander (2011), pp. 19–20. For a discussion on the implementation of the proposals set out in the de Larosière Report with a particular focus on the need to amend the EU primary law, see Siekmann (2009).

[344] These regulations are the following: Regulation (EU) No. 1092/2010 of the European Parliament and of the Council of 24 November 2010 on European Union macro-prudential oversight of the financial system and establishing a European Systemic Risk Board (ESRB Regulation); Regulation (EU) No. 1093/2010 of the European Parliament and of the Council of 24 November 2010 establishing a European Supervisory Authority (European Banking Authority), amending Decision No. 716/2009/EC and repealing Commission Decision 2009/78/EC; Regulation (EU) No. 1094/2010 of the European Parliament and of the Council of 24 November 2010 establishing a European Supervisory Authority (European Insurance and Occupational Pensions Authority), amending Decision No. 716/2009/EC and repealing Commission Decision 2009/79/EC; Regulation (EU) No. 1095/2010 of the European Parliament and of the Council of 24 November 2010 establishing a European Supervisory Authority (European Securities and Markets Authority), amending Decision No. 716/2009/EC and repealing Commission Decision 2009/77/EC; and Council Regulation (EU) No. 1096/2010 of 17 November 2010 conferring specific tasks upon the European Central Bank concerning the functioning of the European Systemic Risk Board. For the purpose of this book and given the equal content of the first articles, we define the last three regulations as 'ESAs Regulations'. Further, there is also the Directive 2010/78/EU of the European Parliament and of the Council of 24 November 2010 amending Directives 98/26/EC, 2002/87/EC, 2003/6/EC, 2003/41/EC, 2003/71/EC, 2004/39/EC, 2004/109/EC, 2005/60/EC, 2006/48/EC, 2006/49/EC, and 2009/65/EC in respect of the powers of the European Supervisory Authority (European Banking Authority), the European Supervisory Authority (European Insurance and Occupational Pensions Authority), and the European Supervisory Authority (European Securities and Markets Authority).

network of supervisors,[345] three micro-supervisory authorities, that is, the EBA, EIOPA, and ESMA, and one macroprudential supervisory body, that is, the ESRB, were established.[346]

The new institutional architecture for the supervision of the financial system comprises the ESRB, as a supranational board with no legal personality entrusted with the general oversight of the financial system in the EU.[347] Its objective is to contribute to the prevention and mitigation of systemic risks in line with the principles of subsidiarity and proportionality laid down in Article 5 TFEU.[348]

2.4.1.1 The ESRB: Objective and Powers

The legal basis for the creation of the ESRB is to be found in Article 114 TFEU[349] where it specifies that the 'Council shall adopt the measures for the approximation of the provisions laid down by law, regulation or administrative action in Member States which have as their object the establishment and functioning of the internal market'. The reference to this Article is noteworthy since—differently from Article 127(5) TFEU—it does not explicitly refer to the stability of the financial system.

The ESRB is primarily deemed to contribute to the functioning of the internal market, and its action shall necessarily contribute to the approximation of Member States provisions. Against this backdrop, some doubts have been raised on the soundness of the ESRB's legal basis.[350]

It is not evident in particular that the Council Regulation (EU) No. 1092/2010 establishing the ESRB can be interpreted as contributing to the approximation of Member States provisions. In addition, it is not clear whether the ESRB's objective and competences are intended to alter the

[345] According to Recital (9) of Regulation (EU) No. 1093/2010 'the ESFS should be an integrated network of national and Union supervisory authorities, leaving day-to-day supervision to the national level'. According to Van Cleynenbreugel (2015), p. 60, this network permits to set up a cooperative structure among different levels of supervision. Therefore, this network is instrumental in including supranational and national authorities in a singularly integrated market system of supervision.

[346] For a general overview of the legal framework of the EU financial supervisory architecture and of the role and competences of ESAs and ESRB, see Papadopoulos (2014).

[347] See Recital (10) and Article 3(1) of Regulation (EU) No. 1092/2010.

[348] For more details, see Erdélyi (2016), pp. 62–63. For a discussion of the principles of subsidiarity and proportionality in the governance of financial supervision in Europe, see Lastra (2003), pp. 54–56.

[349] See Recital (31) of Regulation (EU) No. 1092/2010.

[350] Inter alia, doubts have been expressed by Verhelst (2011), pp. 32–33.

content of Member States provisions in light of its financial stability objective.[351]

It must be noted, however, that the European Court of Justice has interpreted this article in a flexible way.[352] The approximation of Member States provisions does not require that the legislative act should be addressed directly to Member States and does not necessarily need to harmonize rules directly. Article 114 TFEU may be used instead to create an EU body that merely contributes to harmonization of Member State provisions, without doing so itself.[353] The ESRB can therefore be validly constituted if its role is deemed to effectively pull towards this direction.[354]

To pursue the smooth functioning of the internal market and guarantee its objective, the ESRB has been assigned with the following tasks:

1. determining and/or collecting and analyzing all the relevant and necessary information to meet its mandate;
2. identifying and prioritizing systemic risks;
3. issuing warnings where such systemic risks are deemed to be significant and, where appropriate, making those warnings public;
4. issuing recommendations for remedial action in response to the risks identified and, where appropriate, making those recommendations public;
5. issuing a confidential warning addressed to the Council when an emergency situation arises, and providing the Council with an assessment of the situation, in order to enable the Council to adopt a decision addressed to the ESAs determining the existence of an emergency situation;
6. monitoring the follow-up to warnings and recommendations;

[351] Verhelst (2011), p. 32.

[352] See Judgment of the Court (Grand Chamber) of 2 May 2006. United Kingdom of Great Britain and Northern Ireland v European Parliament and Council of the European Union. Regulation (EC) No. 460/2004—European Network and Information Security Agency—Choice of legal basis (Case C-217/04).

[353] In the words of the ECJ 'acts adopted on that legal basis can contain provisions which do not, in themselves constitute harmonisation measures, but which facilitate the approximation of national laws. In particular, nothing in the wording of that article prevents the legislature from creating a Community body entrusted with the task of providing expertise in an area which is already subject to harmonization measures' (See paragraph 29 of Case C-217/04).

[354] Verhelst (2011), p. 32. The argument is further developed in Siekmann (2010), pp. 56–60.

7. cooperating closely with all the other parties to the ESFS, providing the ESAs with the information on systemic risks required for the performance of their tasks;
8. developing in collaboration with the ESAs a common set of quantitative and qualitative indicators to identify and measure systemic risk;
9. participating, where appropriate, in the Joint Committee; and
10. coordinating its actions with those of international financial organizations, particularly the IMF and the FSB, as well as the relevant bodies in third countries on matters related to macroprudential oversight.[355]

All these tasks are consistent with the content of the recommendations laid down in the de Larosière Report. As for the Report, the ESRB macroprudential oversight results mainly in a continuous monitoring and assessment of risks to financial stability that can harm the financial system as a whole. Accordingly, the end products of this supervision are soft-law measures, namely, warnings and recommendations, having the function—via the public disclosure of the acquired information[356]—to increase awareness of authorities and market participants about the risks identified while leaving other competent authorities to take appropriate hard-law measures to address such risks.[357]

There are a number of reasons for why the ESRB has been entrusted with soft-law powers only. On the one hand, as pointed out by Ferran and Alexander (2011), 'soft laws and institutions can exert considerable power and [...] they are not simply symbolic'.[358] This is particularly the case in financial markets, where soft-law instruments 'can be superior to hard law-making processes in meeting the need for regulation that can be changed and adapted in response to the ever-evolving, highly complex interactions'.[359]

[355] See Article 3(2) of Regulation (EU) No. 1092/2010.

[356] Of this opinion: Napoletano (2014), p. 126. However, it must be noted that the choice to provide the ESRB with soft-law powers only was mainly due to political reasons where the ESRB has a coordination function. On the issue, in particular, see Ferrarini and Chiodini (2012), Part II, paragraph 8.04.

[357] See Napoletano (2014), p. 126, arguing that 'it is up to the ESRB, through its warnings and recommendations, to convey the necessary macroprudential messages to the public entities that have the hard power to act'. To do so it is necessary for the ESRB to build up a strong credibility that may allow the Board itself to act as a 'moral authority'. On this issue, see Trichet (2011). For a critical perspective on the ESRB's moral authority, see instead Manger-Nestler (2013), p. 59, where the author questions the concrete achievement of such authoritative power due to the vulnerabilities of its structure.

[358] Ferran and Kern (2011), p. 3.

[359] Idem, p. 7.

Moreover, 'the capacity for soft law to be changed more easily than hard law may foster willingness to "try out" regulatory innovations in circumstances of uncertainty; if the experiment "works", this can, in turn, lead to a stabilisation of expectations in that area'.[360] These reasons strictly adhere to the case of macroprudential instruments which are supposed to be continuously adjusted in order to meet the ever-evolving macroeconomic circumstances of specific market areas.

On the other hand, the peculiar nature of macroprudential policy measures may entail considerable economic consequences for the addressees.[361] For example, requiring a Member State to implement a high LTI ratio cap may exclude the low-income portion of the population from the mortgage market. This, in turn, may result in a dangerous political backlash which may hamper the credibility of the supranational body requiring the adoption of such a macroprudential tool.

At last, the use of soft-law instruments is related to the small dimension of the ESRB. Differently from the ECB, the ESRB has maintained a contained size, while the human resources at its disposal, with particular regard to the Secretariat, are rather limited.[362] Therefore, it is unthinkable entrusting such a small body with hard-law macroprudential powers, since the binding decisions of few officers not only would be able to heavily influence the public policy of countries, supervisory authorities, and European institutions, but also, and more generally, they would directly impinge on the functioning of the financial system as a whole.

As pure soft-law instruments, the ESRB's recommendations and warnings are not binding under EU law.[363] Albeit not binding, recommendations

[360] Idem, p. 7. Similar reasons regarding the predominance of soft law over hard law in International Finance are provided by Brummer (2012), pp. 101–105.

[361] For a review of the literature on this argument, in particular, see Guibourg, Jonsson, Lagerwall, and Nilsson (2015), pp. 34–39.

[362] See European Commission (2014), p. 7.

[363] Pursuant to Article 288 of TFUE, recommendations and opinions issued by EU institutions have no binding force. For an empirical study of the soft-law instruments adopted in the EU, along with its decision-making and implementation, see Falkner, Treib, Hartlapp, and Leiber (2005). For more details on the ESRB's warnings and recommendations, see Lutter, Bayer, and Schmidt (2011), pp. 329–331. In this respect, Napoletano (2014), p. 128, argues that warnings and recommendations serve only 'to call addressees' attention to a situation and so prompt their evaluation of whether to exercise their own competences'. This would imply that these measures are simply a call for action and are issued to signal to Member States or other competent authorities the build-up or the materialization of systemic risks. Conversely, other authors share different views upon the function of ESRB's

and early warnings may have considerable indirect enforcement.[364] Addressees of such recommendations and warnings may decide to not comply with the normative content of the relevant soft-law acts.[365] In this case sufficient justification for inaction should be provided.[366] This flexible 'comply-or-explain procedure' is based on a 'naming and shaming' mechanism, where addressees are incentivized to ensure compliance with the relevant soft-law instruments due to the reputational costs on the markets that possible defections may generate.[367]

2.4.1.2 The Institutional Relationship Between the ESRB and the ECB

It is worth noting that the ESRB presents a basic departure from the original ESRC proposal laid down in the de Larosière Report. While the report, acknowledging the leading role of central banks in ensuring a sound macroprudential system,[368] recommended the ESRC to be part of the ECB, so that the latter would have been directly entrusted with macroprudential responsibilities, the ESRB is designed as a new EU body, formally separate from the ECB and the ESCB.[369]

legal acts. For example, Soares da Silva (2011), p. 11, highlights that the ERSB's legal acts can put real 'pressure into Member States or national supervisory authorities by going public, thus creating, with a bigger or a smaller degree of certainty (depending on the case), a possible negative reaction'. Similarly, the possible exertion of public pressure as means of indirect enforcement of ESRB's recommendations and early warnings is also highlighted by Tröger (2015), p. 584. The efficiency of this indirect enforcement mechanism is further scrutinized by Ferran and Alexander (2011), p. 31, where the authors suggest that consequences of not-compliance can be substantial.

[364] See Ferran and Kern (2011), p. 30.

[365] For a discussion of the act-or-explain mechanism introduced in the ESRB's legal acts, see Hennessy (2014), p. 157, where the author argues that this mechanism can be superior when uncertainty over the right instruments to detect and deflate bubbles is material.

[366] See Article 17(1) of Regulation (EU) No. 1092/2010. For a better understanding of the functioning of the act-or-explain mechanism and how the follow-up compliance assessment is made, see ESRB, Handbook on the follow-up to ESRB recommendations, available online at https://www.esrb.europa.eu/pub/pdf/other/130708_handbook.pdf?4b88b3f49384aa9ff3564fc86f5767fa.

[367] For a critical overview of soft-law enforcement mechanisms in financial markets and the related reputational costs for inaction, see Brummer (2011), pp. 284–290. On the effectiveness of the *comply-or-explain mechanism* to foster better governance of corporate entities, see Abma and Olaerts (2012), pp. 286–299.

[368] de Larosière Report (2009), p. 44.

[369] As indicated in Recital (15) of Regulation (EU) No. 1092/2010, 'the ESRB should be established as a new independent body, covering all financial sectors as well as guarantee

Against this backdrop, the EU lawmakers have decided to establish the ESRB as macroprudential pillar of the ESFS,[370] thereby extending the meaning of financial supervision as to reflect the interconnection between the micro- and macroprudential dimensions of risks in the whole financial system.[371] Leaving aside the reasons behind this institutional choice,[372] as the ECB stays outside the scope of the EFSF, this institutional construction implies a strict separation between macroprudential and monetary policy. This separation is primarily highlighted by the role played by the ECB in the functioning of the ESRB.

Despite the primary objective of the ESCB which is to maintain price stability,[373] in accordance with Article 127(5) of TFEU and Article 3(3) of the ESCB Statute, the ESCB has a role to play in banking supervision, as it must 'contribute to the smooth conduct of policies pursued by the competent authorities relating to the prudential supervision of credit institutions and the stability of the financial system'.[374]

For this purpose, the TFEU acknowledges that

> the Council, acting by means of regulations in accordance with a special legislative procedure, may unanimously, and after consulting the European Parliament and the European Central Bank, confer specific tasks upon the European Central Bank concerning policies relating to the prudential supervision of credit institutions and other financial institutions with the exception of insurance undertakings.[375]

schemes. The ESRB should be responsible for conducting macro-prudential oversight at the level of the Union and should have no legal personality.'

[370] Actually, this is how the ESRB describes itself. See ESRB (2012), p. 43. However, this self-description is questionable given its absence of legal personality and hard-law powers.

[371] See Moloney (2014), p. 1009.

[372] The institutional choice of creating the ESRB as an independent body out of the ECB has been due mainly by the different membership in the EU with respect to the membership of the Monetary Union. As an EU body, the ESRB's action covers all the EU Member States, while the monetary policy of the ECB regards only members of the Euro area. If the ESRB would be a unit of the ECB, the ESRB could have adopted a decision contrasting with ECB monetary policy. This fact could have endangered the credibility of the ECB decisions. However, this is exactly our point. The risk of a decision by ESRB contrasting with ECB monetary policy is a risk (and a contradiction) for the financial system that can hamper both the financial stability and the smooth functioning of the monetary policy transmission channel.

[373] See Article 127(1) and Article 282 TFEU. See also Article 2 of the Statute of the ESCB. The price stability objective of the ESCB will be thoroughly analyzed in Chap. 3 of this book.

[374] The same provision is laid down in Article 3(3) of the Protocol (No. 4) on the Statute of the European System of Central Banks and of the European Central Bank (hereafter: ESCB Statute).

[375] Article 127(6) of TFEU.

On the basis of this provision,[376] in 2010 the Council issued the Regulation (EU) No. 1096/2010 which confers specific tasks to the ECB for the functioning of the ESRB. These tasks simply involve the administrative support of the ESRB's daily business. According to the Regulation (EU) No. 1092/2010, the ECB is mandated to 'provide [only] analytical, statistical, administrative and logistical support to the ESRB, also drawing on technical advice from national central banks and supervisors'.[377]

This technical assistance has been concretized by the establishment of an ESRB Secretariat and the provision of human and financial resources for the fulfillment of its tasks.[378] As such, the Secretariat is the body responsible for the day-to-day business of the ESRB, its tasks spanning from the preparation of ESRB meetings to the collection and processing of statistical data enabling the ESRB to achieve its objective.[379]

[376] However, the conformity of the ECB's involvement in the ESRB Secretariat's tasks—and, thus, the conformity of Article 127(6) TFEU with the establishment of the ESRB Secretariat—is disputable. A too-narrow interpretation of this Article would not allow the ECB to assume responsibility for setting up a Secretariat for the ESRB entrusted with overall macroprudential oversight. For a discussion of this issue in line with the different interpretations of Article 127(6) TFEU, see Siekmann (2010), pp. 66–67; Keune and Looschelders (2015), pp. 260–261. It must be noted that Article 127(6) TFEU is the only potential legal basis in the primary law to entrust the ECB with responsibilities for ensuring the functioning of the ESRB's Secretariat. The Article does not explicitly differentiate between microprudential and macroprudential supervisory tasks but simply sets a boundary for the ECB's (specific) tasks in providing administrative support to the operations of the ESRB Secretariat, where the ECB staff assigned to the ESRB Secretariat can be directly involved in the macroprudential supervision of credit institutions and other financial institutions only where the Council unanimously agrees to give such tasks via special legislative procedure. It must be finally noted that insurance institutions should be in any case out of the scope of such general prudential assignments. Following this view, see Di Noia and Furlo (2012), Part II—7.58.

[377] See Recital (9) of Council Regulation (EU) No. 1096/2010.

[378] See Article 4(4) of Regulation (EU) No. 1092/2010. More in detail, see also Regulation (EU) No. 1096/2010, where the ECB's obligations in supporting the ESRB are further defined.

[379] For details, see Recital (8) and Article 2 of Council Regulation (EU) No. 1096/2010. It must be noted that the ECB and the ESCB are in a unique position to collect statistical data and information, given that Article 5 of the ESCB Statute provides as explicit duty of the ECB and the ESCB the collection of all the necessary statistical information either from the competent national authorities or directly from economic agents. For this reason, the ECB is specifically entrusted to provide the statistical information collected to the ESRB. What seems striking is that the same statistical information would be used for conducting both monetary policy and macroprudential oversight. For a critical assessment of the ESRB's information collection, and on the role of the ECB in providing data for the performance of the ESRB's tasks, see Keller (2013), pp. 489–535. For a better understanding of

2.4.1.3 *The Impartiality of the ESRB in View of the ECB's Independence*

The technical support must not in any way hamper the ECB's independence in the performance of its monetary policy tasks, as well as the independence of the ESRB in the pursuing of its macroprudential objective. As stated in the ESRB Regulation, the technical support 'provided by the ECB to the ESRB, as well as the tasks assigned to the ESRB, should be without prejudice to the principle of the independence of the ECB in the performance of its tasks'.[380]

This principle suggests that the ECB in the pursuit of its monetary policy should not consider the findings and the recommendations issued by the ESRB as well as no macroprudential consideration should interfere with the conduct of its monetary operations. Likewise, a similar independency is guaranteed for the members of the ESRB. Although the ESRB Regulation does not mention the principle of independence, Article 7—entitled 'impartiality' rather than 'independence'—states that the members of the ESRB 'shall not seek nor take instructions from the Member States, the Union institutions or any other public or private body',[381] performing their duties impartially in the sole interest of the Union.

As the ECB is an EU institution, the formal independence of ESRB's members in their decision-making process shall be recognized and shall not be affected by any other consideration than the safeguard of financial stability against systemic risks.[382]

the tasks assigned to the ESRB Secretariat, see Kohtamäki (2012), pp. 127–129; Moloney (2014), pp. 1013–1019.

[380] See Recital (6) of Regulation (EU) No. 1092/2010.

[381] According to the same Article, 'Neither the Member States, the Union institutions nor any other public or private body shall seek to influence the members of the ESRB in the performance of the tasks set out in Article 3(2).'

[382] This opinion is shared by Napoletano (2014), pp. 104–109. However, a different interpretation can be given to the word 'impartiality'. While the normative content of the word 'impartiality', as used in Article 7 of ESRB Regulation, largely reflects the same legal obligations imposed by the independence principle laid down in Article 130 TFEU, one can argue that, in view of the different term used, the word 'impartiality' does not have the same meaning of independence. Under this interpretation, the word impartiality would only refer to the prohibition of any interference by national and private interests without any regard to political interference. Of this opinion, Zilioli (2016), p. 156. However, this stance seems contradicted by the normative content of the Article which is mostly the same as the principle of independence established for the ECB. On the issue, see also the Opinion of the European Central Bank of 26 October 2009 on a proposal for a regulation of the European Parliament and of the Council on Community macroprudential oversight of the financial system and

Regardless of the language used, it is questionable whether the European institutional framework seeks to provide the same level of independence to both institutions.[383] One can argue that the argument suggesting the full independence of the ESRB is contradicted by the composition of the ESRB itself. Apart from the Secretariat, the ESRB comprises a General Board, a Steering Committee, an Advisory Scientific Committee, and an Advisory Technical Committee.[384] While the latter three committees have administrative and advisory functions,[385] the General Board is the body in charge of taking the decisions relative to the ESRB's tasks.[386]

Doubts on the independence of the ESRB may arise because of the composition of the General Board. On the one hand, Article 5 of ESRB Regulation provides that the ESRB is chaired by the ECB's President, while a Vice-Chair is to be elected by and from the members of the General Council of the ECB. On the other hand, Article 6 of ESRB Regulation designates as members of the General Board, *inter alia*, both the President and the Vice-President of the ECB and the Governors of the national central banks, the heads of the ESAs, and representatives of other bodies.[387]

This governance composition could question the independence of the ESRB because the presence of central bankers and heads of other

establishing a European Systemic Risk Board and a proposal for a Council decision entrusting the European Central Bank with specific tasks concerning the functioning of the European Systemic Risk Board (CON/2009/88), which specifically recommends the amendment of Article 7 as to introduce the principle of independence for the ESRB members. For a broader discussion on the issue, see also Kohtamäki (2012), pp. 137–138; Kang (2012), p. 197.

[383] For an overview of the main deficiencies in the independence of the ESRB, see Kang (2012), p. 197.

[384] See Article 4 of Regulation (EU) No. 1092/2010.

[385] See Articles 4(3) and (5) of Regulation (EU) No. 1092/2010.

[386] See Article 4(2) of Regulation (EU) No. 1092/2010.

[387] More in detail, members of the ESRB General Board with voting rights are (a) the President and the Vice-President of the ECB; (b) the Governors of the national central banks; (c) a Member of the Commission; (d) the Chairperson of the EBA; (e) the Chairperson of the ESMA; (f) the Chairperson of the EIOPA; (g) the Chair and the two Vice-Chairs of the Advisory Scientific Committee; and (h) the Chair of the Advisory Technical Committee. Members without voting rights are (a) one high-level representative per Member State of the competent national supervisory authorities and (b) the President of the Economic and Financial Committee.

institutions with different tasks and objectives could somehow bias the macroprudential decisions of ESRB.[388]

However, this does not seem the case. The explicit requirement of *impartiality* on the board members—*and not on the ESRB*—and the voting mechanism, which assigned only one vote to each voting member with no veto power,[389] is intended to guarantee that no EU institution, body, or national authority may interfere in the adoption of the ESRB's macroprudential decisions.[390] The operational independence of the ESRB is therefore ensured by an institutional composition of the ESRB General Board that does not permit the prevalence of other public, private, or political interests over financial stability concerns.

Based on the above considerations, it is easy to recognize a strict separation between the price stability objective of the ECB and the macroprudential responsibilities of the ESRB. Despite the convergence of statistical information collected and the overlap of the members of each board, from a legal perspective, the macroprudential oversight of ESRB and the monetary policy operations of the ECB are strictly separate because of the detachment of the ESRB from the ECB/ESCB framework along with the impartiality and independence guiding their actions.[391]

2.4.1.4 *The Macroprudential Tasks of the ESAs*

At last, the macroprudential role assigned to the ESAs under the EU legislation must be also discussed. On the grounds of the recommendations

[388] Another argument against the full independence of the ESRB is related to the ECB's administrative support in establishing the ESRB Secretariat. The ECB could theoretically influence the work of the ESRB though its involvement in the daily management of the Secretariat's work streams. On the issue, see Kang (2012), p. 197.

[389] For more details, see Article 10 of Regulation (EU) No. 1092/2010. The General Board generally acts by a simple majority of members present with voting rights. In the event of a tie, the Chair of the ESRB shall have the casting vote. However, a majority of two-thirds is required to adopt a recommendation or to make a warning or recommendation public. In any way, a quorum of two-thirds of the members with voting rights is required for any vote to be taken by the General Board. But if the quorum is not met, the Chair of the ESRB may convene an extraordinary meeting at which decisions may be taken with a quorum of one-third.

[390] See again Article 7 of Regulation (EU) No. 1092/2010.

[391] For a critical perspective of such separation, see Beck and Gros (2012), pp. 1–9. The authors suggest that any strict separation is not desirable during a financial crisis when the systemic stability of the financial system represents the biggest threat to a monetary policy that aims at price stability.

laid down by the de Larosière Report,[392] the ESAs not only are represented in the ESRB board by their respective chairperson, but they also contribute to the overall oversight of macroprudential risks. In the exercise of their tasks, the ESAs must take account of any systemic risk posed by financial institutions[393] and develop, along with the ESRB, a common approach to identify and measure systemic risks, including a set of quantitative and qualitative indicators.[394]

To this end, these authorities, in consultation with the ESRB, must develop specific criteria for the identification and measurement of systemic risk and an adequate stress testing regime which shall include macroprudential considerations.[395]

But the macroprudential role of the ESAs extends beyond the general oversight of the financial system. The need to respond effectively to the build-up and materialization of systemic risks enables these authorities to draw up guidelines, recommendations,[396] and warnings[397] to protect financial stability against the threat posed by systemic risks.[398]

Moreover, as a corollary of these tasks, the ESAs Regulations enable the ESAs, upon request from one or more EU or national authorities, or on its own initiative, to conduct an inquiry for macroprudential supervisory purposes.[399] Additionally, the same regulations enable these authorities to temporarily prohibit or restrict certain financial activities,[400] impose certain behaviors on financial institutions, or adopt a binding decision where a competent authority did not take necessary actions to counter an emergency situation that may jeopardize financial stability.[401]

[392] The de Larosière Report (2009), p. 54, recommends that the supervisory authorities should have, inter alia, a competence of binding cooperation and information sharing procedures with the ESRC to ensure adequate macroprudential supervision.

[393] For details, see Articles 1(6) and 22(1) of ESAs Regulations.

[394] See Article 22(2) of ESAs Regulations.

[395] See Article 23 of ESAs Regulations.

[396] See Article 22(3) of ESAs Regulations.

[397] See Article 9(3) of ESAs Regulations. Pursuant to Article 22(1) of ESAs Regulations, the ESAs must 'respond to warnings and recommendations by the ESRB in accordance with Article 17 of Regulation (EU) No 1092/2010'.

[398] However, these powers are strictly circumscribed by Union law as the ESAs must act within the scope of the relevant Union assignments stated in the ESAs Regulation.

[399] See Article 22(4) of ESAs Regulations.

[400] See Article 9(5) of ESAs Regulations. The power to temporarily prohibit or restrict certain financial activities is a proper hard-law measure that ESAs can adopt based on macroprudential considerations.

[401] We refer to the procedure laid out in Article 18 of ESAs Regulations in the event of emergency situations. However, as argued by Weismann (2016), the ESA's power to issue

2.4.2 National Macroprudential Responsibilities

In light of the above arguments, it is apparent that the EU macroprudential architecture is tailored to ensure the assessment and monitoring of systemic risks. Beyond the limited set of (constrained) hard-law powers conferred on the ESAs to counter emergency situations, the ESRB and the ESAs have mainly soft-law instruments at their disposal for ensuring financial stability. The follow-ups of systemic risk monitoring and assessment process mainly result in non-binding measures, such as recommendations and warnings, which should instruct other relevant authorities to take prompt action against the build-up and contagion of systemic risks.[402]

This inquiry should therefore focus on the identification of these additional authorities that are supposed to act by means of hard-law measures to concretize macroprudential policy at EU and national levels. The recognition of additional authorities entrusted with macroprudential responsibilities is needed to better understand how the institutional architecture of macroprudential banking supervision is currently constructed in Europe and, in a later stage, how this institutional framework is intended to interact with the ESCB's conduct of monetary policy.

2.4.2.1 *The National Macroprudential Authorities and the National Designated Authorities Under the CRD and CRD IV*

As a general principle, macroprudential responsibilities have been mainly assigned at the national level. Although the de Larosière Report did not recommend explicitly the setting up of any national macroprudential authority,[403] the ESRB argued that the responsibility for implementing the

real binding decisions is disputed and never used. Even in emergency situations, the first objective of the ESAs is to facilitate and coordinate actions by national competent authorities, without binding decisions. Only where necessary, and following the determination of an emergency situation by the Council, the ESAs may, as a last resort, adopt individual decisions requiring the necessary action including the cessation of wrong practices. This decision should state clearly the reasons on which it is based, informing the addressees of the legal remedies available. In addition, prior to issuing the decision, sufficient time should be given to the addressees to express their view on the issue. For a thorough analysis of this procedure, see Weismann (2016), pp. 132–142. This decision-making power raises also concern because of the adequacy of the *weak* legal basis—namely, Article 114 TFEU—upon which the ESAs were established. For insights on this issue, inter alia, see; Moloney (2010), pp. 1317–1383.

402 See Dragomir (2010), p. 293.

403 Napoletano (2014), p. 148. For an overview of the macroprudential framework envisioned by the de Larosière Report, see Siekmann (2009), pp. 2–5.

macroprudential tools should be primarily entrusted as a national competence. Against this backdrop, at the end of 2011, the ESRB recommended Member States to designate national authorities entrusted with the adoption of macroprudential measures necessary for the maintenance of financial stability.[404]

The newly national macroprudential authority, acting upon its own initiative, or as a follow-up to recommendations or warnings from the ESRB, should be provided with a clear mandate, tasks, powers, instruments, and proper institutional arrangements, specifying further the decision-making process of its governing body.[405] The ESRB suggested that this national authority should have not only the tasks of identifying, monitoring, and assessing systemic risks but also, and more significantly, the tasks of implementing the macroprudential decisions and instruments.[406]

To do this, mechanisms for a strict cooperation with the other authorities involved in the safeguard of financial stability, without prejudice to their respective mandates, have to be established, while the timely collection and exchange of data and information which are deemed relevant for the timely exercise of the macroprudential mandate have to be preserved.[407] In order to provide an effective framework, the ESRB recommended the newly designated authorities to have full control over the macroprudential tools, setting up clear and expeditious procedures, where necessary, for a proper assignment of such tools.[408]

Following these recommendations, almost all of the EU Member States began operationalizing their own national macroprudential regime. The macroprudential responsibilities have been implemented at the national

[404] See Recitals (1) and (2) of Recommendation of the European Systemic Risk Board of 22 December 2011 on the macroprudential mandate of national authorities (ESRB/2011/3).

[405] See Recommendations A, B, and C of Recommendation of the European Systemic Risk Board of 22 December 2011 on the macroprudential mandate of national authorities (ESRB/2011/3). The national macroprudential authority must ensure transparency in its decision-making process and must be accountable to the national parliament. Further, it shall be operationally independent from the political bodies and from the financial industry. For details, see also Recommendation D.

[406] See Recommendation C of Recommendation of the European Systemic Risk Board of 22 December 2011 on the macroprudential mandate of national authorities (ESRB/2011/3). In the pursuing of such tasks, as indicated in the recommendation, national central banks have to play a leading role, but macroprudential policy shall not undermine their independence.

[407] Idem.

[408] Id.

level by either entrusting directly the national central bank with macroprudential tasks or establishing new independent committees, usually devoid of legal personality and composed of all other national financial authorities.

The importance of national responsibilities in macroprudential policy is further underlined in the CRR and in the CRD IV legislation. It is not a case, in fact, that both CRR and CRD IV require Member States to designate some national authorities which have to be legally responsible both for the application and calibration of the harmonized macroprudential tools available under the EU law.

For example, Articles 129, 130, and 136 of CRD IV require Member States to designate the authority in charge of the setting up, calibration, and maintenance of the countercyclical capital buffers. The same requirement holds for the application of the G-SII and O-SII buffers,[409] for the systemic risk buffer,[410] as well as for the Pillar 2 instruments.[411] Similarly, the 'CRR national flexibility measures' are subject to national discretion and are to be applied by the national authority designated by the Member State upon notification to the European Parliament, the Council, the Commission, the ESRB, and the EBA.[412]

In light of the above, it can be easily said that the macroprudential tasks assigned by the European legislation are primarily national responsibilities which are carried out by the national macroprudential committees and by national designated authorities, the latter being responsible, in particular, for the effective application of the macroprudential tools laid down in the EU law.[413]

2.4.2.2 The Macroprudential Tasks of the ECB Within the Single Supervisory Mechanism

In discussing the national macroprudential tasks, it is also necessary to consider the setting up of the Single Supervisory Mechanism (SSM) which has recognized, as of November 2014, some macroprudential competences for the ECB in its capacity of banking supervisor.[414]

[409] See Article 131 CRD IV.

[410] See Article 133 CRD IV.

[411] See Article 104 CRD IV.

[412] See Article 458 CRR.

[413] This is clearly acknowledged in ESRB (2013), pp. 2–3, where two rationales for such institutional architecture are provided.

[414] For a critical discussion on the new role of the ECB as banking supervisor after the establishment of the SSM, see in particular Tröger (2014), pp. 449–497. For an analysis of

These additional tasks are to be interpreted as subordinated to the macroprudential responsibilities assigned to the national designated authorities of participating Member States.[415] One may easily infer such subordination can be deducted from the wording of Council Regulation (EU) No. 1024/2013 of 15 October 2013, conferring specific tasks on the European Central Bank concerning policies relating to the prudential supervision of credit institutions, where Article 1 states that 'This Regulation is also without prejudice to the responsibilities and related powers of the competent or designated authorities of the participating Member States to apply macroprudential tools not provided for in relevant acts of Union law'.

Beyond a general duty of close cooperation with the ESRB in the pursuit of its supervisory role,[416] the primary task assigned to the ECB, within the SSM, in this respect, is just a consultative role in the application of macroprudential tools by national designated authorities. As stated in Article 5 of Council Regulation (EU) No. 1024/2013, national competent authorities can apply the capital-based macroprudential buffers and the other measures aimed at addressing systemic risks, in accordance with the provisions of the CRD IV and CRR, upon notification to the ECB of their intention ten days before such a decision.

Should the ECB object, it must state in writing the reasons of its negative opinion within five days. Then, national authorities have the duty to consider the reasons of the ECB's objection prior to proceeding with their own decision.[417] Although such consultation is in fact compulsory,

the competences shared among the ECB and national competent authorities, see Gortsos (2015), pp. 401–420. For a broader perspective on the European banking supervisory framework, see also Verhelst (2013); Boccuzzi (2016), pp. 23–47; Angeloni (2015).

[415] This opinion is shared, among others, by Sapir (2014), pp. 164–165, where the author explains that the model chosen by regulation for the divisions of macroprudential responsibilities between SSM and national competent authorities is not centralized and the main responsibility for macroprudential measures still lies with national authorities. The same opinion is supported by Alexander (2014), p. 428, where he argues that the ECB cannot be an effective macroprudential supervisor given the lack of powers mostly left to Member States. A different opinion is instead supported by Lastra (2015), pp. 328–329, as the author states that conferral of microprudential and macroprudential powers to the ECB through the Single Supervisory Mechanism has substantially altered the supervisory architecture in Europe, with the risk that the ESRB may become irrelevant.

[416] See Recital 31 and Article 3(1) of Regulation (EU) No. 1024/2013.

[417] See Article 5(1) of Regulation (EU) No. 1024/2013.

national authorities are not required to comply with the ECB's opinion and may decide to apply the objected measures despite a negative judgment. As a result, this consultative task does not allocate a major macroprudential power to the ECB, but more of an advisory function.[418]

One more relevant task assigned to the ECB, within the SSM, is the faculty to act in lieu of the national designated authority in the event of ineffectiveness of the instruments applied. Indeed, the ECB is entrusted with the power to substitute national authorities, if deemed necessary, by applying higher requirements for capital-based macroprudential buffers and stricter measures to counter systemic risks than those applied by national authorities in the cases specifically set out by the relevant Union law.[419]

This faculty of substitution, however, has to be exercised in close cooperation with the national macroprudential authorities of the Member State concerned. The ECB must notify its intention to the national authorities involved ten days before taking such a decision, and—in case of its objection—it must duly consider the reasons of the national authorities before proceeding.[420]

Undoubtedly, this top-up responsibility represents a true macroprudential hard power for the ECB which can decide to tighten macroprudential requirements for banks on its own initiative. However, this ECB's power is restricted in a number of ways. In detail:

1. The provision explicitly provides the power only to tighten—*and not to relax*—macroprudential measures. Therefore, the rationale of giving such a power to the ECB is not related to counter directly the extremes of the financial cycle—by tightening the requirements in good times and relaxing them in bad times—but, rather, to provide a safety valve where the national competent authority does not act

[418] It must be highlighted that such ECB's top-up powers could generate clashes with national competent authorities as they may not share the same view upon the systemic risk arising in the market for certain supervised entities.

[419] See Article 5(2) of Regulation (EU) No. 1024/2013. However, the national authority may propose to the ECB to act in lieu of the ECB 'in order to address the specific situation of the financial system and the economy in its Member State'. See also Article 5(3) of Regulation (EU) No. 1024/2013. For a short analysis of the Article, *inter alia*, see Alexander (2014), p. 426.

[420] Article 5(4) of Regulation (EU) No. 1024/2013.

efficiently by setting up appropriate requirements in times of economic expansions.[421] Under this perspective, the responsibility of conducting the macroprudential policy remains in this case largely a national task, and such an assignment is not intended to shift away major hard-law power at the EU level.

2. The wording of the article seems to suggest that the ECB's faculty can be exercised only *after* a national authority exercises its own macroprudential powers. In other words, it is not clear by the letter of the text whether the ECB could replace the national authorities in the event of inertia or delay in the setting up or calibration of any instrument. A strict interpretation of the article suggests that the ECB could tighten further only those tools already put in place at the national level where they are deemed not sufficient to target systemic risks. Conversely, the ECB would not have any power to implement *ex novo* macroprudential tools not already in place in the Member State.
3. The ECB powers only apply to macroprudential tools provided in the relevant legislation of the Union law, namely, the CRR and the CRD IV.[422] Any other macroprudential instrument is excluded from the scope of the tasks attributed to the ECB under Article 5 of Council Regulation (EU) No. 1024/2013.
4. An extensive interpretation of the Article, which would enable the ECB to intervene in cases of total inaction or delay at the national level, could deprive the provision of any rationale because the central bank would acquire the power to set out and tighten the macroprudential tools at any time without clear constraints. This interpretation contradicts the institutional architecture of the EU macroprudential policy which primarily relies on the discretion exercised at the national level by the designated authorities.[423]

[421] Napoletano (2014), p. 188.

[422] Consistent with this interpretation is Sapir (2014), p. 165. In particular, the ECB, as argued in Darvas and Merler (2013), p. 6, has no power to apply or calibrate tools aimed at controlling borrowers' behavior, such as LTV and DTI ratio caps.

[423] Some authors have advocated different interpretations of the relevant provisions. For example, Napoletano (2014), p. 188, suggests the strict interpretation 'would prevent the ECB from intervening in cases of major national inaction. [...] Accordingly, the regulation must be interpreted to permit ECB intervention in cases of total inaction at national level'. This interpretation does not seem consistent with the competences of the ESRB which shall recommend or warn national authorities to act in case of unjustified inaction. Under this interpretation, the ECB would deprive the ESRB of any role by taking up all the macroprudential tasks currently assigned to different EU and national authorities. This concern is

In view of the above arguments, the SSM framework does not seem to trigger any particular shift in the allocation of macroprudential powers and tasks assigned at EU and national levels.[424] The EU bodies are mainly involved in the general oversight of financial stability, having mostly soft-law instruments for reacting. The implementation of the SSM does not substantially change this structure as top-up powers can only be used as a measure of last resort and after consulting the national authority involved. The bodies in charge of concrete macroprudential policy action—with hard-law powers and regulatory tools at disposal—remain the national authorities as designated by the Member States.

2.4.3 *The Role of the IMF, the FSB, and the BIS*

To conclude this chapter, the role played by the IMF, the FSB, and the BIS within the overall macroprudential framework of EU must also be mentioned. These institutions shared a unique position in helping Member States to establish an effective macroprudential policy, due to their universal membership, their expertise in macroeconomic and financial stability analysis, and their focus on policy coordination across countries.[425]

Hence, it is not the case that in 2011 the G20 leaders called upon these institutions to do further work on the global development of macroprudential policy frameworks. This potential has been clearly acknowledged in the tasks assigned to them which include the macroprudential oversight of the global financial system and the development of strategies and standards

further discussed by Ferran and Babis (2013), pp. 282–283, with particular emphasis on the dominant role the ECB can assume in the decision-making process of the ESRB. On the issue, see also Tröger (2014), p. 468. As set out by Véron (2012), p. 6, the capacity for initiative attributed to national authorities in this matter would be more consistent with the principles suggested by the ESRB in the context of the legislative discussion on capital requirements, and with the deep expertise of national authorities in monitoring local markets.

[424] See *infra* at note 1225 ss. For a proper shift of the macroprudential tasks at the EU level, there should be an operationalization of some of the comments expressed in ESRB (2013). For example, the choice of a centralized or decentralized model for macroprudential policy may directly affect the competences and powers as well as the overall regulatory framework of the macroprudential authorities involved. For a discussion of the centralized and decentralized models for banking supervision, see Sapir (2014), pp. 163–165.

[425] IMF (2013b), p. 38.

needed to address systemic risks.[426] Recognizing their importance, the EU has embedded these international organizations in its macroprudential framework, mainly with functions of policy cooperation.

For example, the ERSB is required to carry out its tasks by cooperating closely with the IMF and the FSB. First evidence of this close cooperation is the fact that high-level representatives from the above international organizations can be invited to attend the meetings of the ESRB General Board, if their activities are related to the macroprudential tasks assigned to the ESRB.[427] Second, the IMF and the FSB are supposed to provide early warnings of macroprudential risks at the global level which are supposed to inform the ESRB in its macroprudential oversight.[428]

On the issue, it must be recalled that the IMF and the FSB were asked by the G20[429] to develop regular early warning exercises (EWEs), whose primary intent is to signal the sources of systemic risk and sectoral vulnerabilities that could lead to a financial crisis, and identify policies aimed at countering them.[430] As a corollary of this supportive function, the ESRB

[426] For details, see G20, Declaration summit on financial markets and the world economy, 15 November 2009, where the G20 leaders ask the IMF to better integrate regulatory and supervisory responses into the macroprudential policy framework and conduct early warning exercises. In addition, it must be recalled that the FSB Charter recognizes, as part of the FSB's mandate, to: '(a) assess vulnerabilities affecting the global financial system and identify and review on a timely and ongoing basis within a macroprudential perspective, the regulatory, supervisory and related actions needed to address them, and their outcomes; (b) promote coordination and information exchange among authorities responsible for financial stability; [...] (h) collaborate with the International Monetary Fund (IMF) to conduct Early Warning Exercises'. Further, the FSB 'should, as needed to address regulatory gaps that pose risk to financial stability, develop or coordinate development of standards and principles, in collaboration with the SSBs and others, as warranted, in areas which do not fall within the functional domain of another international standard setting body, or on issues that have cross-sectoral implications (Article 2)'.

[427] See Article 9(4) of Regulation (EU) No. 1092/2010.

[428] See Recital (7) and Article 3(2) of Regulation (EU) No. 1092/2010.

[429] Again, see G20, Declaration summit on financial markets and the world economy, 15 November 2009. The legal basis for the IMF early warning exercises is laid down in Article IV of the IMF Articles of Agreement, where the IMF is entrusted with two types of surveillance: bilateral surveillance and multilateral surveillance. The former is conducted vis-a-vis IMF Member States and refers to the monitoring of economic and financial policies of each member. The latter is related to the oversight of the international monetary system in order to ensure its effectiveness. IMF early warning exercises fall within the scope of the IMF surveillance responsibility. For further details, see Rendak (2014), pp. 206–215.

[430] The early warning system of the IMF aimed at monitoring low-probability but high-impact risks to the global economy and identifies policies to mitigate them, drawing on a

is required to contribute towards the implementation of the recommendations issued by the IMF, the FSB, and the BIS on macroprudential issues in the EU legislative framework.[431]

For the ESAs a specific requirement is provided in the pursuing of their macroprudential tasks. In developing the criteria for the identification and measurement of systemic risks, the ESAs must fully consider any relevant approach established by the FSB, the IMF, and the BIS. As paradigms of these approaches developed at the global level, it is sufficient to recall the guidance to assess the systemic importance of financial institutions, markets, and instruments; the note on capital and liquidity surcharges, systemic levies, and taxes[432]; and the work made to address data gaps involving foreign currency exposures.[433]

The impact of these works in the development of the EU macroprudential framework is prominent and suggests that an even stronger cooperation between the EU macroprudential bodies and the international institutions dealing with the macroprudential surveillance is to be expected in the following years.

References

Abma, Rients, Olaerts, Mieke (2012). Is the Comply or Explain Principle a Suitable Mechanism for Corporate Governance throughout the EU?: The Dutch Experience, *European Company Law*, Vol. 9, Issue 6.

Acharya, Viral V., Pedersen, Lasse Heje, Philippon, Thomas Richardson, Matthew P. (2010). Measuring Systemic Risk. *AFA 2011 Denver Meetings Paper*, SSRN. Available at: http://ssrn.com/abstract=1573171

Acharya, Viral V., Philippon, Thomas, Richardson, Matthew, Roubini, Nouriel (2009). The Financial Crisis of 2007–2009: Causes and Remedies, *Financial Markets, Institutions & Instruments*, Vol. 18, Issue 2.

Adrian, Tobias, Shin, Hyun Song (2009). The Shadow Banking System: Implications for Financial Regulation, *Federal Reserve Bank of New York Staff Reports*, No. 382.

range of quantitative tools and broad-based consultations. For insights, see IMF (2010). See also Ghosh, Ostry, and Tamirisa (2009); Robinson (2014). For a critical perspective on the assignment of such new IMF's responsibility, see Aiyar (2010), pp. 491–593.

[431] See Recital (8) of Regulation (EU) No. 1092/2010.

[432] See FSB, IMF, and BCBS (2010).

[433] See FSB, IMF, and BIS (2014).

Agresti, Anna Maria, Baudino, Patrizia, Poloni, Paolo (2008). The ECB and IMF Indicators for the Macro-prudential Analysis of the Banking Sector: A Comparison of the Two Approaches, *ECB Occasional Paper Series*, No. 99.

Agur, Itai, Sharma, Sunil (2013). Rules, Discretion, and Macro-prudential Policy, *IMF Working Paper*, No. 65.

Ahmed, Elsayed, Elgazzar, Amr S., Hegazi, Ahmed S. (2005). An Overview of Complex Adaptive Systems, *Mansoura Journal of Mathematics*, Vol. 32, No. 6059.

Aiyar, Shekhar, Calomiris, Charles W., Wieladek, Tomasz (2014). Identifying Channels of Credit Substitution When Bank Capital Requirements Are Varied, *Bank of England Working Paper*, No. 485.

Aiyar, Swaminathan S. Anklesaria (2010). Crisis Prevention through Global Surveillance: A Task Beyond the IMF, *Cato Journal*, Vol. 30, No. 3.

Alawode, Abayomi A., Al Sadek, Mohammed (2008). What Is Financial Stability? *Central Bank of Bahrain Financial Stability Paper Series*, No. 1/March 2008.

Alexander, Kern (2014). The ECB and Banking Supervision: Building Effective Prudential Supervision?, *Yearbook of European Law*, Vol. 33, No. 1.

Alexander, Kern, Moloney, Niamh (eds.) (2011). Law Reform and Financial Markets, *Edward Elgar Publishing*, Cheltenham.

Alford, Duncan (2006). The Lamfalussy Process and EU Bank Regulation: Another Step on the Road to Pan-European Bank Regulation?, *Annual Review of Banking & Finance Law*, Vol. 25.

Allen, Franklin, Babus, Ana (2009). Networks in Finance. In: '*The Network Challenge: Strategy, Profit, and Risk in an Interlinked World*', (eds.) Paul Kleindorfer, Yoram (Jerry) R. Wind, Robert E. Gunther, *Pearson Prentice Hall*.

Allen, Franklin, Babus, Ana, Carletti, Elena (2010). Financial Connections and Systemic Risk, *NBER Working Paper Series*, No. 16177.

Allen, Franklin, Song, Wei-Ling (2005). Financial Integration and EMU, *European Financial Management*, Vol. 11, No. 1.

Amorello, Luca (2016). Europe Goes 'Countercyclical': A Legal Assessment of the New Countercyclical Dimension of the CRR/CRD IV Package, *European Business Organization Law Review*, Vol. 17, Issue 1.

Angelini, Paolo, Stefano Neri, and Fabio Panetta (2011). Monetary and Macroprudential Policies, *Banca d'Italia Working Papers*, No. 801, March 2011.

Angeloni, Ignazio (2014). European Macroprudential Policy from Gestation to Infancy, *Banque de France Financial Stability Review*, No. 18.

Angeloni, Ignazio (2015). Rethinking Banking Supervision and the SSM Perspective, *Conference at the European University Institute*, 23 April 2015, Florence.

Arner, Douglas W, Taylor, Michael W. (2009). The Global Financial Crisis and the Financial Stability Board: Hardening the Soft Law of International Financial Regulation?, *UNSW Law Journal*, Vol. 32, Issue 2.

Arregui, Nicolas, Beneš, Jaromír, Krznar, Ivo, Mitra, Srobona, Santos, Andre Oliveira (2013). Evaluating the Net Benefits of Macroprudential Policy: A Cookbook, *IMF Working Paper*, No. 167.

Atik, Jeffery (2014). EU Implementation of Basel III in the Shadow of Euro Crisis, *Review of Banking and Financial Law*, Vol. 33.

Aziz, Zeti A. (2007). Governor's Opening Speech at the Malaysia Financial Exhibition 2007, Kuala Lumpur, 30 October 2007.

Babis, Valia (2015). Single Rulebook for Prudential Regulation of EU Banks: Mission Accomplished?, *European Business Law Review*, Vol. 26, Issue 6.

Baker, Andrew (2013). The New Political Economy of the Macroprudential Ideational Shift, *New Political Economy*, Vol. 18, Issue 1.

Banco De Portugal (2011). *Explanatory Note by Banco de Portugal: Loan-to-deposit Ratio in the Context of the Portuguese Financial Assistance Programme*, 29 September 2011.

Banco De Portugal (2014a). Strategy and Instruments of Macro-prudential Policy, *Financial Stability Report*, May 2014.

Banco De Portugal (2014b). Macroprudential Policy in Portugal: Objectives and Instruments, 18 December 2014.

Banerjee, Soumya (2011). Macro Prudential Supervision and the Financial Crisis of 2007: The Aegis of the Central Banks. *SSRN*. Available at: http://ssrn.com/abstract=1827088

Bank of England (2009). The Role of Macroprudential Policy, *Discussion Paper*, November 2009.

Bank of England, HM Treasury, FSA (2008). Financial Stability and Depositor Protection: Special Resolution Regime, *Cm 7459*, July 2008.

Banka Slovenjie (2015). Macroprudential Policy for the Banking Sector Strategic Framework, 24 September 2015.

BCBS (2003). The New Basel Capital Accord. *BCBS Consultative Document*, April 2003.

BCBS (2009). Strengthening the Resilience of the Banking Sector, *Consultative Document*, December 2009.

BCBS (2010a). Basel III: A Global Regulatory Framework for More Resilient Banks and Banking Systems, December 2010.

BCBS (2010b). Basel III: International Framework for Liquidity Risk Measurement, Standards and Monitoring, December 2010.

BCBS (2014). Basel III: The Net Stable Funding Ratio, October 2014.

BCBS (2016). Standards Interest Rate Risk in the Banking Book, April 2016.

Beck, Thorsten, Gros, Daniel (2012). Monetary Policy and Banking Supervision: Coordination Instead of Separation, *CEPS Policy Brief*, No. 286.

Begg, Iain (2009). Regulation and Supervision of Financial Intermediaries in the EU: The Aftermath of the Financial Crisis, *Journal of Common Market Studies*, Vol. 47, Issue 5.

Berger, Allen N., Molyneux, Philip, Wilson, John O.S. (2009). The Oxford Handbook of Banking, *Oxford University Press*, Oxford.

Beroš, Marta B. (2010). Europe's Regulatory Reform after the Crisis – A Macroprudential Perspective, *Columbia Journal of European Law Online*, Vol. 16.

Bicu, Andreea, Bunea, Daniela, Wedow, Michael (2014). Initial Considerations Regarding a Macro-prudential Instrument based on the Net Stable Funding Ratio, *ECB Financial Stability Review*, November 2014.

Billio, Monica, Getmansky, Mila, Lo, Andrew W., Pelizzon, Loriana (2010). Measuring Systemic Risk in the Finance and Insurance Sectors, *MIT Sloan School Working Paper*, No. 4774-10.

Billio, Monica, Getmansky, Mila, Lo, Andrew W., Pelizzon, Loriana (2012). Econometric Measures of Systemic Risk in the Finance and Insurance Sectors, *Journal of Financial Economics*, Vol. 104, Issue 3.

BIS (1986). Recent Innovation in International Banking (Cross Report), *CGFS Publications*, No. 1.

BIS (1992). Recent Developments in International Interbank Relations (Promisel Report), *CGFS Publications*, No. 2.

BIS (1997). The Evolution of Central Bank. In: 'The *67th Annual Report, 1st April 1996–31st March 1997*'. Basle, 9 June 1997.

BIS (2010). Macroprudential Policy and Addressing Procyclicality, *BIS 80th Annual Report.*

BIS (2013). Global Systemically Important Banks: Updated Assessment Methodology and the Higher Loss Absorbency Requirement, July 2013.

Bisias, Dimitrios, Flood, Mark, Lo, Andrew W., Valavanis, Stavros (2012). A Survey of Systemic Risk Analytics, *Office of Financial Research Working Paper*, No. 1.

Blancher, Nicolas, Mitra, Srobona, Morsy, Hanan, Otani, Akira, Severo, Tiago, Valderrama, Laura (2013). Systemic Risk Monitoring (——SysMo||) Toolkit—A User Guide, *IMF Working Paper*, No. 168.

Boccuzzi, Giuseppe (2016). The European Banking Union, *Palgrave Macmillan.*

Borio, Claudio (2003). Towards a Macroprudential Framework for Financial Supervision and Regulation?, *BIS Working Papers*, No. 128.

Borio, Claudio (2012). The Financial Cycle and Macroeconomics: What Have We Learnt?, *BIS Working Papers*, No. 395.

Borio, Claudio (2014). Macroprudential Frameworks: (Too) Great Expectations?, *Contribution to the 25th Anniversary Edition of Central Banking Journal* Originally Published on 5 August 2014.

Borio, Claudio, Drehmann, Mathias (2009). Towards an Operational Framework for Financial Stability: "Fuzzy" Measurement and Its Consequences, *BIS Working Papers*, No. 284.

Borio, Claudio, Furfine, Craig, Lowe, Philip (2001). Procyclicality of the Financial System and Financial Stability: Issues and Policy Options, *BIS Paper*, No. 1.

Brummer, Chris (2011). How International Financial Law Works (and How It Doesn't), *The Georgetown Law Journal*, Vol. 99, Issue 2.

Brummer, Chris (2012). Why Soft Law Dominates International Finance – And Not Trade. In: '*International Law in Financial Regulation and Monetary Affairs*', (eds.) Thomas Cottier, John H. Jackson, Rosa M. Lastra, *Oxford University Press.*

Brunnermeier, Markus K, Oehmke, Martin (2013). The Maturity Rat Race, *Journal of Finance*, Vol. 68, No. 2.

Caruana, Jaime (2014). Macroprudential Policy: Opportunities and Challenges. Speech at the Tenth High-Level Meeting for the Middle East and North Africa Region on '*Global Banking Standards and Regulatory and Supervisory Priorities*' Jointly Organized by the BCBS, the BIS's Financial Stability Institute and the Arab Monetary Fund, Abu Dhabi, United Arab Emirates, 9 December 2014.

Caruana, Jaime, Cohen, Benjamin H. (2014). Five Questions and Six Answers about Macroprudential Policy, *Banque de France Financial Stability Review*, No. 18, April 2014.

CGFS (1995). Issues of Measurement Related to Market Size and Macroprudential Risks in Derivatives Markets (Brockmeijer Report), *CGFS Publications,* No. 5.

CGFS (2010). Macroprudential Instruments and Frameworks: A Stocktaking of Issues and Experiences. Report Submitted by the Committee on the Global Financial System, *CGFS Papers*, No. 38.

Chan, Serena (2001). Complex Adaptive Systems, *ESD.83 Research Seminar in Engineering Systems*, October 31, 2001/November 6, 2001.

Chant, John (2003). Financial Stability as a Policy Goal. In: '*Essays on Financial Stability*', *Bank of Canada Technical Report*, No. 95.

Ciani, Daniele, Cornacchia, Wanda, Garofalo, Paolo (2014). The Macroprudential Measures Adopted in Europe for the Real Estate Sector, *Bank of Italy Occasional Paper*, No. 227.

Clement, Piet (2010). The Term "Macroprudential": Origins and Evolution, *BIS Quarterly Review*, March 2010.

Clementi, David (2001). Banks and Systemic Risk – Theory and Evidence, *Speech held at the Bank of England Conference*, London, 23 May 2001.

Coglianese, Cary, Kilmartin, Heather, Mendelson, Evan (2009). Transparency and Public Participation in the Rulemaking Process: Recommendations for the New Administration, *George Washington Law Review, Vol. 77, No. 4.*

Collin, Marianne, Druant, Martine, Ferrari, Stijn (2014). Macroprudential Policy in the Banking Sector: Framework and Instruments, *NBB Financial Stability Review*, Vol. 12, No. 1.

Constâncio, Vítor (2013). The Nature and Significance of Banking Union, *Speech Delivered at the Chatham House Conference: Financial Regulation: Towards a Global Regulatory Framework?*, London, 11 March 2013.

Constâncio, Vitor (2014). Making Macro-prudential policy work, *Speech at High-level Seminar Organized by De Nederlandsche Bank*, 10 June 2014.

Constâncio, Vítor (2015). Macroprudential Policy in Europe: Ensuring Financial Stability in a Banking Union, *Keynote Speech at the Financial Stability Conference*, Berlin, 28 October 2015.

Crockett, Andrew D. (1997). "Why is Financial Stability a Goal of Public Policy?," Economic Review, Federal Reserve Bank of Kansas City, issue Q IV, pages 5–22.

Darvas, Zsolt, Merler, Silvia (2013). The European Central Bank in the Age of Banking Union, *Bruegel Policy Contribution*, Issue 2013/13.

Das, Udaibir S., Quintyn, Marc, Chenard, Kina (2004). Does Regulatory Governance Matter for Financial System Stability? An Empirical Analysis, *IMF Working Paper*, No. 89.

Davis, E. Philip (2001). A Typology of Financial Instability", *Oesterreichische Nationalbank Financial Stability Report*, No. 2.

De Bandt, Olivier, Hartmann, Philipp (2000). Systemic Risk: A Survey, *ECB Working Paper*, No. 35.

Dell'Ariccia, Giovanni, Marquez, Robert (2004). Information and Bank Credit Allocation. *Journal of Financial Economics*, Vol. 72, Issue 1.

de Larosière Report (2009). Report of the High-Level Group on Financial Supervision in the EU, Brussels, 25 February 2009.

De Nicolò, Gianni, Favara, Giovanni, Ratnovski, Lev (2012). Externalities and Macroprudential Policy, *IMF Staff Discussion Note*, No. 12/05.

De Nicolò, Gianni, Lucchetta, Marcella (2010). Systemic Risks and the Macroeconomy, *IMF Working Paper*, No. 29.

De Meester, Bart (2008). Multilevel Banking Regulation: An Assessment of the Role of the EC in the Light of Coherence and Democratic Legitimacy. In: '*Multilevel Regulation and the EU: The Interplay between Global, European and National Normative Processes*', (eds.) Andreas Follesdal, Ramses A. Wessel, Jan Wouters, *Brill.*

Dennis, Kia (2009). Rating Game: Explaining Rating Agency Failures in the Buildup to the Financial Crisis, *University of Miami Law Review*, Vol. 63, Issue 4.

Detken, Carsten, Weeken, Olaf, Alessi, Lucia, Bonfim, Diana, et al. (2014). Operationalising the Countercyclical Capital Buffer: Indicator Selection, Threshold Identification and Calibration Options, *ESRB Occasional Paper Series,* No. 5/June 2014.

Deutsche Bundesbank (2013). Macroprudential Oversight in Germany: Framework, Institutions and Tools, *Deutsche Bundesbank Monthly Report April 2013.*

Di Noia, Carmine, Furlo, Maria Chiara (2012) The New Structure of Financial Supervision in Europe: What's Next?, In: '*Financial Regulation and Supervision: A Post-Crisis Analysis*' (eds. Eddy Wymeersch, Klaus Hopt, and Guido Ferrarini), Oxford University Press.

Domanski, Dietrich, Ng, Tim (2011). Getting Effective Macroprudential Policy on the Road: Eight Propositions, *BIS Paper*, No. 60.

Dombret, Andreas, Lucius, Otto (2013). Stability of the Financial System: Illusion or Feasible Concept?, *Edward Elgar Publishing Ltd.*

Dragomir, Larisa (2010). European Prudential and Banking Regulation and Supervision: The Legal Dimension, *Routledge*, London and New York.

EBA (2014). EBA Opinion on the Macroprudential Rules in CRR/CRD, *EBA Response to the European Commission on Article 513 CRR Call for Advice.* EBA/Op/2014/06.

ECB (2009). The Concept of Systemic Risk, *Financial Stability Review*, December 2009.

ECB (2014). Recent Experience of European Countries with Macro-prudential Policy, *Financial Stability Review*, May 2014.

Erdélyi, Olivia Johanna (2016). Twin Peaks for Europe: State-of-the-Art Financial Supervisory Consolidation Rethinking the Group Support Regime Under Solvency II, *Springer International Publishing.*

Esen, Oğuz, Binatlı, Ayla Oğuş (2012). The Minsky Perspective on Macroprudential Policy, *PERI Working Paper Series*, No. 308.

ESRB (2012). Annual Report.

ESRB (2013). The Consequences of the Single Supervisory Mechanism for Europe's Macro-prudential Policy Framework, *Reports of the Advisory Scientific Committee,* No. 3/September 2013.

ESRB (2014a). Handbook on Operationalising Macro-prudential Policy in the Banking Sector.

ESRB (2014b). Flagship Report on Macro-prudential Policy in the Banking Sector.

ESRB (2015). Report on the Regulatory Treatment of Sovereign Exposures, March 2015.

European Commission (2009a). Communication of the Commission for the Spring European Council of 4 March 2009, "*Driving European Recovery*". COM(2009) 114.

European Commission (2009b). Communication from the Commission of 27 May 2009, "*European Financial Supervision*". COM(2009) 252 final.

European Commission (2014). Report from the Commission to the European Parliament and the Council on the Mission and Organisation of the European

Systemic Risk Board (ESRB), Brussels, 8 August 2014 (COM(2014) 508 final).

Evans, Owen, Leone, Alfredo M., Gill, Mahinder, Hilbers, Paul (2000). Macroprudential Indicators of Financial System Soundness, *IMF Occasional Papers*, No. 192.

Falkner, Gerda, Treib, Oliver, Hartlapp, Miriam, Leiber, Simone (2005). Complying with Europe EU Harmonisation and Soft Law in the Member States, *Cambridge University Press.*

FCA (2014). Guidance on the Financial Policy Committee's Recommendation on Loan to Income Ratios in Mortgage Lending, *Guidance Consultation*, August 2014.

Ferguson, Roger W. (2003). Should Financial Stability Be an Explicit Central Bank Objective? *Paper Presented to the IMF Conference on Challenges to Central Banking from Globalized Financial Markets*, Washington, DC, 17 September 2002.

Ferran, Eilis, Kern, Alexander (2011). Can Soft Law Bodies be Effective? Soft Systemic Risk Oversight Bodies and the Special Case of the European Systemic Risk Board, *University of Cambridge Faculty of Law, Research Paper*, No. 36/2011.

Ferran, Eilis, Babis, Valia (2013). The European Single Supervisory Mechanism, *Journal of Corporate Law Studies*, Vol. 13.

Ferrarini, Guido, Chiodini, Filippo (2009). Regulating Cross-border Banks in Europe: A Comment on the de Larosière Report and a Modest Proposal, *Capital Markets Law Journal*, 2009.

Ferrarini, Guido, Chiodini, Filippo (2012). Nationally Fragmented Supervision over Multinational Banks as a Source of Global Systemic Risk: A Critical Analysis of Recent EU Reforms. In: '*Rethinking Financial Regulation and Supervision in Times of Crisis*', (eds.) Guido Ferrarini, Klaus J. Hopt, Eddy Wymeersch, *Oxford University Press.*

Finance Watch (2015). Finance Watch Response to FSB's Consultation on Adequacy of Loss-Absorbing Capacity of Global Systemically Important Banks in Resolution. Brussels, 30 January 2015.

Financial Stability Forum (2009). Report of the Financial Stability Forum on Addressing Procyclicality in the Financial System, 2 April 2009.

Finanspektionen (2012). The Swedish Mortgage Market, Report 13 March 2012. Ref. 11-6461.

Finanspektionen (2013). The Swedish Mortgage Market, Report 7 March 2013. Ref. 13-2825.

Finanspektionen (2014). The Swedish Mortgage Market, Report 10 April 2014. Ref. 13-7755.

FSB (2014). Adequacy of Loss-Absorbing Capacity of Global Systemically Important Banks in Resolution. *Consultative Document*, 10 November 2014.

FSB, IMF, BCBS (2010). Systemic Surcharges vs. Levies, *Report to the G20*, April 2010.

FSB, IMF, BIS (2011). Macroprudential Policy Tools and Frameworks, *Update to G20 Finance Ministers and Central Bank Governors*, 14 February 2011.

FSB, IMF, BIS (2014). Letter on Progress Regarding Data Gaps in Foreign Currency Exposures, 11 September 2014.

Galati, Gabriele, Moessner, Richhild (2013). Macroprudential Policy – A Literature Review, *Journal of Economic Surveys*, Vol. 27, Issue 5, pp. 846–878.

Galati, Gabriele, Moessner, Richhild (2014). What Do We Know about the Effects of Macroprudential Policy?, *DNB Working Paper*, No. 440.

Garicano, Luiss, Lastra, Rosa M. (2010). Towards a New Architecture for Financial Stability: Seven Principles, *Journal of International Economic Law*, Vol. 13, Issue 3.

Ghosh, Atish R., Ostry, Jonathan D., and Tamirisa, Natalia (2009). Anticipating the Next Crisis, *IMF Finance & Development*, Vol. 46, No. 3.

Gianviti, François (2010). The Objectives of Central Banks. In: '*International Monetary and Financial Law*', (eds.) Mario Giovanoli, Diego Devos, *Oxford University Press*.

Głuch, Daniel, Škovranová, Lucia, Stenström, Mikael (2013). Central Bank Involvement in Macro-prudential Oversight, *ECB Legal Working Paper Series, No. 14.*

Gohari, Behzad, Woody, Karen E. (2014). The New Global Financial Regulatory Order: Can Macroprudential Regulation Prevent Another Global Financial Disaster? *Journal of Corporation Law*, Vol. 40, Issue 2.

Goodhart, Charles (2008). The Background to the 2007 Financial Crisis, *International Economics and Economic Policy*, Vol. 4, Issue 4.

Goodhart, Charles (2009). Procyclicality and Financial Regulation, *Bank of Spain Revista de Estabilidad Financiera*, No. 16.

Goodhart, Charles A.E., Perotti, Enrico (2014). From Tampering to Preventive Policy, *Banque de France Financial Stability Review*, No. 18.

Gorton, Gary, He, Ping (2008). Bank Credit Cycles, *Review of Economic Studies*, Vol. 75, No. 4.

Gortsos, Christos V. (2015). Competence Sharing Between the ECB and the National Competent Supervisory Authorities Within the Single Supervisory Mechanism (SSM), *European Business Organization Law Review*, Vol. 16, Issue 3, pp. 401–420.

Grace, Therese, Hallissey, Niamh, Woods, Maria (2015). The Instruments of Macro-prudential Policy, *Bank of Ireland Quarterly Bulletin 01/January 15.*

Greenwood, Justin, Roederer-Rynning, Christilla (2014). The "Europeanization" of the Basel Process: Financial Harmonization between Globalization and Parliamentarization, *Regulation & Governance*, Vol. 9, Issue 4.

Guibourg, Gabriela Jonsson, Magnus Lagerwall Björn, Nilsson, Christian (2015). Macroprudential Policy – Effects on the Economy and the Interaction with Monetary Policy, *Sveriges Riksbank Economic Review*, Issue 2, pp. 29–46.

Haldane, Andrew G. (2009). Rethinking the Financial Network, *Speech Held at the Financial Student Association, Amsterdam, 28 April 2009.*

Hanson, Samuel G., Kashyap, Anil K., Stein, Jeremy C. (2011). A Macroprudential Approach to Financial Regulation, *Journal of Economic Perspectives*, Vol. 25, No. 1.

Hartlage, Andrew W. (2012). The Basel III Liquidity Coverage Ratio and Financial Stability, *Michigan Law Review*, Vol. 111, No. 3.

Hautsch, Nikolaus, Schaumburg, Julia, Schienle, Melanie (2014). Financial Network Systemic Risk Contributions, *SFB 649 Discussion Paper* 2012-053.

He, Zhiguo, Krishnamurthy, Arvind (2014). A Macroeconomic Framework for Quantifying Systemic Risk, *Chicago Booth Research Paper*, No. 12–37.

Hennessy, Alexandra (2014). Redesigning Financial Supervision in the European Union (2009–2013), *Journal of European Public Policy*, Vol. 21, Issue 2.

Hoggarth, Glenn, Reis, Ricardo, Saporta, Victoria (2001). Costs of Banking System Instability: Some Empirical Evidence, *EFA 2001 Barcelona Meetings, Bank of England Working Papers*, No. 144.

Houben, Aerdt, Kakes. Jan, Schinasi, Garry (2004). Towards a Framework for Financial Stability, *De Nederlandsche Bank Occasional Studies*, Vol. 2, No. 1.

Houben, Aerdt, van der Molen, Remco, Wierts, Peter (2012). Making Macroprudential Policy Operational, *Banque Centrale du Luxembourg, Revue de Stabilité Financière 2012.*

Huang, Rocco, Ratnovski, Lev (2010). The Dark Side of Bank Wholesale Funding, *IMF Working Paper*, No. 170.

Hunt, John P. (2009). Credit Rating Agencies and the Worldwide Credit Crisis: The Limits of Reputation, the Insufficiency of Reform, and a Proposal for Improvement, *Columbia Business Law Review*, Issue 1.

Hüser, Anne-Caroline (2015). Too Interconnected to Fail: A Survey of the Interbank Networks Literature, *SAFE Working Paper*, No. 91.

IMF (2006). Financial Soundness Indicators. *Compilation Guide*, March 2006. Available at: http://www.imf.org/external/pubs/ft/fsi/guide/2006/index.htm

IMF (2010). The IMF-FSB Early Warning Exercise, Design and Methodological Toolkit, September 2010.

IMF (2011a). Changes in Bank Funding Patterns and Financial Stability Risk, *IMF Global Financial Stability Report: Transition Challenges to Stability.*

IMF (2011b). Macroprudential Policy: An Organizing Framework. Available at: https://www.imf.org/external/np/pp/eng/2011/031411.pdf

IMF (2011c). Toward Operationalizing Macroprudential Policies: When to Act?, *IMF Global Financial Stability Report*, September 2011.

IMF (2013a). The interaction of Monetary and Macroprudential Policies, 29 January 2013.

IMF (2013b). Key Aspects of Macroprudential Policy, 10 June 2013.

IMF (2013c). Annual Report on Exchange Arrangements and Exchange Restrictions.

Israël, Jean-Marc, Sandars, Patrick, Schubert, Aurel, Fischer, Björn (2013). Statistics and Indicators for Financial Stability Analysis and Policy, *ECB Occasional Paper Series*, No. 145, April 2013.

Jácome, Luis I., Nier, Erlend W. (2011). Macroprudential Policy: Protecting the Whole, *IMF Finance and Development Issues*. Online. Available at: http://www.imf.org/external/pubs/ft/fandd/basics/macropru.htm

Jahn, Nadya, Kick, Thomas (2012). Early Warning Indicators for the German Banking System: A Macroprudential Analysis, *Deutsche Bundesbank Discussion Paper*, No. 2.

Jeanneau, Serge (2014). Financial Stability Objectives and Arrangements – What's New?, *BIS Paper*, No. 76.

Jeanne, Olivier, Korinek, Anton (2014). Macroprudential Policy Beyond Banking Regulation, *Banque de France Financial Stability Review*, No. 18.

Kacperczyk, Marcin, Schnabl, Philipp (2010). When Safe Proved Risky: Commercial Paper During the Financial Crisis of 2007–2009, *Journal of Economic Perspectives*, Vol. 24, No. 1.

Kang, Teuk Rok (2012). Reform des europäischen Finanzaufsichtssystems als Vorbild für Ostasien (Schriften zum Europäischen und Internationalen Privat-, Bank- und Wirtschaftsrecht, Band 43), *De Gruyter*.

Kannan, Prakash, Rabanal, Pau, Scott, Alasdair (2009). Monetary and Macroprudential Policy Rules in a Model with House Price Booms, *IMF Working Paper*, No. 251.

Kaufman, George G. (2000). Banking and Currency Crises and Systemic Risk: A Taxonomy and Review, *Financial Markets, Institutions & Instruments*, Vol. 9, No. 2.

Kawai, Masahiro, Pomerleano, Michael (2010). Regulating Systemic Risk, *ADBI Working Paper Series*, No. 189.

Kawata, Hiroshi, Kurachi, Yoshiyuki, Nakamura, Koji, Teranishi, Yuki (2013). Impact of Macroprudential Policy Measures on Economic Dynamics: Simulation Using a Financial Macro-econometric Model, *Bank of Japan Working Paper Series*, No. 13-E-3.

Keller, Anat (2013). Collecting Data: How will the ESRB Overcome the First Hurdle Towards Effective Macro-Prudential Supervision?, *European Business Law Review*, Vol. 24, Issue 4, pp. 487–535.

Kellermann, A. Joanne, de Haan, Jakob, de Vries, Femke (2013). Financial Supervision in the 21st Century, *Springer*, Berlin.

Kern, Alexander (2014). In: '*The Rule of Law in Monetary Affairs*, (eds.) Thomas Cottier, Rosa Maria Lastra, Christian Tietjie, Lucia Satragno, *Cambridge University Press.*

Kero, Afroditi (2011). Macroprudential Regulations and the Basel III, *Universitat Pompeu Fabra*. Available at: https://fp7.portals.mbs.ac.uk/Portals/59/docs/MC% 20deliverables/WP8%20AKeroSurvey_MacroprudentialRegulations&BaselIII.pdf

Keune, Christina, Looschelders, Dirk (2015). Rechtliche Grundlagen und Grenzen der EIOPA (Düsseldorfer Reihe), *Verlag Versicherungswirtschaft.*

Knot, Klaas (2014). Governance of Macroprudential Policy, *Banque de France Financial Stability Review*, No. 18.

Kohtamäki, Natalia (2012). Die Reform der Bankenaufsicht in der Europäischen Union, *Mohr Siebeck.*

Kregel, Jan (2014). Minsky and Dynamic Macroprudential Regulation, *PSL Quarterly Review*, Vol. 67, No. 269.

Krishnamurti, Damodaran, Lee, Yejin Carol (2014). Macroprudential Policy Framework: A Practice Guide, *World Bank,* Washington, DC.

Laker, John (1999). Monitoring Financial System Stability, *Speech Held at the 52nd International Banking Summer School*, Melbourne, 1 September 1999 (*Reserve Bank of Australia Bulletin*, October 1999).

Landau, Jean-Pierre (2009). Procyclicality – What It Means and What Could Be Done. *Remarks at the Bank of Spain's Conference on Procyclicality and the Role of Financial Regulation*, Madrid, 4 May 2009.

Lannoo, Karel (2009). The Road Ahead after De Larosière, *CEPS Policy Brief*, No. 195.

Lastra, Maria Rosa (2003). Governance Structure for Financial Regulation and Supervision in Europe, *Columbia Journal of European Law*, Vol. 10, Issue 1.

Lastra, Maria Rosa (2015). Systemic Risk and Macroprudential Supervision. In: '*The Oxford Handbook of Financial Regulation*', (eds.) Moloney Niamh, Eilis Ferran, Jennifer Payne, *Oxford University Press.*

Lim, Cheng Hoon, Columba, Francesco, Costa, Alejo, Kongsamut, Piyabha, Otani, Akira, Saiyid, Mustafa, Wezel, Torsten, Wu, Xiaoyong (2011). Macroprudential Policy: What Instruments and How to Use Them? Lessons from Country Experiences, *IMF Working Paper*, No. 238.

Lutter, Marcus, Bayer, Walter, Schmidt, Jessica (2011). Europäisches Unternehmens- und Kapitalmarktrecht Grundlagen, Stand und Entwicklung nebst Texten und Materialien, *De Gruyter*, Berlin.

Manger-Nestler, Cornelia (2013). Interaction for Monetary and Financial Stability: Central Banks as Main Actors in the Global Financial System. In: "*European Yearbook of International Economic Law 2014*", (eds.) Christoph Herrmann, Markus Krajewski, Jörg Philipp Terhechte, *Springer-Verlag Berlin Heidelberg.*

Masera, Rainer (2014). CRR/CRD IV: The Trees and the Forest, *PSL Quarterly Review*, Vol. 67, No. 271.

Martinez-Miera, David, Suarez, Javier (2012). A Macroeconomic Model of Endogenous Systemic Risk Taking, *CEPR Discussion Paper*, No. DP9134.

Mawdsley, Andrew (2014). The Architecture of Macroprudential Supervision in the EU Regional Model. In: '*Macroprudential Supervision in Insurance*', (eds.) Jan Monkiewicz, Marian Małecki, *Palgrave Macmillan UK*.

McDonnell, Brett H. (2013). Dampening Financial Regulatory Cycles, *Florida Law Review*, Vol. 65, Issue 5.

McDonnell, Brett H. (2014). Designing Countercyclical Capital Buffers, *University of Minnesota Law School, Legal Studies Research Paper Series*, No. 14–16.

Mehrling, Perry (1999). The Vision of Hyman P. Minsky, *Journal of Economic Behavior & Organization*, Vol. 39.

Minsky, Hyman P. (1967). Suggestions for a Cash Flow Oriented Bank Examination. Levy Economics Institute of Bard College, *Hyman P. Minsky Archive, Paper* No. 175.

Minsky, Hyman P. (1970). Financial Instability Revisited: The Economics of Disaster, *Paper Prepared for the Steering Committee for the Fundamental Reappraisal of the Discount Mechanism Appointed by the Board of Governors of the Federal Reserve System*, Levy Economics Institute of Bard College, *Hyman P. Minsky Archive*, Paper No. 80.

Minsky, Hyman P. (1975). Suggestions for a Cash Flow Bank Oriented bank Examination, *Paper Prepared for the Conference on Bank Structure and Competition, Federal Reserve Bank of Chicago*, 1–2 May 1975.

Minsky, Hyman P. (1976). Banking and a Fragile Financial Environment, *Paper Prepared for the American Association Meetings*, Atlantic City, 16 September 1976.

Minsky, Hyman P. (1986). Stabilizing an Unstable Economy, *McGraw-Hill Professional*, New York.

Minsky, Hyman P. (1992). The Financial Instability Hypothesis, Levy Economics Institute of Bard College, *Working Paper* No. 74.

Mishkin, Frederic S. (1999). Central Banking in a Democratic Society, *Springer Science+Business Media*, New York.

Möllers, Thomas M.J. (2010). Sources of Law in European Securities Regulation – Effective Regulation, Soft Law and Legal Taxonomy from Lamfalussy to de Larosière, *European Business Organization Law Review*, Vol. 11.

Moloney, Niamh (2010). EU Financial Market Regulation after the Global Financial Crisis: "More Europe" or More Risks?, *Common Market Law Review*, Vol. 47, Issue 5.

Moloney, Niamh (2014). EU Securities and Financial Markets Regulation, *Oxford University Press*, Oxford.

Murphy, Edward V. (2013). Financial Stability Oversight Council: A Framework to Mitigate Systemic Risk, *Congressional Research Service*, 21 May 2013.

Nagy, Ágnes, Pete, Ştefan, Benyovszki, Annamária, Petru, Tünde Petra, Györfy, Lehel-Zoltán (2010). The de Larosière Report Regarding the new Structure of European System of Financial Supervision, *Theoretical and Applied Economics*, Vol. XVII, No. 11(552).

Napoletano, Giuseppe (2014). Legal Aspects of Macroprudential Policy in the United States and in the European Union, *Banca d'Italia Legal Research Papers*, No. 76.

Narodna Banka Slovenska (2014). Quarterly Commentary on Macroprudential Policy, October 2014.

Nersisyan, Yeva, Wray, Randall L. (2010). The Global Financial Crisis and the Shift to Shadow Banking, *Levy Economics Institute of Bard College Working Paper*, No. 587.

Ng, Tim (2012). Communication on Macroprudential Policies: Work in Progress. *Speech Held at the Conference 'Communications and External Relations for Central Banks'*, Christ's College, Cambridge, 11–14 September 2012.

Nier, Erlend W. (2011). Macroprudential Policy – Taxonomy and Challenges, *National Institute Economic Review*, No. 216.

Noyer, Christian (2014). Macroprudential Policy: From Theory to Implementation, *Banque de France Financial Stability Review*, No. 18.

Oet, Mikhail V., Ong, Stephen J., Gramlich, Dieter (2013). Policy in Adaptive Financial Markets—The Use of Systemic Risk Early Warning Tools. *FRB of Cleveland Working Paper*, No. 13/09.

Osiński, Jacek, Seal, Katharine, Hoogduin, Lex (2013). Macroprudential and Microprudential Policies: Toward Cohabitation, *IMF Staff Discussion Note*, No. 5.

Österreichische Finanzmarktaufsicht & Österreichische Nationalbank (2012). Supervisory Guidance on the Strengthening of the Sustainability of the Business Models of Large Internationally Active Austrian Banks, 14 March 2012.

Padoa-Schioppa, Tommaso (2002). Central Banks and Financial Stability: Exploring a Land in Between. *Paper Presented at the Second ECB Central Banking Conference*, Frankfurt am Main, 24–25 October.

Papadimitriou, Dimitri B., Wray, L. Randall (1997). The Economic Contributions of Hyman Minsky: Varieties of Capitalism and Institutional Reform, *Levy Economics Institute of Bard College Working Paper*, No. 218.

Papadopoulos, Thomas (2014). European System of Financial Supervision, *Max Planck Encyclopedia of Public International Law*, (ed.) Rudiger Wolfrum, *Oxford University Press.*

Papaioannou, Michael G, Park, Joonkyu, Pihlman, Jukka, van der Hoorn, Han (2013). Procyclical Behavior of Institutional Investors during the Recent

Financial Crisis: Causes, Impacts, and Challenges, *IMF Working Paper*, No. 193.

Partnoy, Frank (2010). Overdependence on Credit Ratings Was a Primary Cause of the Crisis. In: '*The Panic of 2008 Causes, Consequences and Implications for Reform*', (eds.) Lawrence E. Mitchell, Arthur E. Wilmarth, *Edward Elgar Publishing*.

Patro, Dilip K., Qi, Min, Sun, Xian (2013). A Simple Indicator of Systemic Risk, *Journal of Financial Stability*, Vol. 9, Issue 1.

Phillips, Ronnie J. (1997). Rethinking Bank Examinations: A Minsky Approach, *Journal of Economic Issues*, Vol. 31, No. 2.

Posner, Elliot (2007). Financial Transformation in the European Union. In: '*European Integration and Institutional Change at Fifty*', (eds.) Sophie Meunier, Kathleen R. McNamara, *Oxford University Press*.

PRA (2014). Implementing the Financial Policy Committee's Recommendation on Loan to Income Ratios in Mortgage Lending, *Policy Statement PS9/14*, October 2014.

Ren, Haocong (2011). Countercyclical Financial Regulation, *World Bank Policy Research Working Paper*, No. 5823.

Rendak, Nadia (2014). Monitoring and Surveillance at the International Monetary System: What Can Be Learnt from the Trade Field? In: '*The Rule of Law in Monetary Affairs World Trade Forum*', (eds.) Thomas Cottier, Rosa M. Lastra, Christian Tietje, *Cambridge University Press*.

Repullo, Rafael (2013). The Procyclical Effects of Bank Capital Regulation, *The Review of Financial Studies*, Vol. 26, Issue 2.

Robinson, David (2014). The IMF Response to the Global Crisis: Assessing Risks and Vulnerabilities in IMF Surveillance, *IEO Background Paper*, No. 9.

Rochet, Jean-Charles (2008). Procyclicality of Financial Systems: Is There a Need to Modify Current Accounting and Regulatory Rules?, *Banque de France Financial Stability Review*, No. 12.

Rodríguez-Moreno, María, Peña, Juan Ignacio (2013). Systemic Risk Measures: The Simpler the Better?, *Journal of Banking and Finance*, Vol. 37, Issue 6.

Rothbard, Murray N. (1995). Classical Economics. An Austrian Perspective on the History of Economic Thought, Vol. II, *Edward Elgar Publishing Company*, Brookfield, Vt.

Ryoo, Sang Chul, Hong, Cheol (2011). Countercyclical Tools: A Comparative Assessment. In: '*Macroprudential Regulation and Policy*', *BIS Papers*, Vol. 60.

Schmidt, Vivien A., Thatcher, Mark (2013). Resilient Liberalism in Europe's Political Economy, *Cambridge University Press*.

Sapir, André (2014). Europe's Macroprudential Policy Framework in Light of the Banking Union. In: '*Macroprudentialism*', (ed.) Dirk Schoenmaker, *CEPR Press*, Washington, DC.

Schaub, Alexander (2005). The Lamfalussy Process Four Years On, *Journal of Financial Regulation and Compliance*, Vol. 13, Issue 2.

Schinasi, Garry J. (2004). Defining Financial Stability, *IMF Working Paper,* No. 187.

Schoenmaker, Dirk (2012). The Missing Link in Banking Union: Macro-prudential Supervision, *DSF Policy Brief*, No. 21.

Schwaab, Bernd, Koopman, Siem Jan, Lucas, André (2011). Systemic Risk Diagnostics Coincident Indicators and Early Warning Signals, *ECB Working Paper Series*, No. 1327.

Schuknecht, Ludger (2002). The Fiscal Costs of Financial Instability Revisited, *ECB Working Paper*, No. 191.

Schüler, Martin, Heinemann, Friedrich (2005). The Costs of Supervisory Fragmentation in Europe, *ZEW Discussion Paper*, No. 05-01.

Schwarcz, Steven L. (2008). Systemic Risk, *Georgetown Law Journal*, Vol. 49.

Schwarcz, Steven L. (2012). Regulating Shadow Banking, *Review of Banking and Financial Law*, Vol. 31, No. 1.

Schwarcz, Steven L. (2014). Banking and Financial Regulation. Chapter for '*The Oxford Handbook of Law and Economics*', (ed.) Francesco Parisi, *Oxford University Press* (2015 forthcoming), Oxford.

Sharp, Richard (2014). The Financial Policy Committee of the Bank of England; An Experiment in Macroprudential Management – The View of an External Member, *Speech Given at the London School of Economics*, London, 4 June 2014.

Servén, Luis (2010). Macroprudential Policies in the Wake of the Global Financial Crisis, In '*The Day After Tomorrow: A Handbook on the Future of Economic Policy in the Developing World*', (eds.) Otaviano Canuto, Marcelo Giugale, *World Bank*, Washington, DC.

Shaffer, Gregory C., Pollack, Mark A. (2010). Hard vs. Soft Law: Alternatives, Complements, and Antagonists in International Governance, *Minnesota Law Review*, Vol. 94.

Shin, Hyun Song (2011). Macroprudential Policies Beyond Basel III. In: '*Macroprudential Regulation and Policy*', *BIS Papers*, Vol. 60.

Siekmann, Helmut (2009). Die Schaffung von Einrichtungen der Finanzaufsicht auf EU-Ebene: Stellungnahme zu dem Vorschlag der Sachverständigengruppe unter dem Vorsitz von Jacques de Larosière, *IMFS Working Paper Series*, No. 24.

Siekmann, Helmut (2010). Das neue Europäische Finanzaufsichtssystem, *IMFS Working Paper Series,* No. 40.

Sinha, Anand (2011). Macroprudential Policies: Indian Experience, *RBI Monthly Bulletin July 2011.*

Siqiwen, Li (2010). Financial Fragility and Securitization: The Discussions with Australian Regulators and Bank Risk Managers. In: '*International Banking in the New Era: Post-crisis Challenges and Opportunities*', *International Finance Review*, Vol. 11.

Smaga, Paweł (2014). The Concept of Systemic Risk, *London School of Economics SRC Special Paper*, No. 5.

Soares da Silva, João (2011). Is the EU Better Prepared for a New Financial Crisis? A Brief Analysis of the New Financial Supervisory Architecture, *Contraditorio Policy Paper*, No. 11/10.

Sowell, Thomas (2007). On Classical Economics, *Yale University Press*, New Haven.

Tarullo, Daniel K. (2014). A Macroprudential Perspective on Regulating Large Financial Institutions, *Banque de France Financial Stability Review*, No. 18.

Thalassinos, Eleftherios, Dafnos, Georgios (2015). EMU and the Process of European Integration: Southern Europe's Economic Challenges and the Need for Revisiting EMU's Institutional Framework. In: '*Societies in Transition, Economic, Political and Security Transformations in Contemporary Europe*', (eds.) Savvas Katsikides, Pavlos I. Koktsidis, *Springer International Publishing*.

The Warwick Commission (2009). The Warwick Commission on International Financial Reform: In Praise of Unlevel Playing Fields, *The University of Warwick*.

The World Bank (2014). World Development Record 2014, Risk and Opportunity: Managing Risk for Development, *World Bank*, Washington, DC.

Tröger, Tobias H. (2014). The Single Supervisory Mechanism – Panacea or Quack Banking Regulation? Preliminary Assessment of the New Regime for the Prudential Supervision of Banks with ECB Involvement, *European Business Organization Law Review*, Vol. 15.

Tröger, Tobias H. (2015). A Political Economy Perspective on Common Supervision in the Eurozone. In: '*Financial Regulation: A Transatlantic Perspective*', (eds.) Ester Faia, Andreas Hackethal, Micheal Haliassos, Katja Langenbucher, *Cambridge University Press*.

Trichet, Jean-Claude (2011). The Conditions for Efficient Global and Regional Macro-supervision – Key Success Factors in International Cooperation, *Speech by Jean-Claude Trichet, President of the ECB, at the Eurofi G20 High Level Seminar*, Paris, 17 February 2011.

Tucker, Paul, Hall, Simon, Pattani, Aashish (2013). Macroprudential Policy at the Bank of England, *Bank of England Quarterly Bulletin*, No. 3.

Tumpel-Gugerell, Gertrude (2009). Recent Advances in Modeling Systemic Risk using Network Analysis, *Introductory remarks to ECB Workshop*, 5 October 2005.

Turner, Philip (2000). Procyclicality of Regulatory Ratios?, *CEPA Working Paper Series III*, No. 13.

Van Cleynenbreugel, Pieter (2015). Market Supervision in the European Union: Integrated Administration in Constitutional Context, *Brill | Nijhoff*.

Verhelst, Stijn (2011). Renewed Financial Supervision in Europe – Final or Transitory? *Egmont – The Royal Institute for International Relations Academia Press*, Brussels.

Verhelst, Stijn (2013). Assessing the Single Supervisory Mechanism: Passing the Point of No Return for Europe's Banking Union, *Egmont – The Royal Institute for International Relations Academia Press*, Brussels.

Véron, Nicolas (2012). Europe's Single Supervisory Mechanism and the Long Journey Towards Banking Union, *Bruegel Policy Contribution*, No. 16.

Visco, Ignazio (2011). Key Issues for the Success of Macroprudential Policies, *Policy Panel on the Macroprudential Policy Framework Bok-BIS Conference*, Seoul, 18 January 2011.

Weismann, Paul (2016). European Agencies and Risk Governance in EU Financial Market Law, *Routledge.*

Whelan, Karl (2009). The ECB Role in Financial Supervision, *UCD Centre for Economic Research Working Paper Series*, No. 15.

Willke, Helmut, Becker, Eva, Rostásy, Carla (2013). Systemic Risk: The Myth of Rational Finance and the Crisis of Democracy, *Campus Verlag GmbH*, Frankfurt.

van den End, Jan Willem, Kruidhof, Mark (2013). Modelling the Liquidity Ratio as Macroprudential Instrument, *Journal of Banking Regulation*, Vol. 14, Issue 2.

Wolfson, Martin H. (2001). Minsky's Theory of Financial Crisis in a Global Context, *Journal of Economic Issues*, Vol. 36, No. 2.

Xingyuan Che, Natasha, Shinagawa, Yoko (2014). Financial Soundness Indicators and the Characteristics of Financial Cycles, *IMF Working Papers*, No. 14.

Yellen, Janet L. (2013). Interconnectedness and Systemic Risk: Lessons from the Financial Crisis and Policy Implications, *Speech at the American Economic Association/American Finance Association Joint Luncheon*, San Diego, 4 January 2013.

Zhou, Chen (2010). Why the Micro-Prudential Regulation Fails? The Impact on Systemic Risk by Imposing a Capital Requirement, *DNB Working Paper* No. 256/July 2010.

Zilioli, Chiara (2016). *The Independence of the European Central Bank and Its Banking Supervisory Competences.* In: '*Independence and Legitimacy in the Institutional System of the European Union*', (ed.) Dominique Ritleng, *Oxford University Press.*

CHAPTER 3

A Legal Approach to Monetary Policy

3.1 Past Experiences and Main Developments in Monetary Policy

After having outlined the legal construction of macroprudential policy in the EU, this analysis should move towards a brief description of what is deemed for monetary policy, especially with regard to the main components of the European monetary policy framework within their legal boundaries. The basic rationale of this chapter is to provide instruments necessary to discuss the institutional construction of the Eurozone and highlight the existing interaction with the macroprudential supervisory framework.

The history of monetary policy has been rather complex. In the last two centuries, because of the evolving political economic circumstances and macroeconomic variables, monetary policy is changed dramatically, and different rules have been used to describe the ultimate target of its policy action.[1]

Central banks appeared in history as commercial lenders to the government and dominant issuers of banknotes.[2] The first central banks were

[1] On the issue, see Taylor (1999a).

[2] Archer (2009), p. 19. The first private institutions to issue notes included *Enskilda Bank of Stockholm*, the *Bank of England*, and the *Berliner Kassenverein*. However, in these periods and in most regions, the state and the municipalities could exert major influence on note-issuing, since private institutions willing to create banknotes needed a permit or a license to do so. It took some time before concentrating the right to issue banknotes in one single institution. The first country to establish a monopoly for banknotes issuance was Austria, where the monopoly was awarded by the State to the *Privilegierte Österreichische*

L. Amorello, *Macroprudential Banking Supervision & Monetary Policy*, https://doi.org/10.1007/978-3-319-94156-1_3

often private institutions to which the government had granted the monopoly rights to issue banknotes in exchange for some services.[3] Over the nineteenth century, with the adoption of the gold standard, a change in the targets of central banks occurred, and consideration of monetary and exchange rate stability became pivotal in the economic debate on the role of central banking. The primary concern of central banks was at that time to safeguard the stability of the system through the maintenance of some exchange rate targets to be achieved by pegging the value of the currency to a certain amount of specie.[4]

But, since the breakdown of the gold standard, different concerns—as, for example, currency convertibility targets, financial stability, and promotion of full employment and discretionary monetary management[5]—were used to define the role of central banks and shaped their institutional and operating developments.

Afterward, as a reaction to the inflationary forces that had destroyed the Bretton Woods System, the target of monetary policy moved to the maintenance of stability in the general level of prices.[6] Since then, across the industrial countries and a large fraction of emerging markets, inflation[7] has become the major—*if not the only*—concern of contemporary central banking, while price stability has been acknowledged as the legal objective of central banks' monetary policy.[8]

Nationalbank in 1841. In Germany, instead, the banknotes monopoly was conferred on the *Reichsbank* only in 1939. In the United States, two different attempts to establish a central bank entrusted with such a monopoly failed in the 18th and 19th, and only in 1913 was eventually possible to establish the Federal Reserve with the right to issue banknotes as legal tender. For details on the history of note-issuing monopoly, see Siekmann (2016), pp. 502–508. The origins and developments of European Central Banks, the Federal Reserve, and the Bank of Japan are further explored in Goodhart (1988), pp. 106–160.

[3] Eichengreen (2008), p. 21.

[4] See Flandreau (2006).

[5] For details, see Santomero, Viotti, and Vredin (2001), pp. 20–21.

[6] Fischer (1995), p. 2.

[7] For an overview of the concepts, causes, and effects of inflation, see Hall (1982) and Hahn (1985). For a survey of the different theories on inflation, see also Frisch (1990).

[8] It must be noted that sometimes the mandate of central banks may refer to other objectives, such as full employment or economic growth. This is the case, for example, of the Federal Reserve in the United States, where Section 2A of the Federal Reserve Act states its objective in terms of maintaining long-run growth of the monetary and credit aggregates commensurate with the economy's long-run potential to increase production, so as to promote effectively the goals of maximum employment, stable prices, and moderate long-term interest rates. However, it is conventional wisdom—particularly in Europe—that the objec-

The following paragraphs intend to provide a brief overview of the contemporary economic developments in monetary policy, discussing the critical objectives and the main findings of contemporary monetary policy. The rationale is to provide a broad economic backdrop that can support, afterward, the reconstruction of the monetary policy framework within its legal constraints.

3.1.1 The Central Bankers' Problem

The contemporary understanding of the central banking role can be interpreted as a reaction to the inflationary acceleration occurred in the United States as of the 1960s. In the following two decades, a number of countries experienced a dramatic rise of inflation along with severe recessions, with an upward pressure on prices in excess of 50% per year for extended periods.[9]

This so-called period of 'Great Inflation' was due mainly to the Bretton Woods System, which was originated in 1944 as an institutional agreement that was responsible for the build-up of inflationary pressure throughout the world economy.[10] At that time, there was a general acceptance by economists that central banks could achieve very low level of unemployment by allowing a permanent level of high inflation.[11]

However, when many countries in the 1970s experienced high levels of both inflation and unemployment, that is, stagflation, economists started

tive of central banks primarily falls within the maintenance of price stability based on the idea that inflation is a pure monetary phenomenon and thus falls are natural responsibility of central banks. See Hidalgo (2003), p. 288. For more insights on this topic, see also Blinder, Goodhart, Hildebrand, Lipton, and Wyplosz (2002), pp. 8–9.

[9] Cecchetti (2000), p. 44.

[10] Hazlitt (1984), p. 159. For a historical account of the Bretton Woods and the Great Inflation, see Bordo and Eichengreen (2013), pp. 449–489. For an explanation on how monetary policymakers led at that time to the Great Inflation, see Mayer (1999); for a description on the effects and consequences of Great Inflation on economic growth, stock prices, and living conditions, see Samuelson (2010).

[11] For more details, see Walsh (1998). This economic view upon a trade-off between inflation and unemployment was supported by new Keynesian economics. For a critical review of the economic literature on this topic, see Santomero and Seater (1978), pp. 499–544. This theory, however, has not been completely abandoned as new studies sought to provide new emphasis on this Keynesian theory. For a sample of this strand of literature, see Ball, Mankiw, and Romer (1988), pp. 1–82.

questioning the reality of such assumption.[12] This experience began to discredit the idea of a stable trade-off between inflation and unemployment, and, as a result, many economists started considering that the rate of unemployment was deemed to be affected by a number of different economic factors unrelated, as it was supposed in the 1960s and 1970s, to the average rate of inflation in the economy.[13]

The adoption of deceptive economic theories paralleled the lack, at that time, of unanimous information on output and inflation, informative inconsistencies which certainly played a role in misleading policymakers to adopt timely adjustments needed to stabilize the system.[14]

As a reaction to such a prolonged period of high inflation, several central banks as of 1979 began to put in place concerted efforts to constrain this inflationary acceleration. The shared response was firstly based on a change in the understanding of the inflationary phenomenon: central bankers and economists acknowledged the idea that a prolonged period of high inflation was inherently unstable and can cause detrimental effects for output growth.[15]

Some empirical studies evidenced a significant negative relationship between GDP growth and high rate of inflation in the long run, calling for a reconsideration of central banking roles and policies.[16] The costs of high inflation, along with the related social losses entailed by these costs, were eventually recognized among central bankers.

Historical evidences have clearly demonstrated how inflation is able to erode savings, discourage investments, stimulate capital flight, obstacle

[12] In the early 1980s, EU governments became increasingly aware that inflation is a 'monetary phenomenon'. On the issue, of particular importance were the two general propositions on monetary policy derived by Taylor (1996), pp. 181–195, stating that 'there is no long-run tradeoff between the rate of inflation and the rate of unemployment. [...] over long periods higher rates of inflation are not associated with lower levels of unemployment, and lower levels of inflation are not associated with higher levels of unemployment. Historical experience with inflation and unemployment provides considerable evidence for this view'.

[13] See Walsh (1998).

[14] For some examples of information inconsistencies that misled policymakers, see Orphanides (2003).

[15] See Mishkin (2009), p. 490.

[16] For example, see Kormendi and Meguire (1985), pp. 141–163. See also Fischer (1993) and Judson and Orphanides (1999), pp. 117–138.

growth, and provoke, eventually, social and political instability.[17] In addition, it is a matter of fact that a high inflation rate is responsible for declines in real incomes since the rise of asset price is generally not accompanied by an equal growth of wages.[18] Furthermore, inflation works as a tax on the monetary basis, thereby gradually eroding the value of the money holdings.[19] As a result, rational investors have to waste substantial time and effort to find a way to reduce these costs.[20]

Starting from these premises, in 1979, John Taylor investigated alternative monetary policy rules targeting inflation more directly.[21] By using a structural econometric model with rational expectations and sticky prices, Taylor discovered a long-run trade-off between output and inflation *variance* that could be exploited to select optimal monetary control rules to stabilize the fluctuations in the level of output and inflation.[22]

This trade-off is defined as a curve (so-called Taylor curve), so that for any given level of output variability, the variability of inflation in the short run depends on the amount of persistence in the GDP gap[23] and on whether the central bank targets a specific inflation rate.[24]

Since then, economists have been challenged with the formulation of policy rules capable to achieve optimality in the trade-off between inflation and output variability.[25] The struggle for optimality has become the major problem of central banking, and most of the monetary economic literature developed in the last three decades has focused on the empirical estimate of the impact of the policy rules on output and prices.[26]

[17] See Jahan (2012).

[18] Cecchetti (2000), p. 47.

[19] It must be noted, however, that inflation can also be used to erode public debt, thereby incentivizing the indebtedness of countries. For example, in the 1970s, the Great Inflation helped to reduce public debt burden in various countries such as the United States, the United Kingdom, and France.

[20] Idem, p. 47.

[21] See Taylor (1979), pp. 1267–1286. The concept of monetary policy rule must be distinguished here from any legal understanding. We use this concept, in this section, to identify the 'prescribed guide for monetary policy', as indicated in Svensson (1999), p. 3.

[22] See Taylor (1979), pp. 1267–1286. For an overview of the output/inflation variability trade-off, cf. also Dittmar, Gavin, and Kydland (1999), pp. 23–29.

[23] The GDP gap (or output gap) is defined as the difference between the real GDP and potential GDP.

[24] For a better explanation of Taylor's findings, see Taylor (1994), pp. 21–38.

[25] Cecchetti (1998), pp. 1–2.

[26] Cecchetti (1997). For a non-exhaustive literature review on the proposals to estimate optimal policy rules, see Salter (2014). For examples of these estimate attempts, in general see Taylor (1999b).

These new understandings led central banks in many countries to move away from past policies aimed at controlling exchange rates or the volume of monetary aggregates, and adopt some forms of inflation targeting.[27] This policy rule can be defined as a monetary policy strategy whose primary objective is to maintain inflation at a constant level or within a band,[28] as to guarantee a more predictable, less discretionary monetary policy steadily focused on price stability.[29]

And it is price stability—quoting the very celebrated lecture held by Milton Friedman in 1981[30]—deemed as the control of the absolute level of prices, which was to become the long-run objective of monetary policy in the following years.

From these premises, it must be noted that a general macroeconomic role of pursuing stabilization policy can be attributed to central bankers. It is not the case, indeed, that a widespread consensus exists today among economists and policymakers that central bankers are the sole policymakers that may help reducing business cycle fluctuations, enabling a smooth real growth.[31] This stabilization objective, however, complements the long-run objective of price stability as long as central banks pursue their long-run policy 'in a manner that contributes to minimizing economic fluctuations'.[32]

As of the early 1990s, the adoption of the inflation targeting has been quite successful around the world. Not only it has been able to substantially reduce past hyperinflation characterizing the industrialized countries, but it also contributed to promote real economic growth and reduce output fluctuations.[33] Accordingly, while inflation has been reduced to levels which are on average consistent with the objective of price stability, the aggregate GDP growth has been relatively stable.[34]

[27] For an overview of policy rules operationalized since the 1970s, see Mishkin (2000a).

[28] This definition is taken from Guender and Oh (2006), p. 373.

[29] Taylor (2013a), p. 335.

[30] See Friedman (1982), pp. 98–118. The lecture was presented on 5 July 1981, at the meetings of the Western Economic Association in San Francisco, California.

[31] See Cecchetti (1998), p. 1; Taylor (1986), p. 159.

[32] Friedman (1982), p. 100.

[33] Mishkin (2000a), pp. 22–23.

[34] As explained by Clarida, Gali, and Gertler (1998), for example, this is the case of the United States.

3.1.2 *The Critical Objective of Inflation Targeting*

As for the case of macroprudential policy, it is widely acknowledged that a monetary policy based on policy rules must comprise a set of key components that are organized to pursue the ultimate objective of inflation targeting. If the failure of past policy rules led central banks to adopt, as a pragmatic response, the inflation targeting, it is necessary to examine in detail what are the key components of such monetary policy regime, starting from the rationale of its objective.

The idea of targeting inflation directly by means of an operating monetary policy framework, as seen above, has been a reaction to the failure of past monetary rules adopted by central banks to control the price level. For example, in the past, some central banks used, as nominal anchor to stabilize the price level, a currency peg tying the domestic currency value to the currency value of another low-inflation country.[35] Other countries, instead, in order to control the inflation rate, adopted policy rules based on monetary targeting which imply targeting directly the volume of money supply.[36]

These policy rules eventually failed in stabilizing prices. In the first case, central banks were constrained by the currency peg in their ability to timely respond to wide-system shocks or changes in the interest rate, whereas, in the second case, the instability of the money demand brought about a factual unfeasibility to control properly the money volume.[37] As a result, targeting inflation more directly became a more promising policy rule for central banks to control the spread of prices and reduce the overall costs associated with high level of inflation.

To set a definition of this policy rule, the IMF internationally recognized that the inflation targeting has to involve 'the public announcement of medium-term numerical targets for inflation with an institutional commitment by the monetary authority to achieve these targets'.[38] Accordingly, within this framework 'monetary decisions are to be guided by the

[35] On the issue, see in particular Martínez (2008), pp. 86–87. In addition, for a historical inquiry, see Vargas-Silva (2010), pp. 432–434. An interesting analysis about currency pegs as price stabilizers is given in Frankel (2011), pp. 1–70.

[36] See Jahan (2012). For a survey on money growth targets, inter alia, see Friedman and Kuttner (1996), pp. 77–146.

[37] See Jahan (2012). For a general survey of the past monetary strategies, see Mishkin (2009).

[38] See IMF (2009).

deviation of forecasts of future inflation from the announced target, with the inflation forecast acting (implicitly or explicitly), as the intermediate target of monetary policy'.[39]

Despite this general characterization, capturing the essence of this policy rule is not an easy task. Although different central banks recognized—*formally or informally*—inflation targeting as own monetary policy rule, divergences in its institutional and operational setting currently exist.[40]

Besides these divergences, however, the economic literature argues that the viability of the inflation targeting policy is based on five structural elements which eventually compose the actual operating strategy of central banking:

1. central banks must announce an explicit quantitative target for medium/long periods;
2. the institutional framework must clearly and unambiguously indicate the central bank's commitment to price stability as the actual long-run target of its monetary policy, preceding all other objectives;
3. central banks must establish an informative strategy consisting in a model and/or a methodology for inflation forecasting that takes into account all possible relevant variables affecting inflation expectations;
4. a transparent procedure must be set up enabling the markets and the general public to be constantly informed about the monetary adjustments undertaken by central banks; and
5. central banks in pursuing the inflation targeting must be subject to increased accountability.[41]

It must be noted that these key elements are tracked within the evolutionary path of the monetarist policy framework established by Milton Friedman years before.[42] Albeit the monetarist school suggests to adopt a long-run target based on monetary growth, it shares the institutional commitment to price stability as the primary long-run goal of central bank's monetary policy.[43]

[39] Idem.

[40] See Bernanke (2003a).

[41] This monetary policy strategy is elaborated by Mishkin (2007), pp. 599–600. The same approach can be found also in Heenan, Peter, and Roger (2006), pp. 3–4.

[42] In particular, see Friedman (1982), p. 101.

[43] Mishkin (2007), p. 609.

The choice of a policy rule based on inflation targeting, instead of monetary aggregates, finds its rationale in the number of advantages that the former is capable to achieve. Among others, policy decisions based on inflation targeting not only are unaffected by the shocks that may distort the stability of the money-inflation relationship, but also they configure 'better' decisions in the sense that are grounded on a range of different macroeconomic variables, and not just monetary aggregates, increasing the reliability and transparency of the decision-making processes.[44]

However, a fundamental position in the explanation of the targeting strategy is assumed by the concept of price stability which describes the monetary standard to which the policy settings have to be calibrated. But defining accurately this concept is not straightforward.

In 1983 Paul Volcker suggested that

> a workable definition of reasonable "price stability" would [...] be a situation in which expectations of generally rising (or falling) prices over a considerable period are not a pervasive influence on economic and financial behavior. [...] "stability" would imply that decision-making should be able to proceed on the basis that "real" and "nominal" values are substantially the same over the planning horizon—and that planning horizons should be suitably long.[45]

Thirty years later, Alan Greenspan identified price stability, more generally, 'when households and business need not factor expectations of changes in the average level of prices into their decisions'.[46] These broad explanations, however, are not sufficient to clarify the functional content of price stability which seems to remain largely vague.

Even more interesting is to identify those elements, as recognized by the economic literature that may enable a detailed reconstruction of the price stability concept. In particular, it is first necessary that central banks recognize price stability as price index stability or low inflation.[47] In the first sense, price stability simply means zero inflation, while the second meaning entails that price stability is achieved through low levels of price increases.[48] On the issue, it is sufficient to mention that the world's major central banks, as the ECB and the Bank of England, incorporate the

[44] On the issue, see the voice *Inflation Targeting* in Snowdon and Vane (2002), pp. 361–365.

[45] Volcker (1983), p. 5.

[46] Greenspan (1994), p. 5.

[47] Svensson (1999), p. 1.

[48] Beyeler (2007), p. 94. See also Fischer (1994), p. 284.

concept of price stability into their current monetary policy strategy[49] with this latter meaning.

After having recognized the notion of price stability as low inflation, it is necessary to establish an appropriate price index along with a numerical level for the quantitative target.[50] As for the case of the ECB, many central banks have adopted an explicit numerical point/range target for inflation,[51] while it is widely accepted that the optimal benchmark for inflation targeting is the consumer price index (CPI).

This approach, however, leaves room to a number of criticalities. In this way, price stability refers just to an average of all prices taken into account by the index. This means that, while the prices of a number of goods may remain stable over a certain period, the prices of other goods could go far above the quantitative target.[52] This average represents just a fictitious number that seeks to include a wide variety of price trends. The issue is further complicated by the fact that this average reflects an extended period of time: it does not refer to a constant level of prices, but, rather, to a temporal average that may hide divergent movements.[53]

This double averaging can triple if one thinks that the average level of prices may change dramatically according to the geographic areas under statistical analysis. The price level may be very different across nearby regions, although, on average, it could meet the quantitative target.[54] In addition, it is interesting to note that price indexes have shown over time considerable problems of measurement bias and errors whose materialization can affect, to some extent, the reliability of the policy rule.[55] Moreover, the notion of price stability needs to establish what is the role that the real

[49] The monetary policy strategy shall not be confused with the monetary policy legal frameworks where this specification, that is, price stability as low levels of inflation increase, is not provided.

[50] Svensson (1999), p. 1.

[51] On the issue, see Jahan (2012).

[52] See Wallis (1960), pp. 146–147, and Anderson (2001).

[53] For this reason, some suggest that an optimal policy should index only the subset of prices that display some stickiness. For details, see Lama and Medina (2007), p. 29.

[54] This is the case, for example, of the economic unions, such as the EMU, where the differential distribution effects of monetary policy cannot be ignored by a central bank. For insights on this criticality, see Barnett (2011), p. 225.

[55] On the issue, see ILO, IMF, OECD, SOEC, UN, WB (2004), pp. 207–214.

variables, such as real output and employment, have to play in the pursuit of the monetary policy objectives.[56]

That said, it is clear that inflation targeting cannot be considered as just a policy rule for the conduct of monetary policy. The above considerations suggest that inflation targeting represents a proper policy framework[57] whose different components must be operationalized in a manner that permits the fulfillment of the acknowledged monetary policy objectives. Concretizing this framework through the adoption of clear and effective monetary instruments and legal boundaries is one of the core issues of modern central banking.

3.1.3 Concretizing Price Stability

After considering the price stability targeting of central banks, a few words must be devoted to explain how the monetary policy strategy of central banks is operationalized. Since central banks cannot directly decide the prices of goods and services in the economy and automatically adjust the inflation level, they need an operating policy framework consisting of operating targets and intermediate variables which may directly affect the general level of prices.

3.1.3.1 The Operational Target of Monetary Policy

The implementation of inflation targeting is first subject to the identification of one operational target to be defined as 'an economic variable, which the central bank wants to control, and indeed can control, to a very large extent on a day-by-day basis through the use of its monetary policy instruments'.[58]

Albeit the operational targets may differ across central banks,[59] Bindseil (2011)[60] recognizes some common features: in particular, (1) it should be

[56] Svensson (1999), p. 1. On the issue, see also Svensson (2002), pp. 261–312; Viñals and Valles (1999).

[57] Bernanke and Mishkin (1997), p. 2.

[58] Bindseil (2004), p. 9.

[59] For an overview of the different operations targets available to central banks, see Berk (2001), pp. 4–7; Walsh (2010), pp. 521–530; Bindseil (2014), pp. 36–38. For a survey on the literature on operational targets of monetary policy, see Friedman (1988), pp. 23–39.

[60] Bindseil (2011), p. 8. See also Lyndgren (1990), p. 308; for a discussion on how the choice of the operating targets may influence the use of monetary policy instruments and affect central bank's balance sheet, see Schaechter (2001), pp. 1–28.

sufficiently controlled by the central bank; (2) it should be capable to influence price stability effectively; (3) it must be decided by the decision-making of the central bank; and (4) it must ensure sufficient guidance to central bank officers on how to implement day-by-day monetary policy.

To put it briefly, a general agreement among central bankers currently exists on the idea that the preferred operational target reflecting these characteristics is the short-term interbank interest rate, with particular regard to the unsecured overnight rate.[61] As a result, major central banks today rely on such short-term rate in the pursuit of the price stability objective.[62]

3.1.3.2 The Instruments of Monetary Policy

Further components of the operational frameworks are the monetary policy instruments intended, as argued above, to control the operational target. Although several monetary policy instruments have been defined in the past,[63] central banks currently rely on three major instruments: (1) market operations, (2) standing facilities, and (3) reserve requirements. These instruments play a key role in stabilizing the short-term interest rates of the interbank market and permit the enlargement of the money supply to the banking system.

1. Market operations can be defined as the central bank transactions with credit institutions at the central bank's own initiative.[64] These transactions involve primarily outright purchases and/or sales of

[61] Among others, see Bindseil (2004), p. 9; Schaechter (2001), p. 3; Hardy (1997), p. 4, arguing that central banks of almost all industrialized countries implement policy by setting as operational target the short-term interbank interest rate.

[62] The short-term interbank interest rate is adopted as an operational target in—inter alia—the United Kingdom, Indonesia, Iran, Russia, Sri Lanka, Australia, and Mexico. Similarly, since 1981, the FED has adopted as operational target the federal fund rate, which is the overnight interest rate on unsecured interbank loans. The operational target of the Eurosystem is the overnight interbank interest rate known as European Overnight Index Average (EONIA). For a brief overview on this topic, see Kaiser, Heilenkötter, Herrmann, and Krämer (2012), pp. 42–45. See also Allanazarova (2010), pp. 15–18.

[63] This is the case of the interest rate ceilings and margin requirements used by central banks as stabilization tools. For an overview of these tools, see Jain and Tomic (1995), pp. 280–295.

[64] This definition is provided by Bindseil (2014), p. 9. For insights on open market operations, see also Axilrod (1997); Edwards (1997), pp. 859–872.

securities, such as treasury bills and other debt securities.[65] Should the central bank decide to buy these assets, it can do so by issuing an equivalent amount of new currency, expanding this way the reserve base and increasing the ability of credit institutions to expand the money supply through new loans.[66]

Conversely, if the central bank decides to sell securities, the reserve base is to be reduced while the credit supply starts to tighten. A sub-category of the open market operations are the lending operations via reverse transactions.[67] In this case, the central bank buys or sells eligible assets under repurchase agreements—so-called repos—or grants credit against eligible assets posted as collaterals.[68]

2. The standing facilities are central bank operations that allow credit institutions to manage liquidity at their own initiative, under the conditions set by the central bank.[69] Two types of facilities are commonly used today: (1) a marginal lending facility and (2) a deposit facility. Through the marginal lending facility, banks can borrow directly from the central bank on an overnight basis against the provision of eligible collaterals at a discount rate specified by the central bank. Via the deposit facility, banks can make overnight deposits with the central bank, which are remunerated at a specific rate.

   Standing facilities are of primary importance for the achievement of the operational target because central banks, by setting the interest rate on the marginal lending facility as the upper ceiling and the rate on overnight deposit as the floor, determine the corridor within which the short-term interbank interest rate can fluctuate.[70]

3. The third monetary policy instrument is the reserve requirements. As argued above, banks must hold a certain level of minimum reserves which are deposited on their account with the central bank.[71] The compliance with the reserve requirements is measured

[65] Bindseil (2014), p. 9.

[66] Labonte (2015), p. 3.

[67] Belke and Polleit (2009), p. 43.

[68] de Haan, Oosterloo, and Schoenmaker (2012), p. 113.

[69] Bindseil (2014), p. 9. For better insights on the standing facilities of central banks, see also Hesse and Braasch (1996), pp. 275–291.

[70] Ulrike (2007), p. 17. In general on this topic, see also Bindseil (2014), pp. 130–142; Bertaut (2002), p. 27; Bindseil and Jabłecki (2011).

[71] For a historical perspective, cf. Galvenius and Mercier (2011), pp. 162–173.

on the basis of end-of-day snapshots, while the requirement may apply to single-day ends or to an average over a certain period.[72]

Central banks can decide, if necessary, to adjust the numerical levels of reserve requirements within the boundaries set by law, thereby affecting the volume of liquidity available into the market, although this instrument has been rarely used over time.[73]

3.1.3.3 The Intermediate Variables of Monetary Policy

In addition to the monetary policy instruments, the so-called intermediate variables—best known in the past as *intermediate objectives*—complete the inflation targeting framework.[74] These intermediate variables are defined as economic variables that can be controlled directly by the central bank and used as the primary indicator of price stability, given a sufficiently stable and predictable interrelationship with the ultimate monetary policy objective.[75] The rationale of these variables is to provide a basic framework that may help responding automatically to possible economic shocks.[76] In fact, as implied by the above considerations, the monetary policy instruments are not directly related to the price stability objective,[77] although they are capable to directly affect the operational target.

Therefore, there is the need to ensure a framework of intermediate variables that can relate the monetary policy instruments to the ultimate objective of monetary policy. However, choosing the accurate variables

[72] Bindseil (2014), p. 38.

[73] Labonte (2015), p. 4.

[74] While in the past these variables were considered proper intermediate targets, over the last decade, many small- and medium-sized economies have considered these variables just as useful informative instruments to central banks. For this reason, we refer to them as *intermediate variables*. For more details, see Bindseil (2004), p. 9; Debelle, Masson, Savastano, and Sharma (1998).

[75] Bindseil (2004), p. 9. For a critical appraisal on the relevance of the intermediate variables for monetary policy, see also Friedman (1984).

[76] Walsh (2010), p. 529.

[77] For more details on this topic, see Mourmouras and Arghyrou (2000), p. 82.

constitutes an intricate policy decision that has not found yet unanimous views in the economic literature.[78,79]

It is generally recognized that an optimal variable should meet the following criteria: (1) it must be sufficiently controllable, in the sense that the central bank must be able to adjust the target should some deviations from the wanted policy path emerge; (2) it must be sufficiently measurable, in order to determine if, and to what extent, the ultimate target of monetary policy is achieved; and (3) it must have predictable effects on the final targets it is supposed to influence directly, so that the central bank may decide the types of policy adjustments needed accordingly.[80] In accordance with these criteria, typical intermediate variables have been mainly monetary aggregates, exchange rates, or long-term interest rates.[81]

To understand the relationship between all these components of the operational framework for targeting inflation, and to describe how the short-term interbank interest rate and the inflation level are so related, it is necessary at this point to shed light on the monetary policy transmission mechanism, and its functioning, by which the operational target, the monetary policy instruments, and the intermediate variables are linked together, along with the ultimate objective of monetary policy.[82]

[78] For a critical survey of the different variables scrutinized by the economic literature, see in particular the Federal Reserve Bank of New York (1990), pp. 20–420. On the same topic, cf. Pindyck and Roberts (1976), pp. 627–650; Belongia and Batten (1992); Gaspar and Abreu (1998). For an overview of the relevant literature, see also Berk (2001), pp. 5–7.

[79] While in the past these variables were considered proper intermediate targets, over the last decade, many small- and medium-sized economies have considered these variables just as useful informative instruments to central banks. For this reason, we refer to them as *intermediate variables*. For more details, see Bindseil (2004), p. 9; Debelle, Masson, Savastano, and Sharma (1998).

[80] Mourmouras and Arghyrou (2000), pp. 82–83.

[81] See Bindseil (2004), p. 9. For an overview of the intermediate variables used by some countries, inter alia, see Berg, Hagan, Jarvis, Steinki, Stone, and Zanello (2003), pp. 45–50; Mehran, Quintyn, Nordman, and Laurens (1996), pp. 72–73. For a discussion on the predictability and controllability of inflation as intermediate variable, see Mishkin (2009), pp. 220–221.

[82] Bindseil (2014), pp. 37–38.

3.2 The Monetary Policy Transmission Channels in a Nutshell

As anticipated in the previous section, central banks are able to affect inflation and real variables, through a number of transmission channels, which jointly constitute the so-called 'monetary policy transmission mechanism'. The monetary policy transmission mechanism can be defined as a combination of different channels through which changes in the short-term interbank interest rate affect aggregate output and prices, and may ultimately achieve the inflation target.[83]

Among others, the transmission mechanism is set to allow central banks to influence, directly or indirectly, a number of macroeconomic variables, such as market interest rates, exchange rates, asset prices, credit growth, and firm balance sheets, any of which represents the pathway of a specific transmission channel.[84] By way of these channels, central bank's policy decisions are capable to determine, in the long run, the nominal or money values of goods and services, that is, the general level of prices. Such outcome on the real economy, however, is not immediate, and, more often, a long, variable, and unpredictable time lag is needed to assess any long-lasting real effects of the policy implementation.[85]

Today the debate on the effective functioning of the monetary policy transmission channels remains a priority among macroeconomists, although its complete understanding remains a complex issue.[86] First, the monetary policy mechanism is not equal everywhere. Different economic substrates, such as the monetary policy regime, the stage of development of financial system, and the features of the real economy, all shape and diversify the construction of the monetary transmission mechanism across various countries.[87] Second, the process of globalization and internationalization of financial markets has produced substantial changes—in the industrialized countries as well as in the emerging economies—which altered the functioning of the transmission channels.[88]

[83] Purvis (1992), pp. 763–765. *Cf.* also: Berk (1998), pp. 148–149.

[84] See Mishkin (1996).

[85] ECB (2000), p. 43.

[86] Lopes (1998), p. 65. See also Mishkin (1995), pp. 3–10.

[87] For examples, in general, see BIS (1995); Cevik and Teksoz (2012), pp. 5–7; Mohanty and Turner (2008).

[88] Kamin (2010), p. 3. See also Issing (2000) and Schmukler (2004).

Nonetheless, in order to avoid uncertainty about timing and effectiveness of their policy actions and maintain, in this way, macro-financial stability,[89] policymakers and central bankers need to have a deep understanding of how, and to what extent, monetary policy decisions are transmitted into the real economy through the transmission channels.

This issue has become even more important after the breakdown of the financial system that poses a challenge to central banks in understanding the role of their policy instruments in the materialization of systemic shocks. Today there is a large consensus in the economic literature that monetary policy may contribute in the build-up of systemic risks to financial stability.[90]

As explained in the following sections, through these transmission channels, central bank's monetary policy decisions may incentivize risk-taking behaviors and start a destabilizing spiral that can ultimately turn into a systemic event. Therefore the understanding of how the transmission mechanism work is a primary question to be discussed, because it permits later to shed light on how monetary policy and macroprudential instruments are intertwined and come to interact to each other.

3.2.1 The Transmission Channels: An Overview

In the last two decades, the economic research has evolved significantly describing the existence of five channels for the transmission of monetary policy.[91] Major efforts have been made to understand how each of these channels is deemed to operate within the context of the New Keynesian theory, which depicts the general equilibrium models largely adopted by central banks in the pursuit of their monetary policy evaluation.[92]

[89] Cevik and Teksoz (2012), p. 3.

[90] Among others, see Adrian and Liang (2014); Bluhm, Faia, and Krahnen (2014); Peydró (2014), pp. 37–47; Dokko, Doyle, Kiley, Kim, Sherlund, Sim, and Van den Heuvel (2009). In general, for a survey of the relevant literature, see Allen and Rogoff (2010).

[91] For a general survey on the monetary policy transmission channels, see Boivin, Kiley, and Mishkin (2010).

[92] Inter alia, *cf.* Leith, Moldovan, and Rossi (2009); Schmidt and Wieland (2012); Ramón Pedrero and Pérez (2005). It should be noted, as a prominent example, that the ECB uses a new Keynesian dynamic stochastic general equilibrium (DSGE) model—widely known as Smets-Wouters model—for its monetary policy analysis. For the technical details of this model, see Smets and Wouters (2003), pp. 1123–1175.

Further, remarkable advancements have been recently made in the development of new dynamic macroeconomic models incorporating several important features, such as the rational formation of expectations, improving the quantitative analysis.[93] Far from being a survey on such macroeconomic literature, this section aims at outlining the core findings of this prominent literature and, thus, describing mechanics and functioning of the transmission channels more generally.

3.2.1.1 Interest Rate, Exchange Rate, and Asset Price Channels

1. The traditional Keynesian macroeconomic theory, as formalized by the *Hicks-Hansen model*,[94] identifies *the interest rate channel* as a monetary policy transmission path. Assuming sticky prices and slow price adjustments to monetary shocks, an expansionary monetary policy, by lowering short-term nominal interest rates, leads to a decline in real interest rates, which in turn lowers the cost of capital. Because of the lower cost of capital, economic agents are willing to increase investment spending, which leads to an increase in aggregate demand and, consequently, in output growth.[95]

   In contrast, a contractionary monetary policy, characterized by a rise in the short-term nominal interest rate, leads to an increase in real interest rates, since 'investors have to arbitrage away differences in risk-adjusted expected returns on debt instruments of various maturities'.[96] Finding that the real cost of capital has increased, investors curb their investment spending, while households, having to bear higher borrowing costs, rationalize their purchases. As a consequence of lower aggregate demand, the aggregate output falls as well.
2. The second transmission channel by which changes in the short-term interest rate affect real variables is the *exchange rate channel*. Similar to the interest rate channel, the economic literature acknowledges the exchange rate channel as a standard component

[93] For an overview of the relevant literature, see Gali and Gertler (2007), pp. 25–45.

[94] This model was developed by Sir John R. Hicks and Alvin H. Hansen as an instrument to formalize the relationship between classical theory and the general theory of employment, interest, and money of John Maynard Keynes. It was published the first time in 1937 in Hicks, John R. (1937), pp. 147–159. For a historical survey of the Hicks-Hansen model in the macroeconomic literature, see in particular De Vroey and Hoover (2005).

[95] Mishkin (1996), pp. 2–4. See also Belke and Polleit (2009), pp. 584–586.

[96] Ireland (2005), p. 3. See also Mukherjee and Bhattacharya (2011), p. 5.

of the monetary policy transmission mechanism in open economies.[97] The functioning of this channel is straightforward: when the domestic real interest rate falls below the real interest rates of foreign counterparts, domestic deposits expressed in the national currency become less attractive with respect to deposits abroad denominated in foreign currencies.

The value of domestic deposits relative to foreign deposits, thus, falls leading to a depreciation of the national currency. With a depreciated national currency, domestic goods are now cheaper than foreign goods, resulting in a boost of net exports. In the end, as the net exports increase, the aggregate output rises accordingly.[98] The opposite also holds true. Should the domestic real interest rate rise above the foreign ones, the ultimate result would be an appreciation of the domestic currency leading to a fall of net exports and, thus, of domestic aggregate output.[99]

3. In the 1960s two other important channels of transmission involving asset prices have been identified by James Tobin and Franco Modigliani.
   (a) The first of these channels is based on Tobin's q-theory of investment[100] which provides a model describing how, and to what extent, monetary policy may affect real economy by means of its effects on equity market value. In his model, Tobin provides a definition of q as the market value of firms divided by the replacement cost of capital.[101] When q is high, the market price of firm is high relative to the replacement cost of capital. Thus, new investment in equipment and plants are cheap with regard to the high market value of firms.

   Against this backdrop, firms are incentivized to issue new equity in order to obtain a high price for it that can be used for new investment spending. The investment spending of the

[97] Inter alia, see Fleming (1962), pp. 369–379; Mundell (1963), pp. 227–257; Smets and Wouters (1999); Benigno and Benigno (2001); Bowman and Doyle (2003).

[98] Mishkin (1996), pp. 5–6.

[99] See Ireland (2005), pp. 3–4.

[100] See Tobin (1969), pp. 15–29.

[101] Tobin and Brainard (1968), pp. 8–9; Tobin (1969), p. 21.

firms rises because they can now purchase a lot of new goods with only a relatively small issue of equity.[102]

What is pivotal in his model, however, is that monetary policy may contribute to increase firm's investment spending and, thus, asset prices.[103] With an expansionary monetary policy firms are supposed to have more money at their disposal than they want. To make this extra money profitable, firms are incentivized to reduce their holding by increasing the investment spending. Thus, since one of the possible investment targets is the stock market, if the demand for equity increases, the market value of assets should move upward.[104]

(b) The other transmission channel involving asset prices is derived from Modigliani's life-cycle theory of consumption.[105] In his model, Modigliani describes the consumer spending as driven by the lifetime resources of consumers,[106] namely, wealth and income. In those countries where a significant component of consumers' wealth is represented by common equity, the level of consumer spending is related to the equity price trends. If equity prices rise, the value of consumers' wealth increases, so that consumers will be incentivized to increase their consumption. As a result, the aggregate output will rise.

Conversely, if equity prices drop down, the consumer wealth falls. In this case, consumers are induced to decrease their consumption with negative consequences for the output growth.[107] Against this backdrop, a further transmission channel can be so defined: an expansionary/contractionary monetary policy is

[102] As argued by Tobin and Brainard (1968), p. 9, 'investment is stimulated when capital is valued more highly in the market than it costs to produce it, and discouraged when its valuation is less than its replacement cost'.

[103] See Tobin (1969), p. 29. For some recent literature on how monetary policy affects Tobin's *q*, see Fariaa, Mollickb, Sachsidac, and Wang (2012), pp. 1–10; Ehrmann and Fratzscher (2004); Ida (2013), pp. 733–740; Basua, Gillmanb, and Pearlmanc (2012), pp. 1057–1074.

[104] See Mishkin (1996), pp. 6–7.

[105] See Ando and Modigliani (1963), pp. 55–84. See also Modigliani (1966), pp. 160–217. For an exhaustive explanation of this transmission channel, instead, see Modigliani (1971), pp. 9–97; Modigliani (1986), pp. 297–313.

[106] Modigliani (1986), pp. 299–300.

[107] This model is elaborated in Modigliani (1971), pp. 9–84. For a simplified explanation of this mechanism, see also Mishkin (1996), p. 7; Ireland (2005), p. 4.

capable to increase/decrease equity prices and, thus, consumers' wealth, thereby affecting consumption and, accordingly, the aggregate output.[108]

3.2.1.2 Credit Channels

Notwithstanding the above transmission channels, as formalized by the economic literature, offer fruitful insights on how monetary policy may affect the general level of prices and, consequently, the real economy, two additional channels of transmission are to be scrutinized in order to complete the picture of the monetary policy transmission mechanism and, further, recognize how monetary policy may contribute to the build-up of systemic risks.

We refer here to the so-called credit channels,[109] which are based on the existence of asymmetric information in financial markets.[110]

1. The first credit channel at issue is the ***bank lending channel*** by which banks contribute to the money aggregates within the economy. Basic assumptions of this model are that (1) there must be certain classes of borrowers, such as small and medium firms, which are fully dependent on banks' lending,[111] and (2) central banks must be able to influence, by conducting monetary policy operations, the credit supply of banks.[112]

   Against this backdrop, open market operations leading to an expansion in the supply of bank reserves and in bank deposits increase the quantity of money supply available for borrowers. Due to the lower interest rates, the increase of money supply leads to an

[108] The economic literature on this additional transmission channel is extensive. For some examples, inter alia, see Deaton (2005), pp. 91–107; Ludvigson, Steindel, and Lettau (2002), pp. 117–133; Di Maggio, Kermani, and Ramcharan (2014); Koivu (2010).

[109] See Mishkin (1996), p. 9. On the credit channel of monetary policy, see, in addition, the following authors: Bernanke and Gertler (1995), pp. 27–48; Ramey (1993), pp. 1–45; Ciccarelli, Maddaloni, and Peydró (2010); Hubbard (1995), pp. 63–77; Hendricks (2011), pp. 403–416.

[110] The asymmetric information featuring these transmission channels are generally described as moral hazard and adverse selection. For more details on this topic, inter alia, see Neyer (2001).

[111] This is the case when there are no other financial institutions that may substitute banks as credit providers.

[112] Kashyap and Stein (1994), p. 5.

increase of loans that, in turn, is supposed to cause a rise in investment and consumer spending.[113] By contrast, when central bank tightens its policy, bank holdings and deposits fall immediately. Within a certain time lag, bank loans follow, and a downward trend of aggregate output appears.[114]

2. The second credit channel at stake operates via the borrowers' balance sheets. This *balance sheet channel* is based on the premise that the greater the net worth of borrowers, the lower is the adverse selection and moral hazard problem in lending to them and, thus, the premium they should pay on their loans.[115]

   Fluctuations in the quality of borrowers' balance sheets influence their investment decisions and spending behaviors.[116] For example, if the net worth of borrowers is lower, banks have at their disposal less collateral for their loans. Facing higher risks, these lenders simply decide to decrease their lending to finance investment and consumer spending. At the same time, since borrowers have lower net worth, but higher moral hazard, they are incentivized to increase their leverage position with related additional risks for banks. However, banks, anticipating that these borrowers will not be likely able to pay back, are rationally induced to decrease the credit supply, thereby negatively affecting the sources of funding available for borrowers' spending.[117]

   Via the balance sheet channel, central banks may therefore affect borrowers' decisions in investment and consumer spending which may finally turn into higher or lower aggregate demand and output growth.

   For example, an expansionary monetary policy, pushing up asset prices, raises borrowers' net worth, with a following increase in investment spending and aggregate demand.[118] Moreover, the same expan-

[113] See Mishkin (1996), p. 9.

[114] Kashyap and Stein (1994), p. 6. Empirical evidences of this are provided by Bernanke and Blinder (1992), pp. 901–921.

[115] Mishkin (1996), p. 10. For an overview of the literature on the balance sheet channel of monetary policy, see Igan, Kabundi, De Simone, and Tamirisa (2013), p. 5.

[116] Bernanke and Gertler (1995), p. 35. See also Holmstrom and Tirole (1997), pp. 663–691. The authors provide evidences that banks with lower net worth, due to a contractionary monetary policy, supply fewer loans. On the issue, see also Favero, Giavazzi, and Flabbi (1999).

[117] See Mishkin (1996), pp. 10–11.

[118] Mishkin (1996), p. 11.

sionary monetary policy stance affects positively the borrowers' net cash flow and reduces interest expenses, so that, in general, the overall quality of borrowers' balance sheets is strengthened even further.[119]

Not to forget that, since the borrowers' liabilities are fixed in nominal terms, an expansionary monetary policy leading to a likely rise of nominal prices decreases the real value of borrowers' liabilities, without lowering, however, the real value of their assets.[120]

3.2.2 *The Dark Side of Monetary Policy Transmission: The Risk-Taking Channel*

Although the literature on the monetary policy transmission mechanism is rather extensive, after the 2007 financial crisis, a new approach has been taken to explore the functioning of the transmission channels. A current stream of economic scholarship, in fact, suggests the existence of a 'dark side' in the smooth functioning of the monetary policy *credit channels*, which questions the stabilizing function carried out by central banks through their monetary policy operations.

More precisely, changes in the operational target not only may affect the credit supply of banks, but they may also affect banks' incentives to take on risks when granting loans.[121] Hence, a negative relationship does exist between the level of short-term interests targeted by central banks and the degree of bank risk-taking.[122]

Because of this relationship, a further transmission channel can be identified in the so-called risk-taking channel of monetary policy.[123] The banking sector is featured by intermediaries that finance themselves by borrowing short. The costs of such financing are strictly tied to changes of the short-term policy rates decided by central bank, and, since these funding costs affect to a great extent banks' decisions on their risk preferences,

[119] Bernanke and Gertler (1995), p. 36. The opposite also holds true. See Mishkin (1995), p. 8, arguing that a contractionary monetary policy 'causes a deterioration of borrowers' balance sheets because it reduces cash flow'.

[120] Mishkin (1996), p. 11.

[121] ECB (2010), p. 90.

[122] Bonfim and Soares (2014), p. 2.

[123] For a detailed analysis of the risk-taking channel of monetary policy, inter alia, see Altunbas, Gambacorta, and Marques-Ibanez (2009); Dell'Ariccia, Laeven, and Suarez (2013); Bianchi (2014), pp. 161–168; Angeloni, Faia, and Lo Duca (2015), pp. 285–307.

variations of central bank's monetary policy have substantial influence on the degree of risk ultimately borne by the banking sector as a whole.[124]

As a result, the understanding of this risk-taking channel complements and encompasses the more traditional credit channels,[125] focusing on the effects that monetary policy operations have on real economy by acting on banks' risk perceptions and risk appetite and, thus, on the degree of risks in their investment portfolios.[126] Different mechanisms have been identified by the economic literature on how the risk-taking channel is deemed to operate.

1. An expansionary monetary policy, by lowering the short-term policy rates, leads to a decrease of the interest rate on bank loans. As the profitability on banks' portfolios declines, highly capitalized banks, looking for higher yielding, are so incentivized to increase their leverage position and, in turn, their risk-taking, while the incentives for monitoring decrease.[127] At the same time, the risk-taking channel operates through the liability side of banks' balance sheet. In an environment of expansionary monetary policy, indeed, lower interest rates decrease also the banks' cost of capital, incentivizing credit institutions to increase their leverage even further.[128] This scenario may feature a relaxation of the credit standards, which can easily turn into an excessive growth of credit supply.[129]
2. Changes in the short-term policy rates impact interest rates on valuations, incomes, and cash flows.[130] More precisely, lower interest rates raise the value of assets and collaterals as well as income and profits, making the banks' balance sheet position stronger. As a consequence, the leverage decreases. And, by relying on a greater sustainability of their financial position and having less perception of risks, banks increase their short-term funding and expand credit for

[124] See Bruno and Shin (2013), pp. 1–2.

[125] Bonfim and Soares (2014), p. 5.

[126] Borio and Zhu (2008), p. 9.

[127] Dell'Ariccia, Laeven, and Marquez (2010), p. 18. Additional evidences are provided in De Nicolò, Dell'Ariccia, Laeven, and Valencia (2010); Buch, Eickmeier, and Prieto (2011).

[128] Dell'Ariccia, Laeven, and Marquez (2010), p. 4.

[129] ECB (2010), p. 90. For a survey on this topic, see Maddaloni and Peydró (2010); Maddaloni and Peydró (2011); Ongena and Peydró (2011), pp. 21–28; Paligorova and Sierra Jimenez (2012), pp. 23–30.

[130] Borio and Zhu (2008), p. 9. See also Gambacorta (2009), pp. 44–45.

riskier investments.[131] This augmented risk tolerance, therefore, inexorably leads to a higher risk-taking which, in turn, is reflected in an expansion of balance sheet and credit supply.

3. The risk-taking channel may operate by distorting the incentives of bank managers in an environment of very low interest rates.[132] As already explained above, the volume of aggregate risky investments increases in times of expansionary monetary policy. Against this backdrop, when the risk in the entrepreneurial sector is very high, investors are more likely to reduce direct investments and hold more bank deposits. This leaves banks with an excess of liquidity to be invested which, in turn, dramatizes the moral hazard problem of banks' managers whose payoffs are linked to the bank activity volume. Therefore, by having a liquidity surplus at their disposals, managers are incentivized to take overly aggressive behaviors by lending too much and assuming excessive risk.[133]

   Some economic literature identifies a further mechanism of the risk-taking channel in the communication policies and the reaction function of central banks[134] (so-called signaling channel). In particular, the level of transparency and commitment of future monetary policy decisions can influence future market behaviors. For example, by increasing the degree of transparency in their policy decisions and, thus, removing uncertainty on future policy rates, central banks can push downward the costs of funding, while a strict ex ante commitment to reduce interest rates can encourage investors to engage in more risk-taking activity.[135]

The above overview on the risk-taking channel reveals a further component of the monetary policy transmission mechanism traditionally left apart. If price stability remains the ultimate target of monetary policy, some of the transmission channels by which inflation targeting is achieved pave the way for the build-up of risk-taking behaviors which may ultimately turn in excessive leverage and credit growth.

[131] Adrian and Shin (2008), p. 9. Adrian and Shin (2010), pp. 418–437. For a thorough analysis of this effect, see also Borio, Gambacorta, and Hofmann (2015), pp. 4–23.

[132] Bonfim and Soares (2014), p. 4.

[133] See Acharya and Naqvi (2010), pp. 349–366.

[134] Borio and Zhu (2008), p. 9.

[135] Idem, p. 9.

When the volume of lending and the leverage ratio of banks increase beyond the breakdown point, the seeds of systemic risk are sowed[136] as clearly demonstrated by the financial crisis in the Euro area. As argued further below, the existence of such risk-taking channel in the monetary policy transmission mechanism highlights the existence of a trade-off between monetary policy and macroprudential policy which may ultimately turn into an institutional paradox.

3.2.3 Transmission Channels Under Financial Distress

So far, we have explored the operational mechanics of monetary policy as a set of instruments deemed to influence the interbank interest rates via the variety of monetary policy transmission channels briefly described above. The traditional wisdom, thus, interprets the 'art of central banking'[137] as all about the decision by policy committees on calibrating policy rates in accordance with the ever-changing macroeconomic conditions.[138]

While this is certainly true for the conduct of monetary policy in good times, in the aftermath of the financial crisis, new monetary policy instruments were deemed to be needed as to maintain the central bank's commitment towards price stability and stimulate the economic recovery.[139]

In periods of severe recession—as was the case in 2007–2008—the maintenance of price stability would require lowering the nominal interest rate below its zero lower bound, that is, central banks would be required to adopt negative policy rates,[140] as to avoid periods of severe deflation. But, given that market interest rates cannot fall below zero (or close to zero) since the agents would rather hold non-interest bearing cash instead of lending,[141] cutting the policy rates at some point is no longer viable.[142]

[136] Deutsche Bundesbank (2015), p. 41.

[137] *The Art of Central Banking* is the title of the milestone book in monetary policy written by Ralph G. Hawtrey in 1932. For an interesting discussion on the nature of monetary policy—that is, if art or science—see Fischer, Fraga, Heikensten, Tietmeyer, and Volcker (2006).

[138] See Joyce, Miles, Scott, and Vayanos (2012), p. F275.

[139] See Bini Smaghi (2009). See also Constâncio (2015).

[140] For a discussion on the feasibility of introducing negative policy rates in the Eurozone and on the functioning of such monetary policy stance, see Bech and Malkhozov (2016), pp. 31–43. See also McAndrews (2015).

[141] Joyce, Miles, Scott, and Vayanos (2012), p. F272.

[142] See Bini Smaghi (2009).

In addition, when the impracticability of cutting further the nominal interest rates is flanked by the breakdown of the financial system—requiring central banks to extend emergency credit in order to preserve its functioning—the relationship between changes in nominal interest rates and market interest rates may result severely impaired.[143] Under these circumstances, the ordinary monetary policy transmission channels described above are no longer able to work properly. As a result, conventional monetary tools turn out to be not sufficient to guarantee the smooth functioning of the monetary policy transmission mechanism.[144]

Although the price stability objective was preserved by the conventional policy stances, the aftermath of the financial crisis required a policy shift in the pursuit of central bank's market operations which may operate as additional stimulus to the recovery.[145] More precisely, when nominal interest rates are already at their zero lower bound, a central bank may decide to neglect the short-term interbank interest rates and implement its monetary policy with three complementary strategies: (1) affecting the expectations on medium- and long-term interest rates, (2) making significant changes in the composition of central bank's balance sheet, and (3) expanding the size of central bank's balance sheet (i.e. *quantitative easing*).[146]

The critical variation, with respect to the conventional interest rate policies, is that these strategies share the same attribute of focusing on central bank's balance sheet to achieve the policy objective, by means of substantial changes in size, composition, and risk profile.[147] Therefore, since the breakdown of the financial system in 2007, major central banks have responded to the escalation of the crisis by entering into a number of

[143] Joyce, Miles, Scott, and Vayanos (2012), p. F272.

[144] Idem, p. F272.

[145] For a brief overview on how the Fed and the ECB changed their conventional monetary policy during the financial crisis, see Cukierman (2013), pp. 374–379.

[146] Bernanke and Reinhart (2004), p. 85. As argued by Noyer (2015), these strategies are due to a shift of monetary policy regime where central banks take a proactive approach to their balance sheets. In fact, an expansion of the liability side of the balance sheet occurs when the central bank actively increases liquidity provision to the banking sector. The purpose of such expansion is to ease pressures on bank funding, reducing its costs, and as a result of this, influence lending behavior. An expansion of the asset side is achieved by massive purchases of securities and other assets. These purchases are intended to lower risk premia, decrease asset yields, trigger portfolio rebalancing, and increase risk-taking behaviors of private actors by influencing their short-term and long-term expectations.

[147] Borio and Disyatat (2009), p. 5.

different unconventional programs,[148] any of which intended to track down one of these complementary strategies.

The primary issue at stake is to identify the additional monetary policy transmission channels by which these so-called 'unconventional monetary policy instruments' are supposed to operate. In this regard, a number of different channels have been recognized by the economic literature.[149] The ones generally deemed as the most relevant for these instruments are the *signaling channel* along with the so-called 'portfolio balance sheet channel'.[150]

As discussed in the previous section, the communication policy and the degree of commitment of central banks are capable to influence public expectations about key variables affecting market prices.[151] This signaling channel, with respect to unconventional monetary policy instruments, may involve expectations on relative scarcities of certain classes of assets or their risk and liquidity profiles.[152] For example, if a central bank announces a long-term purchase of certain classes of risky assets, market participants could react by increasing their confidence in these assets. Accordingly, the announcement of this measure brings about positive effects on risk premia, prices, and trading activity of these assets,[153] pushing up their price, lessening the risk premium, and lowering the long-term interest rates.[154] This leads, in turn, to changes in the expectations of investors, which may increase their demand for this type of asset.[155]

In contrast, the portfolio balance sheet channel is a channel of transmission enabling unconventional central bank's operations to affect indirectly the composition of investors' portfolios.[156] If private investors see the assets (and the liabilities) held by the central bank as perfectly substitutable

[148] Fratzscher, Lo Duca and Straub (2014), p. 5. A description of the quantitative easing programs issued by the Federal Reserve, the Bank of England, the European Central Bank, and Bank of Japan during the recent financial crisis is provided by Fawley and Neely (2013), pp. 51–88.

[149] For example, see Krishnamurthy and Vissing-Jorgensen (2011), pp. 215–287.

[150] Borio and Disyatat (2009), p. 13.

[151] Among others, see Borio and Zhu (2008), p. 9.

[152] Borio and Disyatat (2009), p. 13.

[153] Idem, p. 13. For an empirical assessment, see also Bernanke, Reinhart, and Sack (2004), pp. 10–77; Eggertson and Woodford (2003), pp. 139–233.

[154] Glick and Leduc (2012), p. 2080.

[155] Idem.

[156] Borio and Disyatat (2009), p. 13.

with their own assets, any change in the composition of their portfolios would have for them no effect.

In this case, central banks could not influence the portfolios of rational agents because there would be no incentive for them to change their holdings.[157] Any unconventional policies aiming to change the size and/or composition of central bank's balance sheet would in fact be ineffective.

But if investors realize that there is no perfect substitutability between assets, then some portfolio switches should not be a matter of indifference for them.[158] In this case the imperfect substitutability of assets implies that changes in the relative supply of specific assets, with different durations and liquidity available to investors, may affect the composition of their portfolios and alter their behaviors.[159]

Let's take, as example, a massive purchase by central bank of government bonds held by the private sector. This purchase will force investors who sold the government bonds to replace them in their portfolios with close substitutes, say, long-term high-quality corporate bonds. But this portfolio rebalancing will affect substantially prices and yields of the assets at stake and thus, as a consequence, the real investment decisions.[160]

It must be noted that the signaling channel and the portfolio balance sheet channel do not seem to be the only transmission channels by which unconventional monetary policies operate. A further issue in the functioning of central bank's unconventional operations is related to their impact on the risk-taking channel. The problem at stake is to find evidences that expansionary measures of unconventional monetary policy may contribute directly to the build-up of excessive credit growth and risk-taking by credit institutions.

Predicting the scale and scope of these effects ex ante is not straightforward,[161] and the economic literature on the relationship between unconventional monetary policies and bank risk-taking is still embryonic. Nonetheless, some general considerations, based on a number of recent empirical works, can be sketched out.

[157] Joyce, Miles, Scott, and Vayanos (2012), p. F276.

[158] Idem, p. F276.

[159] Borio and Disyatat (2009), p. 13. See also Bernanke (2010a).

[160] See Bernanke (2010b).

[161] See Powell (2014). Additional problem in the measurement of such risks is due to the complexity of determining whether the risk-taking activities are excessive or not. On this issue, see Claeys and Darvas (2015), p. 5.

1. The easy availability of borrowing due to unconventional monetary policies generally increases asset prices. Bond prices increase due to lower interest rates and risk premiums. Stock prices rise up because of the effects of portfolio rebalancing from bonds to stocks, the reduction in the equity risk premium, and the lower discount rate used to calculate the present value of future profits.[162] Although, in the aftermath of the financial crisis, this increase in asset prices is of great benefit to banks in terms of recapitalization, a prolonged unconventional monetary policy may increase asset prices excessively, and eventually a bubble could emerge.[163]
2. Empirical evidences suggest that low interest rates along with lower asset price volatility, due to unconventional monetary policies, encourage banks to reduce their demand for low-risk low-yield assets and increase their purchases of riskier assets offering higher returns.[164] As long as unconventional monetary policies reduce banks' profits and, thus, the franchise value of banks, banks are less incentivized to monitor borrowers and invest prudently.[165] This could imply excessive risk-taking behaviors by banks.
3. Unconventional monetary measures could increase leverage. For example, as low interest rates reduce the opportunity cost of holding required reserves or collateral, credit institutions, facing binding collateral constraints or reserve requirements, may be incentivized to build a larger portfolio and take higher leverage.[166]

Despite these preliminary results, the contribution of unconventional monetary policies to spur excessive leverage and risk-taking remains largely controversial.[167] The economic assessment of this relationship, however, would be of primary importance to understand the concrete effects that such unconventional measures may have in the build-up of systemic risks.

For now, it is just sufficient to bear in mind the transmission channels through which the unconventional monetary policies operate. As argued in the next chapter, the economic interaction between macroprudential and monetary policy largely lies within the functioning of these transmission channels.

[162] Claeys and Darvas (2015), p. 7.
[163] Idem, p. 7.
[164] Lambert and Ueda (2014), p. 19.
[165] Idem, p. 19.
[166] Chodorow-Reich (2014), p. 165.
[167] See Bean (2013), pp. 2–3.

3.3 Price Stability, Instruments, and Monetary Transmission Mechanisms Under a Legal Perspective

It is a matter of fact that the legal scholarship, when scrutinizing the impact of economics in the construction of law, traditionally tends to prefer a microeconomic view. Historically this choice in the understanding of the correlation between the two fields has been due to several factors. Macroeconomic policies are of scarce relevancy for the traditional tasks performed by lawyers, and their policy implications do not seem to address significantly the general issues arising in the fields of private law, procedural law, administrative law, or regulation.[168]

Another related problem of 'law *in* macroeconomics' is that lawyers usually do not possess that kind of mathematical expertise needed to clearly appreciate concepts and dynamics underlying macro phenomena. By contrast to microeconomic theories, explainable—at least to some extent—by means of logical analogies and practical examples, macroeconomics in general needs some theoretical modeling to analyze aggregate phenomena which, in turn, would be difficult to explain using experience parallels.[169]

However, a major exception to this negligence has been represented by constitutional doctrines which recognize principles and norms in the interest of macroeconomic wisdom. With respect to the construction of the EMU, the German constitutional tradition played a central role.[170] Drawing from the German ordo-liberal thinking,[171] it has profoundly influenced constitutional law at the level of economic policies, framing the European integration process and setting the stage for a new economic ordering based on the key principles of price stability,

[168] Kelman (1993), p. 1215. In addition, as argued by Herdegen (1998), p. 9, freezing institutional rules and fundamental principles on a macroeconomic basis implies a substantial risk related to the subsequent falsification by new empirical analyses or scenarios which were not predicted when the rules were established.

[169] Kelman (1993), p. 1216.

[170] For an analysis of how German constitutional tradition was instrumental in setting up the premises of the EMU, see Feld, Köhler, and Nientiedt (2015), pp. 2–18; Nedergaard (2013), pp. 2–27; Gerber (1994), pp. 25–84.

[171] For a historical account of the German Ordo-liberalism and its ideas, see Vanberg (1998), pp. 172–179; Streit (1994), pp. 508–515; Streit (1992), pp. 675–704; Rieter and Schmolz (1993), pp. 87–114.

central bank independence, state-market relationships, and regulatory state interference in markets.[172]

The entrenchment of overriding macroeconomic principles, such as the commitment to price stability and budgetary discipline, in the Maastricht Treaty has recognized the need to ensure a constitutional order where macroeconomics and law are widely intertwined and cooperate for a common good. And, since this cooperation has been pivotal in the construction of the EU institutional framework, it has a lot to say about the concrete implementation of macroeconomic policymaking in Europe.

As democracies in their institutional settings are characterized—*and bound*—by the domain of constitutional principles and fundamental rights, the implementation of macroeconomic policymaking to be meaningful has to rely on some institutional backdrops enabling the formalization of policies in laws and other legal commitments. In other words, the constitutional provisions frame the way in which policies are carried out through clearly defined procedures, setting the boundaries for their scope and ensuring independent judicial review for any possible violations.[173]

Against this backdrop, the conduct of macroeconomic policies must follow the same institutional pattern. Principles and prohibitions that fund the conduct of macroeconomic policies in a state become in this way the domain of legal scholars, lawyers, and judges,[174] who are supposed to test the legality of the actions taken in the pursuit of the constitutionalized macroeconomic objectives.

As a result, this *juridification* of macroeconomic policies[175] discloses the multidimensional role that law comes to play when dealing with macroeconomics. Not only is its contribution to macroeconomics devoted to constrain the behaviors of lawmakers in the ex ante procedural formation of the policy within the *legal order*. Nor it is only intended to ensure ex post enforcement and interpretation of its binding content. Instead, the

[172] Dullien and Guérot (2012), p. 2.

[173] The aim of the Constitution is therefore to provide the necessary legal basis for a well-functioning democracy. The Constitution serves the purpose to preserve the legal order against excesses and pathologies of administrative bodies through the imposition of procedural and legal constraints. See Rosenfeld (2001), p. 1340.

[174] Salama (2012), p. 150.

[175] On the *juridification* of macroeconomic policymaking, see Salama (2012), pp. 148–150.

law assumes the function of promoting and concretizing the macroeconomic targets underlying previous policymaking choices.[176]

Discussions on the relationship between law and macroeconomics will turn around the optimal institutional and legal structures to achieve macroeconomic objectives, such as unemployment, economic growth, or monetary stability, targeted by the legislature.[177] The legal reasoning will then proceed towards exploring the legal constraints assigned to policymakers in the pursuit of constitutionalized macroeconomic objectives. Finally, the elaboration of macroeconomic concepts and the acknowledgment of their dynamics under a legal perspective will build the premises for a consistent intellectual framework of the relationship between law and macroeconomics.

Against this backdrop, the aim of this section is to analyze the *juridification* of monetary policy—a pivotal component of modern macroeconomic theory—with particular regard to the Eurozone framework. As was the case for the above analysis of the EU macroprudential policy, this section seeks to reinterpret the key components of monetary policy under a possible legal significance.

Understanding how central banking shifts from its economic dimension to a legal operationalization will provide the legal underpinnings of the EU monetary policy framework, and the recent events occurring in the Eurozone may offer a significant speculative framework to address the recognition of monetary policy as a rule-bound system.

[176] This reasoning has been acknowledged in the Order of 14 January 2014—2 BvR 2728/13—where the German Federal Constitutional Court (GFCC) argues that monetary policy shall be distinguished by other policies according to the wording, structure, and purpose of the TFEU, and this delimitation must be determined by looking at the immediate objective of a monetary policy act determined by the primary law, the instruments envisioned to achieve this objective, and its link to other provisions. This interpretation was firstly envisioned by the ECJ in the Pringle case (Case C-370/12), where the judges observe a measure fall within the scope of monetary policy if it attains the price stability objective legally established.

[177] This would be at least the theoretical function of the law and macroeconomics, as described by Salama (2012), pp. 147–148. See also Ramirez (2003), pp. 517–518.

3.3.1 *Price Stability as a Legal Foundation of EU Monetary Policy*

The role of the law parallels the role of money in a free-market economy, where both serve the purpose of guaranteeing an overall stability in the exercise of the individual freedom. As a result, money and law are to be seen as necessary preconditions for the organization of a free-market economy.[178] The construction of monetary policy may therefore be understood as a set of specific institutional arrangements—formal and informal—under which monetary policy decisions can be operationalized to target its specific objectives.[179]

3.3.1.1 Price Stability as a Public Good

The intellectual liaison between the rule of law, the fundamental rights, and the institutional development of monetary policy dates back to the German *Ordo-liberal School* of the 1930s.[180] The main contribution of this school of thought relied on the idea that a proper economic constitution was to be established, in order to set the political prerogatives for the organization and regulation of economic activities.[181] The individual freedom must inform the governance of the economic system by means of a legal order to be constructed around a set of constitutional principles framing the underlying pillar of the macroeconomic constitution of the state.[182]

Ordo-liberals looked at this macroeconomic constitution as the structural institution for the post-war society which only could guarantee and promote a broad range of societal aims and ethical values related to the intellectual defense of a free society and individual liberty.[183]

Among these macroeconomic principles, the notion of price stability assumes a crucial importance in the establishment of this legal order. Along with the principles of competition and fiscal discipline, the transposition of price stability into such institutional legal framework is one of the

[178] Arner (2007), p. 91. See also Mersch (2014).

[179] Parkin (2013), p. 1.

[180] The Manifesto of the German *Ordo-liberal* School can be found in Böhm, Eucken, and Grossmann-Doerth (1989), pp. 15–26.

[181] Mestmäcker (2012), p. 588. According to Böhm (1989), pp. 46–67, an economic constitution is a comprehensive decision concerning the nature and form of the process of socio-economic cooperation. Similar opinions are expressed by Eucken (1952), p. 83; and Gerber (1994), pp. 44–49.

[182] Mestmäcker (2012), p. 588.

[183] Tuori and Tuori (2014), pp. 35–36.

legal cornerstones upon which the ideal macroeconomic constitution is built.[184] As a result, the legal notion of price stability overtakes its economic function: it represents not just the economic long-run target of central bank's monetary policy but an authentic public good to be constitutionally protected in the interest of people.[185]

Today a vast spectrum of countries recognizes—implicitly or explicitly—the legal foundation of their monetary policy in the notion of price stability. Some countries have undertaken proper legal reforms establishing price stability as an explicit objective of central bank's operations.[186] A second group of countries, albeit not recognizing price stability by law, have statutorily assigned to central banks an inflation targeting intended to disclose the implicit central bank's commitment to price stability.[187] At last, an implicit price stability objective can be recognized also for those countries that have maintained their old legal regimes and monetary policy arrangements, as central banks have de facto strengthened their anti-inflationary monetary policy orientations.

3.3.1.2 The Legal Meaning of Price Stability in the EU Framework

Leaving aside any countries' specificities, what is exactly the meaning of price stability under a legal perspective? We answer this question by shedding light upon the construction of the European monetary policy within the legal boundaries of the ESCB and ECB.

The EU Treaties acknowledge the notion of price stability as a general principle inspiring the functioning of the European order.[188] This can be primarily recognized by looking at the Treaty on European Union (TEU) where Article 3(3) sets out the economic duty of the European Union in establishing an internal market. The construction of the internal market is acknowledged to serve a variety of purposes, among which the sustainable

[184] For details, see Tuori and Tuori (2014), p. 28.

[185] See Dyson (2000), p. 216; Lastra (2014), p. 92; Lastra (2015a), p. 313.

[186] This is the case, for example, of the ECB and the ESCB.

[187] An inflation targeting regime has been adopted, *inter alia*, in Brazil, India, Canada, Israel, Japan, Mexico, Russia, and the United Kingdom. For better insights, see Roger (2010). With respect to the inflation targeting experiences in emerging economies, see also Mishkin (2000b).

[188] See Article 3(3) TEU and Article 140(1) TFEU.

development of the European Union. But the TEU recognizes that such a development must be based on the following fundamental pillars: (1) balanced economic growth and (2) price stability.[189] Under this perspective price stability becomes one of the principles that must guide the development of the European market integration and the activities of the Member States and the Union.[190]

The relevancy of price stability as a guiding principle in the construction of the internal market can be better understood by looking at the TFEU. Article 119(2) of TFEU requires that the activities of the Member States and of the Union 'shall include a single currency, the euro, and the definition and conduct of a single monetary policy and exchange-rate policy the primary objective of both of which shall be to maintain price stability'.

This provision specifies the content of price stability by establishing a link between its normative content and the conduct of two particular activities of the Union: monetary policy and exchange rate policy.[191] Leaving aside the exchange rate policy for the purpose of this analysis, it is evident that price stability becomes the overriding *legal* objective that must inform the definition and conduct of the monetary policy in the EU.[192]

A legal relationship is thus established: the monetary policy decisions and operations carried out within the borders of the EU must be aimed at achieving the objective of price stability. The law of the EU, thus, establishes a strict relationship, the existence of which, as argued further below, must guide any legal evaluation on the validity of the monetary policy actions.

[189] See Article 3(3) of TEU.

[190] ECB (2011), p. 14. Against this backdrop, Siekmann (2015a), p. 50, argues that the priority of price stability for the EU's monetary policy is unconditional and remains a strict obligation embedded in the primary law of the Union.

[191] As argued by Siekmann (2015a), pp. 48–49, the concept of monetary policy may be interpreted in both a narrow and a wide sense. The wide sense includes both the narrow meaning of monetary policy and the exchange rate policy. In this Article the term monetary policy shall be understood as referring to its wide sense.

[192] Amtenbrink (2011), p. 23. Among others, see also Smits (1997), p. 184; Herdegen (1998), pp. 15–17; Trybus and Rubini (2012), p. 76. In addition, see also Lenihan (2008), p. 20, where the author recognizes that the maintenance of price stability can be recognized as the Grundnorm or raison d'être of the ESCB. This opinion is developed in Zilioli and Selmayr (2001a), p. 629. For a thorough comment on this Article with respect to the normative content of its price stability objective, see Siekmann (2013), pp. 72–75.

The acknowledgment of price stability as inherently linked, as its own objective, to the definition and conduct of EU monetary policy is thus reinforced by Articles 127(1) and 282(2) of TFEU, both of which explicitly state that the 'primary objective of the ESCB shall be to maintain price stability' and, then, by Protocol No. 4 of TFEU—that is, the 'Statute of the ESCB and of the ECB'—which again allocates by Article 2(1) the objective of price stability to the ESCB.[193]

Notwithstanding these references to price stability as the primary monetary policy objective, the EU Treaties do not provide any clear definition of this notion.[194] Yet, a further legal element can be derived from the text of the TFEU. The concept used in the EU Treaties is to be recognized as referring to *internal* price stability—that is, the volume of goods and services obtainable for one Euro[195]—as opposed to the concept of *external* price stability, related instead to the stability or strength of the currency against competing foreign currencies.[196]

This interpretation is drawn from Article 140 of the TFEU which lays down the economic and monetary conditions that a Member State must fulfill for the adoption of the Euro. The decisions on the fulfillment of these obligations are based on four convergence criteria, among which it is required 'the achievement of a high degree of price stability [...] apparent from a rate of inflation which is close to that of, at most, the three best performing Member States in terms of price stability'.[197]

As a corollary, Article 1 of the Protocol No. 13 of TFEU provides a clearer guide on the interpretation of this criterion which is supposed to be satisfied when 'a Member State has a price performance that is sustainable and an average rate of inflation, observed over a period of one year before the examination, that does not exceed by more than 1½ percentage

[193] The common monetary policy conducted by the ESCB shall prioritize the achievement of price stability and where a conflict occurs against other objectives supported by the ESCB, that is, general economic policy, price stability must prevail. On this topic, see Siekmann (2015a), p. 50. For a comment on this Article with particular respect to price stability as the overriding objective of monetary policy and for further literature, see also Waldhoff (2013), pp. 271–285.

[194] Lenihan (2008), pp. 20–23.

[195] Idem, p. 4.

[196] See Smits (1997), p. 184. See also Gaitanides (2005), pp. 18–20; Stadler (1996), p. 100.

[197] See Article 140(1) TFEU.

points that of, at most, the three best performing Member States in terms of price stability'.

In order to assess the price performance of Member States, the Article continues by stating that 'inflation shall be measured by means of the consumer price index on a comparable basis taking into account differences in national definitions'. Since the inflation has to be measured by looking at the fluctuations of consumer prices only,[198] the interpretation of the convergence criteria suggests that the term price stability solely refers to the notion of *internal* price stability.[199]

Despite this qualitative specification, the EU Treaties do not address the legal understanding of price stability in quantitative terms. To fulfill this missing reference, the Governing Council of the ECB announced in 1998 a quantitative definition of price stability that reads as follows: 'Price stability shall be defined as a year-on-year increase in the Harmonised Index of Consumer Prices (HICP) for the euro area of below 2%. Price stability is to be maintained over the medium term.'[200] In 2003 after reviewing its monetary policy strategy, the Governing Council came back to this definition specifying its commitment to maintain inflation rates below, but 'close to 2% over the medium term'.[201]

Some scholars argue this announcement is not legally binding as it represents just a unilateral and arbitrary setting established by an administrative body of the ECB without any reference to the primary law.[202] In support of this claim, these academics suggest that the term price stability, to be compatible with the language of the EU Treaties, should be interpreted as a change of approximately 0% of the consumer price index.

[198] See *infra* this para.

[199] Lenihan (2008), p. 21. See also Selmayr (1999), pp. 2431–2432.

[200] ECB (1999a), p. 9. The reasons of a quantitative determination of price stability are manifold. The ECB intended to make monetary policy more transparent, providing a quantitative instrument against which the central bank is accountable towards the public. In addition, this quantitative determination provides guidance to the public for forming expectations of future developments of consumer price trends. For details, see ECB, Price Stability—Objective of the Eurosystem, MP.001 08/06.

[201] Press release: The ECB's monetary policy strategy, 8 May 2003. Available online at https://www.ecb.europa.eu/press/pr/date/2003/html/pr030508_2.en.html.

[202] In particular, see Siekmann (2015a), p. 50, questioning the conformity of this quantitative value in view of the language of the EU primary law. Similarly, Smits (1997), p. 185, defining price stability as 'absence of inflation, i.e. a situation in which prices remain, relatively, stable'. As a result, the quantitative target set by the ESCB would not be legally binding. Instead, it would provide only some guidance on the fluctuations in purchasing power which would be compatible with the concept of price stability as envisioned by the EU Treaty.

Even though there are certainly supportive reasons to favor this opinion, our understanding of the *juridification* of monetary policy takes a different perspective on the evaluation of the legal sources binding the ECB. The main question is whether an announcement of the ECB can be considered a source of law or, at least, creating legitimate expectations that are legally protected.

Interestingly, this issue has been addressed at the EU level by the Advocate General of the European Court of Justice (ECJ) in the proceeding issued by the German Federal Constitutional Court (GFCC or *Bundesverfassungsgericht*) for a preliminary ruling on the validity of the decision taken by the ECB on the Outright Monetary Transactions (OMT).[203] In scrutinizing the admissibility of the questions issued by the German Constitutional Court, the Advocate General recognizes legal relevance to the OMT announcement as

> It is a fact that the communications strategy of central banks has become one of the central pillars of contemporary monetary policy. Given the impossibility of predicting rational behaviour on the markets, an effective way of managing expectations and, therefore, of ensuring the effectiveness of monetary policy is to exploit all the possibilities of public communication (communications strategies) open to central banks.[204]

Thus,

> acts of public communication [which] assume special significance for the effectiveness of monetary policy [...] constitutes—having regard not only to its content and the actual effects that it may produce but also to the circumstances in which the measure was adopted—an act of an institution whose validity may be called in question in the framework of proceedings for a preliminary ruling under Article 267 TFEU.[205]

[203] Case C-62/14. Opinion of the Advocate General Cruz Villalón, 14 January 2015. The same reasoning is applied by the GFCC in the Order of 14 January 2014—2 BvR 2728/13, para 34, where the Court recognizes the admissibility of the constitutional complaints regarding the OMT decision of the ECB. Although the decision was just an announcement of a monetary policy act—and not a proper measure—the Court acknowledges the need to grant preventive legal protection against this measure in order to avoid future consequences that cannot be corrected. The Court therefore admits the need to ensure legal protection against these acts of public communication.

[204] Case C-62/14. Opinion of the Advocate General Cruz Villalón, 14 January 2015, para 87.

[205] Case C-62/14. Opinion of the Advocate General Cruz Villalón, 14 January 2015, para 90. It must be noted that Article 267 TFEU states that the ECJ shall have jurisdiction to give

Assuming the legal significance of the ECB's announcements generating immediate rational expectations into the market, the announcement on price stability can be used for setting the legal boundaries of this notion. As a result, some remarkable insights into the legal meaning of price stability follow.

On the one hand, the legal scope of price stability is the Euro area as a whole. This means that monetary policy decisions and operations targeting price stability must be based on price developments occurring in the aggregate economy of the Euro area, while their implementation must be homogeneous in all EU jurisdictions.[206] This backdrop provides an initial requirement for the legal assessment of ECB's monetary policy: the legality of any policy tool—given its subordination to the objective of price stability—is a function of its uniform application across the different jurisdictions.

On the other hand, the definition of inflation provided in Article 1 of the Protocol No. 13 of TFEU, along with the quantitative specification laid down in the ECB's announcements, identifies a specific price index that is to be used to assess the maintenance of the price stability target—that is, the HICP for the Euro area. Compiled by EUROSTAT and the national statistical institutes, the HICP for the Euro area is a weighted average of the individual HICPs of Member States of the Eurozone, calculated yearly.[207] Each country weight is based on its share of private final domestic consumption expenditure in the total of the EMU.[208] Not surprisingly, this index has been legally defined by the

preliminary ruling to the validity and interpretation of acts of the institutions, bodies, offices, or agencies of the Union, interpreting the word 'act' in a very general sense. According to the ECJ's jurisprudence, the acts referred to by Article 267(1) neither have to be binding nor directly applicable (see ECJ, Case C-322/88 Grimaldi, judgment of 13 December 1989, para 8; Case 9/73 Schlüter, judgment of 8 October 1973, para 38). On this issue, see also Wendel (2014), pp. 288–289. Acts which are only preparatory or creating mere expectations in the market can be validly considered by the ECJ for judicial review. For more details, see also Sauer (2015), p. 987.

[206] The homogeneous application of monetary policy shall be distinguished from the heterogeneity of its effects. It is clear, indeed, that the adoption of specific monetary policy instruments may provide different macroeconomic outcome across Member States of a monetary union. On this issue, see Beraja, Fuster, Hurst, and Vavra (2015).

[207] On this topic, see Astin (1999), pp. 123–135; Diewert (2002), pp. 6–68. For a critical survey on the use of the HICP and its measurements bias, see Wynne and Rodriguez-Palenzuela (2004), pp. 79–112; Forsells and Kenny (2002), pp. 3–25.

[208] EUROSTAT (1998).

Council Regulation (EC) No. 2494/95 establishing the statistical bases necessary for arriving at the calculation of comparable indices of consumer prices at the EU level. Along with the related regulations issued in the following years to implement the technical features of such index, it provides a harmonization of the statistical methods to be used across the various countries of the Euro area.

Although the words *below 2%* are not present in the TFEU, some remarks with respect to its legal significance can be provided. If the monetary policy announcements of the ECB can be subject to judicial scrutiny, as they can create legitimate expectations in the market with future consequences that cannot be corrected,[209] one can infer that also this quantitative determination—albeit unilateral and likely arbitrary[210]—can be deemed as part of the price stability definition envisioned in the EU. This quantitative threshold is capable to generate expectations for investors and consumers which may adjust their preferences in view of any price developments.[211] Theoretically, these expectations deserve legal protection, and this entails the ECB should be held accountable for any serious deviations from the quantitative target.[212]

In view of this argument, the words *below 2%* should be identified as the upper bound of the notion of price stability, while the use of the word *increase* implies that deflation—deemed as a prolonged decline in the level of the HICP index—is not consistent with price stability.[213] This explains also why the aim of the Governing Council is to maintain the inflation rate at a level below, but close to 2%: the rationale is to have a sufficient margin of maneuver to mitigate possible risks of deflation.[214]

[209] See *supra* notes 692 and 694.

[210] Siekmann (2015a), p. 50.

[211] For a survey on how consumers and investors can change their preferences based on price expectations, see Armantier, Bruine de Bruin, Topa, van der Klaauw, and Zafar (2011), pp. 1–25.

[212] According to Smits (1997), p. 186, the ECB is free to translate the price stability objective into monetary targets based on its auto-interpretation. However, this auto-interpretation is limited by the legal constraints of its activities. Against this backdrop the ECJ could be theoretically called upon to assess whether the level of price stability achieved is consistently within the limits of the law. For a critical analysis, see also Thiele (2013), pp. 29–33.

[213] Inter alia, see ECB (1999a), p. 46; de Haan, Oosterloo, and Schoenmaker (2012), p. 102; Kieler (2003), p. 6; Scheller (2006), p. 81.

[214] This argument is provided in the ECB's press release 'The ECB's monetary policy strategy', 8 May 2003.

Lastly, from the legal definition of price stability, a forth element must be taken into account, which is also the most relevant for the purposes of this book. Under the EU Treaties, price stability refers to 'consumer price stability'.[215] It follows that the legal concept implicitly should exclude increase/decrease in asset prices and, therefore, any assessment on their procyclical trends to generate bubbles and systemic risks.[216] In light of this argument, the ESCB's monetary policy decisions and operations are not related or bound by an assessment on financial stability. From a legal perspective, this implies that the monetary policy in the EU should be conducted free of any macroprudential considerations.[217]

3.3.2 Testing the Monetary Policy Instruments

After identifying price stability as the primary legal objective of the EU monetary policy, the analysis shall move to the legal requirements featuring the operating policy instruments that can be used to maintain the price stability objective. Central banks cannot directly decide the prices of goods and services in the economy, adjusting automatically the inflation level. Instead, they are required to operationalize a policy framework consisting of policy instruments affecting the general level of consumer prices.[218]

Not surprisingly, it is up to the law defining and implementing such operating framework, bounding the central bank within the strict scope of its statutory target, that is, its price stability objective.

3.3.2.1 The Operational Framework: Monetary Policy Instruments

The legal foundations of the EU monetary policy operating framework are laid down in the abovementioned Statute of the ESCB and ECB. In particular, Article 18(1) of the ESCB Statute states that in the pursuit of its objectives and to carry out its tasks, the ECB and the national central banks may: (1) 'operate in the financial markets by buying and selling outright (spot and forward) or under repurchase agreement and by lending or borrowing claims and marketable instruments, whether in euro or

[215] Article 1 of the Protocol No. 13 of TFEU. See Siekmann (2011a), pp. 1824–1857; Siekmann and Wieland (2013a), p. 6. For a discussion, with further references, on whether asset prices should be introduced in the definition of price stability, see Camba-Mendez (2003), pp. 38–39; de Haan, Eijffinger, and Waller (2005), pp. 74–77.

[216] Siekmann (2011b), p. 20. See also Issing (2008), p. 2.

[217] See Gianviti (2010), p. 469.

[218] See *supra* at notes 548–559.

other currencies, as well as precious metals,' and (2) 'conduct credit operations with credit institutions and other market participants, with lending being based on adequate collateral'.

In addition, in accordance with and in pursuance of its monetary policy objectives, the ECB has the power to require credit institutions established in Member States to hold minimum reserve on accounts with the ECB and national central banks.[219] At last, Article 20 of the ESCB Statute assigned to the Governing Council of the ECB the power to decide, by a majority of two-thirds of the votes cast upon the use of other operational instruments of monetary policy deemed necessary to achieve the objective of price stability. In this case, the Council will define the scope of such instruments if they impose obligations on third parties.[220]

The ESCB Statute is not the only legal instrument in the hands of ECB for the conduct of its monetary policy.[221] As stated in Article 18(2) of the Statute, the ECB is tasked with establishing, in secondary legislation, 'general principles for open market and credit operations carried out by itself or the national central banks, including for the announcement of conditions under which they stand ready to enter into such transactions'.

It follows the competence of the ECB to adopt its own legal acts and monetary policy instruments in line with the principle of limited powers and in conformity with the provisions laid down in the primary law.[222] Accordingly, since 2000 the ECB has issued its guidelines on monetary policy instruments and procedures of the Eurosystem. Amended several times over the last 15 years, the ultimate version of these rules is represented by the Guideline (EU) 2015/510 of 19 December 2014 on the implementation of the Eurosystem monetary policy framework.[223]

Looking at the legal nature of the ECB's guidelines, it must be noted that these have special qualification.[224] These guidelines are tools by which the ECB ensures the integration of national central banks in the EU monetary policy and are instrumental in ensuring compliance of national central banks with the decisions adopted by ECB Governing Council.[225] As a

[219] Article 19(1) of ESCB Statute.

[220] See Article 20 of ESCB Statute.

[221] See Louis (2005a), p. 312.

[222] ECB (1999b), p. 54.

[223] Guideline (EU) 2015/510 of the ECB of 19 December 2014 on the implementation of the Eurosystem monetary policy framework (ECB/2014/60), (OJ L 91, 2.4.2015, p. 3).

[224] ECB (1999b), pp. 56–57.

[225] Smits (1997), p. 104.

result, these guidelines have a legally binding nature as national central banks are required to comply with them.

This binding power is affirmed in Article 1(1) of the Guideline (EU) 2015/510 which provides that these provisions are 'the uniform rules for the implementation of the single monetary policy by the Eurosystem throughout the Member States whose currency is the euro'. The ESCB is thus required to take 'all the appropriate measures to implement Eurosystem monetary policy operations in accordance with the principles, tools, instruments, requirements, criteria and procedures laid down in this Guideline'.[226]

The binding nature of these guidelines is strengthened by the power—conferred to the ECB—to impose sanctions and/or penalties on credit institutions not compliant with the obligations arising from the contractual or regulatory arrangements set out in the guidelines and applied by the ECB or by the national central banks.[227] Hence, these guidelines are structured to have not only internal effects—for the ECB and the ESCB in the conduct of their monetary policy—but also direct effects towards private market participants which, in turn, could invoke judicial relief, at least, theoretically, in the event of a breach of law by the ECB and the other national central banks.[228]

As argued, the ECB's guideline lays out principles, tools, operations, and procedures governing the monetary policy instruments of the Eurosystem. In particular, Article 3 sets out the following tools for the implementation of the EU monetary policy: (a) open market operations, (b) standing facilities, and (c) minimum reserve requirements.

Leaving aside the minimum reserve requirements—whose discipline is detailed in Regulation (EC) No. 2531/98 and Regulation (EC) No. 1745/2003 (ECB/2003/9)—the following table (Table 3.1), as set out in Article 4 of the Guideline, illustrates an overview of major legal characteristics for these instruments.

[226] See Louis (2005a), p. 312. It is interesting to note that the binding nature of such guidelines is not contradicted by the fact that the ECB's Governing Council may change their prescriptive content at any time. It is a general principle of administrative law that an authority can choose its own procedural rules within boundaries established by the Constitution and is deemed to be bound by its own rules until it decides to modify them (*patere legem quam ipse fecisti* or in German *Selbstbindung*). For a discussion of this principle with respect to the Union law, see Schermers and Waelbroeck (2000), p. 84.

[227] Guideline (EU) 2015/510, Part Five.

[228] Louis (2005a), p. 312.

Table 3.1 Main legal features of ECB monetary policy instruments

Categories of the monetary policy operations		*Types of instruments*		*Maturity*	*Frequency*	*Procedure*
		Provision of liquidity	*Absorption of liquidity*			
Open market operations	Main refinancing operations	Reverse transactions	–	One week	Monthly	Standard tender procedures
	Longer-term refinancing operations	Reverse transactions	–	Three months	Monthly	Standard tender procedures
	Fine-tuning operations	Reverse transactions	Reverse transactions	Non-standardized	Non-standardized	Standard tender procedures
		Foreign exchange swaps	Foreign exchange swaps			Standard tender procedures
			Collection of fixed-term deposits			
	Structural operations	Reverse transactions	Reverse transactions	Non-standardized	Non-standardized	Standard tender procedures
		–	Issuance of ECB debt certificates	Less than 12 months	Non-standardized	
		Outright purchases	Outright sales	–	Non-standardized	Tender procedures Bilateral procedures
Standing facilities	Marginal lending facility	Reverse transactions	–	Overnight	Access at the discretion of counterparties	
	Deposit facility	–	Deposits	Overnight	Access at the discretion of counterparties	

3.3.2.2 *Targeting Monetary Policy Instruments: A Look at the Jurisprudence*

In order to get a better insight into the legal nature of the monetary policy instruments, it is essential to make one step further in this analysis. The ECB's guidelines, albeit providing the legal features of the policy tools and the procedures to implement them, do not specify the structural components that may determine whether a specific tool is to be deemed a monetary policy instrument. The issue is particularly important today, as the ECB is adopting a plethora of unconventional measures whose features could fall outside the legal boundaries of monetary policy.[229]

As anticipated above, to shed some light on this matter, the GFCC in February 2014 filed a number of questions for a preliminary ruling to the ECJ[230] concerning the ECB's announcement of a sovereign debt purchase program, referred to as OMT.[231]

By scrutinizing the arguments brought about by the plaintiffs—who claimed the OMT was ultra vires by the ECB and in violation of the constitutional identity of the German Basic Law[232]—the GFCC, in its decision, lists a number of reasons for why the OMT is considered to be illegal. In the words of the GFCC, not only it would affect the competence

[229] For example, as of January 2015 the ECB unleashed a package of unconventional measures to stimulate the Eurozone economy with asset purchase programs and an expanded quantitative easing, having the purpose of incentivizing banks to increase lending. See Decision (EU) 2015/5 of the ECB of 19 November 2014 on the implementation of the asset-backed securities purchase program (ECB/2014/45), OJ L 1, 6.1.2015; Decision (EU) 2015/299 of the ECB of 10 February 2015 amending Decision ECB/2014/34 on measures relating to targeted longer-term refinancing operations; Decision (EU) 2015/774 of the ECB of 4 March 2015 on a secondary markets public sector asset purchase program (ECB/2015/10), OJ L 121, 14.5.2015, p. 20; Decision (EU) 2016/810 of the ECB of 28 April 2016 on a second series of targeted longer-term refinancing operations (ECB/2016/10), OJ L 132, 3.5.2016, p. 107.

[230] See BVerfG, 2 BvR 2728/13 vom 14.1.2014, Absatz-Nr. (1–105). For critical discussions on the judgment of the Court, see Feld, Fuest, Haucap, Schweitzer, and Wieland (2016), pp. 15–32; Petersen (2014), pp. 321–328; Schiek (2014), pp. 329–342; Everson (2015); pp. 474–499; Siekmann (2015b), pp. 101–123; Dahan, Fuchs, and Layus (2015), pp. 137–151.

[231] See ECB Press Release. Technical features of Outright Monetary Transactions. 6 September 2012. Available online at http://www.ecb.europa.eu/press/pr/date/2012/html/pr120906_1.en.html. For an analysis of the effects of ECB's OMT announcement, see Altavilla, Giannone, and Lenza (2014).

[232] For a general discussion of these aspects, see Petersen (2014), pp. 321–327. Siekmann and Wieland (2015), pp. 6–12.

of economic policy reserved to Member States, even violating the prohibition of monetary financing established by the TFEU,[233] but also, and more importantly, it would be inconsistent with the monetary policy framework as established by the primary law of the EU.

In support of this, the GFCC differentiates the measures of economic policy from the ones of monetary policy by elaborating a *legal test* based on the following principles: (a) pursuit of its ultimate and immediate objective, (b) selectivity in its implementation, (c) subjection to conditionality, (d) parallelism with economic policy measures, (e) circumvention of the prohibition of monetary financing.[234]

The Advocate General of the ECJ, Pedro Cruz Villalón, in his legal opinion,[235] discusses these principles again, elaborating a *proportionality test* to evaluate the legal consistency of the monetary policy instruments.[236] This proportionality test is further elaborated by the ECJ in its final judgment[237] where the OMT program—and for extension, any ECB's policy measure—is considered legal insofar as the measure is proportional to the price stability objective.[238]

First of all, the GFCC states that a monetary policy instrument to be legally deemed as such has to achieve directly the objective of price stability, while the sole presence of indirect effects on the stability of the Euro is instead irrelevant for such a qualification.[239] In addition, the German judges argue that an instrument cannot be invoked as of monetary policy if its intermediate objective is to safeguard the current composition of the Euro currency area as this is not a task of monetary policy but one of economic policy.[240]

The Advocate General Cruz Villalón upholds this statement but enlarges the prospective on the definition of monetary policy. In particular,

[233] Article 123(1) of TFEU.

[234] See BVerfG, 2 BvR 2728/13 vom 14.1.2014, Absatz-Nr. (1–105), para 55.

[235] We refer to the legal opinion of the Advocate General Cruz Villalón, Case C-62/14, 14 January 2015.

[236] For a very critical appraisal on the use of proportionality test for assessing the legality of monetary policy instruments, see Feld, Fuest, Haucap, Schweitzer, and Wieland (2016), pp. 17–18.

[237] See Judgment of the Court (Grand Chamber) of 16 June 2015 (request for a preliminary ruling from the Bundesverfassungsgericht—Germany), Peter Gauweiler and Others v Deutscher Bundestag (Case C-62/14).

[238] Idem, para 66.

[239] See BVerfG, 2 BvR 2728/13, para 64.

[240] See BVerfG, 2 BvR 2728/13, para 72.

he emphasizes that an ECB's measure, to form part of monetary policy, must specifically serve the primary objective of price stability.[241] However, by turning around the argument that an economic policy does not become by itself a monetary policy measure just because it could have indirect effects on EU economic policy,[242] the Advocate General takes a functional approach to clarify the nature of monetary policy instruments. As a general principle, he argues that 'if a measure belongs to the category of instruments which the law provides for carrying out monetary policy, there is an initial presumption that such a measure is the result of the Union's monetary policy being carried out'.[243] This presumption, however, can be refuted if the measure is proved to be taken in order to pursue objectives other than price stability.

For the ECJ this functional approach is appropriate to delimit the boundaries of monetary policy, as the monetary policy measure is to be deemed legal as far as its instruments are appropriate to target the price stability objective.[244] As a result, the Court closely supports the preliminary presumption that a measure announced in view of the price stability objective shall fall within the domain of monetary policy.

A second element to be scrutinized with respect to the nature of monetary policy instruments lies in its application. As argued in the previous section, the ECB's monetary policy shall be conducted uniformly across the different EU jurisdictions.[245] In his judgment, the GFCC clearly acknowledges this inherent characteristic of the EU monetary policy. Against this backdrop, in its reasoning, the German court points out that the monetary policy instruments cannot consist of selective measures that are constructed to differentiate between individual Member States.[246]

For the Advocate General, this argument is not convincing per se to demonstrate the economic policy nature of an instrument. In his opinion, a monetary policy instrument could be selective where the monetary policy transmission channel results impaired in some Member States only.[247] The same argument is used by the ECJ to corroborate the legality of the

[241] Opinion of Advocate General Cruz Villalón (Case C-62/14), para 132.

[242] This principle was established by the ECJ in the well-known *Pringle case*. For details, see Case C-370/12 Pringle, ECLI:EU:C:2012:756).

[243] Opinion of Advocate General Cruz Villalón (Case C-62/14), para 130.

[244] Peter Gauweiler and Others v Deutscher Bundestag (Case C-62/14), paras 56 and 64.

[245] See *supra* at note 695.

[246] See BVerfG, 2 BvR 2728/13, para 73.

[247] Opinion of Advocate General Cruz Villalón (Case C-62/14), para 153–154.

OMT program, as the judges argue that under certain circumstances a selective bond-buying program can be necessary to rectify the general disruption of the transmission of monetary policy.[248]

The triviality of this claim—which can be easily understood as a contradiction to the principle of uniform application of monetary policy—seems to be related to the difficulty in establishing a clearer legal definition of 'monetary policy transmission channel', as well as on its features and functioning.

A third relevant element concerns the conditionality of monetary policy instruments. The GFCC argues that an instrument, to be part of monetary policy, must be delinked, and thus, not subject to any economic policy measure and/or intervention in favor of a Member State. Should an instrument be made dependent to the full compliance of requirements laid down in the conditionality of an economic policy program, this would be equivalent to an economic assistance measure.[249] Moreover, the features of a monetary policy instrument cannot replicate and/or multiply the characteristics of a parallel assistance measure issued by another institution tasked with competences of economic policy.[250]

The importance of such statements is acknowledged by the Advocate General, according to whom there is a functional distinction between monetary policy and economic policy that must be maintained when referring to monetary policy and economic policy instruments.[251] The ECB in the pursuit of its monetary policy must detach itself from all direct involvement in the monitoring of any economic assistance program. Otherwise, the instrument, 'inasmuch as it is unilaterally linked to those programmes, [may turn] into something more than a monetary policy measure'.[252]

In its final judgment the ECJ neglects this argument and does not provide a clear guidance on how to identify such a functional distinction. The

[248] Peter Gauweiler and Others v Deutscher Bundestag (Case C-62/14), para 89.

[249] See BVerfG, 2 BvR 2728/13, para 77–78.

[250] See BVerfG, 2 BvR 2728/13 para 76.

[251] Opinion of Advocate General Cruz Villalón (Case C-62/14), para 150.

[252] Idem, para 145. Therefore, although the ECB may participate in financial assistance programs, for the Advocate General Cruz Villalón, it must be clearly borne in mind that no circumstances could make possible for the ECB to take part in the monitoring of the financial assistance program to which the Member State is subject when, at the same time, that state is the recipient of a monetary policy measure.

ECJ simply refers to its precedent *Pringle*,[253] by arguing that a monetary policy measure is not equivalent to an economic policy measure merely because it may have indirect economic policy effects.[254] In this way, the ECJ failed to provide a descriptive analysis of the allocation of competences and responsibilities within the EU, leaving a dangerous uncertainty on what instruments can be legally carried out under the monetary policy framework and what measures can be pursued under the economic policy domain.[255]

The prohibition of monetary financing to public entities, established in Article 123 of TFEU, forbids the implementation of monetary policy instruments aimed to circumvent its normative content. As a result, any instrument structured in a way to result in public deficit financing cannot be validly considered as monetary policy measure.

In order to determine whether an instrument causes such a circumvention, the GFCC establishes a five-tier sub-test based on the following variables: (1) pari passu status of ECB,[256] (2) increased risk of failure or of a debt cut,[257] (3) interference with the price formation on the market,[258] (4) holding until maturity,[259] and (5) encouragement of market participants to purchase newly issued securities.[260]

According to the German judges, a monetary policy instrument to be considered legal under Article 123 TFEU must ex ante exclude purchases of sovereign bonds up to unlimited amounts and the possibility of debt cuts due to defaults. In addition, the instrument, where possible, should not interfere with price formation on the market; as a result, when the monetary policy operation involves purchases of government bonds, there must be substantial time lags between the emission of these assets and their purchase, while no holding of them until maturity would be permitted.[261]

[253] Judgment of the Court (Full Court) of 27 November 2012. Thomas Pringle v Government of Ireland, Ireland and The Attorney General (Case C-370/12), para 56.

[254] Peter Gauweiler and Others v Deutscher Bundestag (Case C-62/14), paras 51 and 52.

[255] Feld, Fuest, Haucap, Schweitzer, and Wieland (2016), pp. 18–19.

[256] See BVerfG, 2 BvR 2728/13, para 88.

[257] See BVerfG, 2 BvR 2728/13, para 89.

[258] Also referred to as 'interference with the market logic'. For details, see BVerfG, 2 BvR 2728/13, para 90 and 92.

[259] See BVerfG, 2 BvR 2728/13, para 90.

[260] See BVerfG, 2 BvR 2728/13, para 93–94.

[261] In agreement with the Judgment of the Court, see Dagenhart (2015), pp. 30–36. For a divergent opinion, see Riso (2015), pp. 19–29.

Against this sub-test, the Advocate General Cruz Villalón elaborates a multidimensional 'proportionality test' to be divided into (a) a *suitability test*, (b) a *necessity test*, and (c) a *stricto* sensu *proportionality test*. In light of the *suitability test*, an instrument, such as the OMT, to be considered legal, must be objectively appropriate to achieve its intermediate objectives. Accordingly, the instrument has to be examined by focusing on the casual connection between the means and the objectives.[262]

The *necessity test*, instead, wishes to assess whether the *means* (*read* instruments) used by the ECB are excessive if compared with other options that would have been available to the central bank. This means that the instrument used must be deemed as strictly necessary to achieve its objectives.[263] Finally, the Advocate General suggests applying a test of *proportionality stricto* sensu to the policy instrument to assess whether the benefits of the policy instrument outweigh its costs.[264]

By applying this multidimensional test to the OMT decision, the Advocate General essentially disbanded the first three components of the GFCC's test, as the pari passu status of the ECB in the purchase of bonds, the risk of cuts in the event of restructuring of a Member State's debt, and the exposition of the ECB to a degree of risk default, in his view, would not represent an encroachment to the EU prohibition of monetary financing to public entities.[265]

However, the Advocate General also suggests that, under this proportionality test, the holding of the bonds purchased until maturity and the time of this purchase could become relevant in the legal assessment of the monetary policy instruments. Should the ECB purchases sovereign bonds under the obligation to hold them until maturity, this could give rise to a significant distortion on the secondary market for government securities, this encroaching upon the prohibition laid down in the Treaty.[266]

At the same time, the principle of proportionality suggests that a monetary policy instrument, to be legal, should be implemented in such a way to permit the actual formation of price of the assets concerned.[267] Paraphrasing Cruz Villalón, this means there must be the possibility for market prices to form in respect to the assets concerned in such a way that

[262] Opinion of Advocate General Cruz Villalón (Case C-62/14), para 171.

[263] Idem, para 177.

[264] Idem, para 185–186.

[265] Idem, para 233–241.

[266] Idem, para 243.

[267] Idem, para 254.

a real difference between the purchase of the asset on the primary market and its purchase on the secondary market exists.[268]

In this regard, the ECJ acknowledges in general the proportionality principle for the identification of the monetary policy instruments in accordance with its relevant case law.[269] In addition, the European judges give broad discretion to the ECB in the preparation and implementation of market operations, based on the technical nature, complex forecasts, and macroeconomic assessments driving its policy decisions.[270]

In view of this broad discretion, the multidimensional test of the Advocate General is poorly scrutinized. The judicial review of the Court becomes rather limited, since it can only assess whether the monetary policy measure does not go manifestly beyond what is necessary to achieve the price stability objective based on the language of the ECB's press release.[271] In view of the ECJ, if the result is positive, then the measure is to be deemed legal, without any further consideration regarding the likely mispricing of the purchased assets or the disruption of the market pricing mechanism.[272]

[268] Idem, para 251–252.

[269] Peter Gauweiler and Others v Deutscher Bundestag (Case C-62/14), para 67. In particular, the Court recognizes that in accordance with Union settled case law, the principle of proportionality requires that acts of the EU institutions be appropriate for attaining the legitimate objectives pursued by the legislation at issue and do not go beyond what is necessary in order to achieve those objectives (see Association Kokopelli (Case C-59/11), EU:C:2012:44, para 38).

[270] Peter Gauweiler and Others v Deutscher Bundestag (Case C-62/14), para 68. To five such a discretion the Court relies on two cases: Afton Chemical v Secretary of State for Transport (C-343/09) EU:C:2010:419 and Billerud Karlsborg and Billerud Skärblacka, (C-203/12), EU:C:2013:664. Both judgments, however, recognize broad discretion to the EU legislature when intervening in areas involving political, economic, and social choices. The legality of extending such a legislative discretion in the area of monetary policy is therefore disputable. The assignment of broad discretion to the ECB entails a considerable amount of trust in the Bank by the ECJ. On this topic, *cf.* Beukers (2014), p. 343; Simon (2015), pp. 1030–1032.

[271] Against this backdrop, Wilkinson (2015), p. 1058, points out that adopts a 'featherweight review' of proportionality, where the ECJ in fact carries out a nominal judicial scrutiny on the basis of conferring a wide margin of discretion to the ECB. For the author, the level of deference of the ECJ implies that no 'manifest error of judgment' of the ECB is found. The ECB therefore would have the only duty to act with care and accuracy. For another critical analysis of such ruling, see Feld, Fuest, Haucap, Schweitzer, and Wieland (2016), pp. 17–18.

[272] Feld, Fuest, Haucap, Schweitzer, and Wieland (2016), p. 29, recognize that the ECJ does not deal with the concerns regarding the formation of prices, even criticizing the very

Finally, the ECJ discusses the encouragement of market participants to purchase newly issued securities after the implementation of the monetary policy instrument, which may turn the ECB into a lender of last resort, circumventing in this way the prohibition of Article 123 TFEU. For the Advocate General and the ECJ, the proportionality test applies also in this case: an instrument would be considered circumventing Article 123 TFEU only if it would result in a disproportionate encouragement to purchase newly issued bonds.[273] Instead, where sufficient safeguards are built to avoid such circumvention, the ECB's purchase programs involving sovereign bonds should be recognized as legal.[274]

This argument is rather weak. The ECJ neglects the unconventional nature of the ECB's purchase program targeting sovereign bonds.[275] This measure is capable to generate negative incentives to Member States, which can be persuaded to increase government debt, thereby affecting their budgetary discipline. Moreover, the massive purchases of government bonds on the secondary market clearly have the equivalent effects of purchases from public authorities and bodies of the Member State, where investors in the primary market will be confident that the ECB will purchase their bonds within a certain period due to the OMT. In this way, market participants will act as simple intermediaries for the time of the OMT implementation, allowing Member States to be indirectly financed by the central bank.[276]

Although the proportionality test used by the Advocate General and backed by the ECJ does not seem to fully address the relevant legal issues

narrow functional approach used for the interpretation of Article 123 TFEU. For Craig and Markakis (2016), p. 37, instead, the ECJ's ruling on the interpretation of Article 123 TFEU should be sufficient to placate the GFCC concerns over the volume of OMT purchases and their impact on price formation.

[273] See Opinion of Advocate General Cruz Villalón (Case C-62/14), para 255–261.

[274] For a discussion on the safeguards envisioned by the ECJ, see Craig and Markakis (2016), pp. 17–19.

[275] Feld, Fuest, Haucap, Schweitzer, and Wieland (2016), p. 28. A different opinion on the nature of the OMT is advocated by Simon (2015), pp. 1034–1038, where the author reconciles the nature of the OMT within the normal open market operations of the ESCB.

[276] The argument is thoroughly elaborated in Wilkinson (2015), pp. 1053–1060; Feld, Fuest, Haucap, Schweitzer, and Wieland (2016), pp. 28–31. Conversely, Simon (2015), p. 1038, argues that this view is difficult to uphold as it would be difficult to determine whether the economic effect of direct and indirect purchases are equivalent.

at stake regarding monetary policy,[277] some important considerations can be drawn. The judgments of the courts prove that understanding the legal components of monetary policy instruments, as for the case of the macro-prudential instruments, is pivotal for a legal assessment of monetary policy. All the monetary policy instruments adopted are rule-bound, and, as such, they must be in conformity with the legal principles and requirements established both by the primary and secondary law, and being discussed in light of the relevant jurisprudence.

3.3.3 *Legal Uncertainties in the Concept of 'Monetary Policy Transmission Mechanism'*

In the judgment before the GFCC, the ECB justified the OMT program on the basis of the disruption to the monetary policy transmission mechanism. In the view of the ECB, its monetary policy was no longer appropriately implemented, as the monetary policy channel linking the policy interest rate and the bank interest rates was impaired. As a result, unfounded fears of investors resulted in unjustified interest spreads. For the ECB, therefore, its unconventional action was justified by the need to neutralize these allegedly irrational market concerns.[278]

However, upholding the arguments filed by the Bundesbank as a response to such claim, the GFCC recognizes such reference to the impairment of monetary policy transmission mechanism was not relevant.[279] Yet, it should be noted that this recognition by the German court is not universal; instead, it simply refers to the specific circumstances where the OMT is supposed to operate.

In particular, the ECB failed to clearly describe the functioning of the monetary policy transmission channels and in which manner such purchase of government bonds would have restored its alleged disruption.[280] Precisely for this reason, the GFCC affirmed that any critical deterioration

[277] We refer in particular to the analysis of the monetary policy transmission mechanism and to the extensive discretion that this proportionality test ensured to the ECB in its policymaking. As the proportionality test is not able to clearly define the legal boundaries of the ECB's competences, lots of uncertainty remains. In line with this view, see Goldmann (2016).

[278] See BVerfG, 2 BvR 2728/13, para 7.

[279] See BVerfG, 2 BvR 2728/13, para 95–98.

[280] The same opinion is shared in Siekmann and Wieland (2013b), p. 50.

of the solvency of a state typically coincides with a corresponding deterioration of the solvency of the national banking sector.[281]

But this effect cannot be mitigated by means of an instrument that is intended to support the restoration of the economic policy of the indebted State. Therefore, the Court implicitly suggested that no direct link exists between the effects of the OMT and the targeted policy rates, while any indirect effect was not sufficient per se to establish the existence of a transmission channel justifying the use of such tool to achieve the monetary policy objective. It is only in this respect that the reference to the disruption of the monetary policy transmission channel seems to be irrelevant.

By contrast, in our understanding of the legal framework of monetary policy, the concept of monetary policy transmission mechanism, along with the related conceptualization of the transmission channels, is pivotal. The task for lawyers and legal scholars working in this field should be to recognize and isolate some basic elements that may reconcile the economic explanation of the monetary policy transmission mechanism with its placement into the legal reasoning.

The need to provide a precise description of the functioning of monetary policy transmission mechanism is also supported by the Advocate General. In the OMT case, he clearly points out the responsibility of the ECB to provide precise information on any significant change in market conditions that give rise to external disruption affecting the monetary policy transmission channels.[282] The detailed description of the nature and extent of such disruption is implicitly subject to the previous definition of the functioning of the monetary mechanism that is supposed to become, in this respect, argument of legal dispute between the parties.

In light of this, the Advocate General seeks to develop a comprehensive understanding of the monetary policy transmission mechanism that might apply to both conventional and unconventional monetary policy measures. He sees the monetary policy transmission mechanism as 'the process through which monetary policy decisions affect the economy in general, and the price level in particular'.[283]

The conduct of ECB's monetary policy is carried out by controlling the monetary base of the Euro area economy. To do so, the monetary policy

[281] See BVerfG, 2 BvR 2728/13, para 97.

[282] See Opinion of Advocate General Cruz Villalón (Case C-62/14), para 166–167.

[283] Idem, note 60. The Advocate General, in particular, adopts the definition of monetary policy transmission mechanism laid down in ECB (2011), p. 62.

transmission mechanism is a process that enables the ECB to send out the appropriate 'impulses' or 'signals', primarily through the setting of policy interest rates. As a result, the orderly transmission of the monetary policy enables these impulses, to be firstly passed on to the financial sector and, at last, to firms and households.[284]

In light of these considerations, the appropriateness of monetary policy measures is a function of their capacity to carry out the desired monetary policy 'impulses' from the policy interest rates to the real sector, ultimately affecting the general level of consumer prices. This appropriateness is important in the legal assessment of monetary policy, as it represents one of the main elements necessary to recognize the nature of the monetary policy instruments.

This reasoning introduces an additional distinction in the central bank's conduct of monetary policy, on the basis of which we may draw a line of separation between conventional and unconventional monetary tools. While conventional monetary policy instruments operate when the monetary policy transmission mechanism works smoothly, and thus the transmission of the signals or impulses through the channels is not impaired, the adoption of unconventional monetary policy measures shall be grounded on the disruption of its orderly functioning, the occurrence of which is due to exogenous factors.[285]

These impulses to the real sector involve a number of different mechanisms and actions by economic agents at various stages of the process.[286] Although a precise elaboration of the relevant impulses or signals is not given, the Advocate General outlines a brief description of the type of impulse that the OMT announcement is supposed to transmit via the monetary policy transmission mechanism. The OMT announcement, as part of the ECB's communication strategy, is interpreted as a way to effectively manage the expectations of rational agents on the markets.[287]

[284] Opinion of Advocate General Cruz Villalón (Case C-62/14), para 112.

[285] Idem, para 121. In the words of the Advocate General, there are different disruptive factors that may compromise the monetary policy transmission channels. In the OMT case, for example, the Advocate General acknowledges this disruptive factor in a relatively sudden and virtually unbearable increase of the risk premia of sovereign bonds. This increase would not reflect the macroeconomic reality of those States and, as a result, it would prevent the ECB from transmitting its signals effectively, thereby fulfilling its price stability mandate.

[286] Opinion of Advocate General Cruz Villalón (Case C-62/14), see note 61. See also ECB (2011), pp. 62–63.

[287] Opinion of Advocate General Cruz Villalón (Case C-62/14), para 87 and 110.

For the Advocate General, the proper monetary policy transmission channel by which the OMT announcement operates is the *signaling channel*, through which, as explained above,[288] public expectations about key variables affecting market prices can be influenced. Hence, in the light of the legal opinion, this channel permits the OMT announcement to achieve its price target.[289]

It follows that the channels by which monetary policy instruments operate assume relevance also under a legal perspective, as their description allows to investigate the linkage existing between the type of instrument adopted and the achievement of the monetary policy objective.

Unfortunately, the ECJ failed to recognize the importance of such transmission mechanism for the identification of monetary policy instruments. The ECJ passively accepts the argument of the ECB on the disruption of the transmission mechanism and does not provide a systematic analysis of the transmission channels by which the OMT program is intended to work.

The absence of such analysis is striking: the 'proportionality' of the monetary policy instruments is dependent upon its effectiveness in maintaining price stability. Without an evaluation of the monetary policy transmission mechanism, it is not possible to determine the ways in which the instrument is deemed to affect the targeted real variables. As a result, it does not seem possible to assess whether the measure is 'proportionate' to achieve its price stability objective.

3.4 Monetary Policy in the Institutional Framework of the EU

According to King (2004), the institutional rationale of monetary policy lies into 'the uncertainty about future social decisions resulting from the impossibility and the undesirability of committing our successors to any given monetary policy strategy'.[290] The impracticability to enforce commitment is related to the fact that, absent any outside enforcer, monetary policy arrangements can always be changed over time. The undesirability

[288] See *supra* at notes 620–621.

[289] On the issue, see Eggertsson and Woodford (2003). According to the authors, central banks' large-scale asset purchase serves as a credible tool to signal their commitment to keep interest rates low.

[290] King (2004), p. 1.

is related to our ignorance in forecasting ex ante all future economic contingencies and, thus, the ideal monetary policy strategies that can best suit future states of the world.[291]

The existence of these two aspects of the collective decisions in monetary policy discloses the potential of monetary institutions: the institutional arrangements in monetary policy are to be constructed in order to reduce the costs of this commitment problem.[292] These two dimensions of the monetary policy institutional problem are certainly not secondary.

If there were just a problem of impossibility to enforce commitment in monetary policy, a government could simply adopt an 'optimal-state-contingent policy reaction function'.[293] In order to avoid any deviation from its predetermined path, the optimal function would be established as a constitutional provision, or more generally into the primary law, so that it could hardly be modified, and only with higher degree of consensus.[294] Yet, the coexistence of the second dimension in the commitment problem reasonably entails that the exercise of some discretion is necessary in order to design optimal monetary strategies. A fixed monetary policy would not perform well in the long period as the macroeconomic contingencies may change unexpectedly and may require different policy calibrations.[295]

In light of these premises, the function of a monetary policy institution becomes clear. The conduct of monetary policy requires the establishment of an institution tasked with 'constrained discretion',[296] that is, through the exercise of certain rights and powers and in compliance with certain duties.[297] In setting the legal framework within which the central bank will operate, the monetary authority will be entrusted with a comprehensive list of functions, rights, powers, and duties which are necessary for the maintenance of the monetary policy objective previously identified.[298] And, while the goal of its monetary policy action will be set into the primary law, its institutional architecture will allow for some periodical changes in its policy path, in order to fit the evolving macroeconomic circumstances.

[291] Idem, p. 1.
[292] Idem, p. 3.
[293] Idem, p. 4.
[294] Idem, p. 4.
[295] Idem, p. 4.
[296] For insights into the notion of 'constrained discretion', see Bernanke and Mishkin (1997); Bernanke (2003b). In general, see also Harris (2012), pp. 95–113.
[297] Gianviti (2010), p. 449.
[298] Idem, p. 450.

The legal construction of monetary policy institutions,[299] such as the ESCB and the ECB, has to reflect this double dimension inherent to the commitment problem. On the one hand, the legal rules governing the dynamics of monetary policymaking are to be designed to constrain the decision-making process within the predetermined monetary policy rule, that is, price stability, making any deviation from this rule-bound path too costly.[300]

In doing so, the acknowledgment of such legal framework committed to price stability imposes well-defined discipline and genuine accountability on the behavior of monetary policy institutions,[301] so that the general public may exercise—at least theoretically—its democratic control over the use of monetary powers by policymakers.[302]

On the other hand, the boundaries of this institutional framework, albeit rigorous, are to be established in order to permit a certain degree of flexibility[303] subject to the overall objective of price stability. This flexibility is inherently related to the use of discretion in the conduct of monetary policy by central bankers. Only if the institutional settings are flexible enough to allow the calibration of the monetary policy responses in relation to changing macroeconomic circumstances, the objective of price stability may be achieved in a sufficiently consistent manner.

A remote equilibrium seems to surface in the relationship between the law and the discretion that central bankers may exercise in the conduct of their monetary policy decisions. And this equilibrium is to be primarily reflected in the institutional framework establishing the formal arrangements of the monetary system.

It is the law that guarantees the optimal balance between objectives, instruments, and discretion in the monetary policy conduct. And to make this possible, the legal provisions must be adapted to order an optimal institutional framework that may reconcile, in a consistent manner, all the components of the monetary policy regime.[304] In line with this assumption, this section aims at analyzing the institutional architecture of the ESCB and of the ECB, as laid down in the EU primary law.

[299] We derive this idea of legal construction of monetary policy institutions from Pistor (2013), pp. 315–330.

[300] King (2004), p. 4.

[301] Bernanke, Laubach, Mishkin, and Posen (2001), p. 22.

[302] For a discussion of this topic, see Rymes (1995–1996), pp. 177–188. See also Levy (1995), pp. 189–210.

[303] On the need of flexibility in the establishment of formal monetary policy institutions, see Rogoff (1986).

[304] See Debelle, Masson, Savastano, and Sharma (1998).

3.4.1 *Features of the European System of Central Banks*

There is a common misconception on the monetary policy assignments of the EU. It is commonly believed that the ECB is the sole European institution responsible for the conduct of monetary policy. Actually this is not true. The articles of the TFEU are very clear on the institutional calibration of the monetary policy tasks. Article 127(1) TFEU states that the primary objective of price stability shall be maintained by the ESCB, while Article 282(1) TFEU establishes that the ESCB is constituted by the ECB, together with the national central banks of all Member States.

In pursuing the objective of price stability, along with the other subordinated objectives assigned,[305] the ESCB shall define and implement the monetary policy of the EU.[306] Although the TFEU defines the ESCB by its tasks, objectives, and components, the legal text makes no reference to its nature.[307]

The nature of the ESCB, however, may be understood as an evolving concept.[308] When the establishment of a new EU legal order was initially thought, the introduction of the word 'system' for the construction of the European central banking was meant to 'describe the existence of the ECB and the NCBs as integral parts of the System, governed by a common set of rules and committed to the objectives and tasks assigned to it'.[309] Since then, the ESCB has developed its own legal dimension whose content can be better understood by using the expression 'cross-border central banking system', introduced in Article 56 of the Statute of the BIS when the ECB decided to become a member and shareholder of the BIS.[310]

[305] As laid down in Article 127(1) TFEU, 'Without prejudice to the objective of price stability, the ESCB shall support the general economic policies in the Union with a view to contributing to the achievement of the objectives of the Union as laid down in Article 3 of the Treaty on European Union. The ESCB shall act in accordance with the principle of an open market economy with free competition, favouring an efficient allocation of resources, and in compliance with the principles set out in Article 119.'

[306] See Article 127(2) of TFEU and Article 3(1) of ESCB Statute.

[307] De Lhoneux (2005), p. 163.

[308] Louis (2005a), p. 312.

[309] See Draft Statute of the European System of Central Banks and of the European Central Bank (Commentary), 27 November 1990. See also Louis (2005a), p. 312; Malaguti (2010), p. 151.

[310] Louis (2005a), p. 312. According to Article 56 of the Statute of the BIS 'central bank means the bank or banking system in any country to which has been entrusted the duty of regulating the volume of currency and credit in that country; or, in a cross-border central

The peculiar nature of the ESCB is reflected also in its status. The ESCB has no legal personality and is not an EU institution.[311] And, a simple public body, or quasi-institution, has to perform the tasks specifically imposed by the EU Treaties. The absence of legal personality holds true also for the narrower group of the Eurosystem,[312] subset constituted solely by the ECB and the national central banks of the Member States whose currency is the Euro. In this regard, two different realities coexist into the ESCB framework.

In this institutional context, the Eurosystem is responsible *stricto* sensu for defining and conducting the monetary policy in the narrow sense, for issuing and managing the Euro, for managing the official foreign reserves of the Member States that have adopted the Euro, and for promoting the smooth operation of payment systems.[313]

banking system, the national central banks and the common central banking institution which are entrusted with such duty'.

[311] Repasi (2013), p. 8. See also, with further references, Lastra (2014), p. 94. It must be noted that there is no consensus on the legal status of the ESCB. In fact, although it is undeniable that the ESCB does not have legal personality and that is governed by the decision-making bodies of the ESCB, it is also true that tasks and powers are assigned under the Treaty to the ESCB itself, and not to the ECB or the national central banks. For details, see Malaguti (2010), pp. 156–157. This consideration leads a number of authors to explore the organic nature of the ESCB and its role in the context of the institutional relationship between the ECB and the national central banks. For example, Weber (1998), p. 1465, advocates the federal structure of the relationship between the ECB and the national central banks, where the latter would be entirely autonomous bodies regulated by domestic laws and only charged by the Treaty with a limited set of tasks related to common monetary policy. Differently, Scheller (2006), p. 42, defines the ESCB as an 'organic link' between the ECB and the national central banks. In his view this link should ensure that the tasks assigned to the ESCB are performed jointly by the national central banks, although the ECB and the national central banks can potentially act in full autonomy. Smits (1997), pp. 24–25, takes a constitutional legal view, arguing that the ESCB constitutes a proper constitutional body, and as a community organ, it is truly the central bank of the EU. Finally, Zilioli and Selmayr (2001a), p. 79, refer to a loyalty obligation of national central banks within the ESCB as to ensure the integrity of the whole system.

[312] See Article 282(1) of TFEU and Article 1 of ESCB Statute. For details, see De Lhoneux (2005), p. 163; Lastra (2014), p. 94; Scheller (2006), p. 44. As argued by Lastra (2014), p. 94, since neither the ESCB nor the Eurosystem has legal personality, they are not holders of rights and obligations. It is instead the ECB that holds all the rights and obligations.

[313] De Lhoneux (2005), p. 165.

This designation of the ESCB dates back to the Inter-Governmental Conference (IGC) negotiating the Maastricht Treaty.[314] The central idea of the participants, at that time, was to promote the establishment of a central bank modeled on the institutional structure of the German Bundesbank and the US Federal Reserve System (Fed).[315]

It comes as no surprise that the ESCB/Eurosystem and the Fed share some common characteristics in their respective governance structures. As for the case of the ESCB, the Fed has no legal personality, while the sole bodies recognized as *legal* persons in the US monetary system are the Board of Governors,[316] the Federal Open Market Committee (FOMC),[317] and the regional Federal Reserve Banks.[318] While the Board of Governors and the FOMC are federal agencies and, thus, public legal persons, the regional Federal Reserve Banks have private ownership and are organized as corporate entities.[319] In addition, similar to the Governing Council of the ECB, the FOMC is the sole body responsible for formulating the monetary policy in the United States.[320]

Notwithstanding the common characteristics with the Fed, it is generally accepted that the ESCB/Eurosystem has been primarily modeled following the institutional architecture of the German Bundesbank.[321] According to the Bundesbank Act (*Bundesbankgesetz or BBankG*) of 1957, the governing bodies of the Bundesbank comprised the Bundesbank Council (*Zentralbankrat*), the Directorate (*Direktorium*), and the Executive Boards (*Vorstände*) of the Land Central Banks (*Landeszentralbanken*).[322]

[314] For an account of the negotiations, refer to *Projet de traité en vue de la mise en place d'une UEM, Conférence intergouvernementale* (Brussels, 10 December 1989).

[315] Gauron (1999), p. 148; Mullins and Saunders (1994), p. 222. See also Wynne (1999), p. 3. For a survey on the key similarities between these central banks, see Apel (2007).

[316] 12 U.S. Code § 241.

[317] The Federal Open Market Committee was formed by the Banking Act of 1933 codified at 12 U.S.C. § 263. It is in charge of overseeing the open market operations, setting the policy interest rates, and overseeing the growth of money supply in the United States.

[318] 12 U.S. Code § 282, 323.

[319] 12 U.S. Code § 282, 323. On this argument, inter alia, see Lastra (2012), pp. 1274–1275.

[320] For a thorough comparison between the Fed and the ESCB, see Gerdesmeier, Mongelli, and Roffia (2007).

[321] For an institutional perspective, inter alia, see de Haan (Eds.) (2000); Howart (2012), p. 132.

[322] For a deeper examination of the early Bundesbank governance, see Deutsche Bundesbank (1957), pp. 4–7.

The Council was the primary policymaking body of the central banks, holding both decision-making power and means of execution,[323] and reflects Germany's federal structure.[324] The Council was composed of the Directorate—made up, in turn, of the president, the vice-president, and no more than eight additional members[325]—and of the nine presidents of the Land Central Banks.[326] While the former were nominated by the German Federal Government (*Bundesregierung*), the latter were elected by the German Federal Council (*Bundesrat*). The Directorate, instead, was responsible for implementing the decisions taken by the Bundesbank Council.[327]

More importantly, the Bundesbank's governance system was the model that inspired the ECB's layout.[328] As a result, the ESCB/Eurosystem was established with the Governing Council and Executive Board of the ECB as governing bodies.[329] According to Article 283 TFEU, the Governing Council comprises the members of the Executive Board of the ECB—the president, the vice-president, and four other members—and the governors of the national central banks of the Member States whose currency is the Euro.[330]

[323] Gauron (1999), p. 148. See Articles 6(1) and 6(2) of BBankG (1957).

[324] Maier and de Haan (2000), p. 8. The idea behind establishing this structure was that a range of opinions represented in the decision-making bodies of the central bank would have substantially contributed to the quality of its monetary policy. See Deutsche Bundesbank, Monthly Report, May 2002, p. 5.

[325] Article 7(2) of BBankG (1957).

[326] Article 6(2) of BBankG (1957).

[327] Article 7(1) of BBankG (1957). With the start of the third stage of the EMU in January 1999, a reform debate on how the Bundesbank has to be restructured in view of its new role in the EMU was launched. The idea was to simplify its structure, reducing in particular the number of decision-making bodies and the number of Land Central Banks. This debate concluded in March 2002 when the Bundestag approved the Seventh Act amending the Bundesbank Act and this was published in the Federal Law Gazette on 28 March 2002. For details, see Bundesbank, Monthly Report, May 2002, p. 8.

[328] Maier and de Haan (2000), p. 8; Lastra (2014), p. 80; Busch (2005), p. 111. Although the governing structure of the ECB resembles the institutional governance of the Bundesbank before the EMU in many aspects, it must be noted that some differences between the two banks remain. Kaltenthaler (2006), p. 169, argues that the ECB has a much more protected mandate than the Bundesbank, due to the fact that the ESCB Statute is clearer in defining objectives and instruments. In addition, the ECB is much more protected by the law with respect to its independence, as this is provided by the TFEU, while the Bundesbank could have its independence altered by a simple act of the German parliament.

[329] Article 8 of ESCB Statute.

[330] See also Article 10(1) of ESCB Statute.

The Governing Council must adopt the guidelines and take the decisions necessary to ensure the performance of the tasks assigned by the primary law to the ESCB/Eurosystem. In addition, it formulates the monetary policy of the Union including, where appropriate, decisions relating to intermediate monetary objectives, key interest rates, and the supply of reserves in the ESCB.[331]

The Executive Board, which is made of persons with recognized experience in monetary and banking matters appointed by the European Council,[332] is tasked with the implementation of the monetary policy decided by the Governing Council. To this purpose, the Executive Board shall give the necessary instructions to national central banks.[333]

The federal nature of ESCB's policymaking is underlined by the fact that the Executive Board of the ECB is in a permanent minority on the Governing Council,[334] as each member of the Governing Council may exercise only one vote.[335] Moreover, all governors of the national central banks have a vote in all policy decisions of the Governing Council which, in turn, shall meet at least ten times a year.[336]

Unless otherwise provided, the Governing Council acts by simple majority of the members having a voting right, although, for the validity of the meetings, a quorum of two-thirds of the ESCB/Eurosystem members is required.[337] Likewise, each member of the Executive Board has one vote, although the Executive Board usually acts, unless otherwise provided, without any required quorum.[338]

One of the most noteworthy attributes of the ESCB/Eurosystem framework is its legal emphasis of the principle of independence. Central bank independence can be regarded as a constitutional instrument that

[331] Article 12(1) of ESCB Statute.

[332] Article 11(2) of ESCB Statute. More precisely, the president, the vice-president, and the other members of the Executive Board shall be appointed by the European Council, acting by a qualified majority, on a recommendation from the Council after it has consulted the European Parliament and the Governing Council.

[333] Article 12(1) of ESCB Statute.

[334] Wynne (2001), p. 741.

[335] Yet, as from the date on which the number of members of the Governing Council has exceeded 21, each member of the Executive Board shall have one vote and the number of governors with a voting right shall be 15. The latter voting rights are assigned following a rotation procedure stated in Article 10(2) of ESCB Statute.

[336] Article 10(2)-(5) of ESCB Statute.

[337] Article 10(2) of ESCB Statute.

[338] Article 11(5) of ESCB Statute.

combines public powers to regulate money with a neutral objective to protect economic rights of citizens, detaching monetary policy from political influence.[339] The need of independence for central banks has been widely discussed in the economic and legal literature,[340] and many authors share the opinion that independent central banks perform relatively better in targeting monetary policy objectives.[341]

This model of full independence of central banks is instrumental in giving priority to a monetary policy aimed at maintaining price stability, as central banks enjoy operational freedom from government interference in monetary affairs within the spectrum of the objectives statutorily assigned.[342] As a result, the Maastricht Treaty incorporated central bank's independence as a bulwark for ensuring that the future EU area would have benefited from price stability.[343]

The independent status of the ESCB is guaranteed by Article 130 TFEU, which reads:

> when exercising the powers and carrying out the tasks and duties conferred upon them by the Treaties and the Statute of the ESCB and of the ECB, neither the European Central Bank, nor a national central bank, nor any member of their decision-making bodies shall seek or take instructions from Union institutions, bodies, offices or agencies, from any government of a Member State or from any other body.[344]

The strength of this provision is straightforward: not only the ESCB is shielded from any interference of political institutions or bodies, but it must also conduct its tasks independently from any other non-political authorities, such as micro- or macroprudential supervisors.[345] In addition, the Article imposes an active duty on EU institutions, bodies, agencies, and members of the governing bodies of EU Members States which are prohibited from

[339] This rationale of central bank independence is provided in Monteagudo (2010), p. 485.

[340] Inter alia, see Monteagudo (2010) pp. 495–505; Lastra (2014), pp. 92–96; Lybek (2005), pp. 133–152; Debelle and Fischer (1994), pp. 195–219; Eijffinger and de Haan (1996); Crowe and Meade (2008); Taylor (2013b), pp. 155–162. For a review of the literature on this topic, see Berger, de Haan, and Eijffinger (2001), pp. 3–40.

[341] For analytical surveys on this topic and related evidences on the performance of independent central banks, with further literature, see Cukierman (1992), pp. 369–432; Alesina and Summers (1993), pp. 151–162; Cukierman (1994), pp. 1437–1448; Loungani and Sheets (1997), pp. 381–399; Daunfeldt and De Luna (2003), pp. 2–13.

[342] Lastra (2014), p. 95; Monteagudo (2010), p. 498.

[343] Lamfalussy (1997).

[344] The same provision is laid down in Article 7 of ESCB Statute.

[345] Lastra (2015b), p. 269.

seeking to influence the members of the decision-making bodies of the ECB or of the national central banks in the performance of their tasks.[346]

The principle of independence of the ESCB is further reinforced by Article 123 TFEU that reads:

> Overdraft facilities or any other type of credit facility with the ECB or with the central banks of the Member States (hereinafter referred to as "national central banks") in favor of Community institutions or bodies, central governments, regional, local or other public authorities, other bodies governed by public law, or public undertakings of Member States shall be prohibited, as shall the purchase directly from them by the ECB or national central banks of debt instruments.

By prohibiting any purchase of debt instrument directly from Member States and any extension of credit support in favor of Member State governments or public undertakings,[347] this provision establishes a clear operational defense for the ESCB in its free choice of the policy desired by representing a severance of monetary links between the central bank and the government.[348] In this way, the conduct of the ESCB should remain shielded from any pressure and/or interference reflecting political economic considerations.

[346] For an in-depth analysis of the independence of the ECB, see Zilioli (2016), pp. 125–143; Siekmann (ed.)(2013), pp. 402–453; Zilioli and Selmayr (2001b), pp. 621–627. See also Siekmann (2015a), pp. 70–71; Dutzler (2003), pp. 88–109. On this topic it is important to recall the judgment of the ECJ in the Commission of the European Communities v. the European Central Bank (C-11/00), so-called Olaf case, where the Commission challenged the validity of the ECB Decision 1999/726/EC of 7 October 1999 on fraud prevention. For a discussion of this case, see Louis (2005a), pp. 324–326. For the judges, the principle of independence aims to shield the ECB from all political pressure in order to enable it effectively to pursue the objectives attributed to its tasks, through the independent exercise of the specific powers conferred on it for that purpose by the EC Treaty and the ESCB Statute (see para 134). It must be noted, however, that this shield against any political influence can in practice fail. In 2011 Lorenzo Bini Smaghi, then ECB Executive Board member, was under political pressure to resign as to make space for a French representative on the Executive Board after the mandate of Jean-Claude Trichet, President of the ECB, expired. Mr. Bini Smaghi was harshly lobbied by European and national politicians, and his resignation was seen as a proof of the large influence that politicians can have on the ECB governance. On this topic, see Ralph Atkins, *Bini Smaghi quits ECB after French pressure*, *Financial Times*, 10 November 2011, article available online at https://next.ft.com/content/1ba7a48c-0bc3-11e1-9310-00144feabdc0.

[347] See Council Regulation (EC) No. 3603/93 of 13 December 1993 specifying definitions for the application of the prohibitions referred to in Articles 104 and 104b (1) of the Treaty (OJ L 332, 31.12.1993, p. 1).

[348] Bini Smaghi and Gross (2000), p. 123. For an in-depth analysis of Article 123 TFEU, see Kämmerer (2013), pp. 150–166.

3.4.2 *ECB and National Central Banks: Centralization or Decentralization in the ESCB?*

The functioning of the ESCB in the conduct of its monetary policy shall be now scrutinized by looking at the operational tasks statutorily assigned to the institutions—namely, the ECB and the national central banks—composing the monetary architecture. Although the construction of ESCB resembles a federalized institution, its internal and operational dynamics reflect a different nature. In light of the TFEU, the ECB is the only institution in the EU with its own legal personality and full independence in the exercise of its powers and in the management of its finances.[349]

The precise position occupied by the ECB within the ESCB is reason of discussion among legal scholars and practitioners.[350] The problem at stake lies in the so-called principle of decentralization which is part of the ESCB legal framework.[351] This principle can be recognized in Article 9(2) of ESCB Statute which entrusts the ECB with ensuring that the tasks conferred upon the ESCB in accordance with the Treaty are implemented either by its own activities or through the national central banks. Moreover, Article 12(2) of ESCB Statute establishes that, 'To the extent deemed possible and appropriate and without prejudice to the provisions of this Article, the ECB shall have recourse to the national central banks to carry out operations which form part of the tasks of the ESCB.'[352]

[349] See Article 282(3) of TFEU and Article 9 of ESCB Statute. This legal personality assigns a special status to the ECB. Of this opinion, see, among others, Lastra (2015b) pp. 268–260. This special status of the ECB was used to question the classification of the ECB as an institution of the European Community. In this sense, see Streinz (2008), para 402; Tohidipur (2006), pp. 179–180. In fact, before the entry into force of the Lisbon Treaty, the ECB was not a formal institution of Union as its legal basis was provided not in the Article establishing the institutions, but in a separate one, that is, Article 8 of the EC Treaty. With the introduction of Article 13 TEU, this debate ended as the ECB was finally recognized as an institution of the EU and this provision does not prohibit a legal body that has institutions itself to be an institution of another legal body. In this sense, see Häde (2011), p. 432; Smits (2003), pp. 23–25.

[350] For in-depth surveys on this topic, among others, see Lastra (2015b), pp. 249–253; Zilioli and Selmayr (2001a), pp. 7–31; Lastra (2000), pp. 167–180; Smits (1997); pp. 92–98.

[351] For a discussion on the principle of decentralization in the Eurosystem, with further references, see Louis (2005a), pp. 324–317. For a critical standpoint on the decentralized structure of the system, see de Haan, Berger, and Inklaar (2004), pp. 71–95.

[352] In addition, the principle of decentralization is further reinforced in the primary law by Article 14(3) of the ESCB Statute which provides that national central banks 'are an integral part of the ESCB and shall act in accordance with the guidelines and instructions of the ECB.'

Defining the concept of decentralization within the scope of the ESCB is not an easy task.[353] However, its relevance should not be underestimated: the recognition of the legal relationship between the ECB and national central banks is a crucial factor determining the concrete dynamics of the monetary policy conduct in the EU. To appreciate the nature of this relationship, three decision-making phases of the monetary policy decision-making process should be distinguished, namely, (1) preparation, (2) judgment, and the (3) operational follow-up.[354]

1. The preparation is highly centralized. In this phase the Governing Council usually disposes a double analysis—so-called Pillar 2—consisting of an economic analysis to identify the short- to medium-term risks to price stability and a monetary analysis to assess medium- to long-term inflation trends.[355] This cross-checking evaluation includes the regular monitoring of a variety of relevant indicators by which a systematic evaluation of all relevant information is pursued.[356] National central banks are not participants in the adoption of monetary policy decisions.[357] The governors of national central banks, when participating in the Governing Council, must act in accordance with the principle of independence laid down in Article 130 TFEU and Article 7 of the ESCB Statute.[358]

[353] See *supra* at notes 800–803, 841.

[354] Moutot, Jung, and Mongelli (2008), p. 39.

[355] On the dual pillars strategy undertaken by the ECB in the preparation stage of its policymaking, see Issing (2006), recalling that the author was the one who introduced and developed this monetary policy strategy for the EMU. For more details, see *infra* Chapter 5.III.2.

[356] Moutot, Jung, and Mongelli (2008), p. 42. Inter alia, the relevant economic indicators are the following: (1) output and its components, (2) demand and labor market conditions, (3) broad range of price and cost indicators, (4) fiscal policies, (5) balance of payments for the Euro area, (6) asset prices and financial yields, and (7) sentiment indicators. The monetary indicators adopted instead are (1) monetary aggregates, (2) credit aggregates, (3) counterparts of M3, (4) loans to the private sector, (5) money-based inflation-risk-indicators, (6) measures of excess liquidity, and (7) indicators of the monetary policy stance and interest rate.

[357] Louis (2014), p. 105. Against this backdrop, Zilioli and Selmayr (2001a), p. 67, refer to the ESCB's decision-making structure as one of decisional centralism.

[358] In accordance with Article 130 TFEU, therefore, the governors of the national central banks, when acting within the Governing Council with respect to the conduct of monetary policy, are personally responsible, and, as such, they must not take any instructions not only

The ECB staff prepares briefs discussing the evolution of the monetary trends and addressing specific topical issues.[359] These staff contributions are not sent directly to the Governing Council. These documents are first considered by the Executive Board[360] which, in turn, plays the role of *trait d'union* between the Council and the staff. After the Governing Council decides, these contributions are usually reframed in the ECB's Monthly Bulletins.

A prominent role in the preparation phase is also assumed by the so-called Eurosystem/ESCB Committees, established pursuant to Article 9 of the Rules of Procedure of the ECB. These Committees are made of up to two members from each of the national central banks and the ECB, appointed by each Governor and the Executive Board, respectively.[361] They are tasked with an advisory role to the decision-making bodies of the ECB, assisting the Governing Council and the Executive Board with expert and/or technical advice.[362] More importantly, these committees represent the *locus* where a significant amount of decentralized data and information at aggregate and disaggregate level can be processed[363] for the ESCB decision-making bodies.

2. The second phase of the monetary policy decision-making process, that is, the judgmental phase, is also highly centralized.[364] Although, from the composition of the Governing Council, one could gather arguments in favor of its decentralized nature,[365] the inherent cen-

from the Union institutions and bodies but also from the national central banks they chair. Against this backdrop, Louis (2005a), p. 105, argues that governors of national central banks are independent experts adopting monetary policy in the sole interest of the Union.

359 Moutot, Jung, and Mongelli (2008), p. 42. On the role of the ECB staff in preparing the decision-making phase of the ECB monetary policy conduct, see also Papademos and Stark (2010), pp. 90–93.

360 See *supra* at note 824.

361 See Article 9(3) of the Rules of Procedure of the European Central Bank (Decision of the ECB of 22 January 2014 amending Decision ECB/2004/2 of 19 February 2004).

362 Moutot, Jung, and Mongelli (2008), p. 38. In line with Article 9(1), the Committees 'shall assist in the work of the decision-making bodies of the ECB and shall report to the Governing Council via the Executive Board'.

363 Moutot, Jung, and Mongelli (2008), p. 38.

364 Louis (2005b), p. 35.

365 For example, some arguments in favor of the decentralized nature of the judgmental phase are laid down in de Haan, Berger, and Inklaar (2004), pp. 71–100.

tralization of this phase is supported by a number of suggestions regarding the functioning of the ECB and its bodies.

In accordance with Article 12(2) of the ESCB Statute, the Executive Board is responsible for the preparation of the meetings of the Governing Council. This responsibility involves drawing up meeting agendas, preparing the necessary documentation for the Governing Council, and making proposals for meeting discussions. The President of the ECB chairs the meetings of the Executive Board and shall ensure compliance with the rules of procedure.[366] In line with Article 12(1) of the ESCB Statute, the Governing Council formulates the monetary policy of the Union. However, the Executive Board has a special role within the Council, not only because its members take the lead in the preparatory work but also for their voting weight in the Governing Council.[367]

After the internal debate, the President seeks the consensus among the members of the Governing Council on monetary policy assessments. Once a decision is taken, an introductory statement is drafted and is presented at a press conference.[368] The Governing Council meets twice a month: at the first meeting, it makes its evaluation on the economic, financial, and monetary developments in the Euro area, assuming its monetary policy decisions. At the second meeting, issues related to the tasks and responsibilities of the ECB and national central banks are usually discussed.[369]

3. The last phase of the monetary policy decision-making process is the operational phase. In contrast to the prior stages, this moment presents a clear decentralized nature. This is because national central banks are closely involved in the implementation of monetary policy, as they act as operational agents executing the monetary policy decisions adopted by the ECB Governing Council.[370]

[366] Articles 13 and 46 of ESCB Statute.

[367] As a matter of fact, with the introduction of the rotation of voting rights, the weight of the votes expressed by the Executive Board members in the decisions of the Governing Council is increased considerably. For details on the allocation of voting rights, see Article 10(2) of the ESCB Statute.

[368] Moutot, Jung, and Mongelli (2008), p. 42.

[369] Idem, p. 40.

[370] In this sense, see Louis (2005a), p. 110; Lastra (2000), p. 168. Some have argued that the implementation of monetary policy decisions via national central banks reflects not only the decentralized structure of the implementation phase of ESCB monetary policy but also

When a policy decision is made, national central banks shall perform their operational functions in accordance with Article 9(2) and Article 12(1) of the ESCB Statute, that is, following the instructions previously set out by the Executive Board to carry out the monetary operations approved. In addition, it is up to the Governing Council undertaking the necessary follow-up actions to ensure compliance with the guidelines and instructions so defined.[371] National central banks can perform non-ESCB functions unless these functions interfere with the objectives and tasks of the ESCB. In this case national central banks act as national agencies.[372]

The decentralization of the operational follow-up is not given for granted. Article 9(2) of the ESCB Statute infers that it is up to the governing bodies of the ECB deciding whether the decentralization of the operational phase is 'possible and appropriate' and, thus, the ECB allocates the ultimate phase of the decision-making process to itself or to the national central banks.[373] This discretion may question the concrete existence of a true decentralization in the implementation phase of the monetary policy decision-making process. Rather than being decentralized, the relationship existing between the ECB and the national central banks seems to be characterized by some sort of 'de-concentration',[374] where the decision-making process can be shifted in its operational moment from the apex of the system, represented by the ECB, to its periphery as a free option of its centralized governing body.

the fragmentation of the Euro area. In this sense, see Padoa-Schioppa (2004), p. 85. Although prior to the crisis a convergence wave in financial conditions and markets was characterizing the EU countries' developments, after the crisis, the fragmentation reappeared. This fragmentation may therefore explain the need to rely on national central banks for the implementation of monetary policy decisions. However, this decentralization shall not encroach upon Article 119 TFEU which requires in any case the ESCB to ensure the singleness of monetary policy across the EU. For details, see Lastra (2015b), pp. 110–111.

[371] Article 14(3) of ESCB Statute.

[372] Article 14(4) of ESCB Statute.

[373] Louis (2005a), p. 314.

[374] Idem, p. 314. Similarly, Zilioli and Selmayr (2001a), pp. 66–67, interpret this relationship in terms of the hierarchical organization of the ESCB incompatible with a federal system, where national central banks are legally subordinated to the ECB and its decision-making bodies.

3.4.3 Monetary Policy and Macroprudential Supervision in the EU: Some Preliminary Conclusions

The institutional framework of monetary policy significantly differs from the institutional settings of the EU macroprudential policy where the allocation of powers reflects the supremacy of national macroprudential authorities over the ECB in its capacity of supervisory authority.

On the one hand, the macroprudential policy regime in Europe remains largely fragmented. The operationalization of macroprudential instruments within jurisdictions is in the hands of national designated authorities, along with national macroprudential authorities, which are primarily responsible for countering systemic risks. The responsibilities allocated at the national level are then complemented by a European layer of supervision. This layer, composed of the ESRB and the ECB in its capacity of banking supervisor within the SSM, does not have concrete powers for targeting financial stability.

The ESRB is entrusted with a general macroprudential oversight of the financial system. Its soft-law instruments are not intended to compel Member States in the maintenance of financial stability but only to caution about the existence of market conditions that may generate systemic events. Similarly, the establishment of the SSM has not changed the macroprudential policy regime in Europe as the top-up power assigned to the ECB could be used only as a measure of last resort and after consulting the national authority involved, within the strict limits imposed by the EU legislation.

Conversely, the ESCB features described in the previous section reveal the inner nature of the relationships existing between the ECB and the national central banks within the monetary policy framework provided by the EU Treaties. Far from being a genuine federal system,[375] the decision-making process of the ESCB remains essentially centralized. Even if in the implementation follow-up the allocation of responsibilities seems to follow a de-concentrated pattern, the national central banks are subject to a discretionary evaluation of the ECB over its feasibility and appropriateness, in line with Article 9(2) of ESCB Statute.

[375] Idem, p. 311; Chalmers, Davies, and Monti (2010), p. 551. See also Zilioli and Selmayr (2001a), p. 57, with further references, where the authors explain that it is misleading to call the ESCB a federal system, although it is structured as a two-level organization, with the ECB level and the level of the national central banks.

A number of provisions in the primary law reveal an important characteristic underlying the legal construction of the ESCB, that is, its hierarchical order behind a federal facade.[376]

The ESCB is constructed by the EU Treaties not only in line with an explicit hierarchical set of objectives[377]—where price stability stands at the apex—but also through a hierarchical composition of its institutional framework, where national central banks, acting as operational agents of the monetary policy of the Union, are legally subordinated to the ECB.[378] It can be argued therefore that the ESCB is characterized by a hierarchical relationship between the center, namely, the ECB, and the periphery, namely, the national central banks—subject to its authority in the conduct of monetary policy.[379]

This parallel—but opposite—construction of the two regimes has some important implications for the interaction of the two policies.[380] Although the two policies have different objectives, their tools and instruments can influence the same variables and, eventually, can provide inconsistent

[376] Chalmers, Davies, and Monti (2010), p. 551; Louis (2005a), p. 311.

[377] See *infra* at note 1220.

[378] De Vicuña (1999), p. 299. It must be noted, however, that this opinion is not unanimously accepted. For example, a different view is provided by Seidel (2012), p. 17. The institutional preeminence of the ECB can be clearly inferred from Article 4 of the ESCB Statute which establishes that the ECB must be consulted in advance (1) on any proposed community act in its fields of competence and (2) by national authorities regarding any draft legislative provision in its fields of competence within certain limits and conditions set out by the Council. In addition, Articles 12(3) and 18(3) of TFEU aim at assigning to the decision-making bodies of the ECB the power to adopt the Rule of Procedure regarding the internal organization of the ECB and the general principles for open market operations carried out by the ECB itself or by the national central banks. On the issue, it shall be noted that any legal act adopted on the basis of the primary law, pursuant to Article 34 of the ESCB Statute, is an act of the ECB and not of the ESCB. Finally, it shall be noted that a further argument in favor of national central banks' subordination is inferred from Article 14(4), according to which: 'National central banks may perform functions other than those specified in this Statute unless the Governing Council finds, by a majority of two thirds of the votes cast, that these interfere with the objectives and tasks of the ESCB. Such functions shall be performed on the responsibility and liability of national central banks and shall not be regarded as being part of the functions of the ESCB.' A hierarchical super-ordination of the ECB can also be found therefore in relation to the functions performed by national central banks out of the scope of the ESCB.

[379] Louis (2005a), p. 311.

[380] Kern (2014), p. 520.

results, should they pull in opposite directions. And if the institutional architecture of macroprudential and monetary policy is not consistent, or at least not coordinated, a risk of policy conflicts may arise.

To better understand how this conflict can be substantial, it is now necessary to scrutinize how the macroprudential policy tools and the monetary policy measures thus far described may influence each other, and how their side effects can impact the same macroeconomic variables. If the risks of conflicts are material, the relevant question will be whether and how the EU institutional architecture may coordinate all the actors involved and disentangle possible policy inconsistencies.

References

Acharya, Viral V., Naqvi, Hassan (2010). The Seeds of a Crisis: A Theory of Bank Liquidity and Risk-Taking over the Business Cycle, *Journal of Financial Economics*. Vol. 106, Issue 2.

Adrian, Tobias, Liang, Nellie (2014). Monetary Policy, Financial Conditions, and Financial Stability, *Federal Reserve Bank of New York Staff Report*, No. 690.

Adrian, Tobias, Shin, Hyun Song (2008). Financial Intermediaries, Financial Stability and Monetary Policy, *Federal Reserve Bank of New York Staff Reports*, No. 346.

Adrian, Tobias, Shin, Hyun Song (2010). Liquidity and Leverage, *Journal of Financial Intermediation*, Vol. 19, No. 3.

Alesina, Alberto, Summers, Lawrence H. (1993). Central Bank Independence and Macroeconomic Performance: Some Comparative Evidence, *Journal of Money, Credit and Banking*, Vol. 25, No. 2.

Allanazarova, Leyli (2010). The Eurosystem Approach to Monetary Policy and Liquidity Management, *Logos Verlag*, Berlin.

Allen, Franklin, Rogoff, Kenneth (2010). Asset Prices, Financial Stability and Monetary Policy. In: '*The Riksbank's Inquiry into the Risks in the Swedish Housing Market*'. Paper Presented at the Swedish Riksbank Workshop on Housing Markets, Monetary Policy and Financial Stability, 12 November 2010.

Altavilla, Carlo, Giannone, Domenico Lenza, Michele (2014). The Financial and Macroeconomic Effects of OMT Announcements, *ECB Working Paper Series*, No. 1707.

Altunbas, Yener, Gambacorta, Leonardo, Marques-Ibanez, David (2009). An Empirical Assessment of the Risk-Taking Channel, Paper prepared for the BIS/ECB Workshop on '*Monetary Policy and Financial Stability*'. Basel, 11 September 2009.

Amtenbrink, Fabian (2011). Central Bank Challenges in the Global Economy. In: '*European Yearbook of International Economic Law 2011*', (eds.), Christoph Herrmann, Jörg Philipp Terhechte, *Springer*, Berlin.
Anderson, William L. (2001). What's Wrong with the CPI?, *The Free Market*, Vol. 19, No. 8.
Ando, Albert, Modigliani, Franco (1963). The Life Cycle Hypothesis of Saving: Aggregate Implications and Tests, *American Economic Review*, Vol. 53, No. 1.
Angeloni, Ignazio, Faia, Ester, Lo Duca, Marco (2015). Monetary Policy and Risk Taking, *Journal of Economic Dynamics and Control*, Vol. 52.
Apel, Emmanuel (2007). Central Banking Systems Compared: The ECB, the Pre-Euro Bundesbank and the Federal Reserve System, *Routledge*.
Archer, David (2009). Roles and Objectives of Modern Central Banks. In: '*Issues in the Governance of Central Banks: A Report from the Central Bank Governance Group*', May 2009.
Armantier, Olivier, Bruine de Bruin, Wändi, Topa, Giorgio, van der Klaauw, Wilbert, Zafar, Basit (2011). Inflation Expectations and Behavior: Do Survey Respondents Act on Their Beliefs?, *Federal Reserve Bank of New York Staff Reports*, No. 509.
Arner, Douglas W. (2007). Financial Stability, Economic Growth, and the Role of Law, *Cambridge University Press*.
Astin, John (1999). The European Union Harmonised Indices of Consumer Prices (HICP), *Statistical Journal of the United Nations Economic Commission for Europe*, Vol. 16, No. 2–3.
Axilrod, Stephen H. (1997). Transformations to Open Market Operations, *IMF Economic Issues*, No. 5, January 1997.
Ball, Laurence, Mankiw, Gregoty, Romer, David (1988). The New Keynesian Economics and the Output-Inflation Trade-off, *Brookings Papers on Economic Activity*, No. 1.
Barnett, William A. (2011). Getting It Wrong. How Faulty Monetary Statistics Undermine the Fed, the Financial System, and the Economy, *The MIT Press*, Cambridge.
Basua, Parantap, Gillmanb, Max, Pearlmanc, Joseph (2012). Inflation, Human Capital and Tobin's q, *Journal of Economic Dynamics and Control*, Vol. 36, Issue 7.
Bean, Charlie (2013). Global Aspects of Unconventional Monetary Policies, Remarks Given at the Federal Reserve Bank of Kansas City Economic Policy Symposium, Jackson Hole, Wyoming, 24 August 2013.
Bech, Morten L., Malkhozov, Aytek (2016). How Have Central Banks Implemented Negative Policy Rates?, *BIS Quarterly Review*, March 2016.
Beukers, Thomas (2014). Bundesverfassungsgericht Preliminary Reference on the OMT Program: "In the ECB We Do Not Trust. What About You", *The German Law Journal*, Vol. 15, No. 2.

Belke, Ansgar, Polleit, Thorsten (2009). Monetary Economics in Globalised Financial Markets, *Springer*, Berlin.

Belongia, Michael T., Batten, Dallas S. (1992). Selecting an Intermediate Target Variable for Monetary Policy When the Goal Is Price Stability, *Federal Reserve Bank of Saint Luis Working Paper Series*, No. 8A.

Benigno, Pierpaolo, Benigno, Gianluca (2001). Monetary Policy Rules and the Exchange Rate, *CEPR Discussion Paper*, No. 2807.

Beraja, Martin, Fuster, Andreas, Hurst, Erik, Vavra, Joseph (2015). Regional Heterogeneity and Monetary Policy, *Federal Reserve Bank of New York Staff Report*, No. 731.

Berg, Andrew, Hagan, Sean, Jarvis, Christopher, Steinki, Bernhard, Stone, Mark, Zanello, Alessandro (2003). Reestablishing a Credible Nominal Anchor After a Financial Crisis. In: '*Managing Financial Crises Recent Experience and Lessons for Latin America*', (eds.) Charles Collyns, G. Russell Kincaid, *International Monetary Fund*, Washington, DC.

Berger, Helge, de Haan, Jakob, Eijffinger, Sylvester C.W. (2001). Central Bank Independence: An Update of Theory and Evidence, *Journal of Economic Surveys*, Vol. 15.

Berk, Jan Marc (1998). Monetary Transmission: What Do We Know and How Can We Use It, *Banca Nazionale del Lavoro Quarterly Review*, Vol. 51.

Berk, Jan Marc (2001). The Preparation of Monetary Policy. Essays on a Multi-Model Approach, *Springer Science+Business Media, B.V.*

Bernanke, Ben S. (2003a). A Perspective on Inflation Targeting, *Remarks at the Annual Washington Policy Conference of the National Association of Business Economists*, Washington, DC, 25 March 2003.

Bernanke, Ben S. (2003b). 'Constrained Discretion' and Monetary Policy, *Remarks Before the Money Marketers of New York University*, New York, 3 February 2003.

Bernanke, Ben S. (2010a). Monetary Policy since the Onset of the Crisis, *Speech at the Federal Reserve Bank of Kansas City Economic Symposium*, Jackson Hole, Wyoming, 31 August 2012.

Bernanke, Ben S. (2010b). The Economic Outlook and Monetary Policy, *Speech at the Federal Reserve Bank of Kansas City Economic Symposium*, Jackson Hole, Wyoming, 27 August 2010.

Bernanke, Ben S., Blinder Alan S. (1992). *The American Economic Review*, Vol. 82, No. 4.

Bernanke, Ben S., Gertler, Mark (1995). Inside the Black Box: The Credit Channel of Monetary Policy Transmission, *Journal of Economic Perspectives,* Vol. 9, No. 4.

Bernanke, Ben S., Laubach, Thomas, Mishkin, Frederic, and Posen, Adam (2001). Inflation Targeting: Lessons from the International Experience, *Princeton University Press.*

Bernanke, Ben S., Mishkin, Frederic S. (1997). Inflation Targeting: A New Framework for Monetary Policy?, *NBER Working Paper Series*, No. 5893.

Bernanke, Ben S., Reinhart, Vincent R. (2004). Conducting Monetary Policy at Very Low Short-term Interest Rates, *American Economic Review: Papers and Proceedings*, Vol. 94, No. 2.

Bernanke, Ben S., Reinhart, Vincent R., Sack, Brian P. (2004). Monetary policy alternatives at the zero bound: An empirical assessment, *Brookings Papers on Economic Activity*, No. 2.

Bertaut, Carol C. (2002). The European Central Bank and the Eurosystem, *New England Economic Review*, Second Quarter 2002.

Beyeler, Michelle (2007). The Paths to Price Stability: An International Comparison, *Berner Studien zur Politikwissenschaft,* Bd. 16, Haupt.

Bianchi, Javier (2014). Discussion of "The Risk Channel of Monetary Policy", *International Journal of Central Banking,* Vol. 10, No. 2.

Bindseil, Ulrich (2004). The Operational Target of Monetary Policy and the Rise and Fall of Reserve Position Doctrine, *ECB Working Paper Series*, No. 372.

Bindseil, Ulrich (2011). Theory of Monetary Policy Implementation. In: '*The Concrete Euro: Implementing Monetary Policy in the Euro Area*', (eds.) Paul Mercier, Francesco Papadia, *Oxford University Press*, Oxford.

Bindseil, Ulrich (2014). Monetary Policy Operations and the Financial System, *Oxford University Press,* Oxford.

Bindseil, Ulrich, Jabłecki, Juliusz (2011). The Optimal Width of the Central Bank Standing Facilities Corridor and Banks' Day-to-day Management, *ECB Working Paper Series*, No. 1350.

Bini Smaghi, Lorenzo, Gross, Daniel (2000). Open Issues in European Central Banking, *Palgrave Macmillan.*

Bini Smaghi, Lorenzo (2009). Conventional and Unconventional Monetary Policy, *Keynote Lecture at the International Center for Monetary and Banking Studies (ICMB)*, Geneva, 28 April 2009.

BIS (1995). Financial Structure and the Monetary Policy Transmission Mechanism, *BIS Papers*, No. 0.

Blinder, Alan S., Goodhart, Charles, Hildebrand, Philipp, Lipton, David, Wyplosz, Charles (2002). How Do Central Banks Talk? Geneva Report on the World Economy, *Centre for Economic Policy Research.*

Bluhm, Marcel, Faia, Ester, Krahnen, Jan P. (2014). Monetary Policy Implementation in an Interbank Network: Effects on Systemic Risk, *SAFE Working Paper*, No. 46.

Böhm, Franz (1989). Rule of Law in a Market Economy. In: '*Germany's Social Market Economy: Origins and Evolution*', (eds.) Peacock Alan, Hans Willgerodt, *Palgrave Macmillan*, London.

Böhm, Franz, Eucken, Walter, Grossmann-Doerth, Hans (1989). The Ordo Manifesto of 1936. In: '*Germany's Social Market Economy: Origins and Evolution*', (eds.) Peacock Alan, Hans Willgerodt, *Palgrave Macmillan*, London.

Boivin, Jean, Kiley, Michael T., Mishkin, Frederic S. (2010). How Has the Monetary Transmission Mechanism Evolved Over Time?, *NBER Working Paper*, No. 15879.

Bonfim, Diana, Soares, Carla (2014). The Risk-Taking Channel of Monetary Policy – Exploring All Avenues, *Bank of Portugal Working Papers*, No. 2.

Bordo, Michael, Eichengreen, D. Barry (2013). Bretton Woods and the Great Inflation. In: '*The Great Inflation: The Rebirth of Modern Central Banking*', (eds.) Michael D. Bordo, Athanasios Orphanides, *The University of Chicago Press.*

Borio, Claudio, Disyatat, Piti (2009). Unconventional Monetary Policies: An Appraisal, *BIS Working Papers*, No. 292.

Borio, Claudio, Zhu, Haibin (2008). Capital Regulation, Risk Taking and Monetary Policy: A Missing Link in the Transmission Mechanism?, *BIS Working Paper*, No. 268.

Borio, Claudio, Gambacorta, Leonardo, Hofmann, Boris (2015). The Influence of Monetary Policy on Bank Profitability, *BIS Working Papers*, No. 514.

Bowman, David, Doyle, Brian (2003). New Keynesian, Open-Economy Models and Their Implications for Monetary Policy, *FRB International Finance Discussion Paper*, No. 762.

Bruno, Valentina, Shin, Hyun Song (2013). Capital Flows and the Risk-Taking Channel of Monetary Policy, *NBER Working Paper*, No. 18942.

Buch, Claudia M., Eickmeier, Sandra, Prieto, Esteban (2011). In Search for Yield? Survey-Based Evidence on Bank Risk Taking, *Deutsche Bundesbank Discussion Paper Series 1: Economic Studies*, No. 10/2011.

Busch, Andreas (2005). Shock-Absorbers Under Stress: Parapublic Institutions and the Double Challenges of German Unification and European Integration. In: '*Governance in Contemporary Germany; The Semisovereign State Revisited*', (eds.) Simon Green, William E. Paterson, *Cambridge University Press.*

Camba-Mendez, Gonzalo (2003). The Definition of Price Stability: Choosing a Price Measure. In: '*Background Studies for the ECB's Evaluation of its Monetary Policy Strategy*', (ed.) Otmar Issing, *European Central Bank*, Frankfurt.

Cecchetti, Stephen G. (1997). Central Bank Policy Rules: Conceptual Issues and Practical Considerations, *NBER Working Paper Series*, No. 6306.

Cecchetti, Stephen G. (1998). Policy Rules and Targets: Framing the Central Banker's Problem, *FRBNY Economic Policy Review*, June 1998.

Cecchetti, Stephen G. (2000). Making Monetary Policy: Objectives and Rules, *Oxford Review of Economic Policy*, Vol. 16, No. 4.

Cevik, Serhan, Teksoz, Katerina (2012). Lost in Transmission? The Effectiveness of Monetary Policy Transmission Channels in the GCC Countries, *IMF Working Paper*, No. 191.

Chalmers, Damian, Davies, Gareth, Monti, Giorgio (2010). European Union Law: Cases and Materials. *Cambridge University Press.*

Chodorow-Reich, Gabriel (2014). Effects of Unconventional Monetary Policy on Financial Institutions, *Brookings Papers on Economic Activity*, Spring 2014.

Ciccarelli, Matteo, Maddaloni, Angela, Peydró, José-Luis (2010). Trusting the Bankers. A New Look at the Credit Channel of Monetary Policy, *Working Paper Series*, No. 1228.

Clarida, Richard, Gali, Jordi, Gertler, Mark (1998). Monetary Policy Rules and Macroeconomic Stability: Evidence and Some Theory, *NBER Working Paper Series*, No. 6442.

Claeys, Grégory, Darvas, Zsolt (2015). The Financial Stability Risks of Ultra-Loose Monetary Policy, *Bruegel Policy Contribution*, Issue 2015/03.

Constâncio, Vítor (2015). Assessing the New Phase of Unconventional Monetary Policy at the ECB, *Remarks at the Annual Congress of the European Economic Association*, University of Mannheim, 25 August 2015.

Craig, Paul P., Markakis, Menelaos (2016). Gauweiler and the Legality of Outright Monetary Transactions, *Oxford Legal Studies Research Paper*, No. 5/2016.

Crowe, Christopher, Meade, Ellen E. (2008). Central Bank Independence and Transparency: Evolution and Effectiveness, *IMF Working Paper*, No. 119.

Cukierman, Alex (1992). Central Bank Strategy, Credibility, and Independence, Theory and Evidence, *The MIT Press*.

Cukierman, Alex (1994). Central Bank Independence and Monetary Control, *The Economic Journal*, Vol. 104, No. 427.

Cukierman, Alex (2013). Monetary Policy and Institutions Before, During, and After the Global Financial Crisis, *Journal of Financial Stability*, Vol. 9.

Dagenhart, Christoph (2015). The Legal Limits of Central Banking. In: '*The ECB's Outright Monetary Transactions in the Courts*', (eds.) Helmut Siekmann, Volcker Vieland, *IMFS Interdisciplinary Studies in Monetary and Financial Stability*, No. 1.

Dahan, Samuel, Fuchs, Olivier, Layus, Marie-Laure (2015). Whatever It Takes? Regarding the OMT Ruling of the German Federal Constitutional Court, *Journal of International Economic Law*, Vol. 18, No. 1.

Deaton, Angus (2005). Franco Modigliani and the Life-cycle Theory of Consumption, *PSL Quarterly Review*, Vol. 58.

Debelle, Guy, Fischer, Stanley (1994). How Independent Should a Central Bank Be? In: '*Goals, Guidelines and Constraints Facing Monetary Policy*', (eds.) Jeffrey Fuhrer, *Federal Reserve Bank of Boston Conference Series*, No. 38.

Debelle, Guy, Masson, Paul, Savastano, Miguel, Sharma, Sunil (1998). Inflation Targeting as a Framework for Monetary Policy, *IMF Economic Issues*, No. 15.

de Haan, Jakob (eds.) (2000). The History of the Bundesbank: Lessons for the European Central Bank, *Routledge International Studies in Money and Banking*.

de Haan, Jakob, Berger, Helge, Inklaar, Robert (2004). Is the ECB Too Decentralized? In: '*European Monetary Integration*', (eds.) Hans-Werner Sinn, Mika Widgrén, Marko Köthenbürge, *CEFifo Seminar Series*.

de Haan, Jakob, Eijffinger, Sylvester C.W., Waller, Sandra (2005). The European Central Bank – Credibility, Transparency, and Centralization, *The MIT Press*, Cambridge.

de Haan, Jakob, Oosterloo, Sander, Schoenmaker, Dirk (2012). Financial Markets and Institutions: A European Perspective, *Cambridge University Press.*

Dell'Ariccia, Giovanni, Laeven, Luc, Marquez, Robert (2010). Monetary Policy, Leverage, and Bank Risk-Taking, *IMF Working Paper*, No. 276.

Dell'Ariccia, Giovanni, Laeven, Luc, Suarez, Gustavo (2013). Bank Leverage and Monetary Policy's Risk-Taking Channel: Evidence from the United States, *IMF Working Paper*, No. 143.

De Lhoneux, Etienne (2005). The Eurosystem. In: '*Legal Aspects of the European System of Central Banks*', *ECB Liber Amicorum Paolo Zamboni Garavelli*, Frankfurt.

De Nicolò, Gianni, Dell'Ariccia, Giovanni, Laeven, Luc, Valencia, Fabian (2010). Monetary Policy and Bank Risk Taking, *IMF Staff Note*, No. 09.

De Vroey, Michel, Hoover, Kevin D. (2005). The IS-LM Model: Its Rise, Fall, and Strange Persistence. History of Political Economy Annual Supplement, *Duke University Press Books.*

Daunfeldt, Sven-Olov, De Luna, Xavier (2003). Central Bank Independence and Price Stability: Evidence from 23 OECD-Countries, *The Swedish Research Institute of Trade, Department of Statistics, Umeå University.*

Deutsche Bundesbank (1957). Report of the Deutsche Bundesbank for the Year 1957. Online. Available at: https://www.bundesbank.de/Redaktion/EN/Downloads/Publications/Annual_Report/1957_annual_report.pdf?__blob=publicationFile

Deutsche Bundesbank (2015). The Importance of Macroprudential Policy for Monetary Policy, *Monthly Report March 2015.*

Diewert, Erwin W. (2002). Harmonized Indexes of Consumer Prices: Their Conceptual Foundations, *ECB Working Paper*, No. 130.

Di Maggio, Marco, Kermani, Amir, Ramcharan, Rodney (2014). Monetary Policy Pass-Through: Household Consumption and Voluntary Deleveraging, *Columbia Business School Research Paper*, No. 14-24.

Dittmar, Robert, Gavin, William T., Kydland, Finn E. (1999). The Inflation Output Variability Tradeoff and Price-Level Targets, *Federal Reserve Bank of Saint Louis Review*, January/February 1999.

Dokko, Jane, Doyle, Brian, Kiley, Michael T., Kim, Jinill, Sherlund, Shane, Sim, Jae, Van den Heuvel, Skander (2009). Monetary Policy and the Housing Bubble, *Finance and Economics Discussion Series FED Working Papers*, No. 49.

Dullien, Sebastian, Guérot, Ulrike (2012). The Long Shadow of Ordoliberalism: Germany's Approach to the Euro Crisis, *European Council on Foreign Relations Policy Brief*, No. 49.

Dutzler, Barbara (2003). The European System of Central Banks: An Autonomous Actor?: The Quest for an Institutional Balance in EMU, *Springer.*
Dyson, Kenneth (2000). The Politics of the Euro-zone: Stability Or Breakdown?, *Oxford University Press.*
ECB (1999a). *Monthly Bulletin January 1999.*
ECB (1999b). Examination of the Various Legal Instruments Available to the European Central Bank, *Monthly Bulletin November 1999.*
ECB (2000). Monetary Policy Transmission in the Euro Area, *Monthly Bulletin July 2000.*
ECB (2010). Monetary Policy Transmission in the Euro Area, A Decade after the Introduction of the Euro, *Monthly Bulletin May 2010.*
ECB (2011). The Monetary Policy of the ECB, Frankfurt am Main.
Edwards, Cheryl L. (1997). Open Market Operations in the 1990s, *Federal Reserve Bulletin*, November 1997.
Eggertsson, Gauti, Woodford, Michael (2003). The Zero Bound on Interest Rates and Optimal Monetary Policy, *Brookings Papers on Economic Activity*, No. 1.
Ehrmann, Michael, Fratzscher, Marcel (2004). Taking Stock: Monetary Policy Transmission to Equity Markets, *ECB Working Paper*, No. 354.
Eichengreen, Berry (2008). Globalizing Capital: A History of the International Monetary System, *Princeton University Press.*
Eijffinger, Sylvester, de Haan, Jakob (1996). The Political Economy of Central Bank Independence, *Princeton University Special Paper in International Economics*, No. 19.
Eucken, Walter (1952). Grundsätze der Wirtschaftspolitik, Hamburg.
EUROSTAT (1998). A Key Instrument: New Monetary Union Index of Consumer Prices (MUICP) Monitoring Inflation in the Euro Zone, *Memo*, No. 8/9.
Everson, Michelle (2015). An Exercise in Legal Honesty: Rewriting the Court of Justice and the Bundesverfassungsgericht, *European Law Journal*, Vol. 21, Issue 4, pp. 474–499.
Fariaa, João Ricardo, Mollickb, André Varella, Sachsidac, Adolfo, Wang, Le (2012). Do Central Banks Affect Tobin's q?, *International Review of Economics & Finance*, Vol. 22, Issue 1.
Favero, Carlo A., Giavazzi, Francesco, Flabbi, Luca (1999). The Transmission Mechanism of Monetary Policy in Europe: Evidence from Banks' Balance Sheets, *NBER Working Paper*, No. 7231.
Fawley, Brett, Neely, Christopher J. (2013). Four Stories of Quantitative Easing, *Federal Reserve Bank of St. Louis Review*, January/February 2013.
Federal Reserve Bank of New York (1990). Intermediate Targets and Indicators for Monetary Policy. A Critical Survey, December 1990. Online. Available at: https://fraser.stlouisfed.org/docs/publications/books/frbny_itimp.pdf
Feld, Lars P., Köhler, Ekkehard A., Nientiedt, Daniel (2015). Ordoliberalism, Pragmatism and the Eurozone Crisis: How the German Tradition Shaped Economic Policy in Europe, *CESifo Working Paper*, No. 5368.

Feld, Lars P., Fuest, Clemens, Haucap, Justus, Schweitzer, Heike, Wieland, Volker Wigger (2016). Dismantling the Boundaries of the ECB's Monetary Policy Mandate, *Kronberger Kreis Studies*, No. 61.

Fischer, Stanley (1993). The Role of Macroeconomic Factors in Growth, *NBER Working Paper Series*, No. 4565.

Fischer, Stanley (1994). Modern Central Banking. In: '*The Future of Central Banking*', (eds.) Forrest Capie, Charles Goodhart, Stanley Fischer, Norbert Schnadt, *Cambridge University Press*.

Fischer, Stanley (1995). Modern Approaches to Central Banking, *NBER Working Paper Series*, No. 5064.

Fischer, Stanley, Fraga, Arminio, Heikensten, Lars, Tietmeyer, Hans, Volcker, Paul A. (2006). Panel Discussion: The Art of Central Banking? Presented at '*Monetary Policy: A Journey from Theory to Practice*', An ECB Colloquium Held in Honor of Otmar Issing. Frankfurt am Main, 16–17 March 2006.

Flandreau, Marc (2006). Pillars of Globalization: A History of Monetary Policy Targets, 1797–1997, *Paper Prepared for the Fourth ECB Central Banking Conference*, Frankfurt-Am-Main, 9–10 November 2006.

Fleming, J. Marcus (1962). Domestic Financial Policies Under Fixed and Under Floating Exchange Rates, *IMF Staff Papers*, Vol. 9.

Forsells, Magnus, Kenny, Geoff (2002). The Rationality of Consumers' Inflation Expectations: Survey-based Evidence for the Euro Area, *ECB Working Paper*, No. 16.

Frankel, Jeffrey A. (2011). A Comparison of Monetary Anchor Options, Including Product Price Targeting, for Commodity-Exporters in Latin America. *Economia – Journal of the Latin American and Caribbean Economic Association*, Vol. 12, No. 1.

Fratzscher, Marcel, Lo Duca, Marco, Straub, Roland (2014). ECB Unconventional Monetary Policy Actions: Market Impact, International Spillovers and Transmission Channels, *Paper Presented at the 15th Jacques Polak Annual Research Conference Hosted by the IMF*, Washington, DC, 13–14 November 2014.

Friedman, Benjamin M. (1984). The Value of Intermediate Targets in Implementing Monetary Policy, *NBER Working Paper Series*, No. 1487 (Also Reprint No. r0595).

Friedman, Benjamin M. (1988). Targets and Instruments of Monetary Policy, *NBER Working Paper*, No. 2668.

Friedman, Benjamin M., Kuttner, Kenneth N. (1996). A Price Target for U.S. Monetary Policy? Lessons from the Experience with Money Growth Targets, *Brookings Papers on Economic Activity*, Vol. 1.

Friedman, Milton (1982). Monetary Policy: Theory and Practice, *Journal of Money, Credit and Banking*, Vol. 14, No. 1.

Frisch, Helmut (1990). Theories of Inflation, *Cambridge University Press*, Cambridge.

Gaitanides, Charlotte (2005). Das Recht der Europäischen Zentralbank, *Mohr Siebeck*, Tübingen.

Galì, Jordi, Gertler, Mark (2007). Macroeconomic Modeling for Monetary Policy Evaluation, *Journal of Economic Perspectives*, Vol. 21, No. 4.

Galvenius, Mats, Mercier, Paul (2011). The Story of the Eurosystem Framework. In: '*The Concrete Euro: Implementing Monetary Policy in the Euro Area*', (eds.) Paul Mercier, Francesco Papadia, *Oxford University Press*, Oxford.

Gambacorta, Leonardo (2009). Monetary Policy and the Risk-Taking Channel, *BIS Quarterly Review*, December 2009.

Gaspar, Vítor, Abreu, Ildeberta (1998). Price Stability and Intermediate Targets for Monetary Policy, *Banco de Portugal Working Paper*, No. 1–99.

Gauron, Andre (1999). Europe Misunderstanding, *Algora Pub.*

Gerber, David (1994). Constitutionalizing the Economy: German Neo-Liberalism, Competition Law and the "New" Europe, *The American Journal of Comparative Law*, Vol. 42, No. 1.

Gerdesmeier, Dieter, Mongelli, Francesco Paolo, Roffia, Barbara (2007). The Eurosystem, the US Federal Reserve and the Bank of Japan. Similarities and Differences, *ECB Working Paper Series*, No. 742.

Gianviti, François (2010). The Objectives of Central Banks. In: '*International Monetary and Financial Law*', (eds.) Mario Giovanoli, Diego Devos, *Oxford University Press.*

Glick, Reuven, Leduc, Sylvain (2012). Central Bank Announcements of Asset Purchases and the Impact on Global Financial and Commodity Markets, *Journal of International Money and Finance*, Vol. 31.

Goodhart, Charles (1988). The Evolution of Central Banks, *The MIT Press*, Cambridge.

Goldmann, Matthias (2016). Constitutional Pluralism as Mutually Assured Discretion: The ECJ, the BVerfG, and the ECB, *Maastricht Journal of European and Comparative Law*, Vol. 1.

Greenspan, Alan (1994). *Testimony before the Subcommittee on Economic Growth and Credit Formulation of the Committee on Banking, Finance, and Urban Affairs*, U.S. House of Representatives, 22 February 1994.

Guender, Alfred V., Oh, Do Yoon (2006). Price Stability through Price-Level Targeting or Inflation Targeting? A Tale of Two Experiments, *Journal of Economics and Business*, Vol. 58, No. 5–6.

Häde, Ulrich (2011). The Treaty of Lisbon and the Economic and Monetary Union. In: '*The European Union after Lisbon*', (eds.) Hermann-Josef Blanke, Stelio Mangiameli, *Springer Berlin Heidelberg.*

Hahn, Frank (1985). Money and Inflation, *The MIT Press*, Cambridge.

Hall, Robert (ed.)(1982). Inflation: Causes and Effects, *The University Chicago Press*, Chicago.
Hardy, Daniel C. (1997). Market Information and Signalling in Central Bank Operations, or, How Often Should a Central Bank Intervene?, *IMF Working Paper*, No. 28.
Harris, Ethan S. (2012). Constrained Discretion: Bernanke's Quest for an Inflation Target. In: '*Ben Bernanke's Fed: The Federal Reserve After Greenspan*', *Harvard Business Press.*
Hazlitt, Henry (1984). From Bretton Woods to World Inflation, *Regnery Gateway*, Chicago.
Heenan, Geoffrey, Peter, Marcel, Roger, Scott (2006). Implementing Inflation Targeting: Institutional Arrangements, Target Design, and Communication, *IMF Working Paper*, No. 278.
Hendricks, Torben W. (2011). Monetary Policy and the Credit Channel, Broad and Narrow, *Eastern Economic Journal*, Vol. 37, Issue 3.
Herdegen, Matthias J. (1998). Price Stability and Budgetary Restraints in the Economic and Monetary Union: The Law as Guardian of Economic Wisdom, *Common Market Law Review*, Vol. 35, Issue 1, pp. 9–32.
Hesse, Helmut, Braasch, Bernd (1996). *"Standing facilities" – als geldpolitisches Instrument einer europäischen Notenbank verzichtbar?* In: 'Neuere Entwicklungen in der Geldtheorie und Geldpolitik. *Implikationen für die Europäische Währungsunion. Festschrift für Norbert Kloten*', *Mohr Siebeck Verlag.*
Hicks, John R. (1937). Mr. Keynes and the "Classics" a Suggested Interpretation, *Econometrica*, Vol. 5, Issue 2.
Hidalgo, Luis Jacome (2003). Central Banks and International Financial Volatility. In: '*Current Developments in Monetary and Financial Law*', Vol. 2, *International Monetary Fund*, Washington.
Holmstrom, Bengt, Tirole, Jean (1997). Financial Intermediation, Loanable Funds, and the Real Sector, *Quarterly Journal of Economics*, Vol. 112, No. 3.
Howart, David (2012). Defending the Euro: Unity and Disunity among Europe's Central Bankers. In: '*European Disunion: Between Sovereignty and Solidarity*', (eds.) Jack Hayward, Rüdiger Wurz, *Palgrave Macmillan.*
Hubbard, P. Glenn (1995). Is There a "Credit Channel" for Monetary Policy?, *Federal Reserve Bank of Saint Louis Review*, May/June 1995.
Ida, Daisuke (2013). Tobin's Q Channel and Monetary Policy Rules under Incomplete Exchange Rate Pass-Through, *Economic Modelling*, Vol. 33.
Igan, Deniz, Kabundi, Alain, De Simone, Francisco Nadal, Tamirisa, Natalia (2013). Monetary Policy and Balance Sheets, *IMF Working Papers*, No. 158.
ILO, IMF, OECD, SOEC, UN, WB (2004). Consumer Price Index Manual: Theory and Practice, August 25, 2004.
IMF (2009). De Facto Classification of Exchange Rate Regimes and Monetary Policy Frameworks, February 25, 2009. Available at: http://www.imf.org/external/NP/mfd/er/index.aspx

Ireland, Peter N. (2005). The Monetary Transmission Mechanism. *Federal Reserve of Boston Working Papers*, No. 06-0, *Paper Prepared for 'The New Palgrave Dictionary of Economics'* (Second Edition), (eds.) Lawrence Blume, Steven Durlauf, *Palgrave Macmillan*.

Issing, Otmar (2000). The Globalisation of Financial Markets. *Speech Held at Ottobeuren*, 12 September 2000. Online. Available at: https://www.ecb.europa.eu/press/key/date/2000/html/sp000912_2.en.html

Issing, Otmar (2006). The ECB's Monetary Policy Strategy: Why Did We Choose a Two Pillar Approach? *Presented at the Conference 'The Role of Money: Money and Monetary Policy in the Twenty-First Century'*, 4th ECB Central Banking Conference, Frankfurt.

Issing, Otmar (2008). Asset Prices and Monetary Policy, *Contribution to Cato Institute 26th Annual Monetary Conference 19 November 2008*, Cato Institute, Washington, DC.

Jahan, Sarwat (2012). Inflation Targeting: Holding the Line. *IMF Finance & Development*. Available at: http://www.imf.org/external/pubs/ft/fandd/basics/target.htm

Jain, Chaman L., Tomic, Igor M. (1995). Essentials of Monetary & Fiscal Economics, *Graceway Publishing Company Inc.*

Joyce, Michael, Miles, David, Scott, Andrew, Vayanos, Dimitri (2012). Quantitative Easing and Unconventional Monetary Policy – An Introduction, *The Economic Journal*, Vol. 122, Issue 564.

Judson, Ruth, Orphanides, Athanasios (1999). Inflation, Volatility and Growth, *International Finance*, Vol. 2, No. 1.

Kaiser, Helmut, Heilenkötter, Anja, Herrmann, Markus, Krämer, Werner (2012). Der Euro-Kapitalmarkt, *Gabler Verlag*.

Kaltenthaler, Karl (2006). The Bundesbank and the Formation of the ECB's Monetary Policy Strategy, *German Politics*, Vol.14, Issue 3, pp. 297–314.

Kämmerer, Jörn Axel (2013). Artikel 123 AEUV. In: '*EWU – Kommentar zur Europäischen Währungsunion*', (ed.) Helmut Siekmann, *Mohr Siebeck*, Tübingen.

Kamin, Steven (2010). Financial Globalization and Monetary Policy, *Board of Governors of the Federal Reserve System, International Finance Discussion Papers*, No. 1002.

Kashyap, Anil K., Stein, Jeremy C. (1994). The Impact of Monetary Policy on Bank Balance Sheets, *NBER Working Paper*, No. 4821.

Kelman, Mark (1993). Could Lawyers Stop Recessions? Speculations on Law and Macroeconomics, *Stanford Law Review*, Vol. 45, No. 5.

Kern, Alexander (2014). In: '*The Rule of Law in Monetary Affairs*, (eds.) Thomas Cottier, Rosa Maria Lastra, Christian Tietjie, Lucia Satragno, *Cambridge University Press*.

Kieler, Mads (2003). The ECB's Inflation Objective, *IMF Working Paper*, No. 91.

King, Mervyn (2004). The Institutions of Monetary Policy, *American Economic Review*, Vol. 94, No. 2.

Koivu, Tuuli (2010). Monetary Policy, Asset Prices and Consumption in China, *ECB Working Paper Series*, No. 1240/September 2010.

Kormendi, Roger C., Meguire, Philip G. (1985). Macroeconomic Determinants of Growth. Cross-Country Evidence, *Journal of Monetary Economics*, Vol. 16, Issue 2.

Krishnamurthy, Arvind, Vissing-Jorgensen, Annette (2011). The Effects of Quantitative Easing on Interest Rates: Channels and Implications for Policy, *Brookings Papers on Economic Activity*, No. 2.

Labonte, Marc (2015). Monetary Policy and the Federal Reserve: Current Policy and Conditions, *Congressional Research Service Report*, 9 February 2015.

Lama, Ruy, Medina, Juan Pablo (2007). Optimal Monetary Policy in a Small Open Economy Under Segmented Asset Markets and Sticky Prices, *IMF Working Paper*, No. 217.

Lambert, Frederic, Ueda, Kenichi (2014). The Effects of Unconventional Monetary Policies on Bank Soundness, *IMF Working Paper*, No. 152.

Lamfalussy, Alexandre (1997). The European Central Bank: Independent and Accountable, *Keynote Speech at the Österreichische Nationalbank*, Vienna, 13 May 1997.

Lastra, Rosa Maria (2000). Division of Responsibilities between the European Central Bank and the National Central Banks within the European System of Central Banks, *Columbia Journal of European Law*, Vol. 6, No. 2.

Lastra, Maria Rosa (2012). The Evolution of the European Central Bank, *Fordham International Law Journal*, Vol. 35, Spring Issue.

Lastra, Maria Rosa (2014). The Role of Central Banks in Monetary Affairs: A Comparative Perspective. In: '*The Rule of Law in Monetary Affairs*', (eds.) Thomas Cottier, Rosa Maria Lastra, Christian Tietjie, Lucia Satragno, *Cambridge University Press.*

Lastra, Maria Rosa (2015a). Systemic Risk and Macroprudential Supervision. In: '*The Oxford Handbook of Financial Regulation*', (eds.) Moloney Niamh, Eilis Ferran, Jennifer Payne, *Oxford University Press.*

Lastra, Maria Rosa (2015b). International Financial and Monetary Law, *Oxford University Press.*

Leith, Campbell, Moldovan, Ioana, Rossi, Raffaele (2009). Optimal Monetary Policy in a New Keynesian Model with Habits in Consumption, *ECB Working Paper Series*, No. 1097.

Lenihan, Niall J. (2008). The Price Stability Mandate of the European System of Central Banks: A Legal Perspective. In: '*Current Development in Monetary and Financial Law*', Vol. 5, *International Monetary Fund*, Washington, DC.

Levy, David A. (1995). Does an Independent Central Bank Violate Democracy? *Journal of Post Keynesian Economics*, Vol. 18, No. 2.

Lopes, Francisco L. (1998). The Transmission Mechanism of Monetary Policy in a Stabilising Economy: Notes on the Case of Brazil. In: '*The Transmission of Monetary Policy in Emerging Market Economies*', *BIS Policy Papers*, No. 3.

Louis, Jean-Victor (2005a). The Economic and Monetary Union: Law and Institutions. In: '*A Review of Forty Years of Community Law: Legal Developments in the European Communities and in the European Union*', (ed.) Alison McDonnell, *Kluwer Law International*.

Louis, Jean-Victor (2005b). Monetary Policy and Central Banking in the Constitution. In: '*Legal Aspects of the European System of Central Banks*'. Liber Amicorum Paolo Zamboni Garavelli. Frankfurt, ECB.

Louis, Jean-Victor (2014). Monetary Union and the Law: Some Comments. In: '*The Rule of Law in Monetary Affairs*', (eds.) Thomas Cottier, Rosa Maria Lastra, Christian Tietjie, Lucia Satragno, *Cambridge University Press*.

Ludvigson, Sydney, Steindel, Charles, Lettau, Martin (2002). Monetary Policy Transmission through the Consumption-Wealth Channel. *FRBNY Economic Policy Review*, May 2002.

Loungani, Prakash, Sheets, Nathan (1997). Central Bank Independence, Inflation, and Growth in Transition Economies, *Journal of Money, Credit and Banking*, Vol. 29, No. 3.

Lybek, Tonny (2005). Central Bank Autonomy, Accountability, and Governance: Conceptual Framework. In: '*Current Developments in Monetary and Financial Law*', Vol. 4, *International Monetary Fund*, Washington, DC.

Lyndgren, Carl-Johan (1990). The Transition from Direct to Indirect Instruments of Monetary Policy. In: '*The Evolving Role of Central Banks*', (eds.) Patrick Downes, Reza Vaez-Zadeh, *International Monetary Fund*, Washington.

Maddaloni, Angela, Peydró, José-Luis (2010). Bank Risk-Taking, Securitization, Supervision and Low Interest Rates: Evidence from the Euro Area and the U.S. Lending Standards, *ECB Working Paper Series*, No. 1248.

Maddaloni, Angela, Peydró, José-Luis (2011). The Low Monetary Rates Paradox, Banking Stability and Credit: Evidence from the Euro Area, *Paper Presented at the 12th Jacques Polak Annual Research Conference Hosted by the IMF*, Washington, DC, 10–11 November 2011.

Maier, Philipp, de Haan, Jakob (2000). How Independent Is the Bundesbank Really? In: '*The History of the Bundesbank: Lessons for the European Central Bank*', (eds.) Jakob de Haan, *Routledge International Studies in Money and Banking*.

Malaguti, Maria C. (2010). The ECB, ESCB and the "Eurosystem". A New Paradigm between the Centre and the Peripheries. In: '*The Road Europe Travelled Along. The Evolution of the EEC/EU Institutions and Policies*', (eds.) Daniela Preda, Daniele Pasquinucci, *P.L.E. Peter Lang*.

Martínez, Guillermo O. (2008). Inflation Targeting, *Proceedings of the Conference 'A Festschrift in Honour of David Dodge's Contributions to Canadian Public Policy Held by the Bank of Canada*, November 2008.
Mayer, Thomas (1999). Monetary Policy and the Great Inflation in the United States, *Edward Elgar Publishing*.
McAndrews, James (2015). Negative Nominal Central Bank Policy Rates: Where Is the Lower Bound?, *Remarks at the University of Wisconsin*, 8 May 2015. Online. Available at: https://www.newyorkfed.org/newsevents/speeches/2015/mca150508.html
Mehran, Hassanali, Quintyn, Marc, Nordman, Tom, Laurens, Bernard (1996). Monetary and Exchange System Reforms in China: An Experiment in Gradualism, *IMF Occasional Paper*, No. 14.
Mersch, Yves (2014). Law, Money and Market: The Legal Dimension of Monetary Policy, *Speech at the Information Club Meeting, Luxembourg*, 31 May 2014.
Mestmäcker, Ernst-Joachim (2012). European Economic Constitution. In: '*The Max Planck Encyclopedia of European Private Law*', Vol. I, (eds.) Jürgen Basedow, Klaus J. Hopt, Reinhard Zimmermann, *Oxford University Press*, Oxford.
Mishkin, Frederic S. (1995). Symposium on the Monetary Transmission Mechanism, *Journal of Economic Perspectives*, Vol. 9, No. 4.
Mishkin, Frederic S. (1996). The Channels of Monetary Transmission: Lessons for Monetary Policy, *NBER Working Paper*, No. 5464 (Also Reprint No. r2054).
Mishkin, Frederic S. (2000a). From Monetary Targeting to Inflation Targeting. Lessons from the Industrialized Countries, *The World Bank Policy Research Working Paper*, No. 2684.
Mishkin, Frederic S. (2000b). Inflation Targeting in Emerging Market Countries, *NBER Working Paper Series*, No. 7618.
Mishkin, Frederic S. (2007). Inflation Targeting: True Progress or Repackaging of an Old Idea? In: '*Swiss National Bank 1907–2007*', (ed.) The Swiss National Bank, Zurich.
Mishkin, Frederic S. (2009). Monetary Policy Strategy, *MIT Press*, Cambridge.
Modigliani, Franco (1966). The Life Cycle Hypothesis of Saving, the Demand for Wealth and the Supply of Capital, *Social Research, Essays in Economic Theory in Honor of Adolph Lowe and Hans Neisser*, Vol. 33, No. 2.
Modigliani, Franco (1971). Monetary Policy and Consumption: the Linkages via Interest Rate and Wealth Effects in the FMP Model. In: '*Consumer Spending and Monetary Policy: The linkages*', *Federal Reserve Bank of Boston Conference Series*, No. 5.
Modigliani, Franco (1986). Life Cycle, Individual Thrift, and the Wealth of Nations, *The American Economic Review*, Vol. 76, No. 3.

Mohanty, Madhusudan, Turner, Philip (2008). Monetary Policy Transmission in Emerging Market Economies: What Is New?, *BIS Papers*, No. 35.

Monteagudo, Manuel (2010). Neutrality of Money and Central Bank Independence. In: '*International Monetary and Financial Law*', (eds.) Mario Giovanoli, Diego Devos, *Oxford University Press.*

Mourmouras, Iannis A., Arghyrou, Michael G. (2000). Monetary Policy at the European Periphery. Greek Experience and Lessons for EU Candidates, *Springer*, Berlin.

Moutot, Philippe, Jung, Alexander, Mongelli, Francesco Paolo (2008). The Workings of the Eurosystem. Monetary Policy Preparations and Decision-making – Selected Issues. *ECB Occasional Paper Series,* No. 79.

Mukherjee, Sanchita, Bhattacharya, Rina (2011). Inflation Targeting and Monetary Policy Transmission Mechanisms in Emerging Market Economies, *IMF Working Paper*, No. 229.

Mullins, Anne, Saunders, Cheryl (1994). Economic Union in Federal Systems, *Federation Press.*

Mundell, Robert A. (1963). The Monetary Dynamics of International Adjustment under Fixed and Flexible Exchange Rates, *Quarterly Journal of Economics*, Vol. 74.

Nedergaard, Peter (2013). The Influence of Ordoliberalism in European Integration Processes – A Framework for Ideational Influence with Competition Policy and the Economic and Monetary Policy as Examples, *MPRA Paper*, No. 52331.

Neyer, Ulrike (2001). Asymmetric Information and the Transmission Mechanism of Monetary Policy, December 2011. Online. Available at: http://repec.org/res2002/Neyer.pdf

Noyer, Christian (2015). The Size of Central Bank Balance Sheet – How Relevant (Important) Is It?, *Speech at the Global Interdependence Center/Bank of France Annual Seminar "New Policies for the Post Crisis Era", Session I "Putting a Context on Monetary Policy – On Both Sides of the Pond",* Paris, 23 March 2015.

Orphanides, Athanasios (2003). The Quest for Prosperity Without Inflation, *Journal of Monetary Economics*, Vol. 50, No. 3.

Padoa-Schioppa, Tommaso (2004). The Euro and Its Central Bank – Getting United after the Union, *The MIT Press,* Cambridge.

Paligorova, Teodora, Sierra Jimenez, Jesus A. (2012). Monetary Policy and the Risk-Taking Channel: Insights from the Lending Behaviour of Banks, *Bank of Canada Review*, Autumn 2012.

Papademos, Lucas D., Stark, Jürgen (2010). Enhancing Monetary Policy, *European Central Bank*, Frankfurt.

Parkin, Michael (2013). Central Bank Laws and Monetary Policy Outcomes: A Three Decade Perspective, *EPRI Working Paper*, No. 1.

Petersen, Niels (2014). Karlsruhe Not Only Barks, But Finally Bites—Some Remarks on the OMT Decision of the German Constitutional Court, *German Law Journal*, Vol. 15, No. 02.

Peydró, José-Luis (2014). Systemic Risk, Monetary Policy and Macroprudential Policy, *Banco de Espana Revista de Estabilidad Financiera*, No. 26.

Pindyck, Robert S., Roberts, Steven M. (1976). Instruments, Intermediate Targets, and Monetary Controllability, *International Economic Review*, Vol. 17, No. 3.

Pistor, Katherina (2013). A Legal Theory of Finance, *Journal of Comparative Economics*. Vol. 41, Issue 2.

Powell, Jerome H. (2014). Monetary Policy Accommodation, Risk-Taking, and Spillovers, *Speech at the Global Research Forum on International Macroeconomics and Finance*, Washington, DC, 14 November 2014.

Puccio, Laura (2012). Pressured Inflicted by the Financial Crisis on the Euro Area. In: '*The Treaty of Lisbon and the Future of European Law and Policy*', (eds.) Martin Trybus, Luca Rubini, *Edward Elgar Publishing*.

Purvis (1992). Monetary Transmission Mechanisms. In: '*The New Palgrave Dictionary of Money and Finance*', (eds.) John Eatwell, Murray Milgate, Peter Newman, *Palgrave Macmillan*.

Ramey, Valerie (1993). How Important Is the Credit Channel in the Transmission of Monetary Policy?, *Carnegie-Rochester Conference Series on Public Policy*, Vol. 39.

Ramirez, Steven A. (2003). The Law and Macroeconomics of the New Deal at 70, *Maryland Law Review*, Vol. 62.

Pedrero Ramón, María Dolores, Pérez Jesús, Vázquez (2005). *The New Keynesian Monetary Model, Does It Show the Comovement between Output and Inflation in the U.S. and the Euro Area? Fundacion BBVA/BBVA Foundation Working Papers*, No. 201030.

Repasi, René (2013). Limits and Opportunities for the ECB in the Multi-tier Governance, *Policy Department C: Citizens' Rights and Constitutional Affairs Note*.

Rieter, Heinz, Schmolz, Matthias (1993). The Ideas of German Ordoliberalism 1938–45: Pointing the Way to a New Economic Order, *The European Journal of the History of Economic Thought*, Vol. 1, Issue 1.

Riso, Luca A. (2015). An Analysis of the OMT Case from an EU Law Perspective. In: '*The ECB's Outright Monetary Transactions in the Courts*', (eds.) Siekmann, Helmut, Vieland, Volcker, *IMFS Interdisciplinary Studies in Monetary and Financial Stability*, No. 1.

Roger, Scott (2010). Inflation Targeting Turns 20. *IMF Finance & Development*, Vol. 47, No. 1.

Rogoff, Kenneth (1986). Social Institutions for Overcoming Monetary Policy Credibility Problems, *Paper Presented at the American Economic Association Meetings*, New Orleans, December 1986.

Rosenfeld, Micheal (2001). The Rule of Law and the Legitimacy of Constitutional Democracy, *Southern California Law Review*, Vol. 74.

Rymes, Thomas K. (1995–1996). Autonomous and Accountable, *Journal of Post Keynesian Economics*, Vol. 18, No. 2.

Salama, Bruno Meyerhof (2012). The Art of Law & Macroeconomics, *University of Pittsburgh Law Review*, Vol. 74.

Salter, Alexander W. (2014). An Introduction to Monetary Policy Rules, *Mercatus Working Paper*, Mercatus Center at George Mason University.

Samuelson, Robert (2010). The Great Inflation and Its Aftermath: The Past and Future of American Affluence, *Random House Trade Paperbacks*.

Santomero, Anthony M., Seater, John J. (1978). The Inflation-Unemployment Trade-Off: A Critique of the Literature, *Journal of Economic Literature*, Vol. 16, No. 2.

Santomero, Anthony M., Viotti, Staffan, Vredin, Anders (2001). Challenges for Central Banking, *Springer*, Berlin.

Sauer, Haiko (2015). Doubtful It Stood ...: Competence and Power in European Monetary and Constitutional Law in the Aftermath of the CJEU's OMT Judgment, *The German Law Review*, Vol. 16, No. 4.

Schaechter, Andrea (2001). Implementation of Monetary Policy and the Central Bank's Balance Sheet, *IMF Working Paper*, No. 149.

Scheller, Hanspeter K. (2006). The European Central Bank: History, Story and Functions, *European Central Bank*, Frankfurt.

Schermers, Henry G., Waelbroeck, Denis F. (2000). Judicial Protection in the EUropean Union, *Kluwer Law International*.

Schiek, Dagmar (2014). German Federal Constitutional Court's Ruling on Outright Monetary Transactions (OMT) – Another Step towards National Closure, *The German Law Journal*, Vol. 15, No. 2.

Schmidt, Sebastian, Wieland, Volker (2012). The New Keynesian Approach to Dynamic General Equilibrium Modeling: Models, Methods and Macroeconomic Policy Evaluation, *IMFS Working Paper Series*, No. 52.

Schmukler, Sergio L. (2004). Benefits and Risks of Financial Globalization: Challenges for Developing Countries, *Federal Reserve Bank of Atlanta Economic Review*, Second Quarter 2004–06.

Seidel, Martin (2012). The Constitutional Design of the European Central Bank, *CESifo DICE Report*, No. 1/2012.

Selmayr, Martin (1999). Wie unabhänig ist die Europäische Zentralbank? Eine Analyse anhand der ersten geldpolitischen Entscheidungen der EZB. *Wertpapier-Mitteilungen*, No. 49.

Siekmann, Helmut. (2011a). Artikel 88. In: '*Grundgesetz-Kommentar*', (ed.) Michael Sachs 6, *Auflage*.

Siekmann, Helmut (2011b). Law and Economics of the Monetary Union, *IMFS Working Papers*, No. 24.

Siekmann, Helmut (ed.) (2013). EWU – Kommentar zur Europäischen Währungsunion, *Mohr Siebeck*, Tübingen.

Siekmann, Helmut (2015a). The Legal Framework for the European System of Central Banks. In: '*Central Banking and Financial Stability in East Asia*', (eds.) Frank Rövekamp, Moritz Bälz, Hanns Günther Hilpert, *Springer International Publishing*.

Siekmann, Helmut (2015b). The Legality of Outright Monetary Transactions of the European System of Central Banks. In: '*Central Banking and Financial Stability in East Asia*', (eds.) Frank Rövekamp, Moritz Bälz, Hanns Günther Hilpert, *Springer International Publishing*.

Siekmann, Helmut (2016). Deposit Banking and the Use of Monetary Instruments. In: '*Money in the Western Legal Tradition Middle Ages to Bretton Woods*', (eds.) David Fox, Wolfgang Ernst, *Oxford University Press*.

Siekmann, Helmut, Wieland, Volcker (2013a). The European Central Bank's Outright Monetary Transactions and the Federal Constitutional Court of Germany, *IMFS Working Paper Series*, No. 71.

Siekmann, Helmut, Wieland, Volcker (2013b). From the OMT Announcement to the 2013 Hearings of the German Constitutional Court. In: '*The ECB and Its Watchers*', *IMFS Interdisciplinary Study 1/2013*, Frankfurt.

Siekmann, Helmut, Wieland, Volcker (2015). The German Constitutional Court's Decision on OMT: Have Markets Misunderstood? In: '*The ECB's Outright Monetary Transactions in the Courts*', (eds.) Siekmann, Helmut, Vieland, Volcker, *IMFS Interdisciplinary Studies in Monetary and Financial Stability*, No. 1.

Simon, Sven (2015). Direct Cooperation Has Begun: Some Remarks on the Judgment of the ECJ on the OMT Decision of the ECB in Response to the German Federal Constitutional Court's First Request for a Preliminary Ruling, *The German Law Review*, Vol. 16, No. 4.

Smets, Frank, Wouters, Raf (1999). The Exchange Rate and the Monetary Transmission Mechanism in Germany, *DNB Staff Reports*, No. 35.

Smets, Frank, Wouters, Raf (2003). An Estimated Dynamic Stochastic General Equilibrium Model of the Euro Area, *Journal of European Economic Association*, Vol. 1, No. 5.

Smits, René (1997). The European Central Bank: Institutional Aspects. *Kluwer Law International,* The Hague.

Smits, René (2003). The European Central Bank in the European Constitutional Order, *Eleven International Publishing*.

Snowdon, Brian, Vane, Howard R. (2002). An Encyclopedia of Macroeconomics, *Edward Elgar Publishing,* Cheltenham, UK and Northampton, USA.

Stadler, Rainer (1996). Der rechtliche Handlungsspielraum des Europäischen Systems der Zentralbanken, *Nomos Verlagsgesellschaft*.

Steven, Ongena, Peydró, Jose Luis (2011). Loose Monetary Policy and Excessive Credit and Liquidity Risk-Taking by Banks. In: '*The Future of Banking*', (ed.) Thorsten Beck, CEPR.

Streinz, Rudolf (2008). Europarecht, *C.F. Müller*, Hüthig Jehle Rehm.

Streit, Manfred (1992). Economic Order, Private Law and Economics – The Freiburg School of Law and Economics in Perspective, *Journal of Institutional and Theoretical Economics*, Vol. 148.

Streit, Manfred (1994). The Freiburg School of Law and Economics. In: '*The Elgar Companion to Austrian Economics*', (ed.) Peter J. Boettke, *Aldershot: Edgar Elgar.*

Svensson, Lars E.O. (1999). Price Stability as a Target for Monetary Policy: Defining and Maintaining Price Stability, *NBER Working Paper Series*, No. 7276.

Svensson, Lars E.O. (2002). Monetary Policy and Real Stabilization. In: '*Rethinking Stabilization Policy*', *A Symposium Sponsored by the Federal Reserve Bank of Kansas City*, Jackson Hole, 29–31 August 2002.

Taylor, John B. (1979). Estimation and Control of a Macroeconomic Model with Rational Expectations, *Econometrica*, Vol. 47, Issue 5.

Taylor, John B. (1986). An Appeal for Rationality in the Policy Activism Debate. In: '*The Monetary Versus Fiscal Policy Debate: Lessons from Two Decades*', Totowa, NJ: Rowman & Allenheld, Publishers.

Taylor, John B. (1994). The Inflation/Output Variability Tradeoff Revisited. In: '*Goals, Guidelines, and Constraints Facing Monetary Policymakers*', (ed.) Jeffrey C. Fuhrer, *The Federal Reserve Bank of Boston Conference Series*, No. 38.

Taylor, John B. (1996). How Should Monetary Policy Respond to Shocks While Maintaining Long-Run Price Stability?—Conceptual Issues. In: *'Achieving Price Stability', Federal Reserve Bank of Kansas City.*

Taylor, John B. (1999a). An Historical Analysis of Monetary Policy Rules. In: '*Monetary Policy Rules*', (ed.) John B. Taylor, *The University of Chicago Press.*

Taylor, John B. (ed.) (1999b). Monetary Policy Rules, *The University of Chicago Press.*

Taylor, John B. (2013a). Monetary Policy During the Past 30 Years with Lessons for the Next 30 Years, *The Cato Journal*, Vol. 33.

Taylor, John B. (2013b). The Effectiveness of Central Bank Independence vs. Policy Rules, *Business Economics*, Vol. 48.

Thiele, Alexander (2013). Das Mandat der EZB und die Krise des Euro, *Mohr Siebeck*, Tübingen.

Tobin, James (1969). A General Equilibrium Approach to Monetary Theory, *Journal of Money, Credit and Banking*, Vol. 1, No. 1.

Tobin, James, Brainard, Williams C. (1968). Pitfalls in Financial Model-Building, *Cowles Foundation Discussion Papers*, No. 244.

Tohidipur, Timo (2006). The Emperor's New Clothes: The ECB and the New Institutional Concept. In: '*The Unity of the European Constitution*', (eds.) Philipp Dann, Michal Rynkowski, *Beiträge zum ausländischen öffentlichen Recht und Völkerrecht, Springer.*

Tuori, Kaarlo, Tuori, Klaus (2014). The Eurozone Crisis. A Constitutional Analysis. *Cambridge University Press*, Cambridge.

Ulrike, Neyer (2007). The Design of the Eurosystem's Monetary Policy Instruments, *Springer*, Berlin.

Vanberg, Viktor J. (1998). Freiburg School of Law and Economics. In: '*The New Palgrave Dictionary of Economics and the Law*', (ed.) Peter Newman, Vol. 2, *Macmillan*, London.

Vargas-Silva, Carlos (2010). Exchange Rates. In: '*21st Century Economics: A Reference Handbook*', (ed.) Rhona C. Free, *SAGE Publications* Inc.

De Vicuña, Antonio Sáinz (1999). Institutional Aspects of the European Central Bank. In: '*Current Developments in Monetary and Financial Law*', Vol. 1, *International Monetary Fund*, Washington.

Vifials, Jose, Valles, Javier (1999). On the Real Effects of Monetary Policy, *Banco de Espana Working Paper*, No. 9917.

Volcker, Paul (1983). Can We Survive Prosperity?, *Speech at the Joint Meeting of the American Economic-American Finance Association*, San Francisco, 28 December 1983.

Waldhoff, Chistian (2013). Artikel 127 AEUV. In: 'EWU – Kommentar zur Europäischen Währungsunion,' (ed.) Helmut Siekmann, *Mohr Siebeck*, Tübingen.

Wallis, W. Allen (1960). Price Stability and Economic Growth. Increasing Understanding of Public Problems and Policies, *Farm Foundation.*

Walsh, Carl E. (1998). The New Output-Inflation Trade-off, *FRBSF Economic Letter*, 6 February 1998.

Walsh, Carl E. (2010). Monetary Theory and Policy, *The MIT Press*, Cambridge.

Weber, Martin (1998). Das Europäische System der Zentralbanken, *Wertpapiermitteilungen.*

Wendel, Mattias (2014). Exceeding Judicial Competence in the Name of Democracy: The German Federal Constitutional Court's OMT Reference, *European Constitutional Law Review*, Vol. 10, Issue 2.

Wilkinson, Michael A. (2015). Euro Is Irreversible – Or Is It: On OMT, Austerity and the Threat of Grexit, *The German Law Journal*, Vol. 16, No. 4.

Wynne, Mark A. (1999). The European System of Central Banks, *Federal Reserve Bank of Dallas Economic Review*, First Quarter 1999.

Wynne, Mark A. (2001). European System of Central Banks. In: '*Handbook of Monetary and Fiscal Policy*', (eds.) Alan A. Rabin, Gleen L. Stevens, *CRC Press.*

Wynne, Mark A., Rodriguez-Palenzuela, Diego (2004). Measurement Bias in the HICP: What Do We Know and What Do We Need to Know?, *Journal of Economic Surveys*, Vol. 18, Issue 1.

Zilioli, Chiara (2016). *The Independence of the European Central Bank and Its Banking Supervisory Competences.* In: '*Independence and Legitimacy in the Institutional System of the European Union*', (ed.) Dominique Ritleng, *Oxford University Press.*

Zilioli, Chiara, Selmayr, Martin (2001a). The Law of the European Central Bank, *Hart Publishing*, Oxford.

Zilioli, Chiara, Selmayr, Martin (2001b). The European Central Bank: An Independent Specialized Organization of Community Law, *Common Market Law Review*, Vol. 37.

CHAPTER 4

Policy Interactions and Conflicts

4.1 Interactions Between Monetary Policy and Financial Stability

In the previous chapter, we argued that lawyers are usually not very familiar with macroeconomics. Lawyers tend to look at models, equations, and other analytical tools as a murky metaphysics practically irrelevant in the legal reasoning of real phenomena. This intellectual barrier is perhaps the major reason of the mutual ignorance of one another,[1] as well as the lack of a proper analytical framework for a joint analysis.

But the last financial crisis proved this lack of mutual understanding is no longer tenable.[2] Lawyers and economists have to jointly recognize that the legal regime shaping the institutional arrangements of the state has prominent macroeconomic effects that cannot be neglected.[3] And this is particularly the case for the legal construction underlying the macroprudential and monetary policy regimes.

The macroprudential and monetary policy frameworks have been analyzed separately thus far. The purpose of the previous chapters was to introduce a general overview of both policies, especially underlying their economic functioning within institutional and legal boundaries set out by EU law. Although quite long, this separate analysis was necessary to

[1] Listokin (2014), p. 2.
[2] Idem, p. 2.
[3] Idem, p. 2.

L. Amorello, *Macroprudential Banking Supervision & Monetary Policy*, https://doi.org/10.1007/978-3-319-94156-1_4

introduce the premises upon which the central theme of this book is developed, that is, the *legal interaction* of the two policies.

These premises are based on the insights that the two policies are not isolated policy areas; instead, they are complementary within the same macroeconomic realm. Therefore, the question at stake is whether—and, should the answer be positive, to what extent—the effects of one policy decision may affect the smooth conduct of the other.

The events surrounding the financial crisis allowed us to better understand the side effects of monetary policy on the financial cycle. In this regard, some scholars have attributed to monetary policy a central role in triggering—and even exacerbating—the burst of the asset bubble in 2007–2009.[4] And the current law and economics debate has shifted towards the question whether a change in the monetary policy objective is now required in order to target both price stability and financial stability.[5]

The growing empirical research on how monetary policy may alter the risk-taking behavior of banks[6] and the path-breaking—but still embryonic—literature on how credit supply may respond to monetary policy and banking regulation[7] seem not only to question the actual consistency of central banks' objectives but also, and more importantly, the institutional separation in the conduct of monetary and macroprudential policy. Not surprisingly, the EU legal and institutional settings offer a fruitful stimulus for reflection upon the problem at stake.

[4] In particular, some authors claim that excessively easy monetary policy by the Federal Reserve in the first half of the decade helped causing the global house price bubble. This opinion is shared, among others, by White (2009), pp. 115–124; Taylor (2009), pp. 1–30; Ahrend, Cournède, and Price (2008), pp. 5–33. Other authors claim that the role of monetary policy in financial bubble should not be overestimated, and other factors, such as mortgage standards, were far more important in the build-up of the crisis. Of this view, in particular, see Dokko, Doyle, Kiley, Kim, Sherlund, Sim, and Van Den Heuvel (2011), pp. 239–283; Bernanke (2010).

[5] For example, see Committee on International Economic Policy and Reform (2011), pp. 1–35. The Committee, composed of Barry Eichengreen, Mohamed El-Erian, Arminio Fraga, Takatoshi Ito, Jean Pisani-Ferry, Eswar Prasad, Raghuram Rajan, Maria Ramos, Carmen Reinhart, Helene Rey, Dani Rodrik, Kenneth Rogoff, Hyun Song Shin, Andres Velasco, Beatrice Weder di Mauro, and Yongding Yu, suggests that financial stability should be an explicit objective of central banks.

[6] See Agur and Demertzis (2012), p. 4.

[7] On the issue, inter alia, see Aiyar, Calomiris, and Wieladek (2014), pp. 1–42.

In view of this, the following chapter describes the economic interaction between monetary policy and financial stability so as to assess whether central bank's decisions, through the transmission channels thus far identified, are capable to induce the build-up of systemic risks and spillovers. In addition, a short introduction of the relevant economic literature on the issue anticipates the analysis of policies' interactions.

4.1.1 An Overview of the Relevant Economic Literature

Only in recent times the empirical literature has begun to analyze the economic interactions, conflicts, and complementarities of monetary and macroprudential policies.[8] The research question behind this strand of literature is whether and to what extent monetary and macroprudential policies have the capacity to affect each other and the economy as a whole.[9] Although the two policies' dynamics have been described separately, the foremost issue is to clarify whether they may coexist independently or whether there are potential risks of conflict that may eventually harm the effectiveness of their operationalization.

Point of departure for such an empirical investigation is the development and adoption of dynamic stochastic general equilibrium (DSGE) models, which permit scholars to set up relatively simple and effective analytical tools to explain aggregate economic phenomena.[10] One of the key advantages of DGSE models is that they can be easily tailored to include more details of the market structure. As a result, it is possible to enrich the model in a way that permits to address a wide variety of monetary policy issues under different macroeconomic scenarios.[11] This pliability also explains why many central banks, such as the ECB,[12] adopt

[8] For a survey of the relevant literature, see Angelini, Nicoletti-Altimari, and Visco (2012).

[9] In general, see Tröger (2015), p. 577.

[10] With regard to monetary policy, the simplest DGSE model is constructed around the interconnections of three blocks: (1) an aggregate demand block, (2) an aggregate supply block, and (3) a monetary policy equation. The equations that define these blocks are derived from so-called micro-foundations, that is, explicit assumptions about the behavior of the economic actors—namely, households, firms, the government, and a central bank—which are supposed to interact in a simplified economy. For further details, see Sbordone, Tambalotti, Rao, and Walsh (2010), pp. 24–25.

[11] Sbordone, Tambalotti, Rao, and Walsh (2010), p. 24.

[12] In particular, the ECB uses mainly two aggregate DSGE models for its policy analysis: (1) the New Area Wide Model (NAWM) and (2) the Christiano, Motto, and Rostagno (CMR) model. For details, see Smets, Christoffel, Coenen, Motto, and Rostagno (2010), pp. 51–65.

sophisticated versions of DGSE models to inform the conduct of their monetary policy strategies.[13]

The quantitative literature modeling both macroprudential and monetary policies can be easily split in two different groups. On the one hand, the DGSE models are used to assess the supposed interactions between monetary policy and many macroprudential time-varying tools, such as the countercyclical capital buffers and the LTV.[14] On the other hand, the economists focus in more detail on the problem of coordination between the two policies at stake.

4.1.1.1 *The Literature on the Interactions Between Monetary Policy and Macroprudential Tools*

Kannan, Rabanal, and Scott (2009)[15] develop a model to study house price booms following financial shocks. Their model shows that a central bank having only a price stability objective via inflation targeting is not able to prevent house price busts. Although house price busts are not primary concerns of monetary policy, the authors argue that the use of extra tools, such as macroprudential capital requirements or provisions, reduces the need for policymakers to adopt aggressive monetary policy strategies, which could be particularly disruptive for the whole macroeconomy. For this reason, the authors advocate a broader framework for monetary policy to optimize the policy response against macro-financial risks.[16]

Along the same line, N'Diaye (2009)[17] shows the macroeconomic benefits of using macroprudential regulatory tools for monetary policy purposes. The macroprudential instruments may support monetary policy in reducing output fluctuations while mitigating the risks of financial instability. In this way central banks can achieve the statutory policy objectives—in

[13] Smets and Wouters (2004), pp. 842–843, claim that DSGE models with sticky prices and wages are sufficiently rich to capture most of the statistical features of the main macroeconomic time series. While the model structure is of much help to capture the parameters and the type of shocks that may affect the economy, its probabilistic nature implies that these models can be easily used to forecast uncertainly and to perform a model and data-consistent analysis.

[14] Angelini, Nicoletti-Altimari, and Visco (2012), pp. 9–10.

[15] See Kannan, Rabanal, and Scott (2009).

[16] Idem, pp. 20–21.

[17] See N'Diaye (2009).

terms of deviation of output and inflation from targets—with smaller adjustments in policy interest rates.[18]

Angeloni and Faia (2013)[19] build an integrated DSGE model to appreciate how monetary policy and bank capital regulation shall be conducted coherently.[20] The model shows that an expansionary monetary policy activates the risk-taking channel, thereby increasing bank leverage and risk-taking. Capital requirements exacerbate these effects. As they amplify the response of output and inflation to other shocks, capital requirements generate unstable dynamics, such as output and inflation volatility, and reduce welfare. Since monetary policy cannot fully neutralize these externalities, the countercyclical capital ratios can provide a stabilizing function for business and credit cycles.[21]

Roger and Vlček (2011)[22] find a trade-off between changes in—*micro- and macroprudential*—regulatory requirements and the transmission of monetary policy. Being affected by a tightening of these requirements, credit institutions have to raise interest rates to generate extra profits. An increase of interest rates has contractionary effects on the real economy, since the financing conditions for firms and households would narrow. The effects of wider interest spreads are similar to the ones of a contractionary monetary policy. Therefore, central banks should quickly react in order to mitigate part of the negative output externalities.[23]

Beau, Clerc, and Mojon (2012)[24] assess whether macroprudential and monetary policies have compounding, neutral, or conflicting effects on financial and price stability. Despite the implementation of macroprudential policy seems to have no harmful effects to monetary policy in the DGSE model they develop, the results recognize possible conflicts between the two policies depending on the nature of economic shocks.

The study of how monetary policy would change if it incorporated financial stability in its mandate is conducted by Agur and Demertzis (2012).[25] The analysis shows that in such a case there are very clear implications for the path of interest rates in the event of negative shocks, since

[18] Idem, p. 21.
[19] Angeloni and Faia (2013), pp. 311–324.
[20] Idem, p. 324.
[21] Idem, p. 312. Additional support to this stabilizing role is given by Suh (2012).
[22] See Roger and Vlček (2011).
[23] Idem, p. 20.
[24] See Beau, Clerc, and Mojon (2012).
[25] See Agur and Demertzis (2012).

a more speedy and aggressive monetary policy would be required. Moreover, Lambertini, Mendicino, and Punzi (2013)[26] show that an interest rate policy targeting only inflation fails to mitigate the extremes of the financial cycle. Conversely, an interest rate policy *leaning* against credit growth improves both macroeconomic conditions and financial stability and, thus, welfare.

The inquiry into the interaction between the two objectives is further elaborated by Maddalonia and José-Luis Peydrò (2013)[27] stating that monetary and macroprudential policies are connected and influence each other. The authors provide evidence on how expansionary monetary policies affect bank stability, and their impact mainly depends on bank balance sheet resilience and on banking prudential framework.[28] This implies that monetary policy should incorporate financial stability objectives, while the overall banking prudential framework should also take into account the spillover effects of the monetary policy environments. As a corollary of this, Antipa and Matheron (2014)[29] find that macroprudential instruments act as a useful complement to—conventional and unconventional—monetary policy, as they mitigate the sharp reduction in investment and output during crises.

For Cesa-Bianchi and Rebucci (2015),[30] when a shock lowers interest rates and, thus, hits the economy, and the policy interest rate is the only monetary policy instrument available, central banks face a trade-off between price stability and financial stability. In order to respond effectively to such a contractionary shock, the authors argue for the need to complement the monetary policy framework with macroprudential tools.

Finally, Levine and Lima (2015)[31] find that an extended monetary policy rule used to counter financial imbalances performs better in terms of maximizing welfare than a standard one, though higher inflation volatility may result. The authors argue that welfare maximization can be achieved if standard monetary policy is conducted along with macroprudential tools, under a partially unified mandate that permits to react simultaneously to credit growth and interest spreads.

[26] Lambertini, Mendicino, and Punzi (2013), pp. 1500–1522.

[27] See Maddaloni and Peydrò (2013), pp. 121–169.

[28] Idem, pp. 157–162.

[29] Antipa and Matheron (2014), pp. 225–239.

[30] See Cesa-Bianchi and Rebucci (2015).

[31] Levine and Lima (2015), pp. 1–36.

4.1.1.2 The Literature on Cooperation Between Monetary Policy and Macroprudential Policy

With respect to the cooperation problems between the two policies, a strand of literature offers interesting insights. Starting from the benefits of macroprudential policy over monetary policy in normal times and in the event of financial shocks, Angelini, Neri, and Panetta (2011)[32] assess the value of cooperation between central banks and authorities in charge of macroprudential policy.

On the one hand, they find that in normal times macroprudential policy provides no additional benefits in terms of macroeconomic stability. This is because monetary policy alone is sufficient to tackle the volatility of the key macroeconomic variables. However, in this scenario a non-cooperative behavior between the central bank and the macroprudential authority may generate conflicting effects, as the policy instruments, acting on closely related variables, may push in divergent directions.[33]

On the other hand, the authors show that macroprudential policy significantly benefits monetary policy in times of financial shocks. As monetary policy alone cannot stabilize macroeconomic variables, the simultaneous adoption of both policies, if properly coordinated, may provide substantial gains in terms of output, credit growth, and inflation stabilization.[34]

In a similar fashion, De Paoli and Paustian (2013)[35] analyze different cooperative and non-cooperative settings between monetary and macroprudential authorities, in order to reduce the costs of macroeconomic fluctuations. The results suggest that there are substantial welfare gains if the two institutions cooperate following productivity and financial shocks. But, if the authorities do not cooperate and act under discretion, assigning to both institutions a conservative policy mandate would be beneficial.[36] In addition a leadership structure where the macroprudential authority moves first would also be preferable.[37]

Gelain and Ilbas (2014)[38] show that considerable gains in terms of credit growth volatility can be achieved from coordination if monetary

[32] See Angelini, Neri, and Panetta (2011).

[33] Idem, p. 21.

[34] Idem, p. 24.

[35] See De Paoli and Paustian (2013).

[36] See Idem, p. 3. See also Rogoff (1985), pp. 1169–1189.

[37] De Paoli and Paustian (2013), p. 33.

[38] See Gelain and Ilbas (2014).

policy and macroprudential policy have common objectives, that is, output gap stabilization. In short when the output gap assumes a prominent role in the macroprudential mandate, the best outcomes can be achieved when a single policymaker—namely, the central bank—has both monetary and macroprudential instruments at disposal. Conversely, if the policy objectives are separated, the macroprudential authority would gain from the absence of coordination,[39] while the central bank would be worse off, giving rise to a trade-off between the gains from both institutions.

4.1.2 *Side Effects in the Monetary Policy Transmission Channels*

Although the economic literature on the issue is broad, experts generally acknowledge a theoretical overlapping between the transmission mechanisms of monetary and macroprudential policies.[40] Macroprudential policy mitigates the procyclicality of the financial system by influencing the financial intermediation process and, thus, by affecting assets, liabilities, and leverage of credit intermediaries.[41] Similarly, to the extent that changes in monetary policy rates are capable to affect the cost of borrowing, domestic asset prices, and exchange rates, the conduct of monetary policy may affect agents' decisions on leverage and on the composition of assets and liabilities.[42]

The previous chapter analyzes the transmission channels of conventional and unconventional monetary policy, including (1) the interest rate channel, (2) the 'exchange rate channel', (3) the 'asset price channels', (4) the 'credit channels', (5) the 'signaling channel', and (6) *the risk-taking channel.* These transmission channels represent the venues in which monetary policy can generate side effects on financial stability, in terms of systemic risks and economic spillovers. This consideration represents the crucial premise upon which one should argue that the optimal conduct of one policy should take into account the positive and negative cross side and spillover effects that it may have on the policy target of the other.[43] In particular:

[39] According to the authors, this is the case because the macroprudential authority would be more effective on fulfilling its objectives and safeguarding financial stability.

[40] For example, see Beau, Clerc, and Mojon (2012), p. 7.

[41] See Shin (2015).

[42] IMF (2013a), p. 9.

[43] Idem, p. 9.

1. The 'interest rate channel' stabilizes inflation through the impact of short-term nominal interest rates on real interest rates, with resulting effects on the cost of capital for borrowers, on their investment decisions and, thus, on aggregate loan demand. But the smooth functioning of this channel may be greatly impaired by the presence of potential systemic risks and, more generally, from events of financial instability.[44] At the same time, the build-up of systemic risks may affect the ability of central banks to influence real interest rates.[45] If the risk premia are distorted by some sources of financial instability, the monetary authority may find it particularly difficult to fix the nominal interest rates at the appropriate level.[46]

   In addition, the smooth functioning of this channel requires that a tightening or loosening of monetary policy is reflected into the prices of financial assets, such as bonds and equities. This implies, for example, that a decrease of policy interest rates should lead to a reduction of borrowing costs and to a reduction of households' incentives to save.[47] Households would be incentivized to invest in assets, to purchase durable goods and housing, and to increase their level of consumption. However, as argued by Gameiro et al. (2011), the build-up of systemic risks and financial instability could generate a higher level of precautionary savings, thus reducing the effectiveness of monetary policy.[48] By the same token, if asset price are volatile, their reaction to changes in the policy interest rate set by central bank will be difficult to predict, thereby disturbing the monetary policy transmission mechanism.
2. The interaction between the two policies is also found through the '*exchange rate channel*'. This channel implies that when the domestic real interest rate falls below the real interest rates of foreign counterparts, domestic deposits expressed in the national currency become less attractive with respect to deposits abroad denominated in foreign currencies. As the domestic currency is now depreciated, domestic goods are cheaper than foreign goods, resulting in a boost of net exports. As the net exports increase, the aggregate output rises accordingly.[49]

[44] Gameiro, Soares, and Sousa (2011), p. 15.
[45] Idem, p. 15.
[46] Idem, p. 15.
[47] Idem, p. 15.
[48] Idem, p. 16.
[49] Mishkin (1996), pp. 5–6.

Conversely, should the domestic real interest rate rise above the foreign ones, as a result of a restrictive monetary policy, this would generate an appreciation of the domestic currency and, therefore, of the domestic goods. This leads to a fall of net exports and, as a result, of domestic aggregate output. And such appreciation can expose banks to systemic risks depending on the local vs. foreign currency composition of their balance sheets.[50]

Increasing the nominal interest rates and appreciating the domestic currency are, of course, powerful instruments to attract capital flows from abroad. However, this monetary policy may simultaneously accelerate excessive borrowing in foreign currency because of the lower interest rates and longer maturities available out of the country compared to the domestic currency loans.[51]

This foreign currency lending may pave the way for exchange rate externalities when a strong exchange rate movement occurs. A sharp depreciation of the domestic currency can prevent borrowers, such as domestic households and non-financial firms, from being able to service their foreign currency loans.[52] The aggregate borrowers' defaults on these loans could eventually create dangerous systemic risks, as financial stability is likely to be jeopardized.

3. Monetary policy is capable to affect stock prices in multiple ways. Through the 'asset price channels', an expansionary/contractionary monetary policy may induce an increase/decline in the value of stocks, thereby affecting consumers' wealth, consumption, and, eventually, the aggregate output. As it affects asset prices, monetary policy is also capable to influence the price of collaterals which, in turn, affects the tightness of borrowing constraints.[53] An expansionary monetary policy with low interest rates therefore can increase the value of collaterals, incentivizing banks to over-borrow and undertake in an over-optimal leverage. In an environment of excessive optimism, this may induce asset prices to escalate in bubble-like fashion.[54] The resulting credit growth and leverage, if excessive, may

[50] Claessens, Ghosh, and Roxana (2014), p. 14.

[51] Yeşin (2013), p. 220.

[52] Idem, p. 222. For more insights on the relationship between systemic risk and monetary policy through the exchange rate channel, see Dell'Ariccia, Laeven, and Marquez (2011). See also Brzoza-Brzezina, Kolasa, and Makarski (2015).

[53] Yesin (2013), p. 220. See also Antipa and Matheron (2014).

[54] See Yellen (2010).

eventually amplify the financial cycle and turn into a build-up of systemic risks.

But the opposite holds true as well. If the central bank engages in a contractionary monetary stance reducing the money supply by means of higher policy rates, as soon as the short-term interbank interest rate goes up, banks are incentivized to reduce their borrowing.[55] As a result of this monetary policy tightening, banks decrease the supply of loans and mortgages to the real economy while the lending rates rise up.[56]

At the same time, since money is now less available in the economy, the price of the assets, such as goods and houses, decreases. With higher lending rates and lower asset prices, this monetary contraction brings about higher default levels of the borrowers, while the effective returns on mortgages for banks decrease.[57] Since the benefits of higher mortgage rates are outweighed by the negative effect of higher levels of loan default, the expected profits of banks sink.[58] This may put downward pressure on banks to change their risk appetite along the financial cycle with serious negative consequences for the stability of the financial system.

4. The interactions occurring in the *credit channels*—that is, the 'bank lending channel' and the 'balance sheet channel'—of monetary policy are even more important than the previous ones.

   Through the 'bank lending channel', central bank's operations boost the supply of bank reserves and bank deposits and generate an expansion of credit supply for borrowers. As the interest rates are lower, this credit expansion boosts lending, thereby supporting further investment and consumption. By contrast, through the balance sheet channel, central bank's monetary policy may lead to an expansion/reduction of asset prices that influence the borrowers' real net worth, thereby affecting the borrowers' investment decisions and consumer spending. In this way, the monetary authority is able to indirectly influence aggregate demand and output growth.

   The presence of systemic risks may significantly influence these monetary policy transmissions. On the one hand, the functioning of

[55] See Goodhart, Tsomocos, and Vardoulakis (2009), paras 2.1.1. and 2.1.2.

[56] Idem.

[57] Idem.

[58] Idem.

the bank lending channel may be weakened by the implementation of macroprudential instruments, such as capital-based tools, liquidity-based caps, and real estate ratios. When systemic risks emerge in an environment of expansionary monetary policy, credit institutions may need to tighten credit conditions to shield their weaker balance sheet position resulting from the emergence of systemic uncertainty and volatility.[59] Against this backdrop, the effect of a loose monetary policy may be significantly hampered, since banks would partially absorb the impact of the credit expansion[60] and households would face tighter borrowing constraints.

The introduction of macroprudential tools can dramatize this effect even further. As explained more in-depth in the next sections, the deployment of capital-based or liquidity-based instruments may push banks to use the extra credit acquired for meeting the higher capital/liquidity requirements instead of providing additional loans to the real economy.[61] On the other hand, changes in the monetary stance can create systemic risks via the borrowers' balance sheet.[62]

When an expansionary monetary stance relaxes the collateral constraints and the borrowers' net worth increase, this could incentivize aggregate borrowers to undertake excessive risks. Conversely, a contractionary monetary policy may adversely affect borrowers' net worth and their debt repayment capacity. By affecting the creditworthiness of borrowers, this monetary stance may eventually lead to higher default rates and, in turn, risks of systemic spillovers.[63]

At last, it should be noted that the decisions upon the conduct of both monetary and macroprudential policies are based on similar information and data.[64] This somehow strengthens the idea of a concrete interaction between the two policies. Not only central banks, as the ECB, use information on the financial cycle and on credit aggregate as important sources for achieving their monetary policy objectives, but also national authorities entrusted with macroprudential responsibilities use monetary policy indicators, such as the state of the business cycle, to inform its policy intervention.[65]

[59] Gameiro, Soares, and Sousa (2011), p. 15.
[60] Idem, p. 15.
[61] CGFS (2012), p. 60.
[62] IMF (2013a), p. 10.
[63] Idem, p. 10.
[64] CGFS (2012), p. 60.
[65] Idem, p. 60.

4.1.3 The Risk-Taking Channel: A Reminder

Although the above analysis clearly demonstrates that cross side effects are significant in all the transmission channels, the interaction between *price stability* and *financial (in-)stability* is particularly noteworthy within the already mentioned *risk-taking channel* of monetary policy. Monetary and macroprudential policies are capable to affect either the demand or supply of credit influencing the decisions and funding costs of financial intermediaries.

The basic functioning of this channel is inherently related to the incentives of credit institutions to take on risks when granting loans. As wholesale borrowers, banks and other financial intermediaries are bound by the cost of their short-term financing, which, in turn, is strictly tied to the changes in the short-term policy interest rates set by the monetary authority.

Since the cost of wholesale financing is capable to affect banks' risk appetite, central bank's decisions on key interest rates influence to a large extent the degree of risk taken on by the community of credit institutions.[66] In other words, through this channel monetary policy actions directly affect the *risk-taking capacity* of the credit institutions, leading to variations in the aggregate volume of credit supply and in the composition of investment portfolio relative to risk.

In line with this, it can be inferred that strong linkages intersect monetary policy, leverage, and credit growth[67] via this risk risk-taking channel. And these linkages could leave room for the build-up of systemic risks and jeopardize, at last, the stability of the financial system. These linkages can be especially found in a low interest rate environment, were an accommodative monetary stance may encourage banks to take on risk on both the asset side and the liability side of the balance sheet.

With respect to the asset side, a low interest rate environment may lead to a decrease of the interest rate on banks' loans, thereby lowering the profitability of its portfolios. Looking for higher yield, credit institutions are incentivized to increase their leverage position and appetite for riskier assets, while the incentives for monitoring decrease. Similarly, lower interest rates, on the liability side, decrease banks' cost of capital, encouraging credit institutions to increase their leverage even further.[68]

[66] For details, see *supra* at notes 607–622.

[67] See Yellen (2010).

[68] See *supra* at note 614.

One of the effects of this policy environment is that very low interest rates may lead to a dangerous underestimation of risks. This is because a loose monetary policy implies substantial changes in capital requirements on the price of risky assets and, thus, on the perception of risks by uninformed investors.[69] Against this backdrop, recent economic literature has found a consistent trade-off: the lower the level of interest rates, the larger the underestimation of risks.[70] The smooth functioning of the risk-taking channel in an environment of low interest rates may lead to risk misperceptions which can ultimately contribute, if extended for a prolonged period, to the build-up of systemic risks leading to a bubble.[71]

Another effect of this environment is reflected into the increased exposure to risks by the same investors. Specifically, investors and borrowers may take advantage from the relaxation of the credit standards determined by a long-lasting accommodative monetary policy. Empirical evidences demonstrate that low interest rates prior to loan origination incentivize banks to give more loans to borrowers with low creditworthiness.[72] In addition, the new loans themselves are more hazardous, as they have a substantially higher per time default probability.[73]

Since the extension of loans to bad borrowers and the higher rates of borrowers' default increase the vulnerability of the financial system to shocks, then the risk-taking channel is presumed to amplify systemic risks to financial stability.[74]

However, these are not the only linkages between monetary policy and financial stability within the risk-taking channel. We have already described the effect of changes in the policy interest rates on valuations, incomes, and cash flows.[75] A loose monetary policy raises the value of assets, collaterals, income, and profits, thereby strengthening the balance sheet of credit institutions. The stronger balance sheet position leads banks to

[69] Dubecq, Mojon, and Ragot (2009), p. 4.

[70] Idem, p. 4.

[71] Idem, p. 5.

[72] Jiménez, Ongena, Peydró, and Saurina (2008), p. 31. This opinion is shared by Maddaloni and Peydró (2010) who analyze the lending standards of US and the Euro area in periods of low interest rates.

[73] Idem, p. 31. Similarly, Altunbas, Gambacorta, and Marques-Ibanez (2010) found that unusually low interest rates over an extended period of time contribute to a sharper rise in expected default probabilities for banks, consistent with an increase of risk-taking levels.

[74] Adrian and Liang (2014), p. 3.

[75] See *supra* at note 616.

increase their short-term borrowing and expand their credit supply for risky investments.

More importantly, this effect can be particularly strong with respect to banks' calculation of the variables needed to determine borrowers' creditworthiness: that is, probabilities of default (PD), loss-given-default (LGD), asset and default correlations, as well as volatilities.[76] Changes in the policy interest rates can modify the estimates of these variables and the potential returns from selling collateral. This, in turn, affects the calculation of the related risk-weights for capital requirements, with subsequent adjustments in the composition of balance sheets and in the leverage conditions.[77]

The resulting estimates influence directly the general risk perceptions of banks and are capable to increase or decrease their risk appetite and, thus, their risk-taking behaviors.[78] The risk-taking activities, after a while, can turn into 'excessive' with the related systemic consequences already analyzed.[79]

The functioning of this *risk-taking channel* in a low interest rate environment cannot neglect the bank managers' incentives to 'search for yield', in order to meet their business targets and their bonus salaries.[80] When the risk in the entrepreneurial sector is very high, investors reduce direct investments and hold more bank deposits. Since these extra-deposits constitute a liquidity surplus to be invested, banks' managers engage in overly aggressive risk-taking behaviors.

Therefore, low interest rates may indirectly dramatize the moral hazard problem of banks' top officers, whose salaries and bonuses are linked to the volume of bank activity. This effect can be even stronger if banks' managers are capable to anticipate the moves of the central bank to relax its monetary stance, as asset prices decrease in the downswing of the financial cycle.[81] Working as an amplifier of leverage incentives, the moral hazard problem may ultimately endanger the ability of banks to contain the build-up of systemic risks.[82]

[76] Gambacorta (2009), p. 44. See also Borio and Zhu (2008), pp. 5–6.
[77] Idem, p. 45.
[78] See Borio and Zhu (2008), pp. 9–13.
[79] Idem, p. 14.
[80] BCBS (2012), p. 14.
[81] BCBS (2012), p. 14. See also Altunbas, Gambacorta, and Marques-Ibanez (2010), p. 9.
[82] Agur and Demertzis (2012), p. 23.

4.2 Interactions Between Macroprudential Policy and Price Stability

In contrast to the strand of literature on the side effects of monetary policy, the research on the transmission mechanism of macroprudential policy and on its related side effects is still in its infancy. A high degree of uncertainty surrounds the impact assessment of macroprudential tools on price stability.[83]

Despite the theoretical unclearness on such specific relationship, current empirical research provides noteworthy evidences of a wide variety of macroeconomic effects that macroprudential tools are deemed to generate. In particular, there is no doubt that macroprudential instruments are capable to affect banks' balance sheets, thereby leading to behavioral adjustments in the conduct of their business activities.[84]

For example, researchers suggest that unanticipated changes in the level of capital requirements not only influence the volume of bank lending, but, more importantly, this has important implications to macroeconomy.[85] When a tightening of capital requirements occurs, banks are likely to adjust not only their equity levels but also their lending decisions and credit conditions.[86]

These behavioral adjustments dampen credit supply to households and non-financial firms, while the spreads on mortgages and corporate bonds

[83] See Giese, Nelson, Tanaka, and Tarashev (2013), p. 15.

[84] Carboni, Pariès, and Kok (2013), p. 101.

[85] See Meeks (2015), pp. 1–31, where the author argues that an increase in the required capital ratio has persistent and negative effects on household and corporate lending growth. This reduction in lending growth negatively influences GDP growth, with corporate bond and mortgage spreads acting to amplify this negative pressure through a financial accelerator channel. Conversely, Karmakar (2013), pp. 1–34, shows that countercyclical capital buffers can make the economy resilient to downturns and, in terms of consumption and welfare, the society is better off under such regulatory regime than the current set of microprudential policies.

[86] Carboni, Pariès, and Kok (2013), p. 101. With respect to the equity levels, Francis and Osborne (2012), pp. 803–816, found that regulatory capital requirements play a substantial role in determining banks' internal target capital ratios, and their results demonstrate that desired capital ratios increase (decrease) as capital requirements increase (decrease). Instead, Bridges, Gregory, Nielsen, Pezzini, Radia, and Amar Spaltro (2014), pp. 3–23, investigate by using a panel regression the effects of a change in bank capital requirements on lending decisions. The authors argue that a tightening of capital requirements may affect lending decisions with heterogeneous responses in different sectors of the economy.

are pushed upwards. Moreover, the housing market activity slows down as the prices of real estate decrease and a growing number of households fall behind on their repayments.[87]

Although the macroprudential policy implementation is usually meant to dampen the extremes of the financial cycle, one can also state that macroprudential tools may have positive and/or negative effects on wider macroeconomic dynamics. The extent of these spillover effects and the impact on real variables may greatly differ and is likely to be dependent on the particular phase of the business cycle.[88]

That said, it comes as no surprise that the real effects of macroprudential policy are likely to interact with the transmission mechanism of monetary policy. By influencing the behavior of banks and other financial intermediaries, macroprudential instruments may lead to significant adjustments of their balance sheets, with non-negligible effects on credit supply, asset prices, and overall credit conditions for borrowers.[89] All these factors are deemed not only to constrain the risks of systemic nature that may arise along the financial cycle, but they also influence in a number of ways the smooth conduct of monetary policy and, in turn, the outlook for inflation and price stability.[90]

The aim of this section is to analyze the theoretical interactions between macroprudential policy and price stability. To be more specific, the following sections explore the monetary policy side effects of (1) system-wide capital-based instruments, (2) time-varying liquidity tools, and (3) real estate instruments. In doing so, we seek to highlight the macroeconomic effects that these categories of macroprudential instruments may have on real variables, giving also some insight into what this means for the optimal monetary policy stance.

[87] Meeks (2015), p. 3.

[88] For details, see Kawata, Kurachi, Nakamura, and Teranishi (2013). In addition, Carboni, Pariès, and Kok (2013), at p. 103, argue that changes to banks' capital and liquidity positions, along with their influence on lending decisions, are likely to have considerable costs for the real economy. But these costs are likely to be offset by the long-term benefits that a macroprudential policy intervention may generate as it reduces the probability of a future crisis.

[89] Carboni, Pariès, and Kok (2013), p. 103.

[90] Idem, p. 103.

4.2.1 *Monetary Policy Scenarios with System-Wide Capital-Based Instruments*

Macroprudential instruments to likely have side effects on price stability are the system-wide capital-based instruments, such as the conservative and countercyclical capital buffers along with the new G-SII and O-SII capital requirements. Broadly speaking, a general tightening of the (micro- and macro-) capital prudential framework is capable per se to influence the impact of monetary policy stances, as the increased pervasiveness and risk-sensibility of the new capital buffers may affect more strongly the behaviors of credit institutions.[91]

By manipulating risk perceptions and its pricing, capital requirements are meant to influence, via the risk-taking channel, 'the mapping of monetary policy impulses into portfolio and lending decisions'.[92] Several papers examine these capital requirements' effects on monetary policy impulses,[93] particularly looking at the procyclical dynamics of the microprudential buffers.[94] Distinctively, system-wide capital buffers may interact with the transmission mechanism of monetary policy in multiple ways.

1. Since these buffers largely affect the price of credit, they may also influence the transmission of the interest rate changes in both the upswing and the downswing of the financial cycle.[95] Following the announcement of these macroprudential requirements, the need to build up these buffers may lead banks to increase their lending margins or find other ways to restrict access to credit.[96] As a result of the tighter lending standards, the lending growth increasingly lowers. The now-constrained credit supply affects the wider economic growth and, in turn, the inflation expectations.[97] This scenario may

[91] Borio and Zhu (2008), p. 17.
[92] Idem, p. 7.
[93] Inter alia, see Angeloni and Faia (2013), pp. 311–324; Havemann (2014).
[94] Angeloni and Faia (2013), at p. 312.
[95] ESRB (2014a), p. 33.
[96] Olsen (2013), p. 5.
[97] See De Carvalho and De Castro (2015), pp. 3–31, who found that macroprudential policy announcements have an impact on the gap between inflation expectations and the inflation target. In this respect, Wadhvani (2014), p. 442, argues that an increase of time-varying capital instruments will operate primarily through the spreads between the lending rate and the central bank's policy rate. Due to this, such an increase could have a costly impact on inflation expectations.

induce the central bank to change its outlook for price stability and adjust the policy interest rates accordingly.

2. A second scenario may involve the exchange rate channel of monetary policy, where lending rates abroad have fallen and are supposed to remain substantially low for a prolonged period of time.[98] Where the higher time-varying capital requirements induce local banks to increase their lending margins in order to build up capital, low interest rates abroad widen the interest rate differential against other countries.[99]

   In this scenario both higher lending margins locally and lower lending rates abroad persuade the central bank to lower the policy interest rates, but by less than the decrease in interest rates abroad. Since after this monetary policy move the domestic currency appreciates, this will result in a stronger exchange rate, which will negatively affect short-term inflation and output growth.[100]

3. A third scenario regards the role of system-wide capital instruments in supporting the transmission mechanism of monetary policy in times of financial distress. The economic literature argues that the time-varying use of capital instruments may reduce the need for central bank's intervention to offset the effects of tighter credit conditions on output in downturns,[101] allowing for a more stable conduct of monetary policy along the whole financial cycle.

   In order to react to the short availability of credit at the downswing of the financial cycle, central banks are likely to support the general economy by cutting policy interest rates. But if some time-varying capital buffers were implemented before the downturn, their calibration in accordance with the macroeconomic scenario

[98] Olsen (2013), p. 5.

[99] Idem, p. 5.

[100] Idem, p. 5.

[101] For example, see Antipa and Matheron (2014), p. 227, arguing that time-varying capital buffers can increase the resilience of the banking system and contribute to the proper transmission of monetary policy. This is because the buffers can help maintain the provision of credit to the economy and reduce the depth of the downturn, thereby reducing the need for central banks to offset the effects of tighter credit conditions on output; Agenor, Alper, and Da Silva (2012), pp. 193–223, who show that combining central bank's interest rate policy and a countercyclical capital requirement may be optimal for promoting overall economic stability. See also N'Diaye (2009), where the author explains that the introduction of a countercyclical capital buffer for banks can allow monetary authorities to achieve the same output and inflation objectives but with smaller adjustments in interest rates.

> could help sustain credit supply to the real economy and reduce the effects of the recession underway. The option to dynamically adjust macroprudential capital buffers may reduce the likelihood of monetary policy being constrained in setting the policy interest rates by the zero lower bound.[102]

It should be noted that the system-wide capital instruments may greatly help transmission of monetary policy also in the upswing of the financial cycle. In this scenario, absent adequate prudential buffers, the erosion of capital driven by lending activities may require banks to reduce credit supply.[103] In contrast, the operationalization of stronger dynamic buffers that may be easily drawn down should negative circumstances arise may help the monetary policy transmission mechanism in maintaining a sufficient provision of credit.[104]

The interaction between monetary policy and these capital-based instruments is not always harmonious and the risk of potential conflicts in conducting the two policies can be more than an abstract hypothesis.[105] The general argument here proposed is that macroprudential capital requirements may affect monetary policy in a number of ways. The side effects of these capital buffers may result economically significant, not only because these instruments may influence monetary policy decisions and inflation forecasts but also because they can be meant as complementary instruments to achieve the ultimate price stability objective.

4.2.2 *Monetary Policy Scenarios with Liquidity Instruments*

The second group of instruments that may have side effects on the monetary policy transmission channels are the liquidity tools, such as the LCR, the NSFR, and the liquidity surcharges. The underlying interactions are not always positive from a monetary policy perspective, and a number of detrimental effects can potentially arise.[106]

[102] Antipa and Matheron (2014), p. 227.

[103] See Antipa and Matheron (2014), p. 227.

[104] IMF (2013a), p. 12. On this topic, in particular, see also Angelini, Neri, and Panetta (2011).

[105] For a general overview of the potential conflicts, see Caruana (2011).

[106] See Bindseil and Lamoot (2011), p. 35.

On the one hand, the implementation of a liquidity buffer requirement, such as the LCR, is capable to influence the asset side of banks' balance sheet.[107] To the extent that this liquidity buffer incentivizes banks to change the composition of their balance sheets and securities holdings, it may also have an impact on the operational conduct of monetary policy.

On the other hand, the adoption of a stable funding requirement, such as the NSFR, may harm the monetary policy transmission mechanism by making credit institutions less sensitive to changes in the monetary policy stance.[108]

Bech and Keister (2013)[109] study how the introduction of a liquidity coverage requirement may affect the operational framework of monetary policy, having particular regard to the central bank's ability to control interest rates through open market operations. The authors use a standard economic model where the central bank may influence the short-term interbank markets using a combination of open market operations and standing facilities.

In the standard scenario without any LCR, the overnight interest rate is solely determined by the quantity of reserves supplied by the central bank, while the typology of operation—that is, interbank lending or standing facilities—utilized to generate these reserves is not significant.[110]

Conversely, when the LCR is implemented, it may 'alter behavior in the interbank market, changing the relationship between market conditions and the resulting interest rate'.[111] This is the case when a LCR shortfall occurs. In this scenario, banks are incentivized to reduce their reliance on short-term financing, as this may negatively impact on the calculation of the LCR. Instead, banks will now seek long-term funding in the market to meet their liquidity needs, since this does not impinge upon the LCR calculation. Against this backdrop, credit institutions will be more likely to borrow from central bank's standing facilities.[112]

[107] ESRB (2014a), p. 111.

[108] Idem, p. 111.

[109] See Bech and Keister (2013), pp. 49–60.

[110] Idem, p. 2.

[111] Idem, p. 2.

[112] Bech and Keister (2013), p. 3. The same argument is developed in ECB (2013), pp. 73–89, and Schmitz (2013), pp. 138–148, where the authors investigate the effect of the LCR introduced by Basel III for the monetary policy in the Euro area. According to Schmitz (2013), in particular, the LCR disincentivizes banks to lend and/or borrow on the unsecured money market. Therefore, more banks will participate in the open market operations of central banks. Similar concerns are expressed in Bindseil and Lamoot (2011), pp. 1–41.

This funding choice boosts the bank's reserve holdings and lowers the need of short-term financing in the interbank market. Due to the lower demand for overnight funds, the overnight rate drops down, while the increased demand for long-term financing is likely to steepen the short end of the yield curve.[113] Against this backdrop, the central bank can no longer apply the standard operating framework of monetary policy.[114]

Along with the liquidity coverage requirement, the regulatory operationalization of the NSFR may considerably alter the operating framework of monetary policy. In order to comply with stable funding requirements, credit institutions need to change the structural composition of their funding. To do so, banks are required to adjust their balance sheets.[115] In turn, these adjustments are likely to affect indirectly the interbank market and the normal course of day-to-day monetary policy operations.

In more detail, the adoption of the NSFR may lead to segmentation of the market by maturity, as banks are incentivized to reduce the portion of their funding with maturities below one year.[116] This effect may amplify the shrinkage of short-term funding markets, with potentially negative effect for the overnight rate and, thus, for the smooth conduct of the market operations by the central bank.[117] In addition, the full implementation of the NSFR may reduce the reaction of the loan supply to monetary shocks.[118] The resulting banks' insensitivity to monetary stances may harm the functioning of the bank lending channel of monetary policy.[119]

In light of the above, it can be argued that the introduction of a liquidity coverage buffer and of a stable funding requirement may have non-negligible consequences that may eventually hamper the effectiveness of central banks' monetary policy, though the extent of these effects may depend upon a number of factors and variables.[120]

[113] For an empirical analysis, see Bonner and Eijffinger (2012a).

[114] See Bonner and Eijffinger (2012b).

[115] Scalia, Longoni, and Rosolin (2013), p. 5.

[116] Idem, p. 12.

[117] Idem, p. 12. For a detailed overview upon the effects of the NSFR on the secured and unsecured money markets, see CGFS (2015), pp. 13–14.

[118] For details, see Giordana and Schumacher (2013), pp. 649–652.

[119] Idem, p. 652.

[120] In particular, Bech and Keister (2013), p. 3, state that relevant factors influencing this interaction are (1) the liquidity surplus/deficit of the banking system, (2) the specific variables used to calculate the LCR requirement, (3) the term of the transaction, and (4) the counterparties involved. In ECB (2013), p. 80, it is argued that these factors include (1) the

A last consideration is needed. One of the reasons justifying the introduction of these liquidity instruments is to set proper prudential arrangements as to discourage banks to excessively rely upon the lender of last resort function of central banks.[121] Therefore, as long as the establishment of the liquidity tools may reduce—ex ante—the risks of excessive maturity mismatch and market illiquidity, their full operationalization may also reduce the ex post need of central bank intervention as the ultimate liquidity backstop.[122]

4.2.3 Monetary Policy and Real Estate Instruments

This latest section reflects upon a further group of instruments that might influence monetary policy decisions, namely, the real estate instruments, such as caps on the LTV and the LTI ratio.

Although the HICP utilized by the ECB to target consumer price growth—and ensuring the maintenance of price stability—does not capture real estate prices, this category of macroprudential instruments may significantly affect variables, such as credit growth, leverage, and collateral values, which are overwhelmingly relevant for monetary policy purposes.[123] This is true not only for the United Kingdom, where the mortgage market is a major driver of the economy, but also in other continental EU countries, such as the Netherlands and Sweden, where mortgage debt levels are particularly high.[124]

initial level of the LCR, (2) the nature of the collateral that is mobilized, (3) haircuts applied in the market, and (4) the extent to which some LCR constraints are binding.

[121] ESRB (2014a), p. 111.

[122] Idem, p. 111. For further details, see also Rochet (2008), p. 49.

[123] ESRB (2014a), p. 56.

[124] For a survey of UK mortgage market, see Bunn, Drapper, Rowe, and Shah (2015), pp. 358–361, where the authors found that the average mortgage debt of a British householder has risen to about £85,000 in 2015. Empirical proofs of mortgage debt relevance for the Netherlands can be found in the research paper of ABN-AMRO: *Mortgage market in the Netherlands*, May 2012, reporting that 'The Netherlands scores high in terms of mortgage debt. In fact, with a mortgage debt stock equalling 108% of gross domestic product, the Netherlands ranks number one in the European Union'. Additional analysis is provided in De Nederlandsche Bank (2015), pp. 7–53. Similarly, in Sweden, household debt in the form of mortgages remains at very high levels—roughly 160% of disposable income on average in 2013—and is expanding, with net credit flows outpacing nominal GDP growth. For analytical surveys of the mortgage market in Sweden, see European Commission, *Country Report*

The real estate market constitutes an important link in the transmission chain of monetary policy. The housing market is strictly intertwined with the householders' capacity to borrow. Where real properties are constructed or purchased by means of mortgages, the cost of borrowing becomes a major component of the overall cost of housing.[125]

A contractionary monetary policy which, for example, increases these costs, and, thus, weakens the housing demand, may lead to a decline in the property prices. As soon as this decline affects the value of collaterals, this negatively influences the capacity of credit institutions in providing loans. In addition, a fall in the property prices worsens the households' perceptions on their wealth.[126] As a result, the overall effect is a lower demand for goods and services with negative implications for inflation and economic growth.[127]

The macroprudential use of LTV and DTI ratio caps may generate very similar effects on the economy. By limiting the house price acceleration and affecting household debt, these regulatory measures can determine comparable changes in aggregate demand with related consequences for inflation expectations and GDP growth.[128]

An example may clarify these effects. In economies with no real estate limits, a positive financial shock may considerably increase residential investment and house prices.[129] In this scenario, consumers are incentivized to borrow more against the rising value of their collateral, and thus to consume more non-durable goods,[130] as they have no regulatory constraints for their borrowing.

Sweden 2015, Including an In-Depth Review on the prevention and correction of macroeconomic imbalances, SWD (2015) 46 final, Brussels, 26 February 2015; Finansinspektionen, The Swedish Mortgage Market, 14 April 2016.

[125] Gerlach (2012), p. 1.

[126] Idem, p. 1.

[127] For an empirical investigation of how these monetary policy-induced fluctuations in house prices affect private consumption and, thus, consumer prices and economic growth, with particular respect to EU countries, see Giuliodori (2005), pp. 519–543. The author found that house prices are significantly affected by changes in the policy interest rates and that residential asset values amplify these effects on consumptions in those countries where housing and mortgage markets are more developed. Similar investigations are conducted by Mishkin (2007), pp. 1–45; Ahearne, Ammer, Doyle, Kole, and Martin (2005), pp. 1–42, Assenmacher-Wesche and Gerlach (2008), pp. 1–33.

[128] Antipa and Matheron (2014), p. 227.

[129] IMF (2008), p. 22.

[130] Idem, p. 22.

However, the resulting price pressure would require a large increase in the policy interest rates, in order to stabilize the growing inflation.[131] On the other hand, the lack of real estate instruments in such economies amplifies the decline in output and consumption following a negative financial shock. To offset the deflationary impact of this shock, the central bank would be required to significantly lower the policy interest rates.[132]

These two scenarios reflect the larger responsiveness of consumption and output to shocks in economies with no caps on LTV or DTI ratios.[133] By contrast, as these macroprudential instruments are capable to slow the rate of house price appreciation, they also reduce the response of residential investment and household consumption to positive financial shocks, thereby allowing monetary policy to be conducted in a far less volatile manner.

In addition, the side effects of LTV and DTI ratio caps can reverberate in a downswing through the transmission mechanism of monetary policy. As evidenced by the 2008 financial crisis,[134] when a large fraction of borrowers have high LTV mortgages, this can disrupt the transmission of the lower policy interest rates made necessary by the aftermaths of the financial burst.[135] When house price falls, these borrowers will not be able to refinance their loans since the value of the mortgages will be likely exceeding the value of the property used as collateral.[136]

As a result, borrowers will not be able to benefit from the lower mortgage rates brought about by the monetary policy easing of the central bank.[137] Conversely, the adoption of an LTV cap can help limit the number of borrowers with excessively high LTV ratios, thereby mitigating the risk of failure to roll over their loans and strengthening the smooth transmission of the expansionary monetary policy after the housing bubble.[138]

It must be recalled that the real estate instruments are powerful tools to mitigate the extremes of the financial cycle. As such, the LTV and DTI

[131] Idem, p. 23.
[132] See Idem, p. 23.
[133] IMF (2013a), p. 13.
[134] For details, see Geanakoplos (2010), pp. 111–112. See also Demyanyk and Hemert (2011), pp. 1848–1880.
[135] IMF (2013a), p. 13.
[136] See Geanakoplos (2010), p. 113.
[137] IMF (2013a), p. 13.
[138] Idem, p. 13.

ratio caps are tailored to contain mortgage defaults and losses sustained by credit intermediaries in the wake of the housing bust, reducing depth and duration of downturns.[139] This function may accordingly reduce the need for an expansionary monetary policy that would be otherwise required in an environment of extreme swings of the credit cycle.[140] The operationalization of the real estate instruments may mitigate the risk of monetary policy hitting the zero lower bound and allows central bank to adopt a less aggressive interest rate policy to counter the recession phase.[141]

4.3 Policy Complementarities and Risk of Conflicts

It is common to find economists arguing that, in most circumstances, macroprudential policy and monetary policy are complementary and tend to move into the same directions.[142] One of the main arguments in favor of this claim is that macroprudential supervision aims at containing excessive risk-taking behaviors featuring the financial cycle, and, as such, its focus is wholly unrelated to the activity occurring into the real economy which, in turn, represents the standard focus of monetary policy.[143]

In line with this view, the risk of conflicts between policy objectives is meant as a 'fringe hypothesis' that can be tackled with some sort of policy coordination. Part of this scholarship recognizes macroprudential policy and monetary policy to support—*and reinforce*—each other,[144] while the negative side effects and spillovers are considered quantitatively negligible.[145]

As the two policies are deemed not conflicting in nature, many suggest that having a standalone institutional framework and a separate set of tools for each policy is optimal to achieve the key macroeconomic objectives of price stability and financial stability. This policy

[139] Idem, p. 14.
[140] See IMF (2008), p. 23.
[141] IMF (2013a), p. 14.
[142] For example, see Caruana (2011). In general, see also Borio and Shim (2007).
[143] Barwell (2013), p. 69.
[144] For example, see N'Diaye (2009).
[145] Inter alia, see Ozkan and Unsal (2014).

recommendation is largely consistent with the 'principle of effective market classification' developed by Nobel laureate Robert Mundell[146] in 1962, which states that each policy instrument should be assigned to the target variable on which its relative effect is higher.[147] According to this principle, the separate allocation of different instruments to independent authorities should allow more efficient adjustment for the smooth conduct of the single policy.[148]

The relationship between macroprudential regulation and monetary policy, however, is not as straightforward as one may believe. Having two separate sets of instruments and institutional arrangements does not prevent the arising of material situations where the two policies may have relevant compounding or conflicting outcomes.[149] In addition, while there are cases where both policies pull in the same direction and are no doubt complementary, conflicts and inconsistencies are far from being unlikely.

For example, when an expansionary monetary policy stance is paralleled by a tightening of the macroprudential requirements, households and firms are incentivized at the same time to borrow more and borrow less,[150] since the two regimes are not aligned. Some tension[151] between the conduct of the two policies may eventually arise, endangering the stabilizing effects of each set of instruments. The resulting inconsistency requires the establishment of proper institutional arrangements that may allow for a rational balance between the respective cross side effects.

Having previously summarized the effects and spillovers of each policy, this section briefly discusses both complementarities and risks of conflict that may arise when macroprudential policy and monetary policy are simultaneously settled. Albeit knowledge and experience on this issue are still embryonic, many studies warn about the risk of misalignments and conflicts between the two policies. This section seeks also to expose why setting up a clearly interdependent framework that may permit a smooth

[146] See Mundell (1962), pp. 70–79.
[147] See Reinert and Rajan (eds.) (2009), p. 85.
[148] Idem, p. 86.
[149] Beau, Clerc, and Mojon (2012), p. 3.
[150] See Bruno, Shim, and Shin (2015), p. 3.
[151] For details, see Antipa and Matheron (2014), pp. 225–239.

interaction between the different sets of tools along the financial cycle is badly needed. At last, the current European credit environment is scrutinized in view of the findings obtained.

4.3.1 Positive Complementarities When the Two Policies Work Smoothly

The assessment of the side effects of one policy needs to integrate the side effects of the other, since cross interactions within various policy transmission channels are inevitable.[152] In turn, these cross interactions may be of two kinds: the first entails positive complementarities, and the latter depicts negative conflicts amid policy effects.

In general, price stability and financial stability are complementary in the long run.[153] In their comparative survey,[154] Bruno, Shim, and Shin (2015) found this is specifically the case when macroprudential and monetary policies pull in the same directions, that is, when both policies are equally expansionary or contractionary. Positive correlations are mainly reflected in the impact of macroprudential and monetary policies on borrowing incentives.

These correlations imply that the side effects of macroprudential and monetary policies may be strategically exploited to complement each other. When the two policies operate smoothly, the compound adoption of both set of tools may be calibrated as to guarantee the full maintenance of the two policy objectives.

On the one hand, the macroprudential authority may contribute to increasing price stability by mitigating the risks of destabilizing credit expansion and asset price growth with a tightening of time-varying tools.[155] Similarly, the adoption of macroprudential real estate tools, such as LTV and DTI limits, may contain the negative effects on borrowers' debt capacity and defaults that a contractionary monetary policy may trigger, protecting in this way the resilience of banks' balance sheets.[156] The resulting reduction of procyclical behaviors and leverage may further

[152] Deutsche Bundesbank (2015), p. 40.

[153] For a survey on the economic literature claiming this complementarity, see *supra* at notes 891–915. Of this opinion, see also Carboni, Pariès, and Kok (2013), p. 107.

[154] See Bruno, Shim, and Shin (2015).

[155] Carboni, Pariès, and Kok (2013), p. 107. On the issue at hand, see also Ghilardi and Peiris (2014).

[156] For details, see Igan and Kang (2011).

address the divergences existing between financial and real variables and clean up the relevant information data sets for monetary policy purposes.[157]

On the other hand, the central bank may reinforce financial stability by mitigating the negative impact of inflation volatility on financial markets, and by reducing the risk of shocks through the management of consumer price expectations.[158] Even more importantly, the central bank via its monetary policy adjustments may discourage procyclical behaviors of credit institutions along the financial cycle and, as a result, mitigate systemic spillovers in the financial system.[159]

The economic literature has observed, however, that these policy alignments are mainly determined by the type of shocks that may occur in the economy and by the ability of each policy to take action.[160] Therefore, it is said that macroprudential and monetary policies are likely to respond in a similar fashion at the occurrence of aggregate demand shocks, while misalignments may result after an aggregate supply shock materializes.[161]

Even if it were the case, it should be noted that positive complementarities can be traced not only when monetary and macroprudential policies are perfectly aligned. Since they are extra tools meant to tackle the systemic externalities arising along the credit cycle, macroprudential instruments can be strategically used to 'lean against' the negative side effects of monetary policy. Mixed policy strategies may exploit the side effects of macroprudential tools to make monetary policy more credible and effective.

To make this clearer, let's assume that the central bank decides for a monetary policy stance that affects the risk preferences of market agents. If the monetary authority lowers the policy interest rates in order to increase lenders' risk-taking capacity, the potential systemic risk spillovers that are likely to arise may be synchronically countered by an upward recalibration of the macroprudential capital buffers or a tightening of the leverage ratio.[162] Likewise, when a relaxation of policy interest rates

[157] Carboni, Pariès, and Kok (2013), p. 107.

[158] Idem, p. 107.

[159] See Idem, p. 107.

[160] See OECD (2011), p. 74. See also Beau, Clerc, and Mojon (2012) and Unsal (2013). In addition cf. again: Ghilardi and Peiris (2014).

[161] OECD (2011), p. 74.

[162] For better insights on the issue, inter alia, see Angeloni and Faia (2009); Agur and Demertzis (2012); Angelini, Neri, and Panetta (2011).

encourages new borrowing and, thus, asset prices rise up, some real estate instruments, such as LTV caps, may address the negative effects that could originate from an extraordinary house price growth.[163] A tightening of such caps may contain the rate of house price appreciation, reducing the likelihood of financial imbalances and bubbles. The adoption of such tools under an expansionary monetary policy environment may also help in containing the feedback loops between credit and house prices.[164]

In general, monetary and macroprudential policies are capable to influence the same macroeconomic variables by means of similar transmission channels. Changes in the policy interest rates by central banks and the implementation of macroprudential tools can increase or decrease the money supply in the economy and the related credit conditions for investors and borrowers. Both policies, therefore, can influence the price of leverage and the quantity of risk raking of credit institutions.[165] Moreover, their correlated conduct may allow monetary policy to be more efficient in responding to macroeconomic changes and shocks. When a positive supply shock drives down market inflation but contemporarily increases asset prices and credit, macroprudential instruments can be deployed to tackle the price boom, allowing the central bank to concentrate on inflation stagnation through a more expansionary policy stance.[166]

In contrast, when capital flows trigger an increase in leverage and exposure to exchange rates, macroprudential policy can be tailored to solely tackle these externalities, while the central bank can freely respond to the inflationary pressure by means of a tighter monetary policy move.[167] Against this backdrop, the side effects of macroprudential instruments may reinforce the monetary policy stance, by giving the central bank a more stable credit environment for its policy decisions.

4.3.2 *Negative Interactions: Misalignments and Conflicts Along the Financial Cycle*

In view of the complementary nature of monetary and macroprudential policies and of their side effects, many scholars have neglected in the past

[163] IMF (2012), p. 10. For an empirical survey, cf. Wong, Fong, Li, and Choi (2011). For a similar assessment, see Crowe, Dell'Ariccia, Igan, and Rabanal (2011).

[164] IMF (2012), p. 10. For further details, see also Leduc and Natal (2015).

[165] Tröger (2015), pp. 577–578.

[166] IMF (2013a), p. 13.

[167] Idem, p. 13.

the potential risks of conflicts that may arise between the two policy objectives.[168] The argument is based on the fact that macroprudential policy solely aims at restraining the financial exuberance of financial players. This exuberance is essentially detached from activity in the real economy which, in turn, is largely within the domain of monetary policy.[169]

This consideration is fundamentally flawed as financial markets and real economy cannot be divorced from each other.[170] Although the procyclical activity of banks is largely concentrated into financial markets, the underlying assets on which the balance sheet expansion is linked are always interrelated to some class of lending to the real economy.[171]

And even if the build-up of excessive leverage is found completely unrelated to activity in the real economy, a number of negative implications can nonetheless arise for households and corporations in terms of gross financial wealth and funding costs.[172] Therefore, although monetary and macroprudential policies may be complementary, risks of conflicts between side effects are far from implausible, as interrelationships between financial stability and real economy are material.

Events of conflicts are related to the inconsistencies that may characterize the adverse effects of one policy over the other, and vice versa, through common transmission channels.

The main issue is to determine when—and under what circumstances—these policy conflicts are likely to arise. In answering this question, the economic literature has found that events of policy tension can concretely materialize when the business and the financial cycles are misaligned,[173] that is, when output and inflation change in opposite directions.[174] In addition, the clash between the two policies is relative to the type and diffusion of shocks that may hit the financial system and the real economy.[175]

One example of this conflict lies in the presence of a productivity shock. On the one hand, a positive productivity boom increases asset prices and credit demand. On the other hand, this shock may cap market goods

[168] Among others, see Caruana (2011).
[169] Barwell (2013), p. 69.
[170] Idem, p. 69.
[171] Idem, p. 69.
[172] Idem, p. 69.
[173] Volz (2015), p. 163.
[174] Rubioa and Carrasco-Gallego (2014), pp. 326–327.
[175] See Beau, Clerc, and Mojon (2012), p. 8.

prices.[176] This scenario is characterized by the likely materialization of an asset bubble, while the objective of price stability could be endangered by a downward pressure on consumer prices.[177] In this scenario, business and financial cycles are not only misaligned but also push in conflicting directions.

Against this backdrop, the macroprudential authority is expected to tighten the regulatory requirements on capital and liquidity in order to restrain the build-up of excessive asset prices and credit growth. But this policy stance may have unintended consequences for the maintenance of price stability: this tightening is likely to further depress business activity in the real economy, causing an even stronger downward pressure on inflation.[178] As such, tightening macroprudential policy requirements may have the side effect of pushing the inflation expectations below the statutory target, thereby endangering the ultimate objective of monetary policy.

At the same time, the central bank would be required to counter the persistent decrease in the level of consumer prices by adopting a more expansionary monetary policy. But the side effects of a policy loosening in this environment may adversely impact the stability of the financial system, since lower interest rates may amplify the credit boom and asset prices growth through, for example, the risk-taking channel. Such an interest rate policy may create incentives for banks to undertake an excess of credit activity which, in turn, would multiply the likelihood of systemic risks and financial imbalances via the multiple monetary policy transmission channels.

In view of these Janus-faced interactions, the two policies would result in being mutually constrained by unavoidable tension. The side effects of monetary and macroprudential policies would shape an inconsistent credit environment where banking intermediaries are simultaneously told to expand and curb their lending activities.

The probability that such an event may occur is not as low as one may expect. Prior to the burst of the 2008 financial crisis, the integration of a number of large developing countries in the global market triggered large supply shocks causing deflationary spirals.[179] Central banks had to maintain

[176] IMF (2012), p. 6.
[177] Beau, Clerc, and Mojon (2012), p. 8.
[178] Idem, p. 8.
[179] Beau, Clerc, and Mojon (2012), p. 8.

policy interest rates at very low levels. This prolonged low interest rate environment is today widely deemed as one of the potential drivers of the asset bubble build-up.[180] The introduction of a set of macroprudential policy instruments would have mitigated the risk-taking effects of such a policy stance, but at the apparent cost of curtailing the central banks' efforts to target the objective of price stability.[181]

It must be noted that the scale of this policy tension under the above circumstances is not uniform. The impact of the policy conflicts may vary substantially and its strength, according to the economic scholarship, would critically depend upon the stage of the business cycle at the time[182] and upon the state of the financial sector as a whole.[183]

4.3.3 *Policy Conflicts in the Eurozone? Some Brief Notes*

We need now to understand whether potential risks of conflicts between monetary and macroprudential policies may actually occur in Europe. Although many argue these conflicts are not a threat to the EU,[184] we are prone to believe that it is too early to estimate whether these risks are material—or may become material—in the near future.

On the one hand, this is due to poor implementation of a comprehensive macroprudential framework in most of the EU countries. As a matter of fact a relevant number of EU countries, such as Italy, Germany, Spain, France, Austria, and Portugal, have implemented scarce macroprudential measures thus far.[185] Although the CRR/CRD IV framework provides for a series of capital-based measures that experience a phase-in implementation, the actual absence of a developed macroprudential framework in many countries does not permit an accurate assessment of the negative cross effects that may arise at the EU level between the two policies.

On the other hand, where a macroprudential policy framework is established, its calibration is currently aligned with the ECB monetary policy stance. This is shown, for example, by the present settings of the

[180] Inter alia, see Holt (2009), pp. 120–129.

[181] For an empirical estimate of such a potential conflict, see, for example, Frait, Malovaná, and Tomšík (2015), pp. 110–120.

[182] See IMF (2012), pp. 10–11.

[183] See Spencer (2014).

[184] For example, see Angelini, Nicoletti-Altimari, and Visco (2012).

[185] ESRB (2015), p. 7. The report provides also a general survey of the stage of implementation of macroprudential instruments in the EU Member States.

countercyclical capital buffer rate. The ECB's expansionary monetary policy seems to be assisted by a very low calibration of the countercyclical capital buffer rate, that is, at 0% everywhere.[186]

Based on this example, it would be possible to argue that the macroprudential instruments set out in EU and the ECB monetary policy stance are currently pulling in the same direction and, as a result of this, policy signals given to the market players are mostly aligned.

But one should critically wonder whether risks of conflicts will arise once the macroprudential policy framework will be better structured and applied by all EU Member States. The potential for misalignments and inconsistencies between the two policies is an eventuality that cannot be disqualified in view of the ever-existing menace of shocks that may hit the economy along the financial and business cycles.

This particularly holds true for the Euro area where monetary policy is statutorily constrained, financial and business cycles are not synchronized across countries, and the lack of an institutionalized fiscal union does not permit to react in real time on economic imbalances at EU and national levels.[187]

Since the reality of such concerns cannot be disregarded, many ECB officers have advocated the need to ensure a clear and well-structured European institutional framework that may properly align the conduct of the two policies and avoid material conflicts.[188] To do this, the overwhelmingly majority of scholars have argued in favor of an institutional construction that may permit a certain degree of policy coordination.

The resolution of potential conflicts is intended to challenge the institutional arrangements of the EMU and EU macroprudential supervisory framework. And, in turn, this challenge calls for the establishment of a functional structure that may adequately cope with the economic interactions existing between the cross side effects of the actions undertaken by monetary and macroprudential authorities.

[186] A countercyclical capital buffer rate of 0% currently applies in all EU countries.
[187] IMF (2013b), p. 17.
[188] For example, see Mersch (2013); Lautenschläger (2014).

4.4 Addressing the Conflicts

It is generally acknowledged that potential risks of conflict between macroprudential and monetary policies result from a lack of cooperation between the central bank and the authorities entrusted with macroprudential competences.[189] The failure to conduct a cooperative strategy would accentuate the variability of policy instruments along with their side effects, with conflicting outcomes in terms of credit growth, output, and inflation.[190]

In line with this argument, the establishment of appropriate arrangements enabling a coordinated strategy is of primary importance for a successful achievement of policy objectives. The negative interactions among the abovementioned cross side effects can be addressed only by harmonizing the conduct of the two policies.[191] This harmonized stance has to be reflected in the institutional framework and must allow for an adequate information sharing and analysis in order to avoid policy overlaps and inconsistencies.[192]

But if *policy coordination* is a key device to address negative misalignments and conflicts, it is also true that the level of cooperation may vary substantially across the financial system.[193] On the one hand, it is lawmakers' responsibility to target the desired level of coordination that is optimal, selecting the most suited cooperation arrangements accordingly. On the other hand, the degree of coordination can be high or low and can require either the establishment of one single institution under whose hat both policies are jointly managed or the organization of two independent authorities with separate objectives.

We describe below three prevalent models that may ensure some degree of coordination between macroprudential and monetary policies.[194] The

[189] Inter alia, see Angelini, Neri, and Panetta (2011), p. 22. See also Rubio and Carrasco-Gallago (2014), pp. 326–336; De Paoli and Paustian (2013), pp. 1–32.

[190] See Angelini, Neri, and Panetta (2011), p. 22.

[191] Kim (2013), p. 4.

[192] Idem, p. 4.

[193] For a quantitative estimate of this variance, see De Paoli and Paustian (2013), pp. 17–31, who compare different ways in which the monetary and macroprudential authority may cooperate.

[194] For a general overview of these institutional models, see Nier, Osiński, Jácome, and Madrid (2011a). For an empirical analysis of such models, see also Nier, Osiński, Jácome, and Madrid (2011b). More precisely, the authors categorize the institutional models on the basis of the following criteria: (1) degree of institutional integration of central bank and

first model is relative to the integration of asset prices into the monetary policy reaction function where a single central bank takes responsibility for both policies. The second model involves the establishment of separate bodies targeting different mandates within the same institution. Here macroprudential and monetary objectives are pursued separately but taking into account possible side effects of one policy over the other. The last model provides for the establishment of two independent institutions statutorily focused on targeting their own policy objective only.

As explained further below, the higher the level of institutional independence, the lower the degree of policy coordination. Therefore, choosing one of the policy options is not neutral.[195] Different outcomes—in terms of policy coordination resulting from any of these alternatives—influence policymakers' preferences for the institutional arrangements that are established at national and supranational levels.

And it is exactly within the context of such institutional preferences and structural settings that the economic interactions between macroprudential and monetary policies turn into 'legal'.

4.4.1 *The Full Integration Model*

The most radical model discussed among scholars is the incorporation of asset prices, along with other financial stability indicators, into the reaction function of the monetary authority. Proponents of this institutional model argue for the introduction of an 'augmented Taylor rule' which shall react automatically to volatility in asset prices and credit growth as it does under the current price stability regimes in the event of output and consumer price variations.[196]

financial regulatory functions; (2) ownership of macroprudential policy; (3) role of the treasury; (4) institutional separation of policy decisions from control over policy instruments; (5) existence of a separate body coordinating across policies to address systemic risk. See also Lastra (2015), pp. 325–328.

[195] Alamsyah (2015), p. 5.

[196] See Reifschneider and Williams (2000), pp. 936–966; Cecchetti, Genberg, Lipsky, and Wadhwani (2000), pp. 70–78; Castro (2011), pp. 228–246; Carré, Couppey-Soubeyran, and Dehmej (2015), pp. 541–572. This rule can be expressed by the following simple formula: $i = r + \pi + \alpha\pi\ (\pi - \pi c) + \alpha y\ (y - y^*) + \alpha s\ (f - f^*)$, where the nominal interest rate of the central bank (i) is equal to the gap between inflation (π) and inflation target (πc), the difference between production (y) and its potential (y^*), and the difference between a financial stability proxy (f) and a measure of the optimal/historical level of this financial stability proxy (f^*), containing information from some asset prices and financial variables. For a description,

The rationale of this view lies in the argument made by some that central banks, instead of pondering to what extent asset price changes reflect changes in the real economy, should look into the implications of asset price movements for credit growth, aggregate demand, and inflationary pressure.[197] Against this backdrop, the central bank would be required to tackle misalignments and financial imbalances by adopting a different interest rate stance than the one presently used under normal circumstances.[198]

The central bank would be entrusted with the responsibility of ensuring a wide macroeconomic stability through a 'leaning against the wind' approach[199] to its monetary policy now adjusted in accordance with this augmented Taylor rule. The interest rate policy of the central bank would be employed not only to maintain the objective of price stability but also to counter bubbles and excessive credit growth. The need for additional countercyclical regulatory measures targeting excessive credit growth will decline.[200] Any coordination problem between the side effects of monetary and macroprudential policies would be ruled out by this operational overlap.

While this full integration may be optimal to tackle the problem of coordination, there is some agreement on the inadequacy of this policy model to ensure macroeconomic stability. Albeit a part of the literature suggests that a central bank could improve economic conditions by responding to asset price bubbles, many authors recognize that an

see also Canuto and Cavallari (2013), p. 3. For a quantitative assessment of the impact of adding asset prices to the standard Taylor rule, see also Siklos, Werner, and Bohl (2004). For a literature review on the augmented Taylor rule, see Käfer (2014), pp. 159–192.

[197] Agénor and Pereira da Silva (2012), p. 207.

[198] Visco (2012), p. 131.

[199] For a survey of this monetary policy approach, see Agur and Demertzis (2012), pp. 3–14; Gambacorta and Signoretti (2014), pp. 146–174.

[200] An empirical justification for such a proposal is provided in Cecchetti, Genberg, Lipsky, and Wadhwani (2000), pp. 72–73. An example of the adoption of such model is offered by the pre-2014 experience of Sweden. At that time, Sweden had no institutional framework for macroprudential policy. In order to reduce pressure on upward inflation, along with house prices and household debt, which were considered too high, the Swedish central bank had to rely exclusively on its monetary policy instruments and therefore raised its policy rate from 0.25% in June 2010 to 2% in July 2011. For details, see the Minutes of the Riksbank's Executive Board's Monetary Policy Meeting of 14 December 2010, available at http://www.riksbank.se/en/Press-and-published/Minutes-of-the-Executive-Boards-monetary-policy-meetings/2010/Minutes-of-the-Executive-Boards-monetary-policy-meeting-on-14December2004/.

extended Taylor rule would not provide better outcomes in terms of general macroeconomic stability.[201]

This is because (1) implementing a sound monetary policy by focusing on highly volatile financial indicators may result tremendously tough[202]; (2) it is scientifically difficult to determine the macroeconomic consequence of asset price variations[203]; and (3) monetary policy tools are not per se sufficient to deal with asset price variations and bubbles.[204] Despite the higher level of coordination, relying only on an augmented monetary policy reaction function incorporating asset prices would provide suboptimal results.

For all these reasons, some authors argue for a less extreme approach in the institutional settings of this model. The central bank should be entrusted with both the objectives of financial and price stability, while monetary and the macroprudential policies should be conducted under the same institutional roof. In view of this proposal, the central bank's board shall become the sole decision-making body in monetary and macroprudential affairs endowed with binding powers and a wide array of monetary and macroprudential tools.[205] This institutional pattern would offer several advantages.

[201] The analytical results on the effects of the augmented Taylor rule in fact do not provide a sufficient justification for its introduction. For example, Kafer (2014), pp. 174–182, explains that there would have been little or no benefit for the ECB in using the augmented Taylor rule as developments across Euro area countries have been too heterogeneous. For the author, house price booms are primarily a national phenomenon; therefore a common monetary policy with an augmented Taylor rule would not have been well suited for the Eurozone to combat excessive credit growth.

[202] See Trichet (2005), pp. 16–17.

[203] Trichet (2005), p. 17.

[204] See Bernanke and Gertler (1999), pp. 17–44. In particular, some empirical studies found the *leaning against the wind* monetary policy too simplistic. For example, Laseen, Pescatori, and Turunen (2015), pp. 1–24, argue that such a policy approach may work only if the entire financial sector is procyclical. However, they found that procyclicality varies across countries and sectors over time. In addition, even in those cases where leverage is procyclical, an increase in the policy interest rates may exacerbate the initial asset price movements. Leaning against the wind without clearly distinguishing why leverage is increasing could lead to policy mistakes that may exacerbate financial stress and trigger a financial crisis.

[205] Inter alia, see Nier, Osiński, Jácome, and Madrid (2011a), p. 9; Brockmeijer (2012), p. 166; Goodhart (2014), p. 14.

1. Due to shared capabilities, technical competencies, and resources, the central bank can exploit its expertise in the analysis of macroeconomic conditions and systemic risks to promote jointly its dual monetary and macroprudential mandate.[206] This model could assure the central bank's board to be constantly informed with an extensive flow of information on the side effects that the implementation of one monetary/macroprudential tool may have on the other policy.[207] This information flow is expected to increase the effectiveness of decision-making process, since central bank's stances should now internalize any potential trade-off between price and financial stability, expected to arise along the credit cycle.[208]
2. This institutional model allows the central bank to have a wide variety of relevant tools—either monetary or macroprudential—at its disposal. This joint control on the instruments would reduce the likelihood of mismatches between policy objectives and powers, strengthening the coherence of central bank's intervention.[209] As the risks of conflicts and misalignments between policy signals to the market are eased, this can ultimately optimize the conduct of both policies.
3. Since monetary and macroprudential policy decisions of the board are directly operationalized by the central bank, the agency costs, which would originate from an institutional separation of the body entrusted with policy implementation, are mitigated. In contrast, a model of separate institutions would incentivize risks of misalignments between decision-making body and implementing agency, with possible negative consequences for policy coordination.[210]

[206] Nier, Osiński, Jácome, and Madrid (2011a), p. 10.

[207] Idem, p. 10.

[208] Idem, p. 10. As argued by Brockmeijer (2012), p. 166, the central bank's management can easily put in place arrangements and incentives to ensure access to relevant data and collaboration between functions that would be difficult if more institutions were involved.

[209] Nier, Osiński, Jácome, and Madrid (2011a), p. 10; Brockmeijer (2012), p. 166. As a corollary of this, ESRB (2014b), p. 15, states that an optimal coordination and balance of monetary and macroprudential policies can be easier if powers lie within the central bank. Against this backdrop, indeed, monetary policy must take account of the financial conditions which affect how monetary impulses are transmitted to the real economy. By the same token, macroprudential policy can respond to monetary policy effectively, since financial risks can arise when monetary policy targets inflation, particularly in an environment of low interest rates.

[210] Nier, Osiński, Jácome, and Madrid (2011a), p. 10.

4. At last, assigning macroprudential responsibilities and powers to the central bank can help reduce the risks of inaction or delay in the policy response.[211] As macroprudential policy generates significant spillovers to the real economy, it is subject to strong political considerations and public pressure. This lobbying activity may eventually frustrate a macroprudential response that, instead, would be required based on the macroeconomic circumstances. Against this backdrop, the central bank, due its high degree of independence, is more willing to resist from political pressure and lobbying, thus more quickly reacting to the extremes of the financial cycle, should it become necessary. [212]

Despite these advantages, the full integration model is not without criticism. While the institutional integration permits to balance the cross side effects of monetary and macroprudential policies, and thus fosters coordination, drawbacks can also be material.

1. The failure to adopt a proper macroprudential policy measure perceived by market participants as needed may negatively influence central bank's credibility on its price and financial stability commitments.[213] This is due to the lack of an accountability framework that sets apart different responsibilities in monetary and macroprudential affairs.[214]
2. Full integration provides no safeguard to challenge the representative view formed within the single institution, while few arrangements are put in place against an aggressive use of one policy over the other.[215] This is especially the case when the central bank gives more weight on one policy objective rather than the other. Based on these preferences, the central bank would be free, for example, to use only monetary policy instruments in spite of the procyclical externalities arising along the financial cycle.[216] This decision would be final, and no other agency and/or body would be able to confront or harmonize such a policy stance.

[211] Brockmejer (2012), p. 168.

[212] Idem, p. 168.

[213] For a detailed analysis on the risks to credibility resulting from such an institutional model, see Deutsche Bundesbank (2015), pp. 68–69.

[214] Nier, Osiński, Jácome, and Madrid (2011a), p. 11.

[215] Idem, p. 10.

[216] For example, see Agur and Sharma (2013), p. 20.

3. The large level of independence assigned to the central bank in the conduct of macroprudential policy may also have downsides. Addressing systemic risks could require some coordination with the body in charge of fiscal policy, such as the finance minister or the government.[217] On the one hand, it may be necessary to enact new legislation, or expand the scope of existing rules, to cope with systemic externalities. On the other hand, the build-up of systemic risks may require a cooperative strategy where fiscal policy should complement macroprudential tools.[218] Since central bank's safeguards are meant to exclude any government interference in its decision-making process, this independence may lead to suboptimal policy responses for the stability of the economy.
4. Finally, the allocation of macroprudential competences to an independent central bank may encroach upon democratic principles of political accountability of economic choices.[219] In any democracy, policy preferences that may affect citizens should be aligned with those of the society and should be operationalized through a democratic process.[220] The full integration model may entail a democratic deficit, as macroprudential policy can have substantial impact on the society at large.[221]

Far from being just a notional proposal, and in spite of these drawbacks, it must be emphasized that this full integration model has been translated into reality in a number of countries. For example, the National Bank of Belgium (NBB) is structured under this model. Its Statute provides that the NBB is not only entrusted with the price stability objective,[222] but it shall also contribute to the stability of the financial system.[223] Against this backdrop, the board of the NBB is in charge of both monetary and

[217] For more details, see Benes, Kumhof, Laxton, Muir, and Mursula (2013).

[218] Nier, Osiński, Jácome, and Madrid (2011a), p. 11.

[219] Mishkin (1999), p. 32.

[220] Kaltenthaler, Anderson, and Miller (2010), p. 1267, where the authors claim that citizens will trust institutions and view them as legitimate if the institutions allow them to help set priorities for policy and those citizens have some ability to sanction policymakers if they refuse to heed citizen's preferences for policy.

[221] Alexander (2014), p. 544. For a discussion of the implication of this democratic challenge with respect to the EU architecture, see Ruser (2015), pp. 83–92; Habermas (2013), pp. 4–13; Majone (1998), pp. 5–28; Follesdal and Hix (2006), pp. 533–563.

[222] Article 12 of the Statute of the National Bank of Belgium, as lastly amended by the Council of Regency of 14 January 2015 and approved by Royal Decree of 10 March 2015.

[223] Article 23 of the Statute of the National Bank of Belgium.

macroprudential policies, and it can adopt all the necessary measures to target the related objectives.

Similarly, in 2012, the Statute of the Bank of Greece was amended as to include a financial stability objective.[224] Article 55A(3) of the Statute provides that the Bank of Greece, along with its monetary policy, shall exercise macroprudential tasks with a view to strengthening the resilience of the financial system and decreasing the build-up of systemic risks. To do that, it shall identify, monitor, and assess such risks and adopt the relevant macroprudential measures provided by law.

Another example of the full integration model is provided by the legislative framework of the Bank of Ireland, where Section 6A(2)(a) of Central Bank Act of 1942, as amended by the Central Bank Reform Act 2010, assigns to the central bank a clear financial stability objective, making it the de facto national macroprudential authority.

4.4.2 *The Partial Integration Model*

One more serious criticality affects the efficiency of the full integration model. When the central bank is statutorily entrusted with a dual mandate on price and financial stability, a time-inconsistency problem materializes.[225]

The classical definition of this problem is offered by Kydland and Prescott (1977),[226] according to whom a policy which is socially optimal *ex ante* and is announced in advance as to influence the expectations of private economic agents may result no longer optimal at a later stage, once the economic agents have adjusted their behavior on the basis of their expectations. Accordingly, policymakers may be tempted to step back from the policy stance previously announced.

In line with this principle, a central bank with both price and financial stability mandates may find it optimal to deliver *ex ante* the social optimal level of inflation, but it does not do so *ex post* because of a shock to financial

[224] This amendment was introduced by a decision of the General Meeting of 24 April 2012, which was ratified by Article 165(7) of Law 4009/2012 (government Gazette A 250/20 December 2012).

[225] Ueda and Valencia (2014), p. 327.

[226] Kydland and Prescott (1977), pp. 472–492. For more details on the time-inconsistency problem of central banks, see also Calvo (1978), pp. 1411–1428; Barro and Gordon (1983), pp. 589–610.

stability that has occurred in the meanwhile.[227] In order to guarantee both policy objectives, the central bank may decide to implement a policy stance which provides suboptimal results, leading to a welfare loss.[228] Moreover, the time-inconsistency problem may jeopardize the credibility of the single authority, while its policy decision-making process may start suffering due to a loss of transparency.[229]

The necessity to mitigate time inconsistencies provides the theoretical underpinnings of the second institutional pattern, that is, the partial integration model,[230] where two separate bodies with different policy objectives are housed within the same authority. At least two alternative structures are possible within this institutional model.

First, a dedicated macroprudential policy committee or board—made up of central bank's officers—can be organized as a specialized subsidiary of the monetary authority.[231] Here, the dedicated committee has primary responsibility for the supervision of systemic risks, while the governing body of the central bank still retains a primary responsibility in decision-making and tool implementation processes.

Second, the macroprudential mandate could be assigned to an independent committee entrusted with overall responsibility for the policy conduct.[232] Having no dependence on the central bank's board due to its self-sufficient governance arrangements, this committee may turn into the exclusive responsible for oversight and policymaking functions. Inter-policy coordination is assured by the composition of the committee (e.g. it is usually chaired by the governor of the central bank), and by dedicated

[227] Ueda and Valencia (2014), p. 330.

[228] An explanatory example is given in Deutsche Bundesbank (2015), at p. 68: 'If monetary policy is responsible for both price stability and financial stability and if the latter is influenced by private-sector debt, for instance, it may initially be desirable for monetary policy to pursue a low inflation rate. However, following the onset of a financial shock, which gives rise to a high level of private-sector debt, for example, monetary policymakers could, under certain conditions, decide to reduce the real debt burden further down the line by allowing a higher rate of inflation.'

[229] IMF (2012), p. 20.

[230] For details, see Nier, Osiński, Jácome, and Madrid (2011a), p. 11. For an overview, see also Nier and Tressel (2011), p. 39.

[231] Nier, Osiński, Jácome, and Madrid (2011a), p. 13.

[232] Idem, p. 14.

procedures of information sharing, joint analysis, and interagency dialogue.[233]

The partial integration model has several advantages for a joint conduct of monetary and macroprudential policies. This institutional pattern may help mitigate the credibility risks posed by the full integration model. As the responsibility of macroprudential oversight—at least, partially—shifts away from the hands of the central bank's board, it is possible to distinguish clear responsibilities for the policy actions, and thus, establish separate accountability arrangements for the conduct of each policy.[234] The introduction of a separate committee dealing with financial stability helps alleviate the risks of unchallenged views within the central bank.[235] As the institutional settings are elaborated to further dialogue and cross-check analysis, macroprudential and monetary policies may benefit from the exchanges of different views and assessments within the single institution.

Also, this institutional framework can increase coordination with fiscal policy, when this is critically needed. The rules of committee composition may require the participation of the finance minister and/or government officers. This involvement can certainly be greatly helpful, in certain circumstances, to take a coherent and effective corrective action against the build-up of systemic risks.[236]

This holds true, for instance, when the macroprudential policy reaction requires the enactment of a law, as well as the application of tax levies. The treasury and/or government participation in the work of the committee may help foster political support in favor of the macroprudential policy stance just adopted, thereby easing the expected lobbying pressure and political filibustering.[237] However, it is difficult to argue that such a model can alleviate the lack of democratic legitimacy of the macroprudential policy decisions, as they will be adopted, as for the full integration model, out of the democratic control of the citizens.

It must be noted that using this institutional pattern would imply a lower level of coordination with monetary policy, if compared to the full

[233] This also holds true with respect to the coordination of macroprudential and microprudential policies. For better insights on this topic, see Osiński, Seal, and Hoogduin (2013), p. 4.

[234] Nier, Osiński, Jácome, and Madrid (2011a), p. 14.

[235] Idem, p. 14.

[236] Idem, p. 11.

[237] Idem, p. 13. See also Nier (2011), p. 201.

integration model. This weakened integration may be the cause of suboptimal outcomes and unintended side effects for the conduct of the two policies. For example, if the central bank's board and the macroprudential committee have divergent views upon a selected issue, this would generate risks of delay in the policy response, eventually affecting the integrity of the following policy actions.[238]

This lower coordination could be mirrored in a greater separation between the decision-making and the implementation phases of macroprudential tools.[239] This is the case if the first institutional variant is statutorily established: while the committee would be in charge of the general macroprudential oversight, the board of the central bank would retain control over the relevant instruments. Under these settings, frictions and conflicts between the committee's stances and the board's actions could not be ruled out.[240]

The participation of the finance minister and/or government officers in the work of the macroprudential committee may pose some critical concerns in spite of the advantages. A strong involvement of the finance minister may call into question the smooth functioning of the committee, as some political bias could impinge upon the achievement of the macroprudential objectives.[241] In other words, the operational conduct of macroprudential policy could be hindered by electoral considerations that would produce inefficient results in terms of financial stability assessment and systemic risk mitigation.

Moreover, if the committee is entrusted with a coordination role among macroprudential, monetary, and fiscal policies, and weak institutional safeguards are established to shield the independence of the central bank in its monetary policy functions, this political influence may also overthrow monetary policy decisions.[242]

Despite the likely amplitude of these downsides, the Bank of England decided to adopt this model. Parallel to the Monetary Policy Committee (MPC) which is responsible for the conduct of monetary policy, the

[238] Idem, p. 14. In addition, cf. IMF (2013a), p. 19.

[239] With respect to the mechanisms that can be used to compensate for such a separation, see Nier, Osiński, Jácome, and Madrid (2011a), pp. 31–32.

[240] Among others, see Nier, Osiński, Jácome, and Madrid (2011b), at p. 22.

[241] Nier (2011), p. 201.

[242] For more details on the issue, see Chwieroth and Danielsson (2013).

Financial Services Act 2012 established the FPC as an independent subcommittee of the courts of directors of the central bank.[243]

Under the roof of the Bank of England, the FPC is entrusted with the primary objective of identifying, monitoring, and taking action to remove or reduce systemic risks in the UK financial system, and a secondary objective of supporting the economic policy of the government.[244] In order to ensure accountability and democratic control of the policy decisions, a number of safeguards are established; the macroprudential measures decided by the FPC are subject to prior scrutiny of the Parliament,[245] while the Treasury has the general power to make recommendations with respect to the responsibility of the FPC in the achievement of its objectives.[246]

From this example it follows that the calibration of appropriate rules—establishing a right balance among the policy interests involved—can significantly mitigate criticalities involving the democratic legitimation of the adopted decisions and the risk of political bias in the decision-making process.

4.4.3 *The Independent Institutions Model*

The last institutional model to be considered involves the setting up of two independent institutions, with clearly defined objectives and tools. Since all the macroprudential tasks are taken out of central bank's perimeter, this institutional pattern is characterized by the higher degree of separation between monetary functions and macroprudential policy.[247]

[243] Section 9B(1) of the Financial Services Act 2012. As stated in this Article, the FPC comprises the Governor of the Bank, the Deputy Governors of the Bank, the Chief Executive of the FCA, one member appointed by the Governor of the Bank after consultation with the Chancellor of the Exchequer, four members appointed by the Chancellor of the Exchequer, and a representative of the Treasury.

[244] Section 9C of the Financial Services Act 2012.

[245] Section 9L of the Financial Services Act 2012. However, a macroprudential measure can be disposed without being scrutinized and approved by the Parliament if the measure contains a statement that the Treasury are of the opinion that, by reason of urgency, it is necessary to adopt the measure without such procedure.

[246] Section 9E of the Financial Services Act 2012. In this regard, the FPC is obliged to respond to any recommendation made by the Treasury, stating the action that the Committee has taken or is committed to take in accordance with the recommendation. If the Committee does not intend to act, it must state clearly the reasons of the inaction.

[247] Nier, Osiński, Jácome, and Madrid (2011a), p. 15.

This partitioning is apparent from the fact that the independent macroprudential authority is the sole entity responsible for both the decision-making stage of the policy strategy and the regulatory application of the macroprudential measures.

Despite the wide range of possible alternatives,[248] two settings are more common. On the one hand, the macroprudential powers can lie within a legally independent institution—such as a designed macroprudential authority—composed of macroprudential experts only. In this case, a series of cooperative arrangements are settled to further constant information sharing with the monetary authority.[249]

On the other hand, a special body—or committee—made up of officers from several regulatory institutions, including the central bank, can be formalized based on this variant, the decision-making powers and implementation tasks are still assigned to the independent body, but the cooperation between monetary and macroprudential policies would be achieved through the multifaceted composition of the committee.[250]

Although the precise settings may vary, the central bank usually retains a key role even under this institutional model. In view of its expertise and technical capability relative to financial and macroeconomic stability, the central bank maintains responsibility to provide comprehensive analysis, data models, and surveys of the financial cycle and, more specifically, of the systemic risks that are likely to materialize.[251]

This institutional model offers a number of advantages in terms of policy optimality. Since the establishment of two independent authorities is based upon the statutory separation of policy objectives, this pattern helps each institution to be focused only on its ultimate and intermediate objectives.[252] Each institution bears sole responsibility for the decisions on the policy strategies and for the control over the policy measures assigned to it under the legal mandate.

This sharp separation decreases the risks of operational overlaps between monetary and the macroprudential tasks, while enhancing the creation of an individual accountability framework for monetary policy on the one hand, and macroprudential policy on the other.[253] In addition, the

[248] Ashley (2014), p. 16.
[249] Idem, p. 16.
[250] Idem, p. 16.
[251] Rhu (2011), p. 122.
[252] Nier, Osiński, Jácome, and Madrid (2011b), p. 26.
[253] Idem, p. 26.

continuous dialogue between independent institutions favors critical thinking and exchange of views on risk assessment, thereby reducing the potential for unchallenged outlooks and hasty policy reactions.

Like the full and partial integration models, this alternative is not free from downsides. A number of reasons suggest that a sharp separation between authorities could provide suboptimal outcomes. In particular:

1. As the collection of data and information utilized for systemic risks analysis is shared among the central bank and the macroprudential authority, their risk assessments and stability surveys could be impaired by such fragmentation.[254] Although specific legal arrangements may substantially increase the exchanges of data and free flow of information, information sharing impediments can be due to a number of reasons, such as competition among institutions, legal obstacles, or inefficient infrastructures.[255]
2. Second, despite the risks of operational overlaps would be reduced by a clear assignment of tasks and tools, it is also true that this institutional set-up substantially decreases coordination between authorities. This implies that the side effects of one policy are likely to be not appropriately scrutinized by the authority in charge of the other policy, leading to greater risk of policy inconsistencies and suboptimal policy mix. This criticality is dramatized by the limitation of powers of the central bank. Under this framework, since the monetary authority has no control over any prudential tool, it might be driven to address systemic externalities, should they take place, through an overly aggressive use of its competences and powers, without considering the countercyclical measures issued in the meanwhile by the macroprudential authority.[256]
3. While independent institutions are assumed to cooperate closely in order to achieve their statutory objectives, questions of democratic

[254] See IMF (2011).

[255] For details, see Nier, Osiński, Jácome, and Madrid (2011b), p. 26. Impediments to data sharing are widely recognized by central banks and supervisory authorities and have been material in a number of countries, including the United States and the EU. For details on this topic, see Irving Fisher Committee on Central Bank Statistics (2015), pp. 7–10, which provides an in-depth analysis of the legal and market obstacles to information flows existing across relevant countries. For additional details, see also Tor and Aviram (2004), pp. 231–279.

[256] Nier, Osiński, Jácome, and Madrid (2011b), p. 27.

guidance and control may be raised even under this model. Without specific safeguards that may hold accountable the authority in charge of macroprudential policy, even this model may neglect the policy preferences of the society and its democratic premises.[257] In addition, although the supervisory responsibility for system risk is shared between two authorities under a cooperative framework, no one is held fully responsible when the cooperation fails or the joint policy conduct proved insufficient to tackle systemic risks.[258]

4. This institutional set-up is likely to dramatize the problem of conflicting opinions and disagreements among bodies featuring the partial integration model. In view of their strong individual independence, monetary and macroprudential authorities have no way to challenge possible divergent opinions or conflicting policy stances under this pattern.[259] This could in turn lead to delays in the policy reaction or further inconsistencies after a joint response.[260]
5. A clear-cut separation between monetary and macroprudential authorities can result in an inefficient dispersion of expertise and human resources. Since few resources are dedicated to strengthen a cooperative strategy between authorities, it would be difficult to combine the macroeconomic expertise of the central bank and the institution-specific knowledge of the macroprudential authority towards a specific policy goal.[261]

As for the case of the partial integration model, many of these criticalities can be addressed by establishing a proper legal framework which allows for a strong coordination among the two authorities. This could be done, by way of example, by assigning a coordinating role to an intermediate committee, or by signing a specific memorandum of understanding aimed at increasing coordination among policies.[262]

[257] An in-depth analysis on the democratic legitimacy of an independent macroprudential authority is provided by Tucker (2016), pp. 94–96.

[258] Nier, Osiński, Jácome, and Madrid (2011b), p. 27.

[259] Idem, p. 27.

[260] Idem, p. 27.

[261] For details, see Nier (2009), p. 14; Carney (2014).

[262] See Nier, Osiński, Jácome, and Madrid (2011b), p. 16. For examples related to the operationalization of such a cooperative framework in Indonesia, Hong Kong, Malaysia, and Australia, see Lim, Ramchand, Wang, Wu (2013), pp. 8–11.

This model has been adopted in a number of EU countries. For example, in Germany, the Act on Monitoring Financial Stability of 28 November 2012[263] established the 'Ausschuss für Finanzstabilität' (Financial Stability Committee) entrusted with soft-law macroprudential powers.[264] In order to foster democratic accountability, three representatives of the Federal Ministry of Finance participate in the Committee.[265] And, in view of setting up a coordination regime with the central bank and enhance consistency with monetary policy, the Committee also includes three representatives of the Deutsche Bundesbank, while specific arrangements are laid down for information exchange with the German central bank.[266]

The need to set up a consistent regime implies the economic interaction of monetary and macroprudential policies is to be reflected in specific legal settings which may allow policymakers to achieve their policy objectives in a consistent manner. As such, the economic interaction needs a proper legal establishment set in accordance with the primary law and the constitutional constraints.

References

Adrian, Tobias, Liang, Nellie (2014). Monetary Policy, Financial Conditions, and Financial Stability, *Federal Reserve Bank of New York Staff Report*, No. 690.

Agénor, Pierre-Richard, Pereira da Silva, Luiz A. (2012). Macroeconomic Stability, Financial Stability, and Monetary Policy Rules, *International Finance*, Vol. 15, Issue 2.

[263] See Gesetz zur Überwachung der Finanzstabilität (*Finanzstabilitätsgesetz*) of 28 November 2012 (Federal Law Gazette I, page 2369) as last amended by Article 2 paragraph 36 of the Act of 1 April 2015 (Federal Law Gazette I, p. 434).

[264] In particular, Section 1 of the Finanzstabilitätsgesetz assigns the following competences to the Committee: (1) discussing the factors that are key to financial stability; (2) strengthening cooperation between the institutions represented on the Financial Stability Committee in the event of a financial crisis; (3) advising on the handling of warnings and recommendations issued by the ESRB; (4) reporting annually to the lower house of Parliament, the Bundestag; and (5) issuing warnings and recommendations. The lack of hard-law measures on macroprudential policy—which are instead delegated to the *Bundesanstalt für Finanzdienstleistungsaufsicht* (BaFin)—can be seen as a safeguard as to ensure that decisions with large distributional effects on the society are not direct responsibility of the Committee.

[265] See Section 1(3) of the Finanzstabilitätsgesetz. In addition, the Committee includes also three members of BaFin, which is the authority directly responsible for the application of the macroprudential measure in the German jurisdiction.

[266] With respect to the transmission and exchange of information and data between the Committee and the German Central Bank, see Section 4(1) of the Finanzstabilitätsgesetz.

Agenor, Pierre-Richard, Alper, Koray, da Silva, Pereira Luiz (2012). Capital Regulation, Monetary Policy, and Financial Stability, *International Journal of Central Banking*, Vol. 9, No. 3, pp. 193–238.

Agur, Itai, Demertzis, Maria (2012). “Leaning Against the Wind” and the Timing of Monetary Policy, *IMF Working Paper*, No. 86.

Agur, Itai, Sharma, Sunil (2013). Rules, Discretion, and Macro-prudential Policy, *IMF Working Paper*, No. 65.

Ahearne, Alan G., Ammer, John, Doyle, Brian M., Kole, Linda S., Martin, Robert F. (2005). House Prices and Monetary Policy: A Cross-Country Study, *Board of Governors of the Federal Reserve System International Finance Discussion Paper*, No. 841.

Ahrend, Rudiger, Cournède, Boris, Price, Rober W. (2008). Monetary Policy, Market Excesses and Financial Turmoil, *OECD Economics Department Working Papers*, No. 597.

Aiyar, Shekhar, Calomiris, Charles W., Wieladek, Tomasz (2014). Identifying Channels of Credit Substitution When Bank Capital Requirements Are Varied, *Bank of England Working Paper*, No. 485.

Alamsyah, Halim (2015). Coordinating Macroprudential and Monetary Policies: Asia Pacific Experiences. *Speech Held at the 2015 SEACEN Policy Summit on “Macroprudential Policies: Practical Implementation”*, 7 September 2015, Kuala Lumpur, Malaysia.

Alexander, Kern (2014). The ECB and Banking Supervision: Building Effective Prudential Supervision?, *Yearbook of European Law*, Vol. 33, No. 1.

Altunbas, Yener, Gambacorta, Leonardo, Marques-Ibanez, David (2010). Does Monetary Policy Affect Bank Risk-Taking?, *BIS Working Paper*, No. 298.

Angelini, Paolo, Stefano Neri, and Fabio Panetta (2011). Monetary and Macroprudential Policies, *Banca d’Italia Working Papers*, No. 801, March 2011.

Angeloni, Ignazio, Faia, Ester (2009). A Tale of Two Policies: Prudential Regulation and Monetary Policy with Fragile Banks, *Kiel Institute for the World Economy Working Paper*, No. 2.

Angeloni, Ignazio, Faia, Ester (2013). Capital Regulation and Monetary Policy with Fragile Banks, *Journal of Monetary Economics*, Vol. 60, Issue 3.

Antipa, Pamfili, Matheron, Julien (2014). Interactions between Monetary and Macroprudential Policies, *Banque de France Financial Stability Review*, No. 18.

Ashley, Dunstan (2014). The Interaction between Monetary and Macro-prudential Policy, *Reserve Bank of New Zealand Bulletin*, Vol. 77, No. 2.

Assenmacher-Wesche, Katrin, Gerlach, Stefan (2008). Ensuring Financial Stability: Financial Structure and the Impact of Monetary Policy on Asset Prices, *IMFS Working Paper Series, No. 16.*

Barwell, Richard (2013). Macroprudential Policy, *Palgrave Macmillan.*

BCBS (2012). The Policy Implications of Transmission Channels between the Financial System and the Real Economy, *BIS Working Paper*, No. 20.

Beau, Denis, Clerc, Laurent, Mojon, Benoit (2012). Macro-prudential Policy and the Conduct of Monetary Policy, *Banque de France Occasional Papers*, No. 8.

Bech, Morten L., Keister, Todd (2013). Liquidity Regulation and the Implementation of Monetary Policy, *BIS Working Papers*, No. 432.

Benes, Jaromir, Kumhof, Michael, Laxton, Douglas, Muir, Dirk, Mursula, Susanna (2013). The Benefits of International Policy Coordination Revisited, *IMF Working Paper*, No. 262.

Bernanke, Ben S. (2010). Monetary Policy and the Housing Bubble, *Speech at the Annual Meeting of the American Economic Association*, Atlanta, Georgia.

Bernanke, Ben S., Gertler, Mark (1999). Monetary Policy and Asset Price Volatility, *Federal Reserve Bank of Kansas City Economic Review*, Fourth Quarter.

Barro, Robert J., Gordon, David (1983). A Positive Theory of Monetary Policy in a Natural Rate Model, *Journal of Political Economy*, Vol. 91, No. 4.

Bindseil, Ulrich, Lamoot, Jeroen (2011). The Basel III Framework for Liquidity Standards and Monetary Policy Implementation, *SFB 649 Discussion Paper*, No. 2011-041.

Bonner, Clemens, Eijffinger, Sylvester (2012a). The Impact of Liquidity Regulation on Interbank Money Markets, *DNB Working Paper*, No. 364.

Bonner, Clemens, Eijffinger, Sylvester (2012b). The Impact of Liquidity Regulation on Monetary-Policy Implementation, *Vox CEPR's Policy Portal.* Online. Available at: http://www.voxeu.org/article/liquidity-coverage-ratios-and-monetary-policy

Borio, Claudio, Shim, Ilhyock (2007). What Can (Macro-)Prudential Policy Do to Support Monetary Policy?, *BIS Working Papers*, No. 242.

Borio, Claudio, Zhu, Haibin (2008). Capital Regulation, Risk Taking and Monetary Policy: A Missing Link in the Transmission Mechanism?, *BIS Working Paper*, No. 268.

Bridges, Jonathan, Gregory, David, Nielsen, Mette, Pezzini, Silvia, Radia, Amar, Spaltro, Marco (2014). The Impact of Capital Requirements on Bank Lending, *Bank of England Working Paper*, No. 486.

Brockmeijer, Jan (2012). The Institutional Settings of Macroprudential Policy. In: '*Putting Macroprudential Policy to Work*', (eds.) Aerdt Houben, Rob Nijskens, Mark Teunissen, *De Nederlandsche Bank Occasional Studies*, Vol. 12–7.

Bruno, Valentina, Shim, Ilhyock, Shin, Hyun Song (2015). Comparative Assessment of Macroprudential Policies, *BIS Working Papers,* No. 502.

Brzoza-Brzezina, Michał, Kolasa, Marcin, Makarski, Krzysztof (2015). Monetary and Macroprudential Policy with Foreign Currency Loans, *ECB Working Paper Series*, No. 1783.

Bunn, Philip, Drapper, Lizzie, Rowe, Jeremy, Shah, Sagar (2015). The Potential Impact of Higher Interest Rates and Further Fiscal Consolidation on Households: Evidence from the 2015 NMG Consulting Survey, *Bank of England Quarterly Bulletin 2015 Q4*.

Calvo, Guillermo (1978). On the Time Consistency of Optimal Policy in the Monetary Economy, *Econometrica*, Vol. 46, Issue 6.

Canuto, Otaviano, Cavallari, Matheus (2013). Asset Prices, Macroprudential Regulation, and Monetary Policy, *The World Bank Economic Premise*, No. 116.

Carboni, Giacomo, Pariès, Matthieu D., Kok, Christoffer (2013). Exploring the Nexus between Macro-prudential Policies and Monetary Policy Measures, *ECB Financial Stability Review*, May 2013.

Carney, Mark (2014). One Mission. One Bank. Promoting the Good of the People of the United Kingdom, *Speech Given at the Mais Lecture at Cass Business School*, City University, London, 18 March 2014.

Caruana, Jaime (2011). Monetary Policy in a World with Macroprudential Policy, *Speech Held at the SAARCFINANCE Governors' Symposium 2011*, Kerala, 11 June 2011.

Castro, Vitor (2011). Can Central Banks' Monetary Policy Be Described by a Linear (Augmented) Taylor Rule or by a Nonlinear Rule?, *Journal of Financial Stability*, Vol. 7.

Carré, Emmanuel, Couppey-Soubeyran, Jézabel, Dehmej, Salim (2015). La coordination entre politique monétaire et politique macroprudentielle, *Revue économique*, Vol. 66, Issue 3.

Cecchetti, Stephen G. (2000). Making Monetary Policy: Objectives and Rules, *Oxford Review of Economic Policy*, Vol. 16, No. 4.

Cecchetti, Stephen G., Genberg, Hans, Lipsky, John, Wadhwani, Sushil (2000). Asset Prices and Central Bank Policy, *International Center for Monetary and Banking Studies*, London.

Cesa-Bianchi, Ambrogio, Rebucci, Alessandro (2015). Does Easing Monetary Policy Increase Financial Instability?, *IMF Working Paper*, No. 139.

CGFS (2012). Operationalising the Selection and Application of Macroprudential Instruments, *CGFS Papers*, No. 48.

CGFS (2015). Regulatory Change and Monetary Policy, *CGFS Papers*, No. 54.

Chwieroth, Jeffrey, Danielsson, Jon (2013). Political Challenges of the Macroprudential Agenda. Vox CEPR's Policy Portal (6 September 2013). Online. Available at: http://www.voxeu.org/article/political-challenges-macroprudential-agenda

Claessens, Stijn, Ghosh, Swati R., Mihet, Roxana (2014). Macro-prudential Policies to Mitigate Financial System Vulnerabilities, *IMF Working Paper*, No. 155.

Committee on International Economic Policy and Reform (2011). Rethinking Central Banking, September 2011.

Crowe, Christopher, Dell'Ariccia, Giovanni, Igan, Deniz, Rabanal, Pau (2011). Policies for Macrofinancial Stability: Options to Deal with Real Estate Booms. *IMF Staff Discussion Note*, No. 2.

De Carvalho, Fabia A., De Castro, Marcos R. (2015). Macroprudential and Monetary Policy Interaction: A Brazilian Perspective, *BCB Working Paper*, No. 405.

Dell'Ariccia, Giovanni, Laeven, Luc, Marquez, Robert (2011). Financial Frictions, Foreign Currency Borrowing, and Systemic Risk, *Paper Presented at the 12th Jacques Polak Annual Research Conference*, Washington, DC, 10–11 November 2011.

De Paoli, Bianca, Paustian, Matthias (2013). Coordinating Monetary and Macroprudential Policies, *Federal Reserve Bank of New York Staff Report*, No. 653.

Demyanyk, Yuliya, Hemert, Otto Van (2011). Understanding the Subprime Mortgage Crisis, *Review of Financial Studies*, No. 24, No. 6.

De Nederlandsche Bank (2015). Dutch Mortgages in the DNB Loan Level Data, *DNB Occasional Studies*, Vol. 13–4.

Deutsche Bundesbank (2015). The Importance of Macroprudential Policy for Monetary Policy, *Monthly Report March 2015*.

Dokko, Doyle, Jane Brian M., Kiley, Michael T., Kim, Jinill, Sherlund, Shane, Sim, Jae, Van Den Heuvel, Skander (2011). Monetary Policy and the Global Housing Bubble, *Economic Policy*, Vol. 26, Issue 66, pp. 237–287.

Dubecq, Simon, Mojon, Benoît, Ragot, Xavier (2009). Fuzzy Capital Requirements, Risk-Shifting and the Risk Taking Channel of Monetary Policy, *Banque De France Document de Travail*, No. 254.

ECB (2013). Liquidity Regulation and Monetary Policy Implementation, *Monthly Bulletin April 2013*.

ESRB (2014a). Handbook on Operationalising Macro-prudential Policy in the Banking Sector.

ESRB (2014b). Allocating Macro-prudential Powers, *Reports of the Advisory Scientific Committee*, No. 5/November.

ESRB (2015). A Review of Macro-prudential Policy in the EU One Year after the Introduction of the CRD/CRR, June 2015.

Follesdal, Andreas, Hix, Simon (2006). Why There Is a Democratic Deficit in the EU: A Response to Majone and Moravcsik, *JCMS: Journal of Common Market Studies*, Vol. 44, Issue 3.

Frait, Jan, Malovaná, Simona, Tomšík, Vladimír (2015). The Interaction of Monetary and Macroprudential Policies in the Pursuit of Central Bank's Primary Objectives, *Czech National Bank Financial Stability Report* 2014/2015.

Francis, William B., Osborne, Matthew (2012). Capital Requirements and Bank Behavior in the UK: Are There Lessons for International Capital Standards?, *Journal of Banking & Finance*, Vol. 36.

Gambacorta, Leonardo (2009). Monetary Policy and the Risk-Taking Channel, *BIS Quarterly Review*, December 2009.

Gambacorta, Leonardo, Signoretti, Federico M. (2014). Should Monetary Policy Lean Against the Wind?: An Analysis Based on a DSGE Model with Banking, *Journal of Economic Dynamics and Control*, Vol. 43.

Gameiro, Isabel Marques, Soares, Carla, Sousa, João (2011). Monetary Policy and Financial Stability: An Open Debate, *Banco de Portugal Economic Bulletin*, Spring 2011.

Ghilardi, Matteo F., Peiris, Shanaka J. (2014). Capital Flows, Financial Intermediation, and Macroprudential Policies, *IMF Working Paper*, No. 157.

Geanakoplos, John (2010). Solving the Present Crisis and Managing the Leverage Cycle, *FRBNY Economic Policy Review*, August 2010.

Gelain, Paolo, Ilbas, Pelin (2014). Monetary and Macroprudential Policies in an Estimated Model with Financial Intermediation, *National Bank of Belgium Working Paper*, No. 258.

Gerlach, Stefan (2012). Housing Markets and Financial Stability, *Speech Held at the National University of Ireland*, Galway, 20 April 2012.

Giese, Julia, Nelson, Benjamin, Tanaka, Misa, Tarashev, Nikola (2013). How Could Macroprudential Policy Affect Financial System Resilience and Credit? Lessons from the Literature, *Bank of England Financial Stability Paper*, No. 21.

Giordana, Gaston, Schumacher, Ingmar (2013). Bank Liquidity Risk and Monetary Policy. Empirical Evidence on the Impact of Basel III Liquidity Standards, *International Review of Applied Economics*, Vol. 27, No. 5.

Giuliodori, Massimo (2005). The Role of House Prices in the Monetary Transmission Mechanism Across European Countries, *Scottish Journal of Political Economy*, Vol. 52, No. 4, pp. 519–543.

Goodhart, Charles (2009). Procyclicality and Financial Regulation, *Bank of Spain Revista de Estabilidad Financiera*, No. 16.

Goodhart, Charles (2014). The Use of Macroprudential Instruments. In: '*Macroprudentialism*', (ed.) Dirk Schoenmaker, *CEPR Press*, Washington, DC.

Habermas, Jurgen (2013). Democracy, Solidarity and the European Crisis. In: '*Roadmap to a Social Europe*', (eds.) Anne-Marie Grozelier, Björn Hacker, Wolfgang Kowalsky, Jan Machnig, Henning Meyer and Brigitte Unger, *Social Europe Report*.

Havemann, Roy (2014). Counter-Cyclical Capital Buffers and Interest-Rate Policy as Complements – The Experience of South Africa, *ERSA Working Paper*, No. 476.

Holt, Jeff (2009). A Summary of the Primary Causes of the Housing Bubble and the Resulting Credit Crisis: A Non-technical Paper, *The Journal of Business Inquiry*, Vol. 8, No. 1.

Igan, Deniz, Kang, Heedon (2011). Do Loan-to-Value and Debt-to-Income Limits Work? Evidence from Korea, *IMF Working Paper*, No. 297.

IMF (2008). The Changing Housing Cycle and the Implications for Monetary Policy, *World Economic Outlook – Housing and the Business Cycle*, Washington, DC.

IMF (2011). Macroprudential Policy: An Organizing Framework. Available at: https://www.imf.org/external/np/pp/eng/2011/031411.pdf

IMF (2012). The Interaction between Macroprudential and Monetary Policies: Background Paper.
IMF (2013a). The interaction of Monetary and Macroprudential Policies, 29 January 2013.
IMF (2013b). European Union: Publication of Financial Sector Assessment Program Documentation—Technical Note on Macroprudential Oversight and the Role of the ESRB, *IMF Country Report,* No. 13/70.
Irving Fisher Committee on Central Bank Statistics (2015). Data-Sharing: Issues and Good Practices, *Report to BIS Governors Prepared by the Task Force on Data Sharing*, January 2015.
Jiménez, Gabriel, Ongena, Steven, Peydró, José Luis, Saurina, Jesús (2008). Hazardous Times for Monetary Policy: What Do Twenty-Three Million Bank Loans Say about the Effects of Monetary Policy on Credit Risk-Taking?, *Banco de Espana Documentos de Trabajo*, No. 0833.
Kafer, Benjamin (2014). The Taylor Rule and Financial Stability: A Literature Review with Application for the Euro Zone, *Review of Economics,* Vol. 65.
Kaltenthaler, Karl, Anderson, Chirstopher J., Miller, William J. (2010). Accountability and Independent Central Banks: Europeans and Distrust of the European Central Bank, *JCMS: Journal of Common Market Studies*, Vol. 48, Issue 5.
Kannan, Prakash, Rabanal, Pau, Scott, Alasdair (2009). Monetary and Macroprudential Policy Rules in a Model with House Price Booms, *IMF Working Paper*, No. 251.
Karmakar, Sudipto (2013). Macroprudential Regulation and Macroeconomic Activity, *MPRA Paper*, No. 52172.
Kawata, Hiroshi, Kurachi, Yoshiyuki, Nakamura, Koji, Teranishi, Yuki (2013). Impact of Macroprudential Policy Measures on Economic Dynamics: Simulation Using a Financial Macro-econometric Model, *Bank of Japan Working Paper Series*, No. 13-E-3.
Kim, Choongsoo (2013). Harmonious Operation of Macroprudential and Monetary Policies, and Challenges, *Speech at the International Seminar on 'Macroprudential and Monetary Policies'*, Bank of Korea, Seoul, 8 April 2013.
Kydland, Finn E., Prescott, Edward C. (1977). Rules Rather than Discretion: The Inconsistency of Optimal Plans. *Journal of Political Economy*, Vol. 87, Issue 3.
Lambertini, Luisa, Mendicino, Caterina, Punzi, Maria Teresa (2013). Leaning Against Boom–Bust Cycles in Credit and Housing Prices, *Journal of Economic Dynamics and Control*, Vol. 37, Issue 8.
Laseen, Stefan, Pescatori, Andrea, Turunen, Jarkko (2015). Systemic Risk: A New Trade-off for Monetary Policy?, *IMF Working Paper Series*, No. 142.
Lastra, Maria Rosa (2015). Systemic Risk and Macroprudential Supervision. In: '*The Oxford Handbook of Financial Regulation*', (eds.) Moloney Niamh, Eilis Ferran, Jennifer Payne, *Oxford University Press.*

Lautenschläger, Sabine (2014). The Interplay between Macro-prudential, Microprudential and Monetary Policies at the ECB, *Speech Held at the Conference on "Macroprudential Policy – Implementation and Interaction with other Policies"*, Stockholm, 13 November 2014.

Leduc, Sylvain, Natal, Jean-Marc (2015). Monetary and Macroprudential Policy in a Leveraged Economy, *Federal Reserve Bank of San Francisco Working Paper*, No. 15.

Levine, Paul, Lima, Diana (2015). Policy Mandates for Macro-prudential and Monetary Policies in a New Keynesian Framework, *ECB Working Paper Series*, No. 1784.

Lim, Cheng Hoon, Ramchand, Rishi, Wang, Hong, Wu, Xiaoyong (2013). Institutional Arrangements for Macroprudential Policy in Asia, *IMF Working Paper*, No. 165.

Listokin, Yair (2014). Law and Macroeconomics, *Stanford Law and Economics Seminar*, *Autumn Quarter 2014*.

Maddaloni, Angela, Peydró, José-Luis (2010). Bank Risk-Taking, Securitization, Supervision and Low Interest Rates: Evidence from the Euro Area and the U.S. Lending Standards, *ECB Working Paper Series*, No. 1248.

Maddaloni, Angela, Peydrò, Josè-Luis (2013). Monetary Policy, Macroprudential Policy, and Banking Stability: Evidence from the Euro Area, *International Journal of Central Banking*, Vol. 9, No. 1.

Majone, Giandomenico (1998). Europe's 'Democratic Deficit': The Question of Standards, *European Law Journal*, Vol. 4, Issue 1.

Meeks, Roland (2015). Capital Regulation and Macroeconomic Activity: Implications for Macroprudential Policy. Online. Available at: https://www.aeaweb.org/conference/2015/retrieve.php?pdfid=1213

Mersch, Yves (2013). Monetary Policy and Financial Stability under One Roof, *Keynote Speech Held at the 6th Policy Roundtable of the European Central Bank: "The Future of Global Policy Coordination"*, 6 September 2013.

Mishkin, Frederic S. (1996). The Channels of Monetary Transmission: Lessons for Monetary Policy, *NBER Working Paper*, No. 5464 (Also Reprint No. r2054).

Mishkin, Frederic S. (1999). Central Banking in a Democratic Society, *Springer Science+Business Media*, New York.

Mishkin, Frederic S. (2007). Housing and the Monetary Transmission Mechanism, *FRB Finance and Economics Discussion Series*, No. 40.

Mundell, Robert A. (1962). The Appropriate Use of Monetary and Fiscal Policy for Internal and External Stability, *IMF Staff Papers*, Vol. 9, No. 1.

N'Diaye, Papa (2009). Countercyclical Macro Prudential Policies in a Supporting Role to Monetary Policy, *IMF Working Paper*, No. 257.

Nier, Erlend W. (2009). Financial Stability Frameworks and the Role of Central Banks: Lessons from the Crisis, *IMF Working Paper*, No. 70.

Nier, Erlend W. (2011). On the Governance of Macroprudential Policies. In: *"Macroprudential Regulatory Policies: The New Road to Financial Stability?"*, (eds.) Stijn Claessens, Douglas D. Evanoff, George G. Kaufman, Laura E. Kodres, *World Scientific Studies in International Economics*, Vol. 17.

Nier, Erlend W., Osiński, Jacek, Jácome, Luis I., Madrid, Pamela (2011a). Institutional Models for Macroprudential Policy, *IMF Staff Discussion Note*, No. 18.

Nier, Erlend W., Osiński, Jacek, Jácome, Luis I., Madrid, Pamela (2011b). Towards Effective Macroprudential Policy Frameworks: An Assessment of Stylized Institutional Models, *IMF Working Papers*, No. 250.

Nier, Erlend W., Tressel, Thierry (2011). The European Systemic Risk Board: Effectiveness of Macroprudential Oversight in Europe. In: '*Euro Area Policies: 2011 Article IV Consultation—Lessons from the European Financial Stability Framework Exercise; and Selected Issues Paper*', (eds.) Thomas Harjes, Nico Valckx, Thierry Tressel, Esther Perez Ruiz, Nandaka Molagoda, Erlend Nier, *International Monetary Fund*, Washington, DC.

OECD (2011). OECD Economic Outlook, Vol. 2011, Issue 1, *OECD Publishing*.

Olsen, Øystein (2013). Macroprudential Regulation and Monetary Policy, *Speech at the Centre for Monetary Economics (CME)/BI Norwegian Business School*, Oslo, 7 October 2013.

Osiński, Jacek (2013). Institutional Needs for Optimal Macroprudential Arrangements. In: '*Macroprudential Frameworks in Asia*', (eds.) Steven Barnett, Rodolfo Main, *International Monetary Fund*, Washington, DC.

Ozkan, F. Gulcin, Unsal, D. Filiz (2014). On the Use of Monetary and Macroprudential Policies for Small Open Economies, *IMF Working Papers*, No. 112.

Reifschneider, David, Williams, John C. (2000). Three Lessons for Monetary Policy in a Low-Inflation Era, *Journal of Money, Credit and Banking*, Vol. 32, No. 4, Part 2.

Reinert, Kenneth A., Rajan, Ramkishen S. (2009). The Princeton Encyclopedia of the World Economy, *Princeton University Press*.

Rhu, Hoo-Kyu (2011). Macroprudential Policy Framework, *BIS Paper*, No. 60.

Rochet, Jean-Charles (2008). Liquidity Regulation and the Lender of Last Resort, *Banque de France Financial Stability Review*, No. 11.

Roger, Scott, Vlček, Jan (2011). Macroeconomic Costs of Higher Bank Capital and Liquidity Requirements, *IMF Working Paper*, No. 103.

Rogoff, Kenneth (1985). The Optimal Degree of Commitment to an Intermediate Monetary Target, *Quarterly Journal of Economics*, Vol. 100.

Rubio, Margarita, Carrasco-Gallego, José A. (2014). Macroprudential and Monetary Policies: Implications for Financial Stability and Welfare, *Journal of Banking & Finance*, Vol. 49.

Ruser, Alexander (2015). By the Markets, of the Markets, for the Markets? Technocratic Decision Making and the Hollowing Out of Democracy, *Global*

Policy Special Issue: "Changing the European Debate: A Rollback of Democracy, Vol. 6, Issue Supplement S1.

Scalia, Antonio, Longoni, Sergio, Rosolin, Tiziana (2013). The Net Stable Funding Ratio and Banks' Participation in Monetary Policy Operations: Some Evidence for the Euro Area, *Banca d'Italia Occasional Paper*, No. 195.

Schmitz, Stefan W. (2013). The Impact of the Liquidity Coverage Ratio (LCR) on the Implementation of Monetary Policy, *Economic Notes, Review of Banking, Finance, and Monetary Economics*, Vol. 42, No. 2.

Shin, Hyun Song (2015). Macroprudential Tools, Their Limits and Their Connection with Monetary Policy. *Panel Remarks at IMF Spring Meeting event: 'Rethinking Macro Policy III: Progress or Confusion?'*, Washington, DC, 15 April 2015.

Siklos, Pierre L., Werner, Thomas, Bohl, Martin T. (2004). Asset Prices in Taylor Rules: Specification, Estimation, and Policy Implications for the ECB, *Bundesbank Discussion Paper Series 1: Economic Studies*, No. 22/2004.

Smets, Frank, Christoffel, Kai, Coenen, Günter, Motto, Roberto, Rostagno Massimo (2010). DSGE Models and Their Use at the ECB, *SERIEs*, Vol. 1, Issue 1–2.

Smets, Frank, Wouters, Raf (2004). Forecasting with a Bayesian DSGE Model: An Application to the Euro Area, *Journal of Common Market Studies*, Vo. 42, No. 4.

Spencer, Grant (2014). Coordination of Monetary Policy and Macro-prudential Policy, *Speech Held at the Credit Suisse Asian Investment Conference*, Hong Kong, 27 March 2014.

Suh, Hyunduk (2012). Macroprudential Policy: Its Effects and Relationship to Monetary Policy, *Federal Reserve Bank of Philadelphia Working Paper*, No. 12–28.

Taylor, John B. (2009). The Financial Crisis and the Policy Responses: An Empirical Analysis of What Went Wrong, *NBER Working Paper Series*, No. 14631.

Tor, Avishalom, Aviram, Amitai (2004). Overcoming Impediments to Information Sharing, *Alabama Law Review*, Vol. 55, No. 2.

Trichet, Jean-Claude (2005). Asset Price Bubbles and Their Implications for Monetary Policy and Financial Stability. In: '*Asset Price Bubbles: The Implications for Monetary, Regulatory, and International Policies*', (eds.) William C. Hunter, George G. Kaufman, Michael Pomerleano, *The MIT Press*, Cambridge.

Tröger, Tobias H. (2015). Regulatory Influence on Market Conditions in the Banking Union: The Cases of Macro-prudential Instruments and the Bail-in Tool, *European Business Organization Law Review*, Vol. 15, Issue 3.

Tucker, Paul (2016). Macroprudential Policy Regimes. In: *"Progress and Confusion: The State of Macroeconomic Policy"*, (eds.) Olivier Blanchard, Raghuram Rajan, Kenneth Rogoff, Lawrence H. Summers, *The MIT Press.*

Ueda, Kenichi, Valencia, Fabián (2014). Central Bank Independence and Macroprudential Regulation, *Economics Letters*, Vol. 125, No. 2.

Unsal, D. Filiz (2013). Capital Flows and Financial Stability: Monetary Policy and Macroprudential Responses, *International Journal of Central Banking*, Vol. 9, No. 1.

Visco, Ignazio (2012). Key Issues for the Success of Macroprudential Policies, *BIS Papers*, No. 60.

Volz, Ulrich (2015). Navigating the Trilemma: Central Banking in East Asia Between Inflation Targeting, Exchange-Rate Management and Guarding Financial Stability. In: '*Central Banking and Financial Stability in East Asia*', (eds.) Frank Rövekamp, Moritz Bälz, Hanns Günther Hilpert, *Springer International Publishing*, Cham.

Wadhvani, Sushil (2014). Inflation Targeting, Capital Requirements and 'Leaning Against the Wind': Some Comments. In: '*Twenty Years of Inflation Targeting Lessons Learned and Future Prospects*', (eds.) David Cobham, Øyvind Eitrheim, Stefan Gerlach, Jan F. Qvigstad, *Cambridge University Press.*

Walsh, Carl E. (2010). Monetary Theory and Policy, *The MIT Press,* Cambridge.

White, Lawrence H. (2009). Federal Reserve Policy and the Housing Bubble, *The Cato Journal*, Vol. 29, Issue 1.

Wong, Eric, Fong, Tom, Li, Ka-fai Choi, Henry (2011). Loan-to-Value Ratio as a Macroprudential Tools – Hong-Kong's Experience and Cross-Country Evidence, *HKMA Working Paper*, No. 01/2011.

Yellen, Janet L. (2010). Macroprudential Supervision and Monetary Policy in the Post-crisis World, *Speech Held at the Annual Meeting of the National Association for Business Economics*, Denver, 11 October 2010.

Yeşin, Pınar (2013). Foreign Currency Loans and Systemic Risk in Europe, *Federal Reserve Bank of St. Louis Review*, May/June.

CHAPTER 5

The Legal Interaction in the EU Institutional Framework

5.1 Defining the Legal Interaction

There is a general consensus among law and economics scholars that institutions in general, and the legal system in particular, are fundamental drivers of economic development.[1] In the words of Nobel laureate Douglass North, institutions represents 'the rules of the game in a society, or, more formally, humanly devised constraints that shape human interaction'.[2] The quality of these institutions[3] ensures the performance of economic dynamics in any given market, as they set up infrastructures and boundaries within which market players interact.

The construction of efficient institutions is essential for a modern economy. This is particularly the case in finance, where the establishment of a rule-bound architecture is a necessary precondition for the functioning of

[1] The law and economics analysis of the institutions lies at the heart of 'Institutional Economics' which pays attention to the relationship between institutions, economics, and public policies. Institutional Economics considers the role of the law in the society as the rules frame the economic, political, and social interactions in the societal order, while economic performances are considered as strictly interdependent on the institutional arrangements set by law. On this topic, inter alia, see Drobak (2008), pp. 1–11; Williamson (2000), pp. 595–613; Posner (1993), pp. 73–87; Coase (1984), pp. 229–231; North (1990), pp. 3–11; Eggertsson (1990), pp. 59–82. For a historical survey of the Institutional Economics, see Hodgson (2004). For a critical review of the relevant literature, see Dellepiane-Avellaneda (2009), pp. 195–224; Madema and Mercuro (2006), pp. 208–283.

[2] North (1990), p. 3.

[3] For a quantitative analysis, see Law and Azman-Saini (2008).

L. Amorello, *Macroprudential Banking Supervision & Monetary Policy*, https://doi.org/10.1007/978-3-319-94156-1_5

the financial system as a whole.[4] This argument exposes a familiar inextricable relationship between law, finance, and market participants.[5] The very existence of financial markets depends upon the legal order that shapes markets' interactions and financial institutions. This means that in the same way a contractual relationship cannot be enforced outside the law, so banks and all other financial institutions cannot perform their own activities without legal formalization. The law creates the market, along with the financial institutions and infrastructure, and allows for the vindication of contractual commitments among financial counterparties.[6]

But the law can be understood as playing an even more significant role in modeling of the financial system. To the extent that financial markets are characterized by transaction costs, market failures, and inherent instability,[7] the law shapes the necessary arrangements that can possibly mitigate these market failures. The law is capable to ensure this function either by turning policy signals into regulatory standards that market participants are required to follow, or by giving market players incentives and new opportunities to adjust their behaviors.[8] Hence, the law generates the financial system not only because it sets the stage for market interactions but also because it influences directly static features and dynamic behaviors of financial agents by concretizing public policies.[9]

In both cases, the legal architecture must ensure both the policymaking processes and the oversight of the follow-up implementation. And where different policies are capable to affect the same variables, as for the case of monetary and macroprudential policies, the legal construction of the related frameworks must promote policy coherence and coordination in

[4] Inter alia, see Drobak (1998), pp. 98–104. See also IBRD, WB, IMF (2005), p. 223.

[5] Bini Smaghi (2007). An ever-growing scholarship exists on this relationship. For some examples, cf. La Porta, Lopez-de-Manes, Shleifer, and Vishny (2002), pp. 1147–1170; Coffee (2001), pp. 1–82.

[6] Pistor (2013), pp. 317–318.

[7] For details on the inherent criticalities of the financial system and their relationship with regulation, see Moloney (2014), pp. 1–8. For an overview of the specific inefficiencies and market failure in Europe, see also the Commission Staff Working Document *Economic Review of the Financial Regulation Agenda* accompanying the document Communication from the Commission to the European Parliament, the Council and the European Economic and Social Committee, and the Committee of the Regions—A reformed financial sector for Europe (COM(2014) 279 final).

[8] See Karmann and Enkhzaya (2006), p. 33.

[9] See Nijsen (2008), pp. 27–40.

order to ensure the stability of the system. It is precisely at this point that an economic interaction needs to become 'legal'.

In line with these premises, the following chapter explores the legal architecture of monetary and macroprudential policies, now deemed as intertwined frameworks. The aim is to figure out whether, and to what extent, the cross side effects of two policies have been acknowledged in drafting the relevant EU texts, and, thus, whether an interaction between them may be found not only in the economic theory but also in the settings of EU law.

5.1.1 *Understanding the Interaction: Why 'Legal'?*

So far we have used the term 'interaction' to portray the economic rapprochement between monetary policy and macroprudential policy. The convergence of the economic dynamics in affecting the same macroeconomic variables is the theoretical foundation upon which the legal dimension of the two policy areas can be redefined. In other words, the cross side effects of monetary and macroprudential policies would imply not only that a considerable degree of coordination is needed in order to ensure high efficiency in the policies' conduct but also the recognition of these effects should inform the construction of the rules governing the policy regimes.[10]

As a result, in order to preserve the credibility of each policy field in achieving its intermediate and ultimate objectives and facilitate policy coordination, the economic interactions underlying the macroprudential and monetary policies must be reflected in the law. Not only the overall legal framework of these areas should be capable to set a harmonized institutional architecture maximizing the policy synergies,[11] but it should also permit to set out a number of coherent strategies aimed at tackling the array of financial imbalances and achieving non-conflicting macroeconomic outcomes.[12]

The occasion for reflecting on this subject is given by the current implementation of the EU macroprudential regime. In light of the SSM operationalization, and because of the adoption of very low interest rates and

[10] For a conceptualization of policy regimes as the governing arrangements for addressing policy problems, inter alia, see May and Jochim (2013), pp. 426–452.

[11] IMF (2013a), p. 19.

[12] See Heath (2014), pp. 1107–1110.

unconventional monetary policies that may possibly result in systemic imbalances, the macroprudential policy agenda has become pivotal in the EU.[13] As argued in the previous chapters, the construction of the European macroprudential regime follows a bottom-up structure where national authorities having macroprudential responsibilities are at the forefront in the regulatory interventions, while the ECB in its capacity of banking supervisor retains a supplementary role for the case of inaction or delay.

Having only soft-law measures at disposal, the ESRB is committed to overseeing systemic risks in the financial markets, with the peculiar responsibility to address recommendations and/or early warnings to other public authorities, if deemed necessary.[14] By contrast, the ECB Governing Council is fully responsible for the monetary policy decisions adopted within the ESCB, while national central banks are only the operational agents involved in their factual implementation.

However, due to the inherent cross dynamics affecting each other's policy, we want to point out that these institutional frameworks are not isolated. As noted in the de Larosière Report,

> Overall cooperation between monetary and regulatory authorities will have to be strengthened, with a view to defining and implementing the policy-mix that can best maintain a stable and balanced macro-economic framework. In this context, it will be important for the ECB to become more involved in over-seeing the macro-prudential aspects of banking activities.[15]

Against this backdrop, the institutional layers of the ESCB and SSM, as defined in terms of governance arrangements and policy tools, have been highly influenced by the economic interaction of the two policies. And because of the need to set out a coherent action aimed at targeting price stability on the one side, and countering systemic risks on the other, the legal settings of the two policy areas are constructed as to reflect, at least partly, this necessity. However, the scale of this legal interaction is not constant. On the contrary, it can diverge due to a number of factors, the most relevant of which are (1) differences in the economic cycles and (2) political preferences and considerations.

Different movements in the financial and business cycles may require a weaker stringency of the legal interaction so as to guarantee some

[13] For a general overview on the EU macroprudential policy agenda and its relationship to monetary policy, see Constâncio (2015).

[14] For details on the role of the ESRB, see *supra* at notes 395–407.

[15] de Larosière Report (2009), p. 15.

sort of 'enhanced flexibility' in the operationalization of the two policies. Moreover, political inputs underpinning the consolidation of the banking supervisory functions may provide different outcomes with respect to the legal frame of the rapprochement between monetary and macroprudential policies.

5.1.2 *Economic Cycles and Legal Constraints*

Before and after the financial burst of 2007–8, the EU countries took serious steps to consolidate their economic and fiscal policies,[16] while the introduction of the Euro, along with the implementation of structural and investment funds of the EU,[17] greatly contributed, to adjust the economic cycles of EU Member States.[18] Due to these efforts, the fluctuations of countries' business cycles over the last two decades have become highly synchronized.[19]

Today differences between countries appear negligible, while considerable correlation can be found in the transmission of shocks across the Euro area.[20] This high degree of business cycles' synchronization helps the ECB to effectively adopt its policy stances, as it ensures homogeneity in the transmission mechanism of monetary policy across the whole Euro area.[21]

[16] For an interesting overview of economic and fiscal reforms put in place by EU Member States, see Grüner (2013), No. 487.

[17] The structural and the investment funds are funds established in the EU to support the economic, social, and territorial cohesion of the European area, as particularly laid down in Article 3 of the TEU and Article 174 of the TFEU, with the aim of generating sustainable and inclusive growth. These funds consist of the European Regional Development Fund (ERDF), the European Social Fund (ESF), the Cohesion Fund (CF), the European Agricultural Fund for Rural Development (EAFRD), and the European Maritime and Fisheries Fund (EMFF). The structural and cohesion policy is a central policy area of the EU and has substantially contributed thus far towards the integration of the EU internal market. For details on this topic, see Bachtler, Mendez, and Wishlade (2016); Baun and Marek (2014).

[18] See Barrell, Gottschalk, Holland, Khoman, Liadze, and Pomerantz (2008).

[19] See Afonso and Sequeira (2010). However, after the financial crisis, structural differences across the Euro area have increased. This has created imbalances in the Euro area and asymmetric shocks have become material. Against this backdrop, the synchronized business cycle of the EU has been heavily affected, and divergences can be found now in the monetary policy transmission across EU countries. For empirical evidences, see Mandler, Scharnagl, and Volz (2016), pp. 1–24.

[20] Giannone, Lenza, and Reichlin (2009), p. 7.

[21] Afonso and Sequeira (2010), p. 21.

By contrast, the fluctuations of financial cycles in the EU are not as much aligned. Macroeconomic data suggest the existence of significant differences in the financial cycles of EU Member States.[22] This heterogeneity is primarily due to the domestic nature of the predominant factors driving the financial sector's cyclical fluctuations, namely, the real estate markets, mortgages, and tax policies.[23]

These divergences entail that the EU countries' financial cycles and the corresponding business cycles are not aligned either. In this respect, the economic literature finds non-negligible differences in the duration of business and financial cycles,[24] as well as in the amplitude of their swings and contractions.[25] In view of this, we may assume that the regulatory construction of macroprudential supervision cannot completely match the EU architecture established for monetary policy. These cycles' divergences require lawmakers to take full account of the divergent architecture of financial supervisory institutions and the diverging wealth and income structure of EU Member States, along with the potential for cross-country movements of financial cycles' fluctuations.[26]

The European legal construction of macroprudential supervision and monetary policy needs to reflect these divergences in the synchronization of the related cycles.[27] While the high degree of homogeneity in business cycles across EU countries should allow for a unified conduct of monetary policy by the apex of the system,[28] the heterogeneous nature of the financial cycles should be mostly reflected in a decentralized supervisory regime that may best capture the country-level cyclical movements of financial variables. And this is why the CRR/CRD IV package and, broadly speaking, the overall EU macroprudential framework have acknowledged, as shown in the previous chapters, a bottom-up approach in assigning supervisory tasks and responsibilities.

[22] Inter alia, see Merler (2015).

[23] Houben and Kakes (2013), p. 12.

[24] See Drehmann, Borio, and Tsatsaronis (2012), pp. 18–19. See also Borio (2012), pp. 3–4.

[25] Drehmann, Borio, and Tsatsaronis (2012), pp. 19–20.

[26] Idem, p. 3.

[27] Houben and Kakes (2013), p. 23.

[28] As argued by Constancio (2014), 'Tailoring monetary policy decisions to specific sectoral or regional differences in credit or asset price developments might have inappropriate side effects in other areas.'

This consideration also leads us to take a closer look at the nature of the relationship between the law and the two policies at stake. Although the objectives of monetary and macroprudential policies are premises upon which reconstructing the related frameworks under a legal perspective, we can argue that a deeper understanding of the dynamics establishing the two institutional structures can be gained by interpreting the relevant laws and regulations as a set of *legal constraints* for the economic cycles.[29]

This perspective suggests that the role of the law is to create a resilient 'containment cage' that allows to restrain the credit cycles and mitigate its negative externalities. The whole legal architecture can therefore be recognized as a unified construction aimed at containing the macroeconomic externalities arising from the variations of the business and financial cycles, architecture which should reflect national and transnational peculiarities of their swings, while enabling policymakers to counter expectable spillovers. National peculiarities must not undermine the path towards a full harmonization of banking regulation across the EU,[30] and must be addressed in a way that does not impinge on the level playing field of financial institutions.

Against this backdrop, our analysis should now turn on the functional role of the law in the policy areas at stake. This functional role may read as follows: the set of *legal constraints* determines how, and to what extent, monetary and macroprudential instruments affect the economy.[31] They do so by creating separate rule-based frameworks aimed at ensuring the orderly management of the corresponding economic cycles. Despite these frameworks are heavily bound by objectives, instruments, and tasks assigned to the competent bodies, they are nonetheless flexible enough to challenge the disruptive fluctuations that may arise.[32]

[29] A similar understanding of the relationship between legal structure and monetary policy is offered by Cecchetti (1999).

[30] Eidenberger, Liebeg, Schmitz, Seliger, Sigmund, Steiner, Strobl, and Ub (2014), p. 85.

[31] For example, see Cheun, von Köppen-Mertes, and Weller (2009). The authors offer an interesting assessment on the impact of the legal constraints on the operational and collateral frameworks of the FED, of the Eurosystem, and of the Bank of England. In particular, the performance of the three central banks is strictly related to the specific characteristics of the legal frameworks of their monetary policy operations.

[32] This flexibility is inherent in the regulatory construction of the two policies. In fact, the regulatory acts issued by both the central banks and the macroprudential authorities theoretically permit to quickly react to negative macroeconomic circumstances by adjusting their strategies and/or adopting tools that may better target the policy objectives. On the one hand, the issuance in 2015 of quantitative easing by the ECB is one example of this flexibility

And, albeit autonomous, these frameworks are closely interrelated: where cyclical movements of the financial and business cycles generate cross side effects, the *legal constraints* permit to dampen the related negative externalities while preserving a consistent balance between the policy objectives. The legal interaction of monetary and macroprudential policies shall accommodate the two policies within a unified institutional system, which potentially addresses the variations featuring the synchronized path of the business cycles and the heterogonous nature of the country-level financial cycles, along with the associated spillover effects, in a timely and consistent manner.

5.1.3 *Lawmakers, Central Bankers, and the Primary Law*

The legal interaction of monetary and macroprudential policies is not only affected by the degree of heterogeneity of the economic cycles. Other relevant elements are in fact constitutional boundaries and the political pressures.[33]

While over the last decades monetary policy has achieved full independence from any political influence in its policymaking process, the macroprudential dimension is heavily politicized. This is due not only to the fact that systemic risks' mitigation occasionally requires coordination with fiscal policy, and therefore with the government.[34] But also, and more importantly, this is related to the political tensions that arise from the distributional effects of some macroprudential instruments.[35]

An example may illustrate this point. Let's assume we are in the upswing of the financial cycle, and a macroprudential tool, such as an LTV cap, needs to be implemented as to mitigate the build-up of real estate prices. Although strictly required on the grounds of the available data, this instrument can be contested by the government, as it may appear unnecessary at that stage of the financial cycle due to the perceived low risks.[36]

The political and societal desire in a boom phase towards an increase of housing for special groups, such as families and young couples, might

in the monetary policy framework. On the other hand, the national flexibility measures that national macroprudential authorities may adopt pursuant to article of Art. 458 CRR are examples of flexibility in the macroprudential architecture.

[33] For details, see Chwieroth and Danielsson (2013).

[34] See *supra* at notes 1106–1107.

[35] Baker (2015), p. 26. See also IMF (2012), p. 5.

[36] Baker, Andrew (2015), p. 19.

constitute a decisive counterforce to the introduction of such tool. The fierce opposition of government and political forces against the macroprudential measure may eventually cause the macroprudential authority to refrain from any intervention, thereby contributing to the dangerous procyclical trend.

This problem is dramatized even further by the difficulties to create a public consensus on macroprudential regulation.[37] In good times, people may not be willing to support the introduction of regulatory instruments that may curb investment opportunities and short-term economic growth.[38] The macroprudential authority may be unwilling to constrain the supply and/or demand of credit, even though this would be socially optimal at the present stage of the financial cycle.[39]

The politicization of macroprudential regulation represents a threat for the statutory independence assigned to the authority in charge of macroprudential policy. As a result, a working macroprudential policy necessarily entails the adoption of some regulatory and institutional arrangements capable to diminish—to the extent possible—the risk of politicization of the agency's technical decisions.[40] This can be done by adopting one of the institutional models that may best capture the policymaking independence and the policy officers' autonomy. For instance, the reliance on the central bank for the conduct of macroprudential strategies may help mitigate this conundrum, should the monetary authority be explicitly entrusted with high levels of independence from external pressures.[41]

This choice is also about politics and may reflect the political preferences on the institutional settings of administrative authorities. Because of this, the underpinnings of the *legal interaction* shall take into account the wide gradation of political involvement that policymakers consider appropriate at any point in time. Accordingly, an ample heterogeneity in the monetary/macroprudential frameworks can be recognized worldwide, as national and supranational regulators used to place different weights on these political influences.

By the same token, the construction of the macroprudential supervisory regime, and, in turn, the interaction with the central bank's operating

[37] See Idem, p. 27.
[38] See Chwieroth and Danielsson (2013).
[39] See IMF (2012), p. 19.
[40] See ESRB (2014b), p. 2. See also Kohn (2015).
[41] For a critical appraisal, see Duff (2014), pp. 183–220.

framework, is largely bound by the constitutional constraints set by the primary law. The primary law sets the limits within which the legislature can delegate power to public authorities, as well as the boundaries of policy objectives, tasks, and powers assigned to public bodies.[42] This is particularly the case for monetary and the macroprudential bodies in the EU. In the legal construction of these policy frameworks, the operational independence of the ECB and of other specialized authorities is a function of how the constitutional constraints are structured as to discipline their statutory actions.[43]

The degree of institutional independence is strictly related to constitutional preferences on the delegation of powers to the administrative bodies. The autonomy of an institutional body largely depends on the specific set of powers, tools, and tasks the legislature can legitimately delegate by law due in view of the constitutional constraints.[44] When the delegation of powers—such as the macroprudential ones—entails the assignment of tasks and instruments that may have significant distributional effects for the entire community, lawmakers must carefully assess the constitutionality of this delegation and its legitimacy in view of the primary law. The legal construction of the related framework will reflect this constitutional tension, while the range of tools, tasks, and powers available to the relevant authority will be restricted accordingly.[45]

[42] For a comparative account on the delegation of powers to public authorities and on the constitutional limits, see Caranta, Andenas, and Fairgrieve (Eds.), in particular, Chaps. 2 (France) and 3 (Germany). For a discussion on the central role that constitutions play in delegating powers to independent bodies, see Lawson (1999), pp. 23–29.

[43] For an in-depth analysis of the constitutional limits imposed by the Treaty to EU public authorities, see Weatherill (2012), pp. 570–582. With respect to the establishment of the ESAs, in particular, Van Cleynenbruegel (2014), p. 81, argues that it reflects a constitutional delegation upward from the Member States to an intermediate supranational body that operates firmly within the legal space established by the EU Treaties.

[44] It is generally argued that governments delegate powers in order to reduce decision-making costs and enhance the credibility of their policies. For an empirical assessment of this argument, see Gilardi (2002), pp. 873–879.

[45] A relevant problem in the past regarding this topic was related to the rules governing the delegation of powers to public authorities in accordance with the EU Treaty. Starting from the well-known '*Meroni case*' (*Meroni & Co., Industrie Metallurgiche, SpA v High Authority of the European Coal and Steel Community* (Case 9–56)), the delegation of powers to an agency could relate only to clearly defined executive powers, while the delegation of broad discretionary powers was considered not permissible. Consistently with the Romano case (*Giuseppe Romano v Institut national d'assurance maladie-invalidité* (Case 98/80)), under the Union law it was deemed illegitimate for a body being empowered by the Council to

The constitutional boundaries have clear implications for the legal design of the macroprudential framework as well as for its interaction with monetary policy. The primary law influences the choice of the institutional model to be adopted.[46] Moreover, macroprudential and monetary policies may impinge upon the legitimacy of the general legal structure in achieving socially optimal outcomes. The following example can better clarify this assumption.

Let's assume that the constitution of one country does not permit to delegate the assignment of real estate instruments—that is, LTV, LTI, or DTI caps—to the authority entrusted with macroprudential powers. Instead, the adoption of these instruments is only possible by an act of the Parliament, which is unwilling however to propose these tools for political opportunism, as they can fiercely restrain the housing market, affecting low-income citizens and voters.[47]

In this scenario, the macroprudential authority has little room for maneuver to constrain the excessive growth of the real estate sector in boom times. Moreover, the constitutional constraints on the regulatory instruments could pressure the central bank to adopt a suboptimal policy stance—for example, by rising up interest rates—in order to contain the spillover effects meanwhile building up in the housing market.[48]

In this example the economic interaction does not work properly, since the legal framework that would ensure monetary and macroprudential policies to cooperate consistently is flawed due to constitutional constraints.

adopt acts having the force of law. However, this strong stance of the European jurisprudence was attenuated in the case 'United Kingdom of Great Britain and Northern Ireland v European Parliament and Council of the European Union' (C-270/12), where the ECJ has argued that a public body established under the Treaty with precisely delineated powers and amenable to judicial review in the light of the objectives established by the delegating authority can be legally established. For the ECJ, only a delegation of powers with a very large measure of discretion will be incompatible with the Treaty (see para 52–54). Instead, the EU legislature—pursuant to Article 114 TFEU—may 'delegate to a Union body, office or agency powers for the implementation of the harmonisation sought', where in particular 'the measures to be adopted are dependent on specific professional and technical expertise and the ability of such a body to respond swiftly and appropriately (para 105)'. For a discussion on the delegation of powers allowed by the Treaty with respect to the ESAs, see Ferran (2015), pp. 81–82; Scholten and van Rijsbergen (2014), pp. 389–405.

[46] See Egawa, Otani, and Sakiyama (2015), pp. 15–16.

[47] This is the case of those countries where macroprudential rules can be only enacted with the approval of the Parliament or where macroprudential policy impinges on policy areas that remain within the government's control. For details, see IMF (2013b), p. 18.

[48] Inter alia, see IMF (2012), p. 19. See also Kohn (2015).

This means that when dealing with the legal construction of the macroprudential supervisory regime, variations in the constitutional boundaries largely affect the related regulatory framework, and this, in turn, may impair the socially optimal rapprochement of monetary and macroprudential actions.[49]

The boundaries set by the primary law in Europe have led the ECB and national central banks, at the outset of the financial crisis, to struggle for integrating macroprudential policies under their roofs.[50] Central bankers have acted as a powerful force in the reorganization of financial supervision in the EU: their concerns on the relationship between monetary policy and financial stability have greatly influenced the structural and institutional contexts in which the macroprudential policies have been operationalized across Europe.[51]

The control over macroprudential instruments have been strongly advocated by central bankers whose policy preferences favored the establishment of a central bank's leading role in the conduct of macroprudential tasks. The resulting decentralized nature of the macroprudential policy framework in the EU can be deemed as an institutional compromise between lawmakers and central bankers within the limits imposed by the EU Treaties.

5.2 The Legal Interaction in the EU Regulatory Architecture

After considering the cross side effects of monetary and macroprudential policies introducing the major factors influencing the regulatory structure of the policy interaction, we turn our attention to how the legal interaction is currently constrained within the EU institutional framework. The purpose of this section is to introduce a dynamic description of how the rapprochement between macroprudential and monetary policies operates and what economic consequences—in terms of policies' efficiency—the resultant legal construction might have.

[49] A similar argument is developed with respect to US Fed's macroprudential reforms by Calomiris (2010). More precisely, the author discusses the opinion shared by many that expanding the role of the Fed as macroprudential supervisor would determine negative outcomes, since it would worsen the politicization vulnerability of the Fed.

[50] For an in-depth analysis of the role played by central banks in the process of creating the EU macroprudential framework, see McPhilemy (2016), pp. 526–544.

[51] Idem, p. 529.

The European institutional model setting up this interaction represents a historical ***unicum***.[52] The nature of the ESCB as a cross-border central banking system, along with the complex layer of multiple supervisory authorities, makes the EU legal interaction a major field of research within the institutional law of the European Monetary and Banking Union.[53] The complexity of the policies' rapprochement is principally due to the bottom-up structure of the macroprudential supervision tasks, where national competent authorities move first. This institutional set-up has to fit within a central banking architecture which is basically top-down, as the ECB board is the body primarily responsible of monetary policy due to its hierarchical dominance within the ESCB.

The specialty of the EU legal interaction can be well understood by looking at the quadripartite relationships[54] settled amid the ESCB, the ESRB, the ESAs, and national competent authorities. In this perspective, the primary and secondary EU legislations, along with the EU soft-law sources,[55] provide for a plethora of arrangements and instruments capable to ensure a positive degree of consistency and coordination in the joint policy action.

The cross side effects of monetary and macroprudential policies are meant to be jointly managed by these bodies, as the legal framework so assembled is intended to synchronize the inter-level governance of policies' spillovers, and tie the legal constraints of business and financial cycles together.

5.2.1 The Institutional Patterns of the Relevant Authorities After the Crisis

Not surprisingly, the EU institutional architecture establishing the interaction between monetary and macroprudential policies is intimately dependent on the economic cycles of EU Members States and on political considerations. On the one hand, the lack of synchronization between business and financial cycles at the EU level, along with the national

[52] Broadly speaking, one can also argue that the entire European Monetary and Banking Union represent a worldwide ***unicum*** for its institutional construction. This opinion is shared, inter alia, by Farina and Tamborini (2001), at pp. 8–9; Tamborini (2004), p. 153.

[53] For more details on the institutional law of the Banking Union, see Theissen (2014); Busch and Ferrarini (eds.) (2015).

[54] For a broad overview on this relationship, see Schoenmaker (2012).

[55] We refer, in particular, to the ESRB recommendations.

peculiarities featuring the EU Member States' financial cycles, has been one of the reasons for building an institutional architecture based on multiple supervisory layers.

On the other hand, political considerations relative to the distributional effects of macroprudential policy caused a large array of instruments to be retained at the national level. Due to these economic and political constraints, the institutional model adopted by the EU architects, after the 2007 financial crisis, represents a hybrid model, whose legal settings share some elements with the aforementioned partial-integration and full-integration models.

The resulting legal interaction is entrenched within a complex framework where multiple bodies—at national and EU levels—are required to harmonize their actions, as to achieve consistency, and avoid potential conflict of interests, in an environment of divergent economic cycles and conservative political bias. The aim of this section is to explain how, and to what extent, the arrangements defined in the EU Treaties and in the EU legislation are capable to provide a consistent framework where the monetary policy and the macroprudential policy may operate without conflicting.[56]

As explained in the previous chapters, the ESCB is unambiguously entrusted with the primary objective of preserving price stability.[57] This primary objective regarding monetary policy is followed by a reference to other objectives, which are subordinated to the achievement of the former. Should a conflict occur between the price stability objective and the other objectives, the latter must prevail.[58]

[56] The relevance of this analysis is clearly acknowledged in Angelini, Neri, and Panetta (2011), at pp. 6–7.

[57] As already noted the overriding importance of price stability is clearly indicated in Article 119(2) and Article 219(1) TFEU, and it is further reiterated in Article 127(1) and 282(2) TFEU. For an in-depth analysis of these Articles with respect to the price stability objective, in particular, see Siekmann (ed.) (2013), pp. 70–77; Waldhoff (2013), pp. 277–285. It must be noted that price stability is not only the primary objective of the ESCB, but it constitutes an overriding objective of the Union, pursuant to Article 119(2) and Article 119(3) TFEU. For details, see Lastra (2015), p. 254.

[58] Teivanen (1997), p. 61. It must be noted, however, that for quite some time in the past, price stability, growth, and full unemployment were considered objectives having the same importance. For details, see Siekmann (2015), at note 35.

With the entry into force of the TFEU, this list of objective includes financial stability.[59] As laid down in Articles 127(5) TFEU and 3(3) of the ESCB Statute, the ESCB shall 'Contribute to the smooth conduct of policies pursued by competent authorities relating to prudential supervision of credit institutions and the stability of the financial system'. The formulation of these Articles implies that financial stability must be pursued primarily by national competent authorities of Member States. The role of the ESCB is only limited to a general contribution in the smooth conduct of macroprudential policies which are mostly assigned to national competent authorities.

These articles of the EU primary law set a solid basis to define and develop the legal interaction between monetary and macroprudential, in view of the whole institutional architecture. The legal relevance of these provisions lies in the word 'contribute', which reveals a double meaning: not only the ESCB should assist national competent authorities in charge of macroprudential policy at national and European levels in the achievement of the financial stability objective, but also it should meet its macroprudential supporting goal in a way that does not conflict with maintaining price stability across the EU. The EU primary law therefore acknowledges a statutory hierarchy of objectives within the ESCB, where price stability and financial stability are not equally important.[60]

This does not mean that the ESCB may neglect the macroprudential objective. The recognition by the TFEU of a role for the ESCB in contributing to financial stability implies that the relationship between price stability and financial stability cannot be underrated.[61] This wording in

[59] Lastra (2015), p. 254, argues that the objective of financial stability indeed was not considered at the time of the adoption of the Maastricht Treaty as relevant as the price stability objective. However, with the burst of the financial crisis, the importance of this objective was reconsidered in light of the negative spillovers that systemic events may have on the internal market. In this context, the Eurosystem Mission Statement clearly states that the aim of the ESCB is to safeguard financial stability and promote European financial integration. The Governing Council of the ECB formulated the Eurosystem's mission statement as follows: 'We in the Eurosystem have as our primary objective the maintenance of price stability for the common good. Acting also as a leading financial authority, we aim to safeguard financial stability and promote European financial integration.' For details, see http://www.ecb.int/ ecb/orga/escb/html/mission/ eurosys.en.html.

[60] For details on the hierarchy of objectives assigned to the ESCB, see Siekmann (2015), p. 49. See also Lenihan (2008), pp. 31–32; Dutzler (2003), p. 35; Zilioli and Selmayr (2001), p. 26; Louis (1995), p. 58; Smits (1997), p. 399.

[61] Gianviti (2010), p. 474; Siekmann (2015), p. 49.

fact implicitly recognizes that serious events of financial instability may affect the implementation of monetary policy, while the maintenance of a sound environment of price stability helps reduce risks to financial stability.[62]

As a result, the objective of safeguarding the stability of the financial system, although subordinated to price stability, is necessarily complementary to it. The ESCB should favor a financial environment allowing for the smooth conduct of monetary policy and macroprudential supervision, where the target of countering system risks becomes instrumental in preserving price stability.[63]

These legal foundations raise a fundamental issue. If the ESCB needs to contribute to the smooth conduct of macroprudential policies pursued by competent authorities at the national level, we need to determine how national competent authorities may interrelate with the ESCB, and, in addition, to what extent they are instrumental in the interaction of monetary and macroprudential policies.

At first glance, in order to determine this interaction, it is worth noting that national authorities in charge of the EU macroprudential policy can be grouped in two different layers. On the one hand, the ECB—in its SSM functions—along with the ESRB constitutes an 'EU macroprudential layer'. On the other hand, the national supervisory authorities within the SSM, and, whether set up, the national macroprudential committees, form a 'national macroprudential layer'.

With respect to the relationship between the ECB (in its monetary policy functions) and the ESRB, the EU macroprudential layer is designed by law under a partial-integration model. The establishment of the ESRB as a separate community body responsible for contributing to the harmonization of macroprudential policies and regulatory acts, in accordance with Article 114 TFEU, is dependent upon the tasks specifically assigned to the ECB on the basis of Article 127(6) TFEU for the operational functioning of the ESRB. In line with this Article, the ECB shall contribute to the effective macroprudential oversight of the EU financial system by providing analytical, statistical, administrative, and logistical support to the

[62] Manger-Nestler (2013), p. 37.

[63] See Zilioli (2013). This is consistent with the suggestions upheld by the de Larosière Report, according to which the ESCB has a key role to play in macroprudential oversight. See de Larosière Report, p. 44. For an in-depth survey of the complementarity of financial stability to price stability, see Cukierman (2011), pp. 87–90.

ESRB, and also drawing on technical advice from national central banks and supervisors.[64]

Article 127(6) TFEU constitutes the legal basis for the conferral on the ECB of the macroprudential tasks specified in Article 5 of Council Regulation (EU) No. 1024/2013, and these additional assignments within the SSM framework are capable to reinforce the interplay between monetary and macroprudential policies at the EU level.[65]

By contrast, the national macroprudential layer is not homogeneous. The institutionalization of the relationship between monetary and macroprudential policies across the EU countries depends upon different legal arrangements that are established as to coordinate the national central banks and the other competent authorities.[66]

On the one hand, some EU Member States, such as France and Germany, have entrusted the national microprudential authorities with macroprudential tasks.[67] Few countries, such as Norway, assigned national macroprudential responsibilities to the Minister of Finance.[68] In all these cases, the legal framework of these Member States has acknowledged the

[64] Recital (6) of Regulation (EU) No. 1092/2010. The tasks conferred upon the ECB for the functioning of the ESRB are laid down in Regulation (EU) No. 1096/2010. For details, see *supra* at notes 420–423.

[65] As better explained in the next section, this is principally due to the decision-making process and to the governance structure of the SSM where the Governing Council, made of central bankers, retains a leading role in the supervisory decision-making and monetary policy considerations can influence the supervisory decisions.

[66] For an in-depth discussion on the legal arrangements established at the national level in view of the need to ensure such coordination, see Lastra (2015), pp. 129–140.

[67] In France the Law No. 2013-672 of 26 July 2013 assigns hard-law macroprudential powers to the *Autorité de Contrôle Prudentiel et de Résolution*, while the *Haut Conseil de stabilité financière (HCSF)*, established as national macroprudential authority, is tasked with the oversight of the financial stability, and it aims to facilitate the cooperation and exchange of information between the institutions that its members represent, including Banque de France. A similar institutional model also holds in Germany. In accordance with the German Banking Act (*Gesetz über das Kreditwesen*), BaFin retains the hard-law macroprudential powers on the application of the relevant tools. However, the Act on Monitoring Financial Stability (*Gesetz zur Überwachung der Finanzstabilität*) provides a legal basis for the *Ausschuss für Finanzstabilität*, which constitutes the German national macroprudential authority entrusted with soft-law powers and information exchange tasks.

[68] In Norway, the legislation provides the macroprudential policy is to be principally conducted by the Minister of Finance (*Finansdepartemendet*), who retains overall responsibility for financial stability and has the power to calibrate the capital requirements for financial institutions. For further details, refer to the *Act on Financing Activity and Financial Institutions (Financial Institutions Act)*, 10 June 1988 No. 40.

full-separation model, where monetary policy and macroprudential policies are conducted separately without any substantial interaction. Usually, this strong separation is mitigated by the coexistence at the national level of a national macroprudential committee, which acts as a point of contact between different national authorities involved in monitoring the financial system, including national central banks.[69]

On the other hand, other EU Member States, such as Italy and Belgium, have adopted a full-integration model, where the national central bank—usually, via the establishment of a separate unit—is also the national macroprudential authority.[70] The legal frameworks of these EU countries ensure a strong interaction between the two policies due to the common decision-making framework, although priority is usually given to the monetary policy objectives set out in the central bank's statute.[71]

The degree of interaction between the two policies at the national level, as well as their interferences, therefore varies in accordance with legal framework adopted by national lawmakers and embedded within the constitutional architecture. The existence of this variance at the national level is important to better clarify the interactions existing within the EU architecture, as it reflects the different degrees of 'contribution' that the ESCB—say, the ECB and national central banks—may offer to the macroprudential policy conduct.

At second glance, both the 'EU macroprudential layer' and 'national macroprudential layer' share horizontal and vertical relationships with the ECB and national central banks. Within the EU layer, the ESRB, albeit formally independent, is horizontally interdependent to the ECB's operational capacity.[72] In addition, the role played by the Governing Council of

[69] See *infra* at notes 1293 ss.

[70] For example, Banca d'Italia has assumed macroprudential functions on the basis of Article 67 of the Italian Banking Act (*Testo Unico Bancario*) without having constituted any macroprudential committee. Instead, it is responsibility of its Governing Council to adopt macroprudential policy measures, having ample discretion on their normative content. For details on Belgium, see *supra* at notes 1111–1113.

[71] For a comparative analysis of the objectives set out in the Statutes of national central banks and on the priority given to price stability when multiple objectives are defined, see Gianviti (2010), pp. 454–463.

[72] The existence of such horizontal interdependency becomes clear when looking at the relevant provisions contained in Council Regulation (EU) No. 1096/2010. The ECB ensures the ESRB Secretariat and, to this purpose, provides human and financial resources for the performance of the tasks of the ESRB (Article 3). In view of this, the ECB ensures the work of the General Board, of the Steering Committee, of the Advisory Technical

the ECB as decision-making body of the SSM demonstrates a certain degree of interdependence between the EU banking supervisor and the ESCB.[73]

Similarly, within the national macroprudential layer, national supervisory authorities in a number of EU Member States are closely interlinked to national central banks.[74] And, though the extent of this linkage may change across Member States, relative to the institutional and legal settings assigned to national supervisory authorities, a certain degree of horizontal coordination always exists.

The vertical relationships between national central banks and authorities entrusted with macroprudential responsibilities are even more critical. For example, the composition of the ESRB's General Board, as well as of its Advisory Technical Committee, reflects a leading role of national central banks in the EU-wide macroprudential oversight.[75] At the same time, as explained further below, the establishment of a Mediation Panel,[76] within the SSM legal framework, intended to solve conflicting views upheld by national central banks and the SSM Governing Council upon supervisory decisions, clearly stresses out a vertical interrelation among these institutions.

Committee, and of the Advisory Scientific Committee of the ESRB. In addition, the ECB, in providing analytical, statistical, administrative, and logistical support to the ESRB (Article 2), collects and processes all the information that are deemed necessary for the achievement of ESRB's objective (Article 5). In addition, this horizontal interdependency can be recognized by looking also at the governance of the ESRB, as the General Board and the Executive Board are dominated by ESCB members.

[73] See *infra* at notes 1238 ss.

[74] For example, this is particularly the case when the national central bank assumes joint responsibility for banking supervision together with a supervisory authority.

[75] On this topic, Visco (2011), at p. 132, argues that at the EU level, the structure of the ESRB is intended to ensure consistency between monetary and macroprudential policies, in view of its 'close relationship with the European System of Central Banks, which represents the backbone of the new institution'. However, there are no evidences that the structure of the ESRB is really able to foster this policy consistency. Instead, as noted in the European Parliament resolution of 11 March 2014 with recommendations to the Commission on the European System of Financial Supervision (ESFS) Review (2013/2166(INL)), as monetary policy can have significant influence on credit and asset price bubbles and therefore a conflict of interests between the monetary policy of the ECB and the ESRB's activity might arise.

[76] The Mediation Panel has been established by Regulation (EU) No. 673/2014 of the European Central Bank of 2 June 2014 concerning the establishment of a Mediation Panel and its Rules of Procedure. For further details, see *infra* at notes 1261 ss.

All this being said, we turn our attention to the EU legal arrangements characterizing both layers. The institutional settings that are meant to shape the legal interactions between the tasks conferred upon the ESCB and national competent authorities—and, thus, the interplay across multiple bodies dealing with macroprudential and monetary policies—are the main subject of next sections.

5.2.2 The Integration of Monetary Concerns in the Macroprudential Supervisory Decisions

At the EU level, the secondary ESCB's objective regarding the contribution to financial stability envisaged in Article 127(5) TFEU is restrained by a number of legal arrangements that are intended, on the one hand, to preside the autonomy of the ECB with respect to the conduct of its monetary policy while, on the other, ensuring an equilibrium between monetary policy functions and banking supervisory tasks assigned to the ECB. The separate allocation of macroprudential responsibilities to the ECB, acting as a banking supervisor within the SSM, allows for a severance between financial stability concerns and the price stability objective.[77]

Although the aims of preserving price and financial stability, along with the related policy instruments, are legally separate in the EU legislation, the likelihood of legal trade-offs and conflicts due to the institutional set up cannot be excluded.[78]

[77] However, it must be here emphasized again that Article 25(2) of Council Regulation (EU) No. 1024/2013 requires the ECB to carry out its supervisory tasks without prejudice to and separately from its tasks relating to monetary policy and any other tasks. In addition, Article 24(4) provides that 'The ECB shall ensure that the operation of the Governing Council is completely differentiated as regards monetary and supervisory functions. Such differentiation shall include strictly separated meetings and agendas'.

[78] The potential of conflicts between monetary and macroprudential policies is recognized in the Recital (14) of the Decision ECB/2014/39 of the European Central Bank of 17 September 2014 on the implementation of separation between the monetary policy and supervision functions of the European Central Bank (ECB/2014/39), according to which 'the ECB is responsible for carrying out monetary policy functions with a view to maintaining price stability in accordance with Article 127(1) TFEU. The objective of its supervisory tasks is to protect the safety and soundness of credit institutions and the stability of the financial system. They should therefore be carried out in full separation from the monetary policy function in order to avoid conflicts of interest and to ensure that each of these policy functions is exercised in accordance with its particular objectives. At the same time, effective

In this respect, the application of the principle of independence, as laid down in Article 130 TFEU, to the ECB is central. Although the interpretation of this Article to the ECB in its monetary policy functions is undisputed, some doubts arise with respect to the ECB acting as banking supervisor. The ECB has advocated a number of times its full independence when performing its banking supervisory tasks,[79] seeking to extend the application of this principle beyond its monetary policy affairs. Part of the legal doctrine supports this claim arguing that the standard of independence applicable to the ECB in both its monetary and supervisory tasks shall be the same.[80] However, this opinion, in light of the structure of the SSM decision-making process and of the institutional relationship with the ESRB, seems highly questionable.

A first important concern regarding the structural separation of the ECB's monetary policy and its macroprudential tasks is related to the fact

separation between the monetary policy and supervisory functions should not prevent the reaping, wherever possible and desirable, of all the benefits to be expected as a result of combining these two policy functions in the same institution, including drawing on the ECB's extensive expertise in macroeconomic and financial stability issues and reducing double work when gathering information'. In view of this, the recital concludes by arguing that 'It is therefore necessary to put in place mechanisms that allow an adequate flow of data and other confidential information between the two policy functions'.

[79] For example, see Opinion of the European Central Bank of 27 November 2012 on a proposal for a Council regulation conferring specific tasks on the European Central Bank concerning policies relating to the prudential supervision of credit institutions and a proposal for a regulation of the European Parliament and of the Council amending Regulation (EU) No. 1093/2010 establishing a European Supervisory Authority (European Banking Authority) (CON/2012/96); Opinion of the European Central Bank of 2 September 2015 on bank resolution (CON/2015/31).

[80] This opinion is advocated, in particular, by Zilioli (2016), pp. 125–179; Ter Kuile, Wissink, and Bovenschen (2015), pp. 155–190. In particular, Zilioli (2016), p. 169, suggests that from a legal point of view, the idea of creating two different levels of independence for the two ECB functions is not tenable as the use of Article 126(7) to set up the supervisory tasks of the ECB cannot be used to diminish the independence granted to the ECB by Article 130 TFEU. As a result, for the author, the independence granted to the ECB by Article 130 TFEU shall also apply to it when performing its supervisory functions. Conversely, Lastra (2015), p. 271, argues that when it comes to supervision, the application of the principle of independence should be different, and the supervisory independence should be constructed in less strict terms than the independence of the ECB in its central banking functions. Consistent with this approach, the GCFC in its Order of 14 January 2014—2 BvR 2728/13, states that 'The constitutional justification of the independence of the European Central Bank is, however, limited to a primarily stability-oriented monetary policy and cannot be transferred to other policy areas (para 59)'.

that the supervisory responsibilities within the SSM are not conducted in full isolation from monetary policy considerations.[81] The mechanism underlying the decision-making process of the SSM leaves room for an integration of monetary policy concerns in the supervisory decisions adopted by the ECB Governing Council in its supervisory capabilities.

Pursuant to Article 26 of Council Regulation (EU) No. 1024/2013, the planning and the execution of the SSM's supervisory tasks is undertaken by the Supervisory Board, which comprises its Chair and Vice-Chair, four representatives of the ECB, and one representative of the NCAs of each participating Member State.[82] Based on the SREP supervisory assessments, the Supervisory Board proposes to the ECB Governing Council complete draft decisions that are to be adopted by the latter via a *non-objection procedure*.[83]

Draft decisions issued by the Supervisory Board may have a micro- or a macroprudential content. As for the latter, for example, the Supervisory Board can decide to apply a higher calibration of the countercyclical capital buffer applied to a certain credit institution, if this is deemed necessary to reduce its leverage.[84] The Regulation provides that the draft decisions are considered adopted unless the ECB Governing Council objects within

[81] In this respect, Constâncio (2013) argues that the separation between the ECB's monetary and supervisory function laid down in the legislation does not mean isolation, as the conferral of supervisory tasks to a central bank is in line with the responsibilities of many other central banks that combine these two functions. Cœuré (2013) confirms this statement claiming that the allocation of macroprudential regulatory instruments under the SSM is therefore an important design feature of the draft legislation, as the ECB, having a clear price stability mandate, will have incentives to intensify the prudential policies seeking to counteract emerging financial imbalances and risks. For Cœuré this would reduce pressures on monetary policy and will provide incentives to conduct supervisory policies in a way that would reduce the likelihood of crises and therefore of lender-of-last-resort interventions.

[82] These members are usually the top executives of the relevant national competent authorities responsible for banking supervision. See ECB (2014a), p. 13.

[83] The full discipline is laid down in Article 26(8) of Council Regulation (EU) No. 1024/2013. In addition, it must be noted the important role played in this process by the Directorate General Macro-Prudential Policy and Financial Stability (DG/MF) of the European Central Bank (ECB), which provides analyses and policy advice on issues relating to financial stability, financial regulation and supervision, as well as financial stability arrangements. Its Macro-Financial Policies Division, in particular, is tasked with the design and coordination of the macroprudential strategies undertaken by the ECB in its capacity of supervisory authority. This ECB Directorate also cooperates with national competent or designated authorities in the design and implementation of macroprudential tools under the SSM framework.

[84] Articles 5(2) and 9(2) of Council Regulation (EU) No. 1024/2013.

a period of time not exceeding ten working days. More importantly, the Governing Council may validate the supervisory decisions, but it is not allowed to change their content.[85]

The ECB Governing Council in pursuing its supervisory functions should neither interfere with, nor be determined by, its tasks relating to monetary policy.[86] As a result, the operations of the ECB Governing Council are completely differentiated by those regarding its monetary policy mandate.[87] This is reflected in the organizational arrangements established to separate meetings and agendas, along with the staff involved in carrying out the supervisory and monetary tasks.[88]

However, although the legal provisions set out in Council Regulation (EU) No. 1024/2013 excludes interferences between supervisory and monetary policy tasks,[89] the ECB Governing Council is allowed to introduce monetary policy concerns when it decides to reject Supervisory Board's draft decisions. The full application of the principle of independence laid down in Article 130 TFEU to the ECB in its capacity of banking supervisor would entail that no other considerations, apart from supervisory concerns, should influence the decision-making process of the SSM.

Moreover, Article 19 the Council Regulation (EU) No. 1024/2013 states that the ECB and the national competent authorities acting within the SSM shall act independently when carrying out their supervisory tasks. As a corollary of this, Article 25 compels the ECB to pursue only the supervisory objectives when acting under its role of banking supervisor, without being interfered by monetary policy considerations. Differently, the independence of the Supervisory Board in conducting its supervisory tasks would be weakened by the introduction of non-supervisory related issues.[90]

[85] ECB (2014a), p. 14.

[86] Article 25(2) of Council Regulation (EU) No. 1024/2013.

[87] Idem.

[88] Article 25(4) of Council Regulation (EU) No. 1024/2013.

[89] For an in-depth analysis of the principle of separation between monetary policy and supervisory functions within the SSM, see Boccuzzi (2016), pp. 37–40. For a critical appraisal, see Baglioni (2016), pp. 35–38.

[90] There is in fact a close association between the principle of independence laid down in Article 19 and the principle of separation set out in Article 25 of Council Regulation (EU) No. 1024/2013. Where other policies not related to the supervisory objectives enlisted in the Regulation are introduced in the decision-making process of the SSM, the independence of its decision-making bodies would be endangered. For further details on this topic, see Boccuzzi (2016), p. 37.

Although the Council Regulation (EU) No. 1024/2013 lays down a clear separation between supervisory and monetary objectives, the same Regulation explicitly acknowledges the interaction between the two policies. A rejection of a supervisory draft decision by the Governing Council can in fact be based on monetary policy concerns. To quote the provision, 'if the Governing Council objects to a draft decision, it shall state the reasons for doing so in writing, in particular stating monetary policy concerns'.[91] This means that, if a Supervisory Board's draft decision aims to apply higher macroprudential requirements, monetary policy concerns of the ECB Governing Council may influence the outcomes of the non-objection procedure.

From an economic point of view, this is utterly consistent with the need to reconcile the side effects of monetary and macroprudential policies for banks and investment firms. If a conflict arises between the two policies, this conflict is addressed within the ECB Governing Council by invalidating the draft decision and, thus, opening a dialogue.[92] The SSM framework therefore does permit to integrate monetary policy considerations within the realm of prudential decisions.[93]

This integration is pivotal, since it defines a primary legal interaction between the effects of monetary policy and the conduct of macroprudential supervision carried out within the supervisory architecture. The SSM legal settings enable the ECB to exploit the operational synergies of monetary and macroprudential policies while maintaining a formal separation between the price stability objective and the banking supervisory tasks.[94] But this also implies that the application of the principle of independence with respect to the SSM is not as rigid as for the case of the ECB in its monetary policy functions, since the decisions of the Supervisory Board is virtually subject to a monetary policy review carried out by the ECB Governing Council.

The macroprudential tasks assigned to the ECB are nevertheless quite limited. The bottom-up approach characterizing the European framework of macroprudential supervision gives preference to the national compe-

[91] Article 26(8) of Council Regulation (EU) No. 1024/2013.

[92] Ter Kuile, Wissink, and Bovenschen (2015), p. 178.

[93] For Baglioni (2016), p. 34, this provision implies that the separation principle—and, by extension, the principle of independence—applied to the ECB in its capacity of banking supervisor is not as rigid as one may expect at first sight. See also Amtenbrink (2015), at note 115, who claims that due to these peculiar governance arrangements, a strict separation of monetary and prudential supervisory tasks within the SSM has not been achieved.

[94] ECB (2014a), p. 19.

tent authorities, which are primarily responsible in applying and implementing the macroprudential measures and strategies. The description of the European macroprudential layer, therefore, is not adequate per se to fully explain the legal interactions between the ECB's monetary policy and the macroprudential supervisory regime. The legal construction of the macroprudential framework should necessarily envisage a further mechanism that may encompass the national competent authorities within the decision-making process of the SSM. As the European business cycle and the EU Member States' financial cycles are not synchronized, divergent opinions upon a draft decision may entail a risk of conflicts between the two policies which demands settlement mechanisms within the constitutional constraints.[95]

In view of this, Council Regulation (EU) No. 1024/2013 establishes a Mediation Panel to resolve differences of views expressed by the national competent authorities with respect to an objection made by the Governing Council to a Supervisory Board's draft decision. The rationale of this Panel is precisely to ensure full separation between monetary policy and supervisory tasks.[96]

But a careful analysis of this body would suggest that its aim is more to permit a rapprochement of monetary policy concerns with the content of supervisory decisions, where the former may jeopardize the latter. Since the risk of conflict with monetary policy is far more likely to occur when the supervisory decisions entail macroprudential measures, our assumption is that the Mediation Panel will be utilized to reconcile the monetary policy stance of the ECB Governing Council with the macroprudential decisions of supervisory bodies.[97]

[95] Tröger (2015), p. 184.

[96] In accordance with the Recital (73) of Council Regulation (EU) No. 1024/2013, in fact, 'With a view to ensuring separation between monetary policy and supervisory tasks, the ECB should be required to create a mediation panel. The setting up of the panel, and in particular its composition, should ensure that it resolves differences of views in a balanced way, in the interest of the Union as a whole.'

[97] Thus far, the Mediation Panel has never been requested by a national competent authority. This is consistent with our assumption; in fact, since the Supervisory Board has only utilized its microprudential powers until now, conflicts with monetary policy have never occurred. As such, the risk of conflict between institution-specific microprudential instruments and monetary policy can be regarded as negligible. By contrast, if in the future the Supervisory Board will submit draft decisions of macroprudential nature, a risk of conflict with the monetary policy stance of the ECB—in its central banking capacity—will be more likely to arise, thereby requiring—if requested by national competent authorities—mediation resolution.

The comprehensive discipline of the Mediation Panel, along with the related rules of procedures, is laid down in the Regulation (EU) No. 673/2014 of the European Central Bank, which entered into force on 2 June 2014.[98] According to the governance arrangements, each EU Member State appoints one member of the Mediation Panel from among the members of the Governing Council and the Supervisory Board, so as to ensure full equilibrium between the members of the ECB Governing Council and the Supervisory Board.[99] Each member is entitled to cast one vote, while the decisions are taken by a simple majority of the panel members.[100] In line with the rules of procedure, when a national competent authority has a different view upon a Governing Council's objection to a draft decision submitted by the Supervisory Board, it can request mediation in order to resolve possible conflicts.[101]

This panel can be better understood as a forum for resolving divergent opinions between national supervisory authorities and the ECB's Governing Council, when considerations of monetary policy may affect the implementation of macroprudential policy decisions.[102] Let's suppose, for example, the ECB Governing Council objects to a Supervisory Board's draft proposal. This draft aimed to increase the level of credit institutions' countercyclical capital buffer on the basis of some 'systemic risk' concerns raised up during the SREP. However, the Governing Council justifies its stance by arguing the rejection is badly needed, at the present stage of the business cycle, since an increase of this buffer would negatively affect the bank's cost of funding and, in turn, endanger the effectiveness of its present expansionary monetary policy.

Against this backdrop, a friction between the macroprudential supervisory action undertaken by the Supervisory Board and the monetary moves of the ECB Governing Council eventually arises. This potential conflict envisages the side effects of one policy over the other and reveals how macroprudential supervision and monetary policy, by affecting the same variables, could possibly pull in opposite directions.

The SSM legal framework establishes the Mediation Panel as an ex post mechanism that may align the two conflicting policies, preserving the

[98] Regulation (EU) No 673/2014 of the European Central Bank of 2 June 2014 concerning the establishment of a Mediation Panel and its Rules of Procedure (ECB/2014/26).

[99] Article 4 of Regulation (EU) No. 673/2014.

[100] Article 7 of Regulation (EU) No. 673/2014.

[101] See ECB (2014b), pp. 5–6.

[102] For details, see Article 8 of Regulation (EU) No. 673/2014.

formal separation between monetary policy and prudential supervision.[103] In our example, the national competent authority has the opportunity to react and challenge the monetary policy reasons carried out by the ECB Governing Council. Therefore, the Mediation Panel represents an ex post *safety valve* that permits to (1) reconcile the side effects of both policies, (2) include national competent authorities within the decision-making process of the SSM, and (3) allow for a consistent rapprochement of monetary and macroprudential policy actions.

The ultimate outcome of this settlement mechanism is an opinion that the Mediation Panel, after considering a legal opinion prepared by a Case Committee,[104] submits to the Supervisory Board and the ECB Governing Council. Albeit the opinion is not binding, the Supervisory Board must carefully take it into account to submit a new draft decision to the EC Governing Council.[105] The ECB Governing Council's final decision, regardless of the outcome of the mediation, will eventually prevail.[106] As a result, the Supervisory Board is recommended to fully appreciate the content of the Mediation Panel's opinion and inform its new draft in accordance with the arbitrated policy rapprochement.

5.2.3 *The Liaison Between National Competent Authorities, Macroprudential Bodies, and Central Banks*

Legal interactions between monetary and macroprudential policies are not peculiarities belonging exclusively to the ECB in its capacity of central bank and banking supervisory authority. As noted above, the European construction addressing the potential conflicts between the two policies is characterized not only by a European dimension but also by a national layer. Having considered the latter, the former deserves special attention, since its legal constituents shape the way in which the economic interactions between the policy objectives are managed by the relevant authorities at the national level.

[103] Huertas (2016), p. 26, who also claims this Mediation Panel could obstruct the ability of the SSM to take decisions quickly.

[104] For more details on the Case Committee, see Article 9 of Regulation (EU) No. 673/2014. In particular, the Case Committee is tasked with the analysis of whether the request for mediation is admissible and legally founded. Based on this assessment, it must prepare a legal opinion to be submitted to the Panel for initiating the mediation procedure.

[105] Article 10 of Regulation (EU) No. 673/2014.

[106] Tröger (2015), p. 185.

It should be noted that the national macroprudential layer is largely dependent upon the implementation by EU Member States of a clear legislative framework for macroprudential policy. The high degree of variance experienced by European countries in the implementation process of the macroprudential framework[107] not only affects the way in which macroprudential policy is conducted at the national level but also shapes the degree of rapprochement between the objectives of monetary and macroprudential policy within each jurisdiction.

To better understand this rapprochement, it is necessary to categorize, at first, the national authorities entrusted with macroprudential responsibilities, and then, identify the institutional liaison existing between the relevant authorities and the respective national central banks. This process of identification primarily relies on the legal provisions of the CRR/CRD IV package, where the CRD IV assigns the implementation power of macroprudential instruments harmonized at the EU level[108] either to the national competent authority of the EU Member State concerned[109]—that is, the national banking supervisor—or to other national authorities designated by the government.[110]

Regarding the latter, for example, Article 136 CRD IV requires each EU Member State to designate a public authority or body—that is, the national designated authority—which must be responsible for setting the countercyclical buffer rate in that jurisdiction. Similarly, Article 133 CRD IV requires each EU Member State to designate the authority in charge of setting the systemic risk buffer and of identifying the list of credit institutions to which it applies. The same holds true for the G-SII and the O-SII buffers.[111]

[107] In this perspective an important contribution for understanding this large variance in the implementation of the macroprudential settings across the EU countries is given in ESRB (2014a).

[108] See *supra* at Chap. 2, Sect. 2.3.2.

[109] The definition of competent authority is laid down in Article 4(1) (40) CRR. Pursuant to it, competent authority means a public authority or body officially recognized by national law, which is empowered by national law to supervise institutions as part of the supervisory system in operation in the Member State concerned.

[110] In most of the cases the national designated authority is the national competent authority. However, the government for a number of political and institutional reasons may decide to delegate these macroprudential powers to other authorities, such as the national macroprudential committee. For this reason, it is important to stress the difference between competent authorities and designated authorities.

[111] For details see Article 131 CRD IV.

Along with the requirement of assigning powers to implement the macroprudential instruments laid down in the CRR/CRD IV framework, EU Member States are also recommended to establish a specialized body, namely, a national macroprudential authority or committee, in charge as a minimum of the general oversight of risks to financial stability in their respective jurisdictions. The ESRB, with its Recommendation ESRB/2011/3,[112] has recommended EU Member States to designate in the national legal framework an authority entrusted with the conduct of macroprudential policy, to be institutionalized either as a single institution or as a board composed of the authorities whose actions have a material impact on financial stability.[113]

These national macroprudential authorities are recommended to be tasked with identifying, monitoring, and assessing systemic risks, along with the competence of implementing policies capable to prevent and mitigate the build-up of systemic risks.[114] The ESRB also recommended EU Member States to empower these new authorities with the control over the relevant macroprudential instruments, as to achieve the financial stability objective.[115]

More importantly, the ESRB Recommendation ESRB/2011/3 draws attention to the need of establishing full equilibrium between the legal settings of monetary and macroprudential authorities. In view of this purpose, the ESRB is committed to directly involve central banks in the conduct of macroprudential policy tasks and 'ensure that the central bank plays a leading role in the macroprudential policy and that macroprudential policy does not undermine its independence in accordance with Article 130 of the Treaty'.[116]

This provision entails that the macroprudential authorities are to be established by national legislations as to permit a consistent interaction with the spillover effects of monetary policy. The legal construction of national macroprudential frameworks should reflect this concern and allow for a rapprochement of the ultimate objectives of the policies at stake, possibly within one of the institutional models which are understood

[112] See Recommendation of the European Systemic Risk Board of 22 December 2011 on the macroprudential mandate of national authorities (ESRB/2011/3) (2012/C 41/01).

[113] Sub-recommendations B.1 and B.2 of Recommendation ESRB/2011/3.

[114] For details, see Sub-recommendation C.1 of Recommendation ESRB/2011/3.

[115] Sub-recommendation C.4 of Recommendation ESRB/2011/3.

[116] See Sub-recommendation B.3 of Recommendation ESRB/2011/3.

to mitigate potential conflicts.[117] Following this recommendation, the majority of EU Member States have decided to implement the normative content of these provisions and put into place such a new institutional dimension. The following table (Table 5.1) offers an overview upon the relevant authorities entrusted with macroprudential powers for each Member State.

Table 5.1 National authorities entrusted with macroprudential powers

Country	*Competent authority*	*Designated authority (for countercyclical capital buffer ('CCB'))*	*Designated authority (for macroprudential tools other than CCB)*	*Macroprudential authority*
Austria	Austrian Financial Market Authority	Austrian Financial Market Authority	Austrian Financial Market Authority	Financial Market Stability Board
Belgium	National Bank of Belgium	National Bank of Belgium	National Bank of Belgium	National Bank of Belgium
Bulgaria	Bulgarian National Bank	Bulgarian National Bank/ Financial Supervision Commission	Bulgarian National Bank/Financial Supervision Commission	Bulgarian National Bank/Financial Supervision Commission
Cyprus	Central Bank of Cyprus	Central Bank of Cyprus	Central Bank of Cyprus	Central Bank of Cyprus
Czech Republic	Czech National Bank	Czech National Bank	Czech National Bank	Czech National Bank
Germany	Federal Financial Supervisory Authority (BaFin)	Federal Financial Supervisory Authority (BaFin)	Federal Financial Supervisory Authority (BaFin)	Financial Stability Committee

(*continued*)

[117] For a description of the partial-integration model and of the independent institutions model, which acknowledge the constitution of a separate committee—either established under the roof of the central bank or fully independent—see *supra* at Chap. 4, Sects. 4.4.1–4.4.3.

Table 5.1 (continued)

Country	*Competent authority*	*Designated authority (for countercyclical capital buffer ('CCB'))*	*Designated authority (for macroprudential tools other than CCB)*	*Macroprudential authority*
Denmark	Danish Financial Supervisory Authority	Danish Ministry of Business and Growth	Danish Financial Supervisory Authority	Systemic Risk Council
Estonia	Financial Supervision Authority	Bank of Estonia	Bank of Estonia	Bank of Estonia
Spain	Bank of Spain	Bank of Spain	Bank of Spain	x
Finland	Finnish Financial Supervisory Authority	Finnish Financial Supervisory Authority	Finnish Financial Supervisory Authority	Finnish Financial Supervisory Authority
France	French Prudential Supervision and Resolution Authority	High Council for Financial Stability	French Prudential Supervision and Resolution Authority	High Council for Financial Stability
Greece	Bank of Greece	Bank of Greece	Bank of Greece	Bank of Greece
Croatia	Croatian National Bank	Croatian National Bank	Croatian National Bank	Financial Stability Council
Hungary	Hungarian National Bank	Hungarian National Bank	Ministry for National Economy	Financial Stability Board
Ireland	Central Bank of Ireland	Central Bank of Ireland	Central Bank of Ireland	Central Bank of Ireland
Italy	Bank of Italy	Bank of Italy	Bank of Italy	x
Lithuania	Bank of Lithuania	Bank of Lithuania	Bank of Lithuania	Bank of Lithuania
Luxembourg	Luxembourg Financial Industry Supervisory Commission	Luxembourg Financial Industry Supervisory Commission	Luxembourg Financial Industry Supervisory Commission	Systemic Risk Committee
Latvia	Financial and Capital Market Commission	Financial and Capital Market Commission	Financial and Capital Market Commission	Bank of Latvia

(*continued*)

Table 5.1 (continued)

Country	*Competent authority*	*Designated authority (for countercyclical capital buffer ('CCB'))*	*Designated authority (for macroprudential tools other than CCB)*	*Macroprudential authority*
Malta	Malta Financial Services Authority	Central Bank of Malta	Central Bank of Malta	Central Bank of Malta
The Netherlands	Dutch National Bank	Dutch National Bank	Dutch National Bank	Financial Stability Committee
Poland	Polish Financial Supervision Authority	Financial Stability Committee	Financial Stability Committee	Financial Stability Committee
Portugal	Bank of Portugal	Bank of Portugal	Bank of Portugal	Bank of Portugal
Romania	National Bank of Romania	National Bank of Romania/ Financial Supervisory Authority	National Bank of Romania/ Financial Supervisory Authority	National Committee for Macroprudential Supervision
Sweden	Financial Supervisory Authority	Financial Supervisory Authority	Financial Supervisory Authority	Financial Stability Council
Slovenia	Bank of Slovenia	Bank of Slovenia	Bank of Slovenia	Financial Stability Board
Slovakia	National Bank of Slovakia	National Bank of Slovakia	National Bank of Slovakia	National Bank of Slovakia
United Kingdom	Prudential Regulation Authority	Bank of England (Financial Policy Committee)	Prudential Regulation Authority/HM Treasury	Bank of England (Financial Policy Committee)

The table shows how national macroprudential frameworks have been established in Europe by adopting variations of two institutional patterns, namely, the *full-integration* or *partial-integration* models.

On the one hand, 17 EU Member States have attributed to their respective central bank a predominant role in conducting macroprudential policy. In these countries national central banks are indicated as the designated authorities for setting and calibrating the macroprudential instruments laid down in the CRR/CRD IV package. In addition, many of these central banks are explicitly identified as national macroprudential authorities by national legislation.

The legal framework of these European countries is tailored to incorporate the full-integration model, whose characteristics are meant to ensure maximum alignment between the cross effects of monetary and macroprudential policies.[118] In these countries the interaction of the two policies is ensured by the central bank's statute and implemented via the decision-making process of its governing board. The statute ensures—at least—a double mandate to these central banks, where the objective of price stability is usually accompanied by the function of promoting the stability of the financial system.[119]

Moreover, the governing boards of the respective central banks have the authority to adopt all the external measures necessary to fulfill their public functions, including those macroprudential in nature as well as the

[118] See *supra* at Chap. 4, Sect. 4.4.1.

[119] Article 12 of the Law of 22 February 1998 Establishing the Organic Statute of the National Bank of Belgium, which ensures that the Bank may contribute to the stability of the financial system having the power to detect, assess, and monitor different factors and developments which may affect financial stability. Similarly, Article 6 of the Central Bank of Cyprus Law of 2007 states that one of the main tasks of the bank is to ensure the stability of the financial system. With respect to similar provisions in other central banks' statutes, see Article 2 of the Act No. 6/1993 Coll. on the Czech National Bank; Articles 2 and 24 of the Bank of Estonia (Eesti Pank) Act (RT I 23.12.2011); Article 7 of the Law of Autonomy of the Banco de Espana (Law 13/1994 of 1 June 1994); Article 6A of the Irish Central Bank Act of 1942 (consolidated version); Article 8 of the Law on the Bank of Lithuania (1 December 1994 No I-678); Article 12 of the Organic Law on the Banco de Portugal (Law No. 5/98 of 31 January 1998 as amended by Decree-Law No. 142/2013); and Article 2 of the National Bank of Slovakia Act No. 566/1992 Coll. In addition, Article 55A of the Statute of the Bank of Greece, by defining its macroprudential tasks, states that 'the Bank of Greece shall exercise, inter alia, its macroprudential task with a view to strengthening the resilience of the financial system and decreasing the build-up of systemic risks. In particular, the Bank shall identify, monitor and assess such risks and adopt the measures provided for by law.' In Italy, Banca d'Italia has not been statutorily entrusted with a financial stability objective. However, Article 1(5) of the Statute of Banca d'Italia provides that the Bank of Italy shall perform the other tasks assigned to it by law and engage in activities instrumental to its functions. To this purpose, Article 53 of the Italian Banking Act ('*Testo Unico Bancario*') entrusts Banca d'Italia to adopt acts of general applicability to mitigate systemic risks, thereby assigning de facto macroprudential powers to the Italian central bank.

monetary tasks explicitly delegated within the ESCB.[120] Without a sharp separation between monetary and the macroprudential institutional layers, this institutional framework should ensure full consistency between the monetary policy stance pursued by the national central bank within the ESCB and its macroprudential policy decisions.

On the other hand, 11 EU Member States have preferred the adoption of a partial-integration model where the macroprudential policy is conducted by an independent body within a cooperative framework with the national central bank.[121] Although these countries show great variation in their legal arrangements,[122] some commonalities can be recognized, the most important of which is the establishment of an independent national macroprudential authority, statutorily entrusted with the general oversight of systemic risks.[123]

Member States adopting this pattern utilize a multilevel structure, where the macroprudential authority is seen as the apex of system and national competent/designated authorities represent operating arms. In

[120] For an overview of these powers, see the following national provisions: Article 29 of the Law of 22 February 1998 Establishing the Organic Statute of the National Bank of Belgium; Article 15 of the Central Bank of Cyprus Law of 2007; Article 15 of the Act No. 6/1993 Coll. on the Czech National Bank, which explicitly states 'The Bank Board shall set monetary and macroprudential policy and the instruments for implementing these policies. It shall decide upon the fundamental monetary and macroprudential policy measures of the Czech National Bank and measures in the area of financial market supervision'; Article 6 of the Statute of Bank of Estonia (Eesti Pank) (Decision No. 3-1 of 28.04.2015); Articles 21 and 22 of the Law of Autonomy of the Banco de Espana (Law 13/1994 of 1 June 1994); Article 18B of the Irish Central Bank Act of 1942 (consolidated version); Article 11 of the Law on the Bank of Lithuania (1 December 1994 No I-678); Article 34 of the Organic Law on the Banco de Portugal (Law No. 5/98 of 31 January 1998 as amended by Decree-Law No. 142/2013); Article 6 of the National Bank of Slovakia Act No. 566/1992 Coll.

[121] For the details of this model, see *supra* at Chap. 4, Sect. 4.4.2.

[122] For an analytical survey of variations and discrepancies in the implementation of the macroprudential policy mandate at the national level, see ESRB (2014a). Although the report is not up to date to the new macroprudential developments in many EU Member States, nonetheless it provides a clear picture of how different countries have established their own macroprudential institutional frameworks differently.

[123] The establishment of an independent macroprudential authority, institutionally separate from the national central bank, finds particular support by the ESRB which indeed recommends Member States to 'entrust the macroprudential authority at a minimum with the tasks of identifying, monitoring and assessing risks to financial stability and of implementing policies to achieve its objective by preventing and mitigating those risks'. In particular, see Recommendations B and C of ESRB Recommendation of 22 December 2011 on the macroprudential mandate of national authorities (ESRB/2011/3).

detail, the national macroprudential authorities—or committees—are principally tasked with detecting the build-up of systemic risks and assessing to what extent these may generate spillover effects to the real economy.[124] Once the potential for systemic imbalances is discovered, the macroprudential authorities are empowered to issue soft-law measures, such as recommendations and warnings to the respective national competent authorities. Based on these advices, national competent authorities are then required to take a stance and implement the relevant hard-law and supervisory measures within their respective regulatory frameworks.

Although the tasks of systemic risks' oversight, along with the control over the relevant macroprudential tools, are institutionally separate from the central bank's mandate, the legal arrangements of this institutional

[124] This main responsibility can be found in all the national legislations establishing national macroprudential authorities in Europe. In Germany, Section 2 of the Act on the Strengthening of German Financial Supervision (*Gesetz zur Stärkung der deutschen Finanzaufsicht, vom 28. November 2012 (BGBl. I S. 2369)*) assigns to the *Ausschuss für Finanzstabilität*—the German Financial Stability Council—the following tasks: (1) the discussion of issues relating to financial stability; (2) strengthening the cooperation of the authorities represented in the committee in the event of financial crisis; (3) cooperate with the ESRB for the issuance of recommendations and warnings on financial stability; (4) issue warnings and recommendations. Similarly, in France, the new Article L631-2-1 of the Monetary and Financial Code (*Code monétaire et financier*), the *Haut Conseil de Stabilité Financière*, conducts the general oversight of the financial stability and the macroprudential policy. In this respect, it must (1) cooperate and exchange information with other institutions represented; (2) identify and assess systemic risks arising in the financial markets and take into account the recommendations issued by the competent European institutions; (3) issue recommendations by itself in order to preserve the stability of the financial system. Another example is provided by the Financial Service Act 2012, which established the Financial Policy Committee as the UK macroprudential authority, and assigned to it, among others, the task of identifying, monitoring, and taking action to remove or reduce systemic risks with a view to protecting and enhancing the resilience of the UK financial system (see PART 1A 9C). In the Netherlands, instead, the *Financieel Stabiliteitscomité* has been created by the Minister of Finance with the authoritative act *Besluit van de Minister van Financiën van 2 november 2012, kenmerk: FM2012/1193M, tot oprichting van het financieel stabiliteitscomité*. Article 4 entrusts the committee, inter alia, with the tasks of exchanging information about the stability of the financial system, discussing possible actions to mitigate these risks, including the options for reinforcing the statutory instruments assigned to the other competent authorities, and issuing warnings and recommendations with respect to the identified risks. Similarly, in Austria, Article 13 of the *Finanzmarktaufsichtbehörden-Gesetz* states the mandate of the *Finanzmarktsta bilitätsgremium* (Financial Market Stability Board), having the primary aim of strengthening financial stability, mitigating the risks of systemically important financial institutions, and addressing the structural and cyclical aspects of systemic risk.

path provide for an integration of the monetary policy concerns in the ongoing macroprudential policy discussions.

The liaison between the two policies is permitted by the composition of the national macroprudential authorities. Governors of the national central banks, along with other national central banks' officials, are major figures in these macroprudential committees,[125] though in some cases the position of chairman is assigned to the Minister of Finance due to the political sensitiveness of the decisions at stake.[126] In addition, the agenda of these national macroprudential authorities usually relies on preparatory work and technical capabilities of national monetary authorities,[127] thereby reinforcing the linkage between the analytical developments of the two policies. Finally, it is worth noting that the legal acts establishing these national macroprudential authorities allows for an enhanced cooperation with the respective national central banks, with particular regard to the exchange of information and aggregate data.[128]

[125] In most of the cases the governors of the national central banks are also chairmen of the national macroprudential authorities. In addition, the majority of the components in the committee are central bank's officers. Then, it can be easily assumed that the monetary policy concerns are widely considered in the discussions on macroprudential policy and its possible side effects.

[126] This is the case, for example, for the *Haut Conseil de Stabilité Financière* in France and for *Comité du Risque Systémique* in Luxembourg. It must be noted, however, that there is only one country, namely, Denmark, where the Ministry is directly in charge of macroprudential policy. In all other cases, the Ministers of Finance, although participating in the work of the macroprudential committees, have limited powers. For an in-depth analysis of the political sensitiveness of macroprudential policy, see Clark and Large (2011), pp. 37–39; Baker (2013), pp. 112–139. See also ESRB (2014b), pp. 12–13.

[127] In this respect, an interesting example is given by the decision-making process of the *Ausschuss für Finanzstabilität* and of the *Haut Conseil de Stabilité Financière*. Section 1(1) of the *Gesetz zur Stärkung der deutschen Finanzaufsicht Vom* entrusted the Bundesbank with a prominent role within the national macroprudential framework. The German Central Bank, in particular, is responsible for analyzing issues related to financial stability and for identifying and assessing systemic risks. In light of this general monitoring, the Bundesbank shall prepare the meetings of the *Ausschuss für Finanzstabilität* and draw up status reports as a starting point for the committee's discussions. Instead, Article L631-2-1 of the *Code monétaire et financier* tasked the Governor of the Banque de France with a leading role in proposing and setting macroprudential measures, such as the countercyclical capital buffer and systemic risk buffer. The *Haut Conseil de Stabilité Financière* can indeed adopt such measures only upon proposal by the central bank's Governor.

[128] By way of example, see Section 4 of *Gesetz zur Stärkung der deutschen Finanzaufsicht*. In addition, see the Memorandum of Understanding between *Finansinspektionen* and the *Riksbank* concerning a council for cooperation on macroprudential policy of 17 January 2012.

The legal settings of the partial-integration model do not allow for that sort of integration between monetary and macroprudential policies characterizing the full-integration path. However, the strict linkages between the authorities concerned, along with the leading role of central banks as participants of the respective national macroprudential committees, promote an operating institutional mechanism that may potentially align divergences between the side effects of macroprudential and monetary policy stances, thereby decreasing the risks of conflicts, policy inconsistencies, and negative spillovers.

5.3 Possible Conflict of Policies as a Problem of Rules?

The European multi-layer construction of the macroprudential architecture, as traced after the 2008 financial crisis, may appear somehow complex. A number of national authorities entrusted with macroprudential tasks and powers seem to overlap a European dimension which, in turn, wishes to retain macroprudential responsibilities. The need to reconcile macroprudential policies across EU Member States with the single monetary policy, conducted entirely under the ECB domain, is an intricate conundrum that requires some safety valves as to address likely policy conflicts.

After recognizing that monetary policy and macroprudential policy jointly affect the same macroeconomic variables through comparable transmission channels,[129] and giving account of the necessity to spot some institutional mechanisms that would permit to manage the cross side effects in a consistent manner, thus aligning divergent policy stances, the main argument of this volume is that these institutional mechanisms are set out by the law and constitute what we have considered 'the legal interaction' between the public policies at stake.

The first part of this chapter has been devoted to portray how this legal interaction is supposed to operate in both the EU and national frameworks. A number of legal mechanisms have been identified, ranging from the decision-making process of the ECB Governing Council within the SSM to the institutional models adopted by the EU Member States as to foster cooperation between national central banks and the national authorities entrusted

[129] Cf. *supra* at Chap. 3, Sects. 3.1.2 and 3.1.3.

with macroprudential powers.[130] Where a monetary policy stance and a macroprudential supervisory decision pull in opposite directions, these mechanisms permit—to some extent—an economic rapprochement of the effects at stake, thereby mitigating the negative spillovers of one policy over the other.

However, the legal dimension highlighted thus far and allowing for such a rapprochement does not seem complete. The legal interaction between macroprudential and monetary policies is nowadays supported by very few instruments which are deemed to simply constrain macroprudential decisions in view of monetary policy considerations. Conversely, the European legal architecture does not permit to question the ECB's monetary policy stance based on systemic risk considerations.

This means, in practice, that the law does not provide any safety valve that would permit to re-focus the EU monetary policy under a financial stability perspective. As better explained below, this criticality accounts for the lack of an integrated institutional construction in the EU that would create a *system of checks and balances* in the policymaking process.

This regulatory gap, along with the fragmentation of macroprudential tasks and powers across different EU and national bodies, leaves room for criticism, since the coherent interplay between macroprudential and monetary policies does not appear sufficiently addressed. But this consideration is also of primary importance since it will allow us to re-discuss, in the following sections, the role of the ESRB as a possible point of contact between monetary policy and macroprudential banking supervision in the EU.

5.3.1 Legal Fragmentation of the European Macroprudential Structure

It appears quite clear from what we have explained so far that the European macroprudential framework is largely fragmented. This core feature of the macroprudential dimension in Europe is primarily reflected in the fragmentation of responsibilities and powers between different institutions at national and EU levels.[131] The large number of authorities involved in

[130] The legal mechanisms leading to an interaction between monetary policy and macroprudential policy have been described in Chap. 5, Sects. 5.2.2 and 5.2.3.

[131] An interesting survey in this regard is provided by Gualandri (2015), pp. 91–102, where the author discusses the assignments of macroprudential competences and powers within the context of the European supervisory architecture. The author finds that the resulting framework appears complex, fragmented, and cumbersome. Due to this it can result

tackling systemic risks requires the EU to set up strong coordination arrangements along with an array of effective cooperative tools that may possibly deal with cross-border criticalities and issues of regulatory arbitrage.[132]

Our main argument, however, is that the fragmented structure of macroprudential supervision may have negative consequences for a coherent interaction with monetary policy. This concern is interlinked to the lack of harmonization at the EU level of a number of macroprudential instruments, that is, real estate macroprudential instruments, such as the LTV, LTI, and DTI caps, and liquidity instruments, such as the NSFR, which remain in the hands of national competent authorities, such as banking supervisors or ministries of finance, with no ties to central banks.[133]

Moreover, the lack of convergent strategies in macroprudential policies across countries, along with the limited capacity of the ECB as a true macroprudential authority within the SSM, adds a further element of complication. Finally, the existence in Europe of multiple institutional models more or less tailored to addressing possible conflicts between monetary and macroprudential policies can dramatize this intricate scenario. To better understand the relevance of such criticalities and how they can negatively impinge upon the interaction with monetary policy, we provide below a brief outline.

As already noted, while national competent authorities are primarily responsible for any macroprudential interventions, the ECB, in its capacity of banking supervisor within the SSM, has just a supplementary role in the event of inaction or delay being able to tighten the macroprudential instruments harmonized at the EU level. National competent authorities are also entirely responsible of the calibration of the non-harmonized

rather ineffective in targeting system risks and ensuring financial stability. As a result, the author advocates the need of corrective actions in the European architecture that may foster a rationalization of the multiple supervisory layers.

[132] In this respect, Osiński (2013), pp. 4–5, claims that 'the result of fragmentation of responsibility may be that some important systemic risks will fall between the cracks and stay unaddressed'. If this fragmentation cannot be avoided, it is necessary to ensure strong coordination mechanisms between the authorities involved, possibly having a leading institution which can be formally accountable for the whole supervisory process. For a recent survey on regulatory arbitrage as a result of the operationalization of different macroprudential policies across countries, see Reinhardt and Sowerbutts (2015), as the authors provide evidences that domestic non-bank sector increases borrowing from foreign banks after home authorities tighten macroprudential capital instruments.

[133] For more details, see *supra* at Chap. 2, Sect. 2.3.3.

macroprudential tools.[134] As these instruments fall out of the scope of the SSM framework, they cannot be tightened by the ECB. For these measures it is not possible to figure out any interaction with monetary policy at the EU level, as the ECB Governing Council has no power to object decisions taken by national competent authorities concerning their implementation.

Certainty, if these tools are implemented by national central banks or national macroprudential committees, the rapprochement of their side effects with monetary policy may be ensured by the participation of central bankers in the national macroprudential decision-making process. Suppose, for example, that a national macroprudential authority is responsible for setting the LTV ratio cap in the national regulatory framework. Where the board of this macroprudential authority includes representatives of the national central bank, these officers can introduce their monetary policy concerns in the relevant discussions, pointing out the spillover effects that this cap may have on the sound implementation of monetary policy.

However, where the responsibility for these tools is assigned to the Minister of Finance or national supervisory authorities, the need for a coherent interaction with the current monetary policy environment may be neglected.[135] As a consequence, a vast array of countercyclical instruments, such as the real estate caps and the liquidity buffers—whose strong effects on credit supply and money growth have been scrutinized above[136]—can be put in place at the national level without any cross-checking with monetary policy targets. If these tools and central banking operations pull into conflicting directions, the lack of a legal process that may allow for some sort of reconciliation between their side effects may favor inconsistent policy outcomes.[137]

[134] For more details on these instruments, see *supra* at notes 347–362.

[135] For example, in Germany, the macroprudential powers have been allocated to BaFin, which has no ties to the national central bank. The national flexibility measures laid down in Article 458 of the CRR are also responsibility of BaFin which exercise its banking supervisory functions irrespective of any monetary policy concern. The same holds true for the macroprudential use of Pillar 2 instruments as laid down in Articles 103 and 105 of the CRD IV. In these cases, the German banking supervisor may impose specific macroprudential requirements that may influence the effectiveness of the credit channels with no consideration for the current monetary policy stance.

[136] For more details, see *supra* at Chap. 4, Sects. 4.2.2 and 4.2.3.

[137] This is well recognized under an economic perspective by Angelini, Neri, and Panetta (2011), p. 22. The arrangements that allow for cooperation should be established for any

A number of measures can be adopted to overcome this concern. For example, the full harmonization of all macroprudential tools at the EU level, along with the operationalization of a cooperative framework bringing together the macroprudential and the monetary authorities, with clear and predefined decision-making procedures where central bankers may have a say in any relevant decision, would help mitigate these risks.

Sweden's experience with the LTV cap in 2010 proves this point. When the *Finansinspektionen* decided to impose in October of that year an LTV cap for new mortgages, in order to contain the boom of borrowers' indebtedness, this cap was judged negatively by central bankers as it would have required changes in the monetary policy stance as to reduce excessive house prices and household debt.[138]

In addition, the introduction of non-harmonized macroprudential tools within the scope of the SSM would permit the ECB Governing Council to resolve—via its non-objection procedure—any conflicting interaction with monetary policy, as it is possible today for the capital-based instruments laid down in the CRR/CRD IV package.[139]

A further element of concern relative to the European macroprudential structure is due to the lack of convergent strategies dealing with the implementation of macroprudential measures across countries. We have discussed how a proper macroprudential regime requires a range of policy strategies which should be specifically tailored to address different typologies of systemic risks by means of predefined policy measures. The establishment of these macroprudential strategies permits to tie ex ante each source of systemic risk to a specific set of macroprudential measures that can be used during the build-up phase of the financial cycle. The systemic risks' assessment is ensured by the aforementioned financial stability indicators[140] which should ensure a timely appraisal of the financial conditions, as to allow the relevant authorities to respond quickly.

macroprudential measure and shall find its primary basis in the legal framework of the relevant authorities.

[138] For more details on this topic, see Ingves and Jansson (2014). The authors describe the 'monetary policy experiment' conducted in Sweden, where the policy interest rate was raised in response to a housing bubble. For them, this monetary policy stance has been quite successful as it has contributed the recovery of Sweden from the financial crisis at a pace similar to that in the United States. On this topic, see also ESRB (2014b), pp. 14–15.

[139] For more insights, see *supra* at Chap. 5, Sect. 5.2.2.

[140] An overview of the relevant indicators is provided *supra* in Table 5.1.

In line with this, EU Member States are recommended to make public their macroprudential strategies as to foster transparency, accountability, and effective communication between the relevant authorities and the market.[141] And several countries have published their policy strategies, providing precise details on the effective implementation of their macroprudential actions. Most of these strategies, however, do not recognize the need of incorporating monetary policy concerns in deciding upon the activation of macroprudential measures.[142] In other words, changes in the monetary policy stance, along with the related financial stability effects, are not widely scrutinized in the decision-making process of national macroprudential authorities, with tangible negative consequences for the interplay with monetary policy. Likewise, in spite of the ESRB's efforts to give some guidance on the minimum content,[143] the absence of joint efforts between EU Member States to design and calibrate these policy strategies in a cooperative fashion is likely to generate risks of negative cross-border spillovers and regulatory arbitrage.[144]

In this respect the national legal frameworks should not only state the obligation of making public such strategies,[145] but specific regulatory pro-

[141] In particular, we refer to Recommendation C of Recommendation of the ESRB of 4 April 2013 on intermediate objectives and instruments of macroprudential policy (ESRB/2013/1), according to which macroprudential authorities are recommended to define a policy strategy that (a) links the ultimate objective of macroprudential policy with the intermediate objectives and the macroprudential instruments under their direct control or recommendation powers; (b) establishes a sound framework for the application of instruments under their direct control, including appropriate indicators to monitor systemic risks and to guide decisions on the application and calibration of the instruments; and (c) establishes an appropriate coordination mechanism with relevant authorities.

[142] Conversely, an interesting example where the monetary policy concerns are incorporated into the macroprudential policy strategy is given by the Bank of Slovenia. In its document entitled *Macroprudential Policy for the Banking Sector Strategic Framework* of 24 September 2015, the Slovenian monetary authority acknowledges that it 'will monitor financial stability consequences of changes in the monetary policy stance following its systemic risk identification and assessment processes and take them into account when deciding on its macroprudential policy stance'.

[143] See again the Recommendation of the ESRB of 4 April 2013 on intermediate objectives and instruments of macroprudential policy (ESRB/2013/1).

[144] Herzberg and Watson (2014), p. 4.

[145] This is in fact recommended by the ESRB which fully acknowledges the benefits related to the public disclosure of the macroprudential policy strategies. More precisely, see Sub-recommendation D.I of Recommendation of the ESRB of 22 December 2011 on the macroprudential mandate of national authorities (ESRB/2011/3).

visions must require national macroprudential authorities to monitor the monetary policy effects on financial stability as part of their systemic risk evaluation process so as to take them fully into account when deciding on their policy actions.

The European system of 'checks and balances' in the credit creation process should be strengthened as to permit the ECB/ESCB to assess the consistency of the policy strategies with the monetary policy stance adopted in Europe. As no mechanism of this sort exists so far, its establishment must be understood as a priority for future legislative reforms aimed at further strengthening the overall European macroprudential dimension.

All this being said, one can argue that the overall European macroprudential structure—and, in particular, its relationship to the monetary policy conduct—is complex and inefficiently developed.[146] A number of reasons would support this critical stance. The intricate architecture composed of multidimensional layers and compound authorities would require hierarchical ordering as to permit enhanced cooperation between national competent and macroprudential authorities and the European institutions.[147] The complexity of the macroprudential supervisory structure might endanger the policy assignments and responsibilities, as multiple authorities may be willing to counter and/or mitigate systemic risks in an uncoordinated fashion, with possible negative spillovers for a coherent deployment of the macroprudential policy strategies. This complexity may then create substantial burden for the smooth interaction of the macroprudential measures with the monetary policy environment, as only few regulatory and institutional arrangements are settled to provide an alignment between the policies at stake.

In this context, we believe that the role of the ESRB should be rediscussed. Since it currently represents the sole independent body in the EU where the ESCB participants, the national competent authorities, and the ESAs are jointly represented, its role should be reaffirmed under a more broadly mandate. The ESRB appears well placed to operate as a point of contact between the macroprudential supervisory and monetary

[146] Among others, this opinion is shared by Schoenmaker (2014), p. 193.

[147] It should be noted that this necessity for enhancing cooperation between central banks and competent/macroprudential authorities was already apparent at the earlier stage of the European macroprudential construction. For an interesting example, see House of Lords (2009), p. 216.

policy frameworks in the EU. Its statutory objective, that is, mitigating systemic risks and fostering financial stability, can no longer ignore the need to balance, within the constitutional constraints set by the EU Treaties, the systemic risk effects of the ECB monetary policy and the macroprudential concerns of national supervisory authorities.

5.3.2 *The Integrated Dimension to Constrain the Crossed Effects of Monetary and Macroprudential Policies*

The other *flip of the coin* of this legal interaction between monetary and macroprudential policies is whether there are some regulatory or institutional *safety valves* in the ESCB legislation which aim at incorporating financial stability considerations into the monetary policy decision-making.

We have seen that Article 127 TFEU separates the price stability objective and the financial stability objective in a hierarchical ordering. The ECB often reiterates how price stability represents the sole operational target of its monetary policy conduct, whose quantitative content should be achieved regardless of any other public policy concern.[148] The ESCB's role of contributing to the stability of the financial system ensured by the national competent authorities, as envisioned in Article 127(5) TFEU, shall not encroach upon the primary objective of monetary policy. And, where conflicts arise between price stability and financial stability, the ESCB must be ready to pursue the former at the expense of the latter.

The choice made by EU lawmakers to prioritize price stability as a primary objective of the ESCB, although constitutionally undisputable, can be no longer tenable in light of the events that have affected the EU finan-

[148] In this regard, the ECB affirms that 'price stability is the best—and, ultimately, the only—contribution that a credible monetary policy can make to economic growth, job creation and social cohesion. This reflects the fact that a policy-maker who controls only one instrument cannot meet, and be held accountable for the fulfillment of, more than one objective. The pursuit of additional objectives would risk overburdening monetary policy, and would ultimately result in higher inflation and higher unemployment. Over the longer term, monetary policy can only influence the price level in the economy; it cannot exert a lasting impact on economic activity. This general principle is referred to as the "long-run neutrality of money". It is against this background that the Treaty provides for a clear and efficient allocation of responsibilities, with monetary policy being assigned the primary objective of maintaining price stability'. For the details, see ECB (2008), p. 34.

cial system after the financial crisis.[149] On the one hand, the unconventional conduct of monetary policy can have serious spillover effects for the stability of financial markets due to its capacity to build-up systemic risks and encourage excessive credit growth.[150] On the other hand, the exclusion of financial stability considerations in the ESCB monetary policy decision-making may result in an unreasonable disregard of the ongoing market conditions, with unintended consequences even for the effectiveness of the central bank's policy decisions.[151]

The need to reconcile the objective of price stability with policy concerns for the stability of the financial system has led the ECB to establish, within its constitutional boundaries, an operational strategy—so-called Pillar 2 strategy—that permit to analyze the immediate risks to price stability, based on the ongoing macroeconomic scenario.[152]

The risk assessment is based on a double analytical cross-checking which comprises an 'economic analysis' and a 'monetary analysis'. The economic analysis is devoted to analyze the array of determinants of price developments over the short to medium period as to capture the interplay of supply and demand in goods, services, and factor markets.[153] The monetary analysis relates to the medium to longer-term horizon and consists of a detailed assessment of monetary aggregates and credit developments to assess their implications for future inflation and economic growth.[154]

This monetary policy strategy is designed to ensure an overall judgment of relevant information which may reveal conditions and circumstances threatening the macroeconomic stability of the Euro area. Although the ECB does not target asset prices directly due to the 'consumer price nature' of its price stability objective, this Pillar 2 strategy pays attention to the volatility of asset price trends which may have serious negative spillovers for market dynamics.

[149] Lastra (2015), p. 255, argues that there is now a consensus that the neglect of financial stability considerations by the ESCB in the years leading up to the crisis was of its main causes. See also Lastra and Wood (2010), pp. 531–550.

[150] We refer to the spillover effects that monetary policy may have in terms of financial instability through its transmission channels. For details, see *supra* at Chap. 4, Sect. 4.1.

[151] Inter alia, see ECB (2011), pp. 55–91.

[152] An in-depth survey is provided in Issing (2006). For a critical perspective, see instead Gerlach, Browne, and Honohan (2004), pp. 389–439. The ECB's strategy for monetary policy is further assessed by de Haan, Eijffinger, and Waller (2005), pp. 27–81.

[153] ECB (2011), p. 9.

[154] Idem, p. 10.

Against this backdrop, monetary policy decisions are not taken in a vacuum but in the context of a broader policy framework that helps mitigate financial stability concerns.[155] The ECB 'closely monitors phenomena—mounting excesses in the creation of money and credit—which, if detected in conjunction with sustained market dynamics, can reveal the nature of the financial facts and provide information on whether these financial facts should be taken into account in tracing out the policy course'.[156] In other words, the Pillar 2 strategy 'takes asset price developments into account to assess developments in asset prices and the degree to which they pose a risk to price stability in a more distant future. This is how elements of the "leaning against the wind" approach have been incorporated in the ECB's strategy'.[157]

The ECB's monetary policy strategy in this way may bring systemic risk considerations into its overall assessment, allowing for systemic monitoring and cross-checking of the whole credit creation process. Despite the EU Treaties establish price stability as the primary objective of the ESCB, the ECB's Pillar 2 strategy introduces an operational mechanism for the assessment of its monetary policy decisions under a financial stability perspective. In view of this strategy, the ECB set up the 'Directorate General Macro-Prudential Policy and Financial Stability' as part of its functional organization. This directorate is then sub-organized into four divisions, namely, the 'Financial Stability Surveillance Division', the 'Financial Regulation Division', the 'Macro-Financial Policies Division', and the 'Macro-prudential Linkages'.[158]

And, while the first two divisions provide mainly analysis and policy advise relating to macroprudential policy decisions of the ECB in its capacity of banking supervisor, the 'Macro-Financial Policies Division' and the 'Macro-prudential Linkages' are responsible to identify and monitor sources of systemic risk in the financial system of the Euro area along with

[155] For details, see Draghi (2015a).

[156] ECB (2011), p. 84.

[157] Idem, pp. 84–85. See also de Haan, Eijffinger, and Waller (2005), p. 75, where the authors explain that the ECB uses asset price developments in its broadly based assessment of the risks for price stability, although its monetary policy does not explicitly target asset prices.

[158] For details on the administrative organization of the ECB, including the 'Directorate General Macro-Prudential Policy and Financial Stability', see the Organization Chart of the ECB, available online at https://www.ecb.europa.eu/ecb/orga/orgachart/html/index.en.html

its potential impact on the stability of the markets. These divisions are likely to have the technical capability to assess cross effects between monetary policy and financial stability and provide a financial stability standpoint to inform the ECB Governing Council.

The Pillar 2 strategy is in line with the constitutional boundaries laid down by Article 127(5) TFEU to the ESCB, as it may help ensure the effectiveness of the macroprudential supervision carried out by the competent authorities. However, although this strategy incorporates financial stability items in its macroeconomic assessments, it does not constitute a strategic policy plan dedicated to weigh up the ECB's monetary policy actions with the ensuing systemic risk spillovers. In other words, it is questionable whether this strategy is sufficient to mitigate risks of conflicts between monetary policy and macroprudential supervision.

As a result, it is fair to say that the overall EU institutional model does not envisage an integrated institutional framework aimed at constraining, where needed, the credit creation process. The embryonic system of '*checks and balances*' managing the cross side effects of monetary and macroprudential policies operates only indirectly, through regulatory instruments that may potentially address the policy conflicts only after they arise. Conversely, they are not designed to prevent them.

5.3.3 *Costs and Benefits of the EU Institutional Model*

To cite Yves Mersch, executive board member of the ECB, the governance of the Euro area can be considered as 'a set of interlocking cogs wheels: they do not all need to be of similar size—that is, we do not necessarily need the same degree of centralisation in each area—but they need to all move in the same direction. If one cog moves in the other direction, the whole machine grinds to a halt'.[159]

This quote remarkably summarizes one of the key findings of this volume: in order to have a consistent interplay of monetary and macroprudential policies, the whole EU institutional architecture should promote a coherent interaction of the related side effects. Since monetary policy and macroprudential policy affect the same variables via common transmission channels, this institutional set-up must allow for an integrated cross-checking of the different policy stances to ensure consistency in the resulting outcomes.

[159] See Mersch (2014).

This consistency can be realized by the operationalization of some legal and regulatory arrangements establishing a mechanism of *checks and balances* for the cross side effects of monetary and macroprudential policies. The optimal governance of the two policies, along with the capacity to produce effective results, is related to a sound legal architecture addressing policy conflicts and negative externalities. Based on this consideration, the institutional model adopted in Europe for tackling these negative spillovers should recognize a *legal interaction* of the two policies within a wider cooperative framework.

As noted in the previous sections, the EU institutional architecture provides for a number of legal instruments that can be used for such a purpose.[160] Nonetheless, we have also anticipated that this institutional model is not sufficient to build up an integrated policy framework where monetary and macroprudential policies may operate in equilibrium.

The present EU monetary policy scenario presents a number of risks in the short-medium period that are related to financial stability. To better understand these risks, we refer to the conclusions elaborated by the German Council of Economic Experts (*Sachverständigenrat zur Begutachtung der gesamtwirtschaftlichen Entwicklung*), in its Annual Economic Report 2015/2016,[161] on the loose monetary policy carried out by the ECB. The economists reflect upon the argument that a prolonged environment of low interest rates is likely to build up risks to financial stability. This is due to the spillover effects of loose monetary policy which undermine the business models of credit and financial institutions, erode the regulatory capital base, and incentivize credit institutions to take on greater risky activities.[162]

In the words of the German Council, 'A sharp rise in interest rates after an extended period of low rates poses the greatest risk of a renewed financial crisis. This could put the solvency of large parts of the banking system at risk […]', since a sudden 'decline in asset prices would also be likely, which could be exacerbated by reduced market liquidity'.[163]

In view of this finding, the German Council recommends the introduction in the EU legislative framework of a number of additional macropru-

[160] For better insights, see *supra* at Chap. 5, Sects. 5.2.2 and 5.2.3.

[161] Sachverständigenrat zur Begutachtung der gesamtwirtschaftlichen Entwicklung (2015). Zukunftsfähigkeit in den Mittelpunkt. Jahresgutachten 2015/16, November 2015 (Hereafter: Annual Economic Report 2015/16).

[162] Annual Economic Report 2015/16, p. 143.

[163] Idem, p. 179.

dential instruments, such as loan to value caps for residential and commercial properties and countercyclical limits for interest rate risks.[164] That is to say that, in conducting its monetary policy, the ECB should be able to compare the benefits of its inflation targeting and the costs of the additional systemic risks that its stance may entail.[165] And this comparison would indicate that the benefits of a long-term loose monetary policy stance do not outweigh the likely costs of its side effects on the overall stability of the financial system.

The German experts therefore support the need of reconfiguring the liaison between monetary and macroprudential policies at the institutional level. Because of the interactions existing between the two policies, 'the relationship between monetary policy and macroprudential policy needs to be clarified in order to avoid conflicting signals. Macroprudential policy alone cannot guarantee the stability of the financial system. The ECB must therefore consider the impact of monetary policy on financial stability in its decisions'.[166]

This policy recommendation recognizes not only a strong concern for the cooperative strategy between the European institutions involved in monetary and macroprudential policies but also—and more broadly—the idea of strengthening the system of *checks and balances* for the cross side effects of the two policies.

The interplay between the two institutional frameworks must be clarified and shall permit to calibrate the ECB monetary policy stance taking fully into account the ensuing systemic risks that may destabilize credit markets.[167] Conversely, the macroprudential policy stance shall be decided in accordance with the monetary policy scenario as to permit a supportive interplay between the interrelated side effects in the policy transmission channels.[168]

[164] See Idem, pp. 199–200.

[165] For an interesting survey of costs and benefits of monetary policy targeting also financial stability, see IMF (2015).

[166] Annual Economic Report 2015/16, p. 200.

[167] Among others, this position is shared in Smets (2014), pp. 263–300. The author, in particular, recognizes the need to maintain price stability as the ultimate objective of monetary policy but keeping an eye on the systemic risks that may materialize. See also Weidmann (2012), p. 50.

[168] For a description on how this can be achieved in a monetary union, see Darracq Paries, Rancoita, and Kok (2015), pp. 158–170.

What seems important to stress is that this system of *checks and balances* requires full institutionalization and cannot be established without a clear recognition in the legislative framework of the EU. This does not necessarily entail changing the ultimate objectives of monetary and macroprudential policies. Nor this stands for the enlargement of the ECB's powers and tasks in order to encompass monetary and macroprudential policies under a single roof, as today strongly advocated by some.[169] Instead, we advance a more viable proposal which would permit to establish a real cross-checking system between the two policies without adjusting the core structure of the existing European and national institutions.

In particular, rethinking the role of the ESRB within the current European regime would give due consideration to the main findings of this volume. If the strong interplay between monetary and macroprudential policies is authentic, and the cross side effects of the two policies are capable to negatively affect each other, we believe there is room to recognize the ESRB as a point of contact between the ESCB and the authorities entrusted with macroprudential powers, provided that the constitutional boundaries set by EU law are fully respected.

5.4 The Legal Limits of the ESRB

The ESRB is a ***unicum*** in the European financial architecture.[170] The legal setting of its macroprudential objective allows the ESRB to capture the build-up of systemic risks in all areas of financial markets, embracing banking, insurance, and capital markets.[171] The absence of any legal personality and the soft-law nature of its macroprudential supervisory powers permit an elastic involvement of the Board any time the development of the financial system may pose risks to its stability.

[169] Inter alia, see Aydin and Volkan (2011).

[170] For details on the specialty of the ESRB's nature, see Ferran and Kern (2010).

[171] Although the macroprudential instruments harmonized at the EU level only apply to banking entities, the ESRB has been actively involved, over the last five years, in detecting systemic risks in all areas of the financial system. To cite some of the important ESRB's contributions in the non-banking sectors, we briefly mention the following: Recommendation of the European Systemic Risk Board of 20 December 2012 on money market funds (ESRB/2012/1); ESRB report on systemic risks in the EU insurance sector, December 2015; ESRB Report on systemic risks in the EU insurance sector, December 2015; Annual ESRB Risk Dashboard where systemic risks evolving from financial markets are assessed and measured.

The scope of ESRB's action is multifaceted and open-end. Its special nature is underscored by the intermediate position held within the legal frameworks of both the ESFS and the ESCB. Although the ESRB is formally part of the ESFS, along with the EBA, the EIOPA, and the ESMA, its operative dependence on the ECB's capabilities and the large audience of EU central bankers in its governing bodies narrow the fragile separation between its macroprudential tasks and the monetary policy responsibilities of the ESCB.

In Chap. 2, Sect. 2.4.1, due consideration has been given to the current settings of the ESRB as established by the relevant EU law. This section makes one step forward in profiling the ESRB reviewing its position as intermediate body between the ESFS and the ESCB, and thus reconsiders, within the constitutional constraints, its policy function in view of the main findings of this volume. If the interactions between monetary and macroprudential policies are material and negative cross side effects of the two policies may pull in opposite directions, the ESRB could be the proper *locus* where these policy conflicts are to be addressed.

To recognize this role, the ESRB's legal boundaries should permit to capture—and eventually address—the systemic risks arising from monetary policy. Albeit enormously sensitive,[172] the reconsideration of the institutional set-up would give the ESRB the advantage of fulfilling its macroprudential tasks in a more articulate manner, without being constrained by the current (*unsustainable*) disconnection from the ECB's monetary policy outlook. Similarly, the ESCB would be persuaded to take fully into account, in its monetary policy strategy, any financial stability considerations, thereby fulfilling its inflation targeting objective by weighting the systemic costs of its monetary decisions.

Rethinking the institutional role of the ESRB would permit to strengthen the *system of checks and balances* that this book advocates as a necessary precondition for the smooth conduct of monetary and macroprudential policies. The economic interplays between these policies would find in this way a clearer recognition by the EU supervisory architecture.

[172] It is important to note that redefining the relationship between the ESRB and the ESCB and assigning a special role to the Board in mitigating systemic risks arising from the ESCB's monetary policy would generate strong resistance by central bankers. This special competence would be interpreted as tightening the independence of the ECB and threatening the autonomy of European central bankers.

5.4.1 *The Absence of Legal Interactions Between the ESCB and the ESRB*

The hierarchical composition of ESCB's institutional framework has been thoroughly scrutinized in the previous chapters. While national central banks are the operational agents of the monetary policy of the EU, the ECB is the institution in charge of the wide monetary policy decision-making process. This implies that, if interactions exist in the legal framework of the two policies, this should be found at the EU level, where the decision-making process of the ESCB takes place. It follows that the sole EU macroprudential body that can play a role in this regard is the ESRB which operates as the apex of the macroprudential institutional architecture in the EU.[173]

Although the relations between this macroprudential body and the ESCB are apparent in view of the logistical and administrative support given by the ECB for the performance of the ESRB's tasks,[174] the legislative set-up of the ESRB explicitly acknowledges its full independence from the ESCB's monetary policy.[175]

The impartiality of the ESRB from EU Member States, EU institutions, or any other public or private body, as envisaged in the Regulation (EU) No. 2010/1092,[176] should be reflected in the widest capability of targeting systemic risks wherever they arise. For this reason, the ESRB by no means should be bound by others in its systemic risk determination, being able to use the legal instruments at its disposal to caution any relevant EU and national authorities whose actions may have implications for financial stability.

[173] Moloney (2014), p. 1009, describes the ESRB as the primary location for macroprudential oversight of the EU financial system.

[174] For details, see Council Regulation (EU) No. 1096/2010 of 17 November 2010 conferring specific tasks upon the European Central Bank concerning the functioning of the European Systemic Risk Board. See also Opinion of the European Central Bank of 4 February 2015 on the review of the mission and organization of the European Systemic Risk Board (CON/2015/4), p. 2.

[175] Article 7(1) of Regulation (EU) No. 1092/2010; cf. also Recital (6) of the same Regulation which explains that 'the support provided by the ECB to the ESRB, as well as the tasks assigned to the ESRB, should be without prejudice to the principle of the independence of the ECB in the performance of its tasks pursuant to the TFEU. For a discussion on this topic, see *supra* at notes 426–437.

[176] In details, we refer once again to Article 7 of Regulation (EU) 2010/1092.

This certainly holds true with respect to the EU Member States, the EU Commission, the EU Council, the ESAs, and all national supervisory authorities. Pursuant to Article 16(2) of Regulation (EU) No. 2010/1092, indeed, the ESRB's warnings and recommendations issued by the ESRB can be addressed to the Union, to one or more Member States, to one or more of the ESAs, or to one or more of the national supervisory authorities.

However, Article 130 TFEU limits the scope of this macroprudential oversight as it excludes the ESCB from the bench of potential ESRB's addressees. By no means can the ESCB be bound by the macroprudential supervision of the ESRB, and it has to fulfill its responsibilities and exercise its powers, without seeking or taking instructions from Member States, other institutions, or bodies, including the ESRB itself.[177]

The normative content of this provision with respect to the relationship between the ESRB and the ESCB is evident if we look at the only source of systemic risk never touched upon by the ESRB's analyses, that is, the systemic risk arising directly by loose monetary policy.

Albeit crucial for ensuring financial stability, systemic risks arising due to monetary policy decisions have been widely neglected—at least thus far—as to reflect the constitutional hierarchy of the policy objectives and comply with the principle of independence granted by the EU Treaty to the ECB in its monetary policy functions.[178]

In this respect, it must be noted that the ESRB has the capacity to issue warnings and recommendations to the ECB in its capacity of banking supervisor.[179] When the ECB holds a position of national competent authority, it is just one of the potential addressees of the ESRB's macroprudential actions. The recognition of this power for the ESRB may question the application of the principle of independence with respect to the ESRB's recommendations and warnings.

[177] Article 130 TFEU and Article 7 of ESCB Statute. For details, cf. Chap. 3, Sect. 3.4.1.

[178] See *supra* at notes 831–840.

[179] This power has been exercised by the ESRB a number of times. For example, the Recommendation ESRB/2014/1 of 18 June 2014 on guidance for setting countercyclical buffer rates (ESRB/2014/1) provides as addressees the 'designated authorities' which are defined by the Recommendation itself as the public authorities or bodies designated by a Member State in accordance with Article 136(1) of Directive 2013/36/EU or the ECB in accordance with Article 9(1) of Regulation (EU) No. 1024/2013. There is no doubt therefore that the ECB, in its capacity of banking supervisor, is a potential addressee of the ESRB recommendations from which it can take instructions.

The issue is whether these recommendations and warnings can be considered as ***instructions*** under the meaning of the EU Treaty that would hinder the independence of the central bank. On the one hand, one may argue that the ESRB legal acts, as soft-law instruments, would not have the legal capacity to influence the ESCB in the performance of its monetary policy tasks. On the other hand, the ESCB would not be obliged to discuss the recommendations and warnings of the ESRB, thereby maintaining the full independence of its decision-making process.

These arguments, however, are not tenable in view of the overall content of Article 130 TFEU. Recommendations and warnings would be capable to influence the exercise of the monetary policy tasks of the ESCB due to the ***comply-or-explain procedure*** incorporated as an indirect enforcement mechanism of these soft-law measures.[180] The ESCB would be obliged, in accordance with the principle of sincere cooperation, to implement the normative content of the ESRB's legal acts, or provide adequate justification for its inaction. This would affect the decision-making process of the ESCB, as the members of the Governing Council would be forced to discuss and incorporate the related macroprudential stance of the ESRB in its monetary policy decisions.

Article 130 TFEU also provides an obligation for the ESRB as the provision explicitly states that any EU bodies—thus, including the ESRB—shall not seek to influence the members of the decision-making bodies of the ESCB when performing the tasks assigned by the Treaty.[181] The ESRB therefore should refrain from issuing any kind of policy recommendation that could directly or indirectly impinge upon the decision-making process of the ESCB.[182]

[180] See *supra* at notes 409–410.

[181] In this respect, the principle of independence laid down in the Treaty works in two ways: it restrains the entities composing the ESCB from taking instructions from other bodies; and it restrains the other bodies from seeking to influence the members of the ESCB. See Smits (1997), p. 161.

[182] As pointed out in the Opinion of the European Central Bank of 4 February 2015 on the review of the mission and organization of the European Systemic Risk Board (CON/2015/4) (2015/C 192/01), the inclusion of the ECB, in its capacity of banking supervisor, as a potential addressee should in no way prejudice the primary objective of the ESCB of maintaining price stability in accordance with Article 127(1) of the Treaty. The opinion clearly draws a line between ECB in its capacity of central bank and the ECB in its capacity of banking supervisor within the SSM, assigning the full independence established by Article 130 TFEU only to the former.

This legal analysis is fully consistent with the provisions set out in the Regulation (EU) No. 1092/2010, which exclude the ECB and the national central banks as potential addressees of the ESRB legal acts.[183] The differential treatment of the ECB in its capacity of banking supervisor—which is instead the addressee of the ESRB legal acts—supports the legal opinion of those suggesting that the principle of full independence, as set out in Article 130 TFEU, applies only to the ECB in the conduct of its monetary policy tasks.[184] In contrast, when acting as a banking supervisor, this independence is to be considered more limited as other bodies, such as the ESRB, are capable to influence, through their soft-law acts, the decision-making of the Supervisory Board.[185]

[183] As pointed out in the Resolution of the European Parliament of 11 March 2014 with recommendations to the Commission on the European System of Financial Supervision (ESFS) Review (2013/2166(INL)), the establishment of the ESRB outside the ECB would, due to Article 130 of the Treaty on the Functioning of the European Union (TFEU), not allow the ESRB to address the ECB in opinions, recommendations, or warnings. However, it should be noted that the ESRB has indirectly targeted systemic risks arising from the stances of monetary policy. For example, with the Recommendation ESRB/2011/1 of 21 September 2011 on lending in foreign currencies, the ESRB acknowledged that an excessive foreign currency lending may trigger systemic externalities due to the trends in the currency exchange rates. As the effects of monetary policy on the exchange rate are widely known, the ESRB in issuing such a recommendation has indirectly targeted the systemic implications of monetary policy via its exchange rate transmission channel. The same argument holds true for Recommendation ESRB/2011/2 on US dollar denominated funding of credit institutions.

[184] For reference on this debate, see *supra* at note 1249.

[185] In line with Article 16 of ESAs Regulations, and similar to the ESRB, the ESAs 'shall, with a view to establishing consistent, efficient and effective supervisory practices within the ESFS, and to ensuring the common, uniform and consistent application of Union law, issue guidelines and recommendations addressed to competent authorities, including the ECB in its capacity of banking supervisor'. It is true that Article 19 of the Council Regulation (EU) No. 1024/2013 provides the principle of independence also for the ECB in its capacity of banking supervisors. According to the wording of this Article, 'The members of the Supervisory Board and the steering committee shall act independently and objectively in the interest of the Union as a whole and shall neither seek nor take instructions from the institutions or bodies of the Union, from any government of a Member State or from any other public or private body.' By the same token, 'The institutions, bodies, offices and agencies of the Union and the governments of the Member States and any other bodies shall respect that independence.' However, the concrete applicability of this Article is questionable in view of the above, as the interactions existing between the ECB, the ESAs, and the ESRB do not seem to support the full independence of the ECB when performing its supervisory functions. On this topic, see Baroncelli (2014), p. 142.

This argument seems decisive. The constitutional constraints set out by the EU Treaty do not recognize any possible instrument that may influence the ECB monetary policy in view of macroprudential considerations. The absence of any public stances by the ESRB on systemic risks arising from monetary policy avoids a constitutional clash between the ESCB's monetary policy decision-making and the ESRB's macroprudential supervision.

The question is whether these constitutional boundaries are fully sustainable in view of the main findings of this volume. In other words, one can wonder whether the existence of strong interactions between monetary and macroprudential policies, and the establishment of poor legal mechanisms aimed at addressing the related cross side effects and conflicts, should lead policymakers to rethink the current institutional set-up of the authorities involved, allowing for a rapprochement of the two policies.

5.4.2 Can the ESRB's Instruments Target Monetary Policy?

Since its establishment at the end of 2010, the ESRB has struggled to expand its expertise in a largely uncharted territory.[186] The lack of a well-defined macroprudential common ground in the economic literature and the absence of a clear consensus on the usefulness of an EU-level macroprudential action among EU countries were critical obstacles in the earlier development of a European macroprudential policymaking.[187]

The scarcity of data availability on credit growth and financial interconnectedness along with the complexity of understanding and measuring financial stability[188] further hindered over the years the oversight capacity of the ESRB. The ESRB had to demonstrate the build-up of a solid practical knowledge in the macroprudential field and ensure continuing coverage of all areas of the financial system.[189] The political sensitiveness of macroprudential policy made the working path of the ESRB particularly

[186] See Draghi (2015b).

[187] See Sapir (2014), pp. 162–163.

[188] For details, see Borio and Shim (2007), p. 17.

[189] For more details, see Mazzaferro (2011), p. 131. This large and challenging mandate required the ESRB to develop in few years a solid background in all areas of the financial system. For Moloney (2014), p. 1015, the ESRB is designated as a reputational body which is deemed to influence policymakers and supervisors through the moral authority associated with the quality and range of its members.

arduous,[190] while the absence of autonomous legal personality and the soft-law nature of its recommendations and warnings further restrained the strength of its policy stances.[191]

Although these criticalities hamper the smooth conduct of its macroprudential oversight, the main shortcomings of the ESRB, which clearly unveil the unaccomplished character of this body, are to be found in the constitutional boundaries set out by the EU Treaty. The institutionalization of this body has neglected the construction of an effective system of 'checks and balances', which would align the cross side effects of monetary and macroprudential policies in a more consistent manner.

The establishment of these safety valves would require the enlargement of the potential addressees of the ESRB's legal acts. In this way, the ESRB would be capable to fully advise and warn the ESCB about any negative financial stability effects that may potentially arise from tightening or relaxing the policy interest rates, or from carrying out its monetary policy instruments.[192] For example, this is particularly the case for market transactions involving sovereign bonds as carried out by the ECB in the burst of the European sovereign debt crisis.[193]

The renewed scope of the ESRB's legal acts would help the monetary authorities to better capture the systemic externalities caused by long-lasting money market operations. In addition, it would help the ESCB to actually weigh costs and benefits of their outright purchase programs, anticipating any negative dynamics that may hamper the functionality of the financial system and the economy as a whole.

The constitutional constraints set out by the EU Treaty prohibit such an enlargement, and any policy proposal in this direction would require a change of the primary law. Moreover, these constitutional boundaries also affect the normative content of recommendations and warnings of the ESRB.

The strength of the ESRB's soft-law instruments is restricted by the impossibility to target risks arising from monetary policy. The ESRB's recommendations and early warnings should be able to target the sources of financial instability wherever they arise. But, given the constitutional con-

[190] See Nyberg (2011), p. 6(8).

[191] For a thorough discussion on the effectiveness of the ESRB's soft-law measures, see *supra* at notes 402–413.

[192] For details on the spillover effects, see *supra* section Chap. 4, Sects. 4.1.2 and 4.1.3.

[193] A discussion of these programs is provided, inter alia, by De Grauwe (2013), pp. 520–535.

straints seen above, this general oversight would encroach upon the principle of independence envisaged for the ESCB by the EU Treaty.

The example of asset encumbrance can help us clarify this idea. Credit institutions finance their business activities using a variety of funding instruments. In order to increase the availability of funding, they more often rely on secured funding sources which, in turn, are dependent on the availability of collateral to back the claims of secured creditors.[194] The reliability on pledging collateral to secured creditors leads to a phenomenon widely known as encumbrance of banks' assets.

Asset encumbrance refers to the unavailability of pledged assets utilized as collateral in secured transactions to be used for other purposes, such as, for example, meeting claims of unsecured creditors in the event of bankruptcy.[195] This phenomenon was particularly material in the EU, where some major banks, as a consequence of investors' risk aversion towards unsecured funding markets and due to the Basel III framework on capital and liquidity, have increased the issuance of covered bonds and other financial instruments that can be utilized as collateral for refinancing operations with central banks.[196]

This phenomenon of asset encumbrance 'increases banks' general funding and liquidity risks in a normal environment since it may reduce the funding headroom of an institution'.[197] This is because

> high levels of encumbrance already used for refinancing reduce the amount of assets that can be transformed into central bank eligible collateral, thus undermining central banks' abilities to provide liquidity assistance— Consequently, the increased role of asset encumbrance in bank funding may reduce the effectiveness of the monetary transmission mechanism. Furthermore, high levels of encumbrance can lead to increased systemic risk in the banking sector and/or increased credit risk for central banks if central banks decide to widen the spectrum of acceptable collateral without applying appropriate haircuts.[198]

[194] CGFS (2013), p. 6.

[195] See Annex—Executive Summary, C 119/9 of Recommendation of the European Systemic Risk Board of 20 December 2012 on funding of credit institutions (ESRB/2012/2). For a thorough analysis of asset encumbrance in Europe, see also EBA (2015).

[196] See Annex—III.1.4, C 119/30 of Recommendation of the European Systemic Risk Board of 20 December 2012 on funding of credit institutions (ESRB/2012/2).

[197] Idem.

[198] Idem.

Moreover, the expansionary outright purchase programs, such as quantitative easing, may increase the scarcity of unencumbered assets in bank's balance sheets, given the outstanding amount of assets pledged as collaterals that are used in unconventional market operations.[199]

The materiality of liquidity funding risk associated with asset encumbrance and the related necessity to apply countercyclical policies on collaterals and haircuts in refinancing operations with central banks would require the ESRB to take action recommending a macroprudential approach in the collateral management of the ECB in order to address any supply-demand imbalances.[200]

Another illustrative example is reflected by the massive amount of sovereign bonds the ESCB purchased in response to the European sovereign debt crisis. The ECB's wide-scale sovereign bond purchases have incentivized governments to ease their fiscal discipline, causing also bonds' mispricing of bonds.[201] These distortions have fostered the infamous nexus

[199] See CGFS (2013), p. 45.

[200] For a better explanation of supply-demand imbalances in collateral management, see CGFS (2013), pp. 15–21. For an empirical survey on the countercyclical use of collateral and margin requirements by central banks, see CGFS (2010). It should be noted that the ESRB has not remained impassive against the potential system risk concerns of monetary policy. For example, the European macroprudential body is quite active in discussing the systemic vulnerabilities arising from the current low interest rate environment. For example, see ESRB General Board meeting in Frankfurt of 25 June 2015, *Press Release*. According to the press statement, 'The ESRB is assessing, from a macro-prudential perspective, potential financial stability effects from the current low interest rate environment and structural changes in the financial sector. A report including potential policy proposals is to be presented to the General Board in mid-2016.' The accommodative monetary policy of the ECB and its negative implications for financial stability are serious fields of analysis for macroprudential purposes, in particular with respect to the soundness of long-term investors, including insurance companies and pension funds, and their ability to generate adequate returns. See also ESRB General Board meeting in Frankfurt of 20 December 2012, *Press Release*. Thus, the systemic risks originating from sudden changes in monetary policy are not negligible in the eyes of the ESRB and require specific measures in order to prevent the build-up of negative spillovers to the real economy. Against this backdrop, the ESRB has signaled—albeit only indirectly—some of the risks to financial stability associated to changes in the monetary policy stance of central banks. One prominent example lies in the Recommendation ESRB/2011/1 of 21 September 2011 on lending in foreign currencies (ESRB/2011/1) (2011/C 342/01), where the ESRB has recognized the negative impact of foreign currency lending on all monetary policy transmission channels. This recommendation acknowledges that a monetary policy stance depreciating the domestic currency could lead to the materialization of credit risks relating to foreign currency loans along with bank funding risks.

[201] On the issue, see Sachverständigenrat zur Begutachtung der gesamtwirtschaftlichen Entwicklung (2015), Chap. 4, Sect. 4.3.

between banks and sovereigns (i.e. *bank-sovereign nexus*),[202] and produce material risks of exposure concentration towards European governments. The systemic risk associated with this nexus depends dangerously upon the creditworthiness of the sovereign.[203]

This risk becomes material when 'a sovereign may, for a significant time, have higher expenditures than tax revenues and go so much into debt that, eventually, it finds it impossible or undesirable to pay its debts as they fall due or, more generally, may not comply with its contractual debt obligations'.[204] At this point, the collapse of the highly exposed banking sector occurs.

As far as the side effects of unconventional monetary policy measures may generate significant risks of concentration for the banking system due to the *bank-sovereign nexus*, the ESRB should be capable to warn about any negative implications for the wide stability of the financial stability. And, in doing so, it should recommend the adoption of some measures, such as countercyclical haircut policies for sovereign bonds used as collateral in the open market operations,[205] which may permit to align the ESCB's independent price stability objective with the public concern on financial stability.

The legal constraints set by Article 130 TFEU would render such recommendations and warnings illegal, as they would influence the decision-making process of the ESCB and encroach upon the scope of the competences legally assigned to the ESRB. This shows that no legal interaction can be found between the ESRB and the ESCB that may permit a rapprochement of the two policies, should they pull in opposite directions. The construction of the EU institutional architecture therefore leaves room for possible conflicts and inconsistencies between the side effects of monetary and macroprudential policies.

[202] For a better understanding of the bank-sovereign nexus in Europe, see Breckenfelder and Schwaab (2015). See also De Bruyckerea, Gerhardtb, Schepensc, and Vander Vennet (2013), pp. 4793–4809; Angelini, Grande, and Panetta (2014); Buch, Koetter, and Ohls (2013).

[203] For a survey of the transmission channels of this nexus, see BCBS (2011).

[204] See ESRB (2015), pp. 44–45.

[205] This policy option is briefly discussed in ESRB (2015), p. 147.

5.4.3 *The General Board as the Locus of Conflict Resolution?*

The Regulation establishing the ESRB provides that the General Board, as EU macroprudential decision-making body, is composed of the President and the Vice-President of the ECB, the 27 Governors of the national central banks, a member of the European Commission, the Chairpersons of the three ESAs, the Chair and two Vice-Chairs of the Advisory Scientific Committee, and the Chair of the Advisory Technical Committee, while a representative of each Member State's relevant national supervisory authority, the President of the Economic and Financial Committee, and the Head of ESRB Secretariat may attend the meetings of the Board without voting powers.[206]

The General Board is chaired at the moment by the President of the ECB, and, typically, decisions are taken by a simple majority of the members attending with voting right the Board's meetings. This procedural rule, however, does not stand for the issuance of recommendations and early warnings, as a two-thirds majority of the votes cast is actually required for their approval.[207]

Although the governance arrangements hereby described are quite relevant for the smooth conduct of the ESRB's macroprudential oversight, the aim of this section is to illustrate one of the main criticalities of the General Board, criticality which is strictly related to the core topic of this volume, that is, the way to address the interactions between monetary and macroprudential policies. The limitation at hand is not the only one related to the decision-making structure of this body. Verhelst (2011), for example, has thoroughly scrutinized the hurdles that potentially affect the effectiveness of the General Board's oversight, such as the lack of coercive power and the non-functional size of the body.[208]

However, the major limitation of the ESRB involves the intractability of monetary policy in Boards' meetings, along with the related systemic risks and the strict interplay with macroprudential policy. The EU Treaties, along with the related constitutional constraints, prohibit not only to

[206] See Article 6 of Regulation (EU) No. 1092/2010. For further specifications on the role and structure of the General Board, see also Articles 2 and 7 of Decision of the European Systemic Risk Board of 20 January 2011 adopting the Rules of Procedure of the European Systemic Risk Board (ESRB/2011/1).

[207] See Article 10(3) of Regulation (EU) No. 1092/2010.

[208] We refer to Verhelst (2011), pp. 28–33.

discuss the implications of monetary policy for financial stability[209] but also the cross-examination of the relevant side effects. In other words, the ESRB General Board is not permitted to introduce monetary policy concerns in its macroprudential oversight, weighting any negative externalities.

The interplay between monetary policy and macroprudential supervision, along with the side effects of one policy over the other, would require the establishment of a proper forum where any material conflicts can be assessed and discussed. At EU and national levels, we have recognized a number of arrangements in the decision-making process of national competent authorities and central banks, which are supposed to account for the need to ensure coordination between non-convergent policy stances.[210] The example of the SSM's decision-making process, where the Governing Council may object a draft decision of the Supervisory Board due to monetary policy concerns, gives evidence of that.

Nonetheless, if the reconciliation between the two policies needs to occur at the highest level of the EU architecture due to the hierarchical structure of the ESCB, one should analyze whether the General Board of the ESRB can be the locus of this policy reconciliation. Differently from the principle of independence assigned to the ESCB by the EU Treaty, the independence of the ESRB is guaranteed only by Article 7 of its founding Regulation.[211] Despite the different legal basis upon which this independence is established, the normative content of the provision does not permit an interpretation that would allow the members of the General Board to introduce monetary policy considerations in the general discussion on macroprudential policy.

The General Board shall refrain from introducing monetary policy considerations during the general meetings, as this could be seen as a way to influence other members of the Board in the performance of their tasks.

[209] As above argued, the ESRB is entrusted with the general oversight of systemic risks in the European Union. The large scope of this mandate seems to include the systemic risk implications of monetary policy, as the EU law does not restrain, nor forbid, such a supervisory analysis.

[210] We have described the legal mechanisms established in the EU framework in Chap. 5, Sects. 5.2.1–5.2.3.

[211] See Article 7 of Regulation (EU) No. 1092/2010. For a comparison of this Article with the principle of independence assigned to the ESCB by the TFEU, see *supra* at note 428.

The members of the ESRB General Board must disregard their monetary policy concerns and, acting impartially, should not defend their macroprudential stances during the meetings of the General Board based on their monetary policy stances. Although this separation is in line with the legal boundaries set out by EU law, it nevertheless represents a critical gap for the decision-making of the ESRB and a strong limitation for its effective macroprudential oversight.

The ESRB could be the optimal forum for addressing negative interactions between monetary and macroprudential policies due to its exceptional composition. The ESRB General Board could easily become the proper resolution forum for the case of conflicts between the ESCB monetary policy conducted and the macroprudential policy carried out at the national level by the authorities entrusted with macroprudential powers.

In this respect, the current legal framework also limits ESRB's ability to fully perform its tasks. Assigning separate functions to strictly independent authorities seems no longer sufficient to ensure efficiency of the policy stances and consistency of the targeted results.[212] Policy coordination in this field may be extremely complex to achieve—particularly in a monetary union—and may result ineffective.[213] Conversely, mitigating the variety of systemic risks requires policymakers to acknowledge a broader perspective in the design of the institutions having macroprudential responsibilities, perspective that should no longer disregard the financial stability implications of risky monetary policy scenarios.

[212] For example, this is recognized by Mersch (2013). For a similar stance, see Smets (2014). Due to the legal constraints posed by the Treaty, the legislative reviews of the ESRB institutional arrangements have always neglected the need to weaken the hard separation between monetary and macroprudential policies in view of a policy rapprochement. Instead, these reviews have mainly focused on the need to enlarge the macroprudential toolbox assigned to the ESRB and on the need to strengthen cooperation among the relevant authorities. For details on some of these proposals, see High-Level Group on the ESRB Review (2013), Contribution to the Review of the ESRB; Report from the Commission to the European Parliament and the Council on the mission and organization of the European Systemic Risk Board (ESRB) {SWD(2014) 260 final}; ESAs Joint Opinion—Review on the functioning of the European Systemic Risk Board (ESRB).

[213] Praet (2011), pp. 4–5.

References

Afonso, António, Sequeira, Ana (2010). Revisiting Business Cycle Synchronisation in the European Union, *ISEG Economics Working Paper*, No. 22/2010/DE/UECE.

Amtenbrink, Fabian (2015). The Metamorphosis of European Economic and Monetary Union. In: '*The Oxford Handbook of European Union Law*', (eds.) Anthony Arnull, Damian Chalmers, *Oxford University Press.*

Angelini, Paolo, Grande, Giuseppe, Panetta, Fabio (2014). The Negative Feedback Loop between Banks and Sovereigns, *Bank of Italy Occasional Paper*, No. 213.

Angelini, Paolo, Stefano Neri, and Fabio Panetta (2011). Monetary and Macroprudential Policies, *Banca d'Italia Working Papers*, No. 801, March 2011.

Aydin, Burcu, Volkan, Engin (2011). Incorporating Financial Stability in Inflation Targeting Frameworks, *IMF Working Papers*, No. 224.

Bachtler, John, Mendez, Carlos, Wishlade, Fiona (2016). EU Cohesion Policy and European Integration: The Dynamics of EU Budget and Regional Policy Reform, *Routledge*, London and New York.

Baglioni, Angelo (2016). The European Banking Union: A Critical Assessment, *Palgrave Macmillan.*

Baker, Andrew (2013). The New Political Economy of the Macroprudential Ideational Shift, *New Political Economy*, Vol. 18, Issue 1.

Baker, Andrew (2015). The Bankers' Paradox: The Political Economy of Macroprudential Regulation, *SRC Discussion Paper*, No. 37.

Barrell, Ray, Gottschalk, Sylvia, Holland, Dawn, Khoman, Ehsan, Liadze, Iana, Pomerantz Olga (2008). The Impact of EMU on Growth and Employment, *European Commission Economic Papers*, No. 318.

Baun, Michael, Marek, Dan (2014). Cohesion Policy in the European Union, *Palgrave Macmillan.*

BCBS (2011). The transmission Channels between the Financial and Real Sectors: A Critical Survey of the Literature, *BIS Working Paper,* No. 18.

Baroncelli, Stefania (2014). The Independence of the ECB after the Economic Crisis. In: '*About the Constitutionalization of European Budgetary Constraints*', (eds.) Maurice Adams, Federico Fabbrini, Pierre Larouche, *Hart Publishing.*

Bini Smaghi, Lorenzo (2007). Legal System and Financial Markets, *Opening Remarks at the Conference 'Legal Issues Related to the Financial Markets'*, Frankfurt am Main, 26 October 2007.

Boccuzzi, Giuseppe (2016). The European Banking Union, *Palgrave Macmillan.*

Borio, Claudio (2012). The Financial Cycle and Macroeconomics: What Have We Learnt?, *BIS Working Papers*, No. 395.

Borio, Claudio, Shim, Ilhyock (2007). What Can (Macro-)Prudential Policy Do to Support Monetary Policy?, *BIS Working Papers*, No. 242.

Breckenfelder, Johannes H., Schwaab, Bernd (2015). The Bank-Sovereign Nexus Across Borders. *SSRN*. Online. Available at: http://ssrn.com/abstract=2611107

Buch, Claudia M., Koetter, Michael, Ohls, Jana (2013). Banks and Sovereign Risk: A Granular View, *Deutsche Bundesbank Discussion Paper*, No. 29/2013.

Busch, Danny, Ferrarini, Guido (eds.) (2015). European Banking Union, *Oxford University Press.*

Calomiris, Charles W. (2010). Reassessing the Fed's Regulatory Role, *Cato Journal*, Vol. 30, No. 2.

Cecchetti, Stephen G. (1999). Legal Structure, Financial Structure, and the Monetary Policy Transmission Mechanism, *NBER Working Papers*, No. 7151.

CGFS (2010). The Role of Margin Requirements and Haircuts in Procyclicality. Report Submitted by a Study Group established by the Committee on the Global Financial System, *CGFS Papers*, No. 36.

CGFS (2013). Asset Encumbrance, Financial Reform and the Demand for Collateral Assets. Report Submitted by a Working Group Established by the Committee on the Global Financial System, *CGFS Papers*, No. 49.

Cheun, Samuel, von Köppen-Mertes, Isabel, Weller, Benedict (2009). The Collateral Frameworks of the Eurosystem, the Federal Reserve System and the Bank of England and the Financial Market Turmoil, *ECB Occasional Paper Series*, No. 107.

Chwieroth, Jeffrey, Danielsson, Jon (2013). Political Challenges of the Macroprudential Agenda. Vox CEPR's Policy Portal (6 September 2013). Online. Available at: http://www.voxeu.org/article/political-challenges-macroprudential-agenda

Clark, Alastair, Large, Andrew (2011). Macroprudential Policy: Addressing the Things We Don't Know, *Group of Thirty Occasional Paper*, No. 83.

Coase, Ronald H. (1984). The New Institutional Economics, *Zeitschrift für die gesamte Staatswissenschaft / Journal of Institutional and Theoretical Economics*, Bd. 140, H. 1.

Coffee, John C. (2001). The Rise of Dispersed Ownership the Roles of Law and the State in the Separation of Ownership and Control, *Yale Law Journal*, Vol. 111, No. 1.

Constâncio, Vítor (2013). Toward the Banking Union, *Speech Held at the 2nd FIN-FSA Conference on EU Regulation and Supervision "Banking and Supervision under Transformation"* Organised by the Financial Supervisory Authority, Helsinki, 12 February 2013.

Constâncio, Vitor (2014). The ECB and Macro-prudential Policy: From Research to Implementation, *Speech held at the Third Conference of the Macro-prudential Research Network*, Frankfurt-am-Main, 23 June 2014.

Constâncio, Vítor (2015). Macroprudential Policy in Europe: Ensuring Financial Stability in a Banking Union, *Keynote Speech at the Financial Stability Conference*, Berlin, 28 October 2015.

Cœuré, Benoît (2013). Monetary Policy and Banking Supervision, *Symposium: "Central Banking: Where Are We Headed?" in Honour of Stefan Gerlach's Contribution to the Institute for Monetary and Financial Stability*, Goethe University, Frankfurt, 7 February 2013.

Cukierman, Alex (2011). Reflections on the Crisis and on Its Lessons for Regulatory Reforms and for Central Bank Policies. In: '*Handbook of Central Banking, Financial Regulation and Supervision After the Financial Crisis*', (eds.) Sylvester Eijffinger, Donato Masciandaro, *Edward Elgar Publishing*.

Darracq Paries, Matthieu, Rancoita, Elena, Kok, Christoffer (2015). Quantifying the Policy Mix in a Monetary Union with National Macroprudential Policies, *ECB Financial Stability Review*, November 2015.

De Bruyckerea, Valerie, Gerhardtb, Maria, Schepensc, Glenn, Vander Vennet, Rudi (2013). Bank/sovereign Risk Spillovers in the European Debt Crisis, *Journal of Banking & Finance*, Vol. 37, Issue 12.

De Grauwe, Paul (2013). The European Central Bank as Lender of Last Resort in the Government Bond Markets, *CESifo Economic Studies*, Vol. 59, No. 3.

de Haan, Jakob, Eijffinger, Sylvester C.W., Waller, Sandra (2005). The European Central Bank – Credibility, Transparency, and Centralization, *The MIT Press*, Cambridge.

de Larosière Report (2009). Report of the High-Level Group on Financial Supervision in the EU, Brussels, 25 February 2009.

Dellepiane-Avellaneda, Sebastian (2009). Review Article: Good Governance, Institutions and Economic Development: Beyond the Conventional Wisdom, *British Journal of Political Science*, Vol. 40, Issue 1.

Draghi, Mario (2015a). The ECB's Recent Monetary Policy Measures: Effectiveness and Challenges, *IMF Camdessus Lecture*, Washington, DC, 14 May 2015.

Draghi, Mario (2015b). Introductory Statement by Mario Draghi, Chair of the ESRB, *Hearing before the Committee on Economic and Monetary Affairs of the European Parliament*, Brussels, 12 November 2015.

Drehmann, Mathias, Borio, Claudio, Tsatsaronis, Kostas (2012). Characterising the Financial Cycle: Don't Lose Sight of the Medium Term!, *BIS Working Papers*, No. 380.

Drobak, John N. (1998). Law Matters, *Washington University Law Review*, Vol. 76, Issue 1.

Drobak, John N. (2008). Introduction: Law & the New Institutional Economics, *Washington University Journal of Law & Policy*, Vol. 26, Issue 1.

Duff, Arthur W.S. (2014). Central Bank Independence and Macroprudential Policy: A Critical Look at the U.S. Financial Stability Framework, *Berkeley Business Law Journal*, Vol. 11, Issue 1.

Dutzler, Barbara (2003). The European System of Central Banks: An Autonomous Actor?: The Quest for an Institutional Balance in EMU, *Springer*.

EBA (2015). EBA Report on Asset Encumbrance, September 2015.

ECB (2008). The ECB's Monetary Policy Strategy and Its Implementation. In: '*Monthly Bulletin 10th Anniversary of the ECB*', Frankfurt am Main.

ECB (2011). The Monetary Policy of the ECB, Frankfurt am Main.

ECB (2014a). *Guide to Banking Supervision,* Frankfurt am Main.

ECB (2014b). Progress in the Operational Implementation of the Single Supervisory Mechanism Regulation, *SSM Quarterly Report*, No. 3.

Egawa, Eri, Otani, Akira, Sakiyama, Toshiyuki (2015). What Determines Institutional Arrangements for Macroprudential Policy?, *IMES Discussion Papers*, No. 2015-E-3.

Eggertsson, Thrainn (1990). Economic Behavior and Institutions, *Cambridge University Press.*

Eidenberger, Judith, Liebeg, David, Schmitz, Stefan W., Seliger, Reinhardt, Sigmund, Michael, Steiner, Katharina, Strobl, Peter, Ub, Eva (2014). Macroprudential Supervision: A Key Lesson from the Financial Crisis, *Oesterreichische Nationalbank Financial Stability Report*, No. 27.

ESRB (2013). The Consequences of the Single Supervisory Mechanism for Europe's Macro-prudential Policy Framework, *Reports of the Advisory Scientific Committee,* No. 3/September 2013.

ESRB (2014a). ESRB Recommendation on the Macro-prudential Mandate of National Authorities (ESRB/2011/3) Follow-up Report – Overall Assessment, June 2014.

ESRB (2014b). Allocating Macro-prudential Powers, *Reports of the Advisory Scientific Committee*, No. 5/November.

ESRB (2015). Report on the Regulatory Treatment of Sovereign Exposures, March 2015.

Farina, Francesco, Tamborini, Roberto (2001). Macroeconomic Stabilization Policies in Europe under the New Regime of Monetary Union, *Quaderni Università degli Studi di Siena Dipartimento di Economia Politica*, No. 301.

Ferran, Eilis, Kern, Alexander (2010). Can Soft Law Bodies be Effective? Soft Systemic Risk Oversight Bodies and the Special Case of the European Systemic Risk Board, *University of Cambridge Faculty of Law, Research Paper*, No. 36/2011.

Ferran, Eilis (2015). European Banking Union: Imperfect, But It Can Work. In: '*European Banking Union*', (eds.) Danny Busch, Guido Ferrarini, *Oxford University Press.*

Gerlach, Stefan, Browne, Frank, Honohan, Patrick (2004). The Two Pillars of the European Central Bank, *Economic Policy*, Vol. 19, No. 40.

Giannone, Domenico, Lenza, Michele, Reichlin, Lucrezia (2009). Business Cycles in the Euro Area, *ECB Working Paper Series*, No. 1010.

Gianviti, François (2010). The Objectives of Central Banks. In: '*International Monetary and Financial Law*', (eds.) Mario Giovanoli, Diego Devos, *Oxford University Press.*

Gilardi, Fabrizio (2002). Policy Credibility and Delegation to Independent Regulatory Agencies: A Comparative Empirical Analysis, *Journal of European Public Policy*, Vol. 9, No. 6.

Grüner, Hans P. (2013). The Political Economy of Structural Reform and Fiscal Consolidation Revisited, *European Commission Economic Papers*, No. 487.

Gualandri, Elisabetta (2015). Single Supervisory Mechanism e politiche macro-prudenziali nell'Unione europea, *Banca Impresa Società*, No. 1/2015.

Heath, Daniel (2014). International Coordination of Macroprudential and Monetary Policy, *Georgetown Journal of International Law*, Vol. 45, Issue 5.

Herzberg, Valerie, Watson, Max (2014). Macroprudential Policies in the Euro Area: Issues for the Next Ten Years, St Antony's College, *University of Oxford Discussion Draft.*

Hodgson, Geoffrey M. (2004). The Evolution of Institutional Economics: Agency, Structure and Darwinism in American Institutionalism, *Routledge*, London.

Houben, Aerdt, Kakes, Jan (2013). Financial Imbalances and Macroprudential Policy in a Currency Union, *DNB Occasional Studies*, Vol. 11, No. 5.

House of Lords (2009). The Future of EU Financial Regulation and Supervision, *14th Report of Session 2008–09.*

Huertas, Thomas F. (2016). Banking Union: The Way Forward. In: '*European Banking Union Prospects and Challenges*', (eds.) Juan E. Costaneda, David G. Mayes, Geoffrey Wood, *Routledge*, London and New York.

IBRD, WB, IMF (2005). Financial Sector Assessment: A Handbook, *International Monetary Fund*, Washington, DC.

IMF (2012). The Interaction between Macroprudential and Monetary Policies: Background Paper.

IMF (2013a). The interaction of Monetary and Macroprudential Policies, 29 January 2013.

IMF (2013b). Implementing Macroprudential Policy – Selected Legal Issues, 17 June 2013.

IMF (2015). Monetary Policy and Financial Stability, *IMF Staff Report*, September 2015.

Ingves, Stefan, Jansson, Per (2014). Monetary Policy Has Had Positive Results in Sweden, *Letter to the Financial Times*, 23 July 2014. Online. Available at: http://www.ft.com/cms/s/0/678a9f46-11c7-11e4-8279-00144feabdc0.html#axzz3w6p RcNuM

Issing, Otmar (2006). The ECB's Monetary Policy Strategy: Why Did We Choose a Two Pillar Approach? *Presented at the Conference 'The Role of Money: Money and Monetary Policy in the Twenty-First Century*', 4th ECB Central Banking Conference, Frankfurt.

Karmann, Alexander, Enkhzaya, Chuluunbaatar (2006). Impact of Institutions on Lending: Informal Constraints and Enforcement of Bank Regulation in Mongolia, *Deutscher Universitaetsverlag*, Wiesbaden.

Kohn, Donald (2015). Implementing Macroprudential and Monetary Policies: The Case for Two Committees, *Remarks Delivered to the Federal Reserve Board's Boston Conference*, 2 October 2015.

La Porta, Rafael, Lopez-de-Manes, Florencio, Shleifer, Andrei, Vishny, Robert (2002). Investor Protection and Corporate Valuation, *The Journal of Finance*, Vol. 57, Issue 3.

Lastra, Maria Rosa (2015). International Financial and Monetary Law, *Oxford University Press.*

Lastra, Maria Rosa, Wood, Geoffrey (2010). The Crisis of 2007–09: Nature, Causes, and Reactions, *Journal of International Economic Law*, Vol. 13, No. 3.

Law, Siong Hook, Azman-Saini, W.N.W. (2008). The Quality of Institutions and Financial Development, *MPRA Paper*, No. 12107.

Lawson, Gary (1999). Delegation and the Constitution, *Regulation*, Vol. 22, No. 2.

Lenihan, Niall J. (2008). The Price Stability Mandate of the European System of Central Banks: A Legal Perspective. In: '*Current Development in Monetary and Financial Law*', Vol. 5, *International Monetary Fund*, Washington, DC.

Louis, Jean-Victor (1995). L'Union économique et monétaire. In: '*Commentaire Megret, Le Droit de la CEE*', *Editions de l'Université de Bruxelles.*

Madema, Steven G, Mercuro, Nicholas (2006). Economics and the Law: From Posner to Postmodernism and Beyond, *Princeton University Press.*

Mandler, Martin, Scharnagl, Michael, Volz, Ute (2016). Heterogeneity in Euro-area Monetary Policy Transmission: Results from a Large Multi-country BVAR Model, *Deutsche Bundesbank Discussion Paper*, No. 3/2016.

Manger-Nestler, Cornelia (2013). Interaction for Monetary and Financial Stability: Central Banks as Main Actors in the Global Financial System. In: "*European Yearbook of International Economic Law 2014*", (eds.) Christoph Herrmann, Markus Krajewski, Jörg Philipp Terhechte, *Springer-Verlag Berlin Heidelberg.*

Mazzaferro, Francesco (2011). Macro-prudential Instruments for Containing Systemic Risk: The ESRB View. In: *'The ESRB at 1', IMFS Interdisciplinary Studies in Monetary and Financial Stability*, Vol. 2012/1.

May, Peter J., Jochim, Ashley E. (2013). Policy Regime Perspectives: Policies and Governing, *Policy Studies Journal*, Vol. 41, Issue 3.

McPhilemy, Samuel (2016). Integrating Macro-prudential Policy: Central Banks as the "Third Force" in the EU Financial Reform, *West European Politics*, Vol. 39, Issue 3.

Merler, Silvia (2015). Squaring the Cycle: Capital Flows, Financial Cycles, and Macro-prudential Policy in the Euro Area, *Bruegel Working Papers*, No. 14.

Mersch, Yves (2013). Monetary Policy and Financial Stability under One Roof, *Keynote Speech Held at the 6th Policy Roundtable of the European Central Bank: "The Future of Global Policy Coordination"*, 6 September 2013.

Mersch, Yves (2014). Law, Money and Market: The Legal Dimension of Monetary Policy, *Speech at the Information Club Meeting, Luxembourg*, 31 May 2014.

Moloney, Niamh (2014). EU Securities and Financial Markets Regulation, *Oxford University Press*, Oxford.

Nijsen, André (2008). Origin and Functionalities of Regulation. In: '*Business Regulation and Public Policy: The Costs and Benefits of Compliance*', (eds.) André Nijsen, John Hudson, Christoph Müller, Kees van Paridon, R. Thurik, *Springer*, Berlin.

North, Douglass (1990). Institutions, Institutional Change and Economic Performance, *Cambridge University Press.*

Nyberg, Lars (2011). The ESRB – Reflections after 9 Months of Operation, *Speech Held at the Conference on the Macro Prudential Oversight of the Financial Sector Arranged by Norges Bank*, Oslo, 27 September 2011. Available at: http://www.riksbank.se/Upload/Dokument_riksbank/Kat_publicerat/Tal/2011/110927e.pdf

Osiński, Jacek (2013). Institutional Needs for Optimal Macroprudential Arrangements. In: '*Macroprudential Frameworks in Asia*', (eds.) Steven Barnett, Rodolfo Main, *International Monetary Fund*, Washington, DC.

Pistor, Katherina (2013). A Legal Theory of Finance, *Journal of Comparative Economics.* Vol. 41, Issue 2.

Posner, Richard A. (1993). The New Institutional Economics Meets Law and Economics, *Journal of Institutional and Theoretical Economics (JITE)*, Vol. 149, No. 1.

Praet, Peter (2011). The (Changing) Role of Central Banks in Financial Stability Policies, *Speech at the 14th Annual Internal Banking Conference held by the Federal Reserve Bank of Chicago and the European Central Bank*, Chicago, 10 November 2011.

Reinhardt, Dennis, Sowerbutts, Rhiannon (2015). Regulatory Arbitrage in Action: Evidence from Banking Flows and Macroprudential Policy, *Bank of England Staff Working Paper*, No. 546.

Sachverständigenrat zur Begutachtung der gesamtwirtschaftlichen Entwicklung (2015). Zukunftsfähigkeit in den Mittelpunkt. Jahresgutachten 2015/16, November 2015.

Sapir, André (2014). Europe's Macroprudential Policy Framework in Light of the Banking Union. In: '*Macroprudentialism*', (ed.) Dirk Schoenmaker, *CEPR Press*, Washington, DC.

Schoenmaker, Dirk (2012). The Missing Link in Banking Union: Macro-prudential Supervision, *DSF Policy Brief*, No. 21.

Schoenmaker, Dirk (2014). Allocating Macroprudential Powers. In: 'Putting. Macroprudential. Policy to Work', (eds.) Aerdt Houben, Rob Nijskens, Mark Teunissen, *De Nederlandsche Bank Occasional Studies*, Vol. 12–7.

Scholten, Miroslava, van Rijsbergen, Marloes (2014). The ESMA-Short Selling Case: Erecting a New Delegation Doctrine in the EU upon the Meroni-Romano Remnants, *Legal Issues of Economic Integration*, Vol. 41, Issue 4.

Siekmann, Helmut (ed.) (2013). EWU – Kommentar zur Europäischen Währungsunion, *Mohr Siebeck*, Tübingen.

Siekmann, Helmut (2015). The Legal Framework for the European System of Central Banks. In: '*Central Banking and Financial Stability in East Asia*', (eds.) Frank Rövekamp, Moritz Bälz, Hanns Günther Hilpert, *Springer International Publishing*.

Smets, Frank (2014). Financial Stability and Monetary Policy: How Closely Interlinked? *International Journal of Central Banking*, Vol. 10, No. 2.

Smits, René (1997). The European Central Bank: Institutional Aspects. *Kluwer Law International*, The Hague.

Tamborini, Roberto (2004). The "Brussels Consensus" on Macroeconomic Stabilization Policies: A Critical Assessment. In: '*Governing EMU Economic, Political, Legal and Historical Perspectives*', (eds.) Francisco Torres, Amy Verdun, Chiara Zilioli, Hubert Zimmermann, *European University Institute*, Florence.

Teivanen, Teivo (1997). The Independence of the European Central Bank: Implications for Democratic Governance. In: '*The Politics of Economic and Monetary Union*', (eds.) Petri Minkkinen, Heikki Patomäki, *Springer US*.

Ter Kuile, Gijsbert, Wissink, Laura, Bovenschen, Willem (2015). Tailor-Made Accountability within the Single Supervisory Mechanism, *Common Market Law Review*, Vol. 52.

Theissen, Roel (2014). EU Banking Supervision, *Eleven International Publishing*, Bruxelles.

Tröger, Tobias H. (2015). A Political Economy Perspective on Common Supervision in the Eurozone. In: '*Financial Regulation: A Transatlantic Perspective*', (eds.) Ester Faia, Andreas Hackethal, Micheal Haliassos, Katja Langenbucher, *Cambridge University Press*.

Verhelst, Stijn (2011). Renewed Financial Supervision in Europe – Final or Transitory? *Egmont – The Royal Institute for International Relations Academia Press*, Brussels.

Van Cleynenbruegel, Pieter (2014). Meroni Circumvented? Article 114 TFEU and EU Regulatory Agencies, *Maastricht Journal of European and Comparative Law*, Vol. 2014/1.

Visco, Ignazio (2011). Key Issues for the Success of Macroprudential Policies, *Policy Panel on the Macroprudential Policy Framework Bok-BIS Conference*, Seoul, 18 January 2011.

Waldhoff, Chistian (2013). Artikel 127 AEUV. In: 'EWU – Kommentar zur Europäischen Währungsunion,' (ed.) Helmut Siekmann, *Mohr Siebeck*, Tübingen.

Weatherill, Stephen (2012). The Constitutional Context of (Ever Wider) Policymaking. In: '*The Oxford Handbook of the European Union*', (eds.) Erik Jones, Anand Menon, and Stephen Weatherill, *Oxford University Press*.

Weidmann, Jens (2012). Managing Macroprudential and Monetary Policy – A Challenge for Central Banks. In: '*The ESRB at 1*', *IMFS Interdisciplinary Studies in Monetary and Financial Stability*, Vol. 2012/1.

Williamson, Oliver E. (2000). The New Institutional Economics: Taking Stock, Looking Ahead, *Journal of Economic Literature*, Vol. 38, No. 3.

Zilioli, Chiara, Selmayr, Martin (2001). The Law of the European Central Bank, *Hart Publishing*, Oxford.

Zilioli, Chiara (2013). The Role of Central Banks in Ensuring Financial Stability, *Remarks at the IMFS Conference on Monetary and Financial Stability Economic and Legal Limits of Central Banking*, 26 November 2013, Frankfurt.

Zilioli, Chiara (2016). *The Independence of the European Central Bank and Its Banking Supervisory Competences.* In: '*Independence and Legitimacy in the Institutional System of the European Union*', (ed.) Dominique Ritleng, *Oxford University Press.*

CHAPTER 6

Some Concluding Remarks

This book sought to dissect the main components of macroprudential policy and analyze them under the realm of law. The identification of these components is instrumental in providing a speculative basis upon which lawyers may discuss the current interplay between macroprudential supervision and monetary policy.

Only pure economists have dealt with such a critical issue so far. A number of econometric models have been developed in order to identify the best possible strategies allowing for a cooperative conduct of the policies at hand. But the present need to construct a functional supervisory architecture would require lawyers to step in this discussion. Although familiarizing with macroeconomic concepts and aggregate phenomena may be a complex task for lawyers, the outbreak of the financial crisis challenged mainstream ideas of the irrelevance of law for macroeconomics.

If close interactions can be clearly identified between macroprudential and monetary policies and related cross side effects can affect the smooth functioning of credit channels, law and economics scholars should jointly look for the optimal institutional architecture that may permit the rapprochement of the two policies and the alignment of the side effects. This is particularly true if one considers the ongoing financial reforms taking place in Europe. The establishment of a multi-layer structure for macroprudential oversight across countries, along with the centralized monetary policy framework of the ESCB, can ignite the debate over the optimal institutional arrangements for ensuring consistency of the policy outcomes.

L. Amorello, *Macroprudential Banking Supervision & Monetary Policy*, https://doi.org/10.1007/978-3-319-94156-1_6

The aim of this volume is to open such a debate in the legal scholarship. Lawyers can play a role in this architectural construction by decomposing macroeconomic concepts and reconstructing them under a legal approach. The understanding of how aggregate phenomena are supposed to work can allow lawyers to propose a menu of policy and regulatory options that may likely mitigate—or better constrain—unintended negative spillovers.

In view of this, after having identified the primary and intermediate objectives of macroprudential and monetary policies along with the transmission channels upon which both policies are meant to operate, this volume stresses the importance of the legal framework for institutions conducting—separately—the two policies. And, in analyzing the interactions between the side effects of macroprudential and monetary policies, this tome seeks to highlight how—and to what extent—the current EU legal framework is capable to manage the policy interactions in a coherent manner.

6.1 Rethinking the Interaction Between Macroprudential Supervision and Monetary Policy

There is no doubt that macroprudential policy and monetary policy are different in nature.[1] As argued in this volume multiple times, the primary and more distinctive feature of the two policies lies in their separate ultimate objectives, namely, price stability and financial stability. The domain of monetary policy in stabilizing inflation is clearly distinguished from the objective of macroprudential policy in tackling systemic risks.

But a number of economic interactions can be clearly identified due to common transmission channels upon which the two policies operate. Similar macroeconomic variables come to be influenced by the operationalization of the two policies by the relevant authorities. Since these interactions can be as strong as to generate inconsistent market signals and conflicting side effects in the attainment of each targeted objective, the actual functioning of monetary and macroprudential policies can be seriously jeopardized.

The institutional architecture set out by law should be constructed in a way that allows for some sort of rapprochement between the policies involved as to ensure consistency in their ultimate outcomes. Legal

[1] See Svensson (2015).

arrangements should be put in place within the whole monetary and financial architecture in order to ensure a coherent system of checks and balances in the credit creation process.

The establishment of a new macroprudential dimension within the EU, characterized by national and EU bodies, institutional powers, and regulatory instruments, requires a thorough analysis of how this new supervisory structure works in respect to the monetary policy of the ESCB and whether any such legal arrangements can be found in the EU legal framework.

The analysis of the European macroprudential policy architecture allows us to identify a bunch of institutional provisions aimed at incentivizing cooperative behavior between the ECB, national central banks, and macroprudential bodies. National central banks are usually represented in the governance structure of national macroprudential authorities, and the deployment of macroprudential instruments is subject to a certain level of control by monetary authorities. National central banks belonging to the ESCB can therefore have a say in the macroprudential policy actions and can influence—to some extent—the policy strategies so deployed.

In this respect, particularly important is the construction of the SSM and the assignment of macroprudential tasks to the ECB in its capacity of banking supervisor. A non-negligible legal interaction at the EU level is ensured by the non-objection procedure of the ECB Governing Council for the approval of supervisory draft decisions. The power of the Governing Council to reject supervisory draft decisions based on monetary policy considerations entails the European legislators acknowledges the need to ensure consistency between the ECB monetary policy and the (macro) prudential actions undertaken under its banking supervisory competences. In this way the interplay between macroprudential supervision and monetary policy is managed by institutionalizing a mechanism that permits—in theory—to restrain negative externalities on monetary policy due to macroprudential decisions.

Albeit this mechanism may seem powerful in view of the supervisory tasks allocated within the SSM structure, it can operate only marginally. Core macroprudential responsibilities assigned at the national level, along with the institution-specific features of the ECB's supervisory decisions, make this interaction asymmetrical and fragile. The centralized nature of the ESCB's monetary policy and the decentralized scope of macroprudential policies across the EU (where Member States have different macroprudential policy stances) prove that this institutional arrangement is not sufficient to ensure a proper system of checks and balances in the smooth operationalization of the policies involved. Inconsistencies and negative spillovers cannot be excluded as the EU framework does not figure out a comprehensive mechanism for a cooperative conduct of the two policies.

In line with the primary law, the ESCB's monetary policy cannot be influenced by financial stability considerations. Although the ECB's Pillar 2 strategy could theoretically embrace some systemic risk analysis, the ultimate objective of price stability, along with the principle of full independence assigned by the TFEU, prohibits any significant interaction. Against this backdrop, the adoption of a loose monetary policy and the deployment of unconventional monetary policy instruments may incentivize without any substantial constraint the build-up of systemic risks, which could eventually harm the normal functioning of the internal market.

The design of the ESRB as the apex of the macroprudential architecture at EU level should have recognized these concerns and provided for an array of institutional arrangements aimed at targeting systemic risks arising from loose monetary policy stances. The concrete institutionalization of the ESRB has neglected this issue. Its soft-law powers by no means can be used to warn the ESCB on systemic risk spillovers that may arise from certain perilous market operations, nor can the ESRB recommend the ECB or national central banks on actions to be taken to mitigate related systemic events. As a result, the ESRB faces a puzzling conundrum: despite being a body responsible for overseeing the stability of the European financial system as a whole, it has no power to target systemic risks underlying central banks' operations.

One can assume that the legal framework of macroprudential supervision and the institutional layer of monetary policy are to be rethought in light of the close interactions previously described. The statutory provisions disciplining the two policies should recognize to some extent the mutual interplay of the side effects. Where these interactions are recognized, sound legal arrangements should be put in place as to ensure coherent cooperative strategies of the authorities involved in the achievement of price stability and financial stability. A coherent system of checks and balances between monetary policy and macroprudential supervision should be better defined as to ensure that any negative effects of one policy over the other can be firstly discussed and then mitigated.

6.2 Expanding the Array of Policy Instruments by Exploiting the Legal Interaction

In this volume we sought to explore the main characteristics of the tools available to both central banks and macroprudential authorities to target their respective intermediate and ultimate objectives. A number of pages have been devoted to highlight the structural components of each policy tool and its legal interpretation. This analysis allowed us to understand how monetary and macroprudential policies are concretely carried on in the financial system and what transmission channels are involved in the policy operationalization.

After shedding light upon the need to ensure sound legal arrangements addressing the interaction between macroprudential and monetary policies, some further remarks on tools and instruments can be made. In particular, our attention can turn to the wide range of (macroprudential and monetary) tools that could theoretically be constructed in the near future on the basis of the findings of this volume.

If close interactions exist between the two policies and legal arrangements come to be operationalized in order to ensure consistency between the related side effects, the intertwined system of checks and balances could be further exploited. The analysis of the interplay between central banks and authorities tasked with macroprudential powers, deemed as a by-law product, can be used to set new or better policy instruments and ensure a good rapprochement of divergent policy stances.

Suppose a central bank decides to adopt new unconventional monetary measures aimed at easing credit conditions for non-financial sector. To do so, it establishes a prolonged program of long-term refinancing operations at a discount rate for banks willing to increase their lending to the real economy.[2] Due to the cheaper costs for their refinancing, banks are incentivized to foster their credit activities, and consumers are attracted by the parallel lower costs of funding.

Credit institutions increase their risk-taking activities on the balance sheet by providing different loan products to the private sector, such as consumer financing and mortgages. These new activities impact different sectors of the markets, such as consumer goods and real estate. And, while the increase of consumer prices is the ultimate target of the central bank, a parallel increase of real estate prices can sow the seeds of a bubble.

[2] For an example of such a monetary policy program, see Decision (EU) 2016/XX of the European Central Bank of 28 April 2016 on a second series of targeted longer-term refinancing operations (ECB/2016/10).

Against this backdrop, the authority entrusted with macroprudential powers should be able to step in and warn the central bank of any negative spillovers that may arise from such a real estate boom driven by the credit easing. In order to ensure a balance between price stability and financial stability, the authority should be also able to recommend the central bank to adjust its long-term refinancing operations, for example, by excluding from this program banks providing this new long-term liquidity to households for real estate purchases.

What it is important to understand is that the possibility to align the two policies depends upon the constitutional constraints and the institutional arrangements in which the central bank and the competent authorities are organized. The law plays a fundamental role in the interactions between economic phenomena. Not only it sets the boundaries for relevant institutions, with respect to their powers and tasks, but it also defines the level of interactions that the two policies may have, thereby calibrating the rapprochement of the policy decisions carried out by the central banks and the authorities dealing with macroprudential supervision.

6.3 A Cornerstone for a 'Law and Macroeconomic' Analysis

A last consideration before concluding this survey. This volume seeks to explore the legal intersection between two public policies widely considered as outstanding sub-categories of macroeconomics. Firstly, we have explained how monetary policy and macroprudential supervision may pull in opposite directions and give rise to inconsistent outcomes in targeting their ultimate objectives. Secondly, we have analyzed the role of the law in ensuring (and restraining) a rapprochement of the policies concerned.

Both monetary and macroprudential policies are meant to affect the same macroeconomic variables, namely, the aggregate demand and aggregate supply of credit. Monetary policy instruments are used to control the money supply and incentivize borrowing. This is intended to boost consumer spending and, as a consequence, ensure a statutory level of consumer price growth.

Similarly, macroprudential policy is intended to constrain the supply of money when an excess of credit may endanger the stability of the financial system. And, while the macroprudential ultimate objective is not a steady increase of consumer prices, its operationalization may largely affect the same transmission channels upon which monetary policy operates. Both policies therefore may directly or indirectly affect the expansion of credit in a given economy and—if not constrained—lead to credit boom-busts dynamics along the business and financial cycles.

From these assumptions, one can easily infer the important role that law, in general, comes to play in macroeconomics. Legal arrangements of different kinds can actually affect the aggregate demand and supply of credit. Regulatory provisions may restrict the wide credit demand and supply when these are excessive in a given market. In contrast, opposite rules can be utilized to boost the inadequate supply of credit, along with consumption and investment during periods of economic recession.

Where different macroeconomic policies may have parallel—but opposite—impact on same aggregate variables, the law has an additional important role to play. Legal arrangements could be put in place, within the constitutional boundaries, in order to discipline any negative interactions between the policies concerned, thereby ensuring consistency of the desired outcomes.

This book aims at representing a path-breaking research into this field. The law can—and shall—provide a robust framework within which the cross side effects of monetary and macroprudential policies can be addressed and disciplined. Lawyers are called to provide a new theoretical basis upon which the field of monetary and macroprudential policies can be explored within their legal construction. And, where new criticalities—or inconsistencies—are found, the legal reasoning should provide new practical solutions making the whole financial architecture better off.

This research presumes the foundation of a *law and macroeconomics analysis* of the policy institutions where aggregate phenomena can be newly rationalized within their institutional and legal foundations. The number of challenges underlying the ongoing development of the European Monetary and Banking Union provides an extraordinary basis for developing this field of study.

On the one hand, the institutional complexity of the EU architecture offers fertile ground for analyzing how separate policies conducted by different authorities are intertwined. On the other hand, the analysis of the EU regulatory framework on monetary and macroprudential policies allows us to investigate the macroeconomic effects of law for the internal market as a whole.

The analysis so provided can be utilized more generally as a benchmark to scrutinize the strict relationship between law and macroeconomic phenomena. Our hope is that this approach—although incomplete and dependent upon a number of assumptions—will spread around in the legal scholarship and represent a rudimental cornerstone for a *'law and macroeconomic analysis'* of policy institutions.

Reference

Svensson, Lars E.O. (2015). Monetary Policy and Macroprudential Policy: Different and Separate, *Federal Reserve Bank of Boston's 59th Economic Conference*, Federal Reserve Bank of Boston, October 2–3, 2015.

Glossary

BaFin	Bundesanstalt für Finanzdienstleistungsaufsicht
BCBS	Basel Committee on Banking Supervision
BIS	Bank for International Settlements
BSC	Banking Supervision Committee
CDS	Credit Default Swap
CEBS	Committee of European Banking Supervisors
CEIOPS	Committee of European Insurance and Occupational Pensions Supervisors
CESR	Committee of European Securities Regulators
CET 1	Common Equity Tier 1
CoVaR	Conditional Value at Risk
CPI	Consumer Price Index
CRD	Capital Requirement Directive
CRR	Capital Requirement Regulation
DSGE	Dynamic Stochastic General Equilibrium
DTI	Debt to Income
EBA	European Banking Authority
ECB	European Central Bank
ECJ	European Court of Justice
ECOFIN	Economic and Financial Affairs Council

L. Amorello, *Macroprudential Banking Supervision & Monetary Policy*, https://doi.org/10.1007/978-3-319-94156-1

ECSC	Euro-currency Standing Committee
EMU	European Monetary Union
EONIA	Euro Over-Night Index Average
ESAs	European Supervisory Authorities
ESFS	European System of Financial Supervision
ESRB	European Systemic Risk Board
ESRC	European Systemic Risk Council
EU	European Union
EWE	Early Warning Exercise
Fed	Federal Reserve Board
FOMC	Federal Open Market Committee
FPC	Financial Policy Committee
FSB	Financial Stability Board
FSR	Financial Stability Report/Review
GDP	Gross Domestic Product
GFCC	German Federal Constitutional Court
G-SIIs	Global Systemically Important Institutions
G30	Group of Thirty
HICP	Harmonized Index of Consumer Price
ICAAP	Internal Capital Adequacy Assessment Process
IMF	International Monetary Fund
IRB	Internal Ratings-Based Approach
ITS	Implementing Technical Standards
LCR	Liquidity Coverage Ratio
LIBOR	London Interbank Offered Rate
LTD	Loan to Deposit
LTI	Loan to Income
LTSF	Loan to Stable Funding
LTV	Loan to Value
NBB	National Bank of Belgium
NSFR	Net Stable Funding Ratio
OMT	Outright Monetary Transactions
O-SIIs	Other Systemically Important Institutions
OTC	Over-the-counter
PRA	Prudential Regulation Authority
RTS	Regulatory Technical Standards
RWA	Risk-Weighted Asset
SII	Systemically Important Institution
SRB	Systemic Risk Buffer

SREP	Supervisory Review and Evaluation Process
SRF	Single Resolution Fund
SRM	Single Resolution Mechanism
SSM	Single Supervisory Mechanism
TFEU	Treaty on the Functioning of the European Union

References

Abma, Rients, Olaerts, Mieke (2012). Is the Comply or Explain Principle a Suitable Mechanism for Corporate Governance throughout the EU?: The Dutch Experience, *European Company Law*, Vol. 9, Issue 6.

Acharya, Viral V., Pedersen, Lasse Heje, Philippon, Thomas Richardson, Matthew P. (2010). Measuring Systemic Risk. *AFA 2011 Denver Meetings Paper*, SSRN. Available at: http://ssrn.com/abstract=1573171

Acharya, Viral V., Philippon, Thomas, Richardson, Matthew, Roubini, Nouriel (2009). The Financial Crisis of 2007–2009: Causes and Remedies, *Financial Markets, Institutions & Instruments*, Vol. 18, Issue 2.

Acharya, Viral V., Naqvi, Hassan (2010). The Seeds of a Crisis: A Theory of Bank Liquidity and Risk-Taking over the Business Cycle, *Journal of Financial Economics*. Vol. 106, Issue 2.

Adrian, Tobias, Liang, Nellie (2014). Monetary Policy, Financial Conditions, and Financial Stability, *Federal Reserve Bank of New York Staff Report*, No. 690.

Adrian, Tobias, Shin, Hyun Song (2008). Financial Intermediaries, Financial Stability and Monetary Policy, *Federal Reserve Bank of New York Staff Reports*, No. 346.

Adrian, Tobias, Shin, Hyun Song (2009). The Shadow Banking System: Implications for Financial Regulation, *Federal Reserve Bank of New York Staff Reports*, No. 382.

Adrian, Tobias, Shin, Hyun Song (2010). Liquidity and Leverage, *Journal of Financial Intermediation*, Vol. 19, No. 3.

Afonso, António, Sequeira, Ana (2010). Revisiting Business Cycle Synchronisation in the European Union, *ISEG Economics Working Paper*, No. 22/2010/DE/UECE.

L. Amorello, *Macroprudential Banking Supervision & Monetary Policy*, https://doi.org/10.1007/978-3-319-94156-1

Agénor, Pierre-Richard, Pereira da Silva, Luiz A. (2012). Macroeconomic Stability, Financial Stability, and Monetary Policy Rules, *International Finance*, Vol. 15, Issue 2.

Agenor, Pierre-Richard, Alper, Koray, da Silva, Pereira Luiz (2012). Capital Regulation, Monetary Policy, and Financial Stability, *International Journal of Central Banking*, Vol. 9, No. 3, pp. 193–238.

Agresti, Anna Maria, Baudino, Patrizia, Poloni, Paolo (2008). The ECB and IMF Indicators for the Macro-prudential Analysis of the Banking Sector: A Comparison of the Two Approaches, *ECB Occasional Paper Series*, No. 99.

Agur, Itai, Demertzis, Maria (2012). "Leaning Against the Wind" and the Timing of Monetary Policy, *IMF Working Paper*, No. 86.

Agur, Itai, Sharma, Sunil (2013). Rules, Discretion, and Macro-prudential Policy, *IMF Working Paper*, No. 65.

Ahearne, Alan G., Ammer, John, Doyle, Brian M., Kole, Linda S., Martin, Robert F. (2005). House Prices and Monetary Policy: A Cross-Country Study, *Board of Governors of the Federal Reserve System International Finance Discussion Paper*, No. 841.

Ahmed, Elsayed, Elgazzar, Amr S., Hegazi, Ahmed S. (2005). An Overview of Complex Adaptive Systems, *Mansoura Journal of Mathematics*, Vol. 32, No. 6059.

Ahrend, Rudiger, Cournède, Boris, Price, Rober W. (2008). Monetary Policy, Market Excesses and Financial Turmoil, *OECD Economics Department Working Papers*, No. 597.

Aiyar, Shekhar, Calomiris, Charles W., Wieladek, Tomasz (2014). Identifying Channels of Credit Substitution When Bank Capital Requirements Are Varied, *Bank of England Working Paper*, No. 485.

Aiyar, Swaminathan S. Anklesaria (2010). Crisis Prevention through Global Surveillance: A Task Beyond the IMF, *Cato Journal*, Vol. 30, No. 3.

Alamsyah, Halim (2015). Coordinating Macroprudential and Monetary Policies: Asia Pacific Experiences. *Speech Held at the 2015 SEACEN Policy Summit on "Macroprudential Policies: Practical Implementation"*, 7 September 2015, Kuala Lumpur, Malaysia.

Alawode, Abayomi A., Al Sadek, Mohammed (2008). What Is Financial Stability? *Central Bank of Bahrain Financial Stability Paper Series*, No. 1/March 2008.

Alesina, Alberto, Summers, Lawrence H. (1993). Central Bank Independence and Macroeconomic Performance: Some Comparative Evidence, *Journal of Money, Credit and Banking*, Vol. 25, No. 2.

Alexander, Kern (2014). The ECB and Banking Supervision: Building Effective Prudential Supervision?, *Yearbook of European Law*, Vol. 33, No. 1.

Alexander, Kern (2015). The Role of Capital in Supporting Banking Stability. In: '*The Oxford Handbook of Financial Regulation*', (eds.) Eilis Ferran, Niamh Moloney, Jennifer Payne, *Oxford University Press.*

Alexander, Kern, Moloney, Niamh (eds.) (2011). Law Reform and Financial Markets, *Edward Elgar Publishing*, Cheltenham.

Alford, Duncan (2006). The Lamfalussy Process and EU Bank Regulation: Another Step on the Road to Pan-European Bank Regulation?, *Annual Review of Banking & Finance Law*, Vol. 25.

Allanazarova, Leyli (2010). The Eurosystem Approach to Monetary Policy and Liquidity Management, *Logos Verlag*, Berlin.

Allen, Franklin, Babus, Ana (2009). Networks in Finance. In: '*The Network Challenge: Strategy, Profit, and Risk in an Interlinked World*', (eds.) Paul Kleindorfer, Yoram (Jerry) R. Wind, Robert E. Gunther, *Pearson Prentice Hall*.

Allen, Franklin, Rogoff, Kenneth (2010). Asset Prices, Financial Stability and Monetary Policy. In: '*The Riksbank's Inquiry into the Risks in the Swedish Housing Market*'. Paper Presented at the Swedish Riksbank Workshop on Housing Markets, Monetary Policy and Financial Stability, 12 November 2010.

Allen, Franklin, Babus, Ana, Carletti, Elena (2010). Financial Connections and Systemic Risk, *NBER Working Paper Series*, No. 16177.

Allen, Franklin, Song, Wei-Ling (2005). Financial Integration and EMU, *European Financial Management*, Vol. 11, No. 1.

Altavilla, Carlo, Giannone, Domenico Lenza, Michele (2014). The Financial and Macroeconomic Effects of OMT Announcements, *ECB Working Paper Series*, No. 1707.

Altunbas, Yener, Gambacorta, Leonardo, Marques-Ibanez, David (2009). An Empirical Assessment of the Risk-Taking Channel, Paper prepared for the BIS/ECB Workshop on '*Monetary Policy and Financial Stability*'. Basel, 11 September 2009.

Altunbas, Yener, Gambacorta, Leonardo, Marques-Ibanez, David (2010). Does Monetary Policy Affect Bank Risk-Taking?, *BIS Working Paper*, No. 298.

Amorello, Luca (2016). Europe Goes 'Countercyclical': A Legal Assessment of the New Countercyclical Dimension of the CRR/CRD IV Package, *European Business Organization Law Review*, Vol. 17, Issue 1.

Amtenbrink, Fabian (2011). Central Bank Challenges in the Global Economy. In: '*European Yearbook of International Economic Law 2011*', (eds.), Christoph Herrmann, Jörg Philipp Terhechte, *Springer*, Berlin.

Amtenbrink, Fabian (2015). The Metamorphosis of European Economic and Monetary Union. In: '*The Oxford Handbook of European Union Law*', (eds.) Anthony Arnull, Damian Chalmers, *Oxford University Press*.

Anderson, William L. (2001). What's Wrong with the CPI?, *The Free Market*, Vol. 19, No. 8.

Ando, Albert, Modigliani, Franco (1963). The Life Cycle Hypothesis of Saving: Aggregate Implications and Tests, *American Economic Review*, Vol. 53, No. 1.

Angelini, Paolo, Grande, Giuseppe, Panetta, Fabio (2014). The Negative Feedback Loop between Banks and Sovereigns, *Bank of Italy Occasional Paper*, No. 213.

Angelini, Paolo, Stefano Neri, and Fabio Panetta (2011). Monetary and Macroprudential Policies, *Banca d'Italia Working Papers*, No. 801, March 2011.

Angelini, Paolo, Nicoletti-Altimari, Sergio, Visco, Ignazio (2012). Macroprudential, Microprudential and Monetary Policies: Conflicts, Complementarities and Trade-offs, *Banca d'Italia Occasional paper*, No. 140.

Angeloni, Ignazio (2014). European Macroprudential Policy from Gestation to Infancy, *Banque de France Financial Stability Review*, No. 18.

Angeloni, Ignazio (2015). Rethinking Banking Supervision and the SSM Perspective, *Conference at the European University Institute*, 23 April 2015, Florence.

Angeloni, Ignazio, Faia, Ester (2009). A Tale of Two Policies: Prudential Regulation and Monetary Policy with Fragile Banks, *Kiel Institute for the World Economy Working Paper*, No. 2.

Angeloni, Ignazio, Faia, Ester (2013). Capital Regulation and Monetary Policy with Fragile Banks, *Journal of Monetary Economics*, Vol. 60, Issue 3.

Angeloni, Ignazio, Faia, Ester, Lo Duca, Marco (2011). Monetary Policy and Risk Taking, *Journal of Economic Dynamics and Control*, Vol. 52.

Antipa, Pamfili, Matheron, Julien (2014). Interactions between Monetary and Macroprudential Policies, *Banque de France Financial Stability Review*, No. 18.

Apel, Emmanuel (2007). Central Banking Systems Compared: The ECB, the Pre-Euro Bundesbank and the Federal Reserve System, *Routledge*.

Archer, David (2009). Roles and Objectives of Modern Central Banks. In: '*Issues in the Governance of Central Banks: A Report from the Central Bank Governance Group*', May 2009.

Armantier, Olivier, Bruine de Bruin, Wändi, Topa, Giorgio, van der Klaauw, Wilbert, Zafar, Basit (2011). Inflation Expectations and Behavior: Do Survey Respondents Act on Their Beliefs?, *Federal Reserve Bank of New York Staff Reports*, No. 509.

Arner, Douglas W. (2007). Financial Stability, Economic Growth, and the Role of Law, *Cambridge University Press*.

Arner, Douglas W, Taylor, Michael W. (2009). The Global Financial Crisis and the Financial Stability Board: Hardening the Soft Law of International Financial Regulation?, *UNSW Law Journal*, Vol. 32, Issue 2.

Arregui, Nicolas, Beneš, Jaromír, Krznar, Ivo, Mitra, Srobona, Santos, Andre Oliveira (2013). Evaluating the Net Benefits of Macroprudential Policy: A Cookbook, *IMF Working Paper*, No. 167.

Ashley, Dunstan (2014). The Interaction between Monetary and Macro-prudential Policy, *Reserve Bank of New Zealand Bulletin*, Vol. 77, No. 2.

Assenmacher-Wesche, Katrin, Gerlach, Stefan (2008). Ensuring Financial Stability: Financial Structure and the Impact of Monetary Policy on Asset Prices, *IMFS Working Paper Series, No. 16*.

Astin, John (1999). The European Union Harmonised Indices of Consumer Prices (HICP), *Statistical Journal of the United Nations Economic Commission for Europe*, Vol. 16, No. 2–3.

Atik, Jeffery (2014). EU Implementation of Basel III in the Shadow of Euro Crisis, *Review of Banking and Financial Law*, Vol. 33.

Aucremanne, Luc, Ide, Stefaan (2010). Lessons from the Crisis: Monetary Policy and Financial Stability, *Economic Review*, Issue I.

Avgouleas, Emilios, Arner, Douglas W. (2013). The Eurozone Debt Crisis and the European Banking Union: A Cautionary Tale of Failure and Reform, *University of Hong Kong Faculty of Law Research Paper*, No. 2013/037.

Aydin, Burcu, Volkan, Engin (2011). Incorporating Financial Stability in Inflation Targeting Frameworks, *IMF Working Papers*, No. 224.

Axilrod, Stephen H. (1997). Transformations to Open Market Operations, *IMF Economic Issues*, No. 5, January 1997.

Aziz, Zeti A. (2007). Governor's Opening Speech at the Malaysia Financial Exhibition 2007, Kuala Lumpur, 30 October 2007.

Babis, Valia (2015). Single Rulebook for Prudential Regulation of EU Banks: Mission Accomplished?, *European Business Law Review*, Vol. 26, Issue 6.

Bachtler, John, Mendez, Carlos, Wishlade, Fiona (2016). EU Cohesion Policy and European Integration: The Dynamics of EU Budget and Regional Policy Reform, *Routledge*, London and New York.

Baglioni, Angelo (2016). The European Banking Union: A Critical Assessment, *Palgrave Macmillan*.

Baker, Andrew (2012). When New Ideas Meet Existing Institutions: Why Macroprudential Regulatory Change Is a Gradual Process. In: '*Great Expectations, Slow Transformations Incremental Change in Post-Crisis Regulation*', (eds.) Manuela Moschella, Eleni Tsingou, *ECPR Press*.

Baker, Andrew (2013). The New Political Economy of the Macroprudential Ideational Shift, *New Political Economy*, Vol. 18, Issue 1.

Baker, Andrew (2015). The Bankers' Paradox: The Political Economy of Macroprudential Regulation, *SRC Discussion Paper*, No. 37.

Ball, Laurence M. (1997). Efficient Monetary Policy Rules, *NBER Working Paper*, No. 5952.

Ball, Ray (2009). The Global Financial Crisis and the Efficient Market Hypothesis: What Have We Learned?, *Journal of Applied Corporate Finance*, Vol. 21, No. 4.

Banco De Portugal (2011). *Explanatory Note by Banco de Portugal: Loan-to-deposit Ratio in the Context of the Portuguese Financial Assistance Programme*, 29 September 2011.

Banco De Portugal (2014a). Strategy and Instruments of Macro-prudential Policy, *Financial Stability Report*, May 2014.

Banco De Portugal (2014b). Macroprudential Policy in Portugal: Objectives and Instruments, 18 December 2014.

Ball, Laurence, Mankiw, Gregoty, Romer, David (1988). The New Keynesian Economics and the Output-Inflation Trade-off, *Brookings Papers on Economic Activity*, No. 1.

Banerjee, Soumya (2011). Macro Prudential Supervision and the Financial Crisis of 2007: The Aegis of the Central Banks. *SSRN*. Available at: http://ssrn.com/abstract=1827088

Bank of England (2009). The Role of Macroprudential Policy, *Discussion Paper*, November 2009.

Bank of England (2015). The Financial Policy Committee's Powers over Housing Tools, *Draft Policy Statement*, February 2015.

Bank of England, HM Treasury, FSA (2008). Financial Stability and Depositor Protection: Special Resolution Regime, *Cm 7459*, July 2008.

Banka Slovenjie (2015). Macroprudential Policy for the Banking Sector Strategic Framework, 24 September 2015.

Barnett, William A. (2006). Is Macroeconomics a Science? Foreword to: '*Money and the Economy*', Serletis, Apostolos. *World Scientific Publishing*.

Barnett, William A. (2011). Getting It Wrong. How Faulty Monetary Statistics Undermine the Fed, the Financial System, and the Economy, *The MIT Press*, Cambridge.

Barrell, Ray, Gottschalk, Sylvia, Holland, Dawn, Khoman, Ehsan, Liadze, Iana, Pomerantz Olga (2008). The Impact of EMU on Growth and Employment, *European Commission Economic Papers*, No. 318.

Barwell, Richard (2013). Macroprudential Policy, *Palgrave Macmillan.*

Baun, Michael, Marek, Dan (2014). Cohesion Policy in the European Union, *Palgrave Macmillan.*

BCBS (2003). The New Basel Capital Accord. *BCBS Consultative Document*, April 2003.

BCSB (2009). Strengthening the Resilience of the Banking Sector, *Consultative Document*, December 2009.

BCBS (2010a). Basel III: A Global Regulatory Framework for More Resilient Banks and Banking Systems, December 2010.

BCBS (2010b). Countercyclical Capital Buffer Proposal, *Consultative Document*, July 2010.

BCBS (2010c). Guidance for National Authorities Operating the Countercyclical Capital Buffer, December 2010.

BCBS (2010d). Basel III: International Framework for Liquidity Risk Measurement, Standards and Monitoring, December 2010.

BCBS (2011). The transmission Channels between the Financial and Real Sectors: A Critical Survey of the Literature, *BIS Working Paper*, No. 18.

BCBS (2012). The Policy Implications of Transmission Channels between the Financial System and the Real Economy, *BIS Working Paper*, No. 20.

BCBS (2013). Basel III: The Liquidity Coverage Ratio and Liquidity Risk Monitoring Tools, January 2013.

BCBS (2014). Basel III: The Net Stable Funding Ratio, October 2014.

BCBS (2016). Standards Interest Rate Risk in the Banking Book, April 2016.

Baroncelli, Stefania (2014). The Independence of the ECB after the Economic Crisis. In: '*About the Constitutionalization of European Budgetary Constraints*', (eds.) Maurice Adams, Federico Fabbrini, Pierre Larouche, *Hart Publishing.*

Basua, Parantap, Gillmanb, Max, Pearlmanc, Joseph (2012). Inflation, Human Capital and Tobin's q, *Journal of Economic Dynamics and Control*, Vol. 36, Issue 7.

Bayoumi, Tamim, Dell'Ariccia, Giovanni, Habermeier, Karl, Tommaso Mancini-Griffoli, Fabián Valencia, and An IMF staff (2014). Monetary Policy in the New Normal, *IMF Staff Discussion Note*, No. 14/3.

Bean, Charlie (2013). Global Aspects of Unconventional Monetary Policies, Remarks Given at the Federal Reserve Bank of Kansas City Economic Policy Symposium, Jackson Hole, Wyoming, 24 August 2013.

Beau, Denis, Clerc, Laurent, Mojon, Benoit (2011). Macro-prudential Policy and the Conduct of Monetary Policy, *Banque de France Occasional Papers*, No. 8.

Bech, Morten L., Keister, Todd (2013). Liquidity Regulation and the Implementation of Monetary Policy, *BIS Working Papers*, No. 432.

Bech, Morten L., Malkhozov, Aytek (2016). How Have Central Banks Implemented Negative Policy Rates?, *BIS Quarterly Review*, March 2016.

Beck, Thorsten, Gros, Daniel (2012). Monetary Policy and Banking Supervision: Coordination Instead of Separation, *CEPS Policy Brief*, No. 286.

Begg, Iain (2009). Regulation and Supervision of Financial Intermediaries in the EU: The Aftermath of the Financial Crisis, *Journal of Common Market Studies*, Vol. 47, Issue 5.

Beukers, Thomas (2014). Bundesverfassungsgericht Preliminary Reference on the OMT Program: "In the ECB We Do Not Trust. What About You", *The German Law Journal*, Vol. 15, No. 2.

Belke, Ansgar, Polleit, Thorsten (2009). Monetary Economics in Globalised Financial Markets, *Springer*, Berlin.

Belongia, Michael T., Batten, Dallas S. (1992). Selecting an Intermediate Target Variable for Monetary Policy When the Goal Is Price Stability, *Federal Reserve Bank of Saint Luis Working Paper Series*, No. 8A.

Benes, Jaromir, Kumhof, Michael, Laxton, Douglas, Muir, Dirk, Mursula, Susanna (2013). The Benefits of International Policy Coordination Revisited, *IMF Working Paper*, No. 262.

Benigno, Pierpaolo, Benigno, Gianluca (2001). Monetary Policy Rules and the Exchange Rate, *CEPR Discussion Paper*, No. 2807.

Benito, Andrew, Thompson, Jamie, Waldron, Matt, Wood, Rob (2006). House Prices and Consumer Spending, *Bank of England Quarterly Bulletin*, Summer 2006.

Bennani, Taryk, Després, Morgan, Dujardin, Marine, Duprey, Thibaut, Kelber, Anna (2014). Macroprudential Framework: Key Questions Applied to the French Case, *Banque de France Occasional Papers*, No. 9.

Beraja, Martin, Fuster, Andreas, Hurst, Erik, Vavra, Joseph (2015). Regional Heterogeneity and Monetary Policy, *Federal Reserve Bank of New York Staff Report*, No. 731.

Berg, Andrew, Hagan, Sean, Jarvis, Christopher, Steinki, Bernhard, Stone, Mark, Zanello, Alessandro (2003). Reestablishing a Credible Nominal Anchor After a Financial Crisis. In: '*Managing Financial Crises Recent Experience and Lessons for Latin America*', (eds.) Charles Collyns, G. Russell Kincaid, *International Monetary Fund*, Washington, DC.

Berger, Helge, de Haan, Jakob, Eijffinger, Sylvester C.W. (2001). Central Bank Independence: An Update of Theory and Evidence, *Journal of Economic Surveys*, Vol. 15.

Berger, Allen N., Molyneux, Philip, Wilson, John O.S. (2009). The Oxford Handbook of Banking, *Oxford University Press*, Oxford.

Berk, Jan Marc (1998). Monetary Transmission: What Do We Know and How Can We Use It, *Banca Nazionale del Lavoro Quarterly Review*, Vol. 51.

Berk, Jan Marc (2001). The Preparation of Monetary Policy. Essays on a Multi-Model Approach, *Springer Science+Business Media, B.V.*

Bernanke, Ben S. (2003a). A Perspective on Inflation Targeting, *Remarks at the Annual Washington Policy Conference of the National Association of Business Economists*, Washington, DC, 25 March 2003.

Bernanke, Ben S. (2003b). 'Constrained Discretion' and Monetary Policy, *Remarks Before the Money Marketers of New York University*, New York, 3 February 2003.

Bernanke, Ben S. (2010a). Monetary Policy since the Onset of the Crisis, *Speech at the Federal Reserve Bank of Kansas City Economic Symposium*, Jackson Hole, Wyoming, 31 August 2012.

Bernanke, Ben S. (2010b). The Economic Outlook and Monetary Policy, *Speech at the Federal Reserve Bank of Kansas City Economic Symposium*, Jackson Hole, Wyoming, 27 August 2010.

Bernanke, Ben S. (2010c). Monetary Policy and the Housing Bubble, *Speech at the Annual Meeting of the American Economic Association*, Atlanta, Georgia.

Bernanke, Ben S., Blinder Alan S. (1992). *The American Economic Review*, Vol. 82, No. 4.

Bernanke, Ben S., Gertler, Mark (1995). Inside the Black Box: The Credit Channel of Monetary Policy Transmission, *Journal of Economic Perspectives*, Vol. 9, No. 4.

Bernanke, Ben S., Gertler, Mark (1999). Monetary Policy and Asset Price Volatility, *Federal Reserve Bank of Kansas City Economic Review*, Fourth Quarter.

Bernanke, Ben S., Laubach, Thomas, Mishkin, Frederic, and Posen, Adam (2001). Inflation Targeting: Lessons from the International Experience, *Princeton University Press*.

Bernanke, Ben S., Mishkin, Frederic S. (1997). Inflation Targeting: A New Framework for Monetary Policy?, *NBER Working Paper Series*, No. 5893.

Bernanke, Ben S., Reinhart, Vincent R. (2004). Conducting Monetary Policy at Very Low Short-term Interest Rates, *American Economic Review: Papers and Proceedings*, Vol. 94, No. 2.

Bernanke, Ben S., Reinhart, Vincent R., Sack, Brian P. (2004). Monetary policy alternatives at the zero bound: An empirical assessment, *Brookings Papers on Economic Activity*, No. 2.

Beroš, Marta B. (2010). Europe's Regulatory Reform after the Crisis – A Macroprudential Perspective, *Columbia Journal of European Law Online*, Vol. 16.

Barro, Robert J., Gordon, David (1983). A Positive Theory of Monetary Policy in a Natural Rate Model, *Journal of Political Economy*, Vol. 91, No. 4.

Bertaut, Carol C. (2002). The European Central Bank and the Eurosystem, *New England Economic Review*, Second Quarter 2002.

Beyeler, Michelle (2007). The Paths to Price Stability: An International Comparison, *Berner Studien zur Politikwissenschaft*, Bd. 16, Haupt.

Bianchi, Javier (2014). Discussion of "The Risk Channel of Monetary Policy", *International Journal of Central Banking*, Vol. 10, No. 2.

Bicu, Andreea, Bunea, Daniela, Wedow, Michael (2014). Initial Considerations Regarding a Macro-prudential Instrument based on the Net Stable Funding Ratio, *ECB Financial Stability Review*, November 2014.

Billio, Monica, Getmansky, Mila, Lo, Andrew W., Pelizzon, Loriana (2010). Measuring Systemic Risk in the Finance and Insurance Sectors, *MIT Sloan School Working Paper*, No. 4774-10.

Billio, Monica, Getmansky, Mila, Lo, Andrew W., Pelizzon, Loriana (2012). Econometric Measures of Systemic Risk in the Finance and Insurance Sectors, *Journal of Financial Economics*, Vol. 104, Issue 3.

Bindseil, Ulrich (2004). The Operational Target of Monetary Policy and the Rise and Fall of Reserve Position Doctrine, *ECB Working Paper Series*, No. 372.

Bindseil, Ulrich (2011). Theory of Monetary Policy Implementation. In: '*The Concrete Euro: Implementing Monetary Policy in the Euro Area*', (eds.) Paul Mercier, Francesco Papadia, *Oxford University Press*, Oxford.

Bindseil, Ulrich (2014). Monetary Policy Operations and the Financial System, *Oxford University Press,* Oxford.

Bindseil, Ulrich, Jabłecki, Juliusz (2011). The Optimal Width of the Central Bank Standing Facilities Corridor and Banks' Day-to-day Management, *ECB Working Paper Series*, No. 1350.

Bindseil, Ulrich, Lamoot, Jeroen (2011). The Basel III Framework for Liquidity Standards and Monetary Policy Implementation, *SFB 649 Discussion Paper*, No. 2011-041.

Bini Smaghi, Lorenzo, Gross, Daniel (2000). Open Issues in European Central Banking, *Palgrave Macmillan.*

Bini Smaghi, Lorenzo (2007). Legal System and Financial Markets, *Opening Remarks at the Conference 'Legal Issues Related to the Financial Markets'*, Frankfurt am Main, 26 October 2007.

Bini Smaghi, Lorenzo (2009). Conventional and Unconventional Monetary Policy, *Keynote Lecture at the International Center for Monetary and Banking Studies (ICMB)*, Geneva, 28 April 2009.
BIS (1986). Recent Innovation in International Banking (Cross Report), *CGFS Publications*, No. 1.
BIS (1992). Recent Developments in International Interbank Relations (Promisel Report), *CGFS Publications*, No. 2.
BIS (1995). Financial Structure and the Monetary Policy Transmission Mechanism, *BIS Papers*, No. 0.
BIS (1997). The Evolution of Central Bank. In: 'The *67th Annual Report, 1st April 1996–31st March 1997*'. Basle, 9 June 1997.
BIS (2009). Monetary Policy Frameworks and Central Bank Market Operations, *MC Compendium*, March 2009.
BIS (2010). Macroprudential Policy and Addressing Procyclicality, *BIS 80th Annual Report*.
BIS (2013). Global Systemically Important Banks: Updated Assessment Methodology and the Higher Loss Absorbency Requirement, July 2013.
Bisias, Dimitrios, Flood, Mark, Lo, Andrew W., Valavanis, Stavros (2012). A Survey of Systemic Risk Analytics, *Office of Financial Research Working Paper*, No. 1.
Blancher, Nicolas, Mitra, Srobona, Morsy, Hanan, Otani, Akira, Severo, Tiago, Valderrama, Laura (2013). Systemic Risk Monitoring (——SysMo||) Toolkit—A User Guide, *IMF Working Paper*, No. 168.
Blejer, Mario I., Ize, Alain, Leone, Alfredo M., Werlang, Sérgio (1999). Inflation Targeting in Practice: Strategic and Operational Issues and Application to Emerging Market Economies, *International Monetary Fund*.
Blinder, Alan S., Goodhart, Charles, Hildebrand, Philipp, Lipton, David, Wyplosz, Charles (2002). How Do Central Banks Talk? Geneva Report on the World Economy, *Centre for Economic Policy Research*.
Bluhm, Marcel, Faia, Ester, Krahnen, Jan P. (2014). Monetary Policy Implementation in an Interbank Network: Effects on Systemic Risk, *SAFE Working Paper*, No. 46.
Boccuzzi, Giuseppe (2016). The European Banking Union, *Palgrave Macmillan*.
Böhm, Franz (1989). Rule of Law in a Market Economy. In: '*Germany's Social Market Economy: Origins and Evolution*', (eds.) Peacock Alan, Hans Willgerodt, *Palgrave Macmillan*, London.
Böhm, Franz, Eucken, Walter, Grossmann-Doerth, Hans (1989). The Ordo Manifesto of 1936. In: '*Germany's Social Market Economy: Origins and Evolution*', (eds.) Peacock Alan, Hans Willgerodt, *Palgrave Macmillan*, London.
Boivin, Jean, Kiley, Michael T., Mishkin, Frederic S. (2010). How Has the Monetary Transmission Mechanism Evolved Over Time?, *NBER Working Paper*, No. 15879.
Bonfim, Diana, Soares, Carla (2014). The Risk-Taking Channel of Monetary Policy – Exploring All Avenues, *Bank of Portugal Working Papers*, No. 2.

Bonner, Clemens, Eijffinger, Sylvester (2012a). The Impact of Liquidity Regulation on Interbank Money Markets, *DNB Working Paper*, No. 364.

Bonner, Clemens, Eijffinger, Sylvester (2012b). The Impact of Liquidity Regulation on Monetary-Policy Implementation, *Vox CEPR's Policy Portal*. Online. Available at: http://www.voxeu.org/article/liquidity-coverage-ratios-and-monetary-policy

Bordo, Michael, Eichengreen, D. Barry (2013). Bretton Woods and the Great Inflation. In: '*The Great Inflation: The Rebirth of Modern Central Banking*', (eds.) Michael D. Bordo, Athanasios Orphanides, *The University of Chicago Press.*

Borio, Claudio (2003). Towards a Macroprudential Framework for Financial Supervision and Regulation?, *BIS Working Papers*, No. 128.

Borio, Claudio (2012). The Financial Cycle and Macroeconomics: What Have We Learnt?, *BIS Working Papers*, No. 395.

Borio, Claudio (2014). Macroprudential Frameworks: (Too) Great Expectations?, *Contribution to the 25th Anniversary Edition of Central Banking Journal* Originally Published on 5 August 2014.

Borio, Claudio, Disyatat, Piti (2009). Unconventional Monetary Policies: An Appraisal, *BIS Working Papers*, No. 292.

Borio, Claudio, Disyatat, Piti (2011). Global Imbalances and the Financial Crisis: Link or No Link?, *BIS Working Papers*, No. 346.

Borio, Claudio, Drehmann, Mathias (2009). Towards an Operational Framework for Financial Stability: "Fuzzy" Measurement and Its Consequences, *BIS Working Papers*, No. 284.

Borio, Claudio, Furfine, Craig, Lowe, Philip (2001). Procyclicality of the Financial System and Financial Stability: Issues and Policy Options, *BIS Paper*, No. 1.

Borio, Claudio, Gambacorta, Leonardo, Hofmann, Boris (2014). The Influence of Monetary Policy on Bank Profitability, *BIS Working Papers*, No. 514.

Borio, Claudio, Shim, Ilhyock (2007). What Can (Macro-)Prudential Policy Do to Support Monetary Policy?, *BIS Working Papers*, No. 242.

Borio, Claudio, Zhu, Haibin (2008). Capital Regulation, Risk Taking and Monetary Policy: A Missing Link in the Transmission Mechanism?, *BIS Working Paper*, No. 268.

Bowman, David, Doyle, Brian (2003). New Keynesian, Open-Economy Models and Their Implications for Monetary Policy, *FRB International Finance Discussion Paper*, No. 762.

Breckenfelder, Johannes H., Schwaab, Bernd (2015). The Bank-Sovereign Nexus Across Borders. *SSRN*. Online. Available at: http://ssrn.com/abstract=2611107

Bridges, Jonathan, Gregory, David, Nielsen, Mette, Pezzini, Silvia, Radia, Amar, Spaltro, Marco (2014). The Impact of Capital Requirements on Bank Lending, *Bank of England Working Paper*, No. 486.

Brockmeijer, Jan (2012). The Institutional Settings of Macroprudential Policy. In: '*Putting Macroprudential Policy to Work*', (eds.) Aerdt Houben, Rob Nijskens, Mark Teunissen, *De Nederlandsche Bank Occasional Studies*, Vol. 12–7.

Brummer, Chris (2011). How International Financial Law Works (and How It Doesn't), *The Georgetown Law Journal*, Vol. 99, Issue 2.
Brummer, Chris (2012). Why Soft Law Dominates International Finance – And Not Trade. In: '*International Law in Financial Regulation and Monetary Affairs*', (eds.) Thomas Cottier, John H. Jackson, Rosa M. Lastra, *Oxford University Press.*
Brunnermeier, Markus K, Oehmke, Martin (2013). The Maturity Rat Race, *Journal of Finance*, Vol. 68, No. 2.
Bruno, Valentina, Shin, Hyun Song (2013). Capital Flows and the Risk-Taking Channel of Monetary Policy, *NBER Working Paper*, No. 18942.
Bruno, Valentina, Shim, Ilhyock, Shin, Hyun Song (2015). Comparative Assessment of Macroprudential Policies, *BIS Working Papers,* No. 502.
Brzoza-Brzezina, Michał, Kolasa, Marcin, Makarski, Krzysztof (2015). Monetary and Macroprudential Policy with Foreign Currency Loans, *ECB Working Paper Series*, No. 1783.
Buch, Claudia M. (2014). Presentation of the 2014 Financial Stability Review, *Speech Delivered at the Unveiling of the Deutsche Bundesbank's Financial Stability Review,* Frankfurt am Main, 25 November 2014.
Buch, Claudia M., Eickmeier, Sandra, Prieto, Esteban (2011). In Search for Yield? Survey-Based Evidence on Bank Risk Taking, *Deutsche Bundesbank Discussion Paper Series 1: Economic Studies*, No. 10/2011.
Buch, Claudia M., Koetter, Michael, Ohls, Jana (2013). Banks and Sovereign Risk: A Granular View, *Deutsche Bundesbank Discussion Paper*, No. 29/2013.
Bunn, Philip, Drapper, Lizzie, Rowe, Jeremy, Shah, Sagar (2015). The Potential Impact of Higher Interest Rates and Further Fiscal Consolidation on Households: Evidence from the 2015 NMG Consulting Survey, *Bank of England Quarterly Bulletin 2015 Q4.*
Busch, Andreas (2005). Shock-Absorbers Under Stress: Parapublic Institutions and the Double Challenges of German Unification and European Integration. In: '*Governance in Contemporary Germany; The Semisovereign State Revisited*', (eds.) Simon Green, William E. Paterson, *Cambridge University Press.*
Busch, Danny, Ferrarini, Guido (eds.) (2015). European Banking Union, *Oxford University Press.*
Busuioc, Madalina (2013). Rule-Making by the European Financial Supervisory Authorities: Walking a Tight Rope, *European Law Journal,* Vol. 19, No. 1.
Calomiris, Charles W. (2010). Reassessing the Fed's Regulatory Role, *Cato Journal*, Vol. 30, No. 2.
Calvo, Guillermo (1978). On the Time Consistency of Optimal Policy in the Monetary Economy, *Econometrica*, Vol. 46, Issue 6.
Canuto, Otaviano, Cavallari, Matheus (2013). Asset Prices, Macroprudential Regulation, and Monetary Policy, *The World Bank Economic Premise*, No. 116.

Carboni, Giacomo, Pariès, Matthieu D., Kok, Christoffer (2013). Exploring the Nexus between Macro-prudential Policies and Monetary Policy Measures, *ECB Financial Stability Review*, May 2013.

Carney, Mark (2014). One Mission. One Bank. Promoting the Good of the People of the United Kingdom, *Speech Given at the Mais Lecture at Cass Business School*, City University, London, 18 March 2014.

Caruana, Jaime (2011). Monetary Policy in a World with Macroprudential Policy, *Speech Held at the SAARCFINANCE Governors' Symposium 2011*, Kerala, 11 June 2011.

Caruana, Jaime (2014). Macroprudential Policy: Opportunities and Challenges. Speech at the Tenth High-Level Meeting for the Middle East and North Africa Region on '*Global Banking Standards and Regulatory and Supervisory Priorities*' Jointly Organized by the BCBS, the BIS's Financial Stability Institute and the Arab Monetary Fund, Abu Dhabi, United Arab Emirates, 9 December 2014.

Caruana, Jaime, Cohen, Benjamin H. (2014). Five Questions and Six Answers about Macroprudential Policy, *Banque de France Financial Stability Review*, No. 18, April 2014.

Camba-Mendez, Gonzalo (2003). The Definition of Price Stability: Choosing a Price Measure. In: '*Background Studies for the ECB's Evaluation of its Monetary Policy Strategy*', (ed.) Otmar Issing, *European Central Bank*, Frankfurt.

Castro, Vitor (2011). Can Central Banks' Monetary Policy Be Described by a Linear (Augmented) Taylor Rule or by a Nonlinear Rule?, *Journal of Financial Stability*, Vol. 7.

Caranta, Roberto, Andenas, Mds, Fairgrieve, Duncan (eds.) (2005). Independent Administrative Authorities, *British Institute of International and Comparative Law, London.*

Carré, Emmanuel, Couppey-Soubeyran, Jézabel, Dehmej, Salim (2015). La coordination entre politique monétaire et politique macroprudentielle, *Revue économique*, Vol. 66, Issue 3.

Cecchetti, Stephen G. (1997). Central Bank Policy Rules: Conceptual Issues and Practical Considerations, *NBER Working Paper Series*, No. 6306.

Cecchetti, Stephen G. (1998). Policy Rules and Targets: Framing the Central Banker's Problem, *FRBNY Economic Policy Review*, June 1998.

Cecchetti, Stephen G. (1999). Legal Structure, Financial Structure, and the Monetary Policy Transmission Mechanism, *NBER Working Papers*, No. 7151.

Cecchetti, Stephen G. (2000). Making Monetary Policy: Objectives and Rules, *Oxford Review of Economic Policy*, Vol. 16, No. 4.

Cecchetti, Stephen G., Genberg, Hans, Lipsky, John, Wadhwani, Sushil (2000). Asset Prices and Central Bank Policy, *International Center for Monetary and Banking Studies*, London.

Cesa-Bianchi, Ambrogio, Rebucci, Alessandro (2015). Does Easing Monetary Policy Increase Financial Instability?, *IMF Working Paper*, No. 139.

Cevik, Serhan, Teksoz, Katerina (2012). Lost in Transmission? The Effectiveness of Monetary Policy Transmission Channels in the GCC Countries, *IMF Working Paper*, No. 191.

CGFS (1995). Issues of Measurement Related to Market Size and Macroprudential Risks in Derivatives Markets (Brockmeijer Report), *CGFS Publications*, No. 5.

CGFS (2010a). Macroprudential Instruments and Frameworks: A Stocktaking of Issues and Experiences. Report Submitted by the Committee on the Global Financial System, *CGFS Papers*, No. 38.

CGFS (2010b). The Role of Margin Requirements and Haircuts in Procyclicality. Report Submitted by a Study Group established by the Committee on the Global Financial System, *CGFS Papers*, No. 36.

CGFS (2012). Operationalising the Selection and Application of Macroprudential Instruments, *CGFS Papers*, No. 48.

CGFS (2013). Asset Encumbrance, Financial Reform and the Demand for Collateral Assets. Report Submitted by a Working Group Established by the Committee on the Global Financial System, *CGFS Papers*, No. 49.

CGFS (2015). Regulatory Change and Monetary Policy, *CGFS Papers*, No. 54.

Chalmers, Damian, Davies, Gareth, Monti, Giorgio (2010). European Union Law: Cases and Materials. *Cambridge University Press.*

Chan, Serena (2001). Complex Adaptive Systems, *ESD.83 Research Seminar in Engineering Systems*, October 31, 2001/November 6, 2001.

Chant, John (2003). Financial Stability as a Policy Goal. In: '*Essays on Financial Stability*', *Bank of Canada Technical Report*, No. 95.

Cheun, Samuel, von Köppen-Mertes, Isabel, Weller, Benedict (2009). The Collateral Frameworks of the Eurosystem, the Federal Reserve System and the Bank of England and the Financial Market Turmoil, *ECB Occasional Paper Series*, No. 107.

Chodorow-Reich, Gabriel (2014). Effects of Unconventional Monetary Policy on Financial Institutions, *Brookings Papers on Economic Activity*, Spring 2014.

Christensen, Ian, Meh, Césaire, Moran, Kevin (2011). Bank Leverage Regulation and Macroeconomic Dynamics, *Bank of Canada Working Papers*, No. 2011-32.

Chwieroth, Jeffrey, Danielsson, Jon (2013). Political Challenges of the Macroprudential Agenda. Vox CEPR's Policy Portal (6 September 2013). Online. Available at: http://www.voxeu.org/article/political-challenges-macroprudential-agenda

Ciani, Daniele, Cornacchia, Wanda, Garofalo, Paolo (2014). The Macroprudential Measures Adopted in Europe for the Real Estate Sector, *Bank of Italy Occasional Paper*, No. 227.

Ciccarelli, Matteo, Maddaloni, Angela, Peydró, José-Luis (2010). Trusting the Bankers. A New Look at the Credit Channel of Monetary Policy, *Working Paper Series*, No. 1228.

Clarida, Richard, Gali, Jordi, Gertler, Mark (1998). Monetary Policy Rules and Macroeconomic Stability: Evidence and Some Theory, *NBER Working Paper Series*, No. 6442.

Claessens, Stijn, Ghosh, Swati R., Mihet, Roxana (2014). Macro-prudential Policies to Mitigate Financial System Vulnerabilities, *IMF Working Paper*, No. 155.
Claeys, Grégory, Darvas, Zsolt (2015). The Financial Stability Risks of Ultra-Loose Monetary Policy, *Bruegel Policy Contribution*, Issue 2015/03.
Clement, Piet (2010). The Term "Macroprudential": Origins and Evolution, *BIS Quarterly Review*, March 2010.
Clementi, David (2001). Banks and Systemic Risk – Theory and Evidence, *Speech held at the Bank of England Conference*, London, 23 May 2001.
Clark, Alastair, Large, Andrew (2011). Macroprudential Policy: Addressing the Things We Don't Know, *Group of Thirty Occasional Paper*, No. 83.
Coase, Ronald H. (1984). The New Institutional Economics, *Zeitschrift für die gesamte Staatswissenschaft / Journal of Institutional and Theoretical Economics*, Bd. 140, H. 1.
Coffee, John C. (2001). The Rise of Dispersed Ownership the Roles of Law and the State in the Separation of Ownership and Control, *Yale Law Journal*, Vol. 111, No. 1.
Coglianese, Cary, Kilmartin, Heather, Mendelson, Evan (2009). Transparency and Public Participation in the Rulemaking Process: Recommendations for the New Administration, *George Washington Law Review, Vol. 77, No. 4.*
Collin, Marianne, Druant, Martine, Ferrari, Stijn (2014). Macroprudential Policy in the Banking Sector: Framework and Instruments, *NBB Financial Stability Review*, Vol. 12, No. 1.
Committee on International Economic Policy and Reform (2011). Rethinking Central Banking, September 2011.
Constâncio, Vítor (2013a). The Nature and Significance of Banking Union, *Speech Delivered at the Chatham House Conference: Financial Regulation: Towards a Global Regulatory Framework?*, London, 11 March 2013.
Constâncio, Vítor (2013b). Toward the Banking Union, *Speech Held at the 2nd FIN-FSA Conference on EU Regulation and Supervision "Banking and Supervision under Transformation"* Organised by the Financial Supervisory Authority, Helsinki, 12 February 2013.
Constâncio, Vitor (2014a). Making Macro-prudential policy work, *Speech at High-level Seminar Organized by De Nederlandsche Bank*, 10 June 2014.
Constâncio, Vitor (2014b). The ECB and Macro-prudential Policy: From Research to Implementation, *Speech held at the Third Conference of the Macro-prudential Research Network*, Frankfurt-am-Main, 23 June 2014.
Constâncio, Vítor (2015). Macroprudential Policy in Europe: Ensuring Financial Stability in a Banking Union, *Keynote Speech at the Financial Stability Conference*, Berlin, 28 October 2015.
Constâncio, Vítor (2015b). The European Crisis and the Role of the Financial System, *Journal of Macroeconomics*, Vol. 39.
Constâncio, Vítor (2015c). Assessing the New Phase of Unconventional Monetary Policy at the ECB, *Remarks at the Annual Congress of the European Economic Association*, University of Mannheim, 25 August 2015.

Correa, Ricardo, Sapriza, Horacio (2014). Sovereign Debt Default, *Board of Governors of the Federal Reserve System International Finance Discussion Papers*, No. 1104.

Cœuré, Benoît (2013). Monetary Policy and Banking Supervision, *Symposium: "Central Banking: Where Are We Headed?" in Honour of Stefan Gerlach's Contribution to the Institute for Monetary and Financial Stability*, Goethe University, Frankfurt, 7 February 2013.

Craig, Paul P., Markakis, Menelaos (2016). Gauweiler and the Legality of Outright Monetary Transactions, *Oxford Legal Studies Research Paper*, No. 5/2016.

Crockett, Andrew D. (1997). "Why is Financial Stability a Goal of Public Policy?," Economic Review, Federal Reserve Bank of Kansas City, issue Q IV, pages 5–22.

Crowe, Christopher, Meade, Ellen E. (2008). Central Bank Independence and Transparency: Evolution and Effectiveness, *IMF Working Paper*, No. 119.

Crowe, Christopher, Dell'Ariccia, Giovanni, Igan, Deniz, Rabanal, Pau (2011). Policies for Macrofinancial Stability: Options to Deal with Real Estate Booms. *IMF Staff Discussion Note*, No. 2.

Cukierman, Alex (1992). Central Bank Strategy, Credibility, and Independence, Theory and Evidence, *The MIT Press.*

Cukierman, Alex (1994). Central Bank Independence and Monetary Control, *The Economic Journal*, Vol. 104, No. 427.

Cukierman, Alex (2011). Reflections on the Crisis and on Its Lessons for Regulatory Reforms and for Central Bank Policies. In: '*Handbook of Central Banking, Financial Regulation and Supervision After the Financial Crisis*', (eds.) Sylvester Eijffinger, Donato Masciandaro, *Edward Elgar Publishing.*

Cukierman, Alex (2013). Monetary Policy and Institutions Before, During, and After the Global Financial Crisis, *Journal of Financial Stability*, Vol. 9.

Dabrowski, Marek (2009). The Global Financial Crisis: Lessons for European Integration, *CASE Network Studies and Analyses*, No. 384.

Dagenhart, Christoph (2015). The Legal Limits of Central Banking. In: '*The ECB's Outright Monetary Transactions in the Courts*', (eds.) Helmut Siekmann, Volcker Vieland, *IMFS Interdisciplinary Studies in Monetary and Financial Stability*, No. 1.

Dahan, Samuel, Fuchs, Olivier, Layus, Marie-Laure (2015). Whatever It Takes? Regarding the OMT Ruling of the German Federal Constitutional Court, *Journal of International Economic Law*, Vol. 18, No. 1.

Das, Udaibir S., Quintyn, Marc, Chenard, Kina (2014). Does Regulatory Governance Matter for Financial System Stability? An Empirical Analysis, *IMF Working Paper*, No. 89.

Darracq Paries, Matthieu, Rancoita, Elena, Kok, Christoffer (2015). Quantifying the Policy Mix in a Monetary Union with National Macroprudential Policies, *ECB Financial Stability Review*, November 2015.

Darvas, Zsolt, Merler, Silvia (2013). The European Central Bank in the Age of Banking Union, *Bruegel Policy Contribution*, Issue 2013/13.

Davis, E. Philip (2001). A Typology of Financial Instability", *Oesterreichische Nationalbank Financial Stability Report*, No. 2.

De Carvalho, Fabia A., De Castro, Marcos R. (2015). Macroprudential and Monetary Policy Interaction: A Brazilian Perspective, *BCB Working Paper*, No. 405.

Deaton, Angus (2005). Franco Modigliani and the Life-cycle Theory of Consumption, *PSL Quarterly Review*, Vol. 58.

Debelle, Guy, Fischer, Stanley (1994). How Independent Should a Central Bank Be? In: '*Goals, Guidelines and Constraints Facing Monetary Policy*', (eds.) Jeffrey Fuhrer, *Federal Reserve Bank of Boston Conference Series*, No. 38.

Debelle, Guy, Masson, Paul, Savastano, Miguel, Sharma, Sunil (1998). Inflation Targeting as a Framework for Monetary Policy, *IMF Economic Issues*, No. 15.

De Bandt, Olivier, Hartmann, Philipp (2000). Systemic Risk: A Survey, *ECB Working Paper*, No. 35.

De Bruyckerea, Valerie, Gerhardtb, Maria, Schepensc, Glenn, Vander Vennet, Rudi (2013). Bank/sovereign Risk Spillovers in the European Debt Crisis, *Journal of Banking & Finance,* Vol. 37, Issue 12.

De Grauwe, Paul (2013). The European Central Bank as Lender of Last Resort in the Government Bond Markets, *CESifo Economic Studies*, Vol. 59, No. 3.

de Haan, Jakob (eds.) (2000). The History of the Bundesbank: Lessons for the European Central Bank, *Routledge International Studies in Money and Banking.*

de Haan, Jakob, Berger, Helge, Inklaar, Robert (2004). Is the ECB Too Decentralized? In: '*European Monetary Integration*', (eds.) Hans-Werner Sinn, Mika Widgrén, Marko Köthenbürge, *CEFifo Seminar Series.*

de Haan, Jakob, Eijffinger, Sylvester C.W., Waller, Sandra (2005). The European Central Bank – Credibility, Transparency, and Centralization, *The MIT Press*, Cambridge.

de Haan, Jakob, Oosterloo, Sander, Schoenmaker, Dirk (2012). Financial Markets and Institutions: A European Perspective, *Cambridge University Press.*

Dell'Ariccia, Giovanni, Laeven, Luc, Marquez, Robert (2010). Monetary Policy, Leverage, and Bank Risk-Taking, *IMF Working Paper*, No. 276.

Dell'Ariccia, Giovanni, Laeven, Luc, Marquez, Robert (2011). Financial Frictions, Foreign Currency Borrowing, and Systemic Risk, *Paper Presented at the 12th Jacques Polak Annual Research Conference*, Washington, DC, 10–11 November 2011.

Dell'Ariccia, Giovanni, Laeven, Luc, Suarez, Gustavo (2013). Bank Leverage and Monetary Policy's Risk-Taking Channel: Evidence from the United States, *IMF Working Paper*, No. 143.

Dell'Ariccia, Giovanni, Marquez, Robert (2004). Information and Bank Credit Allocation. *Journal of Financial Economics*, Vol. 72, Issue 1.

de Larosière Report (2009). Report of the High-Level Group on Financial Supervision in the EU, Brussels, 25 February 2009.

De Lhoneux, Etienne (2005). The Eurosystem. In: '*Legal Aspects of the European System of Central Banks*', *ECB Liber Amicorum Paolo Zamboni Garavelli*, Frankfurt.

De Nicolò, Gianni, Dell'Ariccia, Giovanni, Laeven, Luc, Valencia, Fabian (2010). Monetary Policy and Bank Risk Taking, *IMF Staff Note*, No. 09.

De Nicolò, Gianni, Favara, Giovanni, Ratnovski, Lev (2012). Externalities and Macroprudential Policy, *IMF Staff Discussion Note*, No. 12/05.

De Nicolò, Gianni, Lucchetta, Marcella (2010). Systemic Risks and the Macroeconomy, *IMF Working Paper*, No. 29.

De Paoli, Bianca, Paustian, Matthias (2013). Coordinating Monetary and Macroprudential Policies, *Federal Reserve Bank of New York Staff Report*, No. 653.

De Vicuña, Antonio Sáinz (1999). Institutional Aspects of the European Central Bank. In: '*Current Developments in Monetary and Financial Law*', Vol. 1, *International Monetary Fund*, Washington.

De Vroey, Michel, Hoover, Kevin D. (2005). The IS-LM Model: Its Rise, Fall, and Strange Persistence. History of Political Economy Annual Supplement, *Duke University Press Books.*

Dellepiane-Avellaneda, Sebastian (2009). Review Article: Good Governance, Institutions and Economic Development: Beyond the Conventional Wisdom, *British Journal of Political Science*, Vol. 40, Issue 1.

De Meester, Bart (2008). Multilevel Banking Regulation: An Assessment of the Role of the EC in the Light of Coherence and Democratic Legitimacy. In: '*Multilevel Regulation and the EU: The Interplay between Global, European and National Normative Processes*', (eds.) Andreas Follesdal, Ramses A. Wessel, Jan Wouters, *Brill.*

Demyanyk, Yuliya, Hemert, Otto Van (2011). Understanding the Subprime Mortgage Crisis, *Review of Financial Studies*, No. 24, No. 6.

De Nederlandsche Bank (2015). Dutch Mortgages in the DNB Loan Level Data, *DNB Occasional Studies*, Vol. 13–4.

Dennis, Kia (2009). Rating Game: Explaining Rating Agency Failures in the Buildup to the Financial Crisis, *University of Miami Law Review*, Vol. 63, Issue 4.

Detken, Carsten, Weeken, Olaf, Alessi, Lucia, Bonfim, Diana, et al. (2014). Operationalising the Countercyclical Capital Buffer: Indicator Selection, Threshold Identification and Calibration Options, *ESRB Occasional Paper Series*, No. 5/June 2014.

Daunfeldt, Sven-Olov, De Luna, Xavier (2003). Central Bank Independence and Price Stability: Evidence from 23 OECD-Countries, *The Swedish Research Institute of Trade, Department of Statistics, Umeå University.*

Deutsche Bundesbank (1957). Report of the Deutsche Bundesbank for the Year 1957. Online. Available at: https://www.bundesbank.de/Redaktion/EN/Downloads/Publications/Annual_Report/1957_annual_report.pdf?__blob=publicationFile

Deutsche Bundesbank (2013). Macroprudential Oversight in Germany: Framework, Institutions and Tools, *Deutsche Bundesbank Monthly Report April 2013.*

Deutsche Bundesbank (2014). Compendium "Monetary Policy Frameworks and Central Bank Market Operations", *Outcome of the 'Implementing Monetary Policy' Workshop*, 27–31 January 2014.

Deutsche Bundesbank (2015). The Importance of Macroprudential Policy for Monetary Policy, *Monthly Report March 2015.*

Diewert, Erwin W. (2002). Harmonized Indexes of Consumer Prices: Their Conceptual Foundations, *ECB Working Paper*, No. 130.

Di Maggio, Marco, Kermani, Amir, Ramcharan, Rodney (2014). Monetary Policy Pass-Through: Household Consumption and Voluntary Deleveraging, *Columbia Business School Research Paper*, No. 14-24.

Di Noia, Carmine, Furlo, Maria Chiara (2012) The New Structure of Financial Supervision in Europe: What's Next?, In: *'Financial Regulation and Supervision: A Post-Crisis Analysis'* (eds. Eddy Wymeersch, Klaus Hopt, and Guido Ferrarini), Oxford University Press.

Dittmar, Robert, Gavin, William T., Kydland, Finn E. (1999). The Inflation Output Variability Tradeoff and Price-Level Targets, *Federal Reserve Bank of Saint Louis Review*, January/February 1999.

Dokko, Doyle, Jane Brian M., Kiley, Michael T., Kim, Jinill, Sherlund, Shane, Sim, Jae, Van Den Heuvel, Skander (2011). Monetary Policy and the Global Housing Bubble, *Economic Policy*, Vol. 26, Issue 66, pp. 237–287.

Dokko, Jane, Doyle, Brian, Kiley, Michael T., Kim, Jinill, Sherlund, Shane, Sim, Jae, Van den Heuvel, Skander (2009). Monetary Policy and the Housing Bubble, *Finance and Economics Discussion Series FED Working Papers*, No. 49.

Domanski, Dietrich, Ng, Tim (2011). Getting Effective Macroprudential Policy on the Road: Eight Propositions, *BIS Paper*, No. 60.

Dombret, Andreas, Lucius, Otto (2013). Stability of the Financial System: Illusion or Feasible Concept?, *Edward Elgar Publishing Ltd.*

Draghi, Mario (2015a). The ECB's Recent Monetary Policy Measures: Effectiveness and Challenges, *IMF Camdessus Lecture*, Washington, DC, 14 May 2015.

Draghi, Mario (2015b). Introductory Statement by Mario Draghi, Chair of the ESRB, *Hearing before the Committee on Economic and Monetary Affairs of the European Parliament*, Brussels, 12 November 2015.

Dragomir, Larisa (2010). European Prudential and Banking Regulation and Supervision: The Legal Dimension, *Routledge*, London and New York.

Drehmann, Mathias, Borio, Claudio, Tsatsaronis, Kostas (2012). Characterising the Financial Cycle: Don't Lose Sight of the Medium Term!, *BIS Working Papers*, No. 380.

Drobak, John N. (1998). Law Matters, *Washington University Law Review*, Vol. 76, Issue 1.

Drobak, John N. (2008). Introduction: Law & the New Institutional Economics, *Washington University Journal of Law & Policy*, Vol. 26, Issue 1.

Dubecq, Simon, Mojon, Benoît, Ragot, Xavier (2009). Fuzzy Capital Requirements, Risk-Shifting and the Risk Taking Channel of Monetary Policy, *Banque De France Document de Travail*, No. 254.

Duff, Arthur W.S. (2014). Central Bank Independence and Macroprudential Policy: A Critical Look at the U.S. Financial Stability Framework, *Berkeley Business Law Journal*, Vol. 11, Issue 1.

Dullien, Sebastian, Guérot, Ulrike (2012). The Long Shadow of Ordoliberalism: Germany's Approach to the Euro Crisis, *European Council on Foreign Relations Policy Brief*, No. 49.

Dunstan, Ashley (2014). The Interaction between Monetary and Macro-prudential Policy, *Reserve Bank of New Zealand Bulletin*, Vol. 77, No. 2.

Dutzler, Barbara (2003). The European System of Central Banks: An Autonomous Actor?: The Quest for an Institutional Balance in EMU, *Springer.*

Dyson, Kenneth (2000). The Politics of the Euro-zone: Stability Or Breakdown?, *Oxford University Press.*

EBA (2014). EBA Opinion on the Macroprudential Rules in CRR/CRD, *EBA Response to the European Commission on Article 513 CRR Call for Advice.* EBA/Op/2014/06.

EBA (2015). EBA Report on Asset Encumbrance, September 2015.

ECB (1999a). *Monthly Bulletin January 1999.*

ECB (1999b). Examination of the Various Legal Instruments Available to the European Central Bank, *Monthly Bulletin November 1999.*

ECB (2000). Monetary Policy Transmission in the Euro Area, *Monthly Bulletin July 2000.*

ECB (2008). The ECB's Monetary Policy Strategy and Its Implementation. In: '*Monthly Bulletin 10th Anniversary of the ECB*', Frankfurt am Main.

ECB (2009). The Concept of Systemic Risk, *Financial Stability Review*, December 2009.

ECB (2010). Monetary Policy Transmission in the Euro Area, A Decade after the Introduction of the Euro, *Monthly Bulletin May 2010.*

ECB (2011). The Monetary Policy of the ECB, Frankfurt am Main.

ECB (2013). Liquidity Regulation and Monetary Policy Implementation, *Monthly Bulletin April 2013.*

ECB (2014a). Recent Experience of European Countries with Macro-prudential Policy, *Financial Stability Review*, May 2014.

ECB (2014b). *Guide to Banking Supervision*, Frankfurt am Main.

ECB (2014c). Progress in the Operational Implementation of the Single Supervisory Mechanism Regulation, *SSM Quarterly Report*, No. 3.

Edwards, Cheryl L. (1997). Open Market Operations in the 1990s, *Federal Reserve Bulletin*, November 1997.

Egawa, Eri, Otani, Akira, Sakiyama, Toshiyuki (2015). What Determines Institutional Arrangements for Macroprudential Policy?, *IMES Discussion Papers*, No. 2015-E-3.

Eggertsson, Thrainn (1990). Economic Behavior and Institutions, *Cambridge University Press.*

Eggertsson, Gauti, Woodford, Michael (2003). The Zero Bound on Interest Rates and Optimal Monetary Policy, *Brookings Papers on Economic Activity*, No. 1.

Ehrmann, Michael, Fratzscher, Marcel (2004). Taking Stock: Monetary Policy Transmission to Equity Markets, *ECB Working Paper*, No. 354.

Eichengreen, Berry (2008). Globalizing Capital: A History of the International Monetary System, *Princeton University Press.*

Eidenberger, Judith, Liebeg, David, Schmitz, Stefan W., Seliger, Reinhardt, Sigmund, Michael, Steiner, Katharina, Strobl, Peter, Ub, Eva (2014). Macroprudential Supervision: A Key Lesson from the Financial Crisis, *Oesterreichische Nationalbank Financial Stability Report*, No. 27.

Eijffinger, Sylvester, de Haan, Jakob (1996). The Political Economy of Central Bank Independence, *Princeton University Special Paper in International Economics*, No. 19.

Erdélyi, Olivia Johanna (2016). Twin Peaks for Europe: State-of-the-Art Financial Supervisory Consolidation Rethinking the Group Support Regime Under Solvency II, *Springer International Publishing.*

Enoch, Charles, Luc Everaert, Thierry Tressel, and Jianping Zhou (2013). From Fragmentation to Financial Integration in Europe, Washington, DC, (ed.) *International Monetary Fund.*

Esen, Oğuz, Binatlı, Ayla Oğuş (2012). The Minsky Perspective on Macroprudential Policy, *PERI Working Paper Series*, No. 308.

ESRB (2012). Annual Report.

ESRB (2013). The Consequences of the Single Supervisory Mechanism for Europe's Macro-prudential Policy Framework, *Reports of the Advisory Scientific Committee*, No. 3/September 2013.

ESRB (2014a). Handbook on Operationalising Macro-prudential Policy in the Banking Sector.

ESRB (2014b). Flagship Report on Macro-prudential Policy in the Banking Sector.

ESRB (2014c). ESRB Recommendation on the Macro-prudential Mandate of National Authorities (ESRB/2011/3) Follow-up Report – Overall Assessment, June 2014.

ESRB (2014d). Allocating Macro-prudential Powers, *Reports of the Advisory Scientific Committee*, No. 5/November.

ESRB (2015a). A Review of Macro-prudential Policy in the EU One Year after the Introduction of the CRD/CRR, June 2015.

ESRB (2015b). Report on the Regulatory Treatment of Sovereign Exposures, March 2015.

Eucken, Walter (1952). Grundsätze der Wirtschaftspolitik, Hamburg.

European Commission (2009a). Communication of the Commission for the Spring European Council of 4 March 2009, "*Driving European Recovery*". COM(2009) 114.

European Commission (2009b). Communication from the Commission of 27 May 2009, "*European Financial Supervision*". COM(2009) 252 final.

European Commission (2014). Report from the Commission to the European Parliament and the Council on the Mission and Organisation of the European Systemic Risk Board (ESRB), Brussels, 8 August 2014 (COM(2014) 508 final).

EUROSTAT (1998). A Key Instrument: New Monetary Union Index of Consumer Prices (MUICP) Monitoring Inflation in the Euro Zone, *Memo*, No. 8/9.

Evans, Owen, Leone, Alfredo M., Gill, Mahinder, Hilbers, Paul (2000). Macroprudential Indicators of Financial System Soundness, *IMF Occasional Papers*, No. 192.

Everson, Michelle (2015). An Exercise in Legal Honesty: Rewriting the Court of Justice and the Bundesverfassungsgericht, *European Law Journal*, Vol. 21, Issue 4, pp. 474–499.

Faia, Ester, Schnabel, Isabel (2015). The Road from Micro-prudential to Macro-prudential Regulation. In: '*Financial Regulation. A Transatlantic Perspective*', (eds.) Ester Faia, Andreas Hackethal, Michael Haliassos, Katja Langenbucher, *Cambridge University Press.*

Falkner, Gerda, Treib, Oliver, Hartlapp, Miriam, Leiber, Simone (2005). Complying with Europe EU Harmonisation and Soft Law in the Member States, *Cambridge University Press.*

Fariaa, João Ricardo, Mollickb, André Varella, Sachsidac, Adolfo, Wang, Le (2012). Do Central Banks Affect Tobin's q?, *International Review of Economics & Finance,* Vol. 22, Issue 1.

Farina, Francesco, Tamborini, Roberto (2001). Macroeconomic Stabilization Policies in Europe under the New Regime of Monetary Union, *Quaderni Università degli Studi di Siena Dipartimento di Economia Politica*, No. 301.

Favero, Carlo A., Giavazzi, Francesco, Flabbi, Luca (1999). The Transmission Mechanism of Monetary Policy in Europe: Evidence from Banks' Balance Sheets, *NBER Working Paper*, No. 7231.

Fawley, Brett, Neely, Christopher J. (2013). Four Stories of Quantitative Easing, *Federal Reserve Bank of St. Louis Review*, January/February 2013.

FCA (2014). Guidance on the Financial Policy Committee's Recommendation on Loan to Income Ratios in Mortgage Lending, *Guidance Consultation*, August 2014.

Federal Reserve Bank of New York (1990). Intermediate Targets and Indicators for Monetary Policy. A Critical Survey, December 1990. Online. Available at: https://fraser.stlouisfed.org/docs/publications/books/frbny_itimp.pdf

Feinman, Joshua N. (1993). Reserve Requirements: History, Current Practice, and Potential Reform, *Federal Reserve Bulletin*, June 1993.

Feld, Lars P., Köhler, Ekkehard A., Nientiedt, Daniel (2015). Ordoliberalism, Pragmatism and the Eurozone Crisis: How the German Tradition Shaped Economic Policy in Europe, *CESifo Working Paper*, No. 5368.

Feld, Lars P., Fuest, Clemens, Haucap, Justus, Schweitzer, Heike, Wieland, Volker Wigger (2016). Dismantling the Boundaries of the ECB's Monetary Policy Mandate, *Kronberger Kreis Studies*, No. 61.

Ferguson, Roger W. (2003). Should Financial Stability Be an Explicit Central Bank Objective? *Paper Presented to the IMF Conference on Challenges to Central Banking from Globalized Financial Markets*, Washington, DC, 17 September 2002.

Ferran, Eilis, Kern, Alexander (2010). Can Soft Law Bodies be Effective? Soft Systemic Risk Oversight Bodies and the Special Case of the European Systemic Risk Board, *University of Cambridge Faculty of Law, Research Paper*, No. 36/2011.

Ferran, Eilis, Babis, Valia (2013). The European Single Supervisory Mechanism, *Journal of Corporate Law Studies*, Vol. 13.

Ferran, Eilis (2015). European Banking Union: Imperfect, But It Can Work. In: '*European Banking Union*', (eds.) Danny Busch, Guido Ferrarini, *Oxford University Press.*

Ferrarini, Guido, Chiodini, Filippo (2009). Regulating Cross-border Banks in Europe: A Comment on the de Larosière Report and a Modest Proposal, *Capital Markets Law Journal*, 2009.

Ferrarini, Guido, Chiodini, Filippo (2012). Nationally Fragmented Supervision over Multinational Banks as a Source of Global Systemic Risk: A Critical Analysis of Recent EU Reforms. In: '*Rethinking Financial Regulation and Supervision in Times of Crisis*', (eds.) Guido Ferrarini, Klaus J. Hopt, Eddy Wymeersch, *Oxford University Press.*

Finance Watch (2015). Finance Watch Response to FSB's Consultation on Adequacy of Loss-Absorbing Capacity of Global Systemically Important Banks in Resolution. Brussels, 30 January 2015.

Financial Stability Forum (2009). Report of the Financial Stability Forum on Addressing Procyclicality in the Financial System, 2 April 2009.

Finanspektionen (2012). The Swedish Mortgage Market, Report 13 March 2012. Ref. 11-6461.

Finanspektionen (2013). The Swedish Mortgage Market, Report 7 March 2013. Ref. 13-2825.

Finanspektionen (2014). The Swedish Mortgage Market, Report 10 April 2014. Ref. 13-7755.

Fischer, Stanley (1993). The Role of Macroeconomic Factors in Growth, *NBER Working Paper Series*, No. 4565.

Fischer, Stanley (1994). Modern Central Banking. In: '*The Future of Central Banking*', (eds.) Forrest Capie, Charles Goodhart, Stanley Fischer, Norbert Schnadt, *Cambridge University Press.*

Fischer, Stanley (1995). Modern Approaches to Central Banking, *NBER Working Paper Series*, No. 5064.

Fischer, Stanley, Fraga, Arminio, Heikensten, Lars, Tietmeyer, Hans, Volcker, Paul A. (2006). Panel Discussion: The Art of Central Banking? Presented at '*Monetary Policy: A Journey from Theory to Practice*', An ECB Colloquium Held in Honor of Otmar Issing. Frankfurt am Main, 16–17 March 2006.

Flandreau, Marc (2006). Pillars of Globalization: A History of Monetary Policy Targets, 1797–1997, *Paper Prepared for the Fourth ECB Central Banking Conference*, Frankfurt-Am-Main, 9–10 November 2006.

Fleming, J. Marcus (1962). Domestic Financial Policies Under Fixed and Under Floating Exchange Rates, *IMF Staff Papers*, Vol. 9.

Follesdal, Andreas, Hix, Simon (2006). Why There Is a Democratic Deficit in the EU: A Response to Majone and Moravcsik, *JCMS: Journal of Common Market Studies*, Vol. 44, Issue 3.

Forsells, Magnus, Kenny, Geoff (2002). The Rationality of Consumers' Inflation Expectations: Survey-based Evidence for the Euro Area, *ECB Working Paper*, No. 16.

Frait, Jan, Malovaná, Simona, Tomšík, Vladimír (2015). The Interaction of Monetary and Macroprudential Policies in the Pursuit of Central Bank's Primary Objectives, *Czech National Bank Financial Stability Report* 2014/2015.

Francis, William B., Osborne, Matthew (2012). Capital Requirements and Bank Behavior in the UK: Are There Lessons for International Capital Standards?, *Journal of Banking & Finance*, Vol. 36.

Frankel, Jeffrey A. (2011). A Comparison of Monetary Anchor Options, Including Product Price Targeting, for Commodity-Exporters in Latin America. *Economia – Journal of the Latin American and Caribbean Economic Association*, Vol. 12, No. 1.

Fratzscher, Marcel, Lo Duca, Marco, Straub, Roland (2014). ECB Unconventional Monetary Policy Actions: Market Impact, International Spillovers and Transmission Channels, *Paper Presented at the 15th Jacques Polak Annual Research Conference Hosted by the IMF*, Washington, DC, 13–14 November 2014.

Friedman, Benjamin M. (1984). The Value of Intermediate Targets in Implementing Monetary Policy, *NBER Working Paper Series,* No. 1487 (Also Reprint No. r0595).

Friedman, Benjamin M. (1988). Targets and Instruments of Monetary Policy, *NBER Working Paper*, No. 2668.

Friedman, Benjamin M., Kuttner, Kenneth N. (1996). A Price Target for U.S. Monetary Policy? Lessons from the Experience with Money Growth Targets, *Brookings Papers on Economic Activity*, Vol. 1.

Friedman, Milton (1982). Monetary Policy: Theory and Practice, *Journal of Money, Credit and Banking*, Vol. 14, No. 1.

Frisch, Helmut (1990). Theories of Inflation, *Cambridge University Press*, Cambridge.

FSB (2014). Adequacy of Loss-Absorbing Capacity of Global Systemically Important Banks in Resolution. *Consultative Document*, 10 November 2014.

FSB, IMF, BCBS (2010). Systemic Surcharges vs. Levies, *Report to the G20*, April 2010.

FSB, IMF, BIS (2009a). Macroprudential Policy Tools and Frameworks, *Update to G20 Finance Ministers and Central Bank Governors*, 14 February 2011.
FSB, IMF, BIS (2009b). Guidance to Assess the Systemic Importance of Financial Institutions, Markets and Instruments: Initial Considerations, *Report to the G-20 Finance Ministers and Central Bank Governors*, October 2009.
FSB, IMF, BIS (2011). Macroprudential Policy Tools and Frameworks, *Update to G20 Finance Ministers and Central Bank Governors*, 14 February 2011.
FSB, IMF, BIS (2014). Letter on Progress Regarding Data Gaps in Foreign Currency Exposures, 11 September 2014.
Gaitanides, Charlotte (2005). Das Recht der Europäischen Zentralbank, *Mohr Siebeck*, Tübingen.
Galati, Gabriele, Moessner, Richhild (2013). Macroprudential Policy – A Literature Review, *Journal of Economic Surveys*, Vol. 27, Issue 5, pp. 846–878.
Galati, Gabriele, Moessner, Richhild (2014). What Do We Know about the Effects of Macroprudential Policy?, *DNB Working Paper*, No. 440.
Galì, Jordi, Gertler, Mark (2007). Macroeconomic Modeling for Monetary Policy Evaluation, *Journal of Economic Perspectives*, Vol. 21, No. 4.
Galvenius, Mats, Mercier, Paul (2011). The Story of the Eurosystem Framework. In: '*The Concrete Euro: Implementing Monetary Policy in the Euro Area*', (eds.) Paul Mercier, Francesco Papadia, *Oxford University Press*, Oxford.
Gambacorta, Leonardo (2009). Monetary Policy and the Risk-Taking Channel, *BIS Quarterly Review*, December 2009.
Gambacorta, Leonardo, Signoretti, Federico M. (2014). Should Monetary Policy Lean Against the Wind?: An Analysis Based on a DSGE Model with Banking, *Journal of Economic Dynamics and Control*, Vol. 43.
Gameiro, Isabel Marques, Soares, Carla, Sousa, João (2011). Monetary Policy and Financial Stability: An Open Debate, *Banco de Portugal Economic Bulletin*, Spring 2011.
Garicano, Luiss, Lastra, Rosa M. (2010). Towards a New Architecture for Financial Stability: Seven Principles, *Journal of International Economic Law*, Vol. 13, Issue 3.
Gaspar, Vítor, Abreu, Ildeberta (1998). Price Stability and Intermediate Targets for Monetary Policy, *Banco de Portugal Working Paper*, No. 1–99.
Gauron, Andre (1999). Europe Misunderstanding, *Algora Pub.*
Ghilardi, Matteo F., Peiris, Shanaka J. (2014). Capital Flows, Financial Intermediation, and Macroprudential Policies, *IMF Working Paper*, No. 157.
Ghosh, Atish R., Ostry, Jonathan D., and Tamirisa, Natalia (2009). Anticipating the Next Crisis, *IMF Finance & Development*, Vol. 46, No. 3.
Geanakoplos, John (2010). Solving the Present Crisis and Managing the Leverage Cycle, *FRBNY Economic Policy Review*, August 2010.
Gelain, Paolo, Ilbas, Pelin (2014). Monetary and Macroprudential Policies in an Estimated Model with Financial Intermediation, *National Bank of Belgium Working Paper*, No. 258.

Gerber, David (1994). Constitutionalizing the Economy: German Neo-Liberalism, Competition Law and the "New" Europe, *The American Journal of Comparative Law*, Vol. 42, No. 1.

Gerdesmeier, Dieter, Mongelli, Francesco Paolo, Roffia, Barbara (2007). The Eurosystem, the US Federal Reserve and the Bank of Japan. Similarities and Differences, *ECB Working Paper Series*, No. 742.

Gerlach, Stefan (2012). Housing Markets and Financial Stability, *Speech Held at the National University of Ireland*, Galway, 20 April 2012.

Gerlach, Stefan, Browne, Frank, Honohan, Patrick (2004). The Two Pillars of the European Central Bank, *Economic Policy*, Vol. 19, No. 40.

Giannone, Domenico, Lenza, Michele, Reichlin, Lucrezia (2009). Business Cycles in the Euro Area, *ECB Working Paper Series*, No. 1010.

Gianviti, François (2010). The Objectives of Central Banks. In: '*International Monetary and Financial Law*', (eds.) Mario Giovanoli, Diego Devos, *Oxford University Press.*

Giese, Julia, Nelson, Benjamin, Tanaka, Misa, Tarashev, Nikola (2013). How Could Macroprudential Policy Affect Financial System Resilience and Credit? Lessons from the Literature, *Bank of England Financial Stability Paper*, No. 21.

Gilardi, Fabrizio (2002). Policy Credibility and Delegation to Independent Regulatory Agencies: A Comparative Empirical Analysis, *Journal of European Public Policy*, Vol. 9, No. 6.

Giordana, Gaston, Schumacher, Ingmar (2013). Bank Liquidity Risk and Monetary Policy. Empirical Evidence on the Impact of Basel III Liquidity Standards, *International Review of Applied Economics*, Vol. 27, No. 5.

Giuliodori, Massimo (2005). The Role of House Prices in the Monetary Transmission Mechanism Across European Countries, *Scottish Journal of Political Economy*, Vol. 52, No. 4, pp. 519–543.

Glick, Reuven, Leduc, Sylvain (2012). Central Bank Announcements of Asset Purchases and the Impact on Global Financial and Commodity Markets, *Journal of International Money and Finance*, Vol. 31.

Głuch, Daniel, Škovranová, Lucia, Stenström, Mikael (2013). Central Bank Involvement in Macro-prudential Oversight, *ECB Legal Working Paper Series, No. 14.*

Gohari, Behzad, Woody, Karen E. (2014). The New Global Financial Regulatory Order: Can Macroprudential Regulation Prevent Another Global Financial Disaster? *Journal of Corporation Law*, Vol. 40, Issue 2.

Goodhart, Charles (1988). The Evolution of Central Banks, *The MIT Press*, Cambridge.

Goodhart, Charles (2008). The Background to the 2007 Financial Crisis, *International Economics and Economic Policy*, Vol. 4, Issue 4.

Goodhart, Charles (2009). Procyclicality and Financial Regulation, *Bank of Spain Revista de Estabilidad Financiera*, No. 16.

Goodhart, Charles (2014). The Use of Macroprudential Instruments. In: '*Macroprudentialism*', (ed.) Dirk Schoenmaker, *CEPR Press*, Washington, DC.
Goodhart, Charles, Tsomocos, Dimitris, Vardoulakis, Alexander (2009). Foreclosures, Monetary Policy and Financial Stability, *Paper Presented at the 10th International Academic Conference on Economic and Social Development*, Moscow, 7–9 April 2009.
Goodhart, Charles A.E., Perotti, Enrico (2014). From Tampering to Preventive Policy, *Banque de France Financial Stability Review*, No. 18.
Goodhart, Lucy (2015). Brave New World? Macro Prudential Policy and the New Political Economy of the Federal Reserve, *Review of International Political Economy*, Vol. 22, No. 2.
Goodman, John B. (1991). The Politics of Central Bank Independence, *Comparative Politics*, Vol. 23, No. 3.
Goldmann, Matthias (2016). Constitutional Pluralism as Mutually Assured Discretion: The ECJ, the BVerfG, and the ECB, *Maastricht Journal of European and Comparative Law*, Vol. 1.
Gorton, Gary, He, Ping (2008). Bank Credit Cycles, *Review of Economic Studies*, Vol. 75, No. 4.
Gortsos, Christos V. (2015). Competence Sharing Between the ECB and the National Competent Supervisory Authorities Within the Single Supervisory Mechanism (SSM), *European Business Organization Law Review*, Vol. 16, Issue 3, pp. 401–420.
Grace, Therese, Hallissey, Niamh, Woods, Maria (2015). The Instruments of Macro-prudential Policy, *Bank of Ireland Quarterly Bulletin 01/January 15*.
Gray, Simon (2011). Central Bank Balances and Reserve Requirements, *IMF Working Paper*, No. 36.
Greenspan, Alan (1994). *Testimony before the Subcommittee on Economic Growth and Credit Formulation of the Committee on Banking, Finance, and Urban Affairs*, U.S. House of Representatives, 22 February 1994.
Grégory, Claeys, Darvas, Zsolt (2015). The Financial Stability Risks of Ultra-loose Monetary Policy, *Bruegel Policy Contribution*, Issue 2015/03.
Greenwood, Justin, Roederer-Rynning, Christilla (2014). The "Europeanization" of the Basel Process: Financial Harmonization between Globalization and Parliamentarization, *Regulation & Governance*, Vol. 9, Issue 4.
Gros, Daniel (2013). Banking Union with a Sovereign Virus the Self-serving Regulatory Treatment of Sovereign Debt in the Euro Area, *CEPS Policy Brief*, No. 289.
Grüner, Hans P. (2013). The Political Economy of Structural Reform and Fiscal Consolidation Revisited, *European Commission Economic Papers*, No. 487.
Gualandri, Elisabetta (2015). Single Supervisory Mechanism e politiche macro-prudenziali nell'Unione europea, *Banca Impresa Società*, No. 1/2015.

Guender, Alfred V., Oh, Do Yoon (2006). Price Stability through Price-Level Targeting or Inflation Targeting? A Tale of Two Experiments, *Journal of Economics and Business*, Vol. 58, No. 5–6.

Guibourg, Gabriela Jonsson, Magnus Lagerwall Björn, Nilsson, Christian (2015). Macroprudential Policy – Effects on the Economy and the Interaction with Monetary Policy, *Sveriges Riksbank Economic Review*, Issue 2, pp. 29–46.

Habermas, Jurgen (2013). Democracy, Solidarity and the European Crisis. In: '*Roadmap to a Social Europe*', (eds.) Anne-Marie Grozelier, Björn Hacker, Wolfgang Kowalsky, Jan Machnig, Henning Meyer and Brigitte Unger, *Social Europe Report.*

Häde, Ulrich (2011). The Treaty of Lisbon and the Economic and Monetary Union. In: '*The European Union after Lisbon*', (eds.) Hermann-Josef Blanke, Stelio Mangiameli, *Springer Berlin Heidelberg.*

Haldane, Andrew G. (2009). Rethinking the Financial Network, *Speech Held at the Financial Student Association, Amsterdam, 28 April 2009.*

Hall, Robert (ed.)(1982). Inflation: Causes and Effects, *The University Chicago Press*, Chicago.

Hahn, Frank (1985). Money and Inflation, *The MIT Press*, Cambridge.

Hanson, Samuel G., Kashyap, Anil K., Stein, Jeremy C. (2011). A Macroprudential Approach to Financial Regulation, *Journal of Economic Perspectives*, Vol. 25, No. 1.

Hardy, Daniel C. (1997). Market Information and Signalling in Central Bank Operations, or, How Often Should a Central Bank Intervene?, *IMF Working Paper*, No. 28.

Harris, Ethan S. (2012). Constrained Discretion: Bernanke's Quest for an Inflation Target. In: '*Ben Bernanke's Fed: The Federal Reserve After Greenspan*', *Harvard Business Press.*

Hartlage, Andrew W. (2012). The Basel III Liquidity Coverage Ratio and Financial Stability, *Michigan Law Review*, Vol. 111, No. 3.

Hautsch, Nikolaus, Schaumburg, Julia, Schienle, Melanie (2014). Financial Network Systemic Risk Contributions, *SFB 649 Discussion Paper* 2012-053.

Havemann, Roy (2014). Counter-Cyclical Capital Buffers and Interest-Rate Policy as Complements – The Experience of South Africa, *ERSA Working Paper*, No. 476.

Hazlitt, Henry (1984). From Bretton Woods to World Inflation, *Regnery Gateway*, Chicago.

He, Zhiguo, Krishnamurthy, Arvind (2014). A Macroeconomic Framework for Quantifying Systemic Risk, *Chicago Booth Research Paper*, No. 12–37.

Heath, Daniel (2014). International Coordination of Macroprudential and Monetary Policy, *Georgetown Journal of International Law*, Vol. 45, Issue 5.

Hendricks, Torben W. (2011). Monetary Policy and the Credit Channel, Broad and Narrow, *Eastern Economic Journal*, Vol. 37, Issue 3.

Heenan, Geoffrey, Peter, Marcel, Roger, Scott (2006). Implementing Inflation Targeting: Institutional Arrangements, Target Design, and Communication, *IMF Working Paper*, No. 278.

Hennessy, Alexandra (2014). Redesigning Financial Supervision in the European Union (2009–2013), *Journal of European Public Policy*, Vol. 21, Issue 2.

Herdegen, Matthias J. (1998). Price Stability and Budgetary Restraints in the Economic and Monetary Union: The Law as Guardian of Economic Wisdom, *Common Market Law Review*, Vol. 35, Issue 1, pp. 9–32.

Herzberg, Valerie, Watson, Max (2014). Macroprudential Policies in the Euro Area: Issues for the Next Ten Years, St Antony's College, *University of Oxford Discussion Draft*.

Hesse, Helmut, Braasch, Bernd (1996). *"Standing facilities" – als geldpolitisches Instrument einer europäischen Notenbank verzichtbar?* In: 'Neuere Entwicklungen in der Geldtheorie und Geldpolitik. *Implikationen für die Europäische Währungsunion. Festschrift für Norbert Kloten*', *Mohr Siebeck Verlag*.

Hicks, John R. (1937). Mr. Keynes and the "Classics" a Suggested Interpretation, *Econometrica*, Vol. 5, Issue 2.

Hidalgo, Luis Jacome (2002). Central Banks and International Financial Volatility. In: '*Current Developments in Monetary and Financial Law*', Vol. 2, *International Monetary Fund*, Washington.

Hockett, Robert C. (2013). The Macroprudential Turn: From Institutional "Safety and Soundness" to "Systemic Stability" in Financial Supervision, *Cornell Law Faculty Working Papers*, No. 108.

Hodgson, Geoffrey M. (2004). The Evolution of Institutional Economics: Agency, Structure and Darwinism in American Institutionalism, *Routledge*, London.

Hoggarth, Glenn, Reis, Ricardo, Saporta, Victoria (2001). Costs of Banking System Instability: Some Empirical Evidence, *EFA 2001 Barcelona Meetings*, *Bank of England Working Papers*, No. 144.

Holmstrom, Bengt, Tirole, Jean (1997). Financial Intermediation, Loanable Funds, and the Real Sector, *Quarterly Journal of Economics*, Vol. 112, No. 3.

Holt, Jeff (2009). A Summary of the Primary Causes of the Housing Bubble and the Resulting Credit Crisis: A Non-technical Paper, *The Journal of Business Inquiry*, Vol. 8, No. 1.

Houben, Aerdt, Kakes, Jan (2013). Financial Imbalances and Macroprudential Policy in a Currency Union, *DNB Occasional Studies*, Vol. 11, No. 5.

Houben, Aerdt, Kakes. Jan, Schinasi, Garry (2004). Towards a Framework for Financial Stability, *De Nederlandsche Bank Occasional Studies*, Vol. 2, No. 1.

Houben, Aerdt, van der Molen, Remco, Wierts, Peter (2012). Making Macroprudential Policy Operational, *Banque Centrale du Luxembourg, Revue de Stabilité Financière 2012*.

House of Lords (2009). The Future of EU Financial Regulation and Supervision, *14th Report of Session 2008–09.*

Howart, David (2012). Defending the Euro: Unity and Disunity among Europe's Central Bankers. In: '*European Disunion: Between Sovereignty and Solidarity*', (eds.) Jack Hayward, Rüdiger Wurz, *Palgrave Macmillan.*

Huang, Rocco, Ratnovski, Lev (2010). The Dark Side of Bank Wholesale Funding, *IMF Working Paper*, No. 170.

Hubbard, P. Glenn (1995). Is There a "Credit Channel" for Monetary Policy?, *Federal Reserve Bank of Saint Louis Review*, May/June 1995.

Huertas, Thomas F. (2016). Banking Union: The Way Forward. In: '*European Banking Union Prospects and Challenges*', (eds.) Juan E. Costaneda, David G. Mayes, Geoffrey Wood, *Routledge*, London and New York.

Hunt, John P. (2009). Credit Rating Agencies and the Worldwide Credit Crisis: The Limits of Reputation, the Insufficiency of Reform, and a Proposal for Improvement, *Columbia Business Law Review*, Issue 1.

Hüser, Anne-Caroline (2015). Too Interconnected to Fail: A Survey of the Interbank Networks Literature, *SAFE Working Paper*, No. 91.

IBRD, WB, IMF (2005). Financial Sector Assessment: A Handbook, *International Monetary Fund*, Washington, DC.

Ida, Daisuke (2013). Tobin's Q Channel and Monetary Policy Rules under Incomplete Exchange Rate Pass-Through, *Economic Modelling*, Vol. 33.

Igan, Deniz, Kang, Heedon (2011). Do Loan-to-Value and Debt-to-Income Limits Work? Evidence from Korea, *IMF Working Paper*, No. 297.

Igan, Deniz, Kabundi, Alain, De Simone, Francisco Nadal, Tamirisa, Natalia (2013). Monetary Policy and Balance Sheets, *IMF Working Papers*, No. 158.

ILO, IMF, OECD, SOEC, UN, WB (2004). Consumer Price Index Manual: Theory and Practice, August 25, 2004.

IMF (2006). Financial Soundness Indicators. *Compilation Guide*, March 2006. Available at: http://www.imf.org/external/pubs/ft/fsi/guide/2006/index.htm

IMF (2008). The Changing Housing Cycle and the Implications for Monetary Policy, *World Economic Outlook – Housing and the Business Cycle,* Washington, DC.

IMF (2009). De Facto Classification of Exchange Rate Regimes and Monetary Policy Frameworks, February 25, 2009. Available at: http://www.imf.org/external/NP/mfd/er/index.aspx

IMF (2010a). The IMF-FSB Early Warning Exercise, Design and Methodological Toolkit, September 2010.

IMF (2010b). Central Banking Lessons from the Crisis, *IMF Policy Paper*, 27 May 2010.

IMF (2011a). Changes in Bank Funding Patterns and Financial Stability Risk, *IMF Global Financial Stability Report: Transition Challenges to Stability.*

IMF (2011b). Macroprudential Policy: An Organizing Framework. Available at: https://www.imf.org/external/np/pp/eng/2011/031411.pdf

IMF (2011c). Toward Operationalizing Macroprudential Policies: When to Act?, *IMF Global Financial Stability Report*, September 2011.

IMF (2012). The Interaction between Macroprudential and Monetary Policies: Background Paper.

IMF (2013a). The interaction of Monetary and Macroprudential Policies, 29 January 2013.

IMF (2013b). Key Aspects of Macroprudential Policy, 10 June 2013.

IMF (2013c). Annual Report on Exchange Arrangements and Exchange Restrictions.

IMF (2013d). European Union: Publication of Financial Sector Assessment Program Documentation—Technical Note on Macroprudential Oversight and the Role of the ESRB, *IMF Country Report,* No. 13/70.

IMF (2013e). Implementing Macroprudential Policy – Selected Legal Issues, 17 June 2013.

IMF (2014). Risk Taking, Liquidity, and Shadow Banking Curbing Excess While Promoting Growth, *Global Financial Stability Report (GFSR)*, October 2014.

IMFC (2014). Communiqué of the Thirtieth Meeting of the International Monetary and Financial Committee (IMFC), Washington, DC, October 11, 2014.

IMF (2015). Monetary Policy and Financial Stability, *IMF Staff Report*, September 2015.

Ingves, Stefan (2014). Monetary Policy and Financial Stability in a Globalised World. *Speech at the Stockholm School of Economics, Organized by the Swedish Economic Association*, Stockholm, 28 May 2014.

Ingves, Stefan, Jansson, Per (2014). Monetary Policy Has Had Positive Results in Sweden, *Letter to the Financial Times*, 23 July 2014. Online. Available at: http://www.ft.com/cms/s/0/678a9f46-11c7-11e4-8279-00144feabdc0.html#axzz3w6p RcNuM

Ireland, Peter N. (2005). The Monetary Transmission Mechanism. *Federal Reserve of Boston Working Papers*, No. 06-0, *Paper Prepared for 'The New Palgrave Dictionary of Economics'* (Second Edition), (eds.) Lawrence Blume, Steven Durlauf, *Palgrave Macmillan*.

Issing, Otmar (2000). The Globalisation of Financial Markets. *Speech Held at Ottobeuren*, 12 September 2000. Online. Available at: https://www.ecb.europa.eu/press/key/date/2000/html/sp000912_2.en.html

Issing, Otmar (2003). Monetary and Financial Stability – Is There a Trade-Off? *Speech Held at the Conference on "Monetary Stability, Financial Stability and the Business Cycle"*, Organized by the Bank for International Settlements, 28–29 March 2003, Basel.

Issing, Otmar (2006). The ECB's Monetary Policy Strategy: Why Did We Choose a Two Pillar Approach? *Presented at the Conference 'The Role of Money: Money and Monetary Policy in the Twenty-First Century'*, 4th ECB Central Banking Conference, Frankfurt.

Issing, Otmar (2008). Asset Prices and Monetary Policy, *Contribution to Cato Institute 26th Annual Monetary Conference 19 November 2008*, Cato Institute, Washington, DC.

Israël, Jean-Marc, Sandars, Patrick, Schubert, Aurel, Fischer, Björn (2013). Statistics and Indicators for Financial Stability Analysis and Policy, *ECB Occasional Paper Series*, No. 145, April 2013.

Irving Fisher Committee on Central Bank Statistics (2015). Data-Sharing: Issues and Good Practices, *Report to BIS Governors Prepared by the Task Force on Data Sharing*, January 2015.

Jácome, Luis; Mancini-Griffoli, Tommaso (2014). A Broader Mandate, *IMF Finance & Development*, Vol. 51, No. 2, June 2014.

Jácome, Luis I., Nier, Erlend W. (2011). Macroprudential Policy: Protecting the Whole, *IMF Finance and Development Issues.* Online. Available at: http://www.imf.org/external/pubs/ft/fandd/basics/macropru.htm

Jahan, Sarwat (2012). Inflation Targeting: Holding the Line. *IMF Finance & Development.* Available at: http://www.imf.org/external/pubs/ft/fandd/basics/target.htm

Jahn, Nadya, Kick, Thomas (2012). Early Warning Indicators for the German Banking System: A Macroprudential Analysis, *Deutsche Bundesbank Discussion Paper*, No. 2.

Jain, Chaman L., Tomic, Igor M. (1995). Essentials of Monetary & Fiscal Economics, *Graceway Publishing Company Inc.*

Jeanneau, Serge (2014). Financial Stability Objectives and Arrangements – What's New?, *BIS Paper*, No. 76.

Jeanne, Olivier, Korinek, Anton (2014). Macroprudential Policy Beyond Banking Regulation, *Banque de France Financial Stability Review*, No. 18.

Jiménez, Gabriel, Ongena, Steven, Peydró, José Luis, Saurina, Jesús (2008). Hazardous Times for Monetary Policy: What Do Twenty-Three Million Bank Loans Say about the Effects of Monetary Policy on Credit Risk-Taking?, *Banco de Espana Documentos de Trabajo*, No. 0833.

Jorda, Oscar, Schularick, Moritz, Taylor, Alan M. (2014). Betting the House, *NBER Working Paper*, No. 20771.

Joyce, Michael, Miles, David, Scott, Andrew, Vayanos, Dimitri (2012). Quantitative Easing and Unconventional Monetary Policy – An Introduction, *The Economic Journal*, Vol. 122, Issue 564.

Judson, Ruth, Orphanides, Athanasios (1999). Inflation, Volatility and Growth, *International Finance*, Vol. 2, No. 1.

Kacperczyk, Marcin, Schnabl, Philipp (2010). When Safe Proved Risky: Commercial Paper During the Financial Crisis of 2007–2009, *Journal of Economic Perspectives*, Vol. 24, No. 1.

Kafer, Benjamin (2014). The Taylor Rule and Financial Stability: A Literature Review with Application for the Euro Zone, *Review of Economics,* Vol. 65.

Kaiser, Helmut, Heilenkötter, Anja, Herrmann, Markus, Krämer, Werner (2012). Der Euro-Kapitalmarkt, *Gabler Verlag*.

Kaltenthaler, Karl (2004a). Evolution of the German Bundesbank from Bank Deutscher Länder to Regional Bank of the ECB. In: '*Germany at Fifty-Five*', (ed.) James Sperling, *Manchester University Press*.

Kaltenthaler, Karl (2004b). Policymaking in the European Central Bank – The Masters of Europe's Money, *Rowman & Littlefield Publishers*.

Kaltenthaler, Karl (2006). The Bundesbank and the Formation of the ECB's Monetary Policy Strategy, *German Politics*, Vol.14, Issue 3, pp. 297–314.

Kaltenthaler, Karl, Anderson, Chirstopher J., Miller, William J. (2010). Accountability and Independent Central Banks: Europeans and Distrust of the European Central Bank, *JCMS: Journal of Common Market Studies*, Vol. 48, Issue 5.

Kämmerer, Jörn Axel (2013). Artikel 123 AEUV. In: '*EWU – Kommentar zur Europäischen Währungsunion*', (ed.) Helmut Siekmann, *Mohr Siebeck*, Tübingen.

Kamin, Steven (2010). Financial Globalization and Monetary Policy, *Board of Governors of the Federal Reserve System, International Finance Discussion Papers*, No. 1002.

Kang, Teuk Rok (2012). Reform des europäischen Finanzaufsichtssystems als Vorbild für Ostasien (Schriften zum Europäischen und Internationalen Privat-, Bank- und Wirtschaftsrecht, Band 43), *De Gruyter*.

Kannan, Prakash, Rabanal, Pau, Scott, Alasdair (2009). Monetary and Macroprudential Policy Rules in a Model with House Price Booms, *IMF Working Paper*, No. 251.

Karmakar, Sudipto (2013). Macroprudential Regulation and Macroeconomic Activity, *MPRA Paper*, No. 52172.

Karmann, Alexander, Enkhzaya, Chuluunbaatar (2006). Impact of Institutions on Lending: Informal Constraints and Enforcement of Bank Regulation in Mongolia, *Deutscher Universitaetsverlag*, Wiesbaden.

Kashyap, Anil K., Stein, Jeremy C. (1994). The Impact of Monetary Policy on Bank Balance Sheets, *NBER Working Paper*, No. 4821.

Kaufman, George G. (2000). Banking and Currency Crises and Systemic Risk: A Taxonomy and Review, *Financial Markets, Institutions & Instruments*, Vol. 9, No. 2.

Kawai, Masahiro, Pomerleano, Michael (2010). Regulating Systemic Risk, *ADBI Working Paper Series*, No. 189.

Kawata, Hiroshi, Kurachi, Yoshiyuki, Nakamura, Koji, Teranishi, Yuki (2013). Impact of Macroprudential Policy Measures on Economic Dynamics: Simulation Using a Financial Macro-econometric Model, *Bank of Japan Working Paper Series*, No. 13-E-3.

Keller, Anat (2013). Collecting Data: How will the ESRB Overcome the First Hurdle Towards Effective Macro-Prudential Supervision?, *European Business Law Review*, Vol. 24, Issue 4, pp. 487–535.

Kellermann, A. Joanne, de Haan, Jakob, de Vries, Femke (2013). Financial Supervision in the 21st Century, *Springer*, Berlin.

Kelman, Mark (1993). Could Lawyers Stop Recessions? Speculations on Law and Macroeconomics, *Stanford Law Review*, Vol. 45, No. 5.

Kern, Alexander (2014). In: '*The Rule of Law in Monetary Affairs*, (eds.) Thomas Cottier, Rosa Maria Lastra, Christian Tietjie, Lucia Satragno, *Cambridge University Press*.

Kero, Afroditi (2011). Macroprudential Regulations and the Basel III, *Universitat Pompeu Fabra*. Available at: https://fp7.portals.mbs.ac.uk/Portals/59/docs/MC% 20deliverables/WP8%20AKeroSurvey_MacroprudentialRegulations&BaselIII.pdf

Keune, Christina, Looschelders, Dirk (2015). Rechtliche Grundlagen und Grenzen der EIOPA (Düsseldorfer Reihe), *Verlag Versicherungswirtschaft*.

Kieler, Mads (2003). The ECB's Inflation Objective, *IMF Working Paper*, No. 91.

Kim, Choongsoo (2013). Harmonious Operation of Macroprudential and Monetary Policies, and Challenges, *Speech at the International Seminar on 'Macroprudential and Monetary Policies'*, Bank of Korea, Seoul, 8 April 2013.

King, Mervyn (2004). The Institutions of Monetary Policy, *American Economic Review*, Vol. 94, No. 2.

Knot, Klaas (2014). Governance of Macroprudential Policy, *Banque de France Financial Stability Review*, No. 18.

Kohn, Donald (2015). Implementing Macroprudential and Monetary Policies: The Case for Two Committees, *Remarks Delivered to the Federal Reserve Board's Boston Conference*, 2 October 2015.

Koivu, Tuuli (2010). Monetary Policy, Asset Prices and Consumption in China, *ECB Working Paper Series*, No. 1240/September 2010.

Kormendi, Roger C., Meguire, Philip G. (1985). Macroeconomic Determinants of Growth. Cross-Country Evidence, *Journal of Monetary Economics*, Vol. 16, Issue 2.

Kohtamäki, Natalia (2012). Die Reform der Bankenaufsicht in der Europäischen Union, *Mohr Siebeck*.

Kregel, Jan (2014). Minsky and Dynamic Macroprudential Regulation, *PSL Quarterly Review*, Vol. 67, No. 269.

Krishnamurthy, Arvind, Vissing-Jorgensen, Annette (2011). The Effects of Quantitative Easing on Interest Rates: Channels and Implications for Policy, *Brookings Papers on Economic Activity*, No. 2.

Krishnamurti, Damodaran, Lee, Yejin Carol (2014). Macroprudential Policy Framework: A Practice Guide, *World Bank*, Washington, DC.

Kydland, Finn E., Prescott, Edward C. (1977). Rules Rather than Discretion: The Inconsistency of Optimal Plans. *Journal of Political Economy*, Vol. 87, Issue 3.

La Porta, Rafael, Lopez-de-Manes, Florencio, Shleifer, Andrei, Vishny, Robert (2002). Investor Protection and Corporate Valuation, *The Journal of Finance*, Vol. 57, Issue 3.

Labonte, Marc (2015). Monetary Policy and the Federal Reserve: Current Policy and Conditions, *Congressional Research Service Report*, 9 February 2015.

Laker, John (1999). Monitoring Financial System Stability, *Speech Held at the 52nd International Banking Summer School*, Melbourne, 1 September 1999 (*Reserve Bank of Australia Bulletin*, October 1999).

Lama, Ruy, Medina, Juan Pablo (2007). Optimal Monetary Policy in a Small Open Economy Under Segmented Asset Markets and Sticky Prices, *IMF Working Paper*, No. 217.

Lambert, Frederic, Ueda, Kenichi (2014). The Effects of Unconventional Monetary Policies on Bank Soundness, *IMF Working Paper*, No. 152.

Lambertini, Luisa, Mendicino, Caterina, Punzi, Maria Teresa (2013). Leaning Against Boom–Bust Cycles in Credit and Housing Prices, *Journal of Economic Dynamics and Control*, Vol. 37, Issue 8.

Lamfalussy, Alexandre (1997). The European Central Bank: Independent and Accountable, *Keynote Speech at the Österreichische Nationalbank*, Vienna, 13 May 1997.

Landau, Jean-Pierre (2009). Procyclicality – What It Means and What Could Be Done. *Remarks at the Bank of Spain's Conference on Procyclicality and the Role of Financial Regulation*, Madrid, 4 May 2009.

Lannoo, Karel (2009). The Road Ahead after De Larosière, *CEPS Policy Brief*, No. 195.

Laseen, Stefan, Pescatori, Andrea, Turunen, Jarkko (2015). Systemic Risk: A New Trade-off for Monetary Policy?, *IMF Working Paper Series*, No. 142.

Lastra, Rosa Maria (2000). Division of Responsibilities between the European Central Bank and the National Central Banks within the European System of Central Banks, *Columbia Journal of European Law*, Vol. 6, No. 2.

Lastra, Maria Rosa (2003). Governance Structure for Financial Regulation and Supervision in Europe, *Columbia Journal of European Law*, Vol. 10, Issue 1.

Lastra, Maria Rosa (2012). The Evolution of the European Central Bank, *Fordham International Law Journal*, Vol. 35, Spring Issue.

Lastra, Maria Rosa (2014). The Role of Central Banks in Monetary Affairs: A Comparative Perspective. In: '*The Rule of Law in Monetary Affairs*', (eds.) Thomas Cottier, Rosa Maria Lastra, Christian Tietjie, Lucia Satragno, *Cambridge University Press*.

Lastra, Maria Rosa (2015a). Systemic Risk and Macroprudential Supervision. In: '*The Oxford Handbook of Financial Regulation*', (eds.) Moloney Niamh, Eilis Ferran, Jennifer Payne, *Oxford University Press*.

Lastra, Maria Rosa (2015b). International Financial and Monetary Law, *Oxford University Press*.

Lastra, Maria Rosa, Wood, Geoffrey (2010). The Crisis of 2007–09: Nature, Causes, and Reactions, *Journal of International Economic Law*, Vol. 13, No. 3.

Laurens, Bernard, de la Piedra, Enrique (1988). Coordination of Monetary and Fiscal Policies, *IMF Working Paper*, No. 25, pp. 1–32.

Lautenschläger, Sabine (2014). The Interplay between Macro-prudential, Microprudential and Monetary Policies at the ECB, *Speech Held at the Conference on "Macroprudential Policy – Implementation and Interaction with other Policies"*, Stockholm, 13 November 2014.

Law, Siong Hook, Azman-Saini, W.N.W. (2008). The Quality of Institutions and Financial Development, *MPRA Paper*, No. 12107.

Lawson, Gary (1999). Delegation and the Constitution, *Regulation*, Vol. 22, No. 2.

Leduc, Sylvain, Natal, Jean-Marc (2015). Monetary and Macroprudential Policy in a Leveraged Economy, *Federal Reserve Bank of San Francisco Working Paper*, No. 15.

Leith, Campbell, Moldovan, Ioana, Rossi, Raffaele (2009). Optimal Monetary Policy in a New Keynesian Model with Habits in Consumption, *ECB Working Paper Series*, No. 1097.

Lenihan, Niall J. (2008). The Price Stability Mandate of the European System of Central Banks: A Legal Perspective. In: '*Current Development in Monetary and Financial Law*', Vol. 5, *International Monetary Fund*, Washington, DC.

Levine, Paul, Lima, Diana (2015). Policy Mandates for Macro-prudential and Monetary Policies in a New Keynesian Framework, *ECB Working Paper Series*, No. 1784.

Levitin, Adam J., Wachter, Susan M. (2012). Explaining the Housing Bubble, *Georgetown Law Journal*, Vol. 100, No. 4.

Levy, David A. (1995). Does an Independent Central Bank Violate Democracy? *Journal of Post Keynesian Economics*, Vol. 18, No. 2.

Lim, Cheng Hoon, Columba, Francesco, Costa, Alejo, Kongsamut, Piyabha, Otani, Akira, Saiyid, Mustafa, Wezel, Torsten, Wu, Xiaoyong (2011). Macroprudential Policy: What Instruments and How to Use Them? Lessons from Country Experiences, *IMF Working Paper*, No. 238.

Lim, Cheng Hoon, Ramchand, Rishi, Wang, Hong, Wu, Xiaoyong (2013). Institutional Arrangements for Macroprudential Policy in Asia, *IMF Working Paper*, No. 165.

Listokin, Yair (2014). Law and Macroeconomics, *Stanford Law and Economics Seminar, Autumn Quarter 2014.*

Lopes, Francisco L. (1998). The Transmission Mechanism of Monetary Policy in a Stabilising Economy: Notes on the Case of Brazil. In: '*The Transmission of Monetary Policy in Emerging Market Economies*', *BIS Policy Papers*, No. 3.

Louis, Jean-Victor (1995). L'Union économique et monétaire. In: '*Commentaire Megret, Le Droit de la CEE*', *Editions de l'Université de Bruxelles.*

Louis, Jean-Victor (2005a). The Economic and Monetary Union: Law and Institutions. In: '*A Review of Forty Years of Community Law: Legal Developments in the European Communities and in the European Union*', (ed.) Alison McDonnell, *Kluwer Law International.*

Louis, Jean-Victor (2005b). Monetary Policy and Central Banking in the Constitution. In: '*Legal Aspects of the European System of Central Banks*'. Liber Amicorum Paolo Zamboni Garavelli. Frankfurt, ECB.

Louis, Jean-Victor (2014). Monetary Union and the Law: Some Comments. In: '*The Rule of Law in Monetary Affairs*', (eds.) Thomas Cottier, Rosa Maria Lastra, Christian Tietjie, Lucia Satragno, *Cambridge University Press.*

Ludvigson, Sydney, Steindel, Charles, Lettau, Martin (2002). Monetary Policy Transmission through the Consumption-Wealth Channel. *FRBNY Economic Policy Review*, May 2002.

Loungani, Prakash, Sheets, Nathan (1997). Central Bank Independence, Inflation, and Growth in Transition Economies, *Journal of Money, Credit and Banking*, Vol. 29, No. 3.

Lutter, Marcus, Bayer, Walter, Schmidt, Jessica (2011). Europäisches Unternehmens- und Kapitalmarktrecht Grundlagen, Stand und Entwicklung nebst Texten und Materialien, *De Gruyter*, Berlin.

Lybek, Tonny (2005). Central Bank Autonomy, Accountability, and Governance: Conceptual Framework. In: '*Current Developments in Monetary and Financial Law*', Vol. 4, *International Monetary Fund*, Washington, DC.

Lyndgren, Carl-Johan (1990). The Transition from Direct to Indirect Instruments of Monetary Policy. In: '*The Evolving Role of Central Banks*', (eds.) Patrick Downes, Reza Vaez-Zadeh, *International Monetary Fund,* Washington.

Madema, Steven G, Mercuro, Nicholas (2006). Economics and the Law: From Posner to Postmodernism and Beyond, *Princeton University Press.*

Maddaloni, Angela, Peydró, José-Luis (2010). Bank Risk-Taking, Securitization, Supervision and Low Interest Rates: Evidence from the Euro Area and the U.S. Lending Standards, *ECB Working Paper Series*, No. 1248.

Maddaloni, Angela, Peydró, José-Luis (2011). The Low Monetary Rates Paradox, Banking Stability and Credit: Evidence from the Euro Area, *Paper Presented at the 12th Jacques Polak Annual Research Conference Hosted by the IMF*, Washington, DC, 10–11 November 2011.

Maddaloni, Angela, Peydrò, Josè-Luis (2013). Monetary Policy, Macroprudential Policy, and Banking Stability: Evidence from the Euro Area, *International Journal of Central Banking*, Vol. 9, No. 1.

Maier, Philipp, de Haan, Jakob (2000). How Independent Is the Bundesbank Really? In: '*The History of the Bundesbank: Lessons for the European Central Bank*', (eds.) Jakob de Haan, *Routledge International Studies in Money and Banking.*

Malaguti, Maria C. (2010). The ECB, ESCB and the "Eurosystem". A New Paradigm between the Centre and the Peripheries. In: '*The Road Europe Travelled Along. The Evolution of the EEC/EU Institutions and Policies*', (eds.) Daniela Preda, Daniele Pasquinucci, *P.L.E. Peter Lang.*

Malz, Allan M. (2013). Risk-Neutral Systemic Risk Indicators, *Federal Reserve Bank of New York Staff Reports*, No. 607.

Mandler, Martin, Scharnagl, Michael, Volz, Ute (2016). Heterogeneity in Euro-area Monetary Policy Transmission: Results from a Large Multi-country BVAR Model, *Deutsche Bundesbank Discussion Paper*, No. 3/2016.

Manger-Nestler, Cornelia (2013). Interaction for Monetary and Financial Stability: Central Banks as Main Actors in the Global Financial System. In: "*European Yearbook of International Economic Law 2014*", (eds.) Christoph Herrmann, Markus Krajewski, Jörg Philipp Terhechte, *Springer-Verlag Berlin Heidelberg.*

Masera, Rainer (2014). CRR/CRD IV: The Trees and the Forest, *PSL Quarterly Review*, Vol. 67, No. 271.

Martinez-Miera, David, Suarez, Javier (2012). A Macroeconomic Model of Endogenous Systemic Risk Taking, *CEPR Discussion Paper*, No. DP9134.

Martínez, Guillermo O. (2008). Inflation Targeting, *Proceedings of the Conference 'A Festschrift in Honour of David Dodge's Contributions to Canadian Public Policy Held by the Bank of Canada,* November 2008.

Majone, Giandomenico (1998). Europe's 'Democratic Deficit': The Question of Standards, *European Law Journal*, Vol. 4, Issue 1.

Mazzaferro, Francesco (2011). Macro-prudential Instruments for Containing Systemic Risk: The ESRB View. In: *'The ESRB at 1', IMFS Interdisciplinary Studies in Monetary and Financial Stability*, Vol. 2012/1.

May, Peter J., Jochim, Ashley E. (2013). Policy Regime Perspectives: Policies and Governing, *Policy Studies Journal*, Vol. 41, Issue 3.

Mayer, Thomas (1999). Monetary Policy and the Great Inflation in the United States, *Edward Elgar Publishing.*

Mayer, Christopher J., Pence, Karen M., Sherlund, Shane M. (2008). The Rise in Mortgage Defaults. Divisions of Research & Statistics and Monetary Affairs, Federal Reserve Board, Washington, DC, *Finance and Economics Discussion Series*, No. 58-2008.

Mawdsley, Andrew (2014). The Architecture of Macroprudential Supervision in the EU Regional Model. In: '*Macroprudential Supervision in Insurance*', (eds.) Jan Monkiewicz, Marian Małecki, *Palgrave Macmillan UK.*

McAndrews, James (2015). Negative Nominal Central Bank Policy Rates: Where Is the Lower Bound?, *Remarks at the University of Wisconsin,* 8 May 2015. Online. Available at: https://www.newyorkfed.org/newsevents/speeches/2015/mca150508.html

McDonnell, Brett H. (2013). Dampening Financial Regulatory Cycles, *Florida Law Review*, Vol. 65, Issue 5.

McDonnell, Brett H. (2014). Designing Countercyclical Capital Buffers, *University of Minnesota Law School, Legal Studies Research Paper Series*, No. 14–16.

McPhilemy, Samuel (2016). Integrating Macro-prudential Policy: Central Banks as the "Third Force" in the EU Financial Reform, *West European Politics*, Vol. 39, Issue 3.

Meeks, Roland (2015). Capital Regulation and Macroeconomic Activity: Implications for Macroprudential Policy. Online. Available at: https://www.aeaweb.org/conference/2015/retrieve.php?pdfid=1213

Mehran, Hassanali, Quintyn, Marc, Nordman, Tom, Laurens, Bernard (1996). Monetary and Exchange System Reforms in China: An Experiment in Gradualism, *IMF Occasional Paper*, No. 14.

Mehrling, Perry (1999). The Vision of Hyman P. Minsky, *Journal of Economic Behavior & Organization*, Vol. 39.

Meltzer, Allan H. (2005). Origins of the Great Inflation, *Federal Reserve Bank of St. Louis Review*, Vol. 87, No. 2, Part 2 (March–April 2005).

Merler, Silvia (2015). Squaring the Cycle: Capital Flows, Financial Cycles, and Macro-prudential Policy in the Euro Area, *Bruegel Working Papers*, No. 14.

Mersch, Yves (2013). Monetary Policy and Financial Stability under One Roof, *Keynote Speech Held at the 6th Policy Roundtable of the European Central Bank: "The Future of Global Policy Coordination"*, 6 September 2013.

Mersch, Yves (2014). Law, Money and Market: The Legal Dimension of Monetary Policy, *Speech at the Information Club Meeting, Luxembourg*, 31 May 2014.

Mestmäcker, Ernst-Joachim (2012). European Economic Constitution. In: '*The Max Planck Encyclopedia of European Private Law*', Vol. I, (eds.) Jürgen Basedow, Klaus J. Hopt, Reinhard Zimmermann, *Oxford University Press*, Oxford.

Minsky, Hyman P. (1967). Suggestions for a Cash Flow Oriented Bank Examination. Levy Economics Institute of Bard College, *Hyman P. Minsky Archive, Paper* No. 175.

Minsky, Hyman P. (1970). Financial Instability Revisited: The Economics of Disaster, *Paper Prepared for the Steering Committee for the Fundamental Reappraisal of the Discount Mechanism Appointed by the Board of Governors of the Federal Reserve System*, Levy Economics Institute of Bard College, *Hyman P. Minsky Archive*, Paper No. 80.

Minsky, Hyman P. (1975). Suggestions for a Cash Flow Bank Oriented bank Examination, *Paper Prepared for the Conference on Bank Structure and Competition, Federal Reserve Bank of Chicago*, 1–2 May 1975.

Minsky, Hyman P. (1976). Banking and a Fragile Financial Environment, *Paper Prepared for the American Association Meetings*, Atlantic City, 16 September 1976.

Minsky, Hyman P. (1986). Stabilizing an Unstable Economy, *McGraw-Hill Professional*, New York.

Minsky, Hyman P. (1992). The Financial Instability Hypothesis, Levy Economics Institute of Bard College, *Working Paper* No. 74.

Mishkin, Frederic S. (1995). Symposium on the Monetary Transmission Mechanism, *Journal of Economic Perspectives*, Vol. 9, No. 4.

Mishkin, Frederic S. (1996). The Channels of Monetary Transmission: Lessons for Monetary Policy, *NBER Working Paper*, No. 5464 (Also Reprint No. r2054).

Mishkin, Frederic S. (1999). Central Banking in a Democratic Society, *Springer Science+Business Media*, New York.

Mishkin, Frederic S. (2000). From Monetary Targeting to Inflation Targeting. Lessons from the Industrialized Countries, *The World Bank Policy Research Working Paper*, No. 2684.

Mishkin, Frederic S. (2000b). Inflation Targeting in Emerging Market Countries, *NBER Working Paper Series*, No. 7618.

Mishkin, Frederic S. (2007). Housing and the Monetary Transmission Mechanism, *FRB Finance and Economics Discussion Series*, No. 40.

Mishkin, Frederic S. (2007a). Inflation Targeting: True Progress or Repackaging of an Old Idea? In: '*Swiss National Bank 1907–2007*', (ed.) The Swiss National Bank, Zurich.

Mishkin, Frederic S. (2007b). Globalization and Financial Development. *Remarks Presented at the Econometric Society at Duke University Lecture*, Durham, North Carolina, 23 June 2007.

Mishkin, Frederic S. (2007c). Housing and Monetary Transmission Mechanism, *NBER Working Paper Series*, No. 13518.

Mishkin, Frederic S. (2009). Monetary Policy Strategy, *MIT Press,* Cambridge.

Modigliani, Franco (1966). The Life Cycle Hypothesis of Saving, the Demand for Wealth and the Supply of Capital, *Social Research, Essays in Economic Theory in Honor of Adolph Lowe and Hans Neisser*, Vol. 33, No. 2.

Modigliani, Franco (1971). Monetary Policy and Consumption: the Linkages via Interest Rate and Wealth Effects in the FMP Model. In: '*Consumer Spending and Monetary Policy: The linkages*', *Federal Reserve Bank of Boston Conference Series*, No. 5.

Modigliani, Franco (1986). Life Cycle, Individual Thrift, and the Wealth of Nations, *The American Economic Review*, Vol. 76, No. 3.

Mody, Ashoka, Sandri, Damiano (2011). The Eurozone Crisis: How Banks and Sovereigns Came to Be Joined at the Hip, *IMF Working Paper*, No. 269.

Mohanty, Madhusudan, Turner, Philip (2008). Monetary Policy Transmission in Emerging Market Economies: What Is New?, *BIS Papers*, No. 35.

Möllers, Thomas M.J. (2010). Sources of Law in European Securities Regulation – Effective Regulation, Soft Law and Legal Taxonomy from Lamfalussy to de Larosière, *European Business Organization Law Review*, Vol. 11.

Moloney, Niamh (2010). EU Financial Market Regulation after the Global Financial Crisis: "More Europe" or More Risks?, *Common Market Law Review*, Vol. 47, Issue 5.

Moloney, Niamh (2014). EU Securities and Financial Markets Regulation, *Oxford University Press*, Oxford.

Monteagudo, Manuel (2010). Neutrality of Money and Central Bank Independence. In: '*International Monetary and Financial Law*', (eds.) Mario Giovanoli, Diego Devos, *Oxford University Press.*

Morici, William (2015). Peter Gauweiler et al v. Deutscher Bundestag: The Legal Impetus behind Mario Draghi's Movement for Quantitative Easing. *Cornell*

International Law Journal Online, Vol. 3. Online. Available at: http://cornellilj.org/eu-legal-impetus-behind-quantitative-easing/

Mourmouras, Iannis A., Arghyrou, Michael G. (2000). Monetary Policy at the European Periphery. Greek Experience and Lessons for EU Candidates, *Springer*, Berlin.

Moutot, Philippe, Jung, Alexander, Mongelli, Francesco Paolo (2008). The Workings of the Eurosystem. Monetary Policy Preparations and Decision-making – Selected Issues. *ECB Occasional Paper Series,* No. 79.

Mukherjee, Sanchita, Bhattacharya, Rina (2011). Inflation Targeting and Monetary Policy Transmission Mechanisms in Emerging Market Economies, *IMF Working Paper*, No. 229.

Mullins, Anne, Saunders, Cheryl (1994). Economic Union in Federal Systems, *Federation Press.*

Mundell, Robert A. (1962). The Appropriate Use of Monetary and Fiscal Policy for Internal and External Stability, *IMF Staff Papers*, Vol. 9, No. 1.

Mundell, Robert A. (1963). The Monetary Dynamics of International Adjustment under Fixed and Flexible Exchange Rates, *Quarterly Journal of Economics*, Vol. 74.

Murphy, Edward V. (2013). Financial Stability Oversight Council: A Framework to Mitigate Systemic Risk, *Congressional Research Service*, 21 May 2013.

N'Diaye, Papa (2009). Countercyclical Macro Prudential Policies in a Supporting Role to Monetary Policy, *IMF Working Paper*, No. 257.

Nagy, Ágnes, Pete, Ştefan, Benyovszki, Annamária, Petru, Tünde Petra, Györfy, Lehel-Zoltán (2010). The de Larosière Report Regarding the new Structure of European System of Financial Supervision, *Theoretical and Applied Economics*, Vol. XVII, No. 11(552).

Napoletano, Giuseppe (2014). Legal Aspects of Macroprudential Policy in the United States and in the European Union, *Banca d'Italia Legal Research Papers*, No. 76.

Narodna Banka Slovenska (2014). Quarterly Commentary on Macroprudential Policy, October 2014.

Nedergaard, Peter (2013). The Influence of Ordoliberalism in European Integration Processes – A Framework for Ideational Influence with Competition Policy and the Economic and Monetary Policy as Examples, *MPRA Paper*, No. 52331.

Nersisyan, Yeva, Wray, Randall L. (2010). The Global Financial Crisis and the Shift to Shadow Banking, *Levy Economics Institute of Bard College Working Paper,* No. 587.

Neyer, Ulrike (2001). Asymmetric Information and the Transmission Mechanism of Monetary Policy, December 2011. Online. Available at: http://repec.org/res2002/Neyer.pdf

Ng, Tim (2012). Communication on Macroprudential Policies: Work in Progress. *Speech Held at the Conference 'Communications and External Relations for Central Banks'*, Christ's College, Cambridge, 11–14 September 2012.

Nier, Erlend W. (2009). Financial Stability Frameworks and the Role of Central Banks: Lessons from the Crisis, *IMF Working Paper*, No. 70.

Nier, Erlend W. (2011a). Macroprudential Policy – Taxonomy and Challenges, *National Institute Economic Review*, No. 216.

Nier, Erlend W. (2011b). On the Governance of Macroprudential Policies. In: *"Macroprudential Regulatory Policies: The New Road to Financial Stability?"*, (eds.) Stijn Claessens, Douglas D. Evanoff, George G. Kaufman, Laura E. Kodres, *World Scientific Studies in International Economics*, Vol. 17.

Nier, Erlend W., Jácome, Luis I. (2012). Macroprudential Policy: Protecting the Whole. *IMF Finance & Development.* Available at: http://www.imf.org/external/pubs/ft/fandd/basics/macropru.htm

Nier, Erlend W., Osiński, Jacek, Jácome, Luis I., Madrid, Pamela (2011a). Institutional Models for Macroprudential Policy, *IMF Staff Discussion Note*, No. 18.

Nier, Erlend W., Osiński, Jacek, Jácome, Luis I., Madrid, Pamela (2011b). Towards Effective Macroprudential Policy Frameworks: An Assessment of Stylized Institutional Models, *IMF Working Papers*, No. 250.

Nier, Erlend W., Tressel, Thierry (2011). The European Systemic Risk Board: Effectiveness of Macroprudential Oversight in Europe. In: '*Euro Area Policies: 2011 Article IV Consultation—Lessons from the European Financial Stability Framework Exercise; and Selected Issues Paper*', (eds.) Thomas Harjes, Nico Valckx, Thierry Tressel, Esther Perez Ruiz, Nandaka Molagoda, Erlend Nier, *International Monetary Fund,* Washington, DC.

Nijsen, André (2008). Origin and Functionalities of Regulation. In: '*Business Regulation and Public Policy: The Costs and Benefits of Compliance*', (eds.) André Nijsen, John Hudson, Christoph Müller, Kees van Paridon, R. Thurik, *Springer*, Berlin.

North, Douglass (1990). Institutions, Institutional Change and Economic Performance, *Cambridge University Press.*

Noyer, Christian (2014). Macroprudential Policy: From Theory to Implementation, *Banque de France Financial Stability Review*, No. 18.

Noyer, Christian (2015). The Size of Central Bank Balance Sheet – How Relevant (Important) Is It?, *Speech at the Global Interdependence Center/Bank of France Annual Seminar "New Policies for the Post Crisis Era", Session I "Putting a Context on Monetary Policy – On Both Sides of the Pond"*, Paris, 23 March 2015.

Nyberg, Lars (2011). The ESRB – Reflections after 9 Months of Operation, *Speech Held at the Conference on the Macro Prudential Oversight of the Financial Sector Arranged by Norges Bank*, Oslo, 27 September 2011. Available at: http://www.riksbank.se/Upload/Dokument_riksbank/Kat_publicerat/Tal/2011/110927e.pdf

OECD (2011). OECD Economic Outlook, Vol. 2011, Issue 1, *OECD Publishing.*

Oet, Mikhail V., Ong, Stephen J., Gramlich, Dieter (2013). Policy in Adaptive Financial Markets—The Use of Systemic Risk Early Warning Tools. *FRB of Cleveland Working Paper*, No. 13/09.

Olsen, Øystein (2013). Macroprudential Regulation and Monetary Policy, *Speech at the Centre for Monetary Economics (CME)/BI Norwegian Business School,* Oslo, 7 October 2013.

Orphanides, Athanasios (2003). The Quest for Prosperity Without Inflation, *Journal of Monetary Economics*, Vol. 50, No. 3.

Osiński, Jacek (2013). Institutional Needs for Optimal Macroprudential Arrangements. In: '*Macroprudential Frameworks in Asia*', (eds.) Steven Barnett, Rodolfo Main, *International Monetary Fund*, Washington, DC.

Osiński, Jacek, Seal, Katharine, Hoogduin, Lex (2013). Macroprudential and Microprudential Policies: Toward Cohabitation, *IMF Staff Discussion Note*, No. 5.

Österreichische Finanzmarktaufsicht & Österreichische Nationalbank (2012). Supervisory Guidance on the Strengthening of the Sustainability of the Business Models of Large Internationally Active Austrian Banks, 14 March 2012.

Øystein Olsen: Macroprudential Regulation and Monetary Policy. Speech Held at the Centre for Monetary Economics (CME)/BI Norwegian Business School, Oslo, 7 October 2013.

Ozkan, F. Gulcin, Unsal, D. Filiz (2014). On the Use of Monetary and Macroprudential Policies for Small Open Economies, *IMF Working Papers*, No. 112.

Padoa-Schioppa, Tommaso (2002). Central Banks and Financial Stability: Exploring a Land in Between. *Paper Presented at the Second ECB Central Banking Conference*, Frankfurt am Main, 24–25 October.

Padoa-Schioppa, Tommaso (2004). The Euro and Its Central Bank – Getting United after the Union, *The MIT Press*, Cambridge.

Paligorova, Teodora, Sierra Jimenez, Jesus A. (2012). Monetary Policy and the Risk-Taking Channel: Insights from the Lending Behaviour of Banks, *Bank of Canada Review*, Autumn 2012.

Papademos, Lucas D., Stark, Jürgen (2010). Enhancing Monetary Policy, *European Central Bank*, Frankfurt.

Papadimitriou, Dimitri B., Wray, L. Randall (1997). The Economic Contributions of Hyman Minsky: Varieties of Capitalism and Institutional Reform, *Levy Economics Institute of Bard College Working Paper*, No. 218.

Papadopoulos, Thomas (2014). European System of Financial Supervision, *Max Planck Encyclopedia of Public International Law*, (ed.) Rudiger Wolfrum, *Oxford University Press.*

Papaioannou, Michael G, Park, Joonkyu, Pihlman, Jukka, van der Hoorn, Han (2013). Procyclical Behavior of Institutional Investors during the Recent Financial Crisis: Causes, Impacts, and Challenges, *IMF Working Paper,* No. 193.

Parkin, Michael (2013). Central Bank Laws and Monetary Policy Outcomes: A Three Decade Perspective, *EPRI Working Paper*, No. 1.

Partnoy, Frank (2010). Overdependence on Credit Ratings Was a Primary Cause of the Crisis. In: '*The Panic of 2008 Causes, Consequences and Implications for Reform*', (eds.) Lawrence E. Mitchell, Arthur E. Wilmarth, *Edward Elgar Publishing.*

Patro, Dilip K., Qi, Min, Sun, Xian (2013). A Simple Indicator of Systemic Risk, *Journal of Financial Stability*, Vol. 9, Issue 1.

Petersen, Niels (2014). Karlsruhe Not Only Barks, But Finally Bites—Some Remarks on the OMT Decision of the German Constitutional Court, *German Law Journal*, Vol. 15, No. 02.

Pedrero Ramón, María Dolores, Pérez Jesús, Vázquez (2005). *The New Keynesian Monetary Model, Does It Show the Comovement between Output and Inflation in the U.S. and the Euro Area? Fundacion BBVA/BBVA Foundation Working Papers,* No. 201030.

Peydró, José-Luis (2014). Systemic Risk, Monetary Policy and Macroprudential Policy, *Banco de Espana Revista de Estabilidad Financiera*, No. 26.

Phillips, Ronnie J. (1997). Rethinking Bank Examinations: A Minsky Approach, *Journal of Economic Issues*, Vol. 31, No. 2.

Pindyck, Robert S., Roberts, Steven M. (1976). Instruments, Intermediate Targets, and Monetary Controllability, *International Economic Review*, Vol. 17, No. 3.

Pistor, Katherina (2013). A Legal Theory of Finance, *Journal of Comparative Economics.* Vol. 41, Issue 2.

Posner, Richard A. (1993). The New Institutional Economics Meets Law and Economics, *Journal of Institutional and Theoretical Economics (JITE)*, Vol. 149, No. 1.

Posner, Elliot (2007). Financial Transformation in the European Union. In: '*European Integration and Institutional Change at Fifty*', (eds.) Sophie Meunier, Kathleen R. McNamara, *Oxford University Press.*

Powell, Jerome H. (2014). Monetary Policy Accommodation, Risk-Taking, and Spillovers, *Speech at the Global Research Forum on International Macroeconomics and Finance*, Washington, DC, 14 November 2014.

PRA (2014). Implementing the Financial Policy Committee's Recommendation on Loan to Income Ratios in Mortgage Lending, *Policy Statement PS9/14*, October 2014.

Praet, Peter (2011). The (Changing) Role of Central Banks in Financial Stability Policies, *Speech at the 14th Annual Internal Banking Conference held by the Federal Reserve Bank of Chicago and the European Central Bank*, Chicago, 10 November 2011.

Priego, Francisco Javier, Conlledo, Fernando (2005). The Role of the Decentralization Principle in the Legal Construction of the European System of Central Banks. In: '*Legal Aspects of the European System of Central Banks*'. ECB Liber Amicorum Paolo Zamboni Garavelli, Frankfurt.

Ptak, Ralf (2004). Vom Ordoliberalismus zur Sozialen Marktwirtschaft: Stationen des Neoliberalismus in Deutschland. *VS Verlag für Sozialwissenschaften*, Wiesbaden.

Puccio, Laura (2012). Pressured Inflicted by the Financial Crisis on the Euro Area. In: '*The Treaty of Lisbon and the Future of European Law and Policy*', (eds.) Martin Trybus, Luca Rubini, *Edward Elgar Publishing*.

Purvis (1992). Monetary Transmission Mechanisms. In: '*The New Palgrave Dictionary of Money and Finance*', (eds.) John Eatwell, Murray Milgate, Peter Newman, *Palgrave Macmillan*.

Ramey, Valerie (1993). How Important Is the Credit Channel in the Transmission of Monetary Policy?, *Carnegie-Rochester Conference Series on Public Policy*, Vol. 39.

Ramirez, Steven A. (2003). The Law and Macroeconomics of the New Deal at 70, *Maryland Law Review*, Vol. 62.

Reifschneider, David, Williams, John C. (2000). Three Lessons for Monetary Policy in a Low-Inflation Era, *Journal of Money, Credit and Banking*, Vol. 32, No. 4, Part 2.

Reinert, Kenneth A., Rajan, Ramkishen S. (2009). The Princeton Encyclopedia of the World Economy, *Princeton University Press*.

Reinhart, Carmen M., Rogoff, Kenneth S. (2011). From Financial Crash to Debt Crisis, *American Economic Review*, Vol. 101.

Reinhardt, Dennis, Sowerbutts, Rhiannon (2015). Regulatory Arbitrage in Action: Evidence from Banking Flows and Macroprudential Policy, *Bank of England Staff Working Paper*, No. 546.

Ren, Haocong (2011). Countercyclical Financial Regulation, *World Bank Policy Research Working Paper*, No. 5823.

Rendak, Nadia (2014). Monitoring and Surveillance at the International Monetary System: What Can Be Learnt from the Trade Field? In: '*The Rule of Law in Monetary Affairs World Trade Forum*', (eds.) Thomas Cottier, Rosa M. Lastra, Christian Tietje, *Cambridge University Press*.

Repasi, René (2013). Limits and Opportunities for the ECB in the Multi-tier Governance, *Policy Department C: Citizens' Rights and Constitutional Affairs Note*.

Repullo, Rafael (2013). The Procyclical Effects of Bank Capital Regulation, *The Review of Financial Studies*, Vol. 26, Issue 2.

Rhu, Hoo-Kyu (2011). Macroprudential Policy Framework, *BIS Paper*, No. 60.

Rieter, Heinz, Schmolz, Matthias (1993). The Ideas of German Ordoliberalism 1938–45: Pointing the Way to a New Economic Order, *The European Journal of the History of Economic Thought*, Vol. 1, Issue 1.

Riso, Luca A. (2015). An Analysis of the OMT Case from an EU Law Perspective. In: '*The ECB's Outright Monetary Transactions in the Courts*', (eds.) Siekmann, Helmut, Vieland, Volcker, *IMFS Interdisciplinary Studies in Monetary and Financial Stability*, No. 1.

Robinson, David (2014). The IMF Response to the Global Crisis: Assessing Risks and Vulnerabilities in IMF Surveillance, *IEO Background Paper*, No. 9.

Rochet, Jean-Charles (2008a). Procyclicality of Financial Systems: Is There a Need to Modify Current Accounting and Regulatory Rules?, *Banque de France Financial Stability Review*, No. 12.

Rochet, Jean-Charles (2008b). Liquidity Regulation and the Lender of Last Resort, *Banque de France Financial Stability Review*, No. 11.

Rodríguez-Moreno, María, Peña, Juan Ignacio (2013). Systemic Risk Measures: The Simpler the Better?, *Journal of Banking and Finance*, Vol. 37, Issue 6.

Roger, Scott (2010). Inflation Targeting Turns 20. *IMF Finance & Development*, Vol. 47, No. 1.

Roger, Scott, Vlček, Jan (2011). Macroeconomic Costs of Higher Bank Capital and Liquidity Requirements, *IMF Working Paper*, No. 103.

Rogoff, Kenneth (1985). The Optimal Degree of Commitment to an Intermediate Monetary Target, *Quarterly Journal of Economics*, Vol. 100.

Rogoff, Kenneth (1986). Social Institutions for Overcoming Monetary Policy Credibility Problems, *Paper Presented at the American Economic Association Meetings*, New Orleans, December 1986.

Rosenfeld, Micheal (2001). The Rule of Law and the Legitimacy of Constitutional Democracy, *Southern California Law Review*, Vol. 74.

Rothbard, Murray N. (1995). Classical Economics. An Austrian Perspective on the History of Economic Thought, Vol. II, *Edward Elgar Publishing Company*, Brookfield, Vt.

Rubio, Margarita, Carrasco-Gallego, José A. (2014). Macroprudential and Monetary Policies: Implications for Financial Stability and Welfare, *Journal of Banking & Finance*, Vol. 49.

Ruser, Alexander (2015). By the Markets, of the Markets, for the Markets? Technocratic Decision Making and the Hollowing Out of Democracy, *Global Policy Special Issue: "Changing the European Debate: A Rollback of Democracy*, Vol. 6, Issue Supplement S1.

Rymes, Thomas K. (1995–1996). Autonomous and Accountable, *Journal of Post Keynesian Economics*, Vol. 18, No. 2.

Ryoo, Sang Chul, Hong, Cheol (2011). Countercyclical Tools: A Comparative Assessment. In: '*Macroprudential Regulation and Policy*', *BIS Papers*, Vol. 60.

Sachverständigenrat zur Begutachtung der gesamtwirtschaftlichen Entwicklung (2015). Zukunftsfähigkeit in den Mittelpunkt. Jahresgutachten 2015/16, November 2015.

Schmidt, Vivien A., Thatcher, Mark (2013). Resilient Liberalism in Europe's Political Economy, *Cambridge University Press.*

Salama, Bruno Meyerhof (2012). The Art of Law & Macroeconomics, *University of Pittsburgh Law Review*, Vol. 74.

Salter, Alexander W. (2014). An Introduction to Monetary Policy Rules, *Mercatus Working Paper,* Mercatus Center at George Mason University.

Samuelson, Robert (2010). The Great Inflation and Its Aftermath: The Past and Future of American Affluence, *Random House Trade Paperbacks.*

Santomero, Anthony M., Seater, John J. (1978). The Inflation-Unemployment Trade-Off: A Critique of the Literature, *Journal of Economic Literature*, Vol. 16, No. 2.

Santomero, Anthony M., Viotti, Staffan, Vredin, Anders (2001). Challenges for Central Banking, *Springer*, Berlin.

Sapir, André (2014). Europe's Macroprudential Policy Framework in Light of the Banking Union. In: '*Macroprudentialism*', (ed.) Dirk Schoenmaker, *CEPR Press*, Washington, DC.

Sauer, Haiko (2015). Doubtful It Stood ...: Competence and Power in European Monetary and Constitutional Law in the Aftermath of the CJEU's OMT Judgment, *The German Law Review*, Vol. 16, No. 4.

Sbordone, Argia M., Tambalotti, Andrea, Rao, Krishna, Walsh, Kieran (2010). Policy Analysis Using DSGE Models: An Introduction, *FRBNY Economic Policy Review*, October.

Scalia, Antonio, Longoni, Sergio, Rosolin, Tiziana (2013). The Net Stable Funding Ratio and Banks' Participation in Monetary Policy Operations: Some Evidence for the Euro Area, *Banca d'Italia Occasional Paper*, No. 195.

Schaechter, Andrea (2011). Implementation of Monetary Policy and the Central Bank's Balance Sheet, *IMF Working Paper*, No. 149.

Schaub, Alexander (2005). The Lamfalussy Process Four Years On, *Journal of Financial Regulation and Compliance*, Vol. 13, Issue 2.

Scheller, Hanspeter K. (2006). The European Central Bank: History, Story and Functions, *European Central Bank*, Frankfurt.

Schermers, Henry G., Waelbroeck, Denis F. (2000). Judicial Protection in the EUropean Union, *Kluwer Law International.*

Schinasi, Garry J. (2004). Defining Financial Stability, *IMF Working Paper*, No. 187.

Schiek, Dagmar (2014). German Federal Constitutional Court's Ruling on Outright Monetary Transactions (OMT) – Another Step towards National Closure, *The German Law Journal*, Vol. 15, No. 2.

Schmidt, Sebastian, Wieland, Volker (2012). The New Keynesian Approach to Dynamic General Equilibrium Modeling: Models, Methods and Macroeconomic Policy Evaluation, *IMFS Working Paper Series*, No. 52.

Schmitz, Stefan W. (2013). The Impact of the Liquidity Coverage Ratio (LCR) on the Implementation of Monetary Policy, *Economic Notes, Review of Banking, Finance, and Monetary Economics*, Vol. 42, No. 2.

Schmukler, Sergio L. (2004). Benefits and Risks of Financial Globalization: Challenges for Developing Countries, *Federal Reserve Bank of Atlanta Economic Review*, Second Quarter 2004–06.

Schoenmaker, Dirk (2012). The Missing Link in Banking Union: Macro-prudential Supervision, *DSF Policy Brief*, No. 21.

Schoenmaker, Dirk (2014). Allocating Macroprudential Powers. In: 'Putting. Macroprudential. Policy to Work', (eds.) Aerdt Houben, Rob Nijskens, Mark Teunissen, *De Nederlandsche Bank Occasional Studies*, Vol. 12–7.

Scholten, Miroslava, van Rijsbergen, Marloes (2014). The ESMA-Short Selling Case: Erecting a New Delegation Doctrine in the EU upon the Meroni-Romano Remnants, *Legal Issues of Economic Integration*, Vol. 41, Issue 4.

Schwaab, Bernd, Koopman, Siem Jan, Lucas, André (2011). Systemic Risk Diagnostics Coincident Indicators and Early Warning Signals, *ECB Working Paper Series*, No. 1327.

Schuknecht, Ludger (2002). The Fiscal Costs of Financial Instability Revisited, *ECB Working Paper*, No. 191.

Schüler, Martin, Heinemann, Friedrich (2005). The Costs of Supervisory Fragmentation in Europe, *ZEW Discussion Paper*, No. 05-01.

Schwarcz, Steven L. (2008). Systemic Risk, *Georgetown Law Journal*, Vol. 49.

Schwarcz, Steven L. (2012). Regulating Shadow Banking, *Review of Banking and Financial Law*, Vol. 31, No. 1.

Schwarcz, Steven L. (2014). Banking and Financial Regulation. Chapter for '*The Oxford Handbook of Law and Economics*', (ed.) Francesco Parisi, *Oxford University Press* (2015 forthcoming), Oxford.

Schwarcz, Steven L. (2015). Regulating Financial Change: A Functional Approach, *Minnesota Law Review*, Vol. 100 (forthcoming).

Sharp, Richard (2014). The Financial Policy Committee of the Bank of England; An Experiment in Macroprudential Management – The View of an External Member, *Speech Given at the London School of Economics*, London, 4 June 2014.

Seidel, Martin (2012). The Constitutional Design of the European Central Bank, *CESifo DICE Report*, No. 1/2012.

Selmayr, Martin (1999). Wie unabhänig ist die Europäische Zentralbank? Eine Analyse anhand der ersten geldpolitischen Entscheidungen der EZB. *Wertpapier-Mitteilungen*, No. 49.

Servén, Luis (2010). Macroprudential Policies in the Wake of the Global Financial Crisis, In '*The Day After Tomorrow: A Handbook on the Future of Economic Policy in the Developing World*', (eds.) Otaviano Canuto, Marcelo Giugale, *World Bank*, Washington, DC.

Shaffer, Gregory C., Pollack, Mark A. (2010). Hard vs. Soft Law: Alternatives, Complements, and Antagonists in International Governance, *Minnesota Law Review*, Vol. 94.

Shin, Hyun Song (2011). Macroprudential Policies Beyond Basel III. In: '*Macroprudential Regulation and Policy*', *BIS Papers*, Vol. 60.

Shin, Hyun Song (2015). Macroprudential Tools, Their Limits and Their Connection with Monetary Policy. *Panel Remarks at IMF Spring Meeting event: 'Rethinking Macro Policy III: Progress or Confusion?'*, Washington, DC, 15 April 2015.

Siekmann, Helmut (2009). Die Schaffung von Einrichtungen der Finanzaufsicht auf EU-Ebene: Stellungnahme zu dem Vorschlag der Sachverständigengruppe unter dem Vorsitz von Jacques de Larosière, *IMFS Working Paper Series*, No. 24.

Siekmann, Helmut (2010). Das neue Europäische Finanzaufsichtssystem, *IMFS Working Paper Series*, No. 40.

Siekmann, Helmut. (2011a). Artikel 88. In: '*Grundgesetz-Kommentar*', (ed.) Michael Sachs 6, *Auflage*.

Siekmann, Helmut (2011b). Law and Economics of the Monetary Union, *IMFS Working Papers*, No. 24.

Siekmann, Helmut (ed.) (2013). EWU – Kommentar zur Europäischen Währungsunion, *Mohr Siebeck*, Tübingen.

Siekmann, Helmut (2015). The Legal Framework for the European System of Central Banks. In: '*Central Banking and Financial Stability in East Asia*', (eds.) Frank Rövekamp, Moritz Bälz, Hanns Günther Hilpert, *Springer International Publishing*.

Siekmann, Helmut (2015b). The Legality of Outright Monetary Transactions of the European System of Central Banks. In: '*Central Banking and Financial Stability in East Asia*', (eds.) Frank Rövekamp, Moritz Bälz, Hanns Günther Hilpert, *Springer International Publishing*.

Siekmann, Helmut (2016). Deposit Banking and the Use of Monetary Instruments. In: '*Money in the Western Legal Tradition Middle Ages to Bretton Woods*', (eds.) David Fox, Wolfgang Ernst, *Oxford University Press*.

Siekmann, Helmut, Wieland, Volcker (2013). The European Central Bank's Outright Monetary Transactions and the Federal Constitutional Court of Germany, *IMFS Working Paper Series*, No. 71.

Siekmann, Helmut, Wieland, Volcker (2013b). From the OMT Announcement to the 2013 Hearings of the German Constitutional Court. In: '*The ECB and Its Watchers*', *IMFS Interdisciplinary Study 1/2013*, Frankfurt.

Siekmann, Helmut, Wieland, Volcker (2015). The German Constitutional Court's Decision on OMT: Have Markets Misunderstood? In: '*The ECB's Outright Monetary Transactions in the Courts*', (eds.) Siekmann, Helmut, Vieland, Volcker, *IMFS Interdisciplinary Studies in Monetary and Financial Stability*, No. 1.

Siklos, Pierre L., Werner, Thomas, Bohl, Martin T. (2004). Asset Prices in Taylor Rules: Specification, Estimation, and Policy Implications for the ECB, *Bundesbank Discussion Paper Series 1: Economic Studies*, No. 22/2004.

Simon, Sven (2015). Direct Cooperation Has Begun: Some Remarks on the Judgment of the ECJ on the OMT Decision of the ECB in Response to the German Federal Constitutional Court's First Request for a Preliminary Ruling, *The German Law Review*, Vol. 16, No. 4.

Sinha, Anand (2011). Macroprudential Policies: Indian Experience, *RBI Monthly Bulletin July 2011*.

Siqiwen, Li (2010). Financial Fragility and Securitization: The Discussions with Australian Regulators and Bank Risk Managers. In: '*International Banking in the New Era: Post-crisis Challenges and Opportunities*', *International Finance Review*, Vol. 11.

Smaga, Paweł (2014). The Concept of Systemic Risk, *London School of Economics SRC Special Paper*, No. 5.

Smets, Frank (2014). Financial Stability and Monetary Policy: How Closely Interlinked? *International Journal of Central Banking*, Vol. 10, No. 2.

Smets, Frank, Wouters, Raf (1999). The Exchange Rate and the Monetary Transmission Mechanism in Germany, *DNB Staff Reports*, No. 35.

Smets, Frank, Wouters, Raf (2003). An Estimated Dynamic Stochastic General Equilibrium Model of the Euro Area, *Journal of European Economic Association*, Vol. 1, No. 5.

Smets, Frank, Christoffel, Kai, Coenen, Günter, Motto, Roberto, Rostagno Massimo (2010). DSGE Models and Their Use at the ECB, *SERIEs*, Vol. 1, Issue 1–2.

Smets, Frank, Wouters, Raf (2004). Forecasting with a Bayesian DSGE Model: An Application to the Euro Area, *Journal of Common Market Studies*, Vo. 42, No. 4.

Smits, René (1997). The European Central Bank: Institutional Aspects. *Kluwer Law International*, The Hague.

Smits, René (2003). The European Central Bank in the European Constitutional Order, *Eleven International Publishing*.

Snowdon, Brian, Vane, Howard R. (2002). An Encyclopedia of Macroeconomics, *Edward Elgar Publishing*, Cheltenham, UK and Northampton, USA.

Soares da Silva, João (2011). Is the EU Better Prepared for a New Financial Crisis? A Brief Analysis of the New Financial Supervisory Architecture, *Contraditorio Policy Paper*, No. 11/10.

Sowell, Thomas (2007). On Classical Economics, *Yale University Press*, New Haven.

Spencer, Grant (2014). Coordination of Monetary Policy and Macro-prudential Policy, *Speech Held at the Credit Suisse Asian Investment Conference*, Hong Kong, 27 March 2014.

Stadler, Rainer (1996). Der rechtliche Handlungsspielraum des Europäischen Systems der Zentralbanken, *Nomos Verlagsgesellschaft*.

Steven, Ongena, Peydró, Jose Luis (2011). Loose Monetary Policy and Excessive Credit and Liquidity Risk-Taking by Banks. In: '*The Future of Banking*', (ed.) Thorsten Beck, CEPR.

Streinz, Rudolf (2008). Europarecht, *C.F. Müller*, Hüthig Jehle Rehm.

Streit, Manfred (1992). Economic Order, Private Law and Economics – The Freiburg School of Law and Economics in Perspective, *Journal of Institutional and Theoretical Economics*, Vol. 148.

Streit, Manfred (1994). The Freiburg School of Law and Economics. In: '*The Elgar Companion to Austrian Economics*', (ed.) Peter J. Boettke, *Aldershot: Edgar Elgar.*

Suh, Hyunduk (2012). Macroprudential Policy: Its Effects and Relationship to Monetary Policy, *Federal Reserve Bank of Philadelphia Working Paper*, No. 12–28.

Suàrez, Javier (1988). Risk-Taking and Prudential Regulation of Banks, *Investigaciones Economicas*, Vol. 22, XXII, No. 3.

Svensson, Lars E.O. (1999). Price Stability as a Target for Monetary Policy: Defining and Maintaining Price Stability, *NBER Working Paper Series*, No. 7276.

Svensson, Lars E.O. (2002). Monetary Policy and Real Stabilization. In: '*Rethinking Stabilization Policy*', *A Symposium Sponsored by the Federal Reserve Bank of Kansas City*, Jackson Hole, 29–31 August 2002.

Svensson, Lars E.O. (2015). Monetary Policy and Macroprudential Policy: Different and Separate, *Federal Reserve Bank of Boston's 59th Economic Conference*, Federal Reserve Bank of Boston, October 2–3, 2015.

Tamborini, Roberto (2004). The "Brussels Consensus" on Macroeconomic Stabilization Policies: A Critical Assessment. In: '*Governing EMU Economic, Political, Legal and Historical Perspectives*', (eds.) Francisco Torres, Amy Verdun, Chiara Zilioli, Hubert Zimmermann, *European University Institute*, Florence.

Tarullo, Daniel K. (2014). A Macroprudential Perspective on Regulating Large Financial Institutions, *Banque de France Financial Stability Review*, No. 18.

Taylor, John B. (1979). Estimation and Control of a Macroeconomic Model with Rational Expectations, *Econometrica*, Vol. 47, Issue 5.

Taylor, John B. (1986). An Appeal for Rationality in the Policy Activism Debate. In: '*The Monetary Versus Fiscal Policy Debate: Lessons from Two Decades*', Totowa, NJ: Rowman & Allenheld, Publishers.

Taylor, John B. (1994). The Inflation/Output Variability Tradeoff Revisited. In: '*Goals, Guidelines, and Constraints Facing Monetary Policymakers*', (ed.) Jeffrey C. Fuhrer, *The Federal Reserve Bank of Boston Conference Series*, No. 38.

Taylor, John B. (1996). How Should Monetary Policy Respond to Shocks While Maintaining Long-Run Price Stability?—Conceptual Issues. In: '*Achieving Price Stability*', *Federal Reserve Bank of Kansas City.*

Taylor, John B. (1999). An Historical Analysis of Monetary Policy Rules. In: '*Monetary Policy Rules*', (ed.) John B. Taylor, *The University of Chicago Press.*

Taylor, John B. (ed.) (1999b). Monetary Policy Rules, *The University of Chicago Press.*

Taylor, John B. (2008). The Financial Crisis and the Policy Responses: An Empirical Analysis of What Went Wrong', *NBER Working Paper Series*, No. 14631.

Taylor, John B. (2009). The Financial Crisis and the Policy Responses: An Empirical Analysis of What Went Wrong, *NBER Working Paper Series*, No. 14631.

Taylor, John B. (2013a). Monetary Policy During the Past 30 Years with Lessons for the Next 30 Years, *The Cato Journal*, Vol. 33.

Taylor, John B. (2013b). The Effectiveness of Central Bank Independence vs. Policy Rules, *Business Economics*, Vol. 48.

Teivanen, Teivo (1997). The Independence of the European Central Bank: Implications for Democratic Governance. In: '*The Politics of Economic and Monetary Union*', (eds.) Petri Minkkinen, Heikki Patomäki, *Springer US*.

Ter Kuile, Gijsbert, Wissink, Laura, Bovenschen, Willem (2015). Tailor-Made Accountability within the Single Supervisory Mechanism, *Common Market Law Review*, Vol. 52.

Thalassinos, Eleftherios, Dafnos, Georgios (2015). EMU and the Process of European Integration: Southern Europe's Economic Challenges and the Need for Revisiting EMU's Institutional Framework. In: '*Societies in Transition, Economic, Political and Security Transformations in Contemporary Europe*', (eds.) Savvas Katsikides, Pavlos I. Koktsidis, *Springer International Publishing*.

Theissen, Roel (2014). EU Banking Supervision, *Eleven International Publishing*, Bruxelles.

The Liikanen Report (2012). Final Report of the High-level Expert Group on Reforming the Structure of the EU Banking Sector, Brussels, 2 October 2012.

The Warwick Commission (2009). The Warwick Commission on International Financial Reform: In Praise of Unlevel Playing Fields, *The University of Warwick*.

The World Bank (2014). World Development Record 2014, Risk and Opportunity: Managing Risk for Development, *World Bank*, Washington, DC.

Thiele, Alexander (2013). Das Mandat der EZB und die Krise des Euro, *Mohr Siebeck*, Tübingen.

Thiele, Alexander (2014). Finanzaufsicht Der Staat und die Finanzmärkte, *Mohr Siebeck*, Tübingen.

Tobin, James (1969). A General Equilibrium Approach to Monetary Theory, *Journal of Money, Credit and Banking*, Vol. 1, No. 1.

Tobin, James, Brainard, Williams C. (1968). Pitfalls in Financial Model-Building, *Cowles Foundation Discussion Papers*, No. 244.

Tohidipur, Timo (2006). The Emperor's New Clothes: The ECB and the New Institutional Concept. In: '*The Unity of the European Constitution*', (eds.) Philipp Dann, Michal Rynkowski, *Beiträge zum ausländischen öffentlichen Recht und Völkerrecht, Springer.*

Tor, Avishalom, Aviram, Amitai (2004). Overcoming Impediments to Information Sharing, *Alabama Law Review*, Vol. 55, No. 2.

Trichet, Jean-Claude (2005). Asset Price Bubbles and Their Implications for Monetary Policy and Financial Stability. In: '*Asset Price Bubbles: The Implications for Monetary, Regulatory, and International Policies*', (eds.) William C. Hunter, George G. Kaufman, Michael Pomerleano, *The MIT Press*, Cambridge.

Tröger, Tobias H. (2014). The Single Supervisory Mechanism – Panacea or Quack Banking Regulation? Preliminary Assessment of the New Regime for the Prudential Supervision of Banks with ECB Involvement, *European Business Organization Law Review*, Vol. 15.

Tröger, Tobias H. (2015a). A Political Economy Perspective on Common Supervision in the Eurozone. In: '*Financial Regulation: A Transatlantic Perspective*', (eds.) Ester Faia, Andreas Hackethal, Micheal Haliassos, Katja Langenbucher, *Cambridge University Press.*

Trichet, Jean-Claude (2011). The Conditions for Efficient Global and Regional Macro-supervision – Key Success Factors in International Cooperation, *Speech by Jean-Claude Trichet, President of the ECB, at the Eurofi G20 High Level Seminar*, Paris, 17 February 2011.

Tröger, Tobias H. (2015b). Regulatory Influence on Market Conditions in the Banking Union: The Cases of Macro-prudential Instruments and the Bail-in Tool, *European Business Organization Law Review*, Vol. 15, Issue 3.

Tucker, Paul (2016). Macroprudential Policy Regimes. In: *"Progress and Confusion: The State of Macroeconomic Policy"*, (eds.) Olivier Blanchard, Raghuram Rajan, Kenneth Rogoff, Lawrence H. Summers, *The MIT Press.*

Tucker, Paul, Hall, Simon, Pattani, Aashish (2013). Macroprudential Policy at the Bank of England, *Bank of England Quarterly Bulletin*, No. 3.

Tumpel-Gugerell, Gertrude (2009). Recent Advances in Modeling Systemic Risk using Network Analysis, *Introductory remarks to ECB Workshop*, 5 October 2005.

Tuori, Kaarlo, Tuori, Klaus (2014). The Eurozone Crisis. A Constitutional Analysis. *Cambridge University Press*, Cambridge.

Turner, Philip (2000). Procyclicality of Regulatory Ratios?, *CEPA Working Paper Series III*, No. 13.

Ueda, Kenichi, Valencia, Fabián (2014). Central Bank Independence and Macroprudential Regulation, *Economics Letters*, Vol. 125, No. 2.

Ulrike, Neyer (2007). The Design of the Eurosystem's Monetary Policy Instruments, *Springer*, Berlin.

Unsal, D. Filiz (2013). Capital Flows and Financial Stability: Monetary Policy and Macroprudential Responses, *International Journal of Central Banking*, Vol. 9, No. 1.

Valencia, Fabian (2011). Monetary Policy, Bank Leverage, and Financial Stability, *IMF Working Paper*, No. 244.

Vanberg, Viktor J. (1998). Freiburg School of Law and Economics. In: '*The New Palgrave Dictionary of Economics and the Law*', (ed.) Peter Newman, Vol. 2, *Macmillan*, London.

Van Cleynenbreugel, Pieter (2015). Market Supervision in the European Union: Integrated Administration in Constitutional Context, *Brill | Nijhoff.*

van den End, Jan Willem (2010). Trading Off Monetary and Financial Stability: A Balance of Risk Framework, *DNB Working Papers*, No. 249.

van den End, Jan Willem, Kruidhof, Mark (2013). Modelling the Liquidity Ratio as Macroprudential Instrument, *Journal of Banking Regulation*, Vol. 14, Issue 2.

Vargas-Silva, Carlos (2010). Exchange Rates. In: '*21st Century Economics: A Reference Handbook*', (ed.) Rhona C. Free, *SAGE Publications* Inc.

Verhelst, Stijn (2011). Renewed Financial Supervision in Europe – Final or Transitory? *Egmont – The Royal Institute for International Relations Academia Press*, Brussels.

Verhelst, Stijn (2013). Assessing the Single Supervisory Mechanism: Passing the Point of No Return for Europe's Banking Union, *Egmont – The Royal Institute for International Relations Academia Press*, Brussels.

Véron, Nicolas (2012). Europe's Single Supervisory Mechanism and the Long Journey Towards Banking Union, *Bruegel Policy Contribution*, No. 16.

Van Cleynenbruegel, Pieter (2014). Meroni Circumvented? Article 114 TFEU and EU Regulatory Agencies, *Maastricht Journal of European and Comparative Law*, Vol. 2014/1.

Vifials, Jose, Valles, Javier (1999). On the Real Effects of Monetary Policy, *Banco de Espana Working Paper*, No. 9917.

Visco, Ignazio (2011). Key Issues for the Success of Macroprudential Policies, *Policy Panel on the Macroprudential Policy Framework Bok-BIS Conference*, Seoul, 18 January 2011.

Visco, Ignazio (2012). Key Issues for the Success of Macroprudential Policies, *BIS Papers*, No. 60.

Volcker, Paul (1983). Can We Survive Prosperity?, *Speech at the Joint Meeting of the American Economic-American Finance Association*, San Francisco, 28 December 1983.

Volz, Ulrich (2015). Navigating the Trilemma: Central Banking in East Asia Between Inflation Targeting, Exchange-Rate Management and Guarding Financial Stability. In: '*Central Banking and Financial Stability in East Asia*', (eds.) Frank Rövekamp, Moritz Bälz, Hanns Günther Hilpert, *Springer International Publishing*, Cham.

Vourloumis, Stavros (2012). Reforming EU and Global Financial Regulation: Crisis, Learning and Paradigm Shifts, *Paper Presented at the 4th Biennial ECPR Standing Group for Regulatory Governance Conference 'New Perspectives on Regulation, Governance and Learning 2012'*, University of Exeter, 27–29 June 2012.

Wachtel, Paul (2011). The Evolving Role of the Federal Reserve, *NYU Working Paper*, No. 2451/31339.

Wadhvani, Sushil (2014). Inflation Targeting, Capital Requirements and 'Leaning Against the Wind': Some Comments. In: '*Twenty Years of Inflation Targeting Lessons Learned and Future Prospects*', (eds.) David Cobham, Øyvind Eitrheim, Stefan Gerlach, Jan F. Qvigstad, *Cambridge University Press.*

Waldhoff, Chistian (2013). Artikel 127 AEUV. In: 'EWU – Kommentar zur Europäischen Währungsunion,' (ed.) Helmut Siekmann, *Mohr Siebeck*, Tübingen.

Wall, Larry D. (2010). Prudential Discipline for Financial Firms: Micro, Macro, and Market Structures, *Federal Reserve Bank of Atlanta Working Paper*, No. 2010-09.

Wallis, W. Allen (1960). Price Stability and Economic Growth. Increasing Understanding of Public Problems and Policies, *Farm Foundation*.

Walsh, Carl E. (1998). The New Output-Inflation Trade-off, *FRBSF Economic Letter*, 6 February 1998.

Walsh, Carl E. (2010). Monetary Theory and Policy, *The MIT Press*, Cambridge.

White, Lawrence H. (2009). Federal Reserve Policy and the Housing Bubble, *The Cato Journal*, Vol. 29, Issue 1.

Weatherill, Stephen (2012). The Constitutional Context of (Ever Wider) Policymaking. In: '*The Oxford Handbook of the European Union*', (eds.) Erik Jones, Anand Menon, and Stephen Weatherill, *Oxford University Press*.

Weber, Martin (1998). Das Europäische System der Zentralbanken, *Wertpapiermitteilungen*.

Weidmann, Jens (2012). Managing Macroprudential and Monetary Policy – A Challenge for Central Banks. In: '*The ESRB at 1*', *IMFS Interdisciplinary Studies in Monetary and Financial Stability*, Vol. 2012/1.

Wendel, Mattias (2014). Exceeding Judicial Competence in the Name of Democracy: The German Federal Constitutional Court's OMT Reference, *European Constitutional Law Review*, Vol. 10, Issue 2.

Weismann, Paul (2016). European Agencies and Risk Governance in EU Financial Market Law, *Routledge*.

Whelan, Karl (2009). The ECB Role in Financial Supervision, *UCD Centre for Economic Research Working Paper Series*, No. 15.

Wilkinson, Michael A. (2015). Euro Is Irreversible – Or Is It: On OMT, Austerity and the Threat of Grexit, *The German Law Journal*, Vol. 16, No. 4.

Willke, Helmut, Becker, Eva, Rostásy, Carla (2013). Systemic Risk: The Myth of Rational Finance and the Crisis of Democracy, *Campus Verlag GmbH*, Frankfurt.

Williamson, Oliver E. (2000). The New Institutional Economics: Taking Stock, Looking Ahead, *Journal of Economic Literature*, Vol. 38, No. 3.

Wynne, Mark A. (1999). The European System of Central Banks, *Federal Reserve Bank of Dallas Economic Review*, First Quarter 1999.

Wynne, Mark A. (2001). European System of Central Banks. In: '*Handbook of Monetary and Fiscal Policy*', (eds.) Alan A. Rabin, Gleen L. Stevens, *CRC Press*.

Wynne, Mark A., Rodriguez-Palenzuela, Diego (2004). Measurement Bias in the HICP: What Do We Know and What Do We Need to Know?, *Journal of Economic Surveys*, Vol. 18, Issue 1.

Wolfson, Martin H. (2001). Minsky's Theory of Financial Crisis in a Global Context, *Journal of Economic Issues*, Vol. 36, No. 2.

Wong, Eric, Fong, Tom, Li, Ka-fai Choi, Henry (2011). Loan-to-Value Ratio as a Macroprudential Tools – Hong-Kong's Experience and Cross-Country Evidence, *HKMA Working Paper*, No. 01/2011.

Xingyuan Che, Natasha, Shinagawa, Yoko (2014). Financial Soundness Indicators and the Characteristics of Financial Cycles, *IMF Working Papers*, No. 14.

Yellen, Janet L. (2010). Macroprudential Supervision and Monetary Policy in the Post-crisis World, *Speech Held at the Annual Meeting of the National Association for Business Economics*, Denver, 11 October 2010.

Yellen, Janet L. (2013). Interconnectedness and Systemic Risk: Lessons from the Financial Crisis and Policy Implications, *Speech at the American Economic Association/American Finance Association Joint Luncheon*, San Diego, 4 January 2013.

Yeşin, Pınar (2013). Foreign Currency Loans and Systemic Risk in Europe, *Federal Reserve Bank of St. Louis Review*, May/June.

Zhou, Chen (2010). Why the Micro-Prudential Regulation Fails? The Impact on Systemic Risk by Imposing a Capital Requirement, *DNB Working Paper* No. 256/July 2010.

Zilioli, Chiara, Selmayr, Martin (2001a). The Law of the European Central Bank, *Hart Publishing*, Oxford.

Zilioli, Chiara, Selmayr, Martin (2001b). The European Central Bank: An Independent Specialized Organization of Community Law, *Common Market Law Review*, Vol. 37.

Zilioli, Chiara (2013). The Role of Central Banks in Ensuring Financial Stability, *Remarks at the IMFS Conference on Monetary and Financial Stability Economic and Legal Limits of Central Banking*, 26 November 2013, Frankfurt.

Zilioli, Chiara (2016). *The Independence of the European Central Bank and Its Banking Supervisory Competences*. In: '*Independence and Legitimacy in the Institutional System of the European Union*', (ed.) Dominique Ritleng, *Oxford University Press*.

Zhou, Chen (2010). Why the Micro-Prudential Regulation Fails? The Impact on Systemic Risk by Imposing a Capital Requirement, *DNB Working Paper* No. 256/July 2010.

Index

L. Amorello, *Macroprudential Banking Supervision & Monetary Policy*, https://doi.org/10.1007/978-3-319-94156-1

The manufacturer's authorised representative in the EU is Springer Nature Customer Service Centre GmbH, Europaplatz 3, 69115 Heidelberg, Germany. If you have any concerns regarding our products, please contact ProductSafety@springernature.com

Printed and bound by CPI Group (UK) Ltd, Croydon, CR0 4YY
05/10/2026
02228128-0017